EX LIBRIS

A B Fretz
184

MARCEL PROUST

A BIOGRAPHY

MARCEL PROUST

A BIOGRAPHY
Volume Two

BY
GEORGE D. PAINTER

Et je compris que tous ces matériaux de l'oeuvre
littéraire, c'était ma vie passée.

PROUST, *Le Temps Retrouvé*

VINTAGE BOOKS
A DIVISION OF RANDOM HOUSE
NEW YORK

First Vintage Books Edition, April 1978

Copyright © 1959 by George D. Painter

All rights reserved under International and Pan-American Copyright Conventions.
Published in the United States by Random House, Inc., New York.
Originally published by Chatto and Windus Ltd., London, in September 1959.
Published in hardcover by Random House in April 1978.

Library of Congress Cataloging in Publication Data
Painter, George Duncan, 1914-
Marcel Proust: a biography
Reprint of the ed. published by Chatto & Windus, London.
1. Proust, Marcel, 1871-1922—Biography.
2. Novelists, French—20th century—Biography.
[PQ2631.R63Z78958 1978b]   843'.9'12 [B]   77-090260
ISBN 0-394-72561-1(v. 1)
ISBN 0-394-72562-X(v. 2)

Manufactured in the United States of America

CONTENTS

ACKNOWLEDGMENT

The author and publishers wish to express their grateful appreciation to Princesse Marthe Bibesco, Mr Miron Grindea, Monsieur Pierre Cailler, and to all others who have kindly supplied or own copyright in the illustrations to this volume. They also wish to thank the authors, copyright-owners, and publishers of the works used or quoted in both volumes of the present work. As stated in the Preface to Volume One, only published sources have been used; and these are fully listed and cited in the Bibliography and References to Sources included in Volume Two.

LIST OF PLATES

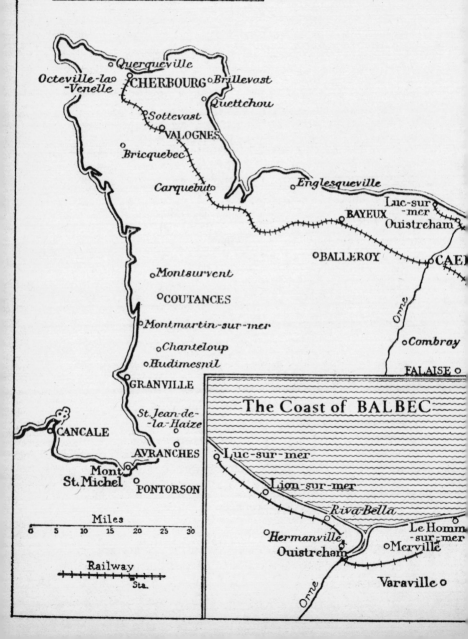

PROUST'

Place names used or adapted by Proust in A la Recherche du Temps Perdu for the stations of the Little Train, or for other features of the country near 'Balbec', are shown in italics.

Querqueville

Octeville-la- -Venelle CHERBOURG *Brillevast*

Quettchou

Sottevast VALOGNES

Bricquebec

Carquebuto *Englesqueville* Luc-sur- -mer

BAYEUX Ouistreham

BALLEROY CAEN

Montsurvent

COUTANCES Orne

Montmartin-sur-mer *Combray*

Chanteloup

Hudimesnil FALAISE

GRANVILLE

St.Jean-de- -la-Haize

CANCALE

AVRANCHES

Mont St.Michel PONTORSON

Miles

0 5 10 15 20 25 30

Railway

Sta.

The Coast of BALBEC

Luc-sur-mer

Lion-sur-mer

Riva-Bella

Le Homm -sur- -mer

Hermanville Merville

Ouistreham

Orne Varaville

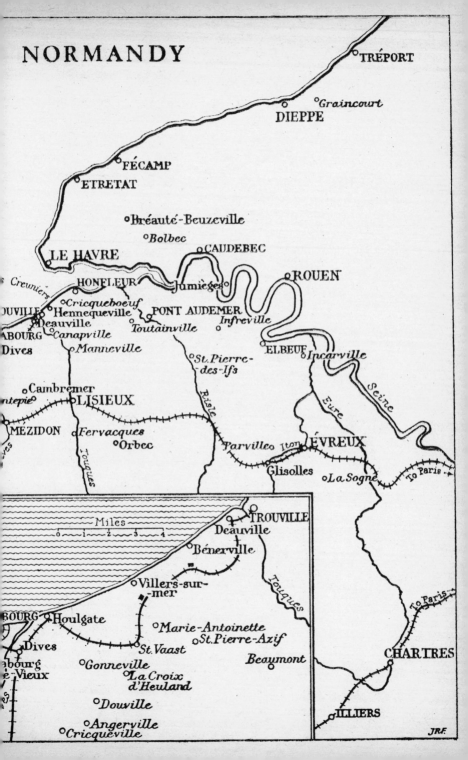

NORMANDY

TRÉPORT

Graincourt

DIEPPE

FÉCAMP

ETRETAT

Bréauté-Beuzeville

Bolbec

CAUDEBEC

LE HAVRE

Creuniers

HONFLEUR

Jumièges

ROUEN

Cricqueboeuf

Hennequeville

PONT AUDEMER

DUVILLE

Deauville

Infreville

ABOURG

Canapville

Toutainville

Dives

Manneville

ELBEUF

Incarville

St. Pierre-
des-Ifs

Seine

Cambremer

ntepie

LISIEUX

Risle

Eure

MEZIDON

Fervacques

Orbec

Parville

Iton

ÉVREUX

Touques

Glisolles

La Sogne

To Paris

Miles

0   1   2   3   4

TROUVILLE

Deauville

Bénerville

Touques

Villers-sur-
mer

BOURG

Houlgate

To Paris

Dives

Marie-Antoinette

St. Pierre-Azif

abourg

Vieux

St. Vaast

Gonneville

Beaumont

CHARTRES

La Croix
d'Heuland

Douville

Angerville

Cricqueville

ILLIERS

JRF.

Chapter 1

VISITS FROM ALBERTINE
(December 1903 – December 1904)

'LIFE has begun again,' Proust had written to Mme de Noailles on 3 December 1903, a week after his father's death. Dr Proust was in his grave at Père Lachaise; but already the absence which at first had seemed calamitous was beginning to appear natural. Little outward change could be seen in Mme Proust: her manner that day was brisk and fortifying, and even the reappearance of her mourning-dress, so recently had she ceased to wear black for her father's and uncle's deaths seven years ago, was hardly noticeable. As before, or still more than before, she ran her son's errands while he slept, and ensured that the servants made no sound until, 'towards six o'clock in the afternoon, or as the common herd would put it, evening', he woke and rang his bell. In moments of leisure she sat in the drawing-room, reading Mme de Sévigné in her ebony Empire armchair, with Lecomte du Nouy's portrait of her husband propped on a black-draped easel beside her. The beautiful Jeanne Proust was now a plain, corpulent, middle-aged lady of fifty-five, with hair beginning at last to grey, and an expression of puzzled serenity which concealed undying grief for her dead and devouring anxiety for her son.

Not unreluctantly Proust imitated his mother: he ceased to weep, and put aside his pangs of genuine sorrow, his remorse for having been, as he confessed to Mme de Noailles, 'the dark side of Father's life'. It was unwise to remark upon the fact. "I don't think Marcel is unduly distressed at his father's death," observed the heartless Antoine Bibesco to a friend, who immediately sneaked; and Antoine, in a well-deserved letter of frantic anger, was told: 'you have committed an unforgivable crime, and I never want to see you again'. But Antoine was no stranger to these paroxysms of rage: he coolly called that very evening to discuss his new play, *Le Jaloux*, and was received as though nothing had happened by a gay and good-tempered Marcel. Even so, incidents of everyday life continued to recall the lost old man. Throughout that December and January

letters of condolence from Anna de Noailles, with their sentiments
and handwriting of 'disciplined tumult', arrived in succession; and
Proust seemed to hear again outside his bedroom door his father's
jovial shout: "Another letter from Mme de Noailles, my boy!",
and his mother's scolding: "Really, my dear, must you spoil Marcel's
pleasure by telling him in advance?"

With a comfortable feeling of obeying his father's last wish,
pleasing his mother, and appeasing his impatient publisher, he fell
again to correcting the proofs of *La Bible d'Amiens*, over which he
had dawdled since July. He made a second resolution for his mother's
sake: 'to enable myself soon to get up at the same time as you, drink
my morning coffee with you, feel that our waking and sleeping hours
are portioned out over one and the same expanse of time, would be, I
mean *will* be, my delight'. Once in December he heroically went to
bed at 1.30 a.m., some nine hours early by his time-scale; but he spent
a sleepless night looking for a safety-pin to fasten the waist of his
drawers, and devising a plan, never to be executed, for 'a new life in
which we shall live to the same time-table, in the same rooms at the
same temperature, in accordance with the same principles and—
though contentment is now, alas, forbidden us—with mutual
approbation'.

In some respects the new régime at 45 Rue de Courcelles was
more liberal than the old. Never in his father's lifetime could Marcel
have received, like the Narrator on the day of Albertine's first visit
in Paris, a young girl in his bedroom; but in December, when the
funeral bakemeats were hardly cold, Marie Nordlinger became a
constant visitor. At first they worked on his Ruskin proofs at the
huge oval dining-room table, the centre of so many 'grand dinner-
parties' since the springtime of Willie Heath, with its red baize cloth
and old-fashioned Carcel oil-lamp, for love of whose soft beams he
extinguished the electric light. In January he was confined to bed
with asthma and lumbago, 'and therefore prevented from having a
young girl to visit me'; but soon he overcame his shyness of being
seen by her in the sacred and chaotic bedroom from which he had
excluded even Emmanuel Bibesco. His bed, when Mlle Nordlinger
entered, was littered with dictionaries, Ruskins and exercise-books;
cheap wooden pen-holders lay fallen on the floor; and Marcel
reclined in a mare's nest of pillows, muffled in pullovers and cotton-
wool, writing sometimes on the rickety bamboo bedside table ('my
shallop'), sometimes, when that was piled too high with books, on

paper held in mid-air. The room was suffocatingly hot; but soon old Félicie brought, with a plate of fancy cakes from Rebattet's, an ice or a glass of orangeade for Marie,[1] and a jug of boiling coffee for Master Marcel. Mlle Nordlinger poured out for him, taking care always to include the skin with the milk, for: "It's the cream, you see," he explained, "it's the best part of the milk!" They fell to work, discussing here a sentence, there a single word, whose possible synonyms Proust had prepared beforehand from his dictionaries. Orders were given that "no one is to be allowed in, except Monsieur Hahn"; and on the one occasion when the inquisitive Antoine Bibesco dared to gate-crash, he was made to rue it.

Towards midnight they began to talk; and Mlle Nordlinger remembered 'his strangely luminous, omnivorous eyes, alight with fun and mimicry, or suddenly suffused unaccountably, unashamedly with tears'. Starting from two Japanese *cloisonné* ear-rings hung on a chain from her neck—"May I touch them? Don't take them off! Where did Reynaldo get them?"—he cross-examined her on the mysteries of her craft. Later she found traces of their conversations in *A la Recherche*; and it is because Mlle Nordlinger worked as an enamellist for Siegfried Bing that the Narrator speaks of 'a crude blue, almost violet, suggesting the background of a Japanese *cloisonné*', or 'the polychrome enamel of pansies'; or of the Prince de Borodino 'embedding glorious images beneath a royal blue enamel in the mysterious, illuminated and surviving reliquary of his eyes'.[2] They exchanged presents: Proust gave her Montesquiou's copy of Whistler's *The Gentle Art of Making Enemies*; and Marie brought her own water-colour of trees at Senlis, painted in 1898, which hung ever after by his bedside until, shortly before his death, Proust gave it to Reynaldo. In witty but sympathetic allusion to his love of the flowers he dared not smell, she gave him a twopenny packet of balsam seeds, a repoussé lily, a hawthorn flower in pink translucent enamel—'your grace is as fresh as a spray of hawthorn,' he had told her five years before. 'The seeds are flowers for the imagination, just as the Japanese dwarf trees at Bing's are trees for the imagination,' he wrote; and the dwarf trees reappeared in

---

[1] Similarly Albertine visualises the ice for which she longs on the morning of her visit to the Trocadéro as coming from Rebattet's (III, 128), and the Narrator offers her orangeade during her visit after the Princesse de Guermantes's soirée (II, 738).

[2] I, 169, 126; II, 132.

Albertine's lyrical monologue on ice-cream.[1] There can be no doubt, indeed, although his relationship with Mlle Nordlinger was one of comradely affection and nothing more, that her idyllic visits during this winter to his mother's home were remembered when, out of many girls and three young men, he created Albertine. But the impressions left by Marie Nordlinger were to be reinforced a few months later by the visits of a young woman with whom his relations were more physical.

Meanwhile, Proust conducted two hot but temporary quarrels. The first was with Antoine Bibesco, shortly before Antoine's departure with Emmanuel on 9 January for two months' leave in Egypt. Proust referred, in a letter to Mme de Noailles, the culprit's cousin, to his '*déboires sentimentaux*' with Antoine. Possibly he was jealous of his friend's prospective visit to Constantinople, where Bertrand de Fénelon still lingered after his transfer to the St Petersburg embassy on 23 November 1903. 'I wish you a very happy stay in Egypt, since I'm certain you'll never get there,' Proust wrote ironically on the eve of Antoine's departure. In fact Antoine went straight to Egypt, but from mid-February till his return to Paris at the end of March was at Constantinople.

The other victim was Constantin de Brancovan, who had rashly promised him the post of literary critic on the *Renaissance Latine*. On reflection Constantin realised that Marcel, being a genius, incessantly ill and now preoccupied with his Ruskin translations, would be totally unsuitable for a task which required a punctual hireling who would write in a manner to which the subscribers were accustomed. Late in December he appointed the versatile Gaston Rageot —'my Usurper,' as Proust called him—and informed Marcel only after the deed was done. Proust was wounded in his pride, his code of friendship, and in the vague longing which pursued him intermittently throughout his life to obtain a regular post as a journalist. He was particularly galled by Constantin's pretence to have acted for his own good ('you have doubted me, Marcel, but I forgive you'), to spare him 'the fatigue, toil and boredom of having to supply a monthly article'. He broke with Constantin in an interview at 45 Rue de Courcelles on 18 January, and on the 20th visited Mme de Noailles to receive her sympathy. But she seemed strangely reluctant to give it, and showed visible irritation when he asked permission to use her telephone, or when, as he left in the small hours, he explained

[1] III, 130.

from the bottom of her staircase that he could not find the switch to put out the electric light. Perhaps there was another reason for Constantin's decision. The *Renaissance Latine* was in some degree a family magazine—'the Brancovan chamber-pot, which the whole family fills so regularly,' said Montesquiou; and Rageot could be relied upon to praise Constantin's sister Anna's work less dithyrambically and more convincingly than Proust.[1]

It is time for a further glimpse of Montesquiou. A year ago, in January and February 1903, he had given a series of seven lectures in the United States, organised by Boni de Castellane's friend Miss Bessie Marbury. She was an intelligent American spinster who lived near Paris with her inseparable companion Miss Elsie de Wolfe (later the famous Lady Mendl of the 1920s); and because Miss de Wolfe was as thin as Miss Marbury was fat, Montesquiou nicknamed them Tanagra and Tonneau Gros. On the liner going over, the Count's tiffs with Yturri were overheard with smothered sniggers by unsympathetic bystanders. His lectures were given to diamonded and tiaraed audiences: "I understand you have a Steel King, an Oil King, a Railway King—but where is your Dream King, your Poetry King?" he began[2]; and he supplemented his earnings by selling *objets d'art* to his new converts. Proust assured him that his voyage was the most epoch-making feat of evangelisation since the Acts of the Apostles, and compared him and Yturri to Saint Paul and Timothy. In this January of 1904 the Count was summoned to Paris from his winter quarters at Nice to fight his second and last duel. Mme Ernesta Stern, an occasional hostess of Proust and Hahn, and a writer of mildly erotic novels, had become one of Montesquiou's *bêtes noires*. In a review of her latest volume he had ungallantly remarked of a chapter entitled 'How to choose a lover': 'this is absurd, because everyone knows she never bothers to choose.' He was challenged by her son Jean, a noted swordsman, and for once it seemed Count Robert had gone too far; but to his great pride he succeeded, by his previous stratagem of whirling his sword like the

[1] In July 1904 occurred a curious incident for which Fernand Gregh never forgave this obedient critic. Rageot had unwarily written a laudatory review of Gregh's new poems, *Les Clartés Humaines*, at a time when Mme de Noailles was consumed with baseless dread lest Gregh might be given the cross of the Legion of Honour before her; and at Constantin's orders he altered his article to a vigorous slating at the very moment of going to press.

[2] Charlus himself makes fun of the Steel King, saying the Iénas' title is no better than his (II, 564).

sail of a windmill, in baffling his opponent for nearly three-quarters
of an hour, and escaped with a mere scratch. The duel was fought on
18 January.

By sheer coincidence it was on that very day that Proust published
in *Le Figaro*, under the pseudonym Horatio,[1] an article entitled
'*Une Fête chez Montesquiou à Neuilly*'. In a brilliant parody of Saint-
Simon's *Mémoires* he evoked a typical fête at the Count's Pavillon
des Muses in the Boulevard Maillot; and the joke pleased him so well
that he included the same material fifteen years later in the much
longer Saint-Simon pastiche in *Pastiches et Mélanges*. Montesquiou
was uncertain whether to be gratified or annoyed. That he should be
treated as one of the great figures of the *grand siècle* was a just tribute
to his genius; but was not the satire a little more edged than could be
accounted for by the exigences of parody? Who on earth was
Horatio? He wrote a haughtily acrid letter to *Le Figaro*, addressed to
'Horatio', which Calmette showed to Proustbut did not print. Soon,
however, Count Robert changed his mind. In March, when Proust
and he were guests at the same dinner-party, he brought the conversation round to Mme de Noailles's short story '*L'Exhortation*',
published in the *Renaissance Latine* of 15 November 1903. "It's
not only sublime, marvellous and ravishing," he cried at the top
pitch of his eldritch voice, underlining his words with extraordinary
gestures, "it is the most beautiful thing I have ever read; indeed,
from all the height of my infallible taste, and all the breadth of my
infinite culture, I can say it is the most beautiful thing that has ever
been written!!" He proceeded to repeat the entire work from
memory, only interrupting himself to murmur aside: "What genius!
What *genius*!!" Outside in the street with Proust, who was acutely
embarrassed by the amazement of passers-by, he pointed to the
heavens and quoted: " 'The sky that evening was of a colour which
no words can describe,' " and stamped on the pavement with body
flung backwards until, as Proust told Mme de Noailles afterwards, 'I
was really afraid he'd sprain his ankles'. Then he changed the subject:
"Are you Horatio, Marcel?" he asked pointblank. Proust denied it.
"Because, as I couldn't discover who wrote the article, I've had a
small edition privately printed—with a few necessary corrections, of
course!" The agitated Marcel could only write to Mme de Noailles:
'What a blow! Not a word about Horatio, mind! *Tombeau, tombeau,*

[1] He had already used it in *Le Figaro* for his '*Salon de la Princesse de Polignac*'
(6 September 1903) and '*Salon de la Comtesse d'Haussonville*' (4 January 1904).

tombeau!' A little later, when Montesquiou found the identity of Horatio, disaster was averted: Proust whitened his lie by explaining that he had promised Calmette to keep the secret of his pseudonym; and Montesquiou, having once professed to take the article as a compliment, could only be doubly pleased to learn that he owed it to his 'dear Marcel'.

Although the *achevé d'imprimer* of *La Bible d'Amiens* was 15 February 1904, it was not too late for Proust to add last-minute corrections. In the small hours of that very day he sent two questionnaires to Mlle Nordlinger on passages which still perplexed him, ending with the ominous words: 'This old man'—meaning Ruskin—'is beginning to bore me.' The actual publication took place in the first week of March, and the book was first briefly mentioned, as 'the elegant and powerful translation which M. Marcel Proust has just given us', in an article on Alphonse Karr in *La Liberté* on 15 March by Robert de Flers. Reviews were for the most part as insensitive as for *Les Plaisirs et les Jours* eight years before. Few among the chorus of indolent reviewers realised that the meeting of Proust and Ruskin had produced a prose and a personality new in French literature, a work in which criticism had become a form of creative imagination, or that a great writer was here on the threshold of self-discovery. *La Bible d'Amiens*, in so far as it was noticed at all, only helped to confirm Proust's reputation as an amateur, a drawing-room dilettante.

Another disappointing feature of the reviews was that Proust's effort to organise them had brought its own punishment. With two unimportant exceptions[1] the book was not reviewed by anyone whom he had not persuaded to do so by entreaty or influence. Even the passing mention by his old friend Robert de Flers was made by request[2]; notices appeared in the *Chronique des Arts* (19 March) and *Le Figaro* (25 March) because Proust was a valued contributor to those papers. Another, in *Arts de la Vie* (March 1904) is to be explained by the fact that the editor Gabriel Mourey, himself a translator and critic of Ruskin, was a friend of Montesquiou, and was to publish the first section of *Sésame et les Lys* in his magazine a year later. Proust conveyed a hint to Léon Daudet that an article

---

[1] The only articles by persons not known to be friends or 'contacts' of Proust were those by Georges Richet in *Revue générale de la Bibliographie française*, 10 April 1904, and by Ernest Gaubert in *Revue universelle*, March 1905.

[2] 'It was nice of you to be so prompt,' Proust wrote in his glowing letter of thanks.

would be an acceptable return for the dedication of '*Ruskin à Notre-Dame d'Amiens*'. 'Never a word, and I still haven't swallowed it,' Proust wrote to Maurice Duplay a year later. He begged Mme de Noailles to ask Abel Hermant, the friend of Constantin de Brancovan, to 'insert ten words in one of his articles', and baited the hook with an invitation for Hermant to dine with his publisher Vallette ('a charming man who knows Henri de Regnier'). Perhaps owing to Proust's unwise quarrel with Constantin, Hermant's tardy compliance in *Gil Blas* on 4 September 1904 was worse than useless: without naming either Proust or his book he maliciously alluded to Mlle Nordlinger in a sentence about 'English gentlewomen who think it their duty to pore over the cornices of St Mark's because these happen to be mentioned by Ruskin.' Proust registered the insult and parodied it for Bloch's vulgar remark about 'drinking sherbet with lovely ladies while pretending to read *The Stones of Venighce* by Lord John Ruskin'.[1] The most satisfying notices, though even these were solicited, came from Proust's cousin-in-law Bergson and the historian Albert Sorel, who showed greater generosity than any of his friends in rallying to the aid of their former pupil. Bergson went so far as to read an official report on the book at the Académie des Sciences Morales on 28 May, remarking that the preface was 'an important contribution to the psychology of Ruskin', and that 'the style is so alive and so original that one would never suspect the work of being a translation'. Sorel gave Proust three whole columns in *Le Temps* on 11 July, including a sentence on his style which, for what it was worth, was perhaps the most penetrating thing said of him before the appearance of *Du Côté de chez Swann*: 'he writes, in moods of revery or meditation, a prose that is flexible, elusive and enveloping, opening on infinite vistas of colours and tones, yet always translucent, reminding one at times of the glass in which Gallé locks away the tendrils and arabesques of his engraving'.[2]

La Bible d'Amiens had originally been designed as a monument

[1] I, 739.
[2] The image drawn from Gallé may well have been suggested to Sorel by Proust himself. Proust shared Montesquiou's regard for Gallé's work and his son's, which he commissioned on several occasions for presents to friends, and twice mentioned with approval in *A la Recherche* (I, 803; II, 392). Proust's gratitude, by a characteristic transition, turned to admiration, and he referred in the preface to *Sésame et les Lys* to Sorel's article as 'perhaps the most powerful pages he has ever written'.

to Proust's voluntary and purposeful surrender to Ruskin, and dates from a period which had ended nearly two years before the publication of the volume. Most of the preface, as we have seen, was written between the summers of 1899 and 1900; the translation was finished in 1901, and the footnotes were added in the spring of 1902. But in the later Postscript to his preface Proust completed the drama by announcing his repudiation of Ruskin; and for the light it throws on the early stages of this liberation and the beginnings of *A la Recherche* his brief afterthought outweighs all the rest.[1]

In his meditation by the shore of Lake Geneva, a real incident of September 1899 which became one of the last-written episodes of *Jean Santeuil*, Proust had penetrated further than ever before into the nature of unconscious memory; but the revelation was premature and incomplete. Unable to advance further by his own power he abandoned his novel and entered, with relief and joy, the promised land of Ruskin, in which the real world is beautiful, and beauty is true and moral. For a time he surrendered completely to Ruskin, or rather to the undiscovered part of himself of which Ruskin first made him conscious. The dead Ruskin was a prophet, a guide, a father: Proust became his disciple, pilgrim and spiritual son. The first signs of a rift in this posthumous relationship came at Venice in May 1900, on the afternoon of thundercloud and storm when Marie Nordlinger read to him from *The Stones of Venice*, in the shelter of Saint Mark's, Ruskin's denunciation of the sins of the Venetians—doubly heinous, said Ruskin, because they were committed in sight of the word of God inscribed in the mosaics of their cathedral. Proust became aware that his union with Ruskin might be one-sided. Whether by a ludicrous coincidence or by a symbolic warning, he stood beneath those very mosaics, while the thunder of a vengeful deity or an angry Ruskin pealed above him; and the dead master denounced him through the young girl's voice for all his sins

---

[1] Possibly, since it continues a train of thought suggested in the last paragraph of the preceding section ('*John Ruskin*', written in the spring of 1900 and first published in the following August), and takes as its text an incident at Venice in May 1900, Proust may have had an inkling even at that early date of the future necessity of the Postscript. The conclusions which it states belong, however, to a period after the completion of the rest of the work; and its writing is firmly dated to May and June 1903 by the publication in the *Revue des Deux Mondes* on 15 June 1903 of Mme de Noailles's poem '*Déchirement*', which appeared, as Proust records, 'almost at the moment when I had finished writing these lines'. (*Pastiches et Mélanges*, p. 195, footnote.)

of sodomy, snobism and sacrilege. For a moment he was tempted to
plead guilty, and Marie Nordlinger saw him overcome by a trance
the opposite of that in which her cousin Reynaldo had found him on
the day of the Bengal roses at Réveillon. However, good sense
prevailed; for sin, in sinful man, is not a forfeiture but a condition of
salvation. He continued and completed his journey through Ruskin;
yet the accusation still rankled, and now in his Postscript he retaliated by accusing his master. He quoted Ruskin's charge against the
Venetians, and described the scene in Saint Mark's, the darkness, the
glowing mosaics and his own tell-tale emotion. But Ruskin, he said,
was mistaken in believing that the sins of Venice were more inexcus-
able because they were committed in the presence of her beautiful
cathedral. In this passage, Proust declared, indeed in the whole of
his life's work, Ruskin was himself guilty of the still more flagrant
sin of idolatry, of worshipping the graven image in preference to the
deity it represented, of pursuing the external beauty of symbols
rather than the truth they conceal. 'The doctrines Ruskin professed
were moral doctrines, not aesthetic, and yet he chose them for their
beauty. And as he wished to present them not as being beautiful, but
as being true, he was forced to lie to himself about the nature of the
reasons which made him adopt them.' Proust proceeded to make the
breach irreconcilable by comparing Ruskin in this respect to the
absurd Montesquiou. He did not venture to name Count Robert,
calling him merely 'one of the most justly celebrated of our contemporaries'; he alleged mendaciously that the sin of idolatry was
to be found 'only in his conversation, not in his books', whereas in
fact it is the fault which vitiates all Montesquiou's works in verse
and prose; and he wreathed the whole so successfully in compliments
that the Count did not take it amiss. 'This incomparable talker,'
Proust instanced, declared a house beautiful because Balzac once
lived in it, thought it a crime to give a passion-flower to a Jew
because its pistils and stamens mimicked the instruments of the
Crucifixion, and went into raptures over the dress of 'a society lady
his friend' (probably Mme Greffulhe) because 'it was in the very
style that the Princesse de Cadignan in Balzac wore when she saw
d'Arthez for the first time'.[1] Here is not only another declaration

---

[1] The same observation is made by M. de Charlus, who shares Montesquiou's
passion for Balzac, on Albertine's grey dress at La Raspelière; but the Narrator,
far from criticising the Baron's remark, silently rebukes Brichot for not appreci-
ating its interest (II, 1054-5).

of independence, another master left behind, but a first step, to be linked with the Saint-Simon parody of the following year, in the transformation of Montesquiou into the comic creation of Charlus.

Proust concludes by explaining that the revelation of Ruskin, through which 'the universe suddenly regained an infinite value in my eyes', is now a thing of the past; he can recall his passion for Ruskin only 'with the memory of facts which tells us "This is what you were," without allowing us to become it again, and assures us of the mere existence of a lost paradise instead of restoring it to us in recollection'. These words, and the whole marvellous passage in which they are embedded, mark a crucial step forward. Proust has now stated the difference between conscious and unconscious memory, and the supreme importance, though he still sees no way of attaining it, of the latter. By explaining the concept of 'idolatry' he has not only freed himself from Ruskin, and from a fault of which he was himself guilty throughout *Jean Santeuil*; he has discovered, though he is not yet aware of it, the theme of his future novel. 'Idolatry', and the casting aside of idolatry which is the only way to salvation, is the very subject of *A la Recherche du Temps Perdu*. The Narrator's vain pursuit of Names of Places and Names of People, of friendship, even of love, is idolatry, a worship of the ephemeral instead of the eternal. Idolatry is Time Lost; the truth behind the locked door of the image is Time Regained; and the key to the door is unconscious memory. *Jean Santeuil* and Ruskin were indispensable blind alleys, explored and left behind; and the way to *A la Recherche*, though long, was now becoming clear.

Copies of *La Bible d'Amiens* were sent to the whole circle of his friends and acquaintances, both sacred and profane, at one extremity to the Abbés Vignot and Hébert, at the other to Mlle de Mornand. Louisa's copy contained a startling inscription which shows, whatever may already have been the freedom of speech customary in their group, that her relations with Proust were taking a new turn. Mornand, he explains, is certainly *not* the present participle of *morner*, 'for this archaic verb had a meaning which I don't exactly remember, except that it was excessively improper.[1] And heaven knows how proper you are! Alas, for those who have had no success

---

[1] The meaning of *morner* (to blunt the point of a lance), if improper at all, is only Freudianly so.

with you—which includes everyone in the world—other women
cease to be attractive. Whence this couplet:

> *He who Louisa cannot win*
> *No refuge has but Onan's sin.'*

In April Mlle de Mornand took steps to save him from this sin.
She gave him two ravishingly pretty photographs of herself, one
signed 'your friend for always', and the other: 'the original, who is
very fond of her little Marcel', and invited him to collect them one
Sunday evening. Louisa was in bed, reading; her white arm, as she
turned the pages, rose like the stem of a lily from the sleeve of her
nightdress; and over her the blue and white canopy of her fourposter
spread like a summer sky striped with cirrus-clouds. As he lay beside
her Proust saw through the open door the crimson wallpaper of the
drawing-room, which seemed, when he looked up again, to turn the
azure bed-curtains green; and when he left, as he pointed out,
Sunday evening had already become Monday morning. Even without the lines which in the published text have been significantly
replaced by rows of dots, the final quatrains of the verses he sent her
in memory of the occasion leave little to the imagination:

> *'Her Sèvres Cupids nothing miss:*
> *Delicious and surprised they view*
> *Two mouths united in a kiss,*
> *Two hearts that are no longer two.*
>
> *The bed is blue, the salon red,*
> *But the azure jewel-case encloses,*
> *While nothing moves, and nought is said,*
> *A pearl whose hue is like a rose's.'*

The message on the photograph, he predicted, 'would have the
power to fix my wandering heart'. But it is unlikely that Mlle de
Mornand had ever heard from other friends in similar circumstances
the image with which he summed up his gratitude. 'I feel, meanwhile,' he said, 'happier than a child that has just been given its first
doll.'

For some time their relationship continued on its new footing.
'Ours was an *amitié amoureuse*,' Mlle de Mornand recalled more than
twenty years later, 'in which there was no element of a banal flirtation
nor of an exclusive liaison, but on Proust's side a strong passion

tinged with affection and desire, and on mine an attachment that was more than comradeship and really touched my heart.' For a year and a half Mlle Nordlinger was not the only girl visitor at 45 Rue de Courcelles. Usually in obedience to a letter or telephone-call, but sometimes inviting herself, Mlle de Mornand came 'so often and so charitably', as he reminded her that July, 'to roast in the suffocating heat of the dining-room, and to bring her ailing little Marcel the consolation of her affectionate smile'. Mme Proust was accustomed to retiring particularly early on the evenings of Louisa's visits, in order to leave the young couple undisturbed; and Marcel went into his mother's room to kiss her goodnight, or listened at her door ostensibly to find whether she was resting comfortably, but no doubt also to make sure that the coast was clear.

His carnal relationship with Louisa was unlikely to last for very long; and its close may be situated towards the July of 1904 when her more serious association with Albufera was in danger, and Proust out of disinterested friendship to them both was doing his best to preserve it. Later allusions in his letters, however, suggest that a limited dalliance continued: in September 1904, for example ('I'm dying to kiss you on both cheeks, and even on the nape of your lovely neck if you'll let me—I'll explain when I see you which part of you I wrote first and then crossed out') or in January 1905, when he makes a daring anatomical pun on the word 'button'. For the suspension of her regular visits which followed the death of his mother in September 1905 there are natural reasons, such as his need for solitude in his grief, his six weeks of confinement in a nursing-home, and Louisa's break with Albufera in the spring of 1906. It is significant, nevertheless, that this intimacy exactly covered the period of his life alone with his widowed mother, except for the first few months, when Mlle Nordlinger filled more platonically the same function. As in other actions of his life Proust was at once proving his mother's love by submitting it to a severe test, and punishing her, with more than a hint of sadism, for a feared or fancied refusal of love. He was arranging for other women, almost before her eyes, to bring him the goodnight kiss she had denied at Auteuil.

In her *amitié amoureuse* with Marcel Mlle de Mornand did not altogether depart from her position as the future original of Rachel-when-from-the-Lord. Proust thought of Louisa when he showed the Narrator astonished by not finding intense pleasure in dining and walking alone with Rachel, or by her seeming 'a mere dust-cloud of

flesh and dress-material', although she had driven Saint-Loup mad
with love.[1] But Mlle de Mornand also has a place among the originals
of Albertine, notably the Albertine who visited the Narrator and
surrendered to his embraces on the foggy evening when he was in
love with Mme de Stermaria; and this is only two pages after a
mention of Rachel's plot to rouse Saint-Loup's jealousy by accusing
the Narrator of 'making furtive attempts to have relations with her
during his absence'.[2] Albertine seems on this occasion to bring the
sea and sunlight of Balbec with her; and Mlle de Mornand was to be
associated a few years later with Trouville and Cabourg, the originals
of Balbec. Proust's silent, immobile love-making with Louisa recalls
the Narrator's with the sleeping Albertine in *La Prisonnière*. '*Louisa
reads herself to sleep*', he had written in his gallant verses on that
night in April,

> '*Lying on her side in bed,*
> *And eyes on book she cannot keep,*
> *But nods and droops her drowsy head*',

and it was in this apparently somnolent state that she had allowed
him to make love to her.

Meanwhile the visits of Mlle Nordlinger continued. Their work
on the proofs of *La Bible d'Amiens* was confined to December 1903
and the second week of February 1904. Early in January they had
already begun the translation of *Sesame and Lilies* for which Proust
signed a contract with the *Mercure de France* in December 1902.[3]
They worked as collaborators. Mlle Nordlinger was to have her
name with Proust's on the title-page and to share the proceeds,
not only from the *Mercure de France* but also from the prior publication of '*Trésors des Rois*' in *Arts de la Vie*, which was arranged with
Gabriel Mourey in May 1904. Proust had translated the beginning
and end of '*Trésors des Rois*' in six exercise-books, leaving blank
or underlining for her advice the phrases he was not sure of understanding. He completed the beginning in January, and had entirely

[1] III, 166, 175.
[2] II, 348.
[3] At first they intended to translate both the first two sections, '*Of Kings'
Treasuries*' and '*Of Queens' Gardens*'. By May 1904, however, they had decided
that the former would suffice, and it was not until February 1905 that Proust
again resolved to add the latter. There was never any question of adding the
third and last section, '*The Mystery of Life*'.

recast it by 7 February; while the end, although he immediately lost the three exercise-books containing it, was finished later in the same month. Mlle Nordlinger's share was the middle, finished late in April and 'turned upside-down', 'with affectionate respect', because he felt her French was too anglicised, by Proust in May. At the end of May he found his lost exercise-books and proceeded to a final revision of the whole, which was no doubt completed in June.

In April Mlle Nordlinger sent the most important of her symbolic gifts, a packet of the Japanese pellets of coloured pith which open, when dropped in a tumbler of water, into exquisite and jewel-like flowers. Proust was then suffering from asthma, and this 'fluviatile and inoffensive spring, these miraculous and hidden flowers' touched him profoundly, amid the desolation of the season he dared not see, with a memory of seasons buried in his childhood. 'Thanks to you,' he wrote, 'my dark electric room has had its Far-Eastern spring'; and he used the Japanese flowers, in the last paragraph of the opening chapter of *Swann*, as a simile for the revelation of unconscious memory, which draws 'all the flowers of Swann's garden, the water-lilies of the Vivonne, the good people of the village and their houses, the church and all Combray and the country round it from my cup of lime tea'.[1]

On 16 April, at the age of eighty, died Comte Thierry de Montesquiou, Count Robert's father and vice-president of the Jockey Club, whom Proust had seen in the street, 'in the days when I was able to go out for walks', and regarded ever after with awe. Like Dr Proust, the fierce old gentleman had viewed a son's eccentricities with mingled contempt, bewilderment and pride: "I didn't do it on purpose," he had sardonically excused himself, when Count Robert reproached him with having 'made me what I am'. He had more than a vestige of his son's wit. "Thank God, they were very light ladies," he said, when run over by two cocottes in a pony-carriage. At the news of his father's operation for stone the year before Count Robert had very decently cancelled a fête in his garden at Neuilly and hurried to his bedside. "I'm sorry to have thrown this stone into your garden," said Count Thierry; whereas Uncle Wladimir de Montesquiou, apprehensively eyeing the very stone in question in its preserving-bottle, remarked simply: "I say, I shall have to be more careful about my health."

[1] I, 47-8.

Ever since her refusal to sympathise in his quarrel with her brother Constantin, Proust had been 'exceedingly but very respectfully annoyed' with Mme de Noailles. On 11 June, however, he received her second novel, *Le Visage émerveillé*, and finished it at the moment before dawn when, looking from his window, he saw a sky still so dimly grey that he could not tell whether the growing light would show it as blue or overcast. His anger vanished in a paroxysm of flattery, which may be defended not so much by his knowledge that for Mme de Noailles, as for Montesquiou, only the topmost pitch of adulation would suffice, as by the fact that her novel had given him a further insight into his own. Through the trellis of her metaphors he glimpsed the landscape, vague and distant, but already bathed in a radiance of joy and familiarity, of *A la Recherche*.

The theme of her novel—it was about a nun falling in love—was no more likely to please him than it gratified her aunt Comtesse Odon de Montesquiou, who exclaimed indignantly: "Why, it's a book against convents!" From the beginning, indeed, her family had shown themselves far from delighted at having a celebrated poetess in their bosom. "So you've written some poetry, countess," the old Marquis de Montsaulnin had remarked, "have you ever thought of making a little volume, just to give to a few of your friends?" But when *Le Cœur Innombrable* appeared her mother-in-law the Duchesse de Noailles burst into tears and sobbed: "Now people will think *I* wrote all that filth!" "She starts quoting Plutarch the moment she comes into the room," complained another relative, "and I can't allow that sort of thing in my house"—an accusation also made by Mme de Gallardon against the Duchesse de Guermantes.[1] Proust cannot have enjoyed the 'daring' theme of Mme de Noailles's novel: he thoroughly approved of the nunneries he had visited at Beaune and in the Netherlands, as manifestations of the aesthetic side of the Church. The cause of 'the ecstasy with which,' he told her, 'every step I have taken in this supernatural landscape has filled me' was her unprecedented attempt to create a whole novel with the fervour and imagery of poetry, to reveal a timeless beauty beneath the momentary surface of the phenomenal world. 'You remove from all things the veil of grey mist which is nothing but the emanation of our own

[1] II, 447. Mme de Gallardon, an ignorant Courvoisier, says 'Aristotle', by mistake for 'Aristophanes'. Mme de Noailles, a Roumanian princess, is 'the young princess from the East' who marries a cousin of Saint-Loup and writes poetry 'as beautiful as Victor Hugo's or Alfred de Vigny's' (II, 107).

mediocrity, and uncover an unknown universe, whose existence we had guessed in our hours of divination, where everything is truth and beauty,' he wrote in words which resemble the Narrator's after the final revelation in *Le Temps Retrouvé*. The phrases he quotes ('on the violet velvet petals [of pansies] is a yellow stain, sleek, alive and glossy, as if a wren's egg had fallen there and broken'—'the light, delicate, green spring-time' and so on) have little intrinsic merit; but he has picked out his own Proustian use of the 'three adjectives'. When he compared her organic unity of colour to a 'spring morning seen from a dining-room with tinted windows and a half-lowered blind, where the garden breezes enter the parlour whose walls are coated with whitewash and sunlight', the discovery of his own method in Mme de Noailles had penetrated to the depths where Aunt Amiot's house at Illiers survived in Time Lost.

The Paris season was over, but the weekly dinners in the country given by Guiche's father Duc Agénor de Gramont were just beginning. His first wife, Princesse Isabelle de Beauvau-Craon, had died bearing his daughter Élisabeth (now Marquise de Clermont-Tonnerre) in 1875; but three years later the impecunious Duc Agénor married Marguerite de Rothschild, the mother of Guiche, and with her untold wealth built the enormous château of Vallières at Mortefontaine. From the three-sided entrance hall the happy visitor could see, far over the trees of the forest of Ermenonville, the spire of Senlis, and to either side the islanded lakes on whose banks Rousseau had wandered. It was the polite thing to say: "You'd think we were in Scotland, yet it's only twenty miles from Paris!" Proust travelled by taxi; and alighting on the hot summer evening of 14 July, wearing top-hat, white tie and tails, he was horrified to find the other guests leaving in tweeds for a pike-fishing expedition on the lake. Guiche had neglected to warn him of the rural protocol of Vallières: diners were expected to arrive in country clothes, with a suitcase containing a mere dinner-jacket. Utterly downcast he advanced to enter his name in the visitors' book, and was encouraged to find that several old acquaintances had just signed in—Comtesse Rosa de FitzJames, the Aimery de La Rochefoucaulds, and the Comte de Cholet, his superior officer at Orleans fifteen years before, who had pretended like Saint-Loup to ignore his salute in the street, but had otherwise been a valued ally. As he hesitated Duc Agénor, recognising one of his son's intellectual friends, remarked with a grin in the words of the Duc de Guermantes on a similar occasion[1]: "Just your name will be sufficient, Monsieur Proust—no need to write a great thought." His evening was ruined, and the sight of thirty fellow-guests at dinner in 'smokings' could hardly add to his despair.

For a few weeks Proust and his friends had been united almost as in bygone years. The Bibesco brothers were still in London at the Roumanian Legation, but Fénelon was back on leave from St Petersburg, and Guiche or Albufera called every day. On the eve of Fénelon's departure Mme Proust allowed Marcel to entertain the group at home, not to dinner, for that would have been a breach of her mourning, but to supper; and soon after the disaster of Vallières there was a dinner with Guiche and the dramatist Tristan Bernard in the Bois de Boulogne. But Proust felt an atmosphere of eternal farewells, for Guiche and Albufera were engaged to be married in the autumn. Guiche's fiancée was none other than Mme Greffulhe's daughter Élaine, and Albufera's—for like Saint-Loup he was to marry a half-Jewish heiress—was Anna, daughter of Prince Victor d'Essling and his wife Paule, born a Furtado-Heine, at whose house in the Rue Jean-Goujon poor Charles Haas had been a constant visitor. "Nothing will be changed, Marcel," protested Albu; but Proust replied: "On the contrary, nothing will ever be the same again." The marriages of Gabriel de La Rochefoucauld and Loche Radziwill were to follow next year. It is a period in Proust's life which is represented in *A la Recherche* by the rumours of impending marriage, not only of Saint-Loup but of the Prince de Foix and his companions, in *Le Côté de Guermantes*.

Albufera might excusably have been on the watch for an opportunity to break with Louisa; but he was more in love than ever, and determined that with her, too, there should be 'nothing changed' by his marriage. Mlle de Mornand was now on holiday at Vichy, whence she allowed disquieting rumours to reach Albu. He called three times on Proust in the week of Vallières to ask his help and advice; and

[1] II, 549. The Duc de Gramont supplied one or two other hints for the Duc de Guermantes. Montesquiou remembered him as a fellow-schoolboy 'with blue eyes and golden, silky hair', in the 1860s at the Jesuit college at Vaugirard; and Basin de Guermantes was just such a boy when at school with his brother Charlus (II, 718; III, 716, 721). The Duc de Guermantes's icy reception of the Bavarian composer M. d'Herweck at the Princesse de Guermantes's soirée (II, 683) was no doubt suggested by Duc Agénor's greeting of the great d'Annunzio a few years later, when he extended two cold fingers of a limp hand and pronounced the words: "Good morning, Monsieur."

Proust duly sent three letters and a telegram to the recalcitrant
Louisa. Before she left Paris, he reproached her, she had 'amused
herself with anchoring Albu in his mistaken ideas'; and he reminded
her how, even as early as the April of 1903, she and Albu had quarrelled in his presence at the Théâtre des Mathurins. Here is the original of the quarrels between Saint-Loup and Rachel in the restaurant
and at the theatre (where, like Louisa at the Mathurins, she has only
a 'walking-on' part), on the day of Mme de Villeparisis's matinée.

When on 17 July Proust dined with Mme de Noailles he thought
again of *Le Visage émerveillé*, but this time with a different aspect
in the foreground. In *La Nouvelle Espérance*, her last year's novel,
the lover of the heroine Sabine had asked: "What do you need to be
happy?"; and Sabine had replied: "Your love, and the possibility of
being loved by everyone else." It is not a modest wish, and its grant-
ing was disastrous. Mme de Noailles was to pursue, like Proust
himself, the changing star of love, ever burning her angelic wings;
but unlike Proust, she could never learn wisdom from suffering, for
she could never reach the hidden depths beneath her vanity. Except
for the saving graces of her ardent love of life, her passionate spon-
taneity, though these only added to the tragedy of her destiny, she
would never be much more, as a poet or person, than a female
counterpart of Montesquiou. Her new novel, Proust knew, was a
roman à clef: the nunnery was a convent school at Évian, its chapel
was that of her mother-in-law's château at Champlâtreux ('you ought
to have a special edition for railway bookstalls,' he told her, 'labelled
Champlâtreux, five minutes' stop'); the enamoured Sister Catherine
was Mme de Noailles herself, and the abbess who persuades her to
give up her lover was the literary hostess, Mme de Noailles's great
friend, Mme Bulteau. But Mme de Noailles did not give up her own
lover, who was none other than Maurice Barrès.

Nothing could have been more unexpected than this illicit union
between the Dreyfusard poetess and the greatest of Dreyfus's
enemies. At the time of Rennes in 1899 Barrès had noted with amusement in his diary the rebuke of Comtesse Jean de Montebello to
Mme de Noailles and her sister Hélène propagandising in her salon:
"Call yourself French! Why, you're a couple of street-urchins from
Byzantium!" Onlookers at their first meeting in the spring of 1903
noted that each of these brilliant people was dazzled by the other:
'they fell madly in friendship at first sight,' said Jacques Émile
Blanche. Their marriage-partners acquiesced: Mme Barrès was

deemed to have taken immensely to Mme de Noailles, and Comte Mathieu was supposed to delight in the company of Barrès. Only the Tharaud brothers, Barrès's secretaries, felt a jealous dislike for Mme de Noailles, which they prudently concealed until after the death of the parties concerned. 'Her body was too long for her legs,' they wrote, 'so that when she stood up she seemed much shorter than when she was sitting down; it was veiled in soft, bright fabrics, so that one was puzzled to know what happened between her tiny feet and her little white neck. . . . When she talked one felt battered by a hail of diamonds; she was an astonishing musical-box which was automatically set in motion the moment there were two or three people to listen.' But the time when Barrès would confess to them: "If only she'd keep quiet I might be able to listen to her!" had not yet come.

Proust had first met Barrès in the summer of 1892, when the tides of Boulangism and Panama were beginning to ebb. Barrès was then a thin, sallow-faced, still-young man of thirty, the nationalist member of the Chamber of Deputies for Nancy, and already a famous writer, commonly known as Prince of the Young. It was in this last capacity that he asked his electoral agent, Léon Yeatman's uncle, to arrange for him to meet some promising young writers; and the guests that evening were accordingly chosen from the group of *Le Banquet*, including Proust, Robert Dreyfus and Gregh. Their reactions to their prince were varied. Gregh, whom Barrès obligingly sent home in his own carriage, was amused and touched (for it was generally felt that Barrès had betrayed literature for politics) to find an open volume of Sainte-Beuve's poems in the side-pocket. Robert Dreyfus wrote for the July *Banquet* a laudatory article on Barrès as a sceptic, in which he attacked the mysticism of Proust's master Paul Desjardins. Proust rebuked him sharply: 'don't you see that Desjardins's faith is a shining light of reason compared with Barrès's scepticism?' As we have seen, the chapter of *Jean Santeuil* which described the first impact on his pupils of M. Beulier (modelled on Proust's revered Darlu) was intended as a counterblast to the opening scene of Barrès's *Les Déracinés*. Proust's uneasy dual attitude to Barrès corresponded to a fundamental division in Barrès himself, between the lyrical individualist and the power-seeking authoritarian. Proust admired the music of Barrès's prose and shared many of his beliefs—his love of France, his support of the persecuted Church as part of the greatness of France, his call to discipline and tradition. Yet by his determination, heroic as it was, to put his doctrines into practice by political action, Barrès was false to his own cause. His art became propaganda, his political faith—horrified as he would have been by the consequences he did not live to see—paved the way for fascism. His unshakeable belief in the guilt of Dreyfus was a symptom that he had come to prefer political expediency to truth and justice.

The rift between Barrès and Proust was not to be bridged by the dinner of 17 July. Proust took the opportunity to clear himself with regard to an anti-Semitic article in *La Libre Parole* during the Affair, in which his name was maliciously included in 'a list of young Jews who abominate Barrès'. "As I couldn't contradict it publicly without saying I wasn't a Jew, which although true would have upset my mother, I thought it useless to say anything," he explained; but it was clear from the expression on Barrès's face that he felt it would have been far from useless. The indomitable young man went on to rebuke the great novelist for a critical reference to Mme de Noailles's Dreyfusism in his glowing review of *Le Visage émerveillé* in *Le Figaro* for 9 July. "You wrote: 'her mistaken belief has been, to use La Fontaine's famous line on the condemnation of Fouquet, that *'misfortune is a kind of innocence'*. But what she really meant was not that misfortune makes a man innocent, but that it's a double misfortune if he's found guilty when he's really innocent!" But Barrès merely gave his abrupt, sardonic laugh, and enquired: "What is the meaning of this sudden explosion of Dreyfusism?" Proust retired in disorder to the fireplace where, beneath a row of Mme de Noailles's favourite Tanagra figurines, he tried to retrieve the evening by a free consultation about his asthma with the young Roumanian doctor Nicolas Vaschide. Vaschide, he decided, was charming, although his medical theories were quite absurd (he took a lady clairvoyant round the hospitals with him to help in his diagnoses), and he was incapable of pronouncing his r's. Proust confided that he had recently visited Dr Merklen, who asserted that his asthma was only a nervous habit, and recommended a stay in Dr Dubois's sanatorium for nervous diseases at Berne: "he'll make you give up the asthma habit, just as they make people give up the morphine habit". Suddenly a crash was heard: Proust had inadvertently toppled over the very best of his hostess's Tanagras. "It's *nelvous*," observed the well-meaning but unhelpful Dr Vaschide. Overwhelmed by the disgrace of his accident Proust avoided Mme de Noailles for over a year; yet she came to treasure the broken figurine even more than its undamaged sisters, and in the exhibition of her relics at the Bibliothèque Nationale in 1953 it appeared as: 'No. 84. Tanagra broken by Marcel Proust.'

On Tuesday, 9 August, when Mme Proust was at Etretat with Robert Proust and her daughter-in-law Marthe, Proust took the train to Le Havre for a cruise on the steam-yacht *Hélène*, owned by Robert de Billy's wife's father, Paul Mirabaud. Proust made himself thoroughly but eccentrically at home in his solitary cabin: he asked for the porthole to be opened, ignited his anti-asthma powders, decided not to undress in the cold sea air, took an ineffective dose of trional, lay sleepless and fully clothed in his bunk till dawn, and finally emerged on the bridge to make the acquaintance of the crew and watch preparations for departure. They steamed along the Normandy coast over a calm, sunlit sea to Ouistreham, where Mme de Billy joined them, pink and charming, in a rowing-boat, and arrived that evening at Cherbourg, 'while a light breeze turned the sapphires of the sea to emeralds and set them in silver'. All day Proust had watched the moving panorama of the seaside resorts of his youth, the Trouville of Marie Finaly, the cliffs of Houlgate, the dunes and Grand Hôtel of Cabourg, from one of those butterfly-white yachts which he had seen and envied many years ago from the shore. The delightful voyage continued; he postponed again and again his secret intention of returning to Paris after the first two days. They lingered on Thursday at Cherbourg, and on Friday sailed by way of Guernsey to Saint-Malo. Three photographs show Proust sitting with Robert and the ladies, beneath a huge awning on the bridge, in the act of talking and gesticulating: he wears a black velvet jacket, a broadbrimmed felt hat, and a gloomy, drooping moustache. M. Mirabaud, 'an enormous Saxon god with blue eyes and flaxen hair', was a martyr to a weak heart, and a patient, like Proust, of Dr Merklen—"he's given me a new lease of life," the old man boasted. They compared notes on one another's ailments, and Proust impressed Billy by giving expert advice; but his keenest conversational pleasure was with the sailors, whom he cross-examined on their mysterious way of life and who, as Billy remembered, 'regretted his sudden departure as much as any of us'. For Proust decided on Saturday to leave next evening. He slept all day on Sunday, took the night train to Paris, and there slept again till Monday evening. The vicious circle of his upside-down life had begun again.

On 16 August, the day after his return, his article '*La Mort des*

Cathédrales' appeared in *Le Figaro*. The Combist movement for the separation of Church and State was now in full career, and the anticlerical Aristide Briand had proposed that, after the withdrawal of state subsidies from the Church, any cathedrals which proved uneconomic to maintain should be secularised and used as museums. Proust pointed out that the cathedrals, 'probably the noblest but indisputably the most original expression of the genius of France', owed their life to the continuance in them of divine worship. To withdraw this would be to kill them, to leave France 'a dry beach strewn with giant chiselled sea-shells, empty of the life which once inhabited them'. 'A performance of Wagner at Bayreuth,' he wrote, 'is a trivial thing compared with the celebration of high mass in Chartres Cathedral.' A Catholic admirer of Proust might regret that he supported the Church for its aesthetic and moral beauty, and wish him more than an *anima naturaliter Christiana*. On the other hand, if Proust had been a full believer he could never have written *A la Recherche*, which is an attempt to find salvation unaided, without the ready-made consolations of religion. But it would be erroneous to explain the limited nature of his Catholic sympathies by his half-Jewish birth: indeed, Proust was in the curious position of defending the Church against his anticlerical Aryan friends. '*La Mort des Cathédrales*' was a sequel to his heated discussion with Lauris and Fénelon in July 1903, and employed the same arguments, often the same words. As then, a memory of Illiers came to the surface: this time it was the way to Méréglise, 'between sainfoin fields and apple orchards, where at almost every step you see a spire soaring on the clear or stormy horizon, transfixing on days of rain and shine a rainbow which, like a mystic aureole reflected from the interior of the church, juxtaposes its rich, distinct, stained-glass colours on the neighbouring sky'.

Towards the middle of September it was agreed that Mme Proust should go on holiday to Trouville, Dieppe or Évian, and be joined later by Marcel. Rarely had his nervous inability to choose been so tormenting; each place had unique advantages—Dieppe would be convenient for Rouen Cathedral, Mme Straus and Charles Ephrussi would provide company at Trouville, at Évian he would feel most at home—and prohibitive disadvantages. He looked further, to Basle, Quimper, Caen, Chamonix (which Albu said was dry, while Billy maintained it was damp), even to Biskra in Algeria. On the 20th Mme Proust cut this Gordian knot by going alone to Dieppe, where

she battled for the last time with seaside wind and cold, still thinking
of her dead mother's delight in bad weather, and waited in vain for
Marcel. He had resolved to stay at home for a final effort to change
his hours by the only possible method: to stay awake for twenty-four
hours, and then go to bed half a day late. By a superhuman effort he
succeeded in rising at 9 a.m.; but the following night he could not
sleep for worrying about Dr Dubois and his sanatorium, the next
day he got up at 4 p.m., the next at 7 p.m. He had by now acquired a
dread, which would be lifelong, of seeing the light of day in times of
illness and unhappiness: 'If I'm to stay indoors and be ill, it's all one
to me at night, because I'm used to it, but in broad daylight, all alone,
and seeing the sunshine outside, it would be too nostalgic.' To avoid
the accusing eye of the sun he continued to rise at sunset. His letters
to his mother on his health had never been so anguished and interminable; but the good lady's replies were as sensible and reassuring
as ever. Her only note of alarm was when, at a moment of 'inexpres-
sible indisposition, despair, inability to move, incredible pulse', he
refused to see his barber, François Maigre (who, like Swann's,[1] was
accustomed to call at the house): 'no more of this looking like a
Frankish king,' she wrote almost sharply, "your hair gets in my eyes
when I think of you!'

Mlle Nordlinger had now almost completed a bronze portrait-
plaque of Dr Proust for his grave at Père Lachaise, which Proust
had persuaded his mother to commission in May, partly in the hope
of persuading his friend and helper to remain in Paris. She had called
with the first model on 8 August, when Proust had been confined to
bed by fever: 'I'll get up for five minutes to shake hands with you,'
he promised, 'and Mother will see you back to Auteuil.' On the
22nd, rather self-consciously, he had visited her for the second
view, without chaperone, in her summer home at Auteuil, 'where
the wasp wanders from rose to rose, drunk with its own mad flight,'
he wrote, confusing his hymenoptera. Then, soon after his mother's
departure for Dieppe, Proust invited Marie to call for a third discussion of the plaque. 'Your idea that your visit would be "improper"
in Mother's absence is perfectly enchanting, and made me laugh a
good deal,' he wrote on 24 September; 'if you were the young man
and I the girl there might be some sense in it—but even so, I managed
to see you alone at Auteuil!' In this situation is visible, as if at a
great distance, the absence of the Narrator's mother at Combray, and

[1] I, 380-1.

the arrival in his home of Albertine. But the year of 'visits from Albertine' was in its decline. On 24 October Mlle Nordlinger left for the United States to organise exhibitions of Japanese prints for her employer Siegfried Bing. Strangely enough, neither Mme Proust nor Marcel were satisfied with the portrait-plaque, though they duly installed it on 25 November, the day before the anniversary of Dr Proust's death, and even the artist herself shared their displeasure. In counterpoint to Lecomte du Nouy, who had painted the Doctor in 1882 as a keen-eyed, affable Holbein, she made him a Pisanello medallion in bronze. To the modern visitor on that utmost height of Père Lachaise, where the four Prousts, mother, father and sons, await the last regaining of Time, she seems to have caught, as successfully as her predecessor, the noble, energetic, Renaissance aspect of Adrien Proust; the handsome, unaged Doctor gazes for ever over the Biblical city of Paris, meditating simultaneously, as in life, on measures for halting a plague and on the portents of tomorrow's weather.

During that autumn Proust conducted a mild flirtation with *Le Figaro's* rival *Gil Blas*, the new daily newspaper owned by Paul Ollendorff, who two years before had failed to publish *La Bible d'Amiens*. On 9 September he tried to persuade Antoine Bibesco to write a publicity-notice in *Gil Blas* for Louisa de Mornand, who began a season at the Vaudeville on 16 September. 'What's needed is something utterly stupid, like "remember this name, it's ripe for stardom", or "the girl's mad about acting, she gives it all she's got" —I think you'd do it marvellously!' But Antoine failed to be moved by this testimonial, and Proust was forced to write the notice himself, and another early in December. He also contributed to the *Gil Blas* of 14 December a review of Fernand Gregh's *Études sur Victor Hugo* over the pseudonym 'Marc Antoine'. His most important contribution to *Gil Blas*, however, was rejected. This was a dialogue, entitled '*Vacances*' and dedicated to Robert de Flers, between a young man representing Proust himself and the ever-recurring Françoise—not the Narrator's servant, but the heroine who had already appeared in *Les Plaisirs et les Jours*, in *Jean Santeuil*, and in the imaginary letters which he had written with Flers for *La Presse* in the autumn of 1899,[1] and who was to become both Swann's Odette

---

[1] These letters, of which the first and third were written by Proust in the character of Bernard d'Algouvres, a society-man, and the second by Flers as his mistress Françoise de Breyves (already the heroine of '*Mélancolique villégiature*

and the Narrator's Albertine in *A la Recherche*. The young man is recovering from an unhappy love-affair, and debates with Françoise, on a September evening during a dinner on the island in the Bois de Boulogne, the possibility of consoling himself in her arms.'*Vacances*', in fact, is a primitive draft of the episode in which the Narrator, on a windy day in the same month of September, visits the island in the Bois, on which he hopes to dine to-morrow with Mme de Stermaria, with Albertine, then a poor second-best.[1]

The first night of Antoine Bibesco's *Le Jaloux* at the Théâtre Marigny[2] on 8 October clashed with the signing of Albufera's marriage-contract, which took place at the mansion of the bride's aunt's husband, Prince Joachim Murat, in the Rue de Monceau opposite Mme Lemaire's. This was the customary occasion for viewing the wedding-presents, prominent among which was Proust's own gift, a column discovered by Mme Proust at Bourcelet's antique-shop and converted into a lampstand. "Although the Murats' is the most magnificent private house in Paris, people will mistake our present for part of the furniture," declared her admiring son. The wedding was celebrated on the 11th; Albu and his bride left for the Bay of Naples; and poor Louisa, enjoying her first real success in Henri Bataille's *Maman Colibri* at the Vaudeville, wrote: 'my head is hard at work, but my heart is suffering.'

The noble fellowship of Proust's friends was dispersing. On 14

[1] II, 386-94.
[2] For two parodies of *Le Figaro's* dramatic criticism written by Proust on this occasion see *Lettres à Bibesco*, pp. 160-6.

---

de Madame de Breyves' in *Les Plaisirs et les Jours*), appeared on 19, 20 September and 12 October 1899 in the newspaper *La Presse*, of which their friend Léon Bailby was the editor. Proust introduced themes repeated from *Jean Santeuil* and reappearing in *A la Recherche*, such as the buzzing of flies suggesting a summer day, the colouring of cream cheese with strawberries, seagulls, jealousy, etc. The idea was a resurrection of a letter-novel planned in 1893 by Fernand Gregh, Daniel Halévy, Louis de La Salle and Proust, in which Gregh played the poet, Halévy the Abbé, La Salle the lover, and Proust himself the lady. No sinister interpretation need be given to any of these minor pieces, for the letter-novel written in collaboration is a recognised form in French literature, and someone, after all, has to write in the character of the heroine. If Flers had anything incriminating on his conscience, he would hardly have collaborated in the *La Presse* letters or accepted the dedication of '*Vacances*'. Nevertheless, in these two last pieces there may well be some connection with Proust's platonic friendship with Flers in 1893, however innocent.

November Guiche married Comtesse Greffulhe's twenty-two-year-old daughter Élaine at the Church of the Madeleine. Her mother was still in the full glory of her beauty; and as the bridal procession descended the steps Élisabeth de Clermont-Tonnerre heard a woman of the people say: "Lord strike me, you'd never believe she was the mother!" Guiche, wrote a reporter, was 'pale, with a gentle smile'—"it's the first time I've known you either pale or gentle," commented Proust, who made his way through the mob of guests to Mme Greffulhe and remarked: "it's my candid opinion that Guiche married your daughter (among other reasons, I quite admit) in the hope of getting your photograph!" The delighted comtesse gave her famous silvery laugh, 'so prettily that I felt tempted to say it ten times over,' and proudly repeated her daughter's latest verses in praise of her beauty. Élaine Greffulhe was a poet, and at the age of five and a half had published remarkable prose-lyrics for which her uncle Montesquiou had written a preface. When Proust asked Guiche what he would like for a wedding-present he jestingly replied: "I think I have everything, except a revolver." Proust took him at his word and gave him the grisly weapon, bought from the best gunsmith in Paris, Gastinne-Renette. It nestled, like a steel jewel, in a leather case painted in gouache by Coco de Madrazo with scenes and words from the bride's childhood poems, with seagulls (*'No more we'll drink the water of the sea, Because our tears have fallen in its waves'*), white ships and mountain-tops (*'The mountains seem like flowers to the ships, The peaks mistake the ships for fountains'*), and a flaming tiger (*' "Why don't people like you any more?" "Because I always eat them at the end of my stories." "Then don't tell me any stories." '*) Proust envied the happiness of the lovers, on honeymoon in the Forest of Fontainebleau at one of the bride's father's châteaux, all the more because the weather had turned bitterly cold. 'Cold weather is the most poignant of all backgrounds for happiness,' he wrote to Guiche, thinking perhaps of Marie de Benardaky and the snow in the Champs-Élysées; 'happiness that's numbed with cold, hunching its shoulders, shrinking back into its core, is for me the intensest of all.'

For Proust there was only the pilgrimage to Père Lachaise on the eve of the year's end of his father's death; and when, on the 28th, the anniversary of his funeral, he asked Mlle de Mornand to visit him 'at a quarter past midnight—I shan't tell Mother I've asked you, so that she'll think you've called on the spur of the moment', it was at her own urgent request, no doubt to talk about Albufera. He was tempted to spend Christmas Eve with the Greghs; but the fog was too thick, and he stayed at home imagining 'the lights of your house through the mist, like a crêche in the darkness'. He had the momentary presence of Fénelon, again on leave, to console him. Next Christmas Day, still more alone, he would be in a nursing-home weeping for his mother's death.

Chapter 2

DEATH OF A MOTHER
(*January – December 1905*)

IT was 1905, and Proust had entered unawares on the last year of
Time Lost. His friends were dispersed by marriage or the diplomatic service, and even Marie Nordlinger was three thousand miles
away in Detroit. He took refuge in work and illness. In principle
he had now accepted the unanimous advice of his doctors ('every
time I visit one the effort costs me several weeks in bed'), that only
a prolonged stay in a sanatorium would enable him to live a normal
life again; but he postponed the evil day, first until April, when his
hay fever would be due, then until autumn, when it would have
departed. All through January he kept to his bed, enjoying the first
fifteen volumes of the Library Edition of Ruskin, a New Year's gift
from Mme Proust; and early in February he began to translate '*Of
Queens' Gardens*', the second part of *Sesame and Lilies*, which a
year before he had decided to omit. Mlle Nordlinger was 'intensely
happy', he was wryly gratified to learn, and had made friends with
the railway-waggon millionaire Charles L. Freer, whose Whistler
collection was the finest in the world.[1] Proust had now banished
from his bedroom the aesthetic souvenirs of beauty of which Ruskin
would have approved, including even his photograph of the Gilded
Virgin of Amiens: 'tell your friend,' he wrote, 'that my room contains
in its intentional nudity only a single reproduction of a work of art—
Whistler's *Carlyle*, whose cloak is as serpentine in its folds as the
gown of Whistler's *Mother*.' He meditated on Ruskin's great
antagonist, of whom he had heard so much from Montesquiou and
Lucien Daudet, but whom he had met only once, on that evening at
Mme Laurent's 'when I made him say a few nice things about Ruskin, and appropriated his elegant grey gloves, which I've lost since'.
Was the opposition between Whistler and Ruskin, Elstir and Bergotte, quite irreconcilable? 'Whistler is right', he concluded, 'when

[1] Mlle Nordlinger had first met Freer in Paris a year before, when he visited
her employer Siegfried Bing.

he says in *Ten O'clock* that Art is distinct from morality; and yet
Ruskin, too, utters a truth, though on a different level, when he says
that all great art is a form of morality.'

On 9 February 1905 Gabriel de La Rochefoucauld married Odile
de Richelieu, an heiress of half-noble, half-Jewish birth.[1] Comte
Gabriel was no exception to the curious trick of destiny which made
so many of Proust's aristocratic friends foreshadow Saint-Loup's
unhappy love-affair, sojourn in the East, and semi-Jewish marriage.
During the year before Gabriel had been in love with a married
woman, and when in August to cure the pangs of jealousy he abandoned her for a trip to Constantinople with the novelist Loti, the
unfortunate lady committed suicide. 'Here is a secret that no one in
the world must know,' Proust wrote on 21 September 1904 to his
mother at Dieppe, 'it was for Gabriel de La Rochefoucauld that
Mme X killed herself.' Much to the indignation of both Proust and
Gabriel it was rumoured that Proust had helped him in his novel
about this tragic affair, *L'Amant et le Médecin*, which appeared in
1905 and scandalised the whole Faubourg Saint-Germain.[2]

In mid-February Proust refused an invitation from the Marquise
de Ludre, explaining that he was about to leave for Dr Dubois's
sanatorium at Berne. Instead, as a farewell to society, but also, he
confessed, by way of displaying his sanity to people who might
otherwise hint that he was being put away in a lunatic asylum, he
decided to give one last party. The 'grand dinners' of the past were
still forbidden in their house of mourning, but Mme Proust reluctantly consented to an afternoon-tea, which she did not honour with
her own presence, at 4 p.m. on 6 March. It was the last and not the
least brilliant of all such gatherings at 45 Rue de Courcelles. 'There
will be extremely few people,' he had reassured Mme Straus; but
these 'extremely few' included the Chevignés, the Ludres, Mme
Lemaire, Mme 'Cloton' Legrand (original of Mme de Villeparisis's

---

[1] Her mother was Alice Heine (1858-1925), who after the death of her husband Duc Armand de Richelieu (1847-80) married Prince Albert of Monaco in
1889, separated from him in 1902, and become one of the originals of the Princesse de Luxembourg in *A la Recherche*.

[2] There is no trace in this facile but workmanlike novel of Proust's influence
as a writer, still less of his actual hand. Proust himself, however, is introduced
rather unfavourably as one of the minor characters, the imaginary invalid Larti,
who has no use for women, quotes Schopenhauer, is about to visit Holland
with his great friend Hermois, and says: "It's no use hoping to get happiness
from love !"

enemy Mme Leroi), Guiche, Albufera and Gabriel de La Rochefoucauld with their mothers and young wives, Proust's adored
Princesse Hélène de Chimay, the Comtesses de Briey and d'Haussonville, and a dozen more. Reynaldo and the Comtesse de Guerne[1]
sang duets, and Proust took the opportunity to cross-examine Loche
Radziwill concerning a press-notice on Louisa de Mornand in the
Écho de Paris which Loche had promised to arrange. But when the
guests were gone and the candles out, while Proust wrote the report
of his party for next day's *Figaro*, choking in a fit of asthma, he
thought with remorse of the dreadful brawl among the servants
which the preparations for his party had caused the day before:
Lucien Henraux had intervened to save the life of Proust's 'faithful
Marie', their cook, who had left on the spot.[2] Worse followed, for
Montesquiou, like the wicked fairy Carabosse, unexpectedly had
wind of the party just in time to learn that he had not been invited.
Proust returned from the *Figaro* office after midnight to find a
scathing letter from Artagnan at his bedside. It was as if he welcomed
the campaign of nagging and reprisal which was to last all that
summer: Marcel mingled unpardonable impertinences with his
apologies, referring to 'that young and charming Clermont-
Tonnerre couple, who couldn't come', and to Montesquiou himself
as 'a fat, pink turbot, whom I might have served up to my guests,
but now can only watch receding behind the glass of the aquarium of
"Too Late" '. 'Your epithets are ill-chosen,' retorted the injured
Count, 'and serve only to dishonour those you purport to praise;
moreover, you seem unaware that the persons to whom you allude
as a "young couple" have children who will shortly be of an age to
partake of Holy Communion.'

Poor Mme Straus had been unable to come to the tea-party.
During the last year or two she had lapsed into a state of vague
neurasthenia from which she was never quite to emerge, and the once
beautiful lady who had so loved society, talk and bright lights was
now condemned intermittently to solitude, silence and darkened
rooms. In April she left for Territet, near Montreux, and was
attended by Dr Widmer, in whose nearby sanatorium called
Valmont Proust had now, for the moment, decided to take his rest-
cure in the autumn. Proust wrote frequently to cheer her with news

[1] Proust thanked her with an eulogistic article on her singing, *La Comtesse
de Guerne*', signed 'Echo', in *Le Figaro* for 7 May 1905.
[2] For a similar catastrophe among the servants of Mme Cottard, cf. I, 597.

and mildly indelicate gossip ('it's not very proper, but then, we're both invalids'). As the guests streamed out from a concert on 27 April he had listened appreciatively to the loud voice of Mme de X (possibly Comtesse Diane de Saint-Paul?), 'who can't open her mouth without saying something unintentionally obscene'. "I don't think any of these pieces quite came off," she bellowed, "so I'm getting Plançon to do it for me—that'll be a real ecstasy! Next Thursday at ten, then—lovers of the noble art who may wish to be present, please note." An eddy of the crowd carried him out of earshot, and when he fought his way back he heard: "say what you like, my dear, Madeleine pays her cook two thousand, but I'd much rather spend it on my tenor. She likes it in her mouth, but I prefer it in my ear. Each to her taste, dear, this is a free country, ain't it?"

He made several half-hearted attempts to see Louisa de Mornand. On 9 March he had not dared, fearing she might be angry at the delay of her press-notice, to take her to a supper-party given by Reynaldo with the music-hall singer Fragson at the Café de l'Univers. Fragson, 'who is charming when you see him at close quarters', sang 'at the top of his voice till half-past three in the morning, when I left with a terrible attack of asthma, after swallowing all the dust and smoke in, so to speak, the Universe!'[1] If, as is possible, Proust and Louisa succeeded in meeting some time in May, this was the final occasion on which their tender relations can have been resumed; but Proust's last allusion to these as a pleasure of the recent past had been on New Year's Day, when Louisa sent him a gold bedside watch with a peacock-blue dial and the motto 'May I only number happy hours'. 'As I contemplated the case, never thinking that such a pretty thing could conceal something prettier still,' he wrote roguishly, 'a certain secret button (no improper suggestion intended!) seemed to invite a gentle pressure; and certainly there never was a button that kept more perfectly its promise of admission to paradise.'

Towards the end of April the second round in Montesquiou's campaign of nagging began. The Count commanded Proust's presence at his lecture 'On Fragments of Hugo's Fin de Satan' at the Théâtre Bour on 21 April, sent Yturri to wake him in the small hours of the afternoon, and wrote an angry letter when, in spite of all his

---

[1] Caricatures in comic papers of the period portray both Fragson and his rival Mayol, whose singing Proust was to admire a few years later, as homosexuals.

menaces, Proust failed to attend: 'your ill health doesn't prevent you from gracing the La Rochefoucauld orangeade,' he complained.[1] Count Robert made fun of Marcel's illegible handwriting, comparing it to the endless cavalcade of insects in the fable of Solomon's interview with Takia, Queen of the Ants, when she paraded her subjects before him. 'After seventy livelong days she announced: "that is all of this species, but there are sixty-nine others to come," whereupon Solomon declared the session closed.' Proust was not amused to find himself playing a mere ant to Montesquiou's Solomon. In return he compared the Count to Jupiter towering over a group of tiny mortals in Gustave Moreau's painting[2]; 'you always take the leading role for yourself,' he grumbled; to which Montes-quiou airily riposted: 'I don't need to *take* the leading role, I already have it!' Early in May, with diabolical generosity, he intimated that since Proust was always too ill to come to his lectures, he would give one in Proust's own home, and allow him a month to round up the guests. After a week of insomnia and much wriggling Proust surrendered, and even showed some enthusiasm for the enormous labours of organising his punishment. The proposed lecture turned into a reading of '*The Handbell*', a savage essay on poor Mme Aubernon from Montesquiou's forthcoming *Professionelles Beautés*, and took place on 2 June in the presence of chosen friends and victims of the deceased lady, including Dr and Mme Pozzi, Mmes Lemaire and Laure Baignères, Albert Flament and Charles Ephrussi. After the function was over Proust stood with Yturri by the street-door bidding goodbye to his guests, while Montesquiou lingered above, still holding forth to those who had not succeeded in escaping. The ailing secretary went upstairs to beg his master to leave, in vain; and when he returned his face was so haggard that Proust could not resist tactlessly exclaiming: "How furious you look!" "No, I'm not furious," Yturri protested with a gentle smile, "I'm only tired." Proust was not to see him again in the land of the living. When even the Count had departed Proust hurried to the offices of *Le Gaulois* and the Paris edition of the *New York Herald* with his account of the evening for next morning's papers, which mendaciously began: 'A few select guests were given the surprise of hearing . . .', and the next two days were spent in a violent fit of asthma.

[1] Hence the ritual orangeade of the Guermantes (II, 31, 513; III, 868).
[2] The Narrator uses the same image of his own father as seen by Mme de Villeparisis (I, 701).

While the genuineness of Proust's ill-health in the first half of 1905 need not be doubted, it is certain that he used it, as so often before and after, for a pretext to ward off the visits of time-wasters like Montesquiou, to excuse his temporary neglect of others of whom he was fond, such as Mme Straus or Louisa, and to free himself for work and solitude. All through his life a period of protracted illness (though it might be as real as it was loudly proclaimed) was generally also a period of absorption in writing. Occasional allusions at this time in letters to less exacting correspondents give a very different picture from the incessant bouts of asthma which kept Count Robert from his door. 'I am leading a blissful life of rest, reading, and studious intimacy with mother,' he told Robert Dreyfus in May. In March, April and May the translation of 'Kings' Treasuries', which he had written from January to June 1904 in collaboration with Marie Nordlinger, appeared in Arts de la Vie. 'I mean this translation to be as faithful as love and pity,' he told the editor Gabriel Mourey. During February and March he translated 'Of Queens' Gardens', with help from Mme Proust, Robert d'Humières, and Ruskin's friend Charles Newton Scott—'the charming old English scholar whom I use as a Mary,' he wrote to the absent Marie Nordlinger. In April, with a renewed burst of energy, he wrote his most important work to date, the prefatory essay to Sésame et les Lys entitled 'Sur la Lecture'.[1]

'My only purpose in this preface', Proust explains, 'is to meditate on the very subject discussed by Ruskin in 'Of Kings' Treasuries', the utility of reading. Hence these pages in which Ruskin is scarcely mentioned constitute, nevertheless, a kind of indirect criticism of his doctrine.' The structure in space and time of the opening pages closely resembles the Combray chapter of Swann. He traverses long-lost Illiers, a boy of twelve again, in the places and hours of a single day's reading, from morning to bedtime, through all the rooms of Aunt Amiot's house to the pond-side and hornbeam spinney of the Pré Catelan. The value of reading in childhood, he suggests, lies not in the book itself (which was only Gautier's Le Capitaine Fracasse) but in the memories unconsciously preserved in it, which are 'so much more precious to our present judgment that, if we happen to turn the same pages today, it is only because they are the sole

[1] It was only in Pastiches et Mélanges (1919) that Proust decided, rather confusingly, to call this essay by the title of his later article in Le Figaro of 20 March 1907, 'Journées de Lecture'.

surviving calendars of vanished days, and in the hope of seeing reflected in them the houses and pools that no longer exist.'[1] Ruskin's doctrine, that reading is valuable because it is 'a conversation with men far wiser and more interesting than those we have the opportunity to meet in everyday life', is in Proust's opinion unsatisfactory, because the difference between a book and a friend is not that the one is wiser than the other, but that in reading we retain the mental power which is peculiar to solitude and is dissipated by conversation. Even so, a book can never tell us what we wish to know, but only rouse in us the desire for knowledge; for 'we cannot receive truth from anyone, but must create it for ourselves', and 'reading is on the threshold of spiritual life: it can lead us in, but does not constitute that life in itself'. In special cases, Proust admits, reading still has its uses. It serves a mind paralysed by idleness or frivolous pleasures as a stimulus to enable it 'to descend spontaneously into its own depths, where the life of the spirit begins'. Another amenity of reading is that one may be encouraged, like Sainte-Beuve pursuing his researches on Port-Royal as far as Utrecht, to travel in quest of a rare book— and here Proust interpolates a magical impression of his own two visits to Holland; and finally, a book may be of value because, like the twin columns in the Piazzetta at Venice, it involuntarily preserves in the present a living fragment of a historic past.

Can this be all that Proust has to say in praise of reading? The beauty and brilliance of his essay have generally distracted attention from its curious bias. Ruskin had written *Sesame and Lilies* as an eulogy of reading: Proust's intention is to warn against its dangers, and '*Sur la Lecture*' is in fact an essay *against* reading. Supposing he had read at Illiers, instead of *Le Capitaine Fracasse*, a masterpiece of a great writer, would his response still have been adequate if he had valued the book only for its power to secrete an unconscious memory of the rooms and gardens in which he read it? A great book is an ocean, but Proust is determined to prove that it is only a diving-board. He does not hint at the true essence of reading, which is surely identical with the purpose of the writer: the communication of the state of vision in which the book was written, so that the writer's revelation becomes the reader's. Such was Proust's own aim in writing *A la Recherche*; and he did not intend his great novel merely to enable his readers to store up unconscious memories of the places

[1] The house is Louis Weil's at Auteuil, demolished in the late 1890s and the pool is that of the Pré Catelan at Illiers, already silted and dry.

in which they read it, nor even to goad idle minds into rejecting the book and thinking for themselves.

'*Sur la Lecture*' is far from representing Proust's normal opinion of the nature of reading: his earlier and later critical essays show that he was supremely able to hold his own vision of truth in abeyance in order to share a great writer's total experience. His preface offers, in fact, neither a general theory of reading nor the record of a permanent personal attitude. Instead, it marks a temporary but deeply motivated revulsion from the act of which it ironically pretends to be a panegyric; and its real meaning only emerges when it is seen as the private and cryptic expression of Proust's approach to literature at one particular period—the spring of 1905—and at no other.

For five and a half years, ever since he abandoned *Jean Santeuil* in the autumn of 1899, Proust had surrendered himself to the most arduous and self-abnegatory of all forms of reading: the translation and interpretation of an admired author. His faithful service to Ruskin was undertaken partly in order to enable him to write a better novel, partly as a punishment for having written a bad one; but now his penance was over, and it was time, he tried to believe, for his reward. Reading was no longer a moral duty, nor a spiritual pleasure, but a snare. 'It becomes dangerous', he warned, 'when we tend to make it a substitute for, rather than an incitement to the personal life of our mind, when truth no longer seems an ideal to be attained only by the inner progress of our thought and the effort of our heart, but a material object deposited between the leaves of books, like honey readymade by others.' The 'personal life of his mind', which he had relinquished but never forgotten during his years of bondage to Ruskin, lay in the writing of the ideal novel of which *Jean Santeuil* had been only the shadow on the walls of the Platonic cave. The secret meaning of '*Sur la Lecture*' is that Proust declares his emancipation not only from Ruskin but from all other authors, and resolves once more to write his novel.

'*Sur la Lecture*' is not only a record of the mental processes by which Proust liberated himself from Ruskin and prepared to resume his novel. It is also, in the narrative digression with which it opens, a preliminary trial for the subject, method and style of the novel itself. Proust had not yet formulated his theory of Time Regained in its mature and final form; yet, by a significant accident, he now found himself for the first time resurrecting Illiers, by means of the unconscious memories latent in *Le Capitaine Fracasse*, from the remote and buried past which he would afterwards call *le Temps Perdu*. Étreuilles in *Jean Santeuil* was Illiers seen directly, still clearly visible and available in the recent past; but in '*Sur la Lecture*' the village lost and found is already recognisable as Combray. More-over, Proust's style has achieved a fundamental advance. The note of *A la Recherche* had already been audible in the Rheims, Amiens and Venice episodes of the *Bible d'Amiens* preface, or indeed, more distantly and by rare snatches, in almost everything he had ever written, from *Jean Santeuil* back to his seventeen-year-old essay in the *Revue Lilas* at Condorcet; but in '*Sur la Lecture*' the full orchestra of his mature prose is used and sustained. The authority and power of the final revelation were still to come; but there is a fore-taste of these in his sense that he is at last saying something of supreme importance, that he is at last on the verge of his inheritance. His feeling of imminent victory was premature, but none the less prophetic.

'*Sur la Lecture*' appeared, as Proust had arranged with Constantin de Brancovan in mid-April, in the *Renaissance Latine* of 15 June. By a fortunate chance Mme de Noailles's third and last novel, *La Domination*, was published on the 9th; and Proust had time to send three letters of frenzied eulogy which on this occasion at least had an ulterior motive. Sure enough, the poetess returned the compli-ment with high praise of '*Sur la Lecture*'; and better still, on 19 June in *Le Figaro* came a favourable review by the influential critic André Beaunier, a friend of the Brancovan group, which, Proust told Mme de Noailles, 'I feel positive you must have dictated.' This indeed was almost the case, for Mme de Noailles had informed him: 'we read your essay with Beaunier yesterday evening', and he recognised in Beaunier's review the very phrases of his benefactress's letter. Proust himself wrote modestly to her of '*Sur la Lecture*': 'it's a kind of indigestible nougat, which has a bit of everything and sticks in your teeth'; and to Mme Straus, just back from Switzerland, 'don't read it, it has sentences a mile long which Dr Widmer would particularly forbid you'. But to trusted comrades he allowed some-thing of his justified satisfaction to appear: 'if you didn't know I'd written it, I believe you'd think it quite original and well thought-out', he told Lauris, who had helped him with friendly advice during the process of composition.

Meanwhile, in the first week of June, Marie Nordlinger arrived from the United States on a flying visit to Paris. Her post at the Art

Nouveau workshops no longer existed: the establishment had closed
during her absence, and her employer Siegfried Bing, once the friend
of Goncourt and Whistler, was a dying man. When she called at 45
Rue de Courcelles for a last consultation on *Sésame et les Lys* she
found Proust in bed, with his pallid face and burning eyes framed
in a formidable black beard. 'His smile had gone, but I heard it still in
his voice,' she recalled forty years after. "Give me a kiss, Marie," he
murmured, "I've thought of you very often. Tell me all that's happened—did you see any beautiful things in America?" But there was
time for nothing but Ruskin, and they worked on the manuscript
until dawn. Marie Nordlinger was to see her friend only once more,
in 1908, an occasion of which we have no record. 'You arrived in
Paris like a Messiah, and left like a demon,' he wrote reproachfully.

On 15 June he visited the Whistler exhibition at the École des
Beaux-Arts, and was impressed to find that so many of the finest
paintings were the property of Mlle Nordlinger's millionaire friend
Charles L. Freer. The experience had another personal aspect: there
were landscapes of 'Venice in turquoise, Holland in topaz, Brittany
in opal'[1]; and it was as if he saw paintings by Elstir of the places he
would never see again. He packed his mother off to see the exhibition
with a long list of everything she must not miss seeing, and subsided
for three days into 'a terrible and indescribable state' of agitation
and asthma. Another lost friend, whom Proust was only seldom to see
again, was in Paris at the same time as Mlle Nordlinger; but to
Bertrand de Fénelon Proust sent merely an icy 'kind regards'
(*amitiés*) through Georges de Lauris.

Louisa de Mornand, still unhappy and ill from her year's parting
with Albufera, had finished a season in Marcel Prévost's *Les Demi-
Vierges* at the Vaudeville on 13 June. Her decision to spend the
summer recess with her mother and sister at the Villa Saint-Jean near
Trouville revived old memories in Proust. He wrote Louisa a series
of letters recommending the places she must visit; and this evocation
of the seacliffs of his youth and the summer of Marie Finaly encouraged the train of thought which led two years later to his decision to
revisit Cabourg, and in this summer of 1905 to his first abortive
work on a novel which introduced those same scenes. The places he
described to Louisa were those of his wagonette-drives in 1892 with
Mme Finaly and her family, from Les Frémonts over the high ground

---

[1] This last picture, Whistler's *La Plage d'Opale*, is recalled in *Du Côté de chez
Swann* when Legrandin says that the Opal Bay is near Balbec (I, 138).

between Trouville and Honfleur, which became in *A l'Ombre* the Narrator's excursions in Mme de Villeparisis's carriage. 'If you visit the humble little church of Cricquebœuf, smothered in its ivy,' he told Louisa, 'give it an affectionate message from me; and say the same to a certain old peartree, broken-backed but untiring, like an aged servant, which holds up with all the strength of its gnarled but still green branches a tiny cottage, in whose only window smile the pretty faces of a group of girls; although,' he added ruefully, 'perhaps they are no longer pretty nor even girls, for all this was a long time ago.' Similarly, on the day of the trip to the ivy-covered church of Carqueville, just before the vision of the three trees near Hudimesnil, the Narrator is attracted by the village girls on the bridge.[1] The valley 'changed by moonlight into an opalescent lake', which he believes Louisa can see from her villa, is one of the 'three views' of Les Frémonts and of La Raspelière[2]; and Proust now recalled the night when he had walked back from Honfleur with Marie Finaly, with her arm round his neck to shield him with her cloak: 'at every step we stumbled into a pool of moonlight,' he told Louisa, without revealing that his companion had been a girl, 'and the valley seemed an endless lake'. Les Creuniers, where Louisa must not fail to walk, because 'all one's sorrows from there seem as small as the absurdly tiny people one sees far below on the sands', is the cliff of the same name near Balbec, which in Elstir's painting resembles a pink cathedral, and to which Andrée takes the Narrator on the day of the game of ferret.[3] As he wrote he saw Marie Finaly's green eyes again, and quoted to Louisa the poem of Baudelaire which he had sung that summer thirteen years ago: '*J'aime de vos longs yeux la lumière verdâtre*'.

On 24 June Proust entertained a party of friends in his bedroom, a rare event since his father's death and his long farewell to friendship. Albufera, Lauris and Robert de Billy were there, but Fénelon, though still on leave, was significantly absent, as was another member of their group. This was the day of Loche Radziwill's marriage-contract. Whatever his inward feelings, Proust had made a creditable display of goodwill in giving his blessing to the marriages of Albu-

[1] I, 715-17.
[2] The Narrator notices it during Cottard's game of écarté with Morel: 'it was almost too dark to see the sea through the windows on the right; but those to the left showed the valley, on which the moonlight had cast a fall of snow' (II, 974).
[3] I, 901, 921-5.

fera, Guiche and Gabriel de La Rochefoucauld; and when, a few
weeks before, Loche Radziwill had announced his intention of
marrying Guiche's nineteen-year-old cousin Claude de Gramont,
he had shown no less altruism in his disapproval. Loche was not in
love, and had no intention of giving up previous entanglements.
"I'm doing it to please my mother," he explained. "You couldn't do
anything more certain to hurt her, sooner or later," Proust retorted,
"and I'm sure your mother is fond enough of you to put her pleasure
in your happiness, and not in your leading a life of self-sacrifice."
For a wedding present he gave Loche a twelfth-century alabaster
figure of Christ, with an appropriate quotation from Ruskin en-
graved on the pedestal: 'You will be happy, but on one condition.'
He sensed some irony in Loche's gift of a tie-pin in the shape of the
Radziwill crest, a hunting-horn: Loche knew perfectly well that tie-
pins were supposed to bring bad luck. "Vigny says that the sound of
the horn is sad in the depths of the wood," Proust remarked, "but
in the depths of my sickbed it sounds sadder still!" His premonition
was soon fulfilled: only a week after his wedding on 27 June Loche
left his wife, and their divorce, pronounced on 17 May 1906, was
perhaps the speediest in the annals of the *Almanach de Gotha*.

The third round of Count Robert's punitive campaign was now
being fought. Twice before, in 1893 and 1899, Proust had both
promised and written an article on his exacting patron, but despite
all his efforts had failed to find a willing editor.[1] On 4 June, as part
of his thanks for the Count's reading from *Professionelles Beautés* on
the 2nd, he had offered to write an essay on the book; and on the
25th he proposed 'for want of a more conspicuous theatre', to place it
in *Arts de la Vie*. But the news which at any other time would have
intensely gratified Count Robert came too late; for the first and last
time in his life he was past caring for the strange discrepancy between
his genius as a poet and its neglect by the critics.

It had generally been assumed that Gabriel d'Yturri, who had now
been Montesquiou's secretary for twenty years, would live to serve
his master for ever. For the past two years, however, his health had
caused some disquiet. "Take care, Yturri," a doctor friend had
warned him, "you have a dreadful smell of rotten apples." But the

[1] A short review of Montesquiou's *Le Pays des aromates* in the *Chronique des
Arts* of 5 January 1901 did not count, as this minor piece (a preface to the
catalogue of an exhibition of perfume-bottles) gave no opportunity for a general
appraisal of Montesquiou's work.

doctor it was who died: "and now he's *feeding* apple-trees," the volatile Yturri would boast, "and I'm still here!"[1] Yturri's smell of apples, which was due to acetone in the breath, is one of the classic symptoms of diabetes, then an obscure and incurable disease; but at first no one was particularly alarmed.

> '*My Yturri, my Gabriel*
> *Often falls ill, always falls well*',

wrote Montesquiou teasingly, and then (for meanness was not among his vices) sent him to spend the winter of 1904-5 in Algeria and Italy. In April Yturri was at Dr Noorden's sanatorium in Frankfort; but hearing of the Count's Good Friday lecture he insisted on returning—'Writing impossible, cured by enthusiasm', he telegraphed—and begged his master not to meet him at the station because, he confessed pathetically, 'I'm ashamed of my ravaged face.' In mid-June, when the icy spring of 1905 changed to a heatwave, poor Yturri began to stifle with the air-hunger which in diabetes marks the beginning of the end. Montesquiou surrendered to him the airiest room in the Pavillon des Muses; and here, on the big rotonda away from the Boulevard Maillot, Yturri received his last visitors, huddled in a silk dressing-gown, wafting the sultry air into his exhausted lungs with a fan, and complaining unjustly to all comers: "Mossou le Connte is leaving me to die like a dog!" Outside Montesquiou would explain to the departing enquirer: "I put my white tie and tails on, and pretend to go out, so that he won't think he's going to die; but he's annoyed if I go out, and still more annoyed if I stay in." On the afternoon of 5 July Yturri uttered his last words to his master. "Thank you for teaching me to understand all these beautiful things," he murmured, gazing at the bric-a-brac around him; then he sank into the final coma and died, watched over by the sleepless Count, at four in the following morning. It was a moment of truth for Montesquiou; for a while his vanity was pierced, and he felt real grief. Élisabeth de Clermont-Tonnerre found him in tears: "whenever I come home I see his little empty cycling-cap, his little empty cap," he sobbed, wringing his hands over his head.

---

[1] This doctor who died was perhaps Proust's own father. Paul Morand reports Proust as telling him in 1917 that Yturri had consulted Dr Proust, who informed Montesquiou: "He's a doomed man, but don't tell him so." "I shall have to tell him," replied the insolent Count, "because I have several messages for him to deliver in the next world."

He visited Yturri's crypt in the Cimetière des Gonards at Versailles daily, seeking comfort in the cool air and scented flowers of the tomb in which one day he would rejoin his friend; until about 10 August he accepted an invitation from the Duchesse de Rohan to recuperate among the pine-trees of her Domaine des Fées, near Bordeaux.

Proust followed the course of Yturri's illness with dismay, and twice sent his mother, willing but sorely distressed by the heat, to the Pavillon des Muses to enquire. He had always liked, as everyone did, the good-hearted, loyal and amusing Yturri; and now it seemed that something of his own life, as well as so much of the Count's, had vanished with him for ever. 'Those simple, every-day gestures of admiration on his part, of trust on yours,' he wrote to Montesquiou, 'are becoming for me, in the far-away, Giottoesque, golden glow in which they lie, almost sacred memories.' 'I know better than anyone else in the world what he means to you,' he wrote again, significantly. Nine years later Proust himself would be overwhelmed by a similar disaster. Meanwhile he rallied to the Count with letters of consolation, to which Montesquiou replied with poignant, unwonted simplicity; and he set to work in the second week of July on his essay for *Arts de la Vie*, which he called (in allusion to its subject, *Professionnelles Beautés*) '*A Professor of Beauty*'.

On 25 July came another death, that of the dear, kind Duchesse de Gramont, *née* Marguerite de Rothschild, Guiche's mother, who in 1893 with her sister Berthe, Princesse de Wagram, had been one of Proust's first hostesses in the Faubourg Saint-Germain.[1] He rose from his sickbed on the 28th to attend her funeral at Saint-Pierre-de-Chaillot, and there met Mme de Noailles, whom he had not seen since Guiche's wedding. She was present as a member of the family,[2] and with her was her mother, the excitable Princesse Rachel de Brancovan, who shocked him by beginning an acrimonious theological argument at the very foot of the altar. The Duchesse de Gramont was a converted Jewess and therefore, declared Princesse Rachel, was by no means certain of going to heaven. Proust went on to visit Dr Brissaud, 'our dear *Médecin malgré lui*', who insisted, like

[1] It was from one of her guests, Comte Léon de Tinseau, 'a sham literary man who was a perfect oaf,' that Proust borrowed the monocle of General de Froberville at Mme de Saint-Euverte's soirée.
[2] Her husband's brother Hélie de Noailles was married to the Duchesse's daughter Corisande.

Professor E, who was modelled on him, on talking literature, but at last deigned to recommend the sanatorium of Dr Sollier; and then he returned to bed with agonised thoughts of the poor Duchesse de Gramont. She shared the doubts of Princesse Rachel, and had died in the conviction that she would not be allowed to meet her beloved daughter Corisande in the next world. This was all too nearly the position between Proust himself, a baptised Catholic, and his mother, still Jewish; and it only made matters worse that neither he nor she believed in a life after death.

It was probably at this time that he held two conversations with Mme Proust which the Narrator has with his grandmother.[1] In the first she asked what he would do if she 'went away for a long time—perhaps for ever?', and he replied, hiding his emotion: "You know what a creature of habit I am. When I'm separated from people I love, I'm unhappy for the first few days—then I grow used to it, I organise my life differently, and I could bear it for months, years, for always." For they had no need, as he remarked in *Contre Sainte-Beuve*, to prove that each loved the other more than anything else in the world: on the contrary, they needed to pretend they were less fond of one another than appearances might suggest, and that whichever might survive the other would be able to go on living. A little later he remarked casually that the latest discoveries of science seemed to proclaim 'the bankruptcy of materialism', and to show that souls were immortal after all, and would be reunited after death. The fact remained, however, that she had asked his permission to die, and he, perforce, had given it.

In Proust's letters of late July and early August 1905 he mentions several times that he is 'working'; and then, for four weeks, there is one of the total gaps in his correspondence which tend to occur when he is absorbed in writing.[2] Veiled hints in his letters suggest that this mysterious new work was nothing less than a first version of the new novel, for which his six years of voluntary exile in the

[1] I, 727-8; in *Contre Sainte-Beuve*, 299-300, he has the same conversation with his mother.

[2] *Sésame et les Lys* was finished and delivered to the *Mercure de France* at the end of June; and when in July, after the arrival of the Library Edition of *Sésame* and of Marie Nordlinger's answers to his questions, he asked for the return of his manuscript, the insertion of a few corrections and additional footnotes can have taken little time. '*Un Professeur de Beauté*' was begun in mid-July, and must have been completed before the end of the month in time for its publication on 15 August.

world of Ruskin had been a preparation. In September 1904 he had informed Mlle Nordlinger of his refusal to translate Ruskin's *Saint Mark's Rest* for a Venetian publisher to whom Barrès had recommended him, 'because otherwise I shall die without ever having written anything by Myself'. In July 1905 he wrote to Antoine Bibesco: 'now that, for the first time after this long lethargy, I have turned my eyes inward towards my own thoughts, I feel how empty my life has been, and see hundreds of characters for a novel, a thousand ideas begging me to give them bodies, like the ghosts in the Odyssey that ask Ulysses for a drink of blood to bring them to life'.

Sufficient evidence exists for a conjectural reconstruction of at least some elements of this unknown novel. The essay '*Sur la Lecture*' may represent a draft for the opening scenes in the village of the Narrator's childhood, since it contains material which had already been used in *Jean Santeuil* and would reappear in *Du Côté de chez Swann*. Proust's letters to Louisa on the Trouville coast would serve as suggestions for episodes at the seaside, at some primitive form of Balbec; and the medical world, absent from *Jean Santeuil* but so prominent in *A la Recherche*, would make a substantial appearance, for he told Mme de Noailles after his visit to Dr Brissaud on 28 July: 'I'm going to write a book about doctors.' A fragment has been published in which the story of Jean and Françoise in *Jean Santeuil*, which became the love of Swann and Odette in *A la Recherche*, is already being told of a hero named Swann and a woman named Carmen. More surprisingly, another fragment shows Swann himself at 'Querqueville' on the seacoast of Normandy for two successive summers, in love like the Narrator with each member of a 'little band' in turn. Anna and Septimie, whom Swann jealously suspects of a Lesbian relationship, are equivalents of Albertine and Andrée, and the other girls, whose names are Maria, Célia and Arabelle, correspond to Gisèle and Rosemonde. Clearly Proust had transferred to Swann, who appears in the third person, a much larger proportion of the material of his own life later shared between Swann and the Narrator in *A la Recherche*; and the section on Swann and Odette in *Du Côté de chez Swann*, in which part of the same story is still told of Swann in the third person, is a surviving relic of the form taken by this intermediate version of his novel. The unexpectedly large part played by Swann suggests that the novel begun in 1905 looked not only forward to *A la Recherche* but backward to

Jean Santeuil. In *Jean Santeuil* the tale is told by and about the novelist C, and the narrator ostensibly closest to Proust himself is only the person who says 'I' in the introduction, who meets C in Brittany and is entrusted with the story of his life, but never appears again. In the 1905 novel Proust may have divided the material of his own life more equally between these two narrators: the novelist C became Swann, and his young friend was recognisable, for the first time, as the Narrator of *A la Recherche*. On this hypothesis the Narrator would begin with his village childhood and continue with his own love in the Champs-Élysées for Gilberte, who in this version may already have been Swann's daughter. He would hear from Swann and retell in the third person the story of Swann's loves not only for Carmen-Odette, but also for the little band; and this story within a story would have the function, as in *A la Recherche*, of foreshadowing the Narrator's own experience of the laws of love and jealousy. The novel would presumably have culminated in a final love-affair of the Narrator; though it is impossible to guess with whom, since the girl who was Charlotte in *Jean Santeuil* and became Albertine in *A la Recherche* was here loved by Swann.

Perhaps Proust himself regarded his 1905 novel only as an experiment, to be abandoned and rewritten as soon as he should find himself at last on the right track. He was writing with the old, ill-advised method of *Jean Santeuil*, in isolated fragments; and even the fragments read like mere notes, rather than considered workings-out of the episodes to which they relate. There is, surprisingly, no discernible advance in aesthetic merit upon *Jean Santeuil*. The Cities of the Plain are apparently still a subsidiary, not, as later, an essential theme. It is unlikely that the Two Ways, or Time Lost and Regained, or unconscious memory were, if they appeared at all, fundamental in the symbolism and structure of the novel; for when they appear three years later in *Contre Sainte-Beuve* it is still only in a tentative and rudimentary form. Indeed, a passage in one of his August letters to Louisa de Mornand at Trouville suggests that he was still using only voluntary and conscious memory as his technique for recovering lost time. Louisa, too, has been recalling the past, 'looking,' he writes, 'into the depths of your heart now calm and clear again, and there discerning ancient images'; and among these is Proust himself —'who means nothing to you, except as one involved in sweet and painful moments of your life ... like the man who held the horse or stood by the carriage-door in some great historic event'. But, he adds, still apparently thinking only of conscious memory, 'our memory often presents us with "views" of the historic events of our own lives, which are not always easy to see clearly, like the views we strain our eyes to make out through the peep-hole in a pencase encrusted with shells, a souvenir of the seaside'.[1]

Early in September Proust's brief work on his novel was interrupted; it was time for the late summer holiday with his mother, which last year owing to his indecision had never taken place. During the year and nine months since his father's death their strange, half-loving, half-hostile relationship had become both closer and more equable. There is no sign of the serious quarrels of the past; Proust stayed more than ever before at home, and visits to friends, dinners at Larue's and evenings in high society were unprecedentedly rare. But his dream of union with his mother, now that his father was for ever out of the way, had failed to come true; it was as though neither of them quite wished it. Mme Proust transferred only a little of her wifely devotion to her son, but kept most of it for her cult of her dead husband. She never abandoned for Marcel's sake her weekly and monthly observance of the days of Dr Proust's stroke, death and funeral, or her insistence that there should be no more grand dinners, and little entertainment of guests, particularly on those fatal days. Marcel, on his side, did not succeed in his resolution to see more of his mother. On the contrary, he allowed his hours to become more unearthly than ever before, until in the spring and summer of 1905 he rose, if at all, at eight or nine in the evening, and Mme Proust was forced to dine at eleven p.m. if she wished to share his daily meal. She showed distress in the heatwave that killed poor Yturri; but otherwise her health had seemed good since a painful attack of nephritis in the winter of 1903-4, which she concealed from Marcel until it was over. When he had mentioned his anxiety to his brother Robert, Mme Proust was annoyed; henceforth he refrained from meddling, and left her health in Robert's hands. Proust has been accused of embittering his mother's life with his meticulous and harrowing letters about his health, and of shortening it by the daily errands which, especially in her last year, she ran for him all over Paris; but both charges are unjust. His complaining letters, whatever gloomy pleasure he may have taken in them, were written to her strict order, and if he neglected them he was sharply rebuked.

[1] Proust used this image of the view in the pencase for the Narrator's boyhood visions of Balbec (I, 389).

Similarly, when Mme Proust delivered a *Bible d'Amiens* in person to the astonished Léon Daudet, or saw Marie Nordlinger back to Auteuil, or journeyed twice in the heat-wave to Neuilly to enquire after Yturri, it was at her own request, not only to satisfy her need to serve, but as an excuse for exercise to reduce her corpulence, and an act of obedience to her dead mother's principles of hygiene. It was in the nature of this proud and formidable lady to rule by self-sacrifice; and when two human creatures live in so complete a state of symbiosis as Proust and his mother, neither can be held responsible, though each is partly the cause, for the actions of the other.

When, about 7 September, they left together for Évian, it was for Marcel's health rather than his mother's. It was agreed that at the end of their holiday she should see him safely installed for his rest-cure; for from Évian both Dr Widmer at Territet and Dr Dubois at Berne would be within easy reach. Only two hours after their arrival, when Proust was fully occupied in being ill himself, his mother had an attack of giddiness and vomiting: with his extensive knowledge of medicine he may have guessed the truth, that these were symptoms of a recurrence of her nephritis, brought on as is often the case by the jolting of a long train journey. Next morning, and every morning for the rest of those terrible few days, she tried to hide her partial paralysis and aphasia, which were two other recognised symptoms of her disease, and insisted on coming downstairs, helped by two servants of the hotel, to sit all day in the lounge. She refused food, and would not admit that she was ill, nor allow the analysis of her urine which would have revealed her condition. Proust telephoned for Mme Catusse, who was staying near by; but on her arrival, somewhat to his irritation, the sick lady only begged her old friend to take her photograph. It was not till later that he could interpret her strange mixture of eagerness, coquetry and reluctance: 'she was torn between the desire to leave me a last image of herself,' he explained to Mme Catusse five years afterwards, 'and the fear that it might be an unbearably sad one'. In his novel it is the grandmother at Balbec who, with the same purpose, persuades Saint-Loup to take her photograph, and is cruelly mocked by the Narrator.[1]

Proust sent for Robert, who decided to bring her back, while there was still time, to the medical facilities of Paris; and next morning, half carried, half dauntlessly walking, she was seen into the

[1] I, 786-7; II, 776-80.

railway-carriage by Mme Catusse. Moved by the wish to die at home
and to spare the distracted Marcel the sight of her agony, she forbade
him to come with her even to the station, and abdicated for ever her
care for her son. "I'm going back to Paris, because I'm useless and
can't help you when you're ill," she declared, almost sternly, as they
parted. For a few days he waited obediently, hoping, as he wrote to
Marie Nordlinger on the 13th, 'that all this will vanish like a bad
dream'; but soon a telegram from Robert summoned him to
Paris.

His mother, he found, showed signs of improvement: "if she gets
over this attack, she'll be as fit as ever," promised Dr Landowski.
Uraemia had been confirmed, but she still refused all food or medicine, and doggedly persisted in dressing and getting up every day.
She kept her lifelong air of absolute calm: 'none of us knows what
she is thinking or suffering,' Proust told Montesquiou, who, still
crushed by his own grief, was temporarily able to notice the sorrows
of other people. Mercifully her disease, instead of inflicting the usual
excruciating pain, took the alternative course of advancing paralysis
and coma. After a few days her apparent improvement ended, and she
began to die. When Dr Merklen called and announced: "Monsieur
Proust, I can recommend only one thing," Proust thought for one
wild moment that he was about to suggest a possible cure; but
Merklen, with a look of genuine sympathy which he always remembered with gratitude, concluded: "and that is, patience and resignation." When she was able to speak the poor lady would play, in a
voice distorted by aphasia, their old game of joking quotations from
the French classics. The nun who nursed her left them together for a
moment, and "*I never saw a better-timed departure,*"[1] she stammered.
"I couldn't bear to be without you," he cried, and "Don't be afraid,
my little boy," she replied, "your mother won't leave you; why, '*a
nice thing it would be, if I was at Étampes and my spelling went to
Arpajon*'."[2] Just before the end, as he fought to suppress his tears,
she frowned, pulled a smiling grimace, and whispered, so that he
guessed rather than heard the quotation from Corneille[3] with which
she had cheered their partings in his childhood: " '*if you're no
Roman, then deserve to be one!*' " In her final coma, as old Félicie told

[1] Molière, *Le Misanthrope*, act 3, scene 5.
[2] Labiche, *La Grammaire*, scene 15, spoken by a father who depends for his
spelling on a learned daughter.
[3] *Horace*, act 2, scene 3.

him afterwards, "Madame trembled like a leaf, although she was quite unconscious, whenever she heard your three rings on the bell, because however quietly you tried to ring that week you have a way which she couldn't mistake for anyone else's". And the nun-nurse remarked to him, with mingled admiration and disapproval, "for her you were still a child of four years old". On 26 September Mme Proust died, and suddenly Time was Lost.

For two days Marcel still had her to himself. She had taken no solid food since their arrival at Évian, and starvation had melted away the heaviness which of late years had made her face plain and middle-aged. The corpse by which he watched was that of a beautiful girl, the very image, he thought, of the portrait painted by Mme Beauvais in 1880. The young mother who had refused and granted his goodnight kiss at Auteuil was restored to him, risen from the abyss of Time. Now he gave her the same kiss again. 'Today I have her still, dead, but accepting my caresses—tomorrow I shall lose her for ever,' he told Mme de Noailles; and Reynaldo Hahn could never forget the horrifying sight of 'Marcel by Mme Proust's deathbed, weeping, and smiling through his tears at her body'.

Because Mme Proust had kept her Jewish religion out of respect for her parents, there was no church service, and the funeral procession, headed by Marcel, Robert, and her brother Georges Weil, left at noon on the 28th directly for Père Lachaise. The usual prohibition of flowers, however, was waived: 'the hearse could hardly be seen for wreaths,' observed the *Figaro* reporter, 'among the finest of which, we noticed, were those from the Marquis d'Albufera, Mme Félix Faure and Mme Gaston Thomson'. One of the most magnificent of all, which the reporter tactfully left unmentioned, came from Louisa de Mornand. Professors Berger, Brouardel, Dentu, Dieulafoy, Fournier, Hartmann and Pozzi attended in memory of her husband their colleague, and from the noble Faubourg the Noailles, Albufera, Chevigné and Grouchy couples came not only out of friendship for Marcel, but because they had been his parents' guests.

For a month Proust disappeared from the world of the living, almost as if he shared his mother's death. In this twilight half-life he lay in bed weeping incessantly and entirely deprived of sleep. The servants, from force of habit, tiptoed about the apartment as before; but he listened to the silence with horror, for it was a spectral relic of his mother, who had trained them not to disturb the sleep that was now forbidden him. Sometimes her bodiless voice murmured

unintelligibly in his ear, from beyond the grave: he had heard it
before, he realised, in the telephone at Fontainebleau nine years
since, when his mother spoke in a tone of mourning from an invisible
world, and he had felt a foreboding of her death. Although he now
thought of her unceasingly, he found to his despair that he could not
remember her face. He recalled that she, too, had known the same
torment, and confided that she could never call up the image of her
beloved mother, his grandmother, except by cruel flashes in sleep.
In his turn he twice suddenly saw her, in an instantaneous waking
vision, as a nightmare figure wrestling with her disease. Sometimes
he dozed; and his mind continued a hideous train of thought far more
terrible than the anguish of waking life, when he still had the protection of his reason. He remembered a moment in the last days before
her death, when she struggled in vain to speak: what had she tried to
say, what command had she left unuttered which might have saved
him?

Towards the end of October he began, by degrees, to sleep again,
at the cost of terrifying dreams. He left his bedroom for the first time
to revisit the empty rooms of their home; but in each one, as he
realised her absence anew, his mother seemed to die again; and he
explored, as he wrote to Mme de Noailles, 'unknown regions of grief,
which reach further and further into infinity with every step I take'.
Outside her bedroom he trod on a creaking board, which she would
hear in the small hours when he returned from an evening in society;
but he listened in vain for the kissing sound which she would then
make with her lips, meaning "Come and embrace me." For the last
time, in death, she had refused her goodnight kiss. At that moment
he decided to leave 'this house which is so sad because it used to be
so happy'; but he would have to wait nearly a year, for their annual
lease would not expire again until 30 September 1906.

Early in November, as if suddenly remembering an appointment,
Proust began to think again of his vow to enter a sanatorium. He had
succeeded, with unceasing feints and retreats, in procrastinating for
a year and a half, ever since Dr Merklen had ordered him to 'unlearn
your asthma'. At first he seemed only to renew his old tactics, plight-
ing his faith to half a dozen different doctors at a time. Dubois and
Sollier were close favourites, until a previous outsider, Dr Déjérine,
last heard of in December 1904, forged to the front. He promised to
cure Proust by three months of complete isolation; and as from
5 December 1905 Proust engaged a private room for three months

in the nursing-home of the Sisters of Sainte-Marie de la Famille in the Rue Blomet, of which Déjérine was the director.

Meanwhile his grief began to wane. He was taken unawares by feelings of possible happiness, followed by instant remorse. He resolved every day to go out for the first time tomorrow; but he was deterred by the memory of his mother meeting him at the door, before the servants could reply to his invariable question: "Is Madame still up?", and gazing anxiously to see whether he had returned in a fit of asthma. 'For grief isn't single,' he told Mme Straus on 9 November, 'because regret takes a different form every moment; suggested by the identity of a present impression with some moment of the past, a new disaster, an unknown sorrow strikes one down, as unbearable as the first onset of bereavement.' Proust's theories of grief and its intermittences, of unconscious memory as a source not only of joy but of anguish, were taught him by experience.

On 4 December, the very eve of his promised entry into the nursing-home in the Rue Blomet, Proust resolved to jilt Dr Déjérine. Sollier, he wildly surmised, might be persuaded to treat him at home, by the simple, well-tried, and totally ineffectual method of changing his hours of meals and sleep. Through Mme Straus he arranged for Sollier to call at 6.30 p.m. on 6 December. The young doctor was charming and optimistic: it was essential for Proust to enter his nursing-home, he explained, but in return he could effect a cure in only six weeks. Whether because he believed in this miracle, or because he felt there was not the least danger of its occurring, Proust allowed himself to be whisked off that very evening to Sollier's sanatorium at Boulogne-sur-Seine, otherwise Billancourt, a rural suburb between the western extremity of the Bois de Boulogne and the river.

Chapter 3

THE WATERSHED
(December 1905 – January 1907)

PSYCHIATRISTS are familiar with the patient who sets impossible conditions for his treatment, abandons it if he sees any risk of being cured, knows enough about the secret causes of his neurosis to be able to parry all attempts to detect them, and begins by establishing a feeling of intellectual superiority over his doctor. So it was to be with Sollier and Proust, who unconsciously preferred his asthma, and the way of life it necessitated, to the health of ordinary beings.

During the first half of 1905 he had conscientiously read up the works of French specialists in nervous ailments, and was interested to learn that the unconscious was responsible for all manner of diseases which hitherto had been supposed to be organic. One of these, according to Dr Brugelmann, was asthma; the very title of Dr Ribot's *Diseases of the Will* was a reproach which struck home; and Camus and Pagnier, in *The Isolation-Treatment in Psychotherapy*, with preface by Dr Déjérine himself, suggested what was in store for him at the Billancourt sanatorium. In a footnote to *Sésame et les Lys* he mentioned all these, and quoted from Dr Dubois's *The Psychoneuroses*, which he had borrowed from Fernand Gregh in 1903: 'Doctors used to say that a pessimist is a man with a bad stomach. Now Dr Dubois says outright that a man with a bad stomach is a pessimist. And it is no longer a question of curing his stomach to change his philosophy, but of changing his philosophy to cure his stomach.' The note of disrespectful irony is evident. It is as though Proust saw his physicians as substitutes for his dead father, saying in the very voice of Dr Proust: "there's nothing wrong with the boy, except lack of will-power"; and he behaved towards them, as to his father, with apparent submission but real evasion.

The charming Dr Sollier made an unfortunate start. In their first conversation after his arrival at Billancourt Proust asked whether he had read Bergson. "Yes, I felt I ought to, because we're both interes-

ted in the same field. But I found him terribly confused and narrow!"
'I felt a Da Vincian smile of intellectual pride passing over my face,'
Proust told Georges de Lauris afterwards, 'and this didn't contribute
to the success of my psychotherapeutic treatment.' Perhaps Proust
had more satisfying discussions with his doctor on a different subject.
He would have heard from Léon Daudet, who had been Sollier's
fellow-student, and like many ardent heterosexuals took a keen
interest in such matters, that Sollier was a specialist in the psycho-
pathology of women, and held advanced views on the statistics of
female homosexuality. "So-called frigidity in women," Sollier would
maintain, "is in three-quarters of all cases a symptom of Lesbianism." Isolation-treatment, indeed, as practised by Dr Sollier, was
delightfully devoid of rigour. Not only was Proust allowed to carry
on his enormous correspondence by dictation; in special cases, as to
Robert de Billy, or Louisa de Mornand, he could still write his own
letters. To Louisa he wrote to warn her against taking a new lover
until she was quite sure of herself—'Don't spoil one happiness until
you have another'—next to arrange a New Year's gift to Albu of a
travelling-watch for his automobile, and again to refuse a gift for
himself: 'unhappy friendships with people who gave me New Year
presents have made me almost superstitious, and in these sad days it
would seem like a bad omen'. The turn of the year, ever since his
love for Marie de Benardaky in the Champs-Élysées, had always
been a melancholy time, and now brought a recrudescence of his
grief for his mother. He remembered her question in his childhood:
"What would you like for a present on New Year's Day?" "I'd like
your love." "Why, you dear old ninny, that isn't a present—you have
that always." But now he had it no longer.

Early in January Dr Sollier became still more gracious. Proust
was now allowed to receive his friends on Tuesdays, Thursdays and
Saturdays from two to four in the afternoon. 'Insist when you arrive,
and if necessary ask to see Dr Sollier himself,' he told Robert de
Billy, who visited him before leaving, towards 9 January, to join the
French delegation at the Algeciras Conference. The isolation-
chamber at Billancourt had become a mere annexe to Proust's
bedroom at 45 Rue de Courcelles, and he was living precisely as
before, with asthma unabated, except that for the first time for five
years he was sleeping at night and breakfasting before noon. 'I'm
not climbing the hill, alas,' he complained to Billy, 'I'm going down it
at a gallop'; but soon the appointed six weeks were over, and about

20 January he returned home, 'fantastically ill'. The faithful Albufera called every day to help with his correspondence; and in February he was at home daily from five to ten to the few chosen friends whom he allowed to know that he was fit to be seen: 'which constitutes a great progress,' wrote Albu to Billy, 'and is an enormous pleasure for us all'.

His sojourn at Billancourt had been not a cure, but a successful and final escape from health. Nevertheless, although its effect on his illness had been, as he unconsciously intended, almost negligible, its symbolic importance was profound and manifold. He had fulfilled his mother's last wish, and also defied her, since his obedience had been useless. At the same time his continued ill health was an act of piety: he would remain for ever in the state in which he had lived with her, whereas if he had become a new man he would have been parted from her eternally. Again, by retiring temporarily from the world of the living he had shared in her death. But the Billancourt cell had been a symbol not only of death but of approaching resurrection. In preparation for his new life of freedom he had retreated into the life before birth, in a strange place where his mother was invisible yet everywhere round him, and the father-figure of Dr Sollier gently invited him to be made new and emerge. When he came out, defenceless, bewildered and in pain, he was reborn, although more than a year would pass before he could gather his strength and establish a new way of life. Already, however, he thought less often of his mother, and only at sudden moments of recollection with the old anguish. Dr Sollier had succeeded in curing him of one thing: not his asthma, but his grief.

In *A la Recherche* his six weeks at Billancourt were magnified into the Narrator's 'long years in a sanatorium, during which I had completely renounced my idea of becoming a writer',[1] which lasted from shortly after his visit to Gilberte de Saint-Loup at Tansonville until the beginning of 1916, and again, 'in a new sanatorium which was no more successful in curing me than the first', for a period of 'many years'.[2] This vast stretching of the thread of time was necessitated technically by Proust's wartime revision of his novel, in which the insertion of the long chapter on the events of the World War caused the revelation of Time Regained at the Princesse de Guermantes's matinée to be transferred from the neighbourhood of 1912 to about the year 1922. Yet the significance of the brief real

[1] III, 723.　　　　　　　　　　[2] III, 854.

and the long imaginary stay in a nursing-home was the same. The six weeks under Dr Sollier marked a fundamental division between the two eras of Proust's life, between the past thirty-four years with his mother and the coming seventeen years without her. Formerly he had lived, like the hero of *Jean Santeuil*, in a present which seemed destined, by the indefinite addition of day to day, to last for ever. When he returned from Billancourt to his empty home his whole previous life had become, by a total break of continuity, the past. On the far side of the barrier was the lost time in which his mother continued to give and withhold her infinite love; on the hither side he was alone in an unreal, ghostly and posthumous present which could be given meaning only by a recovery of the time he had squandered. The year of half-life that followed Billancourt formed a moorland plateau from which the rivers flowed on one side to his childhood, on the other to his death. He had reached the watershed between Time Lost and Time Regained.

For two months, between mid-February and mid-April 1906, Proust once again is lost to view, and the few surviving letters (one each to Mme de Noailles, Mme Catusse and Antoine Bibesco) are written to explain that he is too ill to write. He chose Dr Maurice Bize, who called every Friday, for his new physician. He corrected the proofs of *Sésame et les Lys*, the publication of which had been planned for October 1905, but delayed by his mother's death, and perhaps worked again on his novel.

On 5 May in the *Chronique des Arts* Proust reviewed a translation of Ruskin's *Stones of Venice* by his aunt Mathilde Peigné-Crémieux, Mme Proust's cousin and a sister of Mme Thomson. It was his only article during the prescribed year of his mourning, and no doubt he only allowed himself to write it in the knowledge that it would particularly have pleased his mother. He gave Aunt Mathilde a glowing review for 'this superb translation', but slyly pointed out how greatly her book would have been improved by the addition of footnotes. His passion for Ruskin momentarily revived, though the tables were turned: instead of admiring Venice for Ruskin's sake, he now praised Ruskin for his praise of Venice. 'The skies of Venice and the mosaics of St Mark's,' he wrote, 'take on colours still more miraculous than their own, since these are the hues of a marvellous imagination, carried across the world, as in an enchanted ship, by Ruskin's prose.' As he read the visionary city rose again from the sea of the past, and he thought, towards the end of May, of revisiting this Venice Preserved; 'but Venice is so much a graveyard of happiness for me,' he wrote ruefully to Mme Catusse, 'that I haven't the strength to go back'. For the rest of his life his nostalgia intermittently returned; and the Narrator's many years of longing for the Venice he had not yet seen were experienced by Proust after he had been there, and when he knew in his heart he would never return. Meanwhile, as he planned his imaginary journey, Aunt Mathilde played her part in the reawakening of his desire to live. 'Just recently,' he wrote to Léon Bélugou that summer, 'while reading one of Ruskin's travel books and feeling my heart beating with the desire to see the same places once more, I said to myself: "if I no longer cared for him, would he still be making the world beautiful for me, until I am consumed with longing and desolation whenever I look at a railway-timetable?" Yes, my affection for Ruskin has lasted. Only sometimes nothing chills it so much as reading him.' 'My original love,' he concluded, 'was more involuntary.'

Sésame et les Lys was published on 1 June. Marie Nordlinger had proved adamant in her self-effacing refusal to be treated as his collaborator, and her help, which had meant so much to him not only in itself but as a symbol of friendship and happier days, could be acknowledged only in a footnote. The preface was dedicated to his favourite Princesse Hélène de Chimay, '*Of Kings' Treasuries*' to Reynaldo Hahn, and '*Of Queens' Gardens*' to Suzette Lemaire. He sent a copy to Louisa de Mornand inscribed with Baudelaire's line '*O toi que j'eusse aimée, ô toi qui le savais*'—'*You whom I might have loved, as well you knew*'—and sat back with little hope to await reviews. He was still too downcast to organise, as he had for *La Bible d'Amiens*, the log-rolling publicity which he believed to be his only hope of fame in the world of letters. With an excess of modesty he even begged Calmette not to trouble Beaunier for a review, since that amiable critic had been only too generous the year before; but to his delighted embarrassment a brief notice by Beaunier appeared in *Le Figaro* on 5 June, followed by a front-page article on the 15th.

Since Beaunier's article was his one morsel of satisfaction, it was particularly maddening that Reynaldo, Lucien Daudet and Albufera all failed to notice it. The philistine Albu, who had not yet been persuaded to read even *La Bible d'Amiens*, went so far as to remark: "It's very odd, Marcel, considering Calmette is a friend of yours, that they haven't said a word about your book in *Le Figaro*!" "On the contrary, they've said all too much." "You must be mistaken,

dear boy," replied Albu in the very words of the Duc de Guermantes denying the existence of the Narrator's article on the spires of
Martinville,[1] "because my wife reads *Le Figaro* every morning from
beginning to end, and there's been absolutely nothing about
you!"

'The footnotes to *Sésame* are mere small-talk, and I'd rather do
some really serious work,' Proust told Robert Dreyfus. In fact the
footnotes, however slight their connection may sometimes be with
Ruskin's text, contain some of Proust's most remarkable writing to
date, and even when apparently trivial show his preoccupation with
the 'really serious work' of his novel. His private life, which for
him was so closely connected with his creative writing, persists in
coming to the surface. Without naming the victim he quotes a
Charlus-like remark of Montesquiou on the faithless Delafosse: "To
think that I should be treated so by a person I trimmed into shape as
a topiarist trims a yew-tree!"; and he recalls a saying of his mother,
who continued to the end to discuss the possibility of his marriage:
"I shouldn't mind if you chose someone who'd never heard of
Ruskin, but I couldn't bear it if you married a woman who pronounced 'tramway' 'tramvay'!" The most significant note, however,
is on the organic unity which underlies the apparent deviousness of
Ruskin's construction. In the last paragraph of '*Kings' Treasuries*'
Ruskin gathers together the diverse meanings latent in the Sesame of
his title: it is a seed, a spiritual food, a magic word which opens a
long-hidden, underground treasure-house, and so on. 'He passes
from one idea to another,' comments Proust, 'without any apparent
order. But in reality the fantasy which leads him follows its own
profound affinities, which enforce upon him in spite of himself an
overruling logic. Consequently we find in the end that he has obeyed
a kind of secret plan, which when finally unveiled imposes its retrospective structure upon the work as a whole, so that we now see it
splendidly towering to the final apotheosis.' When he wrote these
words, probably in the spring of 1905, Proust may already have
realised that his novel would demand, what *Jean Santeuil* had lacked,
a majestic unity underlying its diversity, and a fugal or coda-like
regathering of the themes at its conclusion. In his final paragraph,
like Ruskin, he would repeat the keyword of his title, Time, and give
it meanings not far distant from those of Sesame.

In the early summer Proust looked on with mixed feelings at the

[1] III, 583.

last act in the drama of the Dreyfus Affair. Officially Dreyfus was still, in the words of the Rennes verdict in 1899, 'guilty with extenuating circumstances'; but the Appeal Court had been engaged ever since 1903 in a leisurely new review of his case, and the triumph of the Radical bloc in the May elections of 1906 made an early decision so expedient as to be inevitable. The rehabilitation of Dreyfus, however, was no longer an act of justice, but a political manœuvre in the campaign of humiliation against the Church and Army which Ruskin and Orleans had made dear to Proust. 'These elections have been a sad blow to me,' he told Mme Catusse; and to the leftist Reynaldo he grumbled: 'I see all your "unified socialist" friends are in, and you must be as delighted as I'm furious—not that I wouldn't gladly vote for you if you put up as a dear little hunnified socialist, only I'd rather you didn't.' Suddenly, on 13 July, Dreyfus was declared to have been innocent all along, and on the 20th, in a grotesque reversal of his public degradation in the same place eleven years before, he was invested with the cross of the Legion of Honour before the assembled troops at the École Militaire. Proust's revulsion from Dreyfus in the hour of victory is a measure of his former self-identification with Dreyfus in the time of ostracism and martyrdom; it also helps to explain the Narrator's almost neutral attitude to the Affair in *A la Recherche*. 'In these ten years,' he wrote bitterly to Mme Straus, 'we've all had many griefs, disappointments and agonies. And for none of us will the hour ever strike when our griefs will be changed to exultations, our disappointments to un-hoped-for realisations, our agonies into delicious triumphs. I shall get iller and iller, miss my lost ones more and more, and find all I ever dreamed life might give me ever further out of reach. But for Dreyfus and Picquart life has been as providential as a fairy-tale. The reason is that *our* sorrows are based on truths, whether physiological, human or emotional. But their misfortunes were the result of mere mistakes. Blessed are the victims of mistakes, judicial or otherwise! For them alone of mankind there is such a thing as restitution and reparation.' Dreyfus was promoted to the rank of major, in which he served a year for form's sake, and then resigned to live on his ample private means. Picquart, who had been in compulsory retirement since 1898, was more spectacularly made a general, and, on 26 October, War Minister; but eight years of consciousness that in all the French army he was the only man in step had turned his high-souled courage in the heroic age of the Affair to priggish self-satisfaction, and as minister he was neither competent nor popular. Proust wondered whether to favour him with a copy of *Sésame et les Lys*; but, he decided, 'when I think of the difficulty I had in smuggling *Les Plaisirs et les Jours* to him when he was in prison, it seems too easy now'.

As a further stage in his groping return to life he began to plan a summer holiday. At first, remembering his cruise on the *Hélène* two years before, he thought of 'hiring a little yacht', a project which in *A la Recherche* reappeared in the Narrator's intention of buying a yacht for Albertine. A host of bewildering and forbidding possibilities besieged him; and as in former years he would have unburdened his indecision upon his mother, so now he wrote repeatedly and interminably to Mme Straus. He was tempted to return to the Hôtel des Roches Noires at Trouville, but the thought of the mist in the valley, and the thinness of the partitions through which his mother had knocked good-morning in 1894, put him off. Where could he find absence of damp, dust, draughts and trees, abundance of lifts, bathrooms, fires and water-closets, and room for old Félicie whom, as the Narrator took Françoise to Balbec, he was determined to take with him? Knowing her friend as she did, Mme Straus cannot have been surprised to hear that he had resolved to stay at home, 'to rest from my journey, which was as exhausting to plan as it would have been to make', or, a few days later, that he had suddenly left alone for Versailles.

Probably at the suggestion of Reynaldo Hahn, who sometimes stayed there when in the throes of composition, he moved on 6 August into a suite at the Hôtel des Réservoirs. The hotel, an eighteenth-century mansion built for Mme de Pompadour, was separated from the northern wing of the Palace only by the reservoirs which still supplied the fountains and basins of the gardens. From its windows the guests surveyed the Bassin de Neptune and the beech-tree vistas beyond; and should they wish to walk in the park, two private exits led directly upon the gravel alleys and the lawns. Proust's apartment in the annexe was vast, sunless and extremely expensive, with lofty ceilings and innumerable tapestries, paintings and mirrors—'the sort of place where the guide tells you that Charles the Ninth died there, and you cast a furtive look around, longing to get out again into light and warmth and the comfortable present; but I not only can't get out, but even have to make the supreme surrender of sleeping there!' In these melancholy surroundings,

which habit soon changed into a familiar new home, he was to spend
nearly five months.

As a first step he surrounded himself with a band of zealous and
liberally-tipped servants: a hall-porter with powdered white hair,
his wife who made Proust's telephone-calls, a young favourite of
Reynaldo named Léon, another hall-porter whom Proust had
glimpsed previously as a footman of Montesquiou's distant uncle
the Duc de Fezensac, and the head-waiter, Hector, of whom there
may be something in Aimé, his counterpart at Balbec. With his
mind running on servants, Proust mistook a passer-by, who recognised him with frenzied gestures of delight as he drew his curtains
one evening, for his father's alcoholic ex-valet Eugène; but it was
another friend of Reynaldo, an eccentric Austrian painter named
Schlésinger. "Are you in Versailles for the day?" Proust enquired.
"No, I'm staying in the next room to yours," replied Herr Schlésinger, and proceeded to compliment Proust on his new beard: "it suits
you very well, in fact a beard always looks well when one's face is
beginning to show signs of age!" 'And the moral of that is,' Proust
wrote to Reynaldo quoting Pascal, 'that all the misfortunes of man
spring from his inability to live in a room alone!' But Proust himself,
preternaturally free from that inability, was beginning like his Aunt
Amiot at Illiers to create a life of constant drama simply by looking
out of his window.

His uncle Georges Weil was now dying, and one of Proust's
reasons for choosing Versailles was his wish to return the kindness
of this elder brother of his mother, who had called so often in the
evenings after Mme Proust's death to comfort his distracted nephew.
In flat disobedience to Dr Dubois, who had declared a few years
before that his illness was imaginary, Uncle Georges had taken to his
bed in June with uraemia; less fortunate than his sister, who had
died more gently of the same condition, he now experienced the
pain he had so often imagined, and lay in convulsions of ceaseless
agony. One day in mid-August Proust visited Paris to see him for
the last time, too late, for his uncle was already unable to recognise
him. On the way back he had a 'kind of accident' ('I don't like to
talk about it,' he told Mme Catusse) at the Gare Saint-Lazare, and
was rescued by a railway-employee whom he afterwards made vain
efforts to trace. Georges Weil died on the 23rd, and was buried in
the Jewish section of Père Lachaise on the 26th; but the fear of
repeating his unfortunate experience at the railway-station prevented

his nephew from returning to do his duty at the head of the funeral procession.

Another reason for his stay at Versailles was his impending move from 45 Rue de Courcelles, where his lease would expire on 30 September. He decided to leave arrangements for removal in his brother's hands, and to enlist his friends to find him a new home; and from this strategic retreat so near to Paris he would be able to carry on the necessary negotiations by post and telephone. All through September Georges de Lauris and other friends visited possible apartments and described them as vividly as possible by letter. Mme de Noailles was haled from dinner one evening by a telephone caller who introduced himself as the wine-waiter at the Hôtel des Réservoirs: "Monsieur Proust has asked me to ask Madame la Comtesse," he said, "whether she would advise him to take the apartment in the Boulevard Haussmann or the other one." 'My dialogue with this Invisible Man, and the weighty arguments of my well-pondered reply,' she wrote long afterwards, 'were perhaps among the factors which determined Marcel's final decision.' Towards 7 October he took a year's lease, destined to last for twelve and a half years, of the first-floor apartment at 102 Boulevard Haussmann. The house had belonged to his great-uncle Louis Weil; Proust had dined there often with his mother, and watched with her over the old man's death-bed ten years before; perhaps, for it is likely that the incident really occurred, he had also met the lady in pink there. He was even a part-proprietor of the house: Louis Weil had left the property to his nephew Georges and his niece Mme Proust; Georges Weil's share now belonged to his wife Émilie, while Mme Proust's had been divided between Marcel and Robert. Even so, he felt the apartment was beyond his means; but his mother had been there—'I couldn't steel myself to live in a house that mother had never known,' he explained—and it would be 'a transition between the Rue de Courcelles, which for me was the true and dear graveyard where she lay, and some place utterly strange and unknown.' Perhaps, too, he was attracted by its associations not only with Mme Proust, but with Louis Weil, the gay old man who had lived there in such scandalous freedom; and Proust may have foreseen that he would do the same, though mostly on the other side of the border between Paphos and Sodom.

Robert Proust had seen to the removal from 45 Rue de Courcelles, and the family furniture was now inconveniently dispersed between a carpet-store in the Place Clichy, a repository, and the empty ground-floor flat at 102 Boulevard Haussmann. It was time for the brothers to divide this part of their heritage; and for once Marcel's buried jealousy neared the surface, for it was as if he were now called upon to restore to Robert his fair share of their mother's love. His brother's utter unselfishness only thwarted his irresistible need to have a grievance. "Do whatever you please, Marcel," Robert repeated, "anything you decide will be quite perfect"; and when Marcel insisted on being advised he would say only: "Keep what you like, and sell or store the rest." Forgetting that he had taken 102 Boulevard Haussmann for the sake of old memories, he decided that only Robert's cruel refusal to accept his share of their unwieldy chattels had prevented him from economising in a smaller flat. He upbraided his brother: "you have forced me to alter my budget, my investments and my whole life," he said; but Robert's wife Marthe could be induced to covet only a few carpets and tapestries which Proust immediately decided he must keep. In November his little niece Suzy was ill with diphtheria. 'I like to think that perhaps a little of my mother and father survives in her', he declared, 'and it distresses me that she should begin her life so sadly.' But when the possibly plague-stricken Robert visited 102 Boulevard Haussmann, Marcel threatened to have the whole apartment fumigated; and when the hall-porter's wife reported, after telephoning his condolences to Marthe, that 'the lady seemed a bit short', he took severe umbrage. 'She's very nice, however, despite her uncertain temper,' he wrote magnanimously to Mme Catusse, 'and I must confess old Félicie assures me that, without being aware of it, I'm the last word in disagreeableness!'

During the three months from October to December Proust made his new apartment habitable by an infuriating but masterly exhibition of remote control. Becoming more than ever like his Aunt Amiot he succeeded, without leaving his bedroom, in badgering a host of people whom he never saw: Robert, Aunt Émilie, Mme Catusse, the architect, the manager, the concierge Antoine, the installers of electric light and wall-paper, the telephone-company, and the occupant of the flat above, who turned out to be an acquaintance named Arthur Pernolet. For a time he was determined to go to law, if only he could decide with whom: should it be with his aunt, who had improperly let the ground-floor flat to a professional man, Dr Gagey, or with Dr Gagey himself? Or could he persuade M.

Pernolet to be sufficiently aggrieved to do it for him? Early in December he began a lawsuit against the outgoing lady sub-lessor of his own flat, but on second thoughts withdrew it. The most delicious imbroglio of all was over the choice of furniture, in which he had the help of Mme Catusse, an expert on interior decoration. Every epic has its catalogue, the *Iliad* of ships, the *Pharsalia* of snakes; but Proust's catalogue of furniture, in which every single object from 45 Rue de Courcelles is in turn destined for every room in 102 Boulevard Haussmann, or given to servants, to Robert, to Dr Landowski, or sold, or popped into the basement, is an enormity which the biographer must spare the reader.

In the first few weeks of his stay he had risen when the sun was still setting over the green forests of Versailles; but soon it was dark when he awoke, it was therefore pointless to go outside the hotel, and for all those five months he never emerged. While he slept the majestic drama of the Versailles autumn was played unseen: the beech-avenues turned invisibly to gold, shed their leaves, and at last stood branch-deep in the mists of December. 'Am I really at Versailles?' he wrote to his old sweetheart Mme Gaston de Caillavet; 'I haven't left my bed, I haven't seen the palace, the Trianons, or anything; when I open my eyes it's already the dead of night, and I often wonder whether the room I lie in, lit by electricity and hermetically sealed, isn't anywhere in the world rather than at Versailles, where I haven't watched a single dead leaf whirling down over a single fountain!' One morning at sunrise, however, he must at least have looked from his window as he prepared for bed, and have seen the dying splendour of Versailles as an emblem of his own life; for he wrote to Mme Straus of 'these days when the great fall of the leaf outside matches so well all that is withered and dispersed in the heart'. He sent for Dr Bize: "you have a touch of anaemia because you won't open your windows," he was told, "and you're writing far too many letters!"

His isolation at Versailles, however, was neither complete nor uncheered. Something of these autumn months went into the Narrator's idyllic sojourn at Doncières: the season, the mist, the clang our of tramcars, the hotel which was, as Saint-Loup told the Narrator, 'an eighteenth-century palace with old tapestries, a real "historic dwelling" ',[1] the thin bugle-calls from the nearby barracks at dawn, the visits of friends; for Versailles too was a garrison-town and a

[1] II, 71.

peopled solitude. Lauris, Billy, Reynaldo and Mme Catusse came
severally to dinner. "All this talk about meals brought to the annexe
is a myth, they bring everything on the same tray, and it's all frozen
when it arrives," Proust declared; so they dined without him in the
high, white-panelled restaurant of the hotel, with the veined marble
partition down the middle. The head-waiter was instructed to offer
truffled partridges, quails *sur canapé*, the most expensive champagne;
and Proust was furious if his guests ordered anything more modest.
René Peter, a playwright friend of Reynaldo and Debussy and a
native of Versailles, was a constant visitor. They collaborated in a
fairy-tale pantomime, of which Proust supplied the idea and wrote
two of the five acts: where is it now? He thought of writing another
play with Peter, with a preposterous but significant plot, about a
sadistic husband who, though in love with his wife, consorted with
prostitutes, said infamous things about her to them, encouraged them
to answer in kind, and was caught in the act by the injured lady, who
left him, whereupon he committed suicide. As we have seen, this
was an actual occurrence (except for the suicide) in the liaison of his
father's colleague Dr Albert Robin with the courtesan Liane de
Pougy. But the same form of cerebral sadism was a constant element
in Proust's own ambivalent love-hatred for his mother, both in her
lifetime and long after her death, and in the homosexual relationships
with social inferiors with which, by a snobism in every sense inver-
ted, he sought to profane her memory. He had used the theme, long
before the misdemeanour of Dr Robin made it come true, in '*The
Confession of a Young Girl*' in *Les Plaisirs et les Jours*, where the girl
who is so evidently Proust himself kills her mother by allowing her
vice to be detected, and then kills herself; and he was to use it again,
reversing the sexes, in Mlle Vinteuil's desecration of her dead father
at Montjouvain. But early in December, without letting her into the
secret of its plot, he confessed to Jeanne de Caillavet: 'I haven't the
courage to write my play.'

He had still further resources in the hotel itself, where other
Parisians were enjoying the Versailles autumn. He visited the
Comtesse d'Arnoux, whose nephew Henri Bardac was a friend of
Reynaldo and had been studying for the diplomatic service at
Oxford. With her he found a Norpois-like guest, the diplomat Jules
Cambon, 'wrapped in a cloud of silence, old age and mystery, pierced
only by the charm of his cunning eyes, like our Fénelon grown old,
wrinkled and sly'. In the room above his own from August to

October a famous young beauty was staying, Miss Gladys Deacon, the original of the Miss Foster who is Number Three in the list of eligible heiresses discussed by the Prince de Foix and his group at the restaurant in the fog.[1] Her mother's lover, Émile Abeille, had been shot by her father in 1893 as he tried to leap from the window, and had left her 500,000 francs. Boni de Castellane, when he praised her beauty one evening at dinner, was told by the lady sitting next to him: "My dear Boni, I advise you to take jumping lessons." Mme de Clermont-Tonnerre, who was beginning to show signs of preferring intelligent girls to handsome men, thought her 'as beautiful as a Greek warrior, with eyes perhaps too large and blue', and was astonished when Miss Deacon began to talk brilliantly of *The Well-Beloved* and to explain the difference between Hardy and Meredith; while Montesquiou had pronounced her 'absolutely like an archangel!' Proust longed and feared to visit his dazzling neighbour, and was particularly galled when rumours reached him from all sides that he was seeing Miss Deacon every day. Late one evening he mustered all his daring and went up; but Miss Deacon had retired for the night, and he had to be content with a long conversation with her mother. One morning from his bed he glimpsed the lovely heiress in the courtyard, muffled in thick veils and climbing into an automobile. He was fascinated by her from afar for several years to come: 'I never saw a girl with such beauty, such magnificent intelligence, such goodness and charm,' he declared; and in 1910, at Mme de Clermont-Tonnerre's request, he tried half-heartedly and unsuccessfully to make a match between Miss Deacon and the divorced Loche Radziwill. Soon afterwards, however, she met the Ninth Duke of Marlborough, whom she married in 1921 after his long-delayed divorce from the former Consuelo Vanderbilt.

Despite its many logical motives and accidental consolations, however, Proust's incarceration at the Hôtel des Réservoirs remains one of the mysterious episodes of his life. It is not unlikely that he worked again on his novel; and perhaps his very denials at this time of his ability to write should be taken as confessions that he was doing so. 'A minimum of physical wellbeing is necessary not only for working,' he had written in June to Robert Dreyfus, 'but even for receiving poetic impressions from the outside world. And when one's illness ceases for a moment, and such impressions arise, then one enjoys them with the pleasure of a convalescent, without being

[1] II, 404.

able to divert the energy which is unceasingly occupied in repairing
the ravages of malady to make it available for incarnating what one
has felt.' To Marie Nordlinger he wrote from Versailles on 8 December: 'I have put an end to the era of translations, which was favoured
so by Mother; and as for translating myself, I no longer have the
courage.' But there are signs that he was also engaged in a more
sinister occupation.

During the following year it becomes clear that Proust's homosexuality had entered upon a further stage. He was now irrevocably
disillusioned with 'friendship', which for him meant an idealistic
search for happiness from a relationship, whether physical or platonic,
with his social equals—such as Robert de Flers, Reynaldo Hahn or
Lucien Daudet—or with social superiors, who had included the
whole group of young aristocrats whom he turned into Saint-Loup.
But the failure of friendship left his desires unabated; not only the
desire for carnal satisfaction, which he himself believed to be, in this
form, sinful although inescapable, but the nobler desire for reciprocal
kindness and devotion. Proust now proceeded to explore a further
and darker region of the Cities of the Plain, where lover and beloved
are master and servant, where guilt is justified by generosity, and
acceptance is guaranteed by gratitude. Even in the lifetime of his
parents there are traces of these protective and almost paternal
relationships: notably, in 1899, there was a certain 'young Poupe-
tière' to whom, with Mme Proust's knowledge and approval, Proust
gave money and advice. There was now no need for concealment:
his mother's death had given him the freedom of Sodom; and from
1907 to the end of his life a succession of young men of the working-
classes, in the guise of man-servant, secretary or protégé, shared his
very home. The beginnings of this new freedom coincide with the
lifting of the anguish of his grief, and are visible at Versailles, where
it is evident from his letters to Reynaldo that Proust was seeing a
great deal of the young manservant Léon, and of a certain Robert
Ulrich, who intermittently during the next few years acted as his
secretary. For a nameless 'young man aged twenty-five, very
distinguished and pleasing in appearance, good handwriting, book-
keeping fair, charming manners, very serious-minded, but without
further education', he asked Robert de Billy to find a post in his
father-in-law's bank at the modest salary of '100 to 200 francs a
month'; and he continued his efforts to trace his good Samaritan of
the Gare Saint-Lazare.

On 27 December, when Proust had been announcing his imminent
home-coming for the past six weeks and seemed likely to stay at
Versailles for ever, he decided at an hour's notice to return to Paris.
The concierge Antoine and Dr Proust's former manservant Jean
Blanc could not conceal their consternation, for the apartment was
far from ready, and the noisy alterations in Dr Gagey's flat below
would take another month to complete. His new home, which he
had not seen since Louis Weil's death ten years before, consisted,
besides the 'usual offices', of a large bedroom and drawing-room
facing the chestnut-trees of the boulevard, with a smaller bedroom,
a dining-room and an ante-room upon the inner courtyard. Its
appearance was both strange and familiar, for Mme Catusse had used
all her ingenuity in—as Proust put it—her 'symphonic variations'
on his parents' furniture. The floors were still bare, but he refused
to allow the carpets to be laid until he recovered from the insomnia
of arrival; he stopped the hapless Dr Gagey's renovations, and only
consented on entreaty to allow their continuance in the late afternoon. But after a month of these petty obsessions with noise and the
rights of property he was recalled to the real world of love and death,
evil and atonement.

In the early summer of 1906 he had learned of the death of a
certain Monsieur van Blarenberghe, whose wife had been an acquaintance of Mme Proust's. He remembered having dined in society
with their son Henri, and could recall, if he tried, the young man's
vaguely distinguished appearance, his smiling eyes and half-open
mouth as he waited for applause after uttering a witticism. With an
impulse of filial piety Proust wrote a letter of condolence on his dead
mother's behalf, and in September at Versailles received a touching
reply, four months delayed, for Henri van Blarenberghe had been
travelling, under doctor's orders, to forget his grief. His father, he
said, had been 'the centre of his life, the source of all his happiness';
he asked to be allowed to call on Proust, 'to shake your hand and talk
about the past', and signed himself 'very affectionately yours'. It
occurred to Proust that van Blarenberghe was not only an interesting fellow-mourner but also Chairman of the Chemins de Fer de
l'Est, and rather self-seekingly he now wrote to him for help in
tracing his saviour at the Gare Saint-Lazare, 'in whom a friend of
mine is taking an interest', he mendaciously explained; but van
Blarenberghe could tell him nothing, and suggested that he must
have mistaken the name. 'What the year 1907 may have in store for

me I do not know,' the young man added, 'but let us hope it may
bring better things to us both, and that in a few months we may
be able to meet.' This letter was written on 12 January, and Proust
received it, forwarded from Versailles, on the 17th.

On the frosty afternoon of 25 January Proust settled down
luxuriously in bed to enjoy his breakfast coffee and the day's *Figaro*.
He skimmed the news of earthquakes and the latest government
crisis, and was agreeably attracted by the leadline 'Murder by a
Madman', when his pleasure turned to a sacred horror: the madman
was none other than Henri van Blarenberghe, who had killed his
mother the day before. The servants found Mme van Blarenberghe
staggering downstairs, covered with blood: "Henri, what have you
done? What have you done to me?" she cried, raising her arms in the
air, and fell dead. The police broke through the locked door of her
son's room, and found him still conscious on his bed. Henri van
Blarenberghe had stabbed himself several times, and then shot
himself inefficiently through the mouth: the left side of his face was
blown away, his left eye hung on the pillow. The police-inspector
shook him by the shoulder, shouting "Can you hear me? Answer, I
say!"; but the murderer only opened his remaining eye, glared for a
moment, and closed it for ever.

Five days later, on 30 January, Proust was asked by Calmette for
a topical article on the crime[1]: he rested, without thinking of what he
was about to write, until three in the morning, and then worked in
a curious flow of inspiration until halted by writer's cramp and the
din of Dr Gagey's workmen at eight, when he sent Ulrich with the
article to the *Figaro* office. When the proofs arrived at eleven that
evening he had no time to correct them, for he had just thought of
'an ending that was really rather good'. "Tell them they can cut
whatever else they like, but they're not to alter a single word of the
last paragraph," he instructed Ulrich; but when that young person
returned to *Le Figaro* at midnight he found the sub-editor Cardane
in an unaccommodating mood. "Does Monsieur Proust imagine that
anyone will trouble to read his article besides himself, and the few
people who happen to know him?" enquired Cardane, and complained that the new ending was "immoral, in fact it's a panegyric on

---

[1] Since Calmette could not have guessed unaided that Proust was personally
acquainted with van Blarenberghe, or took a special interest in the theme of
matricide, it may be inferred that his invitation had been prompted by Proust
himself.

matricide!" Next morning, in exact contradiction to Proust's entreaty, '*The Filial Feelings of a Matricide*' appeared with the last paragraph omitted but the remainder intact.

Cardane was justified in prophesying the admiration of Proust's friends. Mme Straus's cousin, Ludovic Halévy, had the cuttings mounted and sumptuously bound: "your young friend Proust has written an astonishingly gifted article," he told Robert Dreyfus; and the dear Princesse de Chimay, when Proust told her over the telephone: "I'd rather have written that article of Antoine's than mine,"[1] retorted: "how can you be so *insincere*, Marcel!" and rang off in enthusiastic indignation. Van Blarenberghe's friends, on the other hand, were extremely annoyed. Cardane had been equally shrewd in his diagnosis of the final paragraph, though its omission scarcely affected the meaning of the essay as a whole.[2] Proust's purpose throughout was to show that the wretched van Blarenberghe had only done suddenly and directly what other men do indirectly and by degrees, and that we all kill our mothers. In defending van Blarenberghe he was defending himself; for the past year he had been accusing himself of van Blarenberghe's crime.

After his few months of wild grief in the autumn of 1905 the wound of his bereavement had seemed to heal; yet beneath it a deeper and more terrible wound, the hidden abscess of his guilt, remained. He had wept for his mother's death, but neglected to weep for her life. Their love, certainly, had been real: they were two noble creatures, united in a profound devotion; yet it was, equally, a mockery, for they had also been torn, each by the other, in an unending hostility. Every day for nearly thirty years, when he displayed his asthma, extorted her service, received her visits at his idle bedside, or left her to go with his friends, he had repeated the drama of the goodnight kiss at Auteuil. His mother in turn had been tainted for ever by that symbolic act of denial and surrender: always, whether she indulged his helplessness and soothed his hysteria, or whether she quarrelled with his extravagance, interfered with his

---

[1] An article by her cousin, Antoine Bibesco, on the Emir of Afghanistan, based on his automobile trip to Persia in the previous autumn, appeared in the *Figaro Literary Supplement* on 2 February.

[2] In the omitted ending Proust had written of the special veneration paid by the ancient Greeks to 'the tomb of Oedipus at Colonus and of Orestes at Sparta —that Orestes whom the Furies had pursued to the very feet of Apollo and Athene, crying: "We chase far from all altars sons who slew their mothers" '.

pleasures or showed jealousy of his moments of good health, she
was prompted by anger as well as by love. He saw that, as surely as
Henri van Blarenberghe had killed his mother, so too had he. His
illness, his years on the Guermantes Way, even his homosexuality,
had been not only substitutes for his mother's love but acts of revenge. He had taken her life, not with a dagger, but no less certainly;
and as she swayed in the first onset of vertigo on the stairs at Évian
she might have cried to her son like Mme van Blarenberghe: "What
have you done to me?"

  ' "What have you done to me?" ' he wrote; 'if we allowed ourselves to think of it, there is perhaps no truly loving mother who
could not, on the last day of her life, and often long before, address
this reproach to her son. The fact is that we age and kill the heart
that loves us by the anxiety we cause, by the uneasy tenderness we
inspire and keep in a state of unceasing alarm. If we could see in a
beloved body the slow work of destruction carried out by this
anguished affection, the ravaged eyes, the hair which stayed indomitably black now defeated like the rest and turning white, the hardened
arteries and obstructed kidneys, the courage vanquished by life,
the slow, heavy step, the spirit that knows there is nothing left but
despair, though once it rebounded tirelessly with unconquerable
hopes, the inborn and seemingly immortal gaiety dried up for
ever . . .': if, in a moment of lucid sanity like van Blarenberghe's
when he saw his mother bleeding to death, we could see all these
things, he concluded, then we too would shoot ourselves like him.
'In most men this agonising vision fades all too soon in the returning
dawn of joy in life. But what joy, what reason for living, what life
can bear to look it in the face? Which is true, it or joy? Which is the
Truth?'

  In a pretended generalisation he had described the exact symptoms
of his own mother's slow torment and decline; and conversely he
had condoned van Blarenberghe's matricide, which was also his
own, by making it universal. Cardane was right indeed. In the
preceding passage of his essay Proust compared van Blarenberghe
to the tragic heroes of Sophocles, Shakespeare and Dostoevsky—
to Ajax in his madness slaughtering the shepherds and their sheep,
Oedipus tearing out his eyes at the sight of his mother-wife self-
hanged for his sin, Lear bending over Cordelia dead, Dmitri
Karamazov and the police-captain; and it was as if he saw van
Blarenberghe's crime, and his own insight into its real nature, as an

act of mythological, almost ritual dignity, as a moment of truth. The night on which he wrote '*Filial Feelings of a Matricide*' was a turning-point in Proust's life. For the first time he acknowledged his guilt, and was therefore able to forgive his mother; he had gone back beyond the evening at Auteuil when Time Lost began, into the world outside Time where his novel awaited him. He began to descend from the mountains of his mother's death, the watershed of his life, to make the long journey towards revelation and extinction. Which would come first? In the words of his question, which was the truth, it or joy?

Chapter 4

BALBEC REVISITED
(*February – December 1907*)

THE nervous tension caused by Proust's self-identification with a matricide was soon happily relieved by another, more natural death. Ever since the beginning of his stay at Versailles the mother of Georges de Lauris, whom he had never met, had been ill with a biliary calculus, and Proust had given not only condolence but, with visible pride, expert advice on the choice of a surgeon. On 15 February 1907 the afflicted lady died, and Proust took to himself the healing burden of Lauris's grief. 'When you have become accustomed to the dreadful truth,' he predicted, weeping as he wrote, 'that the time when you still had your mother is banished for ever into the past, you will feel her gently returning to life, coming back to take her place, her whole place, beside you.' 'The eyes of memory,' he wrote again, 'see nothing if we strain them too hard. Only try to live, to survive, leave the beloved images to grow in you without the help of your conscious will, and they will be reborn never to leave you again.' Such was his distress that his friends, Reynaldo, Albu, Maurice Duplay, wrote to console him as well as Lauris, and even the grim Marthe, his sister-in-law, telephoned her concern. Now he could identify himself with a son exempt from blame, and the martyred, accusing ghost of Mme Proust could become the 'beloved image' who was to inhabit *A la Recherche*. But he still continued to receive sympathetic letters from comparative strangers on his Van Blarenberghe article, including one from Mme Claire Dieulafoy ('not the man-woman, but her brother-in-law's wife,' he explained to Reynaldo), which was signed, instead of 'yours very sincerely', with a simple: 'May God have you in his keeping.'

All was now quiet in the flat below, where Dr Gagey had at last moved in; but the apartment adjoining Proust's in the house next door had been leased to a certain Madame Katz, whose new water-closets were being installed within a few inches of his pillow. The concierge Antoine took it upon himself to send the lady a letter pointing out that his sleepless lodger was 'the son of the famous Dr Proust', and to deliver it at one in the morning. Proust's entreaties and tips to the workmen were equally in vain; but providentially it turned out that Mme Katz's son, a judge, was a professional acquaint-ance of Émile Straus. 'If I were you, Marcel, I wouldn't let them raise a hammer till after midnight,' wrote Mme Straus with misplaced irony, for he was now rising a little after mid-day; and she invited M. Katz to lunch for negotiations. Even so the din continued through-out March: 'his cow of a mother is building God knows what,' Proust complained with unwonted discourtesy, 'something as majestic as the Great Pyramid, that I hear but can't see, and which must astound passers-by all the way from the Magasins du Printemps to Saint-Augustin!' Would the water-closets never be finished? 'She's changing the seats—I suppose she found they weren't wide enough.' Dr Bize ordered fresh air, for Proust had not been out of doors since the previous summer. In the earliest days of spring he took his first steps on his balcony, or up and down the pavement outside the house, and saw the sun: "I found it a very beautiful and very strange object," he said.

Meanwhile, in this pale sunlight of convalescence, he wrote a new article for Le Figaro, 'Journées de Lecture', which appeared on 20 March. His subject, once again, was the pleasures of reading; but he now took for his example, instead of Ruskin or the books of his childhood, the just-published memoirs of the Comtesse de Boigne. 'Journées de Lecture' is a practical demonstration of the paradox already announced in 'Sur la Lecture', that light reading is less harm-ful to the creative writer than the works of genius which may deceive him into believing that the truth he seeks has already been found; for most of its material, although the subscribers to Le Figaro could not have guessed it, would reappear in A la Recherche. In the long digression on the telephone-calls which interrupt his reading Proust thought of his conversation with his mother from Fontainebleau in October 1896, which he had already used in Jean Santeuil. The new treatment, however, retains hardly a vestige of the old; it is already in the mature style of his novel, complete with the superb invocation of 'the Ladies of the Telephone', 'the Danaids of the Invisible', 'the Daughters of Night', and 'the murmured words which I longed to kiss in their flight from lips forever turned to dust'. He was to use the whole passage, with only minor changes in wording, for the Narrator's interview from Doncières with his grandmother in Paris, with the

exception of a paragraph on 'the song of a passer-by, the horn of a
cyclist, a distant fanfare of trumpets', which he transferred to
Albertine's telephone-call on the night of the Princesse de Guermantes's soirée.[1] He recalls Bluebeard and Sister Anne on his magic-
lantern at Illiers[2]; and the Nereids who, 'though ravished from their
sea by an ancient sculptor, might think themselves sporting in it still
as they swim through the waves of their marble frieze', are already
the seanymph Glaukonome and her companions at Balbec.[3] A brief
remark on the magic of the names of places and people, which
mysteriously disperses when we experience the reality ('so that true
wisdom would consist in replacing all social relationships and nearly
all travel by study of the *Almanach de Gotha* and the railway
timetable'), contains for the first time the seeds of the same vast
theme in *A la Recherche*: for Proust's novel is the story of how the
enchantments of nature, society and love, symbolised in the names
of Balbec, Guermantes, Gilberte and Albertine, dissolve inevitably
into Time Lost. But the most extensive contributions to *A la Recherche* came from the book which formed the pretext for his
essay.

The five tall volumes of the Comtesse de Boigne's memoirs cover
the same immense period of time as the accompanying portraits,
which begin with a ringletted, pert-lipped, muslin-veiled beauty of
the First Empire, and end sixty years later with a hunched and sallow
octogenarian, like Mme de Villeparisis at Venice. Mme de Boigne
was born in 1781, and contrived, just in time, to be dandled on the
knees of Louis XVI and Marie Antoinette; she played an intimate
part in social and political life under Napoleon, Louis XVIII,
Charles X and Louis-Philippe, began to write her book in 1837, and
died in 1866, leaving her memoirs and all her wealth to her great-
nephew, the Marquis d'Osmond. Proust's interest in her work was
almost filial: the period of her story, the gentlewomanly, pleasantly
astringent prose-style, he felt, would have delighted his mother and
grandmother; and in his novel, as we have already seen, the memoirs
of the non-existent Mme de Beausergent, which next to Mme de
Sévigné's letters are the favourite literature of the Narrator's grandmother, are really those of the Comtesse de Boigne, which both
Mme Weil and Mme Proust had died too soon to read. But the

---

[1] *Jean Santeuil*, vol. 2, 178-81; *Chroniques*, 84-6; *Pléiade*, II, 133-6, 732.
[2] Cf. I, 10.
[3] Cf. I, 705.

fascination of Mme de Boigne was also unexpectedly personal. The Hôtel de Maillé, of which Proust's first home at 9 Boulevard Malesherbes had been an outlying wing, was inhabited by her great-great-nephew and his wife, the Comte and Comtesse François de Maillé; the dowager Duchesse de Maillé, whom he had seen as an aged wall-flower at her last society balls in the 1890s, was her niece; and her heir the Marquis d'Osmond, whose letters and photograph he had recently discovered in the papers of his dead parents, had frequently entertained Dr and Mme Proust as his dinner-guests. Proust introduced M. d'Osmond three times over into his novel; once in his own name as the friend of Charlus and Swann who dies so inconsiderately on the evening when the Duc and Duchesse are to attend a fancy-dress ball; again as the young Marquis de Beausergent in the Princesse de Guermantes's box at the Opera; and yet again as the Duc de Guermantes himself as a boy, for whom his aunt Mme de Beausergent, Mme de Villeparisis's sister, writes her memoirs.[1] Thanks to Mme de Boigne he thought again of the Maillés; and his future Duc and Duchesse de Guermantes could now develop a stage further from the Réveillons, their prototypes in *Jean Santeuil*, to become the nobles in whose house the Narrator lived, whose visitors he could watch from his window, and who were on nodding terms with his parents. The world of Mme de Boigne was familiar in other ways. Again and again in her pages he noticed the names of his friends and hostesses—Breteuil, FitzJames, Greffulhe, Guiche, La Rochefoucauld, Montesquiou, Noailles, Polignac, Potocka; but these were the great-grandparents of the people he knew, and in Mme de Boigne's memoirs the dimension of time seemed at once inexplicably lengthened and vertiginously foreshortened. Sometimes, too, he found a name long extinct and remembered it for his novel: he used Luxembourg for the raffish princess at Balbec, the Balzacian christian name Victurnien for the son of Mme de Surgis to whom M. de Charlus takes a fancy[2]; and he borrowed the title of Duchesse

[1] II, 575-89, III, 300; II, 55-6; III, 715. Proust makes a significant error when he states (*Chroniques*, 89) that his parents' friend, M. d'Osmond, whose portrait as a charming child with blond curls is among the illustrations to the memoirs, was the nephew for whom Mme de Boigne wrote her book. In fact M. d'Osmond was her great-nephew, and the memoirs were written for his father Comte Rainulphe d'Osmond, the Duchesse de Maillé's brother, who predeceased Mme de Boigne in 1862.

[2] II, 698-9. On this occasion M. de Charlus mentions Montesquiou, his own original, as one of the few people in the Faubourg who know their Balzac.

de Duras, borne by Mme Verdurin in her brief second marriage,[1] from the lady who had been in love ninety years before with the great Chateaubriand. His reading of Mme de Boigne, indeed, was perhaps an important factor in his decision to call his heroine Albertine. Albertine's name, like that of Saint-Loup, had many simultaneous sources: he knew it already from Marceline Desbordes-Valmore's poem, from his hostess Albertine de Montebello, from Clomesnil's rival Albertine Groscul, from Princesse Albertine de Broglie, who inherited it from Mme de Staël's daughter, her great-grandmother, and we shall find reason a little later to associate it with several young men. But in the memoirs of Mme de Boigne he found Mlle de Staël herself described at the age of eleven, a century ago, in terms which suggest the precocious Albertine of whom the Narrator hears her aunt Mme Bontemps speaking at Odette's at-home: ' "what's the matter, Albertine?" asked Mme de Boigne—"oh dear, everyone thinks I'm happy, and my heart is full of abysses!" ' And Mme de Boigne might have almost foreseen the enigmatic young girl on the front at Balbec when she wrote, a few years later: 'despite the somewhat daring colour of her hair, and a slight tendency towards freckles, Albertine de Staël was one of the most enchanting people I have ever met, and there was something angelic, pure and ideal in her face which I have never seen in any other'.[2]

Proust sent cuttings of 'Sentiments filiaux' and 'Journées de Lecture' to Marie Nordlinger, asking her to return them 'in case I ever decide to publish a volume of my articles'—a plan to which he was often to revert in the next few years, though it only reached fruition twelve years later, in Pastiches et Mélanges. Georges de Lauris delighted him by reading the latter article to his bereaved father, and by declaring it 'better than Francis Jammes'—an author whom Proust had first read in June 1906, and was to regard later as one of his own precursors. Even Montesquiou wrote to congratulate him, though only by way of a hint that he was still expecting a eulogy of Les Hortensias bleus, the first volume of the extremely expensive de luxe edition of his complete poetical works, for which he had insisted on Proust's taking out a subscription in the previous December. Count Robert called early in April to autograph his latest essays, Altesses sérénissimes, and held forth in a monologue as brilliant as ever. But the signs of approaching old age were visible

[1] III, 955.
[2] Boigne, Mémoires, vol. 1, 256, 413.

beneath the rouge and powder of his cheeks; and was there not a note of malice in Marcel's reassurance: 'it isn't age that gives you the pink, wrinkled face of a moss-rose, a flower which, as well you know, has a beauty of its own!'? The Count took umbrage, and Proust had to find excuses for his simile: 'in the now distant era when we used to meet at Mme Lemaire's on the first fine evenings of spring, and take off our overcoats under the lilacs, I saw you once with an exquisite flower in your button-hole, which you told me was a moss-rose,' he explained; and in the memory at least there was no prevarication, for he had used it long ago in *Jean Santeuil*, in a passage which mentioned Montesquiou by name.[1]

In the spring Proust performed a favour for Maurice Duplay, now director of the Théâtre de Cluny, by recommending a struggling actress, Mlle Macherez, to Louisa de Mornand. Louisa, who was now established in her new liaison with Robert Gangnat, the legal agent of the Société des Auteurs Dramatiques, was generous to 'this little Cinderella, who went home dazzled by your charm'. Perhaps it was at this time that Duplay took Proust to a favourite brothel. The manageress and her staff put on their politest manners, and Proust courteously co-operated, showing absolute belief that one young whore was indeed an actress 'resting', and another was 'a lady in society'. He even gave a family sideboard to 'Toinette', and found her a more respectable post as mannequin at Paquin's. Perhaps this pathetic but by no means ignoble habit of visiting brothels in quest of social relaxation, which belonged also to Swann and the Narrator,[2] was lifelong. As late as 1921 Paul Léautaud recorded Proust's way of driving with Odilon Albaret to one of these establishments, where he would ask two or three of the young ladies to step down, regale them with glasses of milk, and converse for hours in his darkling taxi on love, death and kindred subjects. Another of Duplay's revelations belongs apparently to the period before the death of Proust's parents: he felt 'a tender interest' in a young friend of Duplay's family, Mlle Hélène d'Ideville, 'whose mysterious beauty was like a painting by Leonardo', and who 'inspired in him ideas of marriage'. Here, perhaps, is a faint hint of Albertine in her socially presentable aspect, the niece of Mme Bontemps whom the Narrator's

[1] *Jean Santeuil*, vol. 1, 205. Similarly the Baron de Charlus, after eyeing the Narrator so strangely at Balbec, pretends to be busy arranging 'the moss-rose that hung in his button-hole' (I, 752).

[2] I, 373, 575-8.

mother is prepared to accept, however reluctantly, as her son's
fiancée.

On 11 April Proust made his first appearance in society for nearly
two years by attending the première of Reynaldo Hahn's orchestral
suite *Le Bal de Béatrice d'Este* at the Princesse de Polignac's.
Reynaldo conducted from his seat at the piano, and at his loudest
chords the tottering candlesticks seemed about to fall and set fire to
the paper roses on the dais[1]; but Proust forgot the danger of this
catastrophe when he noticed how Reynaldo's warning forefinger
a moment later 'became a magic baton which flew to the furthest
corner of the orchestra, just in time to wake a little sleeping triangle'.
Most of all, however, he was interested to see, after his long absence,
'how all the people I used to know have aged!' This musical At
Home supplied the first hint of another, at which the Narrator
realised, amid the wreckage of a world grown old around him, that
the recovery of Time Lost would be a race against death.

It was also in the spring of 1907 that Proust conducted his last
friendship with a beautiful young nobleman. The Marquis Illan de
Casa-Fuerte was the son of the Empress Eugénie's niece, the lovely
Flavie de Casa-Fuerte whom Montesquiou had adored nearly twenty
years before. His extraordinary good looks were of the kind which
seem (until, a whole generation late, they suddenly decompose into
old age) to last for ever: 'he was an incarnation of Dorian Gray',
wrote André Germain; and D'Annunzio, who knew him through
Montesquiou, used Illan as a model for Aldo, 'a young, fallen god', in
his novel *Forse chè si*. Proust and Illan had met when the young
marquis was still a schoolboy. Lucien Daudet had taken him one
evening to the Grand Guignol, saying mysteriously: "we shall be
meeting a friend of mine afterwards"; and there, on the pavement
outside the theatre, stood Proust in crumpled evening-clothes and
shaggy top-hat, with drooping moustache and enormous dark-
ringed eyes which seemed, said Illan, 'to eat up the rest of his face'.
They supped at Larue's, where Proust discussed his asthma and
insomnia: "I lie awake until morning, and it's only when I hear our
manservant saying to the cook: 'Hush, you'll wake Monsieur Marcel,'
that I fall into a deep sleep." When Illan began to visit 102 Boulevard

---

[1] Proust remembered this impression for the performance of the Vinteuil
Sonata at Mme de Saint-Euverte's soirée, when the forward young Mme de
Cambremer, much to Général de Froberville's admiration, dashes out to remove
the candlestick (I, 336).

Haussmann he shyly confessed that he, too, suffered from asthma, "particularly from the smell of horses, so I've had to give up riding!" Charmed by his host's lyrical description of the scents of flowers and leaves which caused *his* asthma, Illan declared: "I say, that's poetry!" to which Proust crossly replied: "You mean, it's torture." Next morning Illan received a long letter on 'the appalling attack caused by your perfume' which had followed his visit, together with a parcel containing so many packets of Legras anti-asthma powders that the Marquis, nearly thirty years later, remarked 'I still have several left'. In return Illan sent a pink coral box, in whose colour the coquettish Proust saw 'a delicate tinge of friendship': 'I have seen, desired, mourned it,' he wrote, 'deep in the gulfs of ocean, and high in the skies of summer, where seven o'clock in the evening stripped its last roses of their petals and left them strewn over the fields of the sea.'[1] Proust was equally delighted by his young friend's archaic Christian name. 'When the late Marquis de Casa-Fuerte wished to give his son a christening-gift', he wrote in an unpublished article,[2] 'he found no rarer or sweeter jewel in eleventh-century Spain—not even in the leather of Cordova, or Arab goblets with their pink and yellow-pink reflections—than the forename of Illan, which no one had borne since the capture of Toledo in 1085, and which seemed to have been preserved by a vein of marble lacework in some half-Moslem cathedral, lit by candles unextinguished for nearly a thousand years.' But their relationship was no more than a brief platonic flirtation between an older man and a youth accustomed to admiration from either sex; and if a parallel to Illan exists in *A la Recherche* it is the 'young Létourville' from whom the Narrator, after meeting him at the last matinée of the Princesse de Guermantes, is appalled to receive a letter signed 'your very respectful young friend'.[3]

Proust was fifteen years senior to the boyish marquis; he had abandoned all hope of satisfactory friendship within the aristocracy, and now sought, with the inverse snobism of the heart, only the

[1] An image used by Legrandin at Combray in his rhapsody on the sunsets of Balbec (I, 130).

[2] The passage probably belonged to the digression on Christian names in '*Journées de Lecture*' (an article which is known to have been severely cut), or to its promised sequel '*On Snobism and Posterity*' (cf. *Chroniques*, 87, 90) which was never published, although Proust actually sent it to *Le Figaro*.

[3] III, 927-8.

equally precarious devotion of the working-classes—for the time
being, of his secretary Ulrich. Perhaps it was just as well that Ulrich
was not particularly interested in men, and Proust was not displeased
to discover that he had a mistress, who wrote to him: 'so just one
more little peck, big fond lover, for this tiny morsel of a woman
who isn't the usual sort, oh no, but's thine'. "As you see, she goes
on to quote some poetry, beginning '*Love is such a peculiar feeling,
It's all or it's nothing, is love*' ", Ulrich pointed out: "now that, I'm
quite certain, is by Victor Hugo"; and he added: "as a matter of
fact, she isn't exactly pretty, but I go to bed with her because she's so
extraordinarily intelligent, as you can tell from her letter."

The impact of Illan's beauty on Montesquiou was more serious.
The Count felt, as he had with others of Marcel's friends, such as
Delafosse, Reynaldo Hahn and Lucien Daudet, that here was his
longed-for spiritual heir. André Germain was present at the reception
on a radiant June afternoon, amid the roses of the Pavillon des Muses,
of the Marquis and his young bride Béatrice, on whose forehead
Count Robert imprinted a chaste kiss; and again at the dreadful scene
which marked the inevitable end. A portrait of Illan in the Salon
showed a great deal too much of his neck and shoulders and almost
led, it was rumoured, to his expulsion from his club, the Cercle de
l'Union. Montesquiou cursed painter, portrait and model in a paroxysm of fury which made the gallery and everyone in it tremble.
Even the portrait had an unhappy ending: some years later Illan's
second wife was urged by her maid on no account to enter the drawing-room where it was hung, "because a lady called this morning
and cut Monsieur le Marquis's eyes out!"

The publication of Mme de Noailles's latest poems, *Les Éblouissements*, was now imminent. Already, in '*Journées de Lecture*', Proust
had announced that the new volume would be equal to *Feuilles
d'Automne* and *Les Fleurs du Mal* combined; and then, just as after
giving a stupendous tip to a waiter he always had qualms lest it
might not be quite enough, he telephoned the poetess to enquire
whether there were other works of genius to which she would prefer
hers to be compared. However, his admiration for her writing had
never been more justified. *Les Éblouissements* was the product of her
love for Barrès, a love now ending, for Barrès in a feeling that he
could no longer cope with her interminable effervescence, for Mme
de Noailles in a fury of injured vanity which ravaged the rest of her
life; and these voluptuous, anguished and truly 'dazzling' poems, by

their technical influence during the next few years upon Valéry and Cocteau, were to help to bridge the gap between symbolism and the twentieth century.[1]

Proust's review gave him more than usual trouble. His efforts to get it on the front page, to prevent drastic cutting, or banishment to the *Figaro Literary Supplement*, 'which is a foretaste of eternal oblivion', were in vain. One morning, while he was writing, the inside of his chimney collapsed; the concierge Antoine heroically performed first-aid repairs at the risk of asphyxiation; and then workmen mended the damage all day, in a cloud of plaster and brick-dust, while Proust lugubriously watched them from his bed. He wrote against the grain, for the still-subterranean rising of his own genius was now so far advanced that he would never again submit himself wholeheartedly to the literature of other writers, even of those greater than Mme de Noailles; and his mixed feelings are evident in the discords of irony and impatience which sound beneath the high pitch of his praise. But here and there a remark suggests that the revelation of *A la Recherche* is very near indeed. 'She knows,' he says, 'that a profound idea which has time and space enclosed within it is no longer subject to their tyranny, and becomes infinite in extent and duration'; and 'her metaphors substitute for a description of what exists a resurrection of what we have felt—which is the only reality of any interest'. Remembering the Japanese dwarf trees at Bing's, he sent Ulrich to buy three, which he contemplated at his bedside and used for his review, in words repeated by Albertine in her rhapsody on ice-cream, as a simile of the immensity which can be contained in a single line of poetry.[2] Not only his review, how-ever, but the very words of Mme de Noailles supplied hints for his novel. The poems on gardens, which formed one of the sincerest elements in her inspiration, since they reached back to her childhood

---

[1] To take Valéry only, and to quote only a few of many parallels, such lines as (p. 410):

> '*Tout l'azur chaque jour tombé dans ma poitrine*
> *S'élançait en gestes sans fin . . .*'

contain the essence of *La Jeune Parque*, while the seed of *Le Cimetière marin* is in (p. 5)

> '*Je crois voir, ses pieds nus appuyés sur les tombes,*
> *Un Éros souriant qui nourrit des colombes*'

or in (p. 386)

> '*Hélios . . . Tu me lances tes feux en t'écriant: Va vivre!*'

[2] III, 130; *Chroniques*, 187.

at Amphion and a lost time of innocence, were foreshadowings of
Combray; and he remembered three lines of a poem on Venice—

> '*La Dogana, le soir, montrant sa boule d'or*
> *Semble arrêter le temps et prolonger encor*
> *La forme du soleil qui descend dans l'abîme* . . .

for the scene where the Narrator watches the sun frozen in the act of
setting over the dome of the Salute.[1]

His review appeared on 15 June in the outer darkness of the
Figaro Literary Supplement. He called on Calmette at midnight in the
Figaro offices (where midnight, as for himself, was the equivalent of
high noon elsewhere), and thanked him profusely for printing it at
all. "I should like to have you to dinner," he said unguardedly,
thinking, as he told Mme Straus, "that I might be well enough to
give a dinner in a few years, or before my death, which is perhaps
less distant"; but Calmette urbanely pulled out his notebook,
searched for a vacant date, and asked: "would July the first suit
you?"

The dinner of 1 July in a private room at the Ritz was Proust's
first and last 'grand dinner' for several years; it was also his first
recorded appearance at the hotel in the Place Vendôme from which he
was later to seem so inseparable that people would call him 'Proust
of the Ritz'. The guests, for whom Ulrich was deputed to telephone
all over Paris while his master slept, might well recall to an Anglo-
Saxon reader the words of Blake's *Island in the Moon*—'so all the
people in this book enter'd into the room'. The ladies included the
Comtesses de Brantes, Briey, Haussonville, Ludre and Noailles, and
Élisabeth de Clermont-Tonnerre, who brought her reactionary anti-
Dreyfusist husband Philibert; among the men, besides Calmette
himself, were Albu, Guiche, Jacques Émile Blanche, Proust's former
second Jean Béraud, Beaunier of *Le Figaro* and Emmanuel Bibesco.
The dinner, for which Guiche had chosen the food and wines, went
perfectly; the guests seemed delighted to see their resurrected host,
and old Mme de Brantes was true to form by being charming to
Proust and malicious to everyone else. After dinner came Illan de
Casa-Fuerte and Vicomte Robert d'Humières with their wives, Mme
de Chevigné, the Princesse de Polignac, Gabriel de La Rochefoucauld, Reginald Lister from the British Embassy, whom Proust
had known since the early '90s at Mme Straus's, and Ulrich himself;

[1] III, 1114; *Contre Sainte-Beuve*, 124.

and all adjourned to a gold and cherry-red drawing-room for music. Fauré had promised to play, but had been prevented only the day before by a sudden illness, the beginning of his subsequent deafness; and Proust had turned in desperation to his old friend Risler, who performed piano music by Beethoven, Chopin, Couperin and Fauré, and at Proust's special request the overture to the *Mastersingers* and the Liebestod from *Tristan*. Maurice Hayot, the professor of the violin at the Conservatoire, accompanied by Fauré's favourite pupil Mlle Hasselmans, played Fauré's Violin Sonata, one of the originals of Vinteuil's. Proust noted how Mme d'Haussonville swayed the long aigrette of her head-dress like a metronome, as much as to say "I know this piece backwards!"; and he used his observation for the dowager Marquise de Cambremer's rapture in the Vinteuil Sonata at Mme de Saint-Euverte's.[1] During the interval Élisabeth de Clermont-Tonnerre watched Proust and Mme de Noailles, two strange figures in furs, like a male and female Eskimo, circulating among the guests. "I gave Risler 1,000 francs," he whispered anxiously to the older ladies, "do you think it was enough?"; and "a great deal too much!" they replied in chorus, for he was spoiling their own market.

On 23 July in *Le Figaro* Proust published an obituary on Robert de Flers's grandmother, almost devoid of literary merit, but interesting because he is evidently mourning, in Mme de Rozière's name, for his own grandmother and mother. It is possible that this accidental equation of his beloved dead assisted in a fundamental feature of the structure of his novel—the taking-over by the Narrator's grandmother of many of the functions of Proust's own mother, above all of her death. Perhaps this article also revived his desire to revisit a place where he had grieved, sixteen years before, for his grandmother, and where he would now mourn again for his mother.

Dr Bize insisted that Proust should take a holiday immediately, for he had spent the past two years almost entirely in bed. On 1 August he was still hesitating, as he told Reynaldo, between 'Brittany, Cabourg, Touraine, Germany—and remaining in Paris'; but a few days later he made the choice which determined the future course of his novel and of his life. He had stayed at Cabourg as a child with his grandmother, and again with Mme Proust on his army leave in September 1890; when alone at Cabourg in September 1891 he had been overcome, like his Narrator, by a sudden renewal of

[1] I, 328.

grief for Mme Weil, who had died in January of the previous year; a visit to Cabourg had been vaguely planned for August 1896; in August 1903 his mother had unsuccessfully urged him to go there, because 'you used to find it suited your health so well'; and only a year ago Cabourg had been in his list of possibilities before he finally decided on Versailles. When he left, about 7 August, for this paradise of his past, it was in quest of the sunlit seas of Time Lost and of the two dead women who would watch over him there: 'it was the memory of Mother, who continues to guide me aright, that led me to Cabourg,' he told Mme Catusse. But he also went to meet a destiny which in years to come would complete and destroy the circle of his being.

The visitor who beheld the stately hotels of the Cabourg seafront would hardly guess that here was one of the ancient places of France. The name, by a derivation which Brichot at La Raspelière would certainly have explained if Mme Verdurin had not interrupted him in time, came (like Caithness in Scotland) from the Norse root Cath, a harbour-basin; it was here in 1058 that William of Normandy, the future conqueror of England, hurled the troops of Henri I of France into the sea, while the unhappy monarch, in the words of the minstrel Wace,

> *'Mounting the hill of Bassebourg,*
> *Saw Varaville and saw Cabourg'.*[1]

But the modern Cabourg began in 1853 with the arrival of two Paris financiers in search of a new site for a luxurious watering-place. The railway age had made the Normandy coast accessible to holiday-makers; Dieppe, Trouville and Deauville to the east had already been discovered; but here the adventurers found a virgin expanse of barren dunes and level sea-sands ripe for development. By the 1880s an unreal city of villas and hotels had arisen, in a semicircle whose diameter was the seafront, whose centre was the Grand Hôtel, and whose radii were traced by a fan-work of avenues shaded with limes and Normandy poplars. It was in this hinterland that the Narrator visited Elstir's studio, 'on one of the newest avenues of Balbec, in which his villa was perhaps the most sumptuously ugly of all'.[2] A little past the frontier of the new town, nearly a mile inland from the

[1]   *'Monté fu de suz Basseborc,*
        Vit Varaville e vit Caborc'.

[2] I, 833.

sea, was old Cabourg, a hamlet of thatched cottages and farmhouses, where ducks and hens ran among the fishnets hung to dry. Nevertheless, the equivalent near Cabourg of Balbec-le-Vieux or Balbec-en-Terre was not Cabourg-le-Vieux, but the mediaeval town of Dives, to which the road runs from Cabourg-le-Vieux eastward over the estuary of the little Dives river. Here, not as at Balbec 'more than five leagues away',[1] was the railway-station which served both Cabourg and Dives. The church of Dives was a huge, square-towered, fourteenth-century building which Proust as a boy with his grandmother must have visited, like the Narrator, on alighting from the train before going on to Cabourg or Trouville. The 'half-romanesque, almost Persian'[2] church of Balbec was transferred hither from Saint-Loup-de-Naud; but Dives, too, had its romanesque pillars and sculptured porch, and was famed, like the church of Balbec,[3] for its wooden figure of Christ miraculously cast ashore in A.D. 1001. This legend may have led the boy Proust to expect 'a church receiving at its base the last foam of angry waves'[4]; but the sea had receded long since, and Dives like Balbec-en-Terre was disappointingly far inland. To complete the Narrator's disillusionment Proust transferred to Balbec from his visit to Saint-Malo in the yacht *Hélène* the tramcars, the billiard-room and the statue of Admiral Duguay-Trouin.[5]

Cabourg is a little over 150 miles from Paris: the railway-journey from the Gare Saint-Lazare lasted only five and a half hours, and the 'beautiful, generous, one-twenty-two train' arrived in time for dinner the same evening. For the Narrator's long night-journey to the end of the world Proust thought of his own flight to Brittany with Reynaldo in 1895, and for the mountain valley lit simultaneously by sunrise and moon, of his sleepless train-ride through the gorges of the Yonne to Avallon in 1903. At Mézidon, eighteen miles before Cabourg, the traveller changed from the Paris-Cherbourg express to the local train which meandered, stopping at every village and small seaside-resort, past Cabourg-Dives to Trouville. Mézidon is Doncières in its aspect as junction-town for Balbec; and this 'Transatlantic' to Cabourg and Trouville was none other than the 'Little Train'. Just as the Narrator would set out with Albertine from Balbec, joined at every wayside station by members of 'the faithful', to Douville, the terminus for Mme Verdurin's La Raspelière,

[1] I, 658.   [2] I, 385.   [3] I, 658.
[4] I, 659.   [5] I, 659, 664; II, 772.

so Proust would journey past stations each with a name in '-ville', and symbolising a friend staying nearby, to Louisa de Mornand at Bénerville or Mme Straus's Clos des Mûriers at Trouville. Several of the names of places served by the Little Train at Balbec come from villages in the same district: Saint-Vaast, Douville, Angerville, Saint-Pierre-aux-Ifs are all here. Other names in the same exquisite litany—Hermonville, Saint-Mars-le-Vieux, Toutainville, Montmartin, Incarville, Infreville, Graincourt, Bricquebec, La Sogne, Fervaches—are taken with little or no change from parts of Normandy more or less distant from Cabourg: Proust had only to study his map and choose. A few, such as Hermenonville, Gourville, Marcouville and La Raspelière itself, come from near Illiers: 'these names seemed strange to me,' says the Narrator, 'although if I had read them in a book I should have seen that they had some connection with the names of places near Combray.'[1] We have already found two places in the country of Balbec, Féterne and Rivebelle, on the shores of Lake Geneva near Évian. There is, however, a Riva-Bella eight miles west of Cabourg, reached in Proust's time by a humbler relative of the Little Train known as a steam-tram, which plied through Le Homme-sur-Mer, Merville, Ouistreham, Riva-Bella and Lion-sur-Mer to Luc-sur-Mer. But Rivebelle as a beautiful apparition seen far across the bay from Balbec, enjoying a longer summer because it faces southward, is Le Havre on the opposite side of the Seine estuary, though this is not a holiday town but a busy port; and as a pleasure haunt with a superb restaurant Rivebelle is a synthesis of other resorts to the east of Cabourg, such as Houlgate, Villers-sur-Mer, Deauville or Trouville. The farm-restaurants of La Croix d'Heuland and Marie-Antoinette, with their cider and cherries, which the Narrator frequented with Albertine and the little band,[2] are both within a mile of Saint-Vaast on the Cabourg-Trouville railway. The Narrator praises by name another, more sumptuous farm-restaurant, that of Guillaume-le-Conquèrant at Dives,[3] which served, as Proust thought, the best cider of all.

In this very year Canon Joseph Marquis of Saint-Jacques at

[1] I, 661. Conversely the name Combray itself is that of a village fifteen miles south of Caen: we may be sure that when Proust saw it on his map it chimed with his knowledge of the town called Combres near Illiers, and so gave him the name for the village of the Narrator's childhood.

[2] I, 903-4; II, 837; III, 479.

[3] II, 35.

Illiers, who had taught the boy Marcel Latin and the names of the flowers in his presbytery garden, published his learned monograph *Illiers* in the series of *Archives historiques du diocèse de Chartres*. The good canon's interest in place-names is less exclusive than that of the curé of Combray; but he rather shakily discusses the derivations of Illiers (the Celtic Illia = *ville*), Montjouvin (rejecting a rival's *Mons Jovis*, but supplying no alternative), Tansonville (the *étançons* or props of the nearby bridge over the Thironne), La Rachepelière (from *arrache pieux*, alluding to the exploit of Eudes d'Arrachepel in removing stakes from a moat in a mediaeval siege),[1] and the like. Probably because Proust read this volume during or near the time of his visit to Cabourg, he made the curé of Combray, who is 'spending the last years of his life in writing a great work on Combray and its environs', publish 'a rather interesting little brochure', as the Dowager-Marquise de Cambremer tells the Narrator, on the place-names of Normandy.[2] It was not until twelve years later, however, in 1919, that Proust began his researches for Brichot's brilliant refutation of the poor curé's etymologies at La Raspelière,[3] and corresponded for this purpose with the great French authorities on place-names, Louis Dimier and Henri Longnon.

In the train from Paris that August Proust was joined by Dr Doyen, who remarked, exactly in the manner of Cottard, "Isn't it odd that Mme Greffulhe has never managed to round up such a brilliant salon as Mme Arman de Caillavet!" He stayed at the Grand Hôtel, which like its namesake at Balbec was an enormous edifice on the seafront, with 200 bedrooms, a lift, and a long dining-room from which a succession of plate-glass windows opened directly on the promenade, the sands, and the dazzling sea. Adjoining the hotel to the west was the casino, lined by a row of flagpoles and containing a theatre, a concert-hall, a ball-room and gambling tables. It was near this casino that Charlus eyed the Narrator so strangely, and within it that Bloch's cousin Esther Lévy behaved so scandalously with the actress Léa, the Narrator joined the little band in teasing the dancing-master, and Octave ('In the Soup') played baccarat.[4] To the east was the bathing-establishment of the hotel, where sea-water baths,

---

[1] Cf. II, 963, where M. de Cambremer gives a similar etymology for La Raspelière.

[2] I, 203; II, 809.

[3] II, 887-91, 913, 922.

[4] I, 751; I, 903; II, 902, 853; I, 893; I, 677.

cold showers and perhaps other pleasures were available, for it was
here that the Narrator suspected Albertine of going for the same
illicit purposes as Léa and her friends.[1] On the sands immediately
below the hotel was the bandstand, where the Narrator hears a symphony concert on the morning of his introduction to the Princesse
de Luxembourg.[2] At high tide the music mingled with the waves and
seemed to come from under the sea; and the violins 'hummed like a
swarm of bees that had strayed over the water'.[3]

For the first few days Proust was overcome by renewed grief for
his mother. His 'intermittences of the heart' were more complex than
those of the Narrator on his second arrival at Balbec: the Grand
Hôtel was peopled with memories not only of his mother but of
poor Mme Weil, now seventeen years in her grave, and his two
bereavements joined here into one. It was symptomatic that his first
excursion was to visit the motherless Georges de Lauris and his
widower father at Houlgate, the next station past Dives-Cabourg of
the little train. With unconscious cruelty he insisted on borrowing
Georges's favourite photograph of his dead mother: "I want to look
at it when I'm alone," he said; and he told Lauris that he had never
been so unhappy: 'sorrow isn't meant to be stirred, one needs to keep
still to give it time to settle and become serene and limpid again'.

The penance of grief, however, was not his primary object in
returning to Cabourg. Mme Straus's son Jacques Bizet, his former
schoolfellow, was now the director of a car-hire company, the
Taximètres Unic de Monaco, with branches in Monaco, Paris and
Cabourg. Proust saw the possibility of renewing in Normandy the
visits by automobile to churches and cathedrals which he had enjoyed
with the Bibesco brothers in the spring of 1902. He wrote before
leaving to Emmanuel Bibesco for 'archeologico-spiritual advice', and
again to Émile Mâle, after unsuccessfully sending Ulrich to beg him
to call. At this time he intended to move on to Brittany, and this
abortive plan may have helped in the fusion of Cabourg with Beg-
Meil, and the situation of Balbec in a mysterious borderland between
Normandy and the Atlantic promontories. Another request related
still more directly to his novel, for he asked Mâle to recommend 'an
old, untouched, Balzacian provincial town, which would be still
more fruitful for my dreams than an ordinary cathedral, or even a
sublime one'. Before the end of his first week at Cabourg he had

[1] III, 491.
[2] I, 698.   [3] I, 954; II, 780.

hired his taxi-cab and his three drivers, Jossien, Odilon Albaret, and Agostinelli.

Alfred Agostinelli was a native of Monaco, the son of Eugène Agostinelli, an Italian from Leghorn. His mother, *née* Marie Louise Bensa, of Provençal birth with, it is said, some Arab blood, had already borne ten children to a previous husband named Vittoré, before producing Alfred and his brother Émile. Alfred was a young man of eighteen,[1] whose round face, large, dark-ringed eyes and black moustache gave him a curious, fleeting resemblance to the master to whom he was later to cause such suffering. Agostinelli was photographed that summer, in his black rubber driving-cape and peaked cap, sitting with Albaret in one of the primeval Unic taxis by the public gardens behind the Grand Hôtel: his features show intelligence and ingratiating charm, with a perhaps deceptive hint of softness and indolence, but no sign of evil. It must be said at once that in all the evidence for Proust's relationship with Agostinelli during the next seven years there is nothing for which this honest and amiable young man can be blamed.

The next two months were among the strangest and perhaps the happiest—though he still repeated that he had never been 'so agitated, so sterile, so miserable'—in Proust's life. Every day he hurtled through the Normandy landscape, past frightened villages, immense panoramas of sea, green forests, fruiting hawthorns and apple-trees, beside this sleek and efficient young hireling. Poetic images arose in his mind, roused both by the beauty of Agostinelli's presence and by the mystery of his craft. 'His black rubber cape,' he wrote a few months later, 'and the hooded helmet which enclosed the fullness of his young, beardless face, made him resemble a pilgrim, or rather, a nun of speed.' As he deftly touched first one, then another secret lever, changing the tone and pitch of the engine's droning, he seemed like Saint Cecilia improvising some divine melody on her celestial organ; and the wheel over which he bowed so intently, a cross within a circle, seemed like an emblem carried by a stone saint in a cathedral to display the characteristic of his virtue on earth or the instrument of his death. 'May the steering-wheel of my young mechanic,' Proust prayed in vain, 'remain for ever the symbol of his talent, rather than the prefiguration of his martyrdom!' On they flared: Proust led, he told Lauris, 'the life of a cannon-ball in flight'; and when he alighted from the car, 'a kind of trembling like that of the motor continues to

[1] He was born on 11 October 1888.

hum and vibrate in me, and won't let my hand come to rest and
obey me'. Asthma, despite the rush of wind and clouds of dust, had
left him: at the cost of taking innumerable cups of coffee at wayside
farmhouses, but little or no food, he was staying awake all day.

His first trip was to Caen, through the labyrinth of rivulets and
marshlands west of the Dives, past Varaville and Gonneville to the
watershed above the Orne. The city was invisible in the vast blue
plain below them: its position was marked by the spires of Saint-
Étienne and Saint-Pierre, soon joined by that of Saint-Sauveur and
the towers of La Trinité, which refused inexorably to draw nearer,
yet as the road wound right and left seemed to change places in a
ritual dance. An ancient memory returned to Proust: he saw again
the movement of the village spires round the wide horizon of the
Méréglise way, as they glided into ever-different angles of relationship with the steeple of Saint-Jacques at Illiers. Here at Caen the
shifting spires were at the centre of a circle, at Illiers they had danced
along its circumference; yet the two visions, united across a gulf of
space and time, were miraculously the same. Suddenly he was driving
through the city: the spires of Saint-Étienne, 'towering over us like
giants with their full height, threw themselves so brutally in our way
that we only just had time to avoid colliding with the porch'. A few
days later he visited Bayeux Cathedral, which he preferred to the
churches of Caen, although he complained to Émile Mâle that he had
found the iconography of its sculptures bafflingly obscure. At
Balleroy, ten miles south of Bayeux, he saw the château, built by
Mansard, decorated by Mignard and famous for its tapestries by
Boucher: it was one of the few châteaux of France still inhabited,
like Guermantes by the Duc de Guermantes, by the family to whom
the nearby village had long ago given its name. But Proust was ill-
pleased with the late Comte de Balleroy, who had scattered among
the Bouchers, which his son had framed in red damask, his own
excruciating paintings of hunting-scenes.[1] He called on Marquis
Charles de' Eragues and his wife Henriette, Montesquiou's cousin,

[1] Proust used his memory of Balleroy for the Château de Guermantes. Saint-
Loup informs the Narrator that its tapestries were not mediaeval as he supposed,
but 'by Boucher, bought in the nineteenth century by an art-loving Guermantes,
who had hung beside them the mediocre hunting-scenes which he had painted
himself, in an ugly drawingroom draped with red plush' (II, 14, 15). Mme de
Balleroy is the great-aunt of the Duchesse de Guermantes's niece, who sends
the Narrator a declaration of love to which, crushed by the departure of Albertine, he can make no reply (III, 190, 449).

at their mansion in the market-place of Falaise, with its gardens descending to the rapid stream, and remembered the occasion next year in a charming paragraph of *Contre Sainte-Beuve*.[1] On another day they arrived late at Lisieux, twenty miles south-east of Cabourg and near the small town of Cambremer, which gave its name (pronounced 'Camembert' by the lift-boy) to the Cambremers in *A la Recherche*. When they reached the cathedral night had fallen, and Proust despaired of seeing the porch (through which Henry II of England had passed at his wedding to Eleanor of Guyenne in 1152), with its trees of stone mentioned by Ruskin; but the resourceful Agostinelli played his headlamps from leaf to leaf of the arboreal pillars, and night was turned to day.

Proust had visited Balleroy for the sake of its Bouchers with the artist Paul Helleu, who hoped to convert him to his theory that 'the primitives are worthless, my dear Marcel, because nobody knew how to paint before Rubens', and that painting reached its zenith in the eighteenth century. Helleu's own art was based on this belief, and Degas had called him 'a steam Watteau', a joke which the unfortunate Saniette at La Raspelière transfers to Elstir, saying that he prefers Helleu to Elstir as a moderniser of the eighteenth century.[2] Elstir, in fact, in one of his multitudinous aspects, is based on Helleu, from whose name (as well as Whistler's) his own is taken. The rather anomalous Elstirs which the Narrator sees on his first visit to the Hôtel de Guermantes—the 'man in evening-dress in his own drawing-room', and the same person 'in frock coat and top-hat at a regatta where he was obviously out of place'—were identified by Jacques Émile Blanche as paintings by Helleu.[3] Helleu was staying in Deauville at the time, perhaps in the very studio visited by the Narrator; and in this environment he must have seemed more than ever like his description by Léon Daudet's friend Paul Mariéton: 'he looks like an invitation to a funeral taking a holiday at the seaside'. He was a cadaverous, nervous, yellow-faced, black-bearded man, and always wore black; unlike Elstir, with his 'beautiful Gabrielle', whom Mme

[1] *Contre Sainte-Beuve*, 274-5.
[2] II, 938-9.
[3] II, 420-2. The mythological Elstirs which the Narrator sees on the same occasion, the poet walking with a Muse or riding on the back of a centaur, are pictures by Gustave Moreau, whom Proust had already discussed in similar words in an essay on Moreau written in 1898 (*Contre Sainte-Beuve*, 386-96) and again in his review of *Les Éblouissements* (cf. *Chroniques*, 178-9).

Verdurin called 'lower than the lowest street-woman',[1] he had
married a slim and charming lady who was perfectly presentable in
society and whom he loved devotedly. Proust had met him in the
1890s through Montesquiou, who had made Helleu's fortune in the
Faubourg Saint-Germain (perhaps to his detriment as an artist) by
persuading him to illustrate *Les Hortensias bleus*, and take a hundred
sketches of Comtesse Greffulhe in the intimacy of Bois-Boudran. In
La Bible d'Amiens, after praising Monet's studies of the façade of
Rouen Cathedral, Proust had remarked: 'but for interiors of cathedrals I know of none to equal in beauty those of the great painter
Helleu'. The Narrator's visit to Elstir's studio is based, then, on
Helleu at Cabourg, though the pictures he sees there were suggested
by those of Helleu's betters. Another painter staying at Cabourg,
however, posed during a moment for Elstir. Proust called on the
Bibescos' friend Vuillard in his studio, finding him at work in blue
overalls ('of a rather too pastel shade, I thought,' he wrote to
Reynaldo). Vuillard's opinions were the very opposite of Helleu's:
"a chap like Giotto, d'you see, or then again a chap like Titian, knew
every bit as much as Monet, or then again, a chap like Raphael, d'you
see . . ." he repeated with intensity. 'He's no ordinary man, even if he
does say "chap" every twenty seconds,' was Proust's verdict, and he
made Elstir, discussing the sculptures of the church at Balbec,
deliver the same ideas in similar language: "the chap who carved that
façade of yours," Elstir tells the Narrator, "was every bit as fine a
fellow, you can take it from me, as the people you admire most
nowadays".[2] Another artist, the caricaturist Sem, was staying in the
district, and tried like Helleu to discourage Proust's love of the
Italian primitives. One night Proust brought him over the dark
Normandy roads in his taxi, all the way from Trouville to Cabourg.
At every turning they met a straying cow which threatened to charge
their car: "You invite me for a ride," grumbled Sem, "and then you
expect me to take part in a bull-fight in the heart of the pampas!"

   Proust complained bitterly of the noise and draught of the Grand
Hôtel—'I can't write you a proper letter amid the deafening and
melancholy tumult of this cruel and sumptuous hotel,' he told Émile
Mâle—and of his fellow-guests: 'unspeakable people', 'the common-
est set you could find anywhere', he wrote to Robert de Billy. But
throughout his life it was only in the theatrical but intensely real
environments of a luxury hotel, a society drawing-room or a great

---

[1] II, 940.   [2] I, 841.

restaurant, that he could feel at ease away from his own bedroom. 'This hotel is like a stage-setting for the third act of a farce,' he told Reynaldo; for around him was the delightful and appalling spectacle of Alfred Edwards, the gross, shady, Anglo-Levantine proprietor of *Le Matin*; his mistress, the Lesbian actress Lantelme (who may be compared to Léa at Balbec); his fifth, recently separated wife Misia Godebska; a previous wife, Mme Ralli; the Antarctic explorer Charcot, ex-husband of another ex-wife of Edwards; and Misia's first husband Thadée Natanson, one of Proust's editors on the now defunct *Revue Blanche*, all pretending not to notice one another's presence. One evening the heartening rumour circulated that Misia had shot Edwards stone-dead; but next morning, alas, he was seen to be in the best of health. Proust watched the menagerie around him with relish and entered into its curious pleasures: he attended polo matches, and every evening played baccarat, without success, in the casino.

His daily excursions were not all to gothic churches; along the stations of the little train stretched a garland of friends, the Guiches and Clermont-Tonnerres, Louisa with her new lover Robert Gangnat, and Mme Straus among the roses of her Clos des Mûriers at Trouville. Agostinelli, Albaret and Jossien were not his only male companions: he had dismissed old Félicie and Jean Blanc before leaving Paris, and hired as his manservant a portly young peasant, Nicolas Cottin, who with his wife Céline was to remain in Proust's service for seven years. Nicolas was already showing signs of his besetting fault: 'I have a horrifying suspicion that Nicolas drinks,' Proust wrote to Reynaldo. It may have been in this year that Proust visited the Château of Cantepie near Cambremer, the name of which he adapted for the Forest of Chantepie where M. de Cambremer 'went shooting every day for fifteen years and never wondered how it came by the name', and where the Narrator on his carriage-drives, first with Mme de Villeparisis and then several years later with Albertine, heard the singing birds on a hot day.[1] But from its owners, who were already acquaintances of his, he had borrowed the far more important name of Swann himself. The Swanns were an Anglo-French family whom Proust had met several years before; and they still remember his visit to Cantepie and his enquiring 'if Mr Swann

---

[1] II, 922. The forest is called Canteloup in *A l'Ombre* and Chantepie in *Sodome et Gomorrhe* (I, 720; II, 994-5), but the passage about the birds is identical.

would mind his using his name, which of course he did not mind in the least'.

Towards 20 September, when the Grand Hôtel was about to close for the winter, Proust set off late in a grey afternoon on his last and longest journey of the season with Agostinelli. The Clermont-Tonnerres had offered him a whole wing of their ancestral château at Glisolles near Évreux, promising with touching modesty: "you needn't even set eyes on us if you'd rather not!" Instead he decided to stay for a few days in Évreux itself and visit them from there. Near Évreux the car paused on the brink of a valley filled with white mist; and as they descended into the cold depths Proust felt his asthma, after six weeks' absence, suddenly returning. It was twilight when they reached Évreux, but he hurried to the cathedral, and found the stained-glass windows still lit from outside by the fading dusk: 'they contrived to steal from it jewels of light,' he wrote to Mme Straus, 'a purple that sparkled and sapphires made of fire'. As he told Jacques de Lacretelle many years later, he thought of the windows of Évreux for those of Saint-Hilaire at Combray, particularly for their quality of 'never shimmering more brightly than on days when the sun hardly showed itself, so that if it was dull outside you could be sure there would be fine weather inside'.[1] Then at the Hôtel Moderne he took not only an apartment for himself, but to ensure absolute quiet booked the empty one on the floor above. Here at last he was staying in an 'old Balzacian provincial town'; but Évreux was appallingly noisy, and his asthma grew worse. On the fourth day he set out for the Clermont-Tonnerres' château at Glisolles, an eighteenth-century building in pink sunburnt brick set in the woods and watermeadows of the little River Iton. The marquis and his wife had already given up hope when they heard from their drawing-room the wheels of a motor-car crunching on the gravel drive. "It looks like a taxi," declared Élisabeth. "Don't be absurd, m'dear." "Yes, it is, Philibert, a *red* taxi, and there's someone getting out"; and Proust alighted, panting and beaming, explaining that in order to calm his asthma he had been forced to drink seventeen cups of coffee on the way. He was introduced to their daughters Béatrix and Diane, two little girls with long curls, white frocks and bare arms, and talked about Turner's *Rivers of France*, which he promised to bring next day, and his intention to return to Paris by the valley of the Seine and to visit Monet's water-lily garden at Giverny. Occasionally he

[1] I, 59.

put in compliments on the beauty of their house, which they may
have received like the Cambremers when the Narrator praises the
draughts and broken windows of La Raspelière[1]: "It has the charm,
at once primitive and refined, of a planter's or trout-fisherman's lodge
which is also the studio of two artists," he declared. It was past
midnight when Marquis Philibert guided his tottering steps down
the stone staircase to the garden. "If you don't come again tomorrow
you won't see our roses," complained the marquise; but Proust,
delighted with his ingenuity, replied: "then I'll see them now," and
Agostinelli directed his headlamps on the floodlit rose-beds of
Glisolles. Next day *The Rivers of France* arrived in a parcel with
several enormous Ruskins, but without Proust: distracted by the din
of Évreux ('last night was like a witches' sabbath'), and abandoning
the Seine estuary until next year, he had left suddenly in his taxi for
Paris. There he endured three weeks of asthma and bed, deprived
after a few days, during which he could hire him only twice, of his
delightful companion; for Agostinelli, recalled by an illness of his
brother Émile, had fled like a swallow to his sunny home in Monte
Carlo, and would be seen no more till next summer. For the rest of
the winter Proust was driven on his weekly nights out by Jossien,
of whom he once asked, like the Narrator enquiring after the servant
of Baroness Putbus: "do you think there would be any chance of
one's going to bed with Monsieur Bizet's maid?" Jossien looked
shocked: "you embarrass me, Monsieur," he replied, "because as a
matter of fact she's my sister-in-law."

Towards the end of October Proust wrote the finest of his articles
for *Le Figaro*, '*Impressions de route en automobile*', which appeared
on 19 November. He combined into one five of his summer
journeys with 'my chauffeur, the ingenious Agostinelli'—those to
Caen, Bayeux, Lisieux, Évreux and Glisolles. The description of the
moving steeples of Caen with which the article opens was adapted in
Du Côté de chez Swann to become the Narrator's boyhood essay on
the spires of Martinville seen from Dr Percepied's carriage.[2] This is

[1] II, 944.
[2] *Pastiches et Mélanges*, 92-4, corresponds to *Pléiade*, I, 181-2. The verbal
changes are unimportant, consisting mainly in the omission of phrases which
apply only to Caen and the motor-car, and the whole passage could not have
been written at any earlier period, for it is in Proust's mature style. If there is
any truth in the rumour that the Narrator's essay had already appeared twenty
years earlier in the *Revue Lilas* at the Lycée Condorcet, it must have been in a
very different form.

the article which the Narrator sends to *Le Figaro* a little before his
dinner with Saint-Loup in the fog-bound restaurant in *Le Côté de
Guermantes*, and which remains unpublished until several years later,
after the death of Albertine.[1] Proust himself cannot have had to wait
more than a week or two, if at all. Of all his letters of congratulation
the prettiest, as he told Mme Straus, was from Agostinelli, to whom
Nicolas had sent a copy of the article. The Narrator receives a
similar letter, 'in a working-class hand and charming language', after
the appearance of his essay on the spires of Martinville, and discovers
later that it came from Théodore, the former choir-boy at Combray,
who now lives (like Agostinelli) 'in the South'.[2]

Proust was not yet in love with Agostinelli, or he would not have
acquiesced in their parting for a whole year. No doubt he had taken
pleasure in his charming and youthful company, and perhaps a little
of the Albertine with whom the Narrator drives through the country
near Balbec may come from Agostinelli. But so much of this aspect
of Albertine comes from Marie Finaly in 1892 and Marie de Chevilly
in 1899, and so much more from the girl whom Proust was to meet
at Cabourg in 1908, that little of her is left for Agostinelli. Albertine,
as we shall find, can be identified with Agostinelli (and even then not
entirely) only in 'the agony at sunrise' and in her life as a prisoner
with the Narrator, which corresponds in Proust's life to events
reaching from September 1913 to the spring of 1914. The character
in *A la Recherche* who is based on the Agostinelli of 1907 is, after all,
only the chauffeur whom the Narrator hires to drive himself and
Albertine, and compares to 'a young Evangelist bowed over his
wheel of consecration', in the very words Proust had used of 'the
ingenious Agostinelli' in his *Figaro* article.[3]

At the end of September he had renewed his lease of 102 Boulevard Haussmann, still vowing that he would leave after another year.
On 8 November he had an opportunity of acquiring the whole
building, when his aunt's share, his own and Robert's were put up
for auction. Instead he attended a soirée at Montesquiou's Pavillon

[1] II, 397; III, 567.
[2] III, 591, 701. Théodore in his capacity as a coachman who is a brother of
Mme Putbus's maid (III, 307) resembles Jossien. But perhaps Proust may be
thinking of himself and Agostinelli when he makes the Prince de Guermantes
ask: "Why on earth doesn't X . . . go to bed with his coachman? Who knows,
Théodore might be only too delighted to oblige, and perhaps he's extremely hurt
that his master doesn't make any advances" (III, 306).
[3] II, 1028.

des Muses, where the creeping odour of dead leaves from the garden mingled with the scent of orange-blossom in the drawing-room, and the ghost of Yturri seemed to move among the guests. His aunt outbid her nephews: 'my income is halved,' he lamented to Montes-quiou, and expressed doubts whether he ought not to have visited his lawyer that evening, rather than the Count—'The Cabinet of Ruses, instead of the Pavilion of Muses!' In fact, he was now rich, with an elder son's portion of the accumulated legacies of Louis and Nathé Weil, Dr and Mme Proust, and although he liked occasionally to complain that he was 'ruined', he would always remain wealthy. The fall in his income from the sale of his share in 102 Boulevard Haussmann was no doubt compensated by the rise in his capital.

On 26 December Proust published an anonymous article in *Le Figaro*, signed: D, on the recent death of his old ally, Gustave ('Sword-thrust') de Borda. By a regrettable lapse of taste his farewell to Borda was a parody of the banal society obituaries which Proust himself abominated, and later used for a last turn of the screw in the tragedy of the death of Swann.[1] As a crowning impertinence, when mentioning the ageing Borda's inability in his last years to grace the duelling-ground with his presence, he remarked: 'the last person, if our memory does not deceive us, whom he assisted in the quality of second, was our contributor M. Marcel Proust, who has always preserved a veritable cult for his memory'. A few weeks later Proust engaged in a sequence of very different parodies, which seemed to lead directly away from his novel, yet in fact formed the last turning but one in the circuitous way to *A la Recherche*.

[1] III, 199-200.

Chapter 5

PURIFICATION THROUGH PARODY
(*January – October 1908*)

IN January 1908 all Paris was delighted by one of those monumental frauds which, owing to the impudence of the swindler and
the dignity of the victim, seem more farcical than deplorable. Sir
Julius Wernher, a governor of the great diamond-mining company
of De Beer's, had been approached in London three years before by
a French electrical engineer named Lemoine with the shattering
claim that he had invented a method of making diamonds. All that
was needed was a furnace, a crucible, some common carbon, and a
great deal of money; and after witnessing an experiment in which
Lemoine seemed to produce a tiny but admittedly genuine diamond,
Sir Julius parted by agonising degrees with a total of £64,000. From
time to time Lemoine displayed still more diamonds, but could never
be persuaded to reveal his formula. Sir Julius decided to prosecute.
On 9 January 1908 Lemoine was interrogated in Paris by the magis-
trate Le Poittevin in the presence of his lawyer, who was none other
than the great Labori, the champion of Dreyfus; and the Affair of the
Diamonds immediately became world-famous. Lemoine had plotted
to announce his discovery, to buy De Beer's shares during the
consequent slump, and to make enormous profits when the market
recovered. His diamonds were identified by the jewellers from whom
they had been bought by his wife. The enquiry, and the daily fun,
lasted till the end of March.

At first Proust felt some personal alarm. Ever since the summer
after his mother's death he had been dabbling in the stock market,
often with success, and part of his capital was invested with De
Beer's. But soon the comedy of the situation seized his imagination.
The Affair of the Diamonds was, as he had remarked to Mme Straus
of the Dreyfus Affair, 'just like something in Balzac'; indeed, it was
like something in Flaubert, Michelet, the Goncourt *Journal*, almost
any writer one could imagine; and because it was quite unsuitable for
serious treatment it would certainly have brought out the more

vulnerable sides of them all. Proust had tried his hand at parody twice before, first in '*Mondanité et Mélomanie de Bouvard et Pécuchet*', written in 1895 and included in *Les Plaisirs et les Jours*, and again in his '*Fête chez Montesquiou à Neuilly*' of January 1904; and as it happened, parody was in the air this winter. *A la Manière de . . .*, an amusing but superficial volume of skits by Charles Müller and Paul Reboux (Fernand Gregh's friends and editors of *Les Lettres*), had been one of the successes of the season, and was familiar to readers of *Le Figaro* from a long extract in the issue for 26 January 1908. So it was not 'quite by accident', as Proust recalled long afterwards, that he 'chose this trivial law-suit one evening as the sole theme for a series of fragments in which I would try to imitate the manners of a number of authors'. The first group, consisting of Balzac, Émile Faguet, Michelet, and Edmond de Goncourt, appeared in the *Figaro* literary supplement on 22 February 1908; the second, Flaubert and Sainte-Beuve, on 14 March; and the last, Renan, on 28 March.

Proust's parodies are the funniest and most profound in the French language; they would also be the unkindest, were it not that he does full justice to the genius or talent of his victims, 'paying into other people's accounts,' as he claimed, 'ideas of which a more provident administrator of his own property would have preferred to keep the credit and the signature for himself'. Balzac's grandeur is suggested as unerringly as his ever-latent absurdity and moral vulgarity, and the Flaubert and Renan pastiches contain genuine beauty in a preposterous context. But hostility to his subjects, though all are writers whom he admired, is certainly present, and is keener and deeper than can be accounted for by the mere necessities of parody. 'I found it so amusing to perform literary criticism in action', Proust explained to Robert Dreyfus on 18 March 1908; but his idea of criticism was now, temporarily, very different from the definition he had put forward in *La Bible d'Amiens*. 'To help the reader to receive the full impact of the unique characteristics of a writer,' he had then declared, 'to set before his eyes a series of identical traits, which allow him to realise that these are the essential qualities of the author's genius, should be the first task of every critic.' Now, however, he had undertaken not only to detect those 'unique characteristics', but to make them appear ludicrous. Twelve years later, in his essay '*A propos du Style de Flaubert*' in the *Nouvelle Revue Française* of January 1920, he partly explained his motives. 'For writers intoxicated with Flaubert,' he remarked, 'I cannot recommend too highly the purgative, exorcising virtue of parody; we must make an intentional pastiche in order not to spend the rest of our lives in writing involuntary pastiche.' Perhaps he was serious in pleading his need for this homoeopathic remedy. Proust's Ruskin prefaces, and the *Figaro* articles of 1907, show that throughout the past eight years he had been intermittently in possession of the unique style of *A la Recherche*, not yet in its full power, but already showing little trace of influence from other writers. Nevertheless a curious regression to the derivative prose of *Jean Santeuil*, with its hints of Bourget, Anatole France, and ill-digested Balzac and Flaubert, is visible in the fragments of the lost novel of 1905-8, and is not quite outgrown, a year after the parodies, in the narrative portions of *Contre Sainte-Beuve*. It seems that the danger of imitation, which he had long overcome in other fields, was still formidable when he attempted narrative fiction. But a still deeper motive becomes visible when the parodies are considered in their historical place on Proust's way to *A la Recherche*. They clearly form part of the same series of advances towards free possession of his genius, which began in the summer of 1903 with his rejection of Ruskin, and continued in 1905 with his attack on the very act of reading in 'Sur la Lecture'. There comes a time in the ascent of a great writer when, for the sake of his own future work, he must cease to admire even his greatest predecessors from a position of inferiority. Proust was now reaching the heights from which other summits appeared level with or lower than his own. His parodies were an antidote against the toxins of admiration.

He had risen from the weeping and anguish of the past two years, and now he laughed as if for the first time since the death of his mother. In the most hilarious moments of the Balzac pastiche—'Mme Firmiani sweated in her slippers, which were one of the masterpieces of Polish craftsmanship'—the sound of Proust's solitary glee in his midnight bedroom seems still audible. Not all his jokes were against his subjects. In the courtroom scene of the Flaubert parody, when Lemoine's lawyer Labori is speaking, Proust remembered the same Labori, passionate, noble and boring, at the Zola trial ten years before: 'he had a meridional accent,' he maliciously noted, 'appealed to the generous passions, and incessantly removed his pince-nez; and as she listened Nathalie felt the unrest which is caused by true eloquence; a delicious emotion assailed her, and the cambric on her bosom palpitated like a pigeon about to take flight'. Under the alias of Renan he took the opportunity to suggest his own concealed opinion of the contrast between Mme de Noailles's nostalgia for the innocence of Nature in her writing and her avid pursuit of the pleasures of society in her life—though this had been one of his own sins, the guilt of which he would acknowledge and atone in *A la Recherche*. 'What a false position her poetry must have given her in high society,' muses 'Renan'; 'but she appears to have realised this, and to have led, perhaps not without a certain degree of ennui, an utterly retired and simple life in the little orchard with which she so habitually holds conversations.' He also made fun of himself: 'Renan' quotes Ruskin, 'whom unfortunately we read only in the pitifully platitudinous translation which Marcel Proust has bequeathed to posterity'. The Goncourt pastiche turns on the diarist's gratification when informed by Lucien Daudet[1] that 'an eccentric friend of his named Marcel Proust', ruined by the slump in diamond shares, has committed suicide; Goncourt enjoys a brief vision of popular success from a tragedy on the subject, and is utterly crushed next morning by the news that Proust is still alive and kicking.

Proust's retreat to parody was a relaxation from the tensions of his novel, and a psychological preparation for his final attempt to write it. Nothing, at first sight, could seem more remote from the novel itself; yet in the Lemoine parodies he was in fact moving on several planes in the direction of *A la Recherche*. For the first time he had discovered himself as a comic writer. The Comic Spirit, which is almost entirely absent from *Les Plaisirs et les Jours* and *Jean Santeuil*, arrives in full force in the parodies, and is ever-present in *A la Recherche*, not only in the Narrator's view of the characters and the laws of human frailty which they reveal, but in his ironic attitude to himself, by which Proust redeemed the self-complacency and self-pity which had ruined *Jean Santeuil*. Parody itself, as a means of extracting the essence of other people and making it absurd, became one of the major ingredients of his novel. The Lemoine pastiches are a connecting link between Proust's early habit of performing 'imitations' (in which, as his friends have remarked, he would seem actually to *become* Montesquiou, Mme Lemaire, Mme Arman, or whoever was his victim of the moment), and the spoken words of the characters in *A la Recherche*. Charlus, Mme Verdurin, the Duchesse, Françoise and others do not merely speak as their models spoke:

---

[1] This is not only a compliment to Lucien Daudet, but a touch of verisimilitude, for the Goncourt *Journal* is full of meetings with Lucien and his family.

their conversation is a concentrated exaggeration, a pastiche in fact, of the words and manner of the real people on whom they are based. Charlus talks like Montesquiou, but more intensely so than Count Robert ever did, just as the Balzac parody is more Balzacian than Balzac himself. The parodies were a trial run for this use of pastiche in *A la Recherche*.

Other more direct parallels may be traced between the parodies and the novel. The Faguet is a sketch for certain aspects of Brichot, Mme de Villeparisis criticises the great writers she had known in her youth in the manner of Proust's Sainte-Beuve, Legrandin speaks like Proust's Renan. In the Balzac parody Proust's method of handling the symphonic complexities of a social occasion is a humorous imitation of Balzac's; yet he is now more successful than in similar episodes in *Jean Santeuil* (where he was imitating Balzac in all seriousness), and he was to use the same technique for the matinées and soirées, teas, concerts and dinners of *A la Recherche*. A single sentence of the imitation of Flaubert became one of the chief themes of the Narrator's youth at Combray. When the Narrator reads in an unnamed author, a little before his discovery of Bergotte, of 'a mountainous and fluviatile country, with many sawmills, and with clusters of violet and reddish flowers climbing over low walls'—a landscape in which a little later he imagines himself wandering hand in hand with the Duchesse de Guermantes, who, 'enamoured of me by a sudden caprice', shows him 'flowers leaning their violet and red spindles on low walls'[1]—Proust is thinking of a passage in his own Flaubert pastiche, about 'two clusters of violet flowers, descending to the swift water which they almost touched, along a reddish crumbling wall'. But the Lemoine pastiches actually appear in *A la Recherche* in a symbolic form, the clue to which is the appearance in each of a parody of the Goncourt *Journal*. During his visit to Gilberte at Tansonville the Narrator reads a passage (which is in fact another pastiche by Proust himself) from 'a volume of the unpublished *Journal* of the Goncourts', in which the diarist describes Cottard, Brichot and Swann at one of Mme Verdurin's Wednesdays long ago. The Narrator despairs of writing a great book, because 'Goncourt' has made these people appear more interesting than they ever seemed to himself; yet at the same time he rejects the Goncourt *Journal* and all literature of its kind, since he knows that his own rare glimpses of a reality behind the phenomenal world have been more valuable than

[1] I, 86, 172; II, 13.

anything visible to the 'naturalists' and their school, who can only copy the surface. Proust here called to mind his own situation in the spring of 1908. The Narrator's reading of a Goncourt parody, and Proust's writing of another, are symbolically the same; and both lay in a time of self-doubt and urgency which stood, unrealised, at the threshold of the revelation of Time Regained.

It was not Proust's fault that the Lemoine pastiches came to a temporary end. He had a further supply ready, including one of the dramatic critic Adrien Bernheim—'and even that isn't the lowest I've sunk,' he assured Robert Dreyfus. The Renan had given him particular pleasure: 'it came in such waves that I glued whole new pages on to the proofs,' he told Dreyfus; 'I'd adjusted my inner metronome to his rhythm, and I could have written ten volumes in the same style. You ought to thank me for my discretion in refraining.' He remembered the day nineteen years before when he had visited the serene old apostate and received his blessing. 'For Monsieur Marcel Proust,' Renan had written in the schoolboy's copy of his *Vie de Jésus*, 'whom I ask to keep an affectionate memory of me when I am no longer in this world'; and it is Renan—more even than France, Loti or Barrès, all three of whom were Renan's disciples—who is the chief original of Bergotte as 'the sweet singer with the snowy locks'. At midnight on 11 March Proust sent Ulrich to the *Figaro* offices with the manuscripts of Flaubert, Sainte-Beuve and Renan, and a letter begging Cardane to find room for all three on the following Saturday; but the implacable sub-editor postponed the Renan for a fortnight, till 28 March. A few days later Lemoine was released on bail, and in June the wretched man fled to Constantinople. The Affair of the Diamonds ceased to have news-value, and no more pastiches were required.

Perhaps Proust could publish his parodies as a book? In April he consulted Gaston de Caillavet and his wife in their home at 40 Boulevard de Courcelles, his first recorded visit to these old friends since their marriage in 1893. Remembering Marcel's insistence, in the far-off days when she was a girl and he was in love with her, on making friends with her father's servants, Jeanne teasingly asked his opinion of her present household. "I don't care for the concierge, though I didn't get to know him really well," he replied, "and I thought your page-boy, who's nothing like the one you had in the Rue de Miromesnil, rather mediocre." He was enraptured by this first sight of her pretty, thirteen-year-old daughter Simone, who

when ordered to be nice replied: "I'm doing my best!" It was not,
however, until Mlle de Caillavet was a few years older that he
realised the deeper significance of this offspring of Gilberte and
Saint-Loup. Gaston was thoroughly in favour of the plan to publish
his parodies in volume form, and Jeanne offered to write on his
behalf to Calmann-Lévy; but in the end Proust wrote his own letter,
appealing to an entirely imaginary 'very high credit-balance' for
Les Plaisirs et les Jours, offering to pay for the costs of printing, and
adding with fatal modesty: 'I so hate to bother you that it would
give me more pleasure if you did *not* publish these articles.' It was
hardly surprising that Calmann-Lévy obligingly declined, as also did
the *Mercure de France* and Fasquelle; and the premature appearance
of *Pastiches et Mélanges* was once more averted.

The Lemoine Affair was only one of three scandals which fascinated Proust and all Paris that year. The last act in the decline and fall
of the brilliant Boni de Castellane was now being played, and a
whole epoch of Paris society seemed to end with the vanishing of
his glory. For more than a decade he had received his multitudinous
guests at the top of the red marble staircase in his Palais Rose; to
each new arrival he directed a piercing ray from his lapis-lazuli eyes,
and leaning slightly backwards in the manner of Saint-Loup[1]
extended his gloved hand from a great distance, as if on the end of a
barge-pole. "A nice place you've got here," remarked King Carlos
of Portugal, and Boni replied, with equal truth and chivalry: "if it
please your Majesty, it is the house of Mme de Castellane." To Boni
it seemed unthinkable that the American millionairess to whom he
had given his noble name, and whose wealth he was squandering
with such exquisite taste, should not repay him with eternal gratitude
and overlook his infidelities with prettier women. But his ugly little
wife was about to put her foot down before the last of her fortune
disappeared. "You can't divorce him," their friends exclaimed in
horror; but "I don't see why not," she replied, adding in her still
imperfect accent: "I 'ate 'im, I 'ate 'im!—*Je le hé, je le hé!!*" On 26
January 1906 she left Boni without warning, taking their two sons,
and on 11 April she divorced him. Soon it was clear to everyone that
the former Miss Anna Gould was determined not only to save her
money but to gain a still better title by marrying Boni's cousin, Hélie
de Talleyrand-Périgord, Prince de Sagan, who was nineteen years
her senior. On 2 January 1908, at the funeral of their relative Charles

[1] I, 731.

de Talleyrand-Périgord, the furious Boni clubbed Cousin Hélie with his walking-stick as they emerged from the church. Proust's sympathies lay with Boni: 'Hélie ought to be spelled Élie,'[1] he observed maliciously to Reynaldo, 'like the Prophet, who in similar circumstances flew up into the heavens, a resource which unfortunately wasn't available to our Hélie. But in my opinion Gould for him spells principally Gold.' On 7 July Boni's ex-wife became Princesse Hélie de Sagan: and Boni, left destitute and besieged by creditors, found that by buying and selling antiques, and taking commissions from his fellow-aristocrats for interior decoration, he could still live in modest elegance. A little later Proust was introduced for the first time to Hélie de Talleyrand and the Duc de Brissac, but unluckily confused one with the other. Soon afterwards he happened to meet, as he thought, M. de Brissac, and took the opportunity to make a facetious remark on the new Mme de Talleyrand. "How exquisitely witty, I shall tell my wife," replied the supposed Duc, choking with rage. "But I don't think that could possibly interest Mme de Brissac," said Proust, making the gaffe worse; and it was only after long cogitation that he realised why the inexplicably angry gentleman had been holding a top-hat with the initials T. P. stamped in the lining. He used the incident in *A la Recherche* for the scene between the Narrator and Charlus after Mme de Villeparisis's matinée.[2]

The third scandal of that winter was the Eulenburg Affair in Germany, which combined the most deplorable features of both the Dreyfus Case and the persecution of Oscar Wilde: as in the former the course of justice was perverted by political intrigue, but as in the second the accused man was guilty, and his crime was homosexuality. Kaiser Wilhelm II had long been surrounded by a circle of intimate friends, known to their enemies as the Knights of the Round Table or the Camarilla,[3] who were hated by the Panger-

---

[1] i.e. Elijah.

[2] II, 277-8. The Narrator, seeing a G with ducal coronet in the Baron's top-hat, and forgetting that Charlus is a Guermantes, thinks he has inadvertently taken another guest's property. He then remarks that Saint-Loup is talking to 'that fool of a Duc de Guermantes'. "How very delightful, I shall tell my brother," exclaims the Baron, and the Narrator, supposing that his brother must surely have the same name, enquires: "Do you think that could interest M. de Charlus?"

[3] King Theodosius likewise, as M. de Norpois remarks when dining with the Narrator's parents, is 'surrounded by a camarilla' (I, 461).

manist war party not so much for their morals as for their pacifism
and advocacy of friendship with France. Their leader, Prince
Philip von Eulenburg, a married man in his sixties and the father of
eight children, was attacked in October 1907 along with his dear
friend General Cuno von Moltke (they called one another 'Phili' and
'Tutu') by the right-wing journalist Maximilian Harden. As in the
Wilde Case the accuser was sued for libel, but produced evidence
which resulted in the criminal prosecution of the plaintiff. The
wretched Eulenburg was confronted with a boatman and a milkman,
both now middle-aged, with whom he had had improper relations
long ago in the 1880s. The milkman, as it turned out, was under the
impression that the word Camarilla, which he heard used so often by
Harden's lawyer but could not spell, was a technical term for a
particular perversion. "If the Prince swears he never did Kramilla,"
he averred, "then he's a perjured liar." But although the poor Prince
could never be convicted of Kramilla or anything else, since he
always fainted at the critical moment, his political career was irre-
trievably ruined. The Kaiser abandoned his friends and was left with
the militarists as his sole advisers; and the Eulenburg Affair was thus
among the minor indirect causes of the First World War.

Proust took a keen interest in the Eulenburg Affair. Like many
homosexuals, and like Charlus, he prided himself on his knowledge
of all the prominent, undiscovered inverts of Europe: 'his documentation was remarkable,' says Robert de Billy, who assisted him
in this hobby with inside information gained in his career as a
diplomat. 'What do you think of that homosexuality trial?' Proust
wrote to Billy about 10 November 1907; 'I think they've been
hitting out rather at random, but it's absolutely true of several of the
persons mentioned, notably the Prince, though some of the details
are extremely comic.' The French people looked on with glee,
forgetting that Eulenburg was their friend, and that the existence of
homosexuality is far from impairing the fighting qualities of an
enemy nation. The unhappy Prince was nicknamed 'Eulenbougre',
Berlin became known as Sodom-on-Spree, and Billy told Proust that
'Do you speak German?' was now among the most familiar graffiti in
the public conveniences of Paris. But Proust viewed the Affair with
mingled feelings of grim amusement, scientific interest, and sympathy both human and personal; for the bell that tolled for Eulenburg
tolled also for himself.

Since the beginning of 1908 Proust had been at work on yet

another version of his novel which, as we shall see, included when he abandoned it in the following November scenes at Combray, Balbec (then called Querqueville) and Venice.[1] On 3 February, just before he began the Lemoine pastiches, he wrote to Mme Straus of 'a rather long work to which I should like to devote myself'. On 14 May 1908, a week after Eulenburg's arrest, he spoke to Robert Dreyfus of a plan to write a topical article, in which he would use the Eulenburg Affair as the pretext for a general discussion of homosexuality. The apprehensive Dreyfus advised him to publish, if at all, only in the future collected volume of his essays; but on the 16th Proust suggested the *Mercure de France*, which had already printed in December 1907 and January 1908 two essays on the same theme by Remy de Gourmont, under the facetious title of '*L'Amour à l'envers*'. The article had by now turned into a short story, which must have nothing to do with the Affair, Proust explained, for 'art is too superior to life to be satisfied with copying it'; and his story, if allowed to 'participate in the contingency and unreality of an actual event', 'would seem banal and untrue, and deserve some blow in the face from outraged Existence, like Oscar Wilde saying that the greatest sorrow he had ever known was the death of Lucien de Rubempré in Balzac, and then learning soon afterwards, through his prosecution, that there are sorrows which are still more real'. Professor Vigneron has seen in this project for a short story the origin of *A la Recherche* itself. But the version of his novel on which Proust had now been engaged for several months was only the last in a series begun in the summer of 1905; and the essay discussed with Dreyfus can be identified not with the novel itself, but with the preliminary sketch for the first and second chapters of *Sodome et Gomorrhe* which forms Chapter Twelve, '*La Race Maudite*', of *Contre Sainte-Beuve*.[2]

[1] A letter (discussed by Professor Kolb in *Mercure de France*, 1 August 1956, 750-5) of January 1908 to Auguste Marguiller, sub-editor of the *Gazette des Beaux-Arts*, shows that Proust was then already writing or preparing the incident of his infant brother Robert and the pet goat at Combray, which he later embodied in the last published chapter of *Contre Sainte-Beuve*. Proust asked Marguiller to send on approval some English portrait-engravings including an animal, a genre to which he compares the scene of Robert and his pet. This incident is the first in the list of 'pages written' for the Combray episode in the novel-version of 1908 (*Contre Sainte-Beuve*, 14, 293).

[2] The reference to Wilde and Lucien de Rubempré is expanded in '*Sainte-Beuve et Balzac*' (*Contre Sainte-Beuve*, 217), but Wilde's fall is also mentioned in '*La Race Maudite*' and in *Sodome et Gomorrhe* (*ibid.*, p. 258 = II, 616). Wilde's remark occurs in his dialogue '*The Decay of Lying*', which Proust had read in

In May 1908, therefore, Proust had already begun his essay on the
'accursed race' of inverts, and had decided that elements of his novel
should serve as its text in place of the Eulenburg Affair.

The other purpose of Dreyfus's visit had been to show Marcel
his obituary on Ludovic Halévy—the son of Mme Straus's uncle
Léon, and father of Proust's schoolfriends Élie and Daniel—who had
died on 8 May. Proust thought with nostalgia of the summer
Sundays early in the 1890s at the Halévys' long white country-house
at Sucy, where with Gregh, Louis de La Salle, Jacques Bizet, Robert
Dreyfus and Léon Brunschvicg he had flirted with the host's niece,
Madeleine Breguet (who became Jacques Bizet's first wife and died
under the surgeon's knife of Dr Pozzi) and her charming girl
companions—another model for the 'little band'. "My father was a
Jew, my mother was a Protestant, and they brought me up as a
Catholic—I hope we all meet in the same heaven," M. Halévy used
to say. Proust had intended, if Dreyfus and Beaunier had not fore-
stalled him, to write an obituary of his own: 'it wouldn't have been
as good as Beaunier's,' he told Mme Straus, 'but more precise, and
corroborated by live memories'. Four days later, on 12 May, Robert
de Billy's father-in-law, Paul Mirabaud, the 'blue-eyed Saxon god'
of the yacht *Hélène*, succumbed to the heart-ailment which he had
discussed with Proust during their cruise in 1904. The sea of Time
Lost was rising, drawing so near that it threatened to drown even
the present.

In June Proust meditated another never-to-be-published article,
attacking the recent candidatures for the Académie Française[1] of the
Byzantine historian Gustave Schlumberger, Mme Straus's old enemy,
who had cut her in public ever since their quarrel over the Dreyfus
Affair. Proust breathed horrible threats: 'I'll allude to his big feet,
I'll drop all pretension to good taste, even to good faith.' But in the
end he confined himself to the rather childish revenge of walking
up and down in front of 'this prehistoric buffalo' at Princesse Marie
Murat's soirée, announcing in a loud voice to all and sundry: "I'll say
how d'you do to him when he says it to Mme Straus, not that she
gives a damn about it, but *I do!!*" Mme de Chevigné assured him

---

[1] On 18 March and again on 1 May 1908.

one of the two French translations of *Intentions* published in 1906. 'One of the
greatest tragedies of my life,' says Vivian, 'is the death of Lucien de Rubempré.
It is a grief from which I have never been able completely to rid myself.'

that she felt exactly the same, that she had told M. Schlumberger outright: "now you'll pay for all your mean tricks"; and to emphasise her good will she 'behaved exquisitely to a young girl of whom I'm fond'. Meanwhile 'the buffalo smiled like a ninny every time I walked past, thinking I was going to bow, and his enormous boots made fossil footprints on the carpet'.

The young girl was apparently Mlle de Gontaut-Biron, whom Proust had long admired and now hoped to meet. He waited for a sponsor, acutely embarrassed by Mme Lemaire, who barked: "Suzette, show me this girl Marcel's talking about. H'm, she's extraordinarily ugly, and could do with a good wash!"; while Suzette Lemaire made matters worse by giggling loudly and crying: "Oh no, Mother, she's very pretty—come here, Marcel, look, she's just by the door!" André de Fouquières effected the introduction, but unfortunately was rather drunk, and teased Proust unmercifully: "What d'you say to those tiny cheeks, me lad? Like to pinch them, eh? Or how about a kiss—a really naughty one? Whassat? Want to bite those li'l' ribstone pippins? Qui' right, old man, besides, you're very smart today, got rid of your beard, I see." But Proust, although the young girl's fiancé was present, took his introduction seriously. He wrote pathetically to Lauris, the manuscript of whose novel *Ginette Chatenay* he was now reading, describing his joy at the meeting, and adding: 'you may guess how deep in me is the resonance of words in your novel like "what future does he see for our love?" '

This incident is the original of an episode in the version of Proust's novel then in progress, in which the Narrator attends a soirée given by the Duchesse de Marengo in the hope of meeting a girl whose beauty he admires.[1]

Nearly three years had passed since the death on 6 July 1905 of poor Yturri. Montesquiou had unveiled a statue over his grave, of an angel with finger on lips, trampling on the serpent of envy—'the

[1] *Figaro littéraire*, 16 November 1946. The Narrator listens with Swann to an orchestral suite in which the 'little phrase' is heard, reminding Swann not of the torments of his past love, but of the beauty of the moonlit Bois de Boulogne on the nights when he dined there with Odette and the Verdurins. Proust used elements of this scene four times in *A la Recherche*: the musical evening at Mme de Saint-Euverte's, Swann's remarks on the Vinteuil Sonata when his wife plays it to the Narrator, the soirée at the Princesse de Guermantes's when the Narrator converses with Swann, and the performance of the Vinteuil Septet at Mme Verdurin's in *La Prisonnière*, where he expects to meet Mlle Vinteuil and her friend.

Angel of Silence', he called it—in a tastefully spectacular ceremony
on the following 20 November. For a time the Count was subjected
to illnatured comment. The repulsive Ernest La Jeunesse wrote a
cruel parody of his elegiac manner, with his foible for Latin tags and
rime riche, beginning

> '*Ave, Caesar, morituri*
> *Te salutant!* Mort? Yturri?'

An idiotic rumour arose, because Montesquiou announced to everybody with noble melancholy: "I shan't be able to write any poetry
for years now," that the dead secretary had written his master's
verses for him; and indeed, the poet was to publish only prose until
the First World War, when he burst into rhyme as prolifically as
ever. In this third summer of their eternal parting it was time for a
positively last farewell to Yturri, particularly as the Count had
recently acquired a new secretary, Henri Pinard, to share his life and
—as people noticed—his ever-thickening rouge and powder. On 27
June 1908 he gave a reading of *Le Chancelier des Fleurs*, a memorial
volume in which he told the sad story of Yturri's last days, and
quoted in full his letters of condolence from all the best people. The
guests represented society, royalty, the arts and the Church, and
included Comtesse Greffulhe, Judith Gautier, Mme Arman complete
with Anatole France, Loti, Rodin, Dr Pozzi, the Abbé Mugnier and
Barrès. The Grand Duke Wladimir, uncle of the Tsar and husband
of Mme de Chevigné's inseparable friend the Grand Duchess
Maria Pavlovna, arrived last but one, whereupon Montesquiou
shouted: "Close all the doors!" "But Mme Greffulhe hasn't arrived,"
objected the new secretary, and "She'll be here at her usual time,"
replied her furious cousin. The Grand Duke was heard to enquire:
"Why is she always an hour late? But then, perhaps she hasn't a
clock!"; then he leaned his enormous frame against the wall next
to Rodin ("no, I won't have a chair, I always feel safer in this house
with my back against the wall!"), and the proceedings began. The
air was heavy with the scent of huge lilies, and the drawn curtains
shut out all but the single ray of sunlight in which Montesquiou
nobly stood, reading, reading, reading, and reading, and dropping
each leaf of manuscript into a bronze bowl when finished. "Uniquely
beautiful," murmured Anatole France afterwards as, in the words
of the reporter from *Le Figaro*, 'the motor-cars lined up outside the
silent Pavilion dispersed noisily in the sunlight of a perfect day'.

Proust had not been invited, and rashly complained of it, with the inevitable result that Montesquiou called to give a private recital; and at two in the morning, without pity for the slumbers of Dr Gagey on the floor below, he stamped his heels on the floor and screamed: "and now, Scipio and Laelius, Orestes and Pylades, Cinq-Mars and De Thou, Edmond and Jules de Goncourt, Flaubert and Bouilhet, welcome me, for I am worthy, to your pre-eminent company!!" Proust read the volume, one of a hundred copies privately printed for distribution to the Count's particular friends, at his leisure. He noticed a letter on 'your cruel loss' from the German Ambassador, Prince von Radolin, and remarked bitterly to Reynaldo: 'he'd have done better to keep a little of his sympathy to give to Eulenburg'. But to Montesquiou he wrote, early in July, 'it's just like Bossuet', and added significantly: 'I am struggling, without making progress, on days when I'm not too ill, with a novel which will perhaps give you a little more esteem for me, if you have the patience to read it.' At the same time he also discussed his novel, and his intention of working on it at Cabourg, with his fellow-novelist Lauris.

He arrived at Cabourg on 20 July, but before starting work had two still more urgent matters to settle. First he must review Lucien Daudet's second novel,[1] *Le Chemin Mort*, the discreetly homosexual theme of which may have encouraged his own purpose; but on second thoughts he gave way to prudence, and his article remains unpublished and unknown. The annual problem of his fortnight of military training, which he seems to have succeeded in evading every year since his army service in 1889-90, would have caused him little concern, had it not been more serious this year, when his valet Nicolas Cottin was summoned for 1 August, the same day as himself. Poor Nicolas had a genuine weak chest, and his presence at Cabourg was indispensable to his invalid master. For himself Proust need only write to his father's friend Dr Duplay for a medical certificate[2]; but for Nicolas he asked his aunt Mme Thomson, whose husband was now Navy Minister, to approach General Dalstein, the military governor of Paris. He thought of going still higher, to Picquart himself, who had now been War Minister for nearly two years.

---

[1] The first was *La Fourmilière* (1907), which Proust had dutifully mentioned in his Goncourt pastiche (*Pastiches et Mélanges*, 38).

[2] Proust was transferred to the territorial army reserve on 11 November 1908.

'I'm afraid he's forgotten those who sent him presents and praise
when he was in prison,' he wrote sadly to Mme Catusse; but he
hinted to Reynaldo that any overtures he might feel able to make to
Picquart, 'without turning your hair white about it', would be
gratefully received. He sent Reynaldo 750 francs as alleged profits
in a shares speculation; but Reynaldo, impervious to bribery, insisted
on returning the money, just as he had refused 580 francs forwarded
by Proust with the same excuse from Versailles two years before. To
Nicolas such conduct seemed, on either side, hardly sane, and
whenever his master spent too much money at Cabourg he remarked
with heavy irony: "now we shall have to ask Monsieur Hahn to send
us another lot". Soon Nicolas's ingratitude was punished; despite
General Dalstein's promise a stern summons arrived, and he had to
'do his thirteen days'.

Once more Proust's friends were strung out, like beads on a
rosary, along the line of the Little Train. Loche Radziwill was near
by, with his new friend, the lovely actress Christiane Lorin; at Les
Béquettes near Houlgate was Alexandre de Neufville, whom Proust
had met at the Comte de Saussine's musical salon in 1893; Robert
Gangnat had taken the Chalet Russe at Bénerville for Louisa de
Mornand, her sister Suzanne and her mother; and the Guiches were
in residence at their Villa Mon Rêve, also at Bénerville. One day
Proust lunched there with the Clermont-Tonnerres, and quarrelled
with a retired cavalry officer about literature. "I wouldn't dream of
telling him he was an ass, if we were talking about military strategy,"
he complained in his most mournful tones, "so what right has he to
turn up his nose at such a beautiful book?" But the sight of the little
Clermont-Tonnerre girls soothed his ruffled feelings, as they
demurely drank from their glasses of water, folded their table-
napkins, kissed their Aunt Élaine, and said to him with wide eyes:
"No, Monsieur, we don't remember seeing you at Glisolles." After
lunch he strolled on the lawn, between the beds of sea-geraniums
and the vast glittering of the sea, talking to their mother Élisabeth:
'he unlocked to me the treasures of his memory,' she recalled, 'and
without realising it I was given a private view of his coming novel'.
When he left the thin crescent-moon was shining in the west, and he
quoted his favourite lines of Hugo's '*Booz endormi*', which the
Narrator recites to Albertine on their last drive together through
moonlit Paris[1]:

¹ III, 408.

*'What god, what reaper of the eternal summer
Had left his task and carelessly discarded
This golden sickle in the field of stars?'*

He passed by Louisa's Chalet Russe one evening without calling, on his way back from visiting Robert de Billy at the Finalys' villa, Les Frémonts, at Trouville. Billy hinted that he would like a room at the Grand Hôtel; but Proust had no intention of allowing his solitude to be disturbed, and explained, with the paradoxical and displeasing anti-Semitism which he shared with his mother, that the hotel was full, 'and with what people!—not a soul you could put a name to—and a few Israelite wholesale dealers are the haughty aristocracy of the place'. So Billy, as Proust urged, stayed at Les Frémonts; but Proust's visit to him helped to link the two Balbecs, the Trouville of Marie Finaly in 1892 and the Cabourg of sixteen years later.

Louisa had the four-years-married Albu still on her hook, just as Rachel continued to torment Saint-Loup after his marriage to Gilberte; and before making his promised visit Proust rebuked her sharply by post for her cruelty. He had received, he told her, heart-broken and furious letters from Albu, in the last of which the sufferer complained: 'I've sent her ten telegrams without getting any reply—I don't know even whether she's ill—all I want is to show my affection, but she doesn't answer, however I entreat her.' As a clinching argument Proust reminded Louisa that her birthday was approaching, and Albu might not dare to write, 'although he's gone to such trouble to find a present that would please you'. When Proust at last arrived at the Chalet Russe it was not entirely a courtesy visit. The young Gaston Gallimard, his future publisher, whose mother owned the nearby Manoir de Béneville, happened to be calling on Gangnat and Louisa that afternoon. Gallimard saw a stranger approaching in a threadbare black suit and long velvet-lined cape, with a slightly soiled straw-hat tilted too far down over his forehead, and gathered from his dusty appearance and extreme exhaustion, and his story of the farmhouses at which he had been compelled to stop for coffee and recuperation, the absurd impression that he had walked the ten miles from Cabourg on foot.[1] Louisa joined them. The

[1] 'There was no other way of making the journey at the time,' Gallimard mistakenly explained in his account written fourteen years later; whereas in fact the Mézidon-Cabourg-Trouville railway of the Little Train had been running ever since 1883. Proust no doubt came by train and walked the distance of a little under a mile from Bénerville station.

astonished Gallimard saw the stranger stroking the nape of her
lovely neck, as if soothing a fractious colt, and heard him 'listing all
her faults, of which he seemed to have an expert knowledge, with a
teasing and benevolently interrogative manner, and scolding her in a
calm and controlled voice, but with an authority full of irony and a
patience which surprised me'. Gallimard knew, and saw Proust had
guessed, that Louisa had just been quarrelling with Gangnat: only
Proust and she can have been aware that he was admonishing
her for Albu's sake more than Gangnat's. It was not until the air
was thus cleared that he invited them all to dinner at the Grand
Hôtel.

Proust received his guests, who also included Louisa's sister,
Loche and Christiane, Alexandre de Neufville and others, in the
entrance hall, giving the Bénerville party fascinating word-portraits
and life-stories of the later arrivals. Young Gallimard felt a curious
excitement, as if he were about to witness some extraordinary event:
he was wrong, for nothing happened, yet he was right, for he was
dining at Balbec unawares, with the Narrator of *A la Recherche* and
several of his characters. A guest for whom Proust seemed to feel a
special kindness was an aged marquis, abandoned by his wife and
children, ruined by gambling and women, and crippled by locomotor
ataxia: he walked with sidelong lurches, and when sitting down
would aim elaborately for his chair, hurl himself towards it and miss,
except when Proust guided him. Proust led the conversation to
ground on which the unfortunate nobleman could feel at home, and
the guests, forgetting their embarrassment, found he was witty,
intelligent, and noble indeed. Proust put the marquis twice into *A la
Recherche*. In a curious rejected episode of *A l'Ombre* the Narrator
attends an organ recital in the casino at Balbec, and watches the
grotesque old man painfully climbing and descending, again and
again, 'like a clumsy, centenarian squirrel', to and from his seat on
the organ platform.[1] But in *Sodome et Gomorrhe* he is the impoverished Comte de Crécy, whom the Narrator invites to dinner and en-
courages to talk about wines and genealogy, because 'he considered
our Balbec agapes as an opportunity to converse on subjects which
were dear to him and of which he could not speak to anyone else',[2]

---

[1] I, 980-1. Proust wrote 'quinquagenarian', but it was one of his besetting
delusions (cf. III, 1143, note on 978) that this word meant a person in extreme
old age.
[2] II, 1085.

and who is later revealed by Charlus as the ex-husband of Odette.[1]
Meanwhile the guests devoured their roast chicken, watched
benignly by Proust, who having dined before their arrival sat with
legs crossed and chair turned sideways to the table. The conversation
veered towards travel, someone mentioned Constantinople, and
Proust quoted by heart a page of Loti on that city. "How magnificent," cried Gallimard, "and what an amazing memory you have!"
But Proust only smiled, and said later, as the guests departed: "you
should read the railway-timetable, it's finer still"; and he began to
recite a list of Names of Places.

It was during this visit that Proust met the mysterious young girl
whom he also saw from time to time in Paris, and a year later thought
of marrying. Not even her name is known, although she may be
alive to this day: 'I suppress her identity,' wrote Antoine Bibesco
forty years after, 'as she has begged me not to print her name.' The
evidence on Proust's relations with her is tantalisingly scanty, but
sufficient to show that she was, with Marie Finaly and Agostinelli,
one of the chief originals of Albertine. Her real presence is in Proust's
novel, in the Albertine of the 'little band'; but in his life the biographer can only draw attention, here and there, to her gracious
shadow. He also made the acquaintance of Camille Plantevignes,
a wealthy manufacturer of neck-ties who lived in Paris and was now
on holiday at Cabourg, of his son Marcel, Proust's namesake, who
was about to spend a year in Germany to learn the language, and of
two young men who were Marcel Plantevignes's friends. Meanwhile
he watched the passers-by, known or anonymous, on the promenade.
One evening he saw, silhouetted against the sunset in a pink gown,
the actress Lucy Gérard who had played with Louisa in Marcel
Prévost's *Les Demi-vierges* in 1905: 'I lingered to watch this exquisite
tinge of pink adding the complementary colour of the twilight to the
orange sky,' he told Louisa, 'and only returned to the hotel when I'd
caught cold and seen her fade into the horizon, to the utmost end of
which she glided like an enchanted sail.'

Perhaps it was in this summer that Paul Leclercq, one of Marcel's

[1] Odette, therefore, was perfectly entitled to call herself Odette de Crécy, and
Proust no doubt had in mind the dancer Cléo de Mérode to whom Reynaldo had
introduced him in 1895 and who, as she made a point of explaining, actually
belonged to a branch of the noble Austrian family whose name she bore—
whereas cocottes such as Liane de Pougy or Emilienne d'Alençon took names
which did not belong to them.

playfellows long ago in the Champs-Elysées, called at the Grand
Hôtel after a hot day's bicycling from Honfleur to Cabourg. A heap
of rugs and cushions on a sofa in the entrance-hall began as he
entered to stir, to protrude a hand, a foot, to stand up, and revealed
itself first as 'a sort of dishevelled crossing-sweeper in a huge black
greatcoat', and finally as Marcel. The restaurant was full of bare-
shouldered ladies and tail-coated gentlemen, and Leclercq wore
cycling-breeches and a Norfolk jacket. "Never mind, we'll dine in
my room, and I'll serve you myself so that the waiter shan't see
you," promised Proust; and sure enough he collected each course
from a tray in the lobby of his room, but only when the footsteps of
the waiter had died away in the soft-carpeted corridor. 'He thinks
being seen by a waiter in the wrong clothes would be as important
for me as it would be for him,' thought Leclercq with a pang of
amused affection, and decided that this was true courtesy.

Once more the season was ending. He negotiated unsuccessfully
to stay on in the Grand Hôtel after it closed for the winter, and
thought of revisiting Venice. Providentially the news arrived that
Georges de Lauris had broken a leg in a motor-car accident. Proust
saw the opportunity t combine a dramatic errand of mercy to his
friend with the secluded work and other pleasures which he had
enjoyed in the autumn of 1906, and left immediately for Versailles,
explaining, as he had during the illness of his uncle Georges Weil,
that his sole purpose was to be near the invalid. He travelled in one
of Jacques Bizet's taxis, driven by Agostinelli, and took the round-
about route by the Seine valley, via Pont-Audemer, Caudebec,
Saint-Wandrille and Jumièges, which he had planned the year
before. At Pont-Audemer in the church of Saint-Ouen he found hints
for the stained glass of Saint-Hilaire at Combray; and at the ruined
abbey of Jumièges he saw the Merovingian crypt and the paving of
abbots' tombs which he transferred likewise to Saint-Hilaire.[1]

At the Hôtel des Réservoirs he retired to his bed as before, ill both
with asthma and with the cafeine which he took as an antidote. He
visited Lauris once, in his third-floor bedroom in the Rue Washington, and found him looking the picture of health, but could never
again face the breathless ascent of his stairs; and twice more he came
to Paris to see his Cabourg friends, and enjoyed, as he confided in
Lauris, 'a few small pleasures with a girl who is new and dear to me
and with some young men friends who are new too'. Many as are

[1] I, 59-62, 103.

the possible meanings of '*de petits plaisirs*', Lauris can only have supposed Proust to imply that his 'small pleasures', with the girl at least, were those of love; and it is likely that Proust had in this October the same agreeable surprise as the Narrator, when Albertine in Paris granted him more than she had refused at Balbec. 'Young girls,' he wrote to Lauris early in the following January, 'are almost my only love, as if life weren't complicated enough anyway. You may say marriage was invented for this very purpose, but then the girl ceases to be a girl, one can only possess a girl once. I understand Bluebeard, he was a man who loved young girls.' But at Versailles he had still other enjoyments. Reynaldo stayed in the hotel for a few days and composed a new ballet for the Opéra, *La Fête chez Thérèse*, at his bedside, while Proust played dominoes with Agostinelli and Nicolas. At night, while his servants slept, he worked; and the revelation of Time Regained, gradual and imperfect but true, began to come to him at last.

Chapter 6

BY WAY OF SAINTE-BEUVE
(November 1908 – August 1909)

AFTER HIS three visits to Paris Proust was either too ill, as he alleged to the captive Lauris, or too engrossed in his writing, as may be suspected, to stir from his bed at Versailles. For a few days he lent Agostinelli and his taxi to friends, and then thriftily dismissed chauffeur and vehicle. He was still not sufficiently attached to the young man to invent excuses for keeping him near; and Agostinelli, returning as before like an autumn swallow to Monaco, vanished from his master's life for four years.

Early in November 1908 the re-paving of the Rue des Réservoirs below Proust's apartment drove him back to Paris, where he was afflicted by the noisy moving-in of Dr Williams, a dentist, on the floor above, and suffocated by a leak in his hot-water radiator, which compelled him to the unprecedented step of opening his windows to the winter night. Soon his asthma subsided, and he earnestly quoted to Lauris a maxim adapted by Ruskin from John ix, 4: 'work while you still have light, for soon the night cometh when no man can work'. 'I am already half-immersed in that night,' he added, 'and as I no longer have light I am setting to work.' Nevertheless, whether from dread of the long task ahead, from which only death would release him, or from an instinctive knowledge that the hour of beginning was still not arrived, he again avoided the direct way to his goal. Proust abandoned the 1905-8 novel, including even the promising new version on which he had worked since February in Paris, Cabourg and Versailles. He began to plan a book of very different intention; but in fact a deep intuition had now led him into the last turning of the way to *A la Recherche*.

As early as the previous spring, at the time of the first Lemoine pastiches, he had foreseen the necessity, though not the precise nature, of this new work. When he explained to Robert Dreyfus on 18 March 1908 that he wrote his parodies 'because I'm too lazy to

Mme Proust, in mourning for her husband

The Proust family grave at Père Lachaise

Marie Nordlinger,
Pastel by Frédéric (Coco) de Madrazo

Louisa de Mornand

Proust on the yacht *Hélène*, August 1904, between Mme Robert de Billy and Robert de Billy

Seascape with frieze of girls, Cabourg

The Grand Hôtel, Cabourg

write literary criticism, and because I found it so amusing to perform literary criticism in action', he added: 'but perhaps on the contrary my parodies will force me to write criticism, in order to explain them to people who don't understand them'. Now, towards the end of November 1908, he decided, as he informed Lauris and Mme de Noailles about a month later in almost identical words, to write a study of Sainte-Beuve: he had in mind two possible forms, either an essay in the classical manner like Taine's, or (a new idea which came when the first plan had already failed) an imaginary conversation with his mother, in which he would discuss his unwritten essay with her. But his ostensible subject was only a pretext for a wider theme. In exposing the philistinism of Sainte-Beuve, who was generally accepted as the most infallible of French critics, he would attack the false view of literature by which critics, the reading public, and all but the greatest writers had hitherto been blinded; and in showing the true nature of creative art he would simultaneously prepare the world for his own coming novel, and make the discoveries which would enable him to write it.

By way of preparation, as in 1905 before the composition of 'Sur la Lecture', he entered on a vast course of reading, which included not only the entire works of Sainte-Beuve, but the memoirs of Saint-Simon and of Chateaubriand, both of whom are among the great invisible presences in A la Recherche. Probably it was at this time that Proust wrote the brief fragment 'Chateaubriand', which contains ideas repeated by the Narrator in Le Temps Retrouvé: that Chateaubriand's moments of poetic vision, in which he seems to conquer death and time, are precursors of the theory of unconscious memory —'of the same species as the tasting of the madeleine', says the Narrator—and that such moments are in a sense more important than the great historical events which form the other subject of Mémoires d'Outre-Tombe, since the events are temporal, while the moments are eternal.[1]

In December he added a less avowable aspect of literature to his syllabus, by acquiring four obscene pamphlets at the sale of a respectable Protestant banker. The two 'secret, unclean and stupid Verlaines, of the kind of pornography that mortifies the senses', were Femmes and Hombres: the former a shameless lyric-cycle on the poet's heterosexual orgies, the latter a sodomitic counterpart which

[1] Contre Sainte-Beuve, 407-10; III, 728, 919-20.

reads like a versified prospectus for Jupien's brothel.[1] The others,
a series of seven letters to Stendhal and a memoir on him entitled
H.B., were both by Mérimée. The notorious *H.B.* is a work of
unexpected innocuousness, except for a gross frontispiece added by
the wily publisher, showing Stendhal spying on the infidelity of his
mistress; but its influence on Proust was none the less significant.
He bought his four 'curious' books in quest of inspiration for the
'obscenity' which, as he announced to Lauris and others, he intended
to introduce into both his Sainte-Beuve essay and his novel. The
Narrator's three crucial revelations of sexual deviation are all associated with spying—not, like Stendhal in the scabrous engraving,
through a keyhole, but by a characteristically Proustian symbol
through a window. He becomes aware of Lesbianism by watching
Mlle Vinteuil and her friend through the window at Montjouvain, of
sodomy when he sees the meeting of Charlus and Jupien in the
Duchesse's courtyard, and of solitary pleasure in the upstairs lavatory at Combray, where the Narrator himself is detected from
outside by the flowering currant and the castle-keep of Roussainville.
All these are probably based on real memories, and Proust had
described, some fourteen years before, a similar scene to Stendhal's
in '*Confession d'une Jeune Fille*'; but the earlier impressions were
reinforced and crystallised for his novel by his reading at the crucial
time of Mérimée's *H.B.* Moreover, although the Narrator's posthumous jealousy of Albertine was based on an experience in Proust's
life which lay five years ahead, Proust doubtless did not forget
Stendhal's confession to Mérimée that he 'felt a strange curiosity to
know all my mistress's infidelities, insisted on being told every
detail, and—in spite of the appalling suffering it caused me—took a
certain pleasure in imagining her in all the situations which my
informants described'.

Sainte-Beuve was less slow in coming than Proust pretended.
Again and again he informed Lauris of his inability to set pen to
paper: before the end of 1908 he had already started his essay three

---

1   '*Mes amants n'appartiennent pas aux classes riches,*
        Ce sont des ouvriers faubouriens ou ruraux.
        Leurs quinze et leurs vingt ans sans apprêts sont mal chiches
        De force assez brutale et de procédés gros. . . .'
wrote Verlaine in a catalogue of young men which included, by an odd coincidence, a namesake of Proust's chauffeur: '*Odilon, un gamin, mais monté comme
un homme*'.

times 'in my head', but in January 1909 he alleged his increasing difficulty in remembering either his plan, or the works of Sainte-Beuve which he had read in his course of preparation. The truth was, as we shall see, that he wrote the first two-thirds of *Contre Sainte-Beuve* during this winter and spring, and when in June he at last admitted to Lauris that he had begun to work, his essay was not far from completion.

Meanwhile, recoiling in order to leap better, Proust put his clock a year back by writing yet more pastiches on the Lemoine Affair. The wretched maker of diamonds had fled to Constantinople in the previous June, and on his way was glimpsed incognito in the French embassy at Sofia by Robert de Billy—then *chargé d'affaires* in Bulgaria—as he waited despondently for a visa. In January 1909 Lemoine was tried in his absence. Calmette intimated that further pastiches would be welcome; but Proust had still another motive in his pique at an article in the *Journal des Débats* of 28 September 1908, in which Henri de Régnier had praised other parodists to the skies, but refrained from mentioning his former friend and fellow-member of the Cannibal Academy—'he quoted all our contemporary writers of parody, including several idiots,[1] but never a word about me'. Proust retaliated with a stinging pastiche of Régnier himself, doing full justice to the symbolist rococo of his prose-style, and insinuating that Régnier defrauded the public like Lemoine by manufacturing the false diamonds of literature. A Chateaubriand parody, a Maeterlinck, and a second Sainte-Beuve followed, but remain unpublished.[2] Soon Proust turned from Chateaubriand to an author who was to take an equal but opposite part in the literary sources of *A la Recherche*: 'I'm head over heels in Saint-Simon,' he told Lauris, 'though nothing could be more different from *Mémoires d'Outre-tombe*.' In February Proust wrote to Montesquiou asking to borrow

[1] This is hardly fair: Régnier in fact confined his examples to three verse parodists (Banville, Albert Sorel, and Tristan Bernard) who were by no means idiots; and prose parody was outside his subject.

[2] The Maeterlinck is included in the second of the exercise-books in which Proust wrote *Contre Sainte-Beuve*. The Chateaubriand and second Sainte-Beuve have not yet been reported. A Wellsian parody of Ruskin entitled '*La Bénédiction du Sanglier*', an 'introduction to Giotto's frescoes on the Lemoine Affair' in which the tourist-pilgrim to Paris is advised to travel by aeroplane ('Wilbur's bird'), probably belongs to this period. The brothers Wilbur and Orville Wright had given sensational exhibition flights in France in 1908. See *Nouvelle Nouvelle Revue Française*, 1 October 1953, 762-7.

the Saint-Simon pastiche, '*Fête chez Montesquiou à Neuilly*', which
he had written five years before. This he skilfully embedded, almost
without alteration, in the longer Saint-Simon parody in *Pastiches
et Mélanges*, together with material belonging to the year 1919; but it
was presumably in this February that he inserted the context relating
to the Lemoine Affair. In his Saint-Simon and Chateaubriand
parodies Proust was performing an act of homage as well as reducing
a literary influence to manageable proportions. The two writers had
travelled long before himself the Guermantes and the Méséglise
Ways, the former achieving a devastating vision of the vanity of
human relationships, the latter a recovery of the lost reality of his
own past. Both are invoked in the Narrator's meditations on his
coming novel in *Le Temps Retrouvé*, Chateaubriand, as we have
seen, for his anticipation of the discovery of unconscious memory,
and Saint-Simon when the Narrator resolves to write 'the Saint-
Simon's *Memoirs* of another epoch'.[1]

Early in March he promised, much to the Count's gratification,
a pastiche of Montesquiou himself. He met Jules Lemaître at Mme
Daudet's: "if an author's work can be taken apart and put together
again like that, one hardly dares go on writing—it's not only
extraordinary, it's terrifying!" said Lemaître, and affably urged him
to compose a Mérimée and a Voltaire. The Régnier pastiche appeared
in *Le Figaro* on 6 March; and Proust received a magnanimous note
from his victim, saying: 'I thought it a very good likeness!', and 'a
most intelligent and really pretty letter' from Barrès, remarking that
Proust had discovered 'a formula for criticism based on Buffon's
principle that form and content must not be separated'. Lemoine's
arrest in April happened to be witnessed by a Paris bookseller named
Puzin, whose assistant, however, was unable to give any further
information to reporters. "Lemoine?" the young man repeated,
"who's he?"; and he explained, pointing to a volume of Nietzsche
in his hand: "I never read newspapers, only books!" In a *Figaro*
article on 17 April Robert Dreyfus took the opportunity to mention
Proust's pastiches, 'in which he performs a marriage between the
solid substance of his fancy and the airy inspirations of topicality!',
and invited him to parody Nietzsche. In June Proust wrote for
Dreyfus's benefit an unpublished parody of the popular novelist
Paul Adam; but in July he exclaimed to his friend in unwontedly
strong language, '*Merde pour les pastiches!*'; and a brief '*Explanation*

[1] III, 919, 1044.

by H. Taine of the reasons why your talk of pastiches bores me to distraction' marked the end of the era of parodies. Nevertheless, during these eight months of apparent delay and evasion, he had never ceased to work on *Contre Sainte-Beuve*.

Early in March Proust had confided in Lauris that he hoped, 'if I am still alive', to publish his Sainte-Beuve essay in the autumn, 'because this full trunk in the middle of my brain is getting in my way, and I must decide either to make the journey or to unpack'. On 23 May he asked Lauris an epoch-making question: did the name Guermantes belong to the Pâris family, or was it 'extinct and available for a writer'? The châtelaine of Guermantes, François de Pâris's grandmother the Baronne de Lareinty, was an imposing, sharp-tongued old lady, whom Lauris forty years later remembered in her red armchair by the window, scanning the radiating avenues of the park for arriving guests, and exclaiming crossly when her son seemed indisposed, "He looks the image of a parsley omelette!" The château, a mellow edifice which exists to this day and is illustrated in standard works on French architecture, was built in the reign of Louis XIV for a wealthy financier named Paulin Prondre de Guermantes; for the majestic and poetic name which became a symbol of the last splendours of the French nobility was chosen by Proust, with deliberate irony, from a plebeian parvenu of the seventeenth century, who in turn had borrowed it from the nearby village.[1]

In June, having lamented for seven months his inability to begin, Proust at last declared to Lauris: 'I'm worn out from starting *Sainte-Beuve*—work is in full swing, though the results are deplorable.' This burst of creation was soon interrupted. 'My intention is to try to resume work on *Sainte-Beuve* from tomorrow onwards,' he told Lauris early in July; but in mid-August, when Lauris asked 'Is *Sainte-Beuve* finished?', Proust could still only reply: 'what a hurry you're in! I'll start again when I can.' Already, however, *Contre Sainte-Beuve* as we have it was probably completed, for a week or two later Proust considered his work far enough advanced to justify

[1] Proust alludes to this situation twice in *A la Recherche*, once when th Narrator is disillusioned by learning from Saint-Loup that the Guermantes acquired their château only in the seventeenth century (II, 14), and again when Charlus informs him that Mme de Villeparisis's second husband was 'a certain little Monsieur Thirion', whose stolen name, once the property of a family extinct in 1702, belonged of right only to the small town of Villeparisis near Paris (II, 294). Villeparisis is, in fact, a little town near Meaux, not far from Guermantes itself.

seeking a publisher, and reported to Lauris: 'it's very long, between four and five hundred pages'. There is no record of further additions, and it was in this July, as we shall see, that he began *A la Recherche du Temps Perdu*.

Proust's work during the eighteen months from February 1908 to August 1909 may now be surveyed in chronological order. The new version of his novel, begun in February and abandoned in November 1908, survives in seventy-five unpublished loose leaves. These are said[1] to comprise the visit to Venice, a holiday at a seaside resort as yet unnamed, where the Narrator meets a much reduced little band of only two girls, and a long episode at Combray—a name which now appears for the first time—including the scene of the goodnight kiss and, again for the first time, the symbol of the Two Ways. Swann as the unwelcome visitor is called M. de Bretteville, and his other functions at Combray are filled by the Narrator's uncle; for although Proust had created and named Swann three years before, and had even at one time given to him episodes, such as the love-affair with the little band, which in *A la Recherche* belong to the story of the Narrator, he had not yet introduced him into the primal scenes of his novel. The first of the Ways was already called Méséglise, though the other was not yet Guermantes, but Villebon. Villebon is indeed a village with a fourteenth-century château, seven miles past Saint-Éman to the north of Illiers, and therefore in the same direction as the later Guermantes Way.

On a further twenty leaves of the same paper, and presumably written immediately after, are the three earliest sections of *Contre Sainte-Beuve*: the two prefaces (one to the 'classical essay', and the other to the imaginary conversation), and the essay '*Sur la méthode de Sainte-Beuve*'. This is none other than the 'classical essay in the manner of Taine' which Proust mentioned in December 1908 to Lauris and Mme de Noailles—indeed, he quotes Taine's essay on Sainte-Beuve in the first few paragraphs[2]—and its composition is further dated by the inclusion of the words from Saint John—'work while ye still have light'[3]—which Proust cited to Lauris early in November. The abandonment of his new work on his novel and the beginning of *Contre Sainte-Beuve* can be assigned, therefore,

---

[1] *Contre Sainte-Beuve*, 14. As at present reported, the order of the episodes in this manuscript is curiously reversed.

[2] *Contre-Sainte Beuve*, 133-4.

[3] *Ibid.*, 131.

to early November 1908, more than seven months before Proust's first admission to Lauris, in June 1909, that he had commenced his essay.

Proust's indictment of Sainte-Beuve is a development of his parody of the year before, in which the critic delivers on Proust's Flaubert pastiche the same perfidiously philistine judgements which Sainte-Beuve himself had uttered on Flaubert's *Salammbo*. Sainte-Beuve maintained that the supreme test of critical insight lay in ability to detect genius among one's contemporaries; yet he consistently underrated the truly original writers of his own time, such as Stendhal, Balzac, Baudelaire and Flaubert. Proust diagnoses the causes of this failure in Sainte-Beuve's false view of literature as a pleasant cultural recreation for a person of good breeding, in his journalist's habit of writing with his eye on the average intelligent reader—'he saw Mme de Boigne in her tall four poster, opening *Le Constitutionnel* in the wintry dawn'[1]—instead of looking in his own heart, but most of all in his famous method of using the external features of a writer's life and character to explain his work. 'An author's writing is inseparable from the rest of him,' declared Sainte-Beuve; and Stendhal, he pointed out, mediocre as his novels might be, was the soul of honour to his friends, while Baudelaire, however eccentric his poetry, was a perfect gentleman when one had the privilege of knowing him personally. Proust satirised Sainte-Beuve's method in Mme de Villeparisis's deflating anecdotes of Chateaubriand, Balzac, Vigny and Hugo. "I'm entitled to speak of them," she tells the Narrator at Balbec, "because they used to come to my father's house; and as Monsieur Sainte-Beuve, a man of great intelligence, used to say, one ought to take the word of people who've mixed with them and had the opportunity of forming a more exact opinion of their real worth."[2] And Proust condemns the method of Sainte-Beuve in a formula which applies equally to the understanding of another's work of art and to the now imminent creation of his own: 'a book is the product of a different self from the one we manifest in our habits, in society, in our vices. If we mean to try to understand this self it is only in our inmost depths, by endeavouring to reconstruct it there, that the quest can be achieved.' Sainte-Beuve, he concludes, 'found himself in the presence of reality and received from it a direct sensation' only in his early verses; and Proust ends with a metaphor which reappears in the dying Bergotte's vision of 'a

[1] *Ibid.*, 147, repeated III, 570.   [2] I, 710-11, 721-3.

celestial balance, with his life in one scale and the little patch of yellow wall in the other'[1]: 'the poetry written by a critic outweighs, in the scales of eternity, all the rest of his work'.

Proust's verdict on Sainte-Beuve may well give pause to Proust's would-be biographer. Can it be that he has applied this shallow and falsifying 'method of Sainte-Beuve' to *A la Recherche* itself? Fortunately, however, the biographical approach to a work of art is the direct opposite of Sainte-Beuve's, in which a superficial impression of an author's outward behaviour is used as a corrective to an equally superficial impression of his work. The biographer's task, on the contrary, is to trace the formation and relationship of the very two selves which Proust distinguishes. He must discover, beneath the mask of the artist's every-day, objective life, the secret life from which he extracted his work; show how, in the apparently sterile persons and places of that external life, he found the hidden, universal meanings which are the themes of his book; and reveal the drama of the contrast and interaction between his daily existence and his incommensurably deeper life as a creator. *A la Recherche*, of all great works of art, cannot be fully understood until the life in time of which it is a symbolic reconstruction in eternity is known. So the biographer, if he fails, should blame his own faulty application of the biographical method, his deficiencies of talent and sensibility, but not the method itself. Proust himself was concerned at this time to vindicate his future novel as a work of creative imagination, and to forestall the philistine critics and readers who would mistake it for a *roman à clef*. But in different contexts, and particularly in *Le Temps Retrouvé* itself, he was ready to admit a much closer relation between the self that wrote his novel and 'the one we manifest in our habits, in society, in our vices', and so conceded some truth to Sainte-Beuve's belief that 'an author's work is inseparable from the rest of him'.

The section called *'Conclusion'* in the published *Contre Sainte-Beuve*, and placed at the end of the work, was not so called by Proust, and was neither last to be written nor intended as a conclusion. It alludes to the reading of Régnier and Maeterlinck which resulted, a few weeks later, in Proust's parodies of these authors, and must have been written, towards the end of December 1908, immediately after the essay on Sainte-Beuve's method to which it is a logical sequel. Proust now studies the nature of the true work of art

[1] III, 187.

in contemporary writers such as France, Régnier, Loti or Barrès (omitting to mention that he was now out of sympathy with all these), and the false in Romain Rolland's *Jean Christophe* and the neo-classicist poet Moréas. More important, he investigates artistic truth as it might be revealed in his own work 'if he were able to write', taking for the first time the position of his Narrator, who until the end of *A la Recherche* is a writer *manqué*; and although this is not literally true of Proust himself, who had written incessantly since his schooldays, it is true symbolically, because he had now worked for twenty years without being able to write *A la Recherche*. He claims, 'although, as I'd never been able to work, I could not be a writer', that he possesses two faculties necessary for creation. He can sense beneath the text of great literature the deeper undertone which is the creative self of the writer—'as soon as I began to read an author, I detected under the words the tune of the song, which in each author is different from that of every other'; and this, despite his inability to create, 'enabled me to produce parodies, because once a writer's tune is heard, the words soon follow'.[1] His other gift is the power to 'discover a profound affinity between two ideas or two sensations'; and for the separate being within him who only comes to life at such moments of revelation, 'existing and being happy are one and the same thing . . . it is he, and only he, who ought to write my books'. 'Why,' he asks, 'is reality restored to us by the coincidence of two identical sensations?'—but he can still give no satisfactory answer.

Once again, as in the vision by the Lake of Geneva in *Jean Santeuil* and in certain passages of his Ruskin prefaces, Proust was travelling in the right direction. But his objective 'essay in the manner of Taine' could take him no further. Soon his inspiration and his prose deteriorated, and he wrote in the margin of his manuscript: 'don't leave this horrible style unaltered!'[2] It was now, late in December 1908, when he realised that the problems of the creative imagination could not be satisfactorily handled in this abstract form, that he first thought of an alternative plan and asked the advice of

[1] The idea is an adaptation of Proust's remark to Robert Dreyfus in March 1908 on his Renan parody: 'I set my inner metronome to his rhythm, and the words came in floods.' But it is true of Proust's own work, which had failed because he had not yet fully discovered his own 'tune'. When he found it, in the summer of 1909, he immediately began *A la Recherche*.

[2] *Contre Sainte-Beuve*, 306.

Lauris and Mme de Noailles. His new idea was suggested by a digression in the essay on Sainte-Beuve's method, in which he contrasted the self-satisfaction of the great critic on seeing his weekly article in the Monday morning *Le Constitutionnel* with the more innocent joy of the beginner who—like Proust himself long ago—sees his own first article brought to his bedside by his mother.[1] He now decided to describe such a morning, and to bring the dead Mme Proust to life for a conversation in which, liberated from the rules of conventional criticism, he would unfold his essay to her in the mirror of his own past. For in order to show his view of art springing from its source in his own depths, he must first reconstruct his former and present self around it, complete with the environment of his lost family and the Faubourg Saint-Germain of his youth.

[1] *Contre Sainte-Beuve*, 146-7.

Chapter 7

THE TEA AND THE MADELEINE
(*January – December 1909*)

WITH the new year, after two months of unseasonable warmth and sunlight, came the first snow-fall of the winter. It was on or about 1 January 1909 that Proust returned, late at night, along the snow-covered Boulevard Haussmann, to experience one of the most momentous events of his life. As he sat reading by his lamp, still shivering with cold, Céline urged her master to take a cup of tea, an unfamiliar beverage for this addict of coffee; and when he idly dipped in it a finger of dry toast and raised the sodden mixture to his lips, he was overwhelmed once more by the mysterious joy which marked an onset of unconscious memory. He caught an elusive scent of geraniums and orange-blossom, mingled with a sensation of extraordinary light and happiness. Not daring to move, clinging to the taste on his palate, he pondered, until suddenly the doors of memory opened. The garden of his great-uncle Louis Weil at Auteuil had returned, miraculously preserved by the savour of the rusk soaked in tea which his grandfather Nathé Weil would give him when, a child in the summer mornings of the 1880s, he visited the old man in his bedroom. The experience, for Proust as for the Narrator, was of a familiar kind, which he had known at intervals all through his life. At that moment he saw it only as a symbol of his present theme, the nature of artistic creation; for the act of unconscious memory combined both the aspects of art of which he had written a few days before, the sensation in the depths of the self of a pure reality, and the discovery of an affinity between two feelings. He did not yet realise that this was the missing key, which he had sought ever since the beginning of *Jean Santeuil* in 1895, to the creation of his novel.

He now wrote the preface to the new version of *Contre Sainte-Beuve*. 'Every day,' he began, 'I attach less and less importance to the intellect. Every day I realise more that it is only by other means that a writer can regain something of our impressions, reach, that is, a particle of himself, the only material of art. What the intellect restores to us under the name of the past is not the past . . .' And by way of example he described four instances of involuntary memory, of which the first three, at least, were probably recent: the garden of Auteuil unfolding in his cup of tea, 'like the Japanese paper flowers which only come to life when we drop them in water'[1]; Venice preserved by his stumbling, 'last year, as I was crossing a courtyard', on an uneven paving-stone[2]; the trees near a railway-line, barred with sunlight and shadow, resurrected by the tinkling of a spoon on a saucer[3]; and the never-solved enigma of the group of trees, which would reappear to the Narrator during his drive in Mme de Ville- parisis's carriage near Balbec.[4] Now, at last, Proust interpreted the riddle of unconscious memory correctly: it was reality itself, freed from the mask of time and habit, 'a fragment of pure life preserved in its purity, which we can only know when it is so preserved, because, in the moment when we live it, it is not present to our memory, but surrounded by sensations which suppress it'. The whole vast structure of *A la Recherche* is enclosed in these seven pages of Proust's preface: within a few days he had experienced and sketched out the beginning of his novel in Time Lost and its end in Time Regained.

Such is the bewilderment produced by an unconscious memory before it is identified, Proust remarked in the new preface, that 'for a moment I was like a sleeper who wakes in the night and cannot tell where he is, or in what bed, in what house, what place, what year of his life he may be'. Once again a chance simile in one part of his

---

[1] A simile repeated in *A la Recherche* at the end of the madeleine incident (I, 47-8), and inspired by Marie Nordlinger's gift in April 1904.

[2] Cf. III, 867. There is no need to doubt that this, the first movement in the symphony of incidences of unconscious memory in *Le Temps Retrouvé* which cause the Narrator to begin his novel, actually occurred to Proust. Possibly 'last year' means the autumn of 1908, a time when he was thinking of Venice, and the courtyard may have been at Versailles in the Hôtel des Réservoirs. Neither Proust nor any other visitor could fail to stumble on the pavement of the basilica of Saint Mark, which undulates on the sea of time like the sea on which it is built; and the incident is as exquisitely appropriate to calling up the memory of Venice as it is likely to have occurred in real life.

[3] III, 855, 868. If this, too, is taken from real life, it may belong to one of Proust's two railway-journeys since the death of his mother, to Cabourg in 1907 and 1908. But in an early novel-fragment (1908?) the incident occurs in the Narrator's boyhood, on a train-journey to Combray (*French Studies*, vol. 3, no. 4 (Oct. 1949), 340).   [4] I, 717-19.

essay suggested the plan of the next, and was destined to expand still further in *A la Recherche*. As a prelude to his morning conversation with his mother he now decided to describe the mysteries of his sleep and awakening on that and other mornings: at the outset he would map the country of his unconscious mind, in the depths of which he would then situate the act of criticism and the act of creation.

Early in January 1909 Proust set aside the loose leaves on which he had so far worked, and proceeded to write the new version of his essay in seven school exercise books bound in black plush. The date is confirmed by the fact that the first two contain not only the account of his waking and the conversations with his mother, but the Maeterlinck and Régnier parodies written in the same month.

The first two chapters, '*Sommeils*' and '*Chambres*', contain the meditation on the various forms of sleep, the hallucinatory efforts to discover in which of the bedrooms of his past he has awoken, which later form the opening of *Du Côté de chez Swann*. Next, just as a seedling encloses in small compass the leaves, branches and flowers which will grow far apart in the mature plant, he produced material which would reappear in widely separate parts of *A la Recherche*. A long account of his solitary experiments in sex in the upstairs lavatory at Illiers, one of the passages of obscene beauty which formed part of his plan, is followed immediately by the lilacs of 'the park outside the town', which is not yet called Tansonville, and the tadpoles and mysterious fisherman of the river, which is not yet called the Vivonne.[1] One of the rooms in which he believes he has woken is at 'the château of Réveillon'; and the description of his life there was re-used, at opposite ends of *A la Recherche*, in the nocturnal walks of the Narrator with Gilberte de Saint-Loup at Tansonville.[2]

[1] The lavatory incident is given doubled force in *Swann* by being drastically abbreviated and split into two (I, 12, 158). The lilacs appear, much revised, at I, 135, the tadpoles and fisherman with little alteration at I, 168, 167. The mystery of the fisherman is solved in a rejected fragment: he is none other than the former lover of Mme Putbus's maid; but in *Swann* Proust wisely preferred to leave him as an enigma.

[2] *Contre Sainte-Beuve*, 71-2 = I, 6-7; III, 691-3. It is significant that even in *Jean Santeuil* Proust placed Réveillon (which in fact is a hundred miles, and on the other side of Paris, from Illiers) only a little way from the horizon of Étreuilles. 'I took them round by Montjouvain,' says the Duc de Réveillon (vol. 2, 244), and Henri one day 'has gone to Étreuilles with his father' (vol. 2, 23).

For the first time it is clear that these are the same walks which Jean
Santeuil took at Réveillon with the Duchesse or Henri, and Proust
himself at the real Réveillon of Madeleine Lemaire in the late
summer of 1894; and Gilberte at this moment, alternately matronly
and still young, is a fusion of Mme Lemaire herself fourteen years
before (when Albert Flament had thought Proust 'infatuated' with
her) and her charming daughter Suzette. At this stage in *Du Côté de
chez Swann* the whole Combray episode intervenes, introduced by
Swann's visit, the goodnight kiss, and the tasting of the madeleine.
But Proust had already written a first version of this (though without
the madeleine) in the novel-draft of the previous year; and in *Contre
Sainte-Beuve* he leaps immediately to the moment when he sees,
'above the place I had assigned to my wardrobe, the streak of risen
day',[1] and the kaleidoscope of Time Lost steadies into the grey
daylight of the present.

In Chapter Three, '*Journées*', he is broad awake, yet the real world
reaches his bedside only in the form of a natural metaphor, when the
sound of passing tramcars, 'piercing with the auger of a fife the blue
ice of a chill sunlit day', brings news of the unseen weather in the
streets. The morning belongs to the very January in which Proust
writes, but he has also unconsciously prophesied a future state. On
winter mornings four years later he would listen as now before
the sleep of the day, while in the next room Agostinelli rose for
purposes of his own from the sleep of the night; and when Proust
opened *La Prisonnière* with the beginning of a day with the captive
Albertine, his material was ready to hand in *Contre Sainte-Beuve*.
The description of Great-Uncle Louis's dining-room at Auteuil
likewise reappears in *La Prisonnière*,[2] as does the evocation of the
odour of motor-cars in the street, 'most intoxicating of country
scents in summer', when the same smell of petrol makes the Narrator
long to travel and leave Albertine, a moment before Françoise enters
his bedroom with the news that Albertine, on the contrary, has left
him; but in *Contre Sainte-Beuve* these country thoughts merge into
the cornfields and poppies of the road to Méséglise, and the wind
which seems to bring the Narrator a message from Gilberte. A little
further on, now first used in a serious context, are the 'spindles of red
flowers peering over a sunlit wall' from the Flaubert pastiche, which

[1] *Contre Sainte-Beuve*, 73 = I, 187.
[2] *Contre Sainte-Beuve*, 78-9 = *De David à Degas*, vii-viii. Cf. III, 168,
412.

the Narrator at Combray would associate with the Duchesse de Guermantes.[1]

Chapter Four, '*La Comtesse*', is a sketch for the Narrator's pursuit of the Duchesse de Guermantes, modelled on Proust's wooing of Mme de Chevigné in 1892; but in this primitive and inferior version she is only a countess, becomes his mistress, and visits friends with the mawkish names which Proust had favoured in *Les Plaisirs et les Jours* and *Jean Santeuil*: Princesse d'Alériouvres, Mme de Breyvres. Soon, however, he would find the names of his characters, and therefore be ready to create them. The unnamed concierge of his family works as a tailor in the shop in the countess's courtyard: here is a first faint appearance of Jupien. The family servant is called Françoise, a name which Proust had previously given only to women loved by his heroes.[2]

In Chapter Five, '*L'Article dans* Le Figaro', Proust has at last reached the central episode of the new essay, when his mother brings in the morning's *Figaro* with his article, tactfully leaves him to enjoy it alone, and re-enters for their morning conversation. The subject of the article is not revealed, and no single article of Proust's is intended: the scene represents countless similar occasions from the *Le Banquet* contributions of 1892 onwards. Nowhere else, whether in the surviving letters between mother and son, or in *Jean Santeuil*, or even in *A la Recherche* itself, is the intimacy and wit of their relationship so vividly preserved as in the protracted dialogue of *Contre Sainte-Beuve*. Proust had now brought his mother back to life, to collaborate in his new work as she had in his Ruskin translations, and in *A la Recherche* he would not let her die. The episode is a development of the fortuitous image of a conversation between mother and son in '*Sur la Méthode de Sainte-Beuve*'; and in *A la Recherche* it recurs when the Narrator's mother, some months after the death of Albertine, brings to his bedside his long-delayed article on the spires of Martinville in *Le Figaro*.[3] Soon the pink light of

---

[1] Material from this chapter (*Contre Sainte-Beuve*, 74-85) will be found in order of occurrence at III, 9, 82, 12, 27, 412; I, 145-6, 172.

[2] *Contre Sainte-Beuve*, 91. In the following chapters she is generally called Félicie, after her original in real life, Félicie Fitau; but on pp. 107, 113 she is again Françoise.

[3] *Contre Sainte-Beuve*, 146-7, 95-101 = III, 566-70. As we have seen, however, the Narrator's essay on the spires is an actual extract from Proust's *Figaro* article of 19 November 1907, which was written two years after his mother's death and published within a month or so of its composition.

dawn renews his longing to travel; and he recalls the vision seen by
the Narrator on the night-train to Balbec, and by Proust himself on
the way to Avallon in September 1903, of hills lit by moon and sun,
and the rosy peasant-girl who brings coffee to the train.[1]

In Chapter Six, '*Le Rayon de Soleil sur le Balcon*', the conversation
on the article continues, with a digression on the comedy of Saturday
lunch (displaced in *A la Recherche* from Paris to Combray),[2] and
another on the ray of sunlight on the balcony, and the boy Proust's
first visit to Marie de Benardaky's home, which he used in the Narrator's love for Gilberte.[3] "Don't you agree that the piece about the
telephone isn't too bad?" he asks his mother. Proust is thinking here
both of the telephone-scene in '*Journées de Lecture*' (his *Figaro*
article of 20 March 1907, which Mme Proust never saw), and of the
episode in *Jean Santeuil* where Jean telephones his mother from
Beg-Meil (written at Fontainebleau in October 1896), which Mme
Proust had admired but thought 'terribly sad'. The 'piece about the
telephone' would recur at Doncières.[4]

Chapter Seven, '*Conversation avec Maman*', the last in which the
dialogue is fully sustained, includes four incidents from real life. The
first, on his visits to Venice in May and October 1900, is a preliminary sketch for the Narrator's sojourn in Venice with his mother after
the death of Albertine[5]; the second is the night at Auteuil when his
mother read *François le Champi*, an episode afterwards transferred to
Combray and joined to the story of the goodnight kiss. For two
others, however, no place could be found in *A la Recherche*: one
recalls Mme Proust quoting Molière and Labiche on her deathbed,
to comfort her son; and in the other Reynaldo Hahn sings his setting
of a chorus from Racine's *Esther* at the piano in Marcel's bedroom:
'my father did not dare to applaud; and my mother darted a furtive
glance at him, to enjoy his happiness with a pang of emotion'.[6]
Marcel now plans a new *Figaro* article to be called '*Contre Sainte-
Beuve*,'[7] and summons his mother to hear it.

---

[1] I, 654-8.   [2] *Contre Sainte-Beuve*, 106-7 = I, 101-11.
[3] I, 396-9, 503-4; II, 637.   [4] II, 132-6.
[5] Cf. especially III, 623-5, 652-4. A later passage on Venice as imagined by
his grandmother, *Contre Sainte-Beuve*, 290, corresponds to III, 628-9.
[6] A copy of Reynaldo's song from *Esther*, '*O douce paix*', dated 1896 and
inscribed by him 'To Mme Adrien Proust, in memory of our friends in the *grand
siècle*', was shown in the Proust exhibition at the Wildenstein Gallery (No. 332).
[7] This title, though it apparently occurs only here in Proust's manuscript, is
therefore Proust's own.

In the ensuing studies of Gérard de Nerval, Baudelaire and Balzac, except that in the two latter he intermittently speaks to his mother, Proust reverts to his 'essay in classical form'. He shows that Sainte-Beuve's criticisms of these great writers are untrue not only of them, but of all great art; and conversely, when he refutes Sainte-Beuve by giving his own vision of their genius, his remarks are valid also for great literature in general, and for *A la Recherche* in particular. The writing of *Contre Sainte-Beuve* is symbolised in *A la Recherche* (just as the Lemoine pastiches are represented by the Narrator's disillusioned reading of the Goncourt *Journal* at Tansonville) by the Narrator's meditation on the nature of his coming novel at the Princesse de Guermantes's matinée. It is a consequence of Proust's train of thought at this time—about March and April 1909—that when the Narrator at last steps through the open door of Time Regained he meets Nerval and Baudelaire already there. Nerval's *Sylvie*, he reflects as he waits in the Prince de Guermantes's library,[1] 'contains a sensation analogous to the taste of the madeleine and the warbling of the thrush in Chateaubriand'; and he tries 'to remember the poems of Baudelaire which are based on a similar transposition of sensations, in order to establish my own place in that noble company, and to prove to myself that the work I no longer hesitated to undertake was worth the effort I was determined to consecrate to it'.

From Balzac, however, Proust gained mostly by reaction. 'He's an author you don't care for,' he observes to the dead Mme Proust, 'and you're not altogether mistaken. The vulgarity of his feelings is such that his life was inadequate to refine it.' Perhaps this assertion, which Proust elaborates with relentless documentation throughout the chapter,[2] is itself not quite exempt from the fault it condemns; but he has the grace to point out that Balzac's vulgarity is an indispen-

---

[1] III, 919-20. Proust quotes from Nerval's *Sylvie* a passage which is strikingly close to the theme of the early chapters of *Contre Sainte-Beuve*, and therefore to the opening of *Du Côté de chez Swann*: 'I went back to bed, but could find no rest there. As I lay half-sleeping, half-waking, all my youth returned in my memories. This state in which the mind still fights against the fantastic juxta-positions of dreams often allows one to see, crowded into a few minutes, the most striking pictures of a long period of one's life.' *Sylvie* must have formed part of Proust's reading in November 1908, and is therefore among the immediate sources not only of the second *Contre Sainte-Beuve*, but of *A la Recherche* itself.

[2] Proust himself is here guilty of adopting the 'method of Sainte-Beuve', since he uses Balzac's biography and letters not in order to throw light on the nature of his greatness, but to convict him of vulgarity.

sable condition of his power.[1] Partly, perhaps, because he had not discovered it himself, but had it thrust upon him in the mid-1890s by Reynaldo, Lucien Daudet and Montesquiou, Proust never admired Balzac's genius without reservations. But the vast plan of the *Comédie Humaine*, in which the ever-recurring characters are visible from all aspects at every stage of their lives, as they rise and sink in the infinite dimension of time, was not without influence on *A la Recherche*. The social episodes of Proust's novel in particular are profoundly Balzacian, though with an added angle of vision which is Proust's own. He already had an inkling of the way in which he would transcend his mighty model: he remarks—of an unnamed author, but in words which fit his own achievement in the soirées of *A la Recherche*—that 'his descriptions of evenings in high society are dominated by the mind of the writer, so that our own worldliness is purged, as Aristotle would say; whereas in Balzac's we feel an almost worldly satisfaction in being invited to be present'. A paragraph on Balzac's sudden realisation that all his previous novels had a mysterious interrelationship, and would form part of an enormous work to be called *La Comédie Humaine*, is repeated by the Narrator in his thoughts on Wagner's *Tristan* on the afternoon of Albertine's visit to the Trocadéro, and is not unrelated to Proust's own revelation of the unifying theme of his own novel.[2] At this moment Proust complains of Balzac's unduly materialistic use of two metaphysically significant titles, *Les Illusions Perdues* and *La Recherche de l'Absolu*. From this juxtaposition, and along the connecting link of the French proverb which mistakenly declares that Time Lost cannot be regained—'*Temps perdu ne se retrouve point*'—Proust must have found the title and theme of his novel. The Narrator's quest is for an absolute—Time Lost—which is indeed 'a matter of philosophy', and which both can and must be regained.[3]

Once more Proust's treatise was approaching a dead end. Revived

[1] Similarly the Narrator, in his meditation on the Goncourt *Journal* at Tansonville, reflects that Swann 'would rather have died a thousand deaths than use one of the vulgar expressions with which Balzac's letters are strewn'; and yet Swann, for all his refinement, 'would have been incapable of writing *La Cousine Bette* or *Le Curé de Tours*' (III, 720).

[2] *Contre Sainte-Beuve*, 206 = III, 160.

[3] *Contre Sainte-Beuve*, 207. Compare also Racine's lines in *Phèdre*, which Proust knew so well (act II, scene 5):

'*Et Phèdre au labyrinthe avec vous descendue*
Se serait avec vous retrouvée ou perdue.'

for a few chapters by the dramatic idyll of his waking and the
resurrection of his mother, it had again relapsed into the sterile
'essay in the manner of Taine', with only, for form's sake, an
occasional '*tu*' still addressed to the fading spectre of Mme Proust.
For the second time Proust altered his plan: he would fashion living
symbols of false art and true from the names and places of his
recently discarded novel, and so contrast the lunar desert of his life
in society with the lost sunlight of his childhood. Suddenly—the
date is fixed to May 1909 by his letter to Lauris on François de
Pâris—his critique of Sainte-Beuve was invaded by a legion of
strangely rudimentary Guermantes, still hardly recognisable as their
later selves, but clad at last in the feudal splendour of their names.

Yet again the new section was an unforeseen proliferation of a
single branch of the old. Proust decided to study the various possible
forms of a mis-directed passion for Balzac, as they might be displayed by the different members of the aristocratic family which had
held his imagination ever since the Réveillons of *Jean Santeuil*. The
Comte and Comtesse de Guermantes (for they are not yet Duc and
Duchesse) live in the same mansion as the family of the Narrator
(as he must at last be called, since he now begins to be distinguished
by a larger element of fiction from the Proust of real life). The florist
in the courtyard, like Jupien, has a republican sense of his own
dignity, and addresses his landlord's visitor not as 'Monsieur le
Vicomte' but as plain 'Monsieur Praus': "you may think yourself
lucky it hasn't come to Citizen Praus," cries the furious nobleman
to his guest, in the very words of the Duc de Guermantes.[1] The
count has a brother, the Marquis de Quercy, who in the fullness of
time will become the Baron de Charlus (himself, like Montesquiou, a
fervent Balzac-lover), and an aunt, Mme de Villeparisis, who once
met Balzac ('a very common person, who never had anything
important to say'). Among their set is 'the young Marquise de
Cardaillec, *née* Forcheville', who is a preliminary sketch for Gilberte
as Mme de Saint-Loup: her reverence for the noble caste into which
she has married has an aesthetic fervour which people attribute to
her Forcheville blood, 'whereas I,' says the Narrator, 'knew it was
the Swann in her'.[2] Each of these has an individual attitude towards

[1] *Contre Sainte-Beuve*, 231-2 = II, 32-3.
[2] For a similar misunderstanding by the uninitiate of Gilberte's background,
see III, 960, 1010. Gilberte reads Balzac's *La Fille aux yeux d'or* at Tansonville,
'to keep up with my uncles' (III, 706).

Balzac, which already, however, concerns Proust less for the light
it throws on Balzac, than as a touchstone for the portrayal of his
characters. Sainte-Beuve and Balzac are receding into limbo: it is at
this point that Proust loses interest in the criticism of great art,
because he is so soon to create it. Yet it is strange that the noble
couple should have evolved so little in the fourteen years since *Jean
Santeuil*. The Comte has nothing of the Duc de Guermantes's
'Jupiterian' grandeur, the Comtesse has not acquired Oriane's
brilliance and glamour: they are still as homely, dowdy and stupid
as the Réveillons.[1] Proust even attributes to them the ceremony of
'showing the stereoscope', which in *A l'Ombre* he wisely transferred,
as a culminating bourgeois absurdity, to the Bloch family.[2] Here,
however, real life was odder, though less aesthetically appropriate,
than fiction; for this stereoscope was in fact the pride and joy of
Comte and Comtesse Greffulhe, when they regaled the guests at
Boisboudran with views of their travels in Egypt. "Is it *like?*" Mme
Greffulhe would breathlessly enquire. "But my dear, of course it is,"
cried Comtesse Jean de Montebello, "a photograph is always like!"
"Yes, I know, but is the local colour right?"; and yet another three-
dimensional picture of palms and camels would be popped into the
odious machine.

At this point Proust used the substance of his past and future
novel for a theme which had nothing to do with Balzac, Sainte-
Beuve, or the principles of literary criticism. The Narrator sees M.
de Quercy crossing the courtyard: with his burly frame and dyed

---

[1] Nevertheless, they have several minor characteristics of the Duc and
Duchesse. The Comte, besides his attitude towards the florist, and his patronis-
ing insistence on adjusting the Narrator's father's coat-collar (cf. II, 33),
habitually cries "But she's a cousin of mine!" (cf. II, 534), and has the Duc's
addiction to vulgar colloquialisms and bad French. His library, with its original
editions of writers of the 1840s, inspires the Narrator to the same conclusion as
that produced in *Le Temps Retrouvé* by the sight of *François le Champi* in the
library of the Prince de Guermantes: that if ever he became a collector of first
editions, these should be 'first' not in the bibliographical sense, but as being
those in which he had read the books for the first time in the garden at Combray,
in the days when his father used to cry: "Sit up straight!" (cf. III, 887). As for
the Comtesse, her first name is Floriane, at once like and infinitely unlike Oriane;
she has the Duchesse's intentionally provincial accent, saying: "*Elle est bête
comme eun oie*" (cf. II, 485; III, 43). But when asked if she has seen a certain
picture she is given the Duc's ineffable reply: "If it was there to be seen, I saw
it!" (cf. II, 524).
[2] I, 748.

moustaches, like Charlus at the same moment, he resembles Baron Doasan rather than Montesquiou.[1] Apprehensive, as in *A la Recherche*, lest his invitation should be a mere practical joke, the Narrator attends the Princesse de Guermantes's soirée,[2] and is amiably greeted by his hostess, though strangely ignored by M. de Quercy, who gives him only the little finger of his hand to shake.[3] Now M. de Quercy, ceasing to resemble Doasan, has Montesquiou's pale features and lofty oval forehead, his 'gaze glittering over the noble line of his nose', his gesture of lifting his unruly hair with a delicate hand; and the Narrator is overcome by the revelation that the unhappy nobleman not only looks like a woman but is one, since he belongs to the race of men who love other men. 'A race accursed,' Proust wrote; and the ensuing sentence of nearly fifteen hundred words is the longest he, even he, ever wrote, as if he dared not pause, lest he should come to a full stop indeed. In its anguished cruelty this is Proust's indictment, in its angry sympathy his defence, in its tragic beauty his confession of homosexuality. Here are many of the ideas and even the very words of the more extended natural history of 'the men-women, descendants of those inhabitants of Sodom who were spared by the fire from heaven' in *Sodome et Gomorrhe*. He had reached another of the major themes of his novel, though not for the first time. The whole chapter is no doubt an adaptation of the article in the form of a short story which Robert Dreyfus had dissuaded him from publishing a year before, in May 1908; but the character of M. de Quercy shows little advance beyond the ineffec-

[1] The encounter with the tailor-florist-concierge who will afterwards be Jupien does not occur here; but one cannot be sure that it does not occur in Proust's manuscript, concealed in the printed edition by the three dots with which the paragraph (p. 247) ends, and perhaps revealed by the editorial statement that the tailor's name is Julliot (which is almost Jupien), though he is unnamed in the published fragments.

[2] It is noticeable that the Princesse, not the Comtesse, is given the association with the Guermantes Way at Combray, the stained glass in the window of Gilbert (here called Charles) the Bad, the magic lantern and Geneviève de Brabant, which in *A la Recherche* belongs to the Duchesse; and the Narrator even hopes that the glamour she thus retains will compensate for his disillusionment with the Comte and Comtesse her cousins (*Contre Sainte-Beuve*, 247-8, 252).

[3] In *A la Recherche* this incident of the grudging handshake is transferred to the Narrator's glimpse of M. de Charlus in conversation with Odette at Mme de Villeparisis's matinée (II, 270); though at the Princesse de Guermantes's soirée the Baron's attitude is similarly distant (II, 639, 654).

tual Vicomte de Lomperolles in *Jean Santeuil*: the tremendous
Baron de Charlus still remains to be created. Proust already draws
the strange and moving parallel between the inverts and the Jews,
but does not yet compare them, as in *Sodome et Gomorrhe*, to a third
unjustly despised minority—the Dreyfusards.[1] Invert, Jew, Dreyfusard: was he not all three, triply rejected by his fellow-men? But
Proust's pleasure-pain in feeling solidarity with outcasts came
ultimately from the far-distant, ever-present moment when as a
child he thought himself rejected by his mother. In *Sodome et
Gomorrhe*, but not yet in *Contre Sainte-Beuve*, he dared to tell the last
secret of his guilt: the accursed people of Sodom, he wrote, 'are sons
without a mother, since they are obliged to lie to her all her life
long, and even in the hour when they close her eyes in death'.[2] Had
he lied to spare his mother, or rather to punish her by founding their
love upon a lie? Had he not chosen to lie, and chosen the sin that
compelled him to lie? At moments such as these he looked into the
pit of Sodom, and saw his own wraith imprisoned there.

  Contre Sainte-Beuve was waning to its close. The penultimate
chapter, on the contrast between the poetry of the names of places
and people, and the emptiness of their reality, discusses one of the
chief themes of his novel, yet contains little material which he
thought worth including in *A la Recherche*.[3] But in the last chapter
of the published volume the Narrator and his mother converse once
more, and Proust ends his curious hybrid of critique and novel in a
magnificent dying fall. The Narrator visits Mme de Villeparisis at the
château of Guermantes, which is here modelled on Jumièges as seen
by Proust on his return from Cabourg in the previous autumn.
The pavement of abbots' tombstones will be found again in the
church of Saint-Hilaire at Combray[4]; the vision of the towers of
Guermantes rising over France before those of Chartres or Amiens
had been built would recur to the Narrator as a prelude to his
infatuation for the Duchesse.[5] On a walk with his hostess he sees,
beyond the furthest horizon of woods and fields, 'a tiny blue-grey

[1] *Contre Sainte-Beuve*, 265; II, 619.
[2] II, 615.
[3] However, the ancient lullaby, *Glory to the Lady of Guermantes*, which the
Narrator's nurse sings to him in his childhood, reappears in *Le Côté de Guermantes* (*Contre Sainte-Beuve*, 268 = II, 12), as does the meditation on Fantaisie,
the palace of Louis-Philippe's daughter (*Contre Sainte-Beuve*, 280-2 = II, 536).
[4] I, 103.
[5] *Contre Sainte-Beuve*, 287 = II, 13.

city dominated by twin spires': it is Chartres, 'that irregular, unforgettable, cherished and dreaded face'[1]; he is seized by a memory of partings there with his mother in childhood, and invents an excuse to return home to her. This incident, in which the Two Ways meet, and Time Lost is miraculously glimpsed across the dimension of space, is worthy of A la Recherche. No less mature, though in the field of pure comedy, is the episode (written, however, eighteen months before, in January 1908, as part of the novel-draft from which so much of Contre Sainte-Beuve is adapted) in which his infant brother Robert refuses to leave Combray without his pet goat, ruins the dress in which he is about to be photographed, and complains that "Marcel has had more chocolate blancmange than me!" But there was no room at Combray for such broad humour, nor in all his novel for Robert. Proust suppressed his brother: in Du Côté de chez Swann it is the Narrator who spoils his fine array, embracing the hawthorns of the raidillon[2]; and the mother's words of comfort in the scene of parting—"Regulus, on painful occasions, would show amazing fortitude"—were reserved for the Narrator's first departure to Balbec.[3] His mother, touched by this memory of his grief, asks what he would do if they were parted for ever—so had Mme Proust enquired, a few months before her death, and so would the Narrator's grandmother at Balbec[4]; and he tells her, in the last sentence of the published Contre Sainte-Beuve, that 'materialism is now discredited', and philosophers are beginning to teach 'that souls are immortal, and one day will meet again'. Within a few weeks he would begin the novel in which his mother would live again and never die, and would be absent on the afternoon of the Princesse de Guermantes's matinée only because 'she had to go to a little tea-party at Mme Sazerat's'.[5]

The origins and evolution of Contre Sainte-Beuve can now be seen more clearly. Proust's dissatisfaction with the accepted principles of literature had begun seven years before with his rejection of Ruskin for the sin of idolatry, and continued in 1905 with his attack on reading considered as an interference with individual vision in 'Sur la Lecture'. The Lemoine pastiches of 1908-9 were

---

[1] Such a view of Chartres would be quite possible from the Villebon (i.e. Guermantes) country in the hills to the north of Illiers. Perhaps Proust also had in mind Jude's distant view of 'Christminster' in Hardy's Jude the Obscure.
[2] I, 145. [3] I, 650.
[4] I, 727-8. [5] III, 857.

similarly designed to free him from past admirations for writers
who, although many of them would function as secondary influences
in *A la Recherche*, could no longer be allowed to remain as primary
influences. His parodies were also directed against the misuses of
style as an artifice, an evasion of reality, an ornament for emptiness,
an exploitation of the more easily accessible levels of a writer's
individuality, a concession to the idle reader. But the main object of
Proust's attacks had been himself: his complaints against the work
of other authors were a projection of his disappointment with his
own. A surrender to 'idolatry' (or worship of the graven image in
place of the divinity it symbolises), an inability to penetrate beneath
surface reality, an endeavour to compensate for lack of truth with
beauty of style, had caused the failures of *Jean Santeuil* and the novel-
drafts of 1905-8.[1] The solution was still to seek.

In *Contre Sainte-Beuve* Proust intended to demolish both the
literature which was content with exterior reality, and the critical
philosophy which hitherto had provided its justification. But his
essay was also a quest for the secret key to his unwritten novel. The
plot of the novel, indeed, was already fixed, since he had lived it once
and written it twice without success: what he lacked was the hidden
door to inner reality, which alone could give meaning to the narrative. In the four stages of *Contre Sainte-Beuve* Proust pursued his
search ever deeper. He attempted to find his quarry first in a direct
statement of doctrine; next in the freer region of his lost intimacy
with his dead mother; then in a profounder understanding of the
three great writers—Nerval, Baudelaire and Balzac—who had
trodden the same path before him; and last in the whole world of
his past, which was also the world of his novel. But the secret,
however far he advanced, fled always beyond his grasp.

Like *Jean Santeuil*—though with ten years' store of riper maturity
and keener insight—*Contre Sainte-Beuve* is a marvellous failure.
Both are works of art at a stage only half-way advanced from chaos,
since the finger of the creator has imposed only here and there the
imperfect beginnings of order. The chapters tend to begin from
nowhere and stop without having arrived, to form a series of separate
dead ends rather than stages in a single road. Proust's Ruskin
prefaces and the finest of his *Figaro* articles had shown a mastery of

---

[1] Proust himself wrote in his notes for *Contre Sainte-Beuve*: 'Idolatry in my
preface to *La Bible d'Amiens*. The exact opposite now, and in '*Sur la
Lecture.*'

construction and of his maturest style. *Contre Saint-Beuve*, despite many moments of still higher inspiration, marks a regression in both construction and style. Too often Proust abdicates, and allows the young man who wrote *Jean Santeuil*, or even the schoolboy who 'covered page after page with the speech of the Constable de Bourbon', to wander aimlessly.

Set in this disorderly substratum are many wonderful glimpses of the world of *A la Recherche*; and it was thought, when *Contre Sainte-Beuve* first appeared, that Proust's critique had somehow turned, half-unawares, into his novel; that the appearance of characters and events which are common to both could only be an invasion from the future work. The still fragmentary evidence suggests, however, that many, perhaps all or nearly all, of these are borrowings from the intermediate drafts of 1905-8, and not anticipations of the novel to come. Some episodes had already appeared in *Jean Santeuil*: Combray is the same as Étreuilles, the little girl in the Champs-Élysées belongs to both works, M. de Quercy is an expansion of the Vicomte de Lomperolles, the Comte and Comtesse de Guermantes are still close to the Duc and Duchesse de Réveillon. A list in one of Proust's note-books of 'pages written' for the novel-version of 1908[1] includes incidents which recur in the last two chapters of *Contre Sainte-Beuve*: the hortensias of the Normandy châteaux,[2] the palace of Fantaisie, Robert and the goat, the departure of the Narrator's mother. One of the few published passages from the intermediate novel shows the Narrator with M. de Quercy in a conversation which is a curious compound of interviews in *A la Recherche* with M. de Norpois and the Baron de Charlus, who at this early stage were one and the same character. M. de Quercy, like Norpois (and like Gabriel Hanotaux in 1895) recommends a diplomatic career and pours scorn upon the Narrator's ambition to write; but like Charlus (and like Montesquiou in 1893) he promises, at the price of an absolute but unexplained obedience, a life in common and the key to the secrets of society. Other passages, as has been seen, show Swann in love with Carmen (Odette), and with the little band at Querqueville (Balbec); but Swann, we are told, appears in the unpublished parts of *Contre Sainte-Beuve*, while Querqueville, still more significantly, though it is mentioned only once in passing,[3] is

[1] *Contre Sainte-Beuve*, 14.
[2] *Ibid.*, 274-6.
[3] *Ibid.*, 14, 269.

no doubt the same as the nameless seaside-resort in the draft of 1908.[1]
The Guermantes chapters of *Contre Sainte-Beuve* seem to postulate
a more detailed structure of characters and relationships as already
in existence elsewhere, that is, in Proust's abandoned novel. The
available evidence suggests that in characters, incidents and plot the
fictional part of *Contre Sainte-Beuve* is not so much a voyage of
exploration as a return to a country which Proust had already
discovered. In these respects, as in style and construction, Proust's
essay marks at the most a limited advance, certainly not a break-
through into the unknown. Yet—as will be seen shortly—in other
unobtrusive quarters, of whose full significance Proust was not
aware at the time of writing, *Contre Sainte-Beuve* held the true keys
to *A la Recherche*.

Meanwhile, throughout the stresses of *Contre Sainte-Beuve*,
Proust had kept in touch with his Cabourg friends. From May to
July he negotiated with Camille Plantevignes to obtain a job for a
rustic army-comrade of Georges de Lauris, Nogrette by name.
'Plantevignes of all ages' were so delighted with the young man
for his own sake that Proust felt half-disappointed, lest his own
merit in the case should seem impaired; for 'by pure chance I've been
able to be extremely nice to them, and I know they'd like to do a
great deal for me'. He maintained contact with the mysterious girl of
Cabourg. His remarks to Lauris early in 1909—when he expressed
his sympathy with Bluebeard, because 'he too loved girls', declared
'I love hardly any women but young girls, as if life weren't complicated enough without that', or confessed his sensual enjoyment on
reading how Chateaubriand 'was arrested when in bed with two
women'[2]—show that his thoughts still ran on the 'little pleasures'
he had experienced with her during his flying visits to Paris from
Versailles last October. In July, when he began to plan his annual
return to Cabourg, he confided in Lauris: 'Georges, if I leave Paris,
it will perhaps be with a woman.'[3]

[1] Querqueville, the first form of Balbec, was the seaside resort at which the
love-affair with the little band was experienced by Swann in the novel of 1905;
and it is mentioned also in a later but still primitive episode at Kreuznach, based
on Proust's stays there with his mother in July 1895 and August 1897 (BSAMP,
VIII, 447).

[2] Proust must have read this in the Goncourt *Journal*, 7 October 1866, which
seems to be the only printed source for the tradition.

[3] '. . . *avec une femme.*' The expression is ambiguous; it could mean, equally
well, 'with a wife.'

In the same July came a farcical yet touching encounter with a goddess of his past. Comtesse Greffulhe, in her capacity as president of the Société des Grandes Auditions Musicales de la France, requested 'a few lines, just as you feel, that is, exquisitely poetic!' for her annual concert-fête at Bagatelle in the Bois de Boulogne on 17 July. Proust declined, pleading illness and recent refusals of equally deserving cases (which included her own cousin Montesquiou). But instead of striking him off her list, the sympathetic noblewoman sent him a superb vine, cascading with grapes, in a pot: it was 'a speaking symbol', she declared, and if he would name his day and hour, she would visit his sickbed, 'hoping to find you restored to the very summit of your powers!' Proust, outreached for once, sent the unmanageable vegetable to Marie Nordlinger: 'I thought of throwing in some roses,' he maliciously told Reynaldo, 'so that I could quote Nerval's "*Trellis where vine is intertwined with rose*"; but it occurred to me that Mallarmé's "*When I have sucked the clarity of grapes*" would be more economical, because then there'd be no need for roses.' He swore Reynaldo to secrecy: 'otherwise the Élisabeth would hear in five minutes, because nowadays the moment anybody says anything unkind concerning anyone Montesquiou writes them a letter about it INSTANTANEOUSLY!'

Proust was now working with desperate energy on the last two of the seven black plush exercise-books of *Contre Sainte-Beuve*. His material was getting out of hand: still more characters, with ever less relevance to Sainte-Beuve, forced their way in from his old novel to wait on the brink of the new. In these last, unpublished fragments he wrote about Cottard, and Mme Verdurin's sacred monster Princesse Sherbatoff; he developed M. de Quercy, the future Charlus, and Montargis, the future Saint-Loup; Swann himself reappeared. On 29 June, when the living presence of the seven-years-dead Charles Haas was thus in his mind, he read in an article by Robert Dreyfus in *Le Figaro* of Haas as a brilliant young dandy in 1863, playing in amateur theatricals with the Pourtalès's, the Galliffets and Gaston de Saint-Maurice at the Château de Mouchy, and much to Dreyfus's bewilderment wept as he read. Would Mme Lemaire recognise herself in Mme Verdurin? and was his critique not becoming too much like a novel?

> '*I rather fear my novel on Sainte-Beuve*
> *May not entirely please our friend La Veuve*',

he told Reynaldo. On 6 July the electric light had glared for sixty hours unextinguished in his bedroom, until even the scornful Nicolas remarked with awe: "I think Monsieur must be an old Brahmin!"

It was during these first weeks of July 1909 that Proust began *A la Recherche*: indeed, it is possible that his sixty sleepless hours from 4 to 6 July were caused not by the last throes of *Contre Sainte-Beuve*, but by the first wave of inspiration on which his great novel was launched. Just as in the autumn of 1899 he had renounced the barren *Jean Santeuil* and turned joyfully to Ruskin, so he now abandoned the waning *Contre Sainte-Beuve*; but this time the illumination came from within. It was the most important single event of his life, both for himself and for posterity.

All the material of his novel had long been available to him. He had known its characters and experienced its plot—except for certain episodes which were still in the unknown future—in a period of his life which was now long past. He had even written it twice, in *Jean Santeuil* and in the novel of 1905-7, and much of it (counting the new draft of 1908 and *Contre Sainte-Beuve*) four times over. But the identity of the last catalyst, which would fuse the whole and crystallise its meaning, its metaphysic and its secret structure, remained an impenetrable mystery. The story he had told so often could only display the vanity of human desire; it could only tell the terrible half-truth, that desire is vain not because it is frustrated but because it is fulfilled, and the people and places we love turn to ashes when we possess them. Comparison between *A la Recherche* and the fruitless efforts of Proust's past twenty years of ceaseless writing will show the nature of the revelation which came to him in July 1909. In *A la Recherche*, although he mapped the desert of experience more bitterly and minutely than ever before, he showed that it leads, except for those who stay in it, to the recovery of innocence, that the joy of our vision is not cancelled by the disillusion of its attainment, that the truth of salvation everywhere underlies the truth of sin and despair. Proust had entered, at last and once for all, into Time Regained.

He had found it in real life, precisely as in *A la Recherche*, through the incidents of unconscious memory which form the beginning and end of his novel. He had eaten the madeleine and trodden on the uneven paving-stone; he had forced them to release their messages from Time Lost, of the scented garden at Auteuil and the sunlight of Venice. At the time when they occurred, however, despite the spiritual joy with which they were accompanied, these experiences seemed mere opportune recurrences of similar events which had happened throughout his life, and had been recorded again and again in *Jean Santeuil*. He used them in January 1909, almost perfunctorily, for the second preface to *Contre Sainte-Beuve*, as useful parallels of his thesis in that work, the superiority of instinct over intellect. The profounder revelation came only in July, and was aesthetic rather than spiritual. The event in Proust's real life on which the eating of the madeleine in *A la Recherche* is based is not so much the actual occurrence of January 1909, as the moment of triumph in July when he realised that it was the key to his novel. *A la Recherche* would be a vast unconscious memory, embodying the whole of his past life, and extracting from it the truths which had been invisible in Time Lost.

In order to fit the incident for its new function as the gateway to his novel, he rearranged it. For the humble tea and rusk, which could only recall Auteuil and Nathé Weil, he substituted the lime-tea and madeleine which were associated with Illiers and would create Combray. Instead of Céline Cottin, as in real life, or Félicie Fitau, 'my old cook', as in *Contre Sainte-Beuve*,[1] his own mother brought him the enchanted potion, atoning for the kiss which had destroyed him by the clue to a work of art which would save him.

This new use of a minor incident—like the stone the builders rejected—for a greater purpose was a continuation of the curious instinctive process which we have seen at work in *Contre Sainte-Beuve*. A fortuitous and apparently unimportant image in one chapter would become, as Proust became conscious of its latent meaning, the inspiration for the next section of his essay: a brief digression in the 'classical' discussion of Sainte-Beuve's method suggested the conversation with his mother, the image in the second preface of the sleeper awakening provided his introductory chapters, the critique of Balzac introduced the Guermantes clan. The unconscious creative forces of *A la Recherche* were rising in *Contre Sainte-Beuve*, not in the incidents and characters, which were still unimproved repetitions of his earlier drafts, but in the structural devices which at the time seemed relevant only to his essay. The madeleine incident, which began his novel, was matched by the stumbling on the paving-stone, which ended it. The themes of waking in an unfamiliar room, lying in bed at early morning, longing for travel, the article in *Le Figaro* and the Narrator's conversation with his mother, became architectural motifs which recur throughout *A la Recherche*. During the seven months of

[1] *Contre Sainte-Beuve*, 53.

Contre Sainte-Beuve the hidden power of Time Regained had prepared, unknown to Proust, the symbolic patterns of *A la Recherche*.

The beginning of his novel delayed his departure for Cabourg
several weeks past the usual time. His exhaustion was intensified by
asthma, an abscess in a hollow tooth, and a mysterious fever, for
which Dr Bize ordered fresh air. Suddenly, about 20 August, he left
for Cabourg with Nicolas, and on the train had the unexpected
pleasure of meeting 'Father Plantevignes', with whom he discussed
the virtues of young Nogrette for two livelong hours.

For the sake of warmth and quiet he took a small, airless attic on the
fourth floor of the Grand Hôtel, because it had a fireplace and no
neighbours. Above was the roof, to one side an inner courtyard, and
to the other only Nicolas, who had a palatial room with a private bathroom, 'for which', said Proust, 'I'm his sub-tenant'. Ulrich arrived to
be his secretary; 'though so far,' he told Reynaldo, 'he's given me no
cause to quote *Ulrich, thine eyes have plumbed the ocean's depths*' '.[1]
Last year he had risen early enough to visit the beach before dinner;
but now he worked till far past dawn, rose at sunset, and first appeared
at half-past nine in the vast restaurant whence other diners had long
since fled. One evening he asked the gipsy orchestra 'whether they
knew anything by Reynaldo Hahn?'; and when they obligingly struck
up with Reynaldo's *Rêverie* he dissolved into tears, while twenty
otherwise idle waiters put on expressions of deep concern, and the
head-waiter hurried to fetch him a glass of water. Then he joined the
young sons of his Cabourg friends in the casino next door, where one
of his forms of innocent merriment was to make propaganda for the
poetry of Mme de Noailles. 'The adolescents', as he called them, soon
caught on. A student of mathematics quoted '*as sweet and savage as a
Persian garden*' in the midst of a purely scientific discussion, and
another enquired, in the name of optics, whether the sun could really
'*insert his prism in a stained-glass window*'? The correct answer to
"How was your golf today?"' was " '*The course was full of maddened
butterflies, Like jasmine blossoms poised on fluttering wings*'!" 'Great
loves for you were born in those youthful hearts,' Proust assured the
poetess.

A distressing letter, apparently of this year, from Proust to one of
these 'adolescents' survives: it would be wrong to call it, as it has been
called, a love-letter, still more to identify its insignificant recipient as 'one

[1] Adapted from Musset's sonnet to Ulrich Guttinguer.

who became in the end the very image of Albertine'. The temperature is low, the tone that of Montesquiou's melodious automatic nagging, or of Charlus's note to the headwaiter Aimé at Balbec[1]; this is merely a letter of aggrieved, unimportant, crestfallen platonic friendship, to a young man who has broken his promise to meet Proust on the sea-front from six to seven in the evening. Now Proust will refrain from inviting him to a party he is giving for 'the young people of Cabourg and others'; Alphonse Daudet and Anatole France never treated him like this; the young person has 'passed by and spoiled a famous oppor-tunity of friendship'; Proust will put him in his novel as an example of 'characters that will never know the elegance of missing a dance to give their company to a friend', and meanwhile 'bids him goodbye once and for all'. They probably made it up next morning. But this youth supplied, indeed, one small detail for Albertine at Balbec. 'I guessed your true nature,' says Proust, 'on the day when you told me with such energy: "I can't, because I've got to go to the Feucarts' party" '; and Albertine hurries off to tea at the golf club, crying to Andrée: "But you know Madame Durieux has invited you!"[2]

Another curious incident of the Narrator's first visit to Balbec, the appearance at the Grand Hôtel of the young man who has made him-self 'king of a tiny islet in Oceania' and his mistress the queen,[3] alludes to a person notorious in his time. Jacques Lebaudy, son of the sugar millionaire, acquired a plot of land in the Atlas Mountains, proclaimed himself Emperor of the Sahara, distributed titles of nobility, and made the singer Marguerite Dellier his Empress. In exile in the United States he proposed, like the Pharaohs his peers, to make their daughter his consort; whereupon the Empress shot him dead, and was acquitted by a sympathetic jury.

Proust's companions were not all male. He was now paying homage to Mlles Hélène and Colette, the young daughters of the Vicomte d'Alton, a nephew of the Aimée d'Alton who had been Musset's greatest love after George Sand, and had married the poet's brother after his death. 'Colette is ravishing,' Proust told Jean Louis Vaudoyer a year later, 'and resembles Aimée d'Alton in beauty, though in nothing else, for she is as virtuous as could be.' Proust gave Mlle Colette the gold handbag from Cartier's which the Narrator buys for Albertine, after 'finding out from M. de Charlus what the correct thing was at the moment', to use on the Little Train.[1] Another original of Albertine, according to Mme de Clermont-Tonnerre, was Mlle Bauche, the daughter of a manufacturer of safes and leader of a little band of girls on the Cabourg promenade: 'she had a geranium-pink complexion, and her sporting, unconventional behaviour was just like Albertine's, although'—the Duchesse coyly adds—'the resemblance went no further'. The same informant mentions Proust's visits to Comtesse Berthier and her dazzling daughters Germaine and Yvonne at their Villa Berthier in Cabourg, and how they asked, many years later, whether the famous writer was any relative of their former friend. "He's the very same person." "Impossible! Why, he never even mentioned literature, and he used to make us die laughing with his funny stories!" Perhaps the real Albertine was Colette d'Alton, or another of these girls, or one whose name is still unknown in Proust's story; but whoever she may have been, their relationship was now reaching the extraordinary pitch of possible marriage.

Meanwhile Proust had written, just before leaving for Cabourg, to offer *Contre Sainte-Beuve* to the *Mercure de France*; but Vallette, who in April 1908 had rejected the Lemoine pastiches and a volume of collected articles, declined the new work soon after Proust's arrival. By a lucky chance Calmette happened to be staying near Cabourg, and Proust decided to ask this most obliging of editors to find him a publisher. When the interview took place, however, about 27 August, he resolved to play for still higher stakes: without mentioning *Contre Sainte-Beuve*, he confided that he was now writing a novel. The amiable Calmette immediately offered to print it as a feuilleton serial in *Le Figaro*. It now seemed prudent to keep the very existence of *Contre Sainte-Beuve* a secret; and remembering with panic that he had mentioned it to Beaunier, Proust begged Robert Dreyfus to explain that the work accepted by Calmette was a novel and not the critical essay; for if Beaunier thought it was the latter he might advise against it, since only fiction could be considered suitable for a *Figaro* feuille- ton. Dreyfus thought it pointless to warn Beaunier, and on 3 Septem- ber Proust agreed. He reported to Mme Straus that he had 'just begun —and just finished—a whole long book', and that he was about to set to work again, after the interruption caused by his departure for Cabourg. The book begun was *A la Recherche*, and the book finished was *Contre Sainte-Beuve*. Already he was undecided about the *feuille- ton*: he told Mme Straus that only part of his novel would appear in

[1] II, 1037.

Princesse Marthe Bibesco, *by Boldini*

Proust at the tennis-party, 1891

Simone de Caillavet

Céleste Albaret, Proust's housekeeper

Prince Antoine Bibesco

Prince Emmanuel Bibesco

Marquis Louis d'Albufera,
by *Armand, Duc de Guiche*

Bertrand de Fénelon
(*by courtesy of Princesse Marthe Bibesco*)

Le Figaro, 'because it's too improper and too long', and Dreyfus that he would probably wait until he could finish it in volume form. Another remark at this time to Mme Straus explains Proust's curious illusion, which he expressed to many friends during the coming months, that the novel he had so recently begun would soon be completed. 'Although all of it's written,' he told her, 'a great many things need recasting.' He still regarded *A la Recherche* as a mere revision, under the new inspiration of Time Regained, of the work he had drafted three times since 1905. In a sense he was right; but he did not foresee that the task which now seemed to require only a few months would in fact take thirteen years.

Mme Straus was staying again at her Trouville villa, the Clos des Mûriers; but when she offered to visit her 'little Marcel', he put her off with promises to visit her, and never came. Her afternoon call last year, he explained, had been so spoiled by the draughts of the Grand Hôtel, the din of the orchestra, and her husband's tactful disappearance to pay for their cups of chocolate, that it was only after she departed in her motor-car that he had time to realise: 'I have been with Mme Straus!' He envied her the company of Helleu, and quoted Montesquiou's remark (for Helleu's great-grandfather had been a member of the Council of Five Hundred), that 'few of the descendants of his victims have as much breeding as this descendant of their executioner!' He begged her to keep his presence at Cabourg secret from Guiche and his wife, who were at Bénerville again.

When the season ended and his friends went away Proust hoped, as he had planned the year before, to work on through October and November in the solitude of the empty hotel. But the scheme fell through (the manager desperately pleaded urgent repairs to cracks in the walls), and towards the end of September he returned to Paris. He arranged for a fair copy of the illegible beginning of *A la Recherche* to be made, and invited Lauris to call and read it at his bedside; but as he had not yet confided the secret of his novel to this friend, he pretended that the manuscript would be 'the first paragraph, which is almost a volume in itself, of the first chapter of *Contre Sainte-Beuve*'.

As it happened Proust first read his opening chapter in mid-November to Reynaldo, who was enthusiastically encouraging. The manuscript was now two hundred pages long; and he offered again to read it to Lauris, announcing in the same letter (about 20 November 1909) that he would now return Lauris's set of Sainte-Beuve's *Port-Royal*, 'because I shan't use it for several months'. This marked the final postponement of *Contre Sainte-Beuve*, which he never mentioned again. Instead he borrowed Mâle's *L'Art religieux de la fin du moyen-âge en France*; and his sudden need for this volume suggests that he was now describing Saint-Hilaire at Combray, or the sculptures of Saint-André-des-Champs.[1] Early in December he received Lauris's 'divine letter' on the first manuscript-book of his novel, and sent him the second and third. Lauris never forgot the 'enchanted amazement' with which he had read the first few pages, in his little room opening on the garden in the Rue de Berri, and how 'a whole new world opened' before him.

The contents of the three manuscript-books may be deduced with some certainty, for Lauris commented on Proust's apparent praise of George Sand in the first. 'Don't infer that I like George Sand,' Proust replied, 'it isn't intended as a piece of literary criticism, it's just like that at that time, and the rest of the book will correct it.' The mother's reading of George Sand to the Narrator as a child at Combray occurs near the end of the opening chapter of *Swann*, and is in fact 'corrected' by the meditation on *François le Champi* in the Prince de Guermantes's library.[2] The first manuscript-volume contained therefore in all probability the whole chapter ('*Combray* I'); and the second and third volumes must have comprised all or most of '*Combray* II', which is a little more than twice as long again. This is confirmed by Proust's enquiry, about mid-December, whether Lauris thinks the part he has just read could be published separately, and whether, if he were to die suddenly before finishing his work, Lauris would promise to arrange this; for '*Combray*' in fact forms a separable unity.

Meanwhile, in November, he began to say goodbye to his friends for the sake of his novel: to Louisa de Mornand ('I'm on the point of cloistering myself for a long work'), to Montesquiou ('I have undertaken a kind of novel, the beginning of which will appear soon, perhaps'), to Antoine Bibesco (saying that he hoped to finish by next summer), and to Mme de Noailles ('desiring to put enough of myself into it for you to know and esteem me a little'). On 27 November, by way of a farewell appearance, he took three boxes at the Théâtre des Variétés for Feydeau and Croisset's comedy *Le Circuit*. Marcel Plantevignes and the other two young men of Cabourg were his guests of honour; and to these he added '(because these young people are a little too young for me,' he told Louisa), all the unmarried survivors of his closest friends: Lauris, Emmanuel Bibesco, Reynaldo, François de

[1] I, 59-67, 150-2.   [2] I, 39-43; III, 883-8.

Pâris, Fénelon,[1] Loche Radziwill with Christiane, and Louisa complete with Robert Gangnat.

In his letter of invitation to Lauris he revealed a stranger plan than this. 'A person who is dear to me is connected with them,' he wrote, mentioning the three young men of Cabourg, and added, in the formula with which a Frenchman would hint at a coming engagement: 'Georges, perhaps you will soon be hearing news of me—*vous apprendrez peut-être bientôt de moi du nouveau*'. 'Or rather,' he rectified, already retreating a little, 'I shall ask your advice. To make a very young and charming girl share my terrible life, even if she is not afraid of doing so—would it not be a crime?'

'I nearly married her, but in the end I didn't dare—I wouldn't have had the heart to make a young woman live with anyone so ill and so tiresome,' says the Narrator to Albertine of the imaginary woman for love of whom he is asking her to return with him to Paris.[2] 'No, I've too bad a character,' says the Narrator to Gilberte at Tansonville when she urges him to marry, 'and besides, I was engaged once, but couldn't go through with it.'[3] Proust was no doubt sincere in wishing, or half-wishing, or believing that he half-wished to marry the girl of Cabourg. His plan of marriage, however nebulous, came when the revelation of his novel had ended the sense of exile from humanity which, since the moonlight night at Auteuil in his childhood, he had tried in vain to heal. He saw for a moment a mirage of normal love, placation of his dead mother, liberation from pariah-hood, return to the sacraments of the human condition. Might he not possess all these, and still write his novel, which otherwise could bring salvation only at the price of solitude and death? But the vision of this last chance was illusory: not unheroically he turned his face, went his way, and spoke no more of marriage. What were the feelings of the young girl, who asked Antoine Bibesco 'not to print her name', whether she loved Proust and wished more seriously than he for this impossible union, will perhaps never be known.

[1] Fénelon was transferred from the French Embassy at Washington to the political and commercial section of the Foreign Ministry in Paris on 14 October 1909 until his posting to Rio de Janeiro on 21 May 1912.

[2] II, 1123.

[3] III, 707.

Chapter 8

MADEMOISELLE DE SAINT-LOUP
(*January 1910 – July 1912*)

EARLY in the new year of 1910 Proust read Thomas Hardy's *The Well-Beloved* in a recent French translation,[1] noticing with dismay, as he told Robert de Billy, that it resembled 'just the least little bit, though it's a thousand times better, what I'm writing now'. Proust had detected in Hardy's plot, in which the hero loves at different periods of his life a girl, her daughter, and her daughter's daughter, an affinity with his own; for *A la Recherche* was to be the story of three related loves in three separate epochs, Swann's for Odette and the Narrator's for Gilberte and Albertine, a structure of which a more primitive form had already appeared in *Jean Santeuil*. Hardy's view of love, according to which we pursue not a person, but a fleeting image of our own creation which is the same in all objects of our desire, was equally Proustian, as Hardy himself was to observe sixteen years later.[2] Proust asked Billy to approach his British colleague at Tangiers, Sir Reginald Lister, for information on the private lives of both Hardy and Barrie, apparently wondering whether they shared his own two principal vices: 'are they society men, and do they care for women?' he enquired.[3] *The Well-Beloved*, together with *Jude the Obscure* and *A Pair of Blue Eyes*, remained in Proust's mind throughout the writing of his novel. The Narrator in conversation with the captive Albertine illustrates his theory of the identical nature of all the works of a great artist, 'that unknown quality of a unique world which is perhaps the most authentic proof of genius', by the presence of the little phrase in every composition by Vinteuil, and again by the 'stonemason's geometry of Hardy's

[1] *La Bien-aimée*, tr. E. Paul-Margueritte, published in September 1909. *Jude l'Obscur* appeared in 1901, *Deux yeux bleus* in 1913.

[2] F. E. Hardy, *The Life of Thomas Hardy* (1962), p. 432.

[3] Proust had admired Barrie's *Margaret Ogilvie* in translation three years before. He may have been misled by the theme of mother-domination in Barrie's novel, and by the ironical glimpses of high society, or the intentionally platonic and formalistic representation of the hero's love for women, in Hardy's.

novels'; he invites her to consider the recurrence of the stonemason theme in *Jude*, *A Pair of Blue Eyes*, and *The Well-Beloved*, or 'the parallelism between *The Well-Beloved*, where the hero loves three women, and *A Pair of Blue Eyes*, where the heroine loves three men'.[1] The themes of *The Well-Beloved* are particularly present at the Princesse de Guermantes's matinée. The Narrator becomes suddenly aware of his age, like Jocelyn Pierston seeing his own timeworn face in the mirror[2]; like the Narrator before he stumbles on the paving-stone, Pierston, though for him there is to be no renovation, 'could no longer attach a definite sentiment to images of beauty revealed from the past'.[3] "You mistake me for my mother," says Gilberte,[4] a mistake which frequently occurs in *The Well-Beloved*; Odette's miraculous preservation of her youth is found to be due, like Marcia's, to 'beautifying artifices'[5]; "I wish you would speak to her—I'm sure you would like her," says the second Avice to Pierston of her daughter Avice the third, like Gilberte offering to introduce her daughter to the Narrator[6]; and at the same momentous party the Narrator sees gathered together the mother, daughter and granddaughter whom he has loved or may yet love, in the persons of Odette, Gilberte, and Mlle de Saint-Loup. Furthermore, at the very time when he read *The Well-Beloved*, Proust became aware of a similar situation in his own life.

For nearly ten years he had not seen Mme Arman de Caillavet. They had been estranged by what he referred to as a 'dissension', perhaps not unconnected with his habit of arriving so late at her Wednesdays that the guests, including Anatole France himself, would vanish with cries of "There's Marcel—that means we'll be here till two in the morning!" Mme Arman was sixty-three; she had ceased to dye her hair, which now rolled in noble white billows over her vast white forehead; but Monsieur France, rejuvenated by the self-satisfaction which she had toiled to give him, was only sixty-five and beginning to rove. On 30 April 1909 he sailed with Mme Arman's reluctant blessing for a lecture-tour in South America, guarded by two spies, his treacherous secretary Jean Jacques Brousson and her own manservant François. Perhaps his absence, 'in the antipodes,' she said, laughing wryly, 'surrounded by monkeys and parrots and

[1] III, 376-7.   [2] *The Well-Beloved*, 271.
[3] *Ibid.*, 324.   [4] III, 980.
[5] III, 948; *The Well-Beloved*, 328.
[6] III, 1028; *The Well-Beloved*, 237.

savages', would make him love her more; and besides, she was about
to undergo an operation which would, she hoped, restore her lost
youth and health. France sent many cablegrams but few letters. One
evening, at last, Mme Arman assembled her guests to hear 'a letter
from the Argentine'. " 'Yesterday we gave our first lecture . . .' " she
began. "Charming! Who but M. France could have written that!"
cried an unwary newcomer, only to be crushed by her indignant "Sir,
this letter is not from M. France, but from my manservant François."
But she also received anonymous letters, which spoke of an actress
whom France had met on the boat and followed ever after, and a
newspaper cutting, which mentioned the presence of 'M. and Mme
France' at an official reception. The Abbé Mugnier began to call:
perhaps God would give back her lover, or at least her peace? In July
Brousson returned, unmasked, sacked and revengeful: the actress was
Jeanne Brindeau, a lady of ample and well-preserved charms, and M.
France had just sailed with her for Monte-Video, a city not hitherto
included in his lecture itinerary.

On 28 August France returned crestfallen to captivity. He dis-
missed his concubine with all desirable brutality, and accompanied
Mme Arman to the family estate at Capian for the vintage; but in
October, still the eternal sightseer, he dragged her by motor-car to
Toulouse, Montpellier, Carcassonne, and to Hendaye to call on Loti.
Back at Capian she was cold and ill, so ill that France summoned Dr
Widal (the same whose discovery of the dangers of salt in an invalid
diet came too late to save the life of the Narrator's grandmother[1]) from
Paris. Early in January, after nursing her devotedly, France brought
her back to the Avenue Hoche. "Too old, too old," she lamented to
her daughter-in-law Jeanne; "I'd better die, I haven't the courage to
face what life has in store for me . . . but do stop crying, it upsets me!"
France called, still unforgiven, and feeling that he too had a right to be
ill: "Well, Madame, I'm off, my lumbago's hurting me," he grumbled,
and stumped away. On the 12th, suddenly choking and speechless,
Mme Arman scribbled on her bedside pad: 'Gaston quick, and M.
Fr—', and died, regaining in death for a few ironic hours her promised
youth, like Proust's mother five years before. "I could have stayed,"
wept France, "my lumbago wasn't as bad as all that . . . but when I saw
her again she was dead. Her face was calm, her cheeks were soft, she
looked as beautiful as she was at forty. It's I who am dead, not she—
how could she desert me like this?" As he walked in her funeral

[1] II, 298.

cortège on the 14th he was heard to remark: "Pretty house, that, period 1830!"; but during the service at Saint-Philippe-du-Roule[1] he stood alone, avoiding the accusing glances of the others, and stifling his tears. Clemenceau, Gégé Primoli, the great Réjane, all the stars of her salon were present, including perhaps Proust himself, whose wreath of camelias, arum-lilies, lilac, roses and violets was on the hearse. He remembered how in life she would gaze at the flowers he brought her, bury her face in their fragrance, and ring imperiously for the servants to put them in water. 'Please try to put them near her,' he wrote to Gaston's wife, 'I'm drugging myself in the hope of being able to come to the funeral.'

Now he could ask again for the photograph of Jeanne which he had coveted nineteen years before, when he loved her. It came, and he saw a proud young woman, enthroned at the tennis-party in 1891 between the Dancognée and Daireaux girls, recognisable even now as the Jeanne he still knew. But the gawky, shyly grinning young man, who knelt at her feet and strummed on a tennis-racket for a guitar, was almost past recognition: it was himself, smiling from the depths of Time Lost, before he set foot in Sodom, surrendered to asthma, and wore his mother to her death. 'Was it taken *then*, or last summer? Nothing has changed but myself!' he told Jeanne. Emboldened, he wrote to her daughter Simone, now aged fifteen, who had so enchanted him two years before, and received a charming letter which seemed written in Chinese characters, he teasingly told her, 'as if water-coloured or landscape-gardened rather than written!' For a few weeks grandmother, daughter-in-law and granddaughter were in his thoughts together, just as in *The Well-Beloved*. He asked Mlle Simone, too, for a photograph, urged her to read *The Mill on the Floss*, and added in gloomy jest, alluding to the fate of Tom and Maggie Tulliver: 'no doubt I shall be drowned soon as well!'

The Seine was rising, swollen by the unprecedented rains which had fallen in central France since the day after Mme Arman's funeral. The angry brown river hurtled on, ever higher, carrying trees and dead cattle from the fields to the south, household furniture from the working-class suburbs, and barrels from the Quai de Bercy. By the 26th the metro was flooded, the electric trams had ceased to run, the

---

[1] Mme Arman received burial in the Catholic faith, but her grave was in the little Jewish section of the Montmartre cemetery, beside her parents the Lippmanns, where her husband and son, when their time came, did not choose to join her.

Zouave on the Pont de l'Alma stood breast-high in the roaring torrent, and half Paris was under water. Fifty thousand refugees sheltered in public buildings, while President Fallières tasted soup in improvised kitchens, congratulated the society ladies who cooked it, and talked sympathetically to cheering victims. The bears in the Jardin des Plantes were rescued in imminent danger of drowning; it was feared that the crocodiles might escape from their flooded pools; and the poor giraffe had to be left, knee-deep, to die of exposure. Sewers burst in the streets, or rose hideously in cellars, and rats fled through the boulevards. Plank bridges for pedestrians were built along the main thoroughfares, looters were ducked by infuriated crowds, and the police interrupted, in the nick of time, a lynching on the Pont d'Ivry. The carcase of a bullock was seen hurrying down-stream, with the corpse of its young herdsman still clutching its straw halter. Snow fell, and more rain. On the 28th, when the waters reached their highest point, a vast, malodorous lake stretched from the aban-doned Gare Saint-Lazare far up the Boulevard Haussmann, rippling a little past Proust's apartment. The Parisians, except those who were homeless or ruined, grimly enjoyed a spectacle which had never been equalled since the great flood of 1746; and Proust himself, thrillingly marooned, took some pleasure in a drama which might have been entitled Proust on the Floss.

But when at last the river stayed away from his door, his troubles began—'though I daren't speak of myself when others have suffered so badly'. The cellars of 102 Boulevard Haussmann had to be pumped out; fumes from carbolic and stoves used for disinfection and drying gave him incessant fits of asthma; the wrecked lift must be repaired, and Dr Gagey's drains refitted; and because the workmen hammered all day in his sleep-time, he was compelled to take opium and veronal. He had albumen in his urine. It was 'only after the strangest prodigies, and looking like a mummy in a dress-suit', that he could attend the dress-rehearsal at the Opéra of *La Fête chez Thérèse*, the ballet on which Reynaldo had worked by his bedside at Versailles in October 1908, while he played dominoes with Agostinelli. Three times in February the river rose again above danger-level. "Even the Seine wants to see *Chantecler*," people said; for Rostand's brilliant comedy of the farmyard—in which Montesquiou was enraged to find himself satirised as the Peacock, *'prince of the unexpected adjective'*—was playing at the Porte Saint-Martin. For a time, as if he had not seen enough of streets turned into water-ways, Proust thought of leaving

for Venice; and then from March to June there is one of the characteristic gaps in his correspondence which mark a period of total absorption in his writing. In April he informed Mme Straus ('as if I hadn't
told you often enough!') that he was 'finishing a long work, which
may still take several months'. Proust was isolated by his novel still
more completely than by the great flood.

He was isolated, but not alone. At any moment of the day or night
two familiar demons could be brought to his bedside by the triple peal
of his bell. "There's your pal Valentin ringing," said Nicolas Cottin,
with heavy irony, calling his master by the baptismal first name which
Proust never used—"you won't let him put you in a state, will you,
dear?" "Céline, I can feel a gale blowing," Proust complained,
"you've left your larder door open again!" Nicolas was tall and
rotund, thicklipped and cleanshaven, with low forehead, narrow eyes,
and an expression of crafty stupidity; Céline was a jolly blonde; both
were still in their late twenties. The Cottins regarded their strange
employer with less respect than they displayed in his presence, but
perhaps with less contempt than they pretended when alone together.
Proust shed the loose leaves of his novel on the floor in the small
hours: it was one of Nicolas's duties to jab them in order with paper-
fasteners, and sometimes even to take down fresh passages from
dictation. "His rigmaroles are as big a bloody bore as he is," he told
Céline, "but mark my words, when he's dead he'll be a success all
right." The usual pay for a married couple was 150 francs monthly,
and Proust characteristically gave them double. But their service was
not without its rigours: Céline went to bed at 9.30 p.m., for she must
be up to give Monsieur his dawn coffee; while Nicolas, who was on
duty till 4 a.m., had become almost as nocturnal as his master, and
acquired a weak chest which Céline attributed to the suffocating heat
of Proust's bedroom. Proust dined at nine in the evening, on three
croissants from the Gare Saint-Lazare, boiling café au lait in a wadded
coffeepot, œufs Béchamel—"the sauce used to get in his beard!"—
fried potatoes in a little silver vegetable-dish, and stewed fruit according to season—"the same every day for weeks, and how we got tired
of stewed apples!" Often Monsieur Hahn would call, and play a few
dazzling notes on the grand-piano in the drawing-room before bursting in. "He's like the wind," Céline would say, and "He's like a
hurricane, Céline," Proust would reply. She remembered Albufera,
Antoine Bibesco and Loche Radziwill as the next most regular callers.
Monsieur never gave orders, except when he was angry, but always

said: "Would you be so obliging as to—"; and when he was too asthmatic to speak he would write notes, which Nicolas kept:

> *'Since you preserve these missives for all time,*
> *Dear Nicolas, I'm forced to write in rhyme. . . .*
> *If not too weary is your wrist,*
> *Nicolas the nationalist,*
> *Bring me milk-coffee steaming hot. . . .'*

Proust called Céline 'the War-monger', because she once defiantly declared: "I'd love to see what war is like"—a wish destined to be granted.

In June Proust was lured from solitude by a new revelation of high art. Diaghilev and the Russian Ballet had first exploded upon Paris for an all-too-brief season in May 1909. In 1910 all Paris had awaited them for a year, and their triumph was instant and tremendous. Proust went with Reynaldo and the art-critic Jean Louis Vaudoyer to the opening night at the Opéra on 4 June, when *Schéhérazade* was first performed. The stage was a dazzling green tent with shadowy blue doors and a vast orange carpet: 'I never saw anything so beautiful,' he told Reynaldo. Nijinsky, a boy of eighteen, entered with an eery, animal crouch as the negro slave, and whirled away with Ida Rubinstein, the Sultan's favourite wife; an orgy such as the Paris Opéra had never before witnessed was interrupted by the Sultan's return, everyone was hewn to pieces with scimitars, Nijinsky writhed in his unbelievable horizontal death-leap, and the audience became raving mad. 'I don't know how you could possibly see Nijinsky miming,' Proust objected on reading Reynaldo's critique in *Le Journal*, 'because there were always two hundred persons dancing in front of him.' *Schéhérazade*, it is true, was a violent sensation rather than a masterpiece; but the impact was made, and greater things followed in the succeeding years.

Meanwhile Proust and several of his friends discovered that among the most intoxicating charms of the Russian Ballet was the personal relationship which was permitted with the artists. Proust was not to become a habitué until the following year; but he met Nijinsky, and did not care for him, and Bakst, whom he 'admired prodigiously', feeling that the great designer had made a point of being particularly charming—'it's true he's charming to everybody, but I thought I detected a *nuance*!' Montesquiou was seen at every performance with his gold-headed cane, and worshipped the boyish Ida Rubinstein with an adoration he had felt for no woman since the heyday of the Marquise de Casa-Fuerte seventeen years before. Reynaldo was com-

missioned to compose a ballet to a scenario by Cocteau, *Le Dieu Bleu*,
for next season, and was invited to St Petersburg for the end of the
winter. Cocteau, to whom Diaghilev one day would issue the momentous command: "Amaze me!", was first amazed by Diaghilev: the
taxi which Diaghilev had so kindly lent him on the way home from
Larue's seemed to take an extraordinarily long time over the journey,
and at last deposited the bewildered stripling in the courtyard of the
Hôtel des Réservoirs at Versailles. Vaudoyer, a romantically melancholy young man with pendulous moustaches, quoted Gautier's lines
'*I am the spectre of the rose You wore last evening at the ball*' in his essay
'*Variations on the Russian Ballet*' in the *Revue de Paris*, and wrote to
Bakst suggesting that the poem might make a promising subject for a
ballet. Already the camp-following of artists and intellectuals which
formed an indispensable part of the Diaghilev circus was beginning to
gather. Some, like Cocteau and Hahn, would bring their art, others,
like Montesquiou and Vaudoyer, their publicity; some, like Proust
himself, would give only their kindling admiration and conversation;
but all would contribute to the incessant cross-fertilisation, devised by
the strange and cunning genius of Diaghilev, by which the marvellous
organism of the Ballets Russes grew and ripened, and for lack of
which, many years after, it would wither away for ever.

In the next few years Proust frequented the Ballets Russes each
summer. He was 'almost terrifying under the lights of the Opéra,' his
future friend Edmond Jaloux remembered, 'with his fur coat, puffed
face and black-rimmed eyes'; and to Jacques Porel he seemed 'like a
yesterday's gardenia'. Above in the master's box sat the magician
Diaghilev, scrutinising his dancers through a tiny mother-of-pearl
lorgnette, and Misia Edwards beside him, with a tall white Persian
aigrette in her head-dress. For a time Misia had struggled to regain the
formidable Edwards from his mistress, the actress Lantelme; and we
have seen Proust confronted by the grim farce of their triangular
agonies at the Grand Hôtel of Cabourg in 1907. 'I had contrived to
get a photograph of Lantelme,' she wrote in her memoirs; 'it adorned
my dressing-table, and I made desperate efforts to look like her, dress
my hair in the same way, wear the same clothes.' Proust used this
situation for Gilberte's jealousy of Rachel and Saint-Loup at Tansonville: Gilberte has 'come across photographs of Rachel', and imitates
her hair-style and dress 'in the hope of pleasing her husband'.[1] But
Lantelme was drowned from Edwards' yacht in highly suspicious

[1] III, 682-3, 702.

circumstances in July 1911—"I hope she can swim," said Forain, on
first seeing his next mistress, the singer Lina Cavalieri—and Misia was
now the companion, later the wife, of the Spanish artist José Maria
Sert. "How very Spanish," remarked Degas on viewing one of his
huge and hideous frescoes in his Paris studio, "and in such a quiet
street, too!"; but Proust admired his costumes for *La Légende de
Joseph*, the Diaghilev ballet of 1914, and compared to them the
Fortuny and Carpaccio gowns which the Narrator buys for the captive Albertine.[1] Here at the Ballets Russes Misia became 'the ravishing
Princess Yourbeletieff' of Proust's novel, with her 'immense trembling aigrette, the like of which the Parisian ladies had never seen,
though they all tried to imitate it'.[2] "Are you a snob?" Misia asked
Proust; and he indignantly replied that, although he still saw an
occasional duke or prince, his favourite companions were a valet
(Nicolas) and a chauffeur (Odilon): "valets," he said, "are better
educated than dukes, and the chauffeur is more distinguished". Misia
asked him to share her box at the Opéra, and he wrote in accepting,
with thoughts of the final chapter of *Le Temps Retrouvé*: 'I find it
extremely interesting to see how people's faces grow older.'

After the ballet Proust and the dancers adjourned to supper at
Larue's, where Diaghilev devoured beefsteaks with Nijinsky, while
Proust wrote his letters sipping a humble whipped chocolate, and
Cocteau repeated the magnificent gesture of Saint-Loup, originated
in 1902 by the long-lost Fénelon. Proust recorded the occasion in
doggerel verses:

> *To cover my shoulders with satin-lined mink,*
> *Without spilling one drop from his huge eyes' black ink,*
> *Like a sylph to the ceiling, or on snow a thin ski,*
> *Jean leaped on the table and dropped by Nijinsky.'*

Proust constructed Octave, the young dandy 'son of a rich manufacturer', whom the little band at Balbec nickname 'In the Soup', from
various youths in his Cabourg circle: from the artist Léonce de
Joncières, 'that amiable juvenile lead among the Tapirs, a belated
prolongation of Léandre or Octave'—those heroes of sentimental
comedy in the eighteenth century—'the most idiotic person I have
ever seen', as he wrote to Reynaldo, and from Marcel Plantevignes,
son of the manufacturer of neckties. But in his later aspect as the
genius whose 'little sketches, with his own costumes and décor, which

[1] III, 369, 647. In fact the costumes were by Bakst.   [2] II, 743; III, 236-7

have brought about in contemporary art a revolution at least equal to that achieved by the Ballets Russes' are 'perhaps the most extraordinary masterworks of our time', Octave is the Cocteau who created in 1917 and 1919 the revolutionary *Parade* and *Les Mariés de la Tour Eiffel*; while Andrée as Octave's fiancée is probably Jeanne, sister of Paul Iribe with whom Cocteau founded the avant-garde periodical *Le Mot* in 1916, Cocteau's temporary fiancée, and a heroine of *Le Grand Écart*.[1]

Still hoping for the indispensable publicity of serialisation, still believing that the end of his book was already in sight, Proust had recently sent his Combray chapter to *Le Figaro*. But the amiable editor, who a year before had positively begged for the new novel, was now disquietingly coy. 'Someone has managed to *alienate Calmette*, who used to like me so much,' he wrote to Antoine Bibesco about 20 May. In fact Calmette was genuinely impressed, but must have thought a fragment so dense in texture and so apparently destitute of action quite impossible as a feuilleton for his newspaper. Towards the end of June Proust called at one o'clock in the morning —'a most melancholy pilgrimage,' he told Lauris—to collect his rejected manuscript from the *Figaro* office.

As holiday-time approached he thought for a moment of persuading Lauris to accompany him to 'Paul Desjardins's lay abbey'. Desjardins, his revered philosophy teacher twenty years before, had recently founded the famous '*décades*', the discussion groups held for ten days each summer in the mediaeval abbey of Pontigny near Auxerre, which have been carried into our own time by Desjardins's daughter Anne Heurgon. Seventeen years ago with Willie Heath, and again in 1903 with Lauris himself, Proust had vaguely planned to found a secular monastery for writing and meditation. Might not Pontigny be the fulfilment of his dream?

Instead, on the afternoon of 17 July, assisted by the entire family of the concierge Antoine, Proust suddenly fled to Cabourg with Nicolas, reaching the Grand Hôtel on the stroke of midnight. His luggage had an unfamiliar air: it turned out to consist of the pretty hats of a lady who, at that very moment, would be gazing in horror at his cosy nightshirts somewhere in Brittany. The distracted Antoine had muddled the trunks at the Gare Saint-Lazare, and for twenty-four hours Proust was unable to go to bed, while poor Nicolas, very understandably, seized the occasion to go out and get drunk. After a

[1] I, 878; III, 604-7.

few days, however, Proust began to work. In the silence of the night
his exultant cries to the absent Reynaldo of "O my Bunibuls, don't
you agree that's rather nice!" disturbed his sleeping neighbours. He
thought of summoning Ulrich to be his secretary, but discovered that
the young man was in hiding after a thwarted attempt at abduction.

It is not unlikely that in the appropriate environment of Cabourg
Proust now wrote of Balbec. During the eight months since the completion of the Combray chapter in November 1909 he would have
had ample time to dispose of the Narrator's love for Gilberte in the
Champs-Élysées and his visits to Odette's salon. Much of the material
for the first visit to Balbec in *A l'Ombre* had already been worked over.
At the time, perhaps as early as 1905, when Swann was to be the third-
person hero of much of his novel, he had shown him in love with the
little band at Querqueville; the night-journey, and the rosy peasant-
girl selling coffee, had appeared in *Contre Sainte-Beuve*, as also had
passing allusions which show that the Narrator's friendship with
Montargis (Saint-Loup) at the same Querqueville (Balbec) had
formed part of the earlier version of his novel. The little band known
to Swann had borne mawkish names reminiscent of *Les Plaisirs et les
Jours*, such as Arabelle, Célie, Solange; while Albertine and Andrée
had appeared as Anna and Septimie, already suspect of a Lesbian
intimacy which belongs to the second visit to Balbec in *Sodome et
Gomorrhe*. Albertine and Andrée were not to be rechristened until
some years later. But it is probable that the lovely name of Gisèle
belongs to this summer, and that Proust took it from Diaghilev's
revival that June of the old romantic ballet, which Proust reproached
Reynaldo, in a letter from Cabourg, for calling 'the celebrated and
insipid *Giselle*'.

Despite Calmette's refusal, which forced him to abandon hope of
serial publication in a daily newspaper, Proust still thought of finding
a welcome in a monthly magazine; but within a month of arrival at
Cabourg he had advanced so far that too little time seemed left even
for this. He asked Vaudoyer on 18 August 'whether a periodical like
the *Grande Revue* would publish the greater part of my novel; but it
will be finished so soon that I feel it's now too late to think of a
magazine, which would necessarily involve a long delay'.

Meanwhile Proust was enacting some of the situations of his novel.
Towards eleven in the evening he entered the casino and made for the
baccarat table, where he was immediately surrounded by a band of
pretty girls in holiday dresses. His cousin Valentine Thomson, who

happened to be in Cabourg with her married sister Marguerite, watched with sympathetic concern as he shyly produced handfuls of twenty-franc gold pieces for the gay young creatures to gamble away. "They'd like anyone as sweet as you without all that money," she reproached him; but: "Poor young things," he explained, "it amuses them, and besides, they're so nice!" 'Marcel looked like an oriental sorcerer, with his black beard and black-rimmed eyes,' Mlle Thomson recalled long afterwards; and when *Al'Ombre* appeared she recognised the girls of Cabourg in the 'little band' of Balbec. One evening she walked arm in arm with Proust and Calmette, who was staying at the Villa des Tamaris at Houlgate. Suddenly Calmette pointed to her cousin and said: "Did you know that this chap's a genius? He's written a solid, magnificent thing." Valentine turned to Marcel, whose excessive humility was a family joke, expecting to see him protest and dissolve into confusion; but he was smiling remotely, with a look of assurance, although deeply moved, and the young woman realised that Calmette had not exaggerated.

In September, as the end of his holiday drew near, Proust gave the two d'Alton girls their annual present. This year it was a watch each, in periwinkle-blue enamel, on a neck-chain of gold, for which the Paris jeweller Cartier demanded the enormous sum of 4000 francs; so Proust arranged through Reynaldo's sister Maria, and with the expert advice of the elegantly impoverished Boni de Castellane, to buy the trinkets elsewhere at half the price. But the gifts to the two sisters were aimed only at one, apparently at Colette the elder. 'Perhaps you remember,' he wrote to Maria six years later, in the dark days of the war, when he consulted her on the Narrator's presents to Albertine, 'how once long ago you helped me to have fashionable trifles made for two girls, to one of whom I enjoyed giving them.'

Another gift had to be found at the same time, for Georges de Lauris had announced—'in a letter which might have been signed by Fromentin's Dominique or M. de Nemours in *La Princesse de Clèves*', as Proust remarked acidly to Reynaldo—his forthcoming marriage to Madeleine de Pierrebourg, the divorced wife of Proust's still earlier friend, Louis de La Salle. Lauris, after nine long years, was one of the last bachelor survivors of the group of noble young friends from whom Saint-Loup was created; his intimacy had been particularly precious of late, when Proust had made him, as a fellow-novelist, his chief confidant for the writing of *Contre Sainte-Beuve* and the beginning of *A la Recherche*: and Proust could not help feeling a secret

bitterness at the coming end of an old comradeship. But he wrote a
charming letter of congratulation: he had admired the bride for many
years, and 'it would need a Mantegna to paint these nuptials of the
Knight of the Ideal and the Rose Princess!' As a wedding-present
Lauris suggested a clock for his study mantelpiece—'one whose
chimes will tell me to write only books that will please you': 'and that,'
Proust commented with the same note of acrimony to Reynaldo,
'rather complicates one's choice.'

At the beginning of October Proust returned from Cabourg,
lamenting to Mme Catusse that he had only once been well enough to
go on the beach. His mother's friend could not know that his incarceration was voluntary, and the sunlight on the sea had shone still
more brilliantly in the pages he wrote than outside his shuttered
windows and drawn blinds. He hoped to finish his novel soon, he told
her, 'but the book lengthens ahead of me'; for the process of expansion
and enrichment of his prearranged plan had now begun, and would
continue until the day of his death. Now, while he worked through
the hours before and after dawn, or slept from noon until late in the
evening, he was no longer disturbed by the traffic of the Boulevard
Haussmann, or the clatter of his servants and neighbours; for during
his absence he had the famous cork walls installed in his bedroom, a
device borrowed, according to Mme de Noailles, from Henry Bern-
stein. On his nights out, charioted by Odilon Albaret in his taxi, he
visited Félix Mayol's concert-hall. Again, as on his return from
Cabourg in 1907, he was fascinated by the shameless strutting and
swaying of that effeminate singer, which reminded him of the dancing
of the lovely Cléo de Mérode, by his facial likeness to the plump-
cheeked Nicolas, and by the almost beautiful vulgarity of his song
Viens poupoule, which the Narrator, when bringing the news of M. de
Charlus's pretended duel, finds Morel singing at Doncières.[1] 'Mayol
is *sublime*,' he told Reynaldo.

[1] II, 1065. The Narrator, when he brings Albertine captive to Paris, is likewise
reminded of a former autumn when, after returning from a holiday, he went to
hear Mayol, 'in order to regain contact with the forgotten pleasures of Paris',
and finds himself humming Mayol's songs. Although tempted to go again he
refrains, 'fearing the motley crowd at the café-concert might rouse Albertine's
desires and regrets' (III, 1065-7). Charlus, however, was of a different mind:
when the young bus-conductor, asked whether he is fond of concerts, confides
that he 'goes to the Concert Mayol sometimes', the Baron exclaims: "I don't care
for Mayol. I can't bear his effeminate manner, and I hate that sort on principle"
(II, 1188).

Lauris's marriage on 27 October, at which Bertrand de Fénelon was best man, was followed by two deaths. Earlier in the year Proust had warned Louisa de Mornand that she was in danger of losing Robert Gangnat, who had discovered her affair with a well-known actor, and that the man's wife was having her followed in order to secure evidence for divorce. On 29 October this inextricable knot was cut by Gangnat's sudden death; his funeral was attended by his colleagues in the Society of Dramatic Authors, many of whom— Robert de Flers, Gaston de Caillavet, Francis de Croisset, Hervieu, Hermant—were friends of Proust; and Proust sent his condolences to Gangnat's mother: 'an absurd thing to do,' he told Flers, 'because I don't even know her, and no doubt she'll never see my letter, but I couldn't help myself.' To Louisa he wrote with sympathy barbed with bitter phrases: she had stirred in Albufera and Gangnat 'perhaps the two purest, most chivalrous, greatest devotions that any woman has yet inspired'; but 'I don't know how you will conduct your life hence-forth, or whether your friends of tomorrow will be worthy of these two men'. He himself had felt for her—'you whom I loved so much, Louisa'—'that which cannot be forgotten, and nothing can efface'; but—'goodbye, dear favourite friend of long ago!' he concluded. On 7 November died Robert Dreyfus's elder brother Henri, who under the stage-name of Fursy had been a popular comedian, specialising in monologues. Proust remembered him in the Champs-Élysées nearly twenty-five years ago, benevolently watching their games. Thinking of his own bereavement and his own writing, he urged Robert to continue with his literary work; for 'in so doing you will live in a region of yourself where the barriers of Time and the body cease to exist, where there is no death because there is no Time and no body, and we live blissfully in the immortal company of those we love'.

In the summer of 1909 Montesquiou had fled from the Pavillon des Muses, with its mournful memories of the dead Yturri. His new secretary Henri Pinard took him to view a charming property at Le Vésinet, an outlying residential suburb ten miles north-west of Paris. "This is just what M. le Comte needs," said the painted secretary, and "If it isn't mine tomorrow, I shall die!!" declared the Count. His farewell fête at the Pavillon des Muses took place on 16 June 1909; of the nine celebrated actresses who were to represent the Nine Muses Ida Rubinstein (Terpsichore) and Segond-Weber (Thalia) failed to turn up; and although Montesquiou obligingly took the part of Thalia himself, the occasion was not altogether a success. So the Count

moved to the Palais Rose, as he called it after the former mansion ot
the ruined Boni; though when people asked the reason for the name,
he would fix them in the eye and pronounce: "I call it the Palais Rose
because it is a palace, and because it is rose-pink."

At two o'clock in the morning of 12 December 1910 Proust rose
and dressed, and worked until dawn on his novel. The winter sun was
bright that day, although, as his shutters had been closed for months,
he would not have known it if Céline had not told him; and feeling a
sudden impulse to see the Palais Rose he ordered his taxi and emerged,
for the first time for several years, into the air of morning. On the way
he noticed a florist, and bought bouquets of out-of-season sweet-peas
for his host; but soon, overcome by their deadly perfume, he turned
back in a fit of asthma. He was to make further attempts to reach the
Palais Rose, but never succeeded; and many other persons likewise
found the pleasure of seeing the Count too dearly bought by the long
journey to Vésinet. Montesquiou's star was waning: at last, quite
literally, he had gone too far.

In February 1911, when Reynaldo was at St Petersburg with
Diaghilev and the dancers, Proust felt a sudden craving for music.
Subscribers to a curious invention known as the theatrophone could
ask the company's private exchange for any concert, opera or play on
the current list, and listen to the actual performance on their own
telephone. Lying in bed with the supernatural black trumpet pressed
to his ear, Proust heard *Pelléas et Mélisande* from the Opéra Comique
on the 21st. He repeated the experience on following evenings, and
when there was no performance sang the part of Pelléas to himself,
until he felt, as he told Reynaldo, the same bewitchment as when he
went every night to hear Mayol! He was haunted ever after by the
moment when Pelléas emerges from the subterranean cavern to the
air of the sea and the scent of roses. "It's just like *Pelléas*," says the
Narrator to Mme de Cambremer at Balbec, when she tells him of the
fragrance of roses borne on the sea-breeze at La Raspelière; "the scent
of roses is so strong in the score that I have asthma whenever I hear
it!" As a kind of penance Proust transferred to this pretentious lady
his own inadequate first-thoughts as expressed to Reynaldo, when he
was irrelevantly struck by the elements of Wagner, and even
Massenet, in the innovating genius of Debussy; and it is Mme de
Cambremer, not the Narrator, who 'began to hum something which
I suppose she mistook for Pelléas's farewell'.[1]

[1] II, 813-15. When the Narrator listens to the street-cries on the morning of

Reynaldo had arrived at a tragicomic crisis in the history of the Ballets Russes. At the end of January Nijinsky had danced in *Giselle* wearing an extraordinarily short tunic, designed by Benois and abbreviated by Bakst on the instructions of Diaghilev; and beneath this tunic he had been induced to discard an indispensable article of protective clothing. The Dowager-Empress could scarcely believe what she saw, or thought she saw; and although protocol demanded that she should pretend to have seen nothing, the revelation of Nijinski's protuberances was taken as a personal insult to the imperial family. He was dismissed immediately. On both sides the incident was a ludicrous but sinister pretext for a final rift. The court circles which controlled the Imperial Ballet were anxious to be rid of Diaghilev, feeling that he had turned the Maryinsky Theatre into a mere winter home for his private troupe; while Diaghilev, conversely, instead of being dependent on the services of dancers on summer leave from the Imperial Ballet, could now organise the Ballets Russes as an independent and permanent company. Proust sent his sympathy to Bakst and 'Vestris', as he insisted on nicknaming Nijinsky; but on hearing that the scandal had been a put-up job he withdrew his good wishes to the young dancer: 'he only interested me as a victim,' he told Reynaldo, 'and if he hasn't been victimised, then' (using his favourite rude word) '*merde* to him.'

In May 1911, a livid, bearded, fur-coated wallflower on a little gilt chair, Proust sat at the annual ball given by the newspaper *L'Intransigeant*, pursuing with his reproachful nocturnal eyes the fleeing Princesse Marthe Bibesco. Born a Lahovary, she had married her cousin Prince Georges Bibesco in 1905 at the age of sixteen; she was a cousin-german of Antoine and Emmanuel Bibesco and of Mme de Noailles, and was linked through her husband's family or her own with Mme Greffulhe, Montesquiou, Guiche, and half the noble Faubourg. In Paris this astonishingly young tree-nymph from Roumania, with her violet-green eyes and talent budding into power, was received as a reigning beauty and a genius; truly, for she was both, but to her own annoyance, for her wish was not to be discovered by others, but to find herself. Proust and Guiche saw her from afar at the Opéra in 1908, at a performance of *Tristan* sung by Litvinne and Van Dyck, and asked who she could be. "She's my cousin," said

---

Albertine's visit to the Trocadéro (III, 117), the monotonous song of the snail-seller reminds him of *Pelléas et Mélisande*.

Emmanuel to Marcel; and turning to Guiche he added: "She's your cousin." "You mean yours?" "No, yours—mine too, of course!" Emmanuel, that entwiner of destinies, sent Marcel her newly published first book, *Les Huit Paradis*, pretending it came from herself. Proust wrote to Emmanuel in the Bibesco slang of his longing to:

> *'Tell to the Princess, be it said,*
> *Her beauty and her genius* (sic) . . .
> *She whom at* Tristan, *by Van Dyck,*
> *My eyes had much preferred unwed . . .'*

But the Princess, who had heard the words beauty and genius too often, was not amused; and for opposite reasons she resented still more the uncanny divination with which, in the letter he wrote her a few days later, Proust praised her book, spoke of 'the childlike gaiety which alone can aid you to bear the weight of your perpetual thought', and warned her. So, at the ball three years later, his insistent and uneasy presence reminded her (for she was perhaps the first person to sense something supernatural in him), of a fantastic figure in a Hoffmann fairytale of her childhood, the night-owl Councillor Drosselmayer, whose apparition inside the grandfather-clock terrifies little Clara:

> *'The clock is humming*
> *At midnight's tread,*
> *The Owl is coming,*
> *The King has fled!'*

She danced ever away from his melancholy eyes, till Fénelon, suborned, danced her towards him. Was she writing another book, Proust asked. She was writing, she replied, a book about happiness, *Alexandre Asiatique*, the story of Alexander the Great considered as a symbol of the greatest possible earthly bliss. Proust seemed appalled; one should seek, he murmured, not for happiness, but for disaster! "I have never made any money on the stock-exchange," he added, "but the important thing in gambling is to lose." The Princess beckoned to Fénelon and danced away. Proust had understood her already; but the 'Labourer of the eleventh hour', as the Bibesco brothers and Fénelon called this latecomer to their group, understood him afterwards with a poetic truth which no critic has equalled. 'He possessed the keys of a world into which I refused to follow him that evening,' she wrote after his death, 'but into which he has led me since.' Proust and Princesse Marthe Bibesco were two natives of the same land; and their touching of finger-tips at the ball was more deeply significant than the embraces of those who danced together till dawn.

On 21 May 1911 Proust attended the dress-rehearsal of D'Annunzio's play *Le Martyre de Saint-Sébastien*, with décor by Bakst and music by Debussy, at the Théâtre du Châtelet. During the last act he sat next to Montesquiou: 'wired to the dynamos of your enthusiasm by the electrode of your wrist,' he told the Count later, 'I was convulsed in my seat, as if it had been an electric chair!'[1] Montesquiou regarded the whole occasion as a spectacular private party. He had known Gabriele d'Annunzio since the days of poor Yturri (whom D'Annunzio used to call 'the other Gabriel'), and had suggested the subject of his play. The saint, pierced by the arrows of the heathen—was he not the emblem of Count Robert, wounded by the incomprehension of critics and the treachery of friends? And the lovely boy of Perugino's *Saint Sebastian* in the Louvre, appealing in his distress to the protection of some higher being—was he not the disciple Count Robert had sought in vain, and the very image of Mme Rubinstein? Proust, too, was impressed by Ida Rubinstein: 'she's a cross between Clomesnil and Maurice de Rothschild,' he told Reynaldo, 'and her legs are sublime'. Various members of the noble audience offered their condolences for the ill-health which, they thought, prevented him from visiting them. Like the Narrator at the end of his novel, he found them changed for the worse: 'even the nicest ones,' he complained to Mme Straus, 'have taken to intelligence, which in society people is a mere co-efficient of stupidity, raising it to hitherto unknown powers. Only those who've had the sense to stay silly are still bearable!'

Proust left for his earliest and longest visit to Cabourg on 11 July. At first, unprecedentedly, the sea air failed to relieve his asthma, and in the darkling hour between sunset and electric light he listened from his bed to the fat members of a ladies' brass-band on the beach, playing waltzes on horns and cornets, 'till I'm ready to jump into the sea for melancholy!' He had toyed with the idea of bringing a young man whom he had met once at Constantin Ullmann's to act as his secretary. The young person's task, he explained, would be to take down the portion of his novel which was still in rough draft from dictation by

[1] 'At this moment,' says the Narrator, walking home from Mme de Villeparisis's matinée arm in arm with Charlus, 'I felt my arm jerked violently, as if by an electric shock' (II, 292).

shorthand, and to make a typewritten copy—or, if he happened to
know neither shorthand nor typing, to copy it from dictation in long-
hand. However, even the humble Nicolas was fit to do the latter, and
when Proust found that a lady shorthand-typist was now attached to
the Grand Hôtel, it seemed pointless to hire Constantin's friend at all.
He sent an honorarium of 300 francs for his wasted hopes, but even so
—'because I don't want to force you not to come, if you'd rather
come'—half-invited him to Cabourg, with a salary of 400 francs a
month, 250 more for meals, 'a nice room in my own apartment', and
free mornings and afternoons. The unnamed youth was Albert Nahmias, who became Proust's occasional secretary in the following
winter. Proust turned to the hotel typist, an English lady named Miss
Hayward, who gave every satisfaction except for her insular insistence
on free week-ends. Soon he was able to write to Calmette: 'I have
already dictated almost a quarter of "your" novel to a typist, and even
this quarter, or rather fifth, is the length of a whole volume.'

The Plantevignes had deserted Cabourg for Chamonix, and are
heard of no more; but the invariable d'Altons were present. Proust
attended the Golf Club ball at the casino on 16 August, was received
by the Vicomte d'Alton in his capacity as president of the club, and
watched Mlle Colette lead off the first dance with Alexandre de Neufville. He bowed to the Duc de Morny, whom he had met before
through Reynaldo, 'but he stared at me with an air of such utter
stupefaction that I refrained from insisting further'. The beautiful
Maurice de Rothschild was there, 'but, nice as he's been to me, I must
say he was absolutely impossible, and his wife was sheer torture'. One
of Proust's favourite stories was of Montesquiou's request to Maurice
de Rothschild for the loan of some diamonds to wear at a fancy-dress
ball. Count Robert was outraged to receive only a very small brooch
with the message: 'Please take great care of it, as it is a family jewel.' 'I
was quite unaware that you had a family,' he replied haughtily, 'but I
did think you had some jewels.'

Again Proust indulged in flutters at baccarat, and lost more heavily
than ever, although this year he entrusted his bets to the banker. His
only consolation was to quote to his friends (like the Narrator's
mother in her letter from Combray during the captivity of Albertine,[1]
and his own mother in the past) Mme de Sévigné's words on her erring
son Charles: 'he has found a way of losing without gambling, and
spending without having anything to show for it'. The young Jacques

[1] III, 141.

Porel, son of the great Réjane, was astounded to see him on the golf-course in his archiepiscopal violet velvet cloak, tottering and pale; but his interest was more in the players than in the game, the object of which he believed to be to get round in the greatest possible number of strokes. Andrée, in *A l'Ombre*, does a creditable round of seventy-seven: "That's a record," cries Albertine; but Octave 'In the Soup' remarks with negligent vainglory: "I scored eighty-two yesterday!"[1]

A few days after the Golf Club ball Calmette called to stand him a drink. "I'd rather have offered you one myself," Proust gently complained. "What does it matter, so long as we're together?" replied Calmette amiably. He had recently foiled another attempt of the army to call Proust up for a fortnight's training[2]; yet Proust sensed in him the wry embarrassment of a kindhearted editor towards a rejected contributor. 'I believe he can't bear the sight of me,' he told Reynaldo.

At the beginning of August Proust read excerpts from Maeterlinck's *On Death* in *Le Figaro*, and was shocked by what seemed to him a grossly material and negative conception of death and infinity. 'Death manifests itself in a way which is terribly positive,' he wrote to Lauris, and recalled how in conversation with Georges he had made fun of Maeterlinck's 'forty horsepower Infinite and motor-cars with the tradename Mystery'.[3] In this context he gave another glimpse of the progress of his novel: what he had written about death[4], he said, was finished long ago, and Lauris would be able to read it in the volume of 800 pages which he was now having transcribed for publication.

Proust returned to Paris towards the end of September, and immediately engaged in a grandiose speculation on the stock exchange, a continuation in a graver form, as he told Robert de Billy, of his gambling-fever in the baccarat-room at Cabourg: 'it may be that the stagnation of my solitary life is attracted by its opposite pole'.

[1] I, 878.

[2] At this setback the French army gave up the unequal struggle which had lasted for twenty years. Proust was informed on 6 September 1911 that his name was removed from the army reserve list, 'for reasons of health'.

[3] Similarly the Narrator, while playing *Tristan* on the piano on the afternoon when Albertine has gone to the Trocadéro, and wondering whether a great artist's originality may not be a mere illusion due to his technical skill, ironically longs for 'some downright material machine for exploring the infinite, some apparatus of 120 horsepower, registered trademark Mystery!' (III, 162). Maeterlinck's argument is that, since death consists in our removal from a finite world to an infinite one, we can look forward to an existence of infinite possibilities, far richer than our life on earth.

[4] Cf. I, 44, 82, 670-2.

Similarly Dostoevsky, laden with guilt and about to stake his salvation on the hope of becoming a great novelist, challenged destiny on
the green-baize tables of Baden-Baden. Proust bought gold shares to
the value of nearly 300,000 francs by the operation known as a time-
bargain, in which the shares are to be paid for at a future date at a sum
fixed beforehand. Gold had fallen, and Proust, in his capacity as a
'bull', hoped when the inevitable rise came to sell at a handsome
profit. At each month's end the 'bull' may either 'liquidate', or 'carry
over' until next month; but in the latter case, if his shares have continued to fall, he must pay a 'difference' to compensate their loss in
value. Alas, gold continued inexplicably to slump; at the end of
January 1912 Proust had to pay a large 'difference', and another on 29
February of this ill-omened leap-year. On 4 March he liquidated the
whole transaction, with a loss of 40,000 francs, and next day, as if he
alone had been holding it down, gold began to rise.

For these speculations Proust employed the young Albert Nahmias, whose father was the financial correspondent of *Le Gaulois*.
Their relationship soon became affectionate: the letter in which he
ordered 'liquidation' begins: '*Mon petit Albert*' and ends with '*ten-
dresses*'. He also engaged Albert to supervise the typing of his novel,
recommending him to use Miss Hayward of Cabourg, who was then
wintering in Paris.[1] This new instalment of his typescript completed
the first half of his novel, which he then hoped to publish in two large
volumes. Meanwhile he began to revise this version for a second and
final typescript to be submitted to a publisher in the autumn: 'I am
finishing the last pages of my first chapter for the typist,' he told
Robert de Billy in February 1912.

By way of atoning for his broken promise to publish Proust's novel
as a serial, Calmette had offered to recommend it to the publisher
Fasquelle, and to print suitable extracts in *Le Figaro* by way of
advance publicity. The first of these appeared on 21 March, with the
topical title (not of Proust's choosing, as he angrily explained to
Lauris, Montesquiou and Vaudoyer), '*Au Seuil du Printemps*' (*On the
Threshold of Spring*). This description of the hawthorns of Tansonville, round which he had ingeniously woven excerpts from the moon-

---

[1] He asked for the first page of the new instalment to be numbered 560: this
section was presumably, therefore, the last in the volume which he had told
Lauris would amount to 800 pages; and the two manuscript-books, one red and
one blue, of which it consisted, probably contained the early version of the
Narrator's first visit to Balbec, from what later became *A l'Ombre des Jeunes
Filles en Fleurs*.

lit evenings of Swann's visit and the family walk, the hawthorns on the altar in the church, and the Narrator's farewell to his beloved flowers, was one of Proust's recent additions, although he had used the same memories sixteen years before in *Jean Santeuil*. 'It's an extract, re-arranged,' he told Lauris, who had read the original Combray chapter in November 1909, 'of a part of my book which you haven't yet seen, though it comes from the same chapter which you already know.'[1] He particularly hoped for the approval of Montesquiou. But the Count's praise was grudging and barbed: he referred to the mingling of sexual and religious imagery in the hawthorn episode as 'a hotchpotch of litanies and lechery', compared the whole article to Renan's *Souvenirs d'enfance et de jeunesse* (a great work, but one which Proust had no intention of emulating), and sent a picture-postcard of a gigantic haw-thorn at Artagnan. Proust replied ruefully but affably. For lechery and litanies, he said, he knew nothing to beat Fauré's *Romance sans Paroles*, 'which is the sort of music a pederast might hum when raping a choir-boy'; it was all too true that his articles would make people mistake his novel, 'which is so closely constructed and concentric', for mere *Memories of my Childhood*; and it was just like Montesquiou to have a hawthorn 'bigger than anyone else's and four times the size of mine'!

Reynaldo's mother, Mme Carlos Hahn, died on 25 March. She had written to Proust on New Year's Day, already ailing, during an absence of her son in Monte Carlo and Algeria, with news of 'Rey-naldo, our dear travelling pigeon'; and he had expressed in return his feelings of 'affectionate and filial respect'. It was about this time that he discovered the notebook in which his own mother had recorded the last illnesses of her parents and husband: 'narratives of such anguish,' he told Mme de Noailles, 'that one can hardly bear to go on living after reading them'. He quoted to Reynaldo, and perhaps now inserted in his novel, the words with which his mother had awakened him on the morning of his father's stroke.[2]

Proust's letters during these months in which he revised his novel for publication are full of hidden allusions to his work. He was fascinated by a satirical essay in Montesquiou's new volume, *Brelan de Dames*, on the blue-stocking Marquise de Blocqueville: 'I've often been puzzled,' he told the Count in March, 'to know why ladies like

---

[1] '*Au Seuil du Printemps*' is made up from *Pléiade*, I, 112, 114, 35, 114-15' 138-40, 144, in that order.

[2] II, 335. Cf. vol. 1, *supra*, p. 335.

Mmes de Blocqueville, Beaulaincourt, Janzé, Chaponay, could never
attract the same social élite (*gratin*) to which persons of less exalted
origin find it so easy to treat themselves.' This was the situation of
Mme de Villeparisis and her 'Three Fates', of whom these ladies were
the originals.[1] He asked the Count to write poems on 'gowns, hats,
wraps, apartments, shoes, jewellery', because 'I'd so enjoy comparing
them with a chapter of my book on the same subject'—a reference,
no doubt, to the Narrator's admiration for Odette and her clothing,
when he watches her in the Bois or visits her salon. A few months
before, in December 1911, he had visited the exhibition of Chinese
painting at Durand-Ruel's with Lucien Henraux, and collected hints
for his novel from Georges Rodier, a dilettante whom he had known
long ago at Mme Lemaire's. 'He was aged, unrecognisable under his
hat, eaten away, like unevenly melted honeycomb', he told Reynaldo.
Proust described to him a black hat worn by Clomesnil when he saw
her in the Bois twenty-three years before. "I know just what you
mean," cried Rodier, "a hat *à la Rembrandt!*"; and in his novel Odette
is seen 'walking up the rue d'Abbatucci' in a cape trimmed with skunk,
a Rembrandt hat, and a bunch of violets in her corsage.[2] Indiscreetly
he revealed that Clomesnil was not the only original of Odette ('I wish
I hadn't mentioned the subject, for Laure Hayman's sake,' he told
Reynaldo afterwards); but fortunately Rodier began to talk about
Cocteau. "What I fear for him is society, he goes into society too
much, if he goes into society he's lost!!", he repeated, like Legrandin
meeting the Narrator on the way to Mme de Villeparisis's matinée[3];
'but I saw he spoke,' Proust commented, 'not as a man about town
deploring the cause of his weakness, but as a recluse giving the recipe
for his virtue'.

One afternoon in April 1912 he rose from bed, wrapped his fur coat
over his nightshirt, and drove by taxi to Rueil in search of apple-
blossom. It was six o'clock when the car halted on a muddy road; the
sky was grey after rain, and twilight was falling; gardeners were
eyeing him and his chauffeur with astonished mistrust, mistaking
them, he realised with horror, for the motor-bandits Bonnot and

---

[1] The Narrator asks the same question of M. de Charlus at the Verdurins'
soirée, after the performance of the Vinteuil Septet; but 'he not only did not give
me the solution of this little social problem, but seemed to be unaware of its very
existence' (III, 293).

[2] I, 240.

[3] II, 153-4.

Garnier! But there, row after row, were the apple-trees which the Narrator sees on his second visit to Balbec, at the moment when his anguish for his dead grandmother is turning to a desire for renewed pleasures with Albertine: 'As far as the eye could reach they were in full bloom, scandalously luxurious, wearing ball-dresses with their feet in the mire, and taking no precautions against spoiling the most marvellous pink satin ever seen.'[1]

Comtesse Greffulhe had been sending Proust invitations, on and off, ever since her present of the potted vine two years before; and it is a measure of his revulsion from society that he had not seen her since Guiche's wedding in 1904. At last she succeeded, little knowing that he came for his novel's sake rather than hers, in attracting him to her box at the Opéra, on 9 May, the first night of the season of the Italian company from Monte Carlo. He met there for the first time the famous Mme Standish, the former friend of Edward VII: 'I thought her, making all necessary allowances for her age, amazing in her mummi-fied elegance, her artifical simplicity,' he told Robert de Billy, 'though the apple-trees in their flounces were even better dressed than Mme Standish.'[2] To the dazzling apparition of the Princesse and Duchesse de Guermantes at the Opéra in *Le Côté de Guermantes* he added the contrast between the flamboyant costume of Mme Greffulhe and the austere chicness of Mme Standish. The Duchesse at this moment, birdlike with her beaked nose, muslin plumage and swan's wing fan, is primarily Mme de Chevigné, as Proust had seen her at the theatre twenty years before, and described in the May 1892 number of *Le Banquet*[3]; but in the 'positively British precision' of her dress, which the Princesse considers 'too tailor-made',[4] she is also Mme Standish, who modelled her clothes on Queen Alexandra's and was nicknamed 'Missis' by the Faubourg. He sought instruction on the technical terms of their clothing from Jeanne de Caillavet, whom he had noticed in the audience, and from Mme Straus, not daring to ask Mme Greffulhe outright—'because if my characters turn out to poison people or commit incest later on, they'll think I mean them!' On second thoughts, however, he called several times on Mme Greffulhe, and on 27 June attended the last soirée of the season at her daughter the Duchesse de Guiche's, 'to refresh my memory of people's faces',

[1] II, 781.
[2] Mme Standish (1847-1933) was then sixty-four.
[3] *Les Plaisirs et les Jours*, 74-5.
[4] II, 54.

and saw both ladies again. He alludes to this occasion when, at the Princesse de Guermantes's soirée, the Narrator unexpectedly remarks that Mme Standish is 'a far greater lady than the Duchesse de Doudeauville',[1] or tells of the Duchesse and Princesse de Guermantes an anecdote which Proust repeated to Jeanne de Caillavet a few days later of Mme Greffulhe and Mme Standish.[2]

Proust's renewed interest in Gaston's wife, however, was motivated by deeper causes than her presence at the Opéra or her knowledge of fashions in ladies' dresses. A second extract from his novel, 'Un Rayon de Soleil sur le Balcon', was to appear in Le Figaro on 4 June: it was the story of his love for Marie de Benardaky in the Champs-Élysées, much abridged and not yet wholly revised, but with the episode of the sunlight on the balcony already in its final form.[3] Gilberte was not only Marie, but also Jeanne: 'it's a memory of a childhood love-affair of mine,' he confided to her, 'not my love for you, it was before that—but still, you'll find amalgamated in it something of my feelings when I wasn't sure whether you'd be at the tennis-court'. It was twenty-two years since he had made friends with Gaston de Caillavet, the first original of Saint-Loup, and fallen in love with Jeanne, his fiancée. If he gazed into the well of Time Lost their young faces looked up at him, beside his own, although in this world he could only visit a middle-aged couple in the Avenue Hoche. But Time is not always a thief and destroyer, and now performed the miracle of the Two Ways, creating youth from age, one person from two loves, the last unifying theme of a great novel.

One evening towards the end of April, for the first time since Mme Arman's death and the great flood, Proust had called on the Caillavets. "Have Monsieur and Madame gone to bed?" he asked, for it was half-past eleven, "can they see me?" They had not the heart to refuse. "Madame," he began, "will you give me an enormous joy? I have not met your daughter for a very long time, perhaps I may never come here again, and when she is old enough to go to the ball I shall be too ill to go out. And so, Madame, I beg of you, let me see Mademoiselle Simone this evening." "But, Marcel, she went to bed hours ago." "Madame, I entreat you, go and see. If she's still awake, you can explain to her." Simone de Caillavet came down, a girl of sixteen, with

<hr>

[1] II, 661.
[2] II, 1185; cf. supra, vol. 1, p. 152.
[3] Chroniques, 100-5. Cf. I, 395, 416-17, 413, 416, 398, 402, 411, 396, 404-5, 396-7.

her father's eyes, with cheeks, Proust told her mother, 'like petals of an unknown flower', and a smile which he did not forget. 'I'm in love with your daughter,' he wrote to Jeanne, with an exaggeration which became truth in the world of his book; 'how cruel she is to be kind, for it's her smile that made me fall in love, and has given its meaning to all her person, and if she had been sulky I wouldn't have lost my peace!' Was there any hope of her coming to Cabourg? He had met her cousin there last year, 'little Prémonville, who promised to ask his botany master for information'—about the flowers of Combray, no doubt—'which turned out to be no use', and 'seemed to be in love with her, as I am now'. Proust arranged to call again on his way to the Duchesse de Guiche's soirée, and did not. But it is because Gaston's wife and daughter were in his mind on that occasion that, in the last scene of his novel, Gilberte says: "I'll bring my daughter to you, she's over there talking to little Mortemart and other infants of no importance. I'm sure she'll make such a nice friend for you." And Mlle de Saint-Loup, 'a young girl of about sixteen, whose tall figure measured the lapse of time which I had refused to see', is none other than Simone de Caillavet walking towards him across her parents' drawing-room. 'I thought her beautiful indeed,' says the Narrator, 'radiantly smiling, still full of hopes, made out of the very years I had lost, she resembled my youth.'[1]

[1] III, 1028, 1031-2.

Chapter 9

AGONY AT SUNRISE
(*August 1912 – August 1913*)

PROUST had almost convinced himself that his losses on the stock exchange would prevent him from visiting Cabourg. It was not until 7 August that he decided economy had gone far enough, ordered Nicolas to pack for the afternoon train, and released Céline to her native Burgundy. For the sake of quiet, perhaps also with a view to possible guests, he took five adjoining rooms on the top floor of the Grand Hôtel.

Once again he was surrounded by friends. The Strauses were at Trouville, the Guiches at Bénerville, Calmette, Mme Scheikévitch and Mme Gross (a friend of the Daudets) at Houlgate; and in Cabourg itself he had Reynaldo's friend Henri Bardac, Vaudoyer, the future surrealist poet Philippe Soupault, and young Albert Nahmias. His health and hours had improved, and he hoped once more, after four summers in which he had rarely left the hotel, to enjoy the pleasures of motoring in Normandy. But his ardour was chilled by a series of disasters: on the 11th Nahmias ran over a poor little girl, who died two days later, on the road to Caen; on the 25th Bardac killed another outright; and a few days later two local taxis were wrecked in a collision. In the end he prudently hired the hotel omnibus—'it's enormous and far from elegant,' he told Mme Straus, 'but it's safe, and the driver is very careful and clever'. Perhaps he made one of his mysterious flying visits to Brittany, for he wrote to Reynaldo in mid-August: 'I'm thinking of taking a house at dear little Beg-Meil in September, but it looks a very ugly one to me.'

This summer marked the zenith of his friendship with Albert Nahmias. He introduced Albert to Mme Gross, who declared: "Why, you're the image of Maurice Bernhardt!" "Ought I to regard that as an honour, Monsieur Proust," asked the disconcerted young man, "or as the contrary?"[1] Antoine Bibesco, in a conversation nearly forty

[1] On the whole it was probably meant as a compliment. Sarah Bernhardt's son was considered a little flighty, but charming and devoted to his mother.

years later, remembered Marcel's description of Albert on the front at
Cabourg in the dusk, 'dressed all in fal-lals—*tout de fanfreluches
habillé*', walking with his lovely sisters Anita and Estie, and declared
that these formed the original 'little band', and that Albert was
Albertine. No doubt there is some element of truth in this, although
the little band and Albertine had many models, and there is no important aspect of either which cannot be traced to others. But it seems
probable that the relationship between Proust and Albert Nahmias
was neither profound nor painful, for Proust had been particularly
cheerful since the spring, in the autumn he was engrossed in negotiations for his novel, and early in 1913 he became far more deeply
interested in another young man. Perhaps Anita and Estie were among
the girls with whom ('just to get the rust out of my joints,' he told
Reynaldo apologetically) he danced every other evening in the casino.

Philippe Soupault, then a boy of fifteen, met Proust one evening on
the terrace of the Grand Hôtel. A few minutes after the red sun disappeared into the western sea his strange host emerged, carrying a
sunshade, and subsided into a wicker armchair past which the waiters
walked on tiptoe. "Sunlight is bad for me," he explained; "once I
came out when it was quite dark, and then the sun began to shine. It
wasn't night at all, it was only a cloud! I suffered terribly." He had
known the boy's mother in his schooldays. "I met her at a dancing
class in the Rue de la Ville-l'Evêque, and your Aunt Louise, wasn't
that her name? I can see her eyes now, the only eyes I've ever known
that were *really* violet." Soupault disagreed. "You don't think so? Ah
well, the sun must have been to blame, as always!" The boy had
already begun his career as a writer, and said so, blissfully unaware
that his host was another. Proust smiled gently.

Mme Scheikévitch, one of the most intelligent and influential of a
new generation of hostesses, had seen Proust at Mme Lemaire's in
1905, and was sufficiently impressed to question Reynaldo, the Yeat-
mans and others who knew him; but their opinions tallied in only one
point: "there's no one in the least like him!" More recently Reynaldo
had announced that Proust was writing a great novel, and asked her to
recommend it to her friend Adrien Hébrard, the editor of *Le Temps*,
whom she addressed as 'Nounou'. She called at the Grand Hôtel one
August evening with Calmette, and found Proust tottering under the
chandeliers of the casino, battered straw hat in hand, wearing a winter
overcoat, a voluminous dinner-jacket, several woollen waistcoats, and
the grim black beard which he grew and shaved off so unpredictably—

'he seemed to put it on and take it off again like a comedian in a provincial music-hall,' said Cocteau. Calmette had a private word with his contributor: "Agreed, my dear fellow, I've spoken to Chevassu, you'll be in the Supplement," he cried, and vanished into the baccarat room.

That night, and on many others, Mme Scheikévitch and Proust talked long on the terrace under the stars. She mentioned his novel, too soon, for he interrupted with a deluge of compliments, and paid attention only when she changed the subject to Russian literature, which she had read in the original ever since her childhood in Moscow. "I worship Dostoevsky," said Proust. His face was emaciated, his eyes dark-ringed; he spoke of asthma, fumigations, the misery of never daring to smell a flower, the ignorance of people in high society, with examples. He gave astonishing imitations, and lapsed into harsh, helpless laughter. Pageboys arrived with news of engagements—with whom?—which he had sent them to arrange or cancel, or with letters which he stuffed unopened, after glancing at the handwriting on the envelopes, into his overcoat pockets crammed with unread newspapers and boxes of pills. At the moment of parting she ventured to say: "I've read everything you've published so far!"; and Proust, with a look of extreme disbelief, sat down again to put her through an examination which, she tells us, 'although it was full of catch-questions, I passed with honours'. She mentioned Hébrard, and this time Proust rose to the bait. "Reynaldo told me you'd recommended Suarès to him." "Yes, and Nounou thought Suarès would insist on doing something quite unheard of, but when he asked what he wanted to write, Suarès just said: 'I don't mind, what would you like?'!" On their next meeting they were already friends, and Proust tried to explain his novel; but she felt she was 'being shown the back of a tapestry, and would never understand the picture until I could see it from the front'. She spoke of her unhappy marriage with the son of the painter Carolus-Duran, which ended in attempted suicide and divorce, and wrung Proust's heart by telling how poor Mme Arman, in her grief for Monsieur France's infidelity, had called and said: "I want you to tell me just how you shot yourself."

Towards the end of the month, when Mme Scheikévitch left for Paris, rain fell every day, drumming on Proust's roof and pattering down his chimney; but the fine weather returned in September, together with a letter from his new friend on his latest article in *Le Figaro*—'it's organised and dense', she wrote. The article was

'*L'Église de Village*', a group of extracts from his Combray chapter on the church of Saint-Hilaire, and appeared on 3 September.[1] In his gratitude he paid her the supreme compliment of quoting the lines of Baudelaire which he associated with Marie Finaly, about the sunlight on the sea, and '*the greenish light of your long eyes*'. 'Fortunately I soon forget people I like,' he cautiously added; but Marie Scheikévitch was destined to be a lifelong friend to himself and his novel.

About 16 September Proust at last called on Mme Straus at Trouville. He asked her advice on his annual present to the d'Alton girls, to whom this year he had promised fur coats. Then she took him in her automobile to Honfleur, through the upland lanes which he had seen twenty years ago with Marie Finaly, ten years ago with herself and Fénelon. "It's my donkey-cart," she remarked, and "It's a magic coach for exploring the past," he replied. Two days later he returned to Paris, full of hope and energy, to face one of the great crises of his life. The new, corrected typescript of the first half of his novel was now ready for the press; he was determined to find a publisher in the autumn—preferably Fasquelle—and to see this first of two volumes (as he mistakenly believed) published early in the next spring.

The novel now consisted of two approximately equal halves, which together amounted to little more than a third of *A la Recherche* in its final form. The first half existed in three states: first, the original manuscript, secondly, the unrevised typescript begun by Miss Hayward at Cabourg in August 1911 and completed under the supervision of Albert Nahmias early in 1912; and thirdly the revised typescript made in the summer of 1912, which Proust now intended to submit to Fasquelle. The two typescripts each comprised about 700 pages, ending with the Narrator's return from his first visit to Balbec: they contained, that is, the equivalent of what afterwards became *Du Côté de chez Swann* and *A l'Ombre des Jeunes Filles en Fleurs*. *Swann* itself was to be enlarged in proof, notably in the episode of Swann's jealousy of Odette, but the additions were apparently of no great extent. *A l'Ombre*, however, amounted to less than half of its final length, the most surprising difference being the omission of all mentions of Albertine and the little band, who as yet did not appear until the

---

[1] *Chroniques*, 114-22. The passages which Proust interwove to form his article occur in their final revised and enriched form as follows: I, 63, 48, 62-3, 59-61, 63-4, 715 (here Proust quite unsuitably transfers to Saint-Hilaire his description of the ivy-covered church of Carqueville, which the Narrator sees near Balbec during a drive in Mme de Villeparisis's carriage), 64-7.

second half of the novel. This still existed only in the original rough manuscript, which Proust vaguely hoped to revise while the first volume was being printed, and to publish either simultaneously, or at latest in the next autumn. But this disaster, which would have left his novel immeasurably poorer in content, structure and texture, was to be averted by destiny, and by Proust's own steering of destiny.

At first he could only wait in growing distress. Calmette, who had promised to forward the typescript to his friend Fasquelle, and declared that Fasquelle would be only too glad to publish it intact as a personal favour to himself, —"absolutely, my dear fellow!"—had shown no sign of life since their meeting in August. Towards the middle of October Proust began to enlist the help of all possible friends. He asked Mme Straus to remind Calmette of his promise. The enigmatic editor told her he had spoken to Fasquelle, to whom Proust had only to deliver the typescript; but to Proust himself he remained strangely silent. Proust duly obeyed, and called at the *Figaro* office to thank Calmette. "Tell him I'm not in," said the editor, and left his grateful letters unanswered. Proust turned next to Lauris, Reynaldo, and Antoine Bibesco, who warned him that Fasquelle would refuse to publish the two separate volumes of the work simultaneously, that he would insist on omissions, that his favourite maxim was: "I can't have anything interfering with the *action*!" Could it be that Calmette was lying low out of embarrassment, because he had promised more than he could fulfil? Proust had set his heart upon Fasquelle, who was the publisher of Flaubert, Zola, and Rostand, and a specialist in the high-class bestsellers of whom Proust himself, for no ignoble motive, longed to be one. 'Wide publicity is a precious thing,' he had remarked pathetically to Vaudoyer last April, 'because it's only in the audience which it provides that chance can bring our words to the fraternal, forever unknown heart which will feel them as we have felt.' And to Mme Straus he confided his hope that Fasquelle would bring him 'a wider public, the sort of people who buy a badly printed volume before catching a train'. But now, as his hopes of Fasquelle waned, he decided to find a second string.

In February 1911 Antoine Bibesco had persuaded him to subscribe to the *Nouvelle Revue Française*, the brilliant literary magazine founded by Gide and Jacques Copeau in 1909, in which Gide's *Isabelle* was then appearing. 'Gide's story isn't bad,' he grumbled to Lauris, 'but it doesn't exactly bowl one over!' He was piously shocked to hear from Antoine in July 1912—a little late in the day—that Gide and his friend Henri Ghéon were practising homosexuals: 'which makes Ghéon's hypocrisy in his article on *Le Martyre de Saint-Sébastien* all the more revolting,' he told Reynaldo.[1] At Cabourg he complained to Vaudoyer of attacks in the NRF for September 1912 on Maeterlinck, and (again by Ghéon) on Cocteau as a mere 'boulevard' writer. Yet his failure to find a good word for the sour grapes of the NRF did not prevent him from deeply admiring other writers in that brilliant group, such as Jammes, Valéry Larbaud and Claudel. The NRF had recently launched their own publishing house, under the editorial direction of Gide, Copeau and Jean Schlumberger and the business management of Gaston Gallimard. Now, late in October, Antoine Bibesco offered to recommend his novel to Copeau, and Proust immediately felt that here, among the moderns of a new generation rather than with the best-selling Fasquelle, might be his spiritual home.

While still in doubt he wrote to Louis de Robert, his friend in the heroic days of the Dreyfus Affair. In the spring of 1911 Proust had renewed contact, feeling that they again had much in common; for Robert was now an invalid, and had written a talented novel about his own life, *Le Roman du Malade*, which had been successfully published by Fasquelle after its appearance as a *Figaro* serial. 'I've written a long book which I call a novel because it hasn't the casual element of memoirs,' he confided, pointing out that Robert, too, had produced 'a book that isn't a novel'. Did Robert think it might be wiser to renounce Fasquelle, and that 'a purely literary publisher such as the *Nouvelle Revue Française* might be more likely to persuade readers to accept a work which is completely different from the classical novel?' Robert thought the NRF's public would be too limited, but wrote a glowing letter of recommendation to Fasquelle.

Nevertheless, Proust allowed Antoine to make him an appointment with Copeau, to whom he explained his complex difficulties, and offered to submit the unrevised typescript (for the other was still with Fasquelle) to the NRF. Copeau advised him to apply direct to Gallimard, to whom Proust wrote accordingly on 2 November, recalling their friendship with the dead Robert Gangnat, and their meeting in Gangnat's villa at Bénerville in August 1908. He revealed frankly that his novel was already with Fasquelle, and offered, if the NRF would accept it, to pay the expenses of publication. Moreover,

[1] In his article on D'Annunzio's play (NRF for July 1911) Ghéon had perfidiously drawn attention to its epicene implications.

he confessed, his novel was 'extremely indecent'; indeed, part of the
second volume would be a study of homosexuality. The old gentleman named M. de Fleurus or de Guray in the unrevised typescript—
'I've changed the names several times'—who appeared at Combray
as the supposed lover of Mme Swann, and was met by the hero at the
seaside towards the end of the first volume, would turn out to be a
pederast! 'I think the character is rather an original one,' Proust added
consolingly, 'he's the virile pederast, in love with virility, loathing
effeminate young men, in fact loathing all young men, just as a man
who has suffered through women becomes a misogynist.' 'The
metaphysical and moral viewpoint', it was true, 'is predominant all
through the book'; but 'all the same, the old gentleman seduces a male
concierge and keeps a pianist'.[1] Gallimard replied that if their opinion
of the book was favourable, and Proust could obtain his release from
Fasquelle, the NRF would be able to publish the first volume in two
months' time, about 15 February. He offered to call for the typescript.
'You don't know how heavy it is,' replied Proust, and promised to
send it; but Gallimard, on second thoughts, referred him back to
Copeau.

Again Proust felt the need of the intervention of friends. He handed
over his typescript to Antoine Bibesco, together with a manifesto in
which he called his novel, apparently for the first time, *A la Recherche
du Temps Perdu*.[2] He explained his work ('I hope you can make them
understand my explanation,' he added) in terms paraphrased from *Le
Temps Retrouvé*: it would employ not only plane psychology, but also
psychology in space and time[3]; voluntary memory, being a function
of the intellect and the sense of sight, can give us only the untruthful
surface of the Past, whereas a scent or a taste involuntarily regained
revive in us its extratemporal essence[4]; his book is a sequence of
novels of the unconscious, and the artist should seek the primary
material of his work in involuntary memories only; style is a question
not of technique, but of vision.[5] Armed with all this Antoine and
Emmanuel gave a dinner in mid-November to Copeau, Gide and Jean
Schlumberger, the reading committee of the NRF, and left the type-

[1] In this unrevised version Proust had not given M. de Charlus his final name;
Morel, who was then called Bobby Santois, was not yet a violinist but (like his
chief original, Léon Delafosse) a pianist; and Jupien, called Julliot or Joliot, was
still a concierge.

[2] However, it seems possible that Proust had already chosen his title in
November 1909, when he asked Lauris 'not to reveal the subject or the title'.

[3] III, 1031.   [4] I, 44; III, 872.   [5] III, 895.

script with Gide. But by this second attempt to find a publisher Proust only doubled the anguish of waiting.

Du Côté de chez Swann ends with a passage, unique in Proust's novel, in which the Narrator emerges for a moment from the gulf of Time to observe the present in which he writes. 'On one of the first mornings of this November' he visits the Bois de Boulogne on his way to Trianon, hoping to see elegant ladies in their carriages, as in the year when he loved Gilberte and walked there with Mme Swann. To his horror, the carriages have turned to motor-cars 'driven by moustached mechanics'; the ladies are wearing—in the fashion of 1912—Greco-Saxon tunics and enormous hats 'covered with aviaries and vegetable-gardens'; and the gentlemen, worse still, instead of their former grey toppers wear no hats at all. It is twenty years too late. The sun goes in, he sees in the Avenue des Acacias the wandering spectres, grown old and terrible, of the ladies he had known, and the Bois has become a place of desolation and despair. Traces of Proust's intention to make this journey are visible in his letters of October 1912 to Mme Straus: he feels nostalgia for autumn, he says, and despite insomnia and fever would like to take her to tea at the Trianon Palace Hôtel at Versailles. But the motives of his expedition included not only his longing for autumn leaves and for tea with Mme Straus, but his decision to end the Gilberte episode in his novel with a comparison between the Bois of 1888, when he lay in wait there for Léonie Clomesnil, and the Bois of 1912. His journey may have taken place in Odilon Albaret's taxi a day or two after 10 November, when he told Mme Straus: 'the last dead leaves have fallen before I could see them ... if I'd been well I'd have gone to the Trianon Palace, where I sent Albaret to reconnoitre; for it's a good thing to publish one's impressions of the past, but to experience new ones is better still.'[1]

In these long weeks of waiting Proust called frequently on Mme Straus for tea and sympathy. More than once he had to complain of the unkindness of her husband. "There's one good thing about old So-and-So," remarked M. Straus pointedly, when he found 'dear Marcel'

---

[1] Similarly, the Narrator speaks (I, 422) of 'the spectacle of autumn, which ends so swiftly, before we can see it, and brings a nostalgia for dead leaves that turns to a fever and prevents us from sleeping'; and on his way back he is only prevented from calling on Odette by the realisation that she and the style of her drawing-room would have changed like everything else. As will be seen later, Proust intended this new episode as a finale to '*Chez Madame Swann*', the first chapter of what is now *A l'Ombre*, and did not transfer it to its present position at the end of *Swann* until September 1913.

lolling exhausted in his drawing-room, "he always has the decency to
stand up when I come in!" On 17 December she invited Proust with
Calmette, Hervieu and her son Jacques Bizet to her box for the first
night of *Kismet* (by Edward Knoblauch, translated by Jules Lemaître)
at the Théâtre Sarah Bernhardt. Proust escorted her backstage to congratulate the star, Lucien Guitry, and while they talked hid modestly
by an aged gentleman, 'trembling and sweetfaced', he thought, 'like
an old man in the *Oresteia*'. He recognised Lemaître himself, transformed by old age and the illness of which he was to die twenty
months later; but he was still more astonished when, behind the beard
and invalid features superimposed upon the Marcel whom he had met
as a schoolboy twenty-four years before, Lemaître recognised *him*.
Meanwhile the irascible Jacques Bizet had smacked the face of Comte
Hubert de Pierredon, with whom, despite the efforts of Calmette and
Hervieu to smoothe things over, he fought a duel on the 20th. Proust
felt he would have made a better peacemaker, and told Mme Straus
how once, in the good old days, he had prevented a duel between
Guiche and Albufera. When he returned home, as the final calamity of
this imperfect evening, Nicolas pointed out that he was wearing a
mere dinner-jacket over his white waistcoat.

At last, about 23 December, the NRF replied by rejecting both his
novel and an extract which he had offered Copeau for their magazine.
'I read it with sustained interest,' wrote Copeau of the latter; but the
novel, as Proust learned later, had scarcely been read at all. It was only
to oblige the Bibesco brothers that the NRF had consented to the
enormous breach of etiquette of considering a book which was
already with another publisher. They knew Proust only as 'a snob, a
literary amateur, the worst possible thing for our magazine', said
Gide, who had met him in the alien world of the salons twenty years
before. He wrote for *Le Figaro*, dedicated his book to Calmette, involved himself with the best-selling Fasquelle, and condemned his
own work by offering to pay for its publication. Gide, idly opening the
first volume of the typescript, found himself with extreme distaste
among the pepsin and Vichy water bottles of Aunt Léonie's bedroom,
was shocked by what he wrongly considered a solecism about 'the
vertebrae in her forehead',[1] and read no further; while Schlumberger
pointed out that this novel of 1400 pages would overstrain the

---

[1] I, 52. Proust, by a superb and entirely justified use of the trope known as
metonymy, called the frontal bones in Aunt Léonie's forehead 'vertebrae' in
order to suggest that they looked like vertebrae.

resources of their newly born publishing house. The book was clearly impossible. When the typescript was returned Proust convinced himself, quite mistakenly, that the parcel had never even been opened, and Albaret's fiancée Céleste Gineste, who had helped in its despatch, declared that the string was still tied with her own special knots.

While he still had hopes of the NRF, Proust had not dared to press Fasquelle too hard: 'I've tried to chloroform the situation,' he told Gallimard. But he was delighted to hear through Cocteau, early in November, that Edmond Rostand had only refrained from sending a telegram of congratulation on his *Figaro* article of 3 September because he assumed, knowing of Proust's friendship for his enemy Montesquiou,[1] that his compliments would be unwelcome. Rostand offered to write to Fasquelle, and his son Maurice actually did so. Calmette, overwhelmed to hear in Mme Straus's box at *Kismet* that Proust had tried to see Fasquelle in the daytime, and in vain, did his best to arrange an appointment in the evening; but the publisher did not reply. 'It was so easy to write my novel,' Proust told Louis de Robert with pathos, 'but how difficult it will be to publish it!'

Only a few days after his rejection by the NRF, about 28 December, Proust received his first direct communication from Fasquelle. The letter was courteous, sensible and firm: he 'could not undertake to publish a work of such length, and so different from what the public is accustomed to read'. Proust, with typical fairmindedness, was touched to see that Fasquelle had read his book with care and taken him seriously: 'I think he's wrong,' he told Louis de Robert magnanimously, 'but there's such a thing as being intelligently wrong.' However, three months of anxiety and intrigue had gone for nothing, and all was to begin again.[2]

Robert had already suggested his friend Humblot, the director of Ollendorff's and the publisher of Proust's friends Barrès, Régnier and Hermant, as a possible alternative to Fasquelle. Early in January he informed Humblot that Proust was a great writer, to publish whom would be one of the greatest honours of his career. A few days later Proust sent Humblot the typescript returned by Fasquelle, refraining,

---

[1] Montesquiou had revenged himself for the portrayal of his august person as the Peacock in *Chantecler* by writing an essay called '*Le Météore*'—'The Shooting Star'—on Rostand's rise to fame and the failure of this last play.

[2] On the other hand Fasquelle spoke so enthusiastically to Reynaldo of Proust's *Figaro* articles, which he had rejected in 1909, that Proust thought of offering them to him again, but did not do so.

on Robert's advice but against his own judgement, from mentioning
its rejection by Fasquelle or his readiness to pay the costs of publication.

On the night of 14 January Proust called on Calmette at the *Figaro*
office with a black moiré cigarette case from Tiffany's, with Calmette's
monogram in brilliants, as a thank-offering for his incomplete and
unsuccessful kindness. He dropped the dainty parcel in the editor's
in-tray, shyly murmuring: "It's such a small thing, I hardly dare ..."
Calmette gave an affectionate shrug of the shoulders; without mentioning gifts, novels, gratitude or Fasquelle, without seeming to
notice the package, he spoke only of the imminent election for the
Presidency of the Republic—"I hope Poincaré will get in," he remarked in his warm, modulated voice, "but then again, perhaps it will
be Deschanel"—and ushered Proust to the door.

To another of his benefactors Proust was less forthcoming.
Maurice Rostand, fired by Cocteau's enthusiasm, asked to be allowed
to meet him, but was offered only a rendezvous in front of Notre-
Dame at six o'clock in the morning, which he declined. This extraordinary proposal answered, however, to a real desire. On 17 January
Proust had told Mme Straus of his longing to see the St Anne portal of
Notre-Dame, 'where a human spectacle more charming than the one
to which we are accustomed nowadays has been on view for the last
eight centuries'. The St Anne portal, furthest to the right of the three
which form the front entrance to the cathedral, contains scenes from
the life of the Virgin which Proust no doubt needed for Elstir's
explanation of the porch at Balbec in *A l'Ombre*. He made the excursion towards the 20th, wearing his fur coat over his night-shirt. The
Last Judgement over the adjacent centre portal also caught his eye;
and this lonely man, mistrustful of love, was deeply moved to see the
carving of a married couple, in fear of being parted for all eternity,
facing Christ the Judge with hand clasped in hand.[1]

Towards 10 February Louis de Robert received Humblot's answer.
'My dear fellow,' wrote this candid publisher, 'I may perhaps be dead
from the neck up, but rack my brains as I may I can't see why a chap
should need thirty pages to describe how he turns over in bed before
going to sleep.' 'Fortune has knocked at your door and passed you
by,' Robert grimly retorted, and insisted on Humblot's writing 'a more
decent letter, fit for me to show my friend'. But Proust guessed the
truth, and compelled Robert to show him the original which, much

[1] I, 840-1.

hurt, he rightly declared to be 'stupid and vulgar'. He now knew that he must give up all hope of finding a publisher who would take his novel for its own sake.

Proust indomitably began negotiations for the fourth time. His imprisonment in the ivory tower of his cork-lined bedroom prevented him from interviewing publishers; he felt, too, a sacred dread of even writing directly to beg these indifferent strangers to fulfil the deepest desire of his life. He looked for a new mediator, and found René Blum, whom he had known in the golden days of 1902 with Fénelon, Guiche, Lauris and the Bibesco brothers at the Café Weber. René, with his ironically affectionate smile, was known as 'the Blumet' in distinction from his more famous elder brother Léon, Proust's companion of *Le Banquet*. He was now the editorial secretary of the newspaper *Gil Blas*, for which he had just asked through Antoine Bibesco for an extract from Proust's novel, and was an intimate friend of the intelligent and energetic young publisher Bernard Grasset, who had produced Lauris's *Ginette Chatenay* in 1910. About 20 February Proust wrote to Blum asking him to propose to Grasset the publication of his novel at author's expense, the publisher to take a percentage of the published price, and the author to pay for publicity. A few days of gentlemanly bargaining followed: Grasset proposed to allow Proust half the published price, but Proust would take only three-sevenths; Grasset offered special royalties for de luxe copies, which Proust waived altogether; Grasset was willing to resign the translation rights of 500 francs for each translation, but Proust accepted only half. Finally it was agreed that the first edition should consist of 1200[1] copies at the published price of 3.50 francs, on which Proust was to receive a royalty of 1.50 francs per copy. On 11 March the contract was signed. The words 'author's expense', which had so deeply shocked the NRF, had acted on Grasset like a magic spell.[2] He

[1] This was later increased to 1750 copies.

[2] In justice to Grasset it must be recognised that Proust, although he thought he had been generous to his publisher and intended to be so, had in fact driven a hard bargain. Grasset at first proposed to sell this long volume of over 700 pages at 10 fr., allowing Proust 4 fr., and his profits were greatly curtailed by Proust's insistence (in the hope of wider circulation) on the low price of 3.50 fr. Again, Proust thought he was allowing Grasset 2 fr. per copy; but as the whole-sale price was only 2.10 fr. Grasset's real profit was a mere 60 centimes, and his gain on the whole edition would be the derisory sum of 720 fr. Grasset gained nothing from Proust's concession over the translation rights, as no translation was made until after the novel had passed to another publisher.

confessed later that he had published *Du Côté de chez Swann* without reading it.

Meanwhile Proust was treading a still more dolorous way than the road to publication, and carrying a heavier burden than his novel. During the eighteen months from January 1913 to June 1914 he suffered an agony at sunrise, and made captive in his apartment a male Albertine who fled from him and died.

For many years he had become immune to the exaltation and anguish of passionate love. The period when he was always in love had coincided with the years when he was always in society, and ended with the shock of the Dreyfus Case, the close of youth, the revelation of Ruskin, and the turn of the century. To Clément de Maugny in July 1899 he had written prophetically of 'storms that will never come again'; and he had last used such words as *chagrin, tristesse, peine*—which for him were synonyms of love—for his platonic relationships with Fénelon and Antoine Bibesco in 1902. Since then his needs for affection and physical pleasure had been satisfied—whether with women such as Louisa and the young girl of Cabourg, or with his young men of the working classes—without strong feeling or apparent suffering. During those years the deepest layers of his nature had been occupied first by grief for his mother, afterwards by the creation of his novel. But now the ghost of Mme Proust was temporarily laid, and his novel seemed complete. Without knowing it he was again, and for the last time, vulnerable to love.

One day in January 1913 Alfred Agostinelli, whom Proust had not seen since his return from Versailles in October 1908, called at 102 Boulevard Haussmann. "I've lost my job, Monsieur Proust," he announced, "and I've come to ask you to take me as your chauffeur." Proust objected that this would be unfair to Albaret, and then, struck by a fatal inspiration, suggested that the young man might care to become his secretary, and type the manuscript of the second half of his novel. Agostinelli mentioned that he now had a wife, the very Anna of whom Proust had heard five years before, as a mistress whom he hoped to marry; then, said Proust, she must come too. Anna turned out to be ugly and tiresome—"I can't think what he saw in her," Proust declared afterwards; but he was touched by her devotion to Alfred, and Alfred's to her. He allowed them a great deal of money, out of kindness, and then more still, in the hope of winning their affection, and because they spent it so fast. If he one day gave them fifty francs, he said, they would squander twenty on peaches, twenty on taxis, and next morning they would be penniless. Nor were their outlays always on this modest scale: "if I told you the way they lived, you *wouldn't believe me*," he lamented later to Émile Straus. Anna was madly jealous, and Agostinelli was assiduously unfaithful to her— "fortunately she never found out, or she'd have killed him," said Proust; and yet, "in all my life I've never seen a couple so tenderly united, so truly living each for the other". Anna did not conceal her dislike for Proust, who could not help returning it. Within a few weeks the situation had become impossible, unbearable and inescapable. About 12 February he wrote mysteriously to Mme de Noailles of 'sorrows (*chagrins*) which now discourage me'; and these cries of unexplained distress to his friends were to continue until the final tragedy.

Real life was less well constructed than his novel, and Proust began to experience *La Prisonnière* before he reached his agony at sunrise. The approach of spring, no less than the desire to escape from his captivity, made him long like the Narrator for Italy. He proposed to Mme de Noailles that they should go to Florence together, and suggested a meeting in Rome to Robert de Billy, who was now first secretary in the embassy there. When René Blum left on 25 February for a stay in Dr Widmer's sanatorium at Valmont, he thought of joining him, 'to change my hours', in order to go on and see Florence by daylight. Instead, with the inducement of keeping an eye on Agostinelli, he 'changed his hours' at home, and stayed awake during the day, but found this did not enable him to sleep at night. 'I think all the torments I suffer now might be a little less cruel,' he told Mme Straus early in March, 'if I told them to you. And they are of a kind which is sufficiently general and human to interest you, perhaps.'

The preoccupations of this spring were reflected in '*Vacances de Pâques*', the fourth and last extract from his novel in *Le Figaro*, which appeared on 25 March. He chose the passages from *Du Côté de chez Swann* and *Le Côté de Guermantes* in which the Narrator as a child longs for Florence, and remembers his longing several years later, when he is in love with the Duchesse de Guermantes. He introduced these with a prelude on the vernal sounds of tramcars and street-cries, which he now heard from his bed in the morning as he listened for the voice of Agostinelli; and he here used images first sketched in *Contre Sainte-Beuve* in the spring of 1909, and later splendidly elaborated in *La Prisonnière*.[1] He had not given up hope of publishing extracts in

[1] *Chroniques*, 106-13. Cf. I, 387-92; II, 143, 148; III, 9, 12, 116, 168, 409-10; *Contre Sainte-Beuve*, 74, 76, 79.

the *Nouvelle Revue Française*, although its editors had despised and
rejected his novel; and it was to their address, although his admiration
was sincere, that he inserted laudatory allusions to Claudel, Jammes,
Ghéon and Larbaud in the same article.

Immediately after signing his contract with Grasset on 11 March
Proust had paid a first instalment of 1730 francs for printing costs,
promising another on receipt of the first complete author's copy.
Once again the golden spell worked swiftly. The first galley-proofs
arrived early in April, and by the 13th he was receiving daily batches,
the margins of which he blackened with corrections and additions,
glueing ever more insertions to top, bottom and sides. 'I've written a
whole new book on the proofs,' he told Louis de Robert. His compunction lest he should ruin Grasset with this extra expense was
relieved by the arrival early in May of the first forty-five revise galleys,
together with a bill of 595 francs for excess corrections.

The last of the first galleys arrived at the same time, and necessitated
a momentous decision. There were 95 in all, each of 8 pages, reaching
to near the end of the first visit to Balbec and making a total, allowing
for about five remaining galleys still to come, of approximately 800
pages instead of the 650 or 700 which he had estimated. Grasset
objected, for technical and commercial reasons, since a volume of such
inordinate size would be physically impossible and would reduce his
profits on the whole work; and Louis de Robert thoroughly alarmed
Proust by arguing that the public would refuse to read him unless he
drastically shortened its length. He pleaded to be allowed to publish it
unmutilated, in two parts cased in a cardboard box; but Grasset
refused. He thought of omitting the Balbec chapter and stopping at
the end of '*Chez Mme Swann*', making a total which he variously
estimated as 660 or 680 pages, but which in fact would have been
about 650. Even this sacrifice was not enough: a little over 500 pages
was declared to be the maximum. This would comprise about a third
of the novel, and he reverted accordingly to the alternative plan,
which he had mentioned to Gallimard in the previous November, of
dividing *A la Recherche* into three volumes. Page 500 fell towards the
end of the first stage of the Narrator's love for Gilberte, when he plays
with her in the Champs-Élysées in the snow, and the fateful 1st of
January approaches, just before M. de Norpois 'came to dinner for the
first time'. In search of an effective ending he transferred the magnificent episode of the sunlight on the balcony to this point; but when
the proofs embodying this correction arrived, early in September, he

found a still better plan. Reinstating 'the sunlight on the balcony' to
its former position, just after the Narrator's first meeting with Gilberte
in the Champs-Élysées, he ended the volume with the description of
his visit to the Bois de Boulogne in November 1912, which had
hitherto formed the end of '*Chez Mme Swann*'. *Du Côté de chez Swann*
had thus reached its final form.

The publication of what afterwards became *A l'Ombre des Jeunes
Filles en Fleurs* was thus delayed, not as it then seemed for twelve
months, but in fact for nearly six years. But the disappointment which
to Proust appeared at the time disastrous was to reveal itself as providential. The future *A l'Ombre*, like its successors, was as yet imperfect in content, style, structure and scale. It still lacked many of the
finest and most indispensable episodes, such as the Narrator's 'irregular progress of oblivion' of Gilberte, or the appearance of Albertine
and the little band, which was then intended for the summer after
Mme de Villeparisis's matinée, during the second of three visits to
Balbec. Its insufficient length, for it was afterwards more than doubled
in size, would have left the remainder of *A la Recherche* top-heavy.
The further experience of love and anguish, which would give Proust
essential maturity and material, was still to come. The premature
publication of *A l'Ombre* in 1913, still more that of *A l'Ombre* with the
equally deficient *Le Côté de Guermantes* in 1914, which was to be
averted by the outbreak of war, would have left the greatness of *A la
Recherche du Temps Perdu* as we now know it irremediably com-
promised.

Meanwhile, amid the distractions of publication and unhappy love,
Proust had forgotten last summer's promise of fur wraps to the
d'Alton girls. During April and May he negotiated under Mme
Straus's guidance with the furrier Corby, deciding at last, as one
wanted a white fur and the other a dark, on white fox and grey: 'I don't
like the sound of "mock ermine",' he told her, 'it savours of betrayal.'
The first and second Balkan wars had been raging, with unprecedented
and ill-omened slaughter, since the autumn of 1912. Once again he
speculated on a falling market in the expectation of a rise which never
came, paying his losses at the end of each month. He had staked
several hundred thousand francs; and his 'liquidation' payment at the
end of April was particularly heavy, since at that very moment the
Austrian ultimatum to Montenegro for the evacuation of Scutari had
roused fears of a European conflict. 'I'm a lovesick but ruined specu-
lator,' he wrote to Mme Straus, in words which suggest that he had by

now carried out his hint, made early in March, of confiding in her the reasons for his misery.

At this time he learned that Louis de Robert, like himself, was ill, isolated and unhappily in love, though with a woman. Remembering the great days when he had reconciled Louisa to Albufera, he offered to help: 'I have made peace between friends, lovers, even married couples,' he boasted, 'I have given prestige in the eyes of a coquette to the wretched lover she disdained.' He volunteered to visit the lady, as he had proposed to tackle Louisa at Vichy in 1904. 'When our squandered kindness fails, we must do the opposite, and cease to be kind,' he recommended, and promised to make her 'long to love you, and fear that it may be already too late.' But Robert declined this recipe of doubtful efficacy.

Maurice Rostand had continued in vain to send enthusiastic letters. At last, one evening in May, Proust invited the young man with Marie Scheikévitch to midnight supper at Larue's after the Russian Ballet. Mme Scheikévitch wore a bouquet of red roses on her bosom, as if still stained with blood from her attempted suicide; and Proust, moved by this tragic image, remembered the crimson-breasted doves seen with Reynaldo and Pierre Lavallée in the Jardin des Plantes, eighteen years before, and thought of calling his second volume '*Les Colombes poignardées*'. He ordered enormous strawberries, the most ruinously expensive champagne, and borrowed from the head waiter, who thanked him profusely, several hundred-franc notes of which he gave one as a tip. They deposited Mme Scheikévitch half-asleep at her front door, and went on to 102 Boulevard Haussmann where, in the antiquated lift, Proust suddenly became aware that his guest wore perfume, and buried his face in a huge pocket handkerchief. Maurice waited in the smaller of the two drawing-rooms, among the dust-covers covered with dust, watched steadily by the portrait of a young man in immaculate evening dress, faintly moustached and faintly smiling, with luminous eyes. It was Blanche's painting of his host in 1892; and Maurice, trying to connect it with the spectral marionette in the next room, whose dinner-clothes seemed, he thought, to have been crumpled on purpose by a mad valet, noticed that the eyes were the same. He entered the cork-lined bedroom, where he found his host lying on the bed, amid drugs, invitations, prescriptions, neckties and pyramids of books. Proust began to read aloud from sheets of proof: "For a long time," he said, "I used to go to bed early . . ."

Proust's visit to Cabourg this year was late and brief. He lingered in Paris until August, immobilised by misery and illness. Partly because the subject was too painful, partly because his present life was bringing him new material for it, he felt unable to revise the proofs for the second half of his chapter about Swann in love with Odette, for which Grasset was beginning to press him. Poor Ulrich turned up one afternoon, out of work and starving. Proust telephoned Jacques Bizet's wife, asked her to find him a post as chauffeur, and declared: "I shan't be leaving Paris this year"; but an hour later he suddenly made his decision and fled to Cabourg with Agostinelli by motor-car, leaving Nicolas and Anna to follow next day. On the journey Agostinelli missed the way, and they arrived at the Grand Hôtel at five o'clock in the morning, in the first light of dawn.

For a few days Proust felt at home, and dutifully read his proofs. Then he spoke mysteriously of making a flying visit to Paris and returning; but he postponed this plan from day to day, and announced to Nicolas one Monday afternoon, as he set off with Agostinelli to Houlgate, that he had decided not to leave Cabourg before the end of the week. But when they reached Houlgate, according to Proust's account to Lauris a week later, Agostinelli said: "I can't bear to see you looking so sad. You'd better take the plunge, and catch the Paris train at Trouville without going back to the hotel!" Proust sent a message to Nicolas ordering him to pack and return immediately; Agostinelli added a note to Anna asking her to go with Nicolas: and the eloping couple fled to Paris.

The real situation behind this enigmatic crisis can only be guessed. Perhaps Proust's retreat to Paris with Agostinelli, like the Narrator's with Albertine, marks the point at which the lover first decided to make the beloved a prisoner in his home. It may also be that Proust's sufferings were hitherto caused only by his efforts to resist or conceal his own love, and to gain Agostinelli's; and the young man's behaviour at Cabourg, like Albertine's at Balbec, brought on the first pangs of jealousy and the need to remove him from temptation. But these possibilities do not explain why Proust should wish to visit Paris only for a few days, still less why he should arrange for Nicolas and Anna to follow only a few hours behind them. It is as though he were drawn to Paris by some anxiety unconnected with Agostinelli, which he hoped to allay, without relinquishing his watch upon the young man, and then return to the pleasures of Cabourg.

In the dawn which follows Albertine's terrible revelation on the little train of her intimacy with Mlle Vinteuil's friend, the Narrator

accounts for his unhappiness and his desire to take her with him to
Paris by a characteristic fiction. "When I came to Balbec," he tells her,
"I left behind a woman I was going to marry, who was ready to
sacrifice everything for me. For the last week I've been asking myself
day after day whether I'd have the courage not to send her a telegram
to say I was coming back. I've had that courage, but it made me so
unhappy I thought I would kill myself."[1] In his letter to Lauris
Proust gave exactly the same version of the reasons for his return:
'When I went to Cabourg,' he wrote, 'I left behind me a woman whom
I see rarely in Paris, but at least I know she's there, and at Cabourg I
felt far away and anxious. So I decided to put in a few days in Paris.'
Strange as it seems, it is probable that the story which the Narrator
told Albertine as a lie was at least partly true when Proust told it to
Lauris in real life; for this woman existed, and Lauris himself was one
of the few friends in whom Proust had confided about her. 'Would it
not be a crime,' he had asked Lauris four years before, when he was
thinking of marrying the mysterious girl of Cabourg, 'to make a
charming young girl share my dreadful life?'; and these are almost the
very words of the Narrator when he tells Albertine: "I nearly married
her, but I hadn't the heart to make a young woman live with someone
so ill and troublesome."[2] It is likely that the words Proust used to
Lauris and in his novel were also spoken to Agostinelli at Cabourg.
He may have fled to Paris in the desperate hope of curing his new love
for Agostinelli by reviving his old love for the young girl, or of using
her as a stratagem to compel Agostinelli to submission. However this
may be, the crisis at Cabourg was the equivalent in Proust's life of the
Agony at Sunrise. It marked the point of no return in his life as in his
novel; and it was the moment at which the girl of Cabourg united with
Agostinelli to form Albertine.

[1] II, 1118.   [2] II, 1123.

Chapter 10

AGOSTINELLI VANISHES
(September 1913 – July 1914)

PROUST reached Paris luggageless, without so much as a night-shirt in which to take to his bed, and instantly resumed work on his proofs. Ominously, he now inserted 'small details of the utmost importance which tighten the knots of jealousy round poor Swann'. He had lost weight alarmingly in the past months of distress, and Dr Bize ordered him to regain it by resting. Meanwhile he shaved his beard, revealing for the remainder of his life the moustached and age-less face of the lost young man of whom he wrote.

Early in September he sent a spare set of proofs to Lucien Daudet, who thus became the first person after Louis de Robert to read the whole volume. Robert, with the best of intentions, had plagued him with stupid objections: the book was too long-winded, the title too boring, the scene between Mlle Vinteuil and her friend too improper; why not just publish the *Combray* chapter separately? But Lucien read *Swann* with rapture far into the night, and his verdict, to Proust's great relief, was not only enthusiastic, but showed genuine under-standing. Proust gratefully accepted Lucien's offer to review him. A week or two later he sent proofs to Cocteau; Jean, too, was dazzled and dazzling, and promised a review.

The final instalment of the third and last complete set of proofs arrived towards the end of September, the whole volume went to press early in October,[1] and *Du Côté de chez Swann* was published on Friday, 14 November 1913.

---

[1] The last sheet of the second set, in which the volume ended with 'the sunlight on the balcony', was printed on 1 September; and it was therefore a little after this date that Proust inserted, from the end of '*Chez Mme Swann*', the episode in the Bois de Boulogne which formed the new ending. Meanwhile he had already received, corrected and returned most of the earlier sheets of the second set, from which the third set was printed from 31 July onwards. The last surviving portion of this third set, p. 432 (36 pages before the end of *Un Amour de Swann*), was printed on 28 August. Allowing time for Proust to correct and return the last of the second set and for the rest of the third set to be printed

Proust succeeded in arranging notices in nearly all the important
Paris newspapers. Most were written by friends, or commissioned by
editors who happened to be his friends. Mme Scheikévitch persuaded
Hébrard to send Élie Joseph Bois to interview him for *Le Temps*; and
Bois's description of 'the bedroom where the shutters are nearly
always closed', and the 'two admirable eyes, alive and feverish, darting
their rays beneath a forehead curtained with shaggy hair', gave the
Paris public their first glimpse of Proust's environment and appearance. But the supposed 'interview', as published in *Le Temps* of 12
November, was not what it seemed, for in fact Proust handed to Bois
a copy of the very manifesto which he had given Antoine Bibesco
exactly a year ago to show to Gide and Copeau. This was reproduced
almost word for word, with the addition of an occasional 'So you see',
or 'How shall I put it?', and a tribute to Calmette of which Hébrard
cut all but the opening words. 'I owe it to M. Calmette,' Proust wrote
with bitter nostalgia and exaggeration, 'that I ever knew the joy of a
young man who sees his first article in print. And then again, through
enabling me by way of my articles to return the visits of people whom
I then found it hard to do without, he helped me to make the transition
from life in society to life in solitude.'

Swann was dedicated 'to M. Gaston Calmette, as a token of profound and affectionate gratitude'; yet Proust felt deeply hurt by
Calmette's year-long silence, his ill-kept promise to win Fasquelle, his
disregard of the cigarette-case from Tiffany's, his reluctance to print
more than the four extracts from *Swann*. On 12 November he wrote
Calmette an aggrieved letter: he was heartbroken that *Le Temps* had
cut his eulogy, and sad ('but less so') that no advance notice had
appeared in *Le Figaro*; would Calmette arrange for one, preferably
without using the adjectives 'subtle' or 'delicate'? Calmette, with his
characteristic gentle smile, handed the missive to Robert Dreyfus and
said: "I'm sure you'll be very pleased to give Marcel Proust a specially
kind notice!" Dreyfus did so, on 16 November. In Calmette's own
copy Proust wrote: 'I have often felt that you care little for my
writings. But should you ever have time to read a few pages of my

therefrom, it seems probable that he received the latter towards the end of
September, and that the volume went to press about the beginning of October.
A few leaves exist of a fourth and fifth set of proofs, printed 13-27 October,
but there is no evidence that these sets were ever complete. Owing to the delay
caused by these late alterations the *achevé d'imprimer* of the published volume is
8 November—less than a week before publication.

novel, especially in the second part,[1] I think you would at last make my acquaintance.' Calmette did not reply—'silence with him does duty equally well for gratitude and for many other feelings,' Proust told Dreyfus—but he did not neglect *Swann*. At Lucien's instigation the Empress Eugénie sent him a letter through her secretary: 'it would be *personally agreeable* to Her Imperial Majesty if M. Daudet's article could be published without omissions and in a prominent position.' Calmette obeyed, on 27 November, and on 8 December appeared yet another review by Francis Chevassu, the editor of the *Figaro* Literary Supplement. Meanwhile René Blum printed an advance notice in *Gil Blas* on 9 November, and a long extract from the soirée at Mme de Saint-Euverte's on the 18th.

Lucien Daudet's article was one of the most intelligent Proust ever received in his lifetime, and called attention to vital features of his work which are still not universally appeciated by Proustian critics. 'It evokes the author's presence for those who know him,' he wrote, 'and is capable of reconstituting it for those who do not ... it attains an extraordinary moral grandeur . . . Monsieur Proust's analysis is so perfectly incorporated with a prodigious sensibility that the two qualities become indistinguishable ... in the distant future it will seem one of the most astonishing manifestations of intelligence in the twentieth century.' *A la Recherche*, he concluded with an image worthy of Proust himself, would take its place with the great classics of the past, 'because every masterpiece is the cry of a precursor, and rallies beyond time, in the black frost of eternity, its companions yet to come'.

Cocteau's article appeared on 23 November in *Excelsior*, the editor of which, Pierre Lafitte, was a Cabourg acquaintance of Proust's, and had invited him to choose his own reviewer. Like Lucien, Cocteau saw *Swann* as a new classic; he spoke of the 'cousinship of master-pieces', and wrote: '*Swann* is a gigantic miniature, full of mirages, superimpositions of gardens, plays on space and time, broad cool touches in the style of Manet.' Maurice Rostand in *Comœdia* on 26 December told a charming anecdote of 'my partner in a tango the other evening, who talked about Odette de Crécy and quoted, almost accurately, more than thirty lines of *Swann*', but marred all, with an excess of zeal which infuriated Proust, by comparing him to Pascal, Shelley, Leonardo de Vinci, Goethe, Plato, Dostoevsky and Shake-speare. Jacques Émile Blanche in the *Écho de Paris* of 15 April 1914,

[1] '*Un Amour de Swann*.'

called *Swann* 'the book of insomnia, of a mind working in silence and darkness, but overflowing with life, diverse and one'. Each of the four made it clear that he was a personal friend of Proust: 'I think,' wrote Maurice Rostand, 'that if I had not the great pride and honour of being a friend of the author, I should be unable to rest till I had met him.' The public may have suspected, wrongly, that these reviewers admired this unknown novelist because they were his friends, whereas in fact they were his friends because they admired him.

The loyal Albufera, 'who never reads anything', made his inevitable *gaffe* in the manner of the Duc de Guermantes.[1] "My dear Louis, have you read my book?" enquired Marcel on the telephone. "Read your book? Have you written a *book*?" "Yes, of course, Louis, and I even sent you a copy." "Ah, my dear old Marcel, if you sent it me, I've certainly read it. I was just not quite sure whether it ever reached me!"

Paul Souday, whom Proust had seen in 1900 despised and glowering in the Café Weber, was now the official critic of *Le Temps*, and had been asked by Hébrard, again at Mme Scheikévitch's instigation, 'to give special attention to Marcel Proust's novel'. *Du Côté de chez Swann*, Souday declared on 10 December, was 'not positively boring, though a bit banal'; it 'swarmed with grammatical errors'; the chapter on Swann in love was nothing but 'an enormous digression', and Swann's passion for a cocotte showed 'a naïveté improbable in a Parisian of such extensive experience'. However, he admitted, 'Marcel Proust undoubtedly has a great deal of talent, though for that precise reason it will be deplored that he has spoiled such fine gifts by so many faults'; the novel contained 'precious elements with which he might have made an exquisite slim volume'; and Souday awaited the sequel 'with sympathy, and the hope that it will have a little more order, brevity, and a more chastened prose style'. Grasset telephoned Proust in such agitation that Nicolas exclaimed: "I thought war must have broken out!"; and Proust sent Souday a cutting letter in defence of his grammar. But by deigning to notice *Swann* at all this favourite critic of the philistine middle classes probably brought Proust more readers than any other reviewer; and Souday himself remained under the lifelong impression that he had 'discovered' Proust.

Swann was selling satisfactorily, and early in December Grasset decided to print a second edition, for which he offered to pay the expenses and give Proust a royalty of ten per cent. Grasset was alive to the publicity-value of literary prizes. 'I hear he fought a duel,' Proust

[1] II, 524; III, 583.

told Lucien, 'because the Academy gave a prize to Romain Rolland instead of to one of his authors'; and in his first negotiations with René Blum in February 1913 Proust had offered 'to put in for the Goncourt Prize or some other, if it would please Grasset', though not for the *Vie Heureuse* (which had an all-lady jury), 'because of the extreme licence and indecency of certain passages'. Grasset now asked him to apply for both. As it happened, Proust was too late for the *Vie Heureuse*, for the list was already closed, although he found he would have been ardently supported by Mme de Pierrebourg, Lauris's mother-in-law, who belonged to the committee. Louis de Robert recommended him to two members of the Goncourt Academy, Zola's disciple Paul Margueritte, and Rosny *aîné*, whom Proust had met at Cabourg in 1910, and suggested that he should send his book to Colette. But Proust, much as he admired her, had not seen Colette since Mme Arman's great quarrel with her in 1896 (which had led, because he tried to reconcile each party to the other, to his falling in disgrace with both), and felt it would be unethical to make up their difference with so ulterior a motive. Time was too short for further canvassing, and the Goncourt Prize was awarded on 3 December to a nonentity, as usual, although yet another novel of genius, Alain-Fournier's *Le Grand Meaulnes*, was among the official candidates. Rosny obligingly put in a minority vote of one for Proust, who was well pleased. 'Perhaps when they see my book was discussed by the jury,' he wrote hopefully to Robert, 'some people will think of reading it, and who knows whether among these there may not be some friend of my thoughts who otherwise would never have known them?'

Having longed for the NRF as for a promised land, and seen himself sternly barred at the threshold ('I felt I 'had come unto mine own, but mine own received me not',' he had told Copeau in the words of John i, 11), Proust was doubly hurt by Ghéon's review in the *Nouvelle Revue Française* of 1 January 1914. *Swann*, wrote Ghéon, contained 'poetry of the highest beauty, psychology of the newest, irony of the most original, a picture of "society" that no one had ever drawn before'; but it was 'a work of idle leisure, without organisation, form or selection, in short, the very opposite of a work of art'. He believed, or pretended to believe, that *Temps Perdu* meant only wasted time, not the Past. Proust angrily corrected him, and was dissatisfied with Ghéon's lame excuse, that he liked *Swann* so much that he had felt afraid to let himself go! But behind the scenes of the NRF the tide was turning. Reading between the lines of Ghéon's review, Gide began to mistrust his hasty judgement of twelve months before. Cocteau, too, told him that he had made a serious mistake, and must read *Swann* again, or rather, for the first time. During the first fortnight of January Gide and his colleagues did so, and the scales fell from their eyes.

'My dear Proust,' wrote Gide, with seductive but sincere repentance, about 13 January, 'for several days I have never left your book; I am supersaturating myself in it with rapture, revelling in it. The refusal of this book will always be the gravest mistake the NRF ever made—and (for I have the shame of being largely responsible for it) one of the most stinging regrets, nay, remorses, of my whole life.' Two months later[1] the editorial committee of the NRF sat in full sanhedrin and offered, 'with unanimity and enthusiasm', said Gide, to publish the remaining two volumes of *A la Recherche* and buy back the rights in the first volume from Grasset. The heartfelt apology, the entreaty for forgiveness, the full reparation which the injured dream of but rarely receive, had come beyond all hope to Proust.

He replied with dignified joy and gratitude, but asked for time to consider, and declared that he would not accept the offer if he found that it would hurt Grasset. He sent his contract to Émile Straus, who specialised in the legal problems of authors: could he break it without being liable to prosecution? Knowing that the Princesse de Polignac was a friend of Grasset, he asked Reynaldo, who was to see her on 3 April, to persuade her to sound the publisher informally on his behalf. On the same day, however, he received a letter from Grasset enquiring when he proposed to publish his second volume. He therefore countermanded his request to Reynaldo, and wrote to Grasset on the 4th, revealing his wish to transfer his novel to the NRF; 'I leave it to you to decide whether or not it suits you to grant it,' he said. In his alarm Grasset made the tactical error of trying to hold Proust to the terms of their contract, instead of appealing to his feelings. Proust showed that he was pained, and Grasset wrote again more wisely; Proust must do as he thought best, he released him from the contract, he wanted him to stay only of his own free will. Defeated in this contest of magnanimity, Proust told Gide ruefully that he would have to remain with Grasset.

This was not the first reversal of his defeats in December 1912. Fasquelle, seeing the unexpected success of *Swann*, had recently made overtures through Maurice Rostand for the publication of the remain-

[1] And not in January 1914, as has hitherto been thought, owing to Gide's faulty recollection.

ing volumes; but Proust had seen no reason to exchange one commercial publisher for another. The NRF's approach was far more
tempting, for he regarded that brilliant and idealistic group as his
spiritual home; but he refused for motives of honour, perhaps also of
pride, in order to spurn them in turn and wait till they called him
again. Yet his position with regard to Grasset was irremediably false.
Grasset had consented to publish his novel for hire, unread, rather
than for its own sake. He was a publisher of scrupulous honesty and
high aims, but impelled, unlike the NRF, by ambition for the rise of
his struggling firm more than by selfless love of literature or faith in
the genius of his authors. Proust's fancied concessions in the matter of
royalties had left him, as was no doubt his unconscious intention, with
the impression that he owed nothing to Grasset. He seized every
opportunity of believing that Grasset had the better of him: 'He's had
me for a mug again—*j'ai été poire de nouveau,*' he told Vaudoyer
inelegantly in December 1913.

Proust's campaign for his novel was now satisfactorily over: he had
been reviewed widely and favourably, had made the Goncourt
Academy aware of his existence, gained devoted readers known and
unknown, and seen Fasquelle and the NRF repent their errors in vain.
Even the sales were well above the average for a first novel by an
unestablished author. Third and fourth editions were called for in
January, and two more were to follow before the outbreak of war.
Grasset himself showed his true opinion by his unwillingness to
release Proust (for if he had not regarded him as a valuable asset, the
NRF's offer would have seemed a heavensent opportunity to get rid
of him), and by agreeing to print the remaining volumes at his own
expense and with increased royalties. The mysterious chain-reaction
which turns a *succès d'estime* into a bestseller had not taken place; but
the common idea that the first publication of *Swann* was a failure, that
it passed unnoticed or was a disappointment to Proust himself, is
incorrect.

In February 1914, constrained by his political subsidisers to act out
of character, Gaston Calmette had begun a ruthless campaign in *Le
Figaro* against the progressive and Germanophile Minister of Finance,
Joseph Caillaux, and his proposed income-tax. Calmette threatened to
publish Caillaux's love-letters to the mistress he had later married; and
on 16 March Mme Caillaux called at the *Figaro* office, produced a
revolver and shot him. "Don't touch me, I'm a lady!" she cried, while
Calmette's friends wept, and the gentle editor bled to death. The thugs

of *L'Action Française*, led by the truculent Léon Daudet, raised street-riots with shouts of "Down with Caillaux!" and Barrès, meeting Daudet at Calmette's funeral, ironically enquired: "How the deuce did this happen to *him*, and not to *you*?" To Proust afterwards, as to many others, it seemed that the murder of Calmette, like a ritual sacrifice of a good man performed in vain, was the first warning of world war. The angel of death was abroad; but Proust, in this new era of violence, was to be revisited sooner than other men by that dark angel.

It is a measure of Proust's iron courage and inflexible ambition for his book that throughout these eight months of tireless manœuvre he was enduring the last agonies of his doomed love for Agostinelli. Thinking of his mother and his own coming into the world he compared his novel to a child, long borne in his own body, long protected in helpless infancy; yet he did his duty by *Swann* half mechanically, without joy, like a parent distracted by an adulterous passion. In letters about his book to Louis de Robert, Vaudoyer, Mme de Noailles, Montesquiou, Lucien Daudet, Mme Scheikévitch, Gabriel Astruc, René Blum and Mme Straus he could not resist alluding to the 'immense grief' which had deprived him, he said, of all the pleasure he hoped from its publication. He did not reveal the nature of his suffering; but Montesquiou guessed, and wrote one of the letters of genuine, winning sympathy with which this saturnine man revealed, sometimes, the goodness that still lingered in his corroded heart.

Proust's tortures, like the Narrator's with the captive Albertine, were twofold. The first was jealousy—but of whom and what? Was Agostinelli an invert, seeking relief from his employer's tyranny in less exacting encounters with younger men? It is possible, though there is no evidence to show it. But Proust's remark to Émile Straus, that Agostinelli loved his 'wife' Anna but was unfaithful to her—'which she didn't know, for she was madly jealous and would have killed him' —seems to suggest a more natural explanation: that Agostinelli's infidelities to wife and master were with women, and the pleasures which Proust dreaded because he could not give them were those of normal love. Perhaps Proust hurried Agostinelli to Paris in August 1913 because he had detected him in a seaside flirtation, and realised that not only the humble Anna but all women were his rivals. It was perhaps with the intention of having Agostinelli followed, as does Charlus with Morel,[1] and the Narrator (or so Albertine suspects)[2]

---

[1] III, 216-17.   [2] III, 334.

with Albertine, that Proust asked Albert Nahmias whether he had
'ever, for any reason, had anyone shadowed, and if so, have you kept
the addresses of the detectives or maintained contact with them?' His
second torment, like the Narrator's, was the knowledge that Agostinelli's captivity was nearing its end. Tried too far, despite his
affection for this marvellous master, his gratitude for so much moral
and financial kindness, the young man was planning to escape and live
his own life in freedom.

There are happier incidents of Albertine's imprisonment which
belong to Agostinelli's. The bathroom with frosted glass from which
the Narrator listens to his beloved singing at her morning ablutions[1]
was the one recorded by Cocteau at 102 Boulevard Haussmann, where
Proust stood in his violet waistcoat, eating noodles, after a reading
from *Swann*, and no doubt it was Agostinelli whom Proust heard
there humming '*For melancholy is but folly*'. The pianola on which
Albertine plays Rameau and Borodin was bought by Proust that
autumn, not without difficulty in obtaining the 'rolls' he most desired:
'This is the first request we have had for this piece from any of our
fifteen thousand subscribers during the past ten years,' replied the
indignant makers, when he asked them for the piano transcription of
Beethoven's Fourteenth Quartet.[2] Albertine, bending over the keys
as formerly over the handlebars of her bicycle, is compared to Saint
Cecilia at her organ; again Proust is thinking of Agostinelli whom he
had likened in his motor-rides from Cabourg six years before, bowed
upon his steering-wheel and touching the levers which changed the
speed and tone of the engine, to 'Saint Cecilia improvising on a still
more immaterial instrument'.[3] Albertine, says the Narrator, 'had
become extremely intelligent. She used to say, though quite mistakenly: "I'm horrified to think that without you I should still be
stupid. Don't deny it, you have opened a world of ideas to me that I
never dreamed of, and whatever I've become I owe to you alone".'[4]
The same apparent change had occurred in Agostinelli, and the same
pathetic words were no doubt spoken by him. 'He was an extraordinary person,' Proust told Émile Straus, 'and possessed perhaps the

[1] III, 10-11.
[2] M. de Charlus shares their attitude when he rebukes Morel for playing the
piano transcription of Beethoven's Fifteenth Quartet: "nothing is less suitable
for the piano," he declares (II, 1009).
[3] III, 383; *Pastiches et Mélanges*, 96.
[4] III, 64.

greatest intellectual gifts I have ever known'; and to Gide he wrote of his 'delicious intelligence', 'this merit so marvellously incompatible with his station in life, which I discovered with amazement, though it added nothing to my affection for him, except that I enjoyed making him aware of it'.

We have seen, however, that the customary total identification of Albertine with Agostinelli goes beyond the facts. She already exists, long before Proust's first meeting with Agostinelli in 1907, in the heroine of 'Avant la Nuit' in 1893, in the Françoise and Charlotte of Jean Santeuil in 1897, and in the 1905-6 version of his novel when the little band was wooed by Swann; and in all these the hero is tortured by jealousy of her Lesbianism. In A la Recherche, until the last episode of her story, she is based primarily upon female originals. In the first holiday at Balbec Albertine's chief model is Marie Finaly, in her visits to the Narrator's home she resembles Louisa de Mornand and Marie Nordlinger, and during the second visit to Balbec she is the young girl of Cabourg in 1908 and 1909. It is intrinsically probable, though factual evidence is lacking, that in all these episodes she is reinforced by Proust's memories of young men, particularly by the obscure incidents of 1892-3 and 1897-8, and by Albert Nahmias in 1911-12; but there is no aspect of her here—except perhaps the Narrator's jealousy—which cannot be explained by Proust's known relations with young women. Albertine becomes Agostinelli for the first time in the Agony at Sunrise and the captivity in Paris. Yet even here her origins remain complex and divided. By no possible process of 'transposition' can such themes as the project of marriage, the choice of Fortuny gowns, the Narrator's motionless lovemaking with the sleeping Albertine, be derived from Proust's relationship with a vigorous young chauffeur. All these come from his abortive engagement to the young girl of Cabourg. In his 'little pleasures' with her in Paris during the autumn of 1909 he no doubt displayed the passive and contemplative sexual behaviour which (as is shown also in his affair with Louisa de Mornand) he preferred with women, but not, it may be presumed, with young men; and the marine imagery with which the Narrator 'embarks on the sea of Albertine's sleep'[1] is a memory of their summers of 1908 and 1909 at Cabourg.

The main narrative of La Prisonnière and Albertine Disparue—the flight to Paris, the captivity, the escape, the death, the Narrator's posthumous jealousy and slow oblivion—indubitably retells the true

[1] III, 72.

story of Proust's love for Agostinelli. Yet it is as certain as it is strange
that the earliest plot of *A la Recherche*, in the version finished six
months before Agostinelli's unexpected reappearance in January
1913, followed a similar course. She was already intended at this same
point of the novel, after the last return from Balbec, to become the
Narrator's great love; the Narrator's jealous surveillance and cross-
examinations were sketched out, twenty years before, in '*Avant la
Nuit*' and in *Jean Santeuil*, parts IX and X; the scene in *Du Côté de
chez Swann* between Mlle Vinteuil and her friend at Montjouvain was
already designed to provoke, later in the novel, a revelation resem-
bling the Agony at Sunrise; the process of oblivion was foretold in
miniature by the Narrator's earlier love for Gilberte and Swann's for
Odette; and Albertine's death, the only possible end to so desperate a
love, was already adumbrated by the suicide of the Lesbian heroine of
'*Avant la Nuit*'. It is as though Proust imposed upon his love for
Agostinelli the pre-existing pattern not only of his total previous
experience of love in his own life, but of the climax of his novel.
Agostinelli was conducted along the road to his tragic end by the
ineluctable mechanism of a work of art; he was killed by *A la
Recherche*; and when he seemed to become a free agent, like Albertine
in her flight to Touraine, he journeyed to his death. *A la Recherche* is
a work consecrated by two human sacrifices, the deaths of Mme
Proust and Agostinelli, for which Proust himself, in his own mind and
in fact, was partly responsible.[1]

Soon after the return from Cabourg Agostinelli decided, and Anna
agreed, that there was no future in his luxurious servitude to Proust.
He had become a chauffeur when the motor-car still attracted the
enterprise and mechanical ingenuity of the élite among the young of
the working classes: he may be compared to the intelligent engineer
Straker in *Man and Superman*. But the heroic age of the automobile
was ending, and many of its protagonists were already numbered
among the first pioneers—some among the first martyrs—of the air.
In 1913, known to French aeronautical historians as '*l'Année glorieuse*',
the aviators of France flew by hops from Nancy to Cairo, crossed the
Mediterranean to Algeria non-stop, made a speed record of 126
m.p.h., a height record of 20,000 feet, and looped the first loop. Aerodromes were opened near Paris, notably at Issy and Buc, and

[1] Cf. III, 496, 501. 'When I juxtaposed the deaths of my grandmother
and Albertine I felt that my life was defiled by a double murder,' says the
Narrator.

frequented by pupils, spectators, joy-riders, and the idle rich.[1] Agostinelli began to visit Buc and make friends with the airmen. A curious
incident in *Albertine Disparue*, so irrelevant that it seems to be an
undigested fragment from real life, no doubt belongs to this period.
Albertine declares that she has visited an airfield, where one of the
aviators is her friend; and Andrée (who here, and perhaps not in-
frequently elsewhere, seems to represent Anna) was so dazzled by the
compliments he paid Albertine, that she wanted to go up in his aeroplane.[2]

Before long, whether through his spies or because the young man
naïvely confided in him, Proust discovered Agostinelli's new interest,
and on several occasions accompanied him. 'Often,' says the Narrator,
'I liked to arrange that our outings should end—and it was also agreeable to Albertine, so devoted to every kind of sport—at one of these
aerodromes.' He was reminded by the aeroplanes—moored, departing, arriving, dragged to the starting-point by teams of mechanics—of
boats for hire on the beach at Cabourg; but here the element on which
the trippers sailed was the infinite sky. 'Soon the engine was started,
the machine began to move and gather impetus, and then abruptly to
rise, at a steep angle, in the tense and apparently immobilised ecstasy
of a horizontal speed suddenly transformed into a majestic and
vertical ascent'; while Albertine, like Agostinelli, 'beside herself with
joy, kept asking the mechanics to explain everything'.[3] Proust made
the acquaintance of two of Agostinelli's friends at Buc, Kasterine and
Sentmitchof, and wrote to Albert Nahmias to ask for a recommendation for 'a young man'—presumably Agostinelli himself—'who
believes he has made several inventions in the field of the aeroplane'.

It was probably in October 1913, when Proust's mysterious lamen-
tations to his friends recommenced, that Agostinelli announced his
intention to learn to fly. Possibly he would have been willing to train
at Buc, without entirely deserting his master; and it was perhaps only

---

[1] 'Although she is fifty-three,' wrote the diplomat Paléologue on 14 October
1913 of Cocteau's friend the Grand-Duchess Anastasia, 'she lives openly with
an Argentinian blackguard, dances at Magic City with all comers till two in the
morning and associates with the scum of the aerodromes.'

[2] III, 612. 'She no doubt hoped to turn my suspicions away from women,'
says the Narrator, 'because she thought I was less jealous of men.' Here is an
instance of 'transposition' which strongly suggests (because we can be quite
sure the aviator was a man) that Proust was chiefly jealous of Agostinelli's
relations with women.

[3] III, 105-6.

in the face of Proust's determined opposition that he realised that a complete break would be inevitable. This point may have been reached in mid-November, at the very time when *Du Côté de chez Swann* was published, when Proust told his friends that he was too unhappy to feel any pleasure at the appearance of his novel. The Narrator, weary of his sufferings, longs to see Venice and forget Albertine; and Proust asked Vaudoyer to recommend 'a quiet, isolated house in Italy', and confided to Mme Scheikévitch that she could wish him nothing but 'a kind of numbness which does not come'. In the first week of December Agostinelli fled. The date is fixed by a letter from Francis Jammes, comparing *Swann* to Shakespeare and Balzac, and speaking of its 'Tacitean phrases', which Proust received on 9 December: 'it would have given me such pleasure a month earlier,' he told Lucien Daudet, 'but as fate would have it, it arrived on a day when I was completely insane with misery'. Partly from a pathetic desire to find tranquillity and freedom in his old home, and in the bosom of his numerous family, partly because here was one of the chief aviation centres in France, Agostinelli sought refuge on his native Riviera. He took with him the money he had saved from Proust's gifts, which was amply sufficient for his plans.

In the first rage of betrayal, and with eery foresight, Proust cruelly wrote: 'you can tell your wife that if (which heaven forbid) you should have an aeroplane accident, she will find in me neither a protector nor a friend, and will never get a halfpenny from me'. In 1907, possibly divining in Agostinelli the passion for speed which is sometimes a disguised love of death, Proust had written with a similar presentiment: 'may the steering-wheel of my young mechanic remain for ever the symbol of his talent, rather than the prefiguration of his martyrdom!' Perhaps he now felt the base but irresistable wish, which many a desperate lover has known, to be freed from his torment by the death of the beloved. 'If Albertine could have been the victim of an accident and lived,' says the Narrator, 'I should have had an excuse for hurrying to her side; if she had died, I should have recovered my freedom to live.' And he remembers that Swann had felt the same desire to be freed from Odette by her death. 'If he had still been alive I could have informed him, a little later, that his wish was not only criminal, but absurd, that the death of the woman he loved would have freed him from nothing.'[1] Next, just as the Narrator dispatches Saint-Loup to Touraine to bribe Mme Bontemps and bring back Albertine, he sent

[1] III, 475-6; I, 355.

Albert Nahmias to persuade Agostinelli to return. The telegrams survive, dated from 8 December 1913 onwards and of extraordinary length, in which he advised Albert on the correct strategy for tackling the fugitive and his relatives, but forbade him, unlike the Narrator, to give money.

Agostinelli did not remain silent, and the tone of his letters is no doubt audible in the simple, dignified and affectionate letters of Albertine to the Narrator.[1] Proust had already been struck by his talent as a letter-writer in November 1907, when the young man's congratulations on 'Impressions de route en automobile' had been 'the prettiest I received'. The words in which Albertine describes their last ride together, on the evening when they returned from Versailles—when they hear a sound like 'the droning of a wasp' in the sky, and Albertine says: "Look, there's an aeroplane, it's high up, very high," —may well be Agostinelli's: 'be sure that I for my part shall not forget our drive in that double twilight (since night was near, and we were about to part), and it will not fade from my memory until my night has fallen for ever.' 'I have letters from him,' Proust assured Gide afterwards, 'which are those of a great writer.' On 5 March, as Proust wrote a letter to Henry Bordeaux hinting of his anguish, he heard a lady neighbour 'indefatigably playing', instead of the airs from Massenet's Manon which torment the Narrator after Albertine's escape,[2] the Appassionata of Beethoven; 'but she does not render its sadness,' he added.

But the fugitive did not return. Proust suspected that Anna was mainly to blame: 'I did all I could to prevent him from flying,' he told Émile Straus, 'but his wife was convinced he was going to make a million.' However, it was not until nearly four months after his escape, when the flying season began again, that Agostinelli took the decisive step. Towards the end of March 1914 he enrolled at the flying school of the Garbero brothers at La Grimaudière near Antibes, under the absurd and pathetic pseudonym of Marcel Swann. Among his colleagues were Kasterine and Sentmitchof, his friends at Buc. During the next two months his progress was rapid, and on Saturday, 30 May 1914, at five o'clock in the afternoon, he made his second solo flight, carrying with him the 7000 francs which still remained from his master's gifts.

Joseph Garbero, the chief instructor, had warned the daring novice

[1] Albertine writes five letters, all quoted in full (III, 421, 452, 468, 477-8).
[2] III, 452.

to keep within the aerodrome; but Agostinelli, rashly exulting in the liberation of flight, ventured north-eastward over the sea.[1] He prepared to fly back, but forgot the necessity to gain height and speed for the turn; his monoplane stalled and crashed, along the dipping right wing, into the sea several hundred yards from land. The horrified watchers on the shore saw the young man standing on his seat in the sinking wreck, waving and shouting for help. Agostinelli had never learned to swim; and as a rowing-boat drew near, the plane and the tragic aviator sank.

Proust learned the disaster that evening in a despairing telegram from Anna, and read further details on page 7 of next morning's *Figaro*. A posthumous letter arrived from the dead Agostinelli, and Proust may well have felt, like the Narrator when Françoise brings him the letters posted by Albertine just before her riding accident, that he 'had in his eyes the look of a man whose mind is unbalanced'.[2] A day or two later Agostinelli's step-brother Jean Vittoré called at 102 Boulevard Haussmann, and Proust burst into tears in his arms.

Boats had searched till nightfall on Saturday, but the currents were strong and the body could not be found. On Sunday evening the wrecked aeroplane was hauled to the surface, empty. The Agostinellis issued a description of the drowned man, moved chiefly, as Proust darkly suspected, by desire of the money he had upon him: he was dressed in khaki overalls, a brown rubber helmet, a grey shirt, black trousers, and wore a gold signet-ring marked AA.[3] Anna repeatedly attempted suicide; and Proust, forgetting his threats, took her under his protection, and asked Émile Straus to put in a word for her with Prince Albert of Monaco. He was astonished to learn from the grasping family that she was not Agostinelli's legal wife, but only his mistress; however, in the same spirit of justice, he apologised to Émile Straus and through him to the Prince, but pointed out firmly that Anna was none the less deserving, since 'her love for the deceased and his relations with her were more affectionate than is the case in many lawful unions'.

On Sunday 7 June a fishing-boat found the corpse near Cagnes, six

[1] Proust alludes secretly to the death of Agostinelli, when he makes the Narrator at Balbec burst into tears on first seeing an aeroplane, 'which glided for a few moments over the sea' (II, 1029).

[2] III, 477.

[3] The mysterious rings which Albertine leaves behind her, each bearing a flying eagle, are likewise marked with her monogram (III, 63, 165, 463).

miles north-east from the scene of the crash, still in its khaki overalls,
floating and decomposed. The funeral was at Nice next day; Anna,
heavily veiled and supported by Émile and Agostinelli's father, was
chief mourner; and the bearers were Hector and Joseph Garbero,
Kasterine, and the dead man's other fellow-pupils. Proust sent a 400-
franc wreath, 'as beautiful as could be, but they wished it had been of
artificial flowers,' he complained afterwards. Such was the end of the
brave, intelligent and well-meaning young man who was Proust's
greatest love.

In his grief Proust descended into asthma and incessant fumigations, 'which help me to breathe, but would prevent anyone else,' he
told Gide on 20 June, to ward off a proposed visit of condolence. Anna
stayed at 102 Boulevard Haussmann at his invitation from about mid-
June until early in July; they had both loved the same man, and were
partners in suffering. 'As in the phenomenon of supersaturation,' he
told Montesquiou, 'everything that hitherto was fluid and bearable
grips me in an eternal vice. I only have the strength to restore to his
poor widow the courage I lack for myself.' And to Lucien Daudet he
wrote later: 'I knew what it was to hope, every time I took a taxi, that
an oncoming motor-bus would run me over.' In this burning summer,
while the doomed young men of Europe played their last games of
tennis and love before nightfall, Proust watched with horror, like the
Narrator, 'the declining sun coating the verticality of houses with a
tawny distemper'. 'How slow the day is to die on these immeasurable
evenings of summer!'[1]

Jealousy and separation had not impaired Proust's resolution in the
publication and launching of *Swann*; no more could death and bereavement hinder the preparation of his next volume. On 4 April, when he
made his unsuccessful proposal to Grasset to transfer his novel to the
NRF, he answered Grasset's enquiry as to the date for the publication
of his second volume. Before deciding in June 1913 to end the first
volume with the episode of Gilberte in the Champs-Élysées he had
already received galley-proofs equivalent to about 280 further pages,
comprising the remainder of the Gilberte story ('*Chez Mme Swann*')
and the whole of the first visit to Balbec. These, however, he must
revise and enlarge, and at least two further sets of proofs would be
required. The remainder of the volume, which at this time comprised
the Narrator's love for the Duchesse de Guermantes, the visit to
Doncières, and Mme de Villeparisis's matinée, was for the most part in

[1] III, 479, 481.

typescript[1]; the rest of the typing, the revision, printing and proof-correction of this section would take 'several months'. He therefore suggested October 1914 as a target-month for publication.

As before, he decided to publish extracts from his forthcoming volume; but now, after the success of *Swann*, there was no risk of refusal from unwilling editors, no need to disguise his fragments as topical articles for *Le Figaro*. In April Gide had invited him to contribute long excerpts to the *Nouvelle Revue Française*; and about 7 May Proust sent Rivière, as the first of two instalments, an abridged version of the first visit to Balbec, cut up and pasted together from last year's galleys. This comprised the night-journey, the arrival, the rides in Mme de Villeparisis's carriage, and the meetings with Saint-Loup and the Baron de Charlus, and was published in the NRF for 1 June 1914. Towards the end of May Proust asked Grasset to print second proofs from last year's corrected galleys of '*Chez Mme Swann*' and the first visit to Balbec, and sent the typescript for the remainder of his second volume (which he then intended to call *Le Côté de Guermantes*) for the printing of first proofs. As his second instalment for the NRF was now urgently required, he asked for the typescript to be printed first; and this was done, in 28 galleys numbered 1 to 28 and equivalent to about 224 pages, from 6 to 11 June. The preceding section ('*Chez Mme Swann*' and the first visit to Balbec) was then reprinted in 38 galleys numbered 29 to 66, equivalent to about 304 pages, from 12 to 22 June. From galleys 1 to 18 he made an abridged version of the first half of *Le Côté de Guermantes* as we now know it, comprising the move of the Narrator's family to the Hôtel de Guermantes, the gala at the Opéra Comique[2], the Narrator's love for the Duchesse, the autumn at Doncières,[3] and the visit with Saint-Loup to Rachel's villa, but omitting the matinée at Mme de Villeparisis's, which occupied galleys 19 to 28. He added the episode of the grandmother's stroke in the Champs-Élysées and her illness, which he had hitherto intended to place in his third volume between the Princesse de Guermantes's soirée and the last visit to Balbec. He had now decided that it should come immediately after Mme de Villeparisis's matinée and form the conclusion of his second volume, although he had not included it in

[1] It will be noticed that poor Agostinelli had in fact made some progress with the task of typing for which he was engaged in January 1913, since in the autumn of 1912 Proust's typescript had ended with the first visit to Balbec.

[2] Transferred in the final version of 1920 to the Opéra.

[3] Saint-Loup's garrison-town is nameless in this early version.

the material sent to Grasset. The new extracts were sent to Rivière about 13 June, and appeared in the NRF for 1 July.

Only '*Chez Mme Swann*' now remained unused. Proust's old friend Robert de Flers had replaced poor Calmette as editor of *Le Figaro*, and offered to publish it as a *feuilleton* serial in ten instalments. '*Odette mariée*: a long story by the author of that beautiful and great book, *Du Côté de chez Swann*' was announced as a coming attraction on the front page of *Le Figaro* on 15 July. But '*Odette mariée*' never appeared, *Le Côté de Guermantes* in this primitive and imperfect form was not published in October; and Proust was only one of many millions whose innocent hopes in that hot and ordinary July were not to be granted.

Chapter 11

THE DEATH OF SAINT-LOUP
(*August 1914 – January 1916*)

THE sky above Paris had never seemed so blue and crystalline—
for the factories were closed, and their chimneys had ceased to
smoke—as on the Sunday of Mobilisation Day, 3 August 1914, when
Proust saw his brother Robert off to Verdun at the Gare de l'Est.
Batteries of 75's had parked overnight in the Tuileries gardens, and
cavalry bivouacked on the boulevards, with their horses tethered to
the chestnut trees. The good Abbé Mugnier sat amid the tobacco-
smoke and clinking glasses of a café outside the Gare du Nord, hearing
confessions: "Quick, Monsieur l'Abbé, my train's nearly due out!"
Ferdinand Bac visited Colonel Walewski, once Proust's captain at
Orleans, now commander of the Versailles garrison, and offered his
services in vain. "To Berlin!" cried the marching soldiers; but Mme
Lemaire, grimly painting three white roses in a glass vase, remarked to
Henri Bardac: "I've heard all that before, in 1870."

Bac called on Comte Greffulhe at 8 rue d'Astorg, passing in the
courtyard a group of young men in caps and trilbies, sitting on suit-
cases, whom he seemed vaguely to know, and who seemed to know
him: they were the Count's footmen, about to leave for the war. He
entered the open door of the deserted mansion, climbed the state
staircase; and there, in his study at the end of the vast libary,[1] silhouetted black against the delicious sunlight of the summer garden, with its
flowers and birds and peace, was M. Greffulhe, ringing, ringing and
shouting: "Pierre — Jean — Jules! — Where's everybody? Why
doesn't anyone come?" The butler brought cold lunch from the
restaurant at the corner, and shook hands with his feudal master: "I
can't clear up, Monsieur le Comte," he explained, "I've got to go to
Belfort, you'll never see me again, we can't surrender a fortress, so
we'll have to blow ourselves up." "I shall be all alone," cried M.
Greffulhe, "but let Them come, They'll find me here, I'm not the sort

[1] The very library in which the Narrator sees *François le Champi* and meditates on Time Regained.

that runs away." Next day the streets were empty, and the Metro
stopped; the young men, and the husbands, had gone to the Battle of
the Frontiers.

The catastrophe of war was aggravated for Proust by upheavals in
his household. He had quarrelled with Céline and dismissed her some
months before,[1] but kept Nicolas; while Céline's place was filled by
Odilon's wife Céleste, who came in from their home in the working-
class suburb of Levallois, 'to run errands and do a little sewing'. Now
Odilon was called up, and Proust arranged for Céleste to live in: "I've
known you so long, Odilon," he said, "and your wife has only to take
one of the servants' rooms." A few days later Nicolas had to go;
Proust engaged a former valet, who likewise was summoned to the
front; and a sickly youth recommended by Coco de Madrazo ('the
door opened, and in walked Galloping Consumption in person,' he
told Reynaldo) lasted no longer. Proust lingered in Paris, convinced
that he must protect Robert's wife, and his ten-year-old niece Suzy;
but late in August, liberated by their departure to Pau, he began to
think of Cabourg.

During the first three weeks of war three German armies had
poured across Belgium. On the 23rd they broke the French line at
Charleroi, and next day forced the British retreat from Mons: the way
to the capital was open, and 1870 seemed come again. On they flared,
and in the next twelve days covered all but thirty of the hundred and
eighty miles from the frontier to Paris.

The French public was kept unaware of disaster, although some
noticed (like the Narrator)[2] that the sites of German defeats were
drawing ever nearer; but on the 28th the famous communiqué,
announcing that 'our line extends from the Somme to the Vosges',
revealed that Paris was in danger. On the 29th distant guns were
heard; on the 30th a solitary Taube dropped five bombs on the city;
and on 2 September Von Kluck reached Senlis, only twenty-five miles
away. Amiens, Laon, Coucy, Rheims, Saint-Leu-d'Esserent, Senlis!
—the holy places of Proust's Ruskin pilgrimages twelve years before

[1] Perhaps the quarrel was connected with Agostinelli and Anna, and perhaps
Françoise's hostility to Albertine was suggested by Céline's to Agostinelli. The
break took place some time later than November 1913, when Céline was in
hospital for an operation, and Proust sent her a copy of *Du Côté de chez Swann*
inscribed: 'Greetings to the temporary invalid from the perpetual invalid.'
Céleste helped at this time to send out the presentation copies of *Swann*.

[2] III, 750.

had all, within a few days, been desecrated by the enemy. On the night of the 2nd the government left for Bordeaux, and General Galliéni ominously promised he would defend Paris 'to the end'. A million people, women, children, the old, the infirm, the rich and the frightened, fled from the doomed city. Proust was both infirm and rich, though no coward; he stuck it out till the 4th, and then left for Cabourg.

Céleste not only agreed to come with him, but jestingly proposed to disguise herself as a man, an offer which he prudently rejected. The train took twenty-two hours instead of the peace-time five, and was crammed with fellow-fugitives. On the way he thought with anguish of Robert at Verdun, of his friends in danger, of poor Agostinelli. Agostinelli! Seven years ago at Cabourg, a young man of nineteen, a Saint Cecilia in his black cape, he had driven his sleepless master through the landscapes of peaceful Normandy; a year ago he had said: "I can't bear to see you looking so sad," and returned to captivity in Paris; and now he had ceased to exist, and his drowned body was corrupting far away into dust. Would not his ghost meet the master who had slain him, at Cabourg? Proust murmured to himself a favourite line of Verlaine: '*Ah! quand refleuriront les roses de septembre?* —When will September's roses flower again?'[1] At the Grand Hôtel he occupied room No. 147; and Céleste, revisiting the spot in 1953, recognised the little circular window at the end of the corridor, to which he would walk every evening in his dressing-gown, and watch the sun sinking below the sea-horizon.

He emerged at last from the Grand Hôtel to visit the hospital of Cabourg, now crowded with hundreds of wounded soldiers from the Marne. To his relief he found that most were only lightly injured: they ate, slept, walked and laughed. He went every day with gifts, fifty packs of playing-cards, sets of draughts, boxes of chocolates. Some of his new friends were coloured troops from Morocco and Senegal. One day he heard a tactless lady visitor greet her patient with: "Good morning, nigger!", to which the outraged black replied: "Me nigger, you old cow!!"; and he used the incident for Odette's anecdote of Mme Blatin viewing the Cinghalese in the Jardin d'Acclimatation.[2]

One day, when Proust was too ill to see them, Mme Greffulhe called with 'a gentleman', whom he learned later to have been Montesquiou. The Palais Rose had been commandeered by the Army, and the home-

[1] Verlaine, *Sagesse*, III, iii.
[2] I, 536.

less Count Robert had taken refuge in a hotel at Trouville. "We're all
St Francises of Assisi now," he cried, as he trudged up the path of the
Villa Mon Rêve at Bénerville to see Mme de Clermont-Tonnerre,
carrying his own small suitcase and grey with dust; "I wanted to stay
at home, and let the Germans shoot the author of twenty volumes on
his own doorstep! Now, if I'm spared, perhaps I shall die the author of
thirty volumes.[1] I couldn't bear to bury my pastels and hide my porce-
lain; so I offer my Palais Rose to Destiny." Isadora Duncan the dancer
saw him pacing the seafront beneath her windows at the Hôtel de
Normandie, and asked the Count to give her a baby, 'to soothe my
nerves'; but he preferred to solace his own sorrows over bowl after
bowl of humble mussels with Mme de Clermont-Tonnerre. Meanwhile Mme Straus, 'with the aid,' she said, 'of various duchesses who
have strayed to this coast, and resident cocottes who are a great deal
more efficient', was organising soup-kitchens for Belgian refugees.
Montesquiou sighed for Artagnan: "I'd have peace and quiet there, I
could eat my own eggs!" Soon, in the castle of his musketeer ancestor,
he was hard at work producing war-elegies, with a fecundity he had
never known since the death of Yturri. "If you hear me groaning," he
told his servants, "it means I'm writing poetry and mustn't be disturbed."

Proust visited Mme Straus at the Clos des Mûriers, and for the last
time saw M. Straus pruning his beloved roses, like M. Verdurin at La
Raspelière. He engaged in a good-humoured disputation with a
fellow-guest, the great Réjane (Berma herself), on the war-time ban-
ning of Wagner, which he deplored; "she called me a Boche, and
nearly pushed me into a rosebush". About 12 October, all his money
spent on gifts for the soldiers, he returned to Paris. On the train he
was seized by an appalling attack of asthma, and Céleste, thinking
him on the point of death, forced her way past the angry guard
into the luggage-van to fetch his medicine. At Cabourg, where he
had dreaded the revival of memories of Agostinelli, he had seemed,
as he told Lucien Daudet, 'to feel a little less grief, and feared I was
beginning to forget; but when I came home I was glad to find this
was only a false alarm'. The 'intermittent progress of oblivion' had
begun.

Meanwhile the vast events had occurred which made Germany's
ultimate defeat inevitable, but also ensured that the war would last for

---

[1] As indeed he did.

several years. After sacking Senlis on 2 September, Von Kluck turned
left to the Marne: in the next fortnight the remaining French armies
must be surrounded, in a gigantic Sedan, and the six-weeks war of the
Schlieffen Plan be punctually over. But a new French army, based on
Paris, had been formed under General Maunoury (brother of the
surgeon who operated on Proust's Aunt Amiot); and the British
Expeditionary Force, which was thought broken and scattered far to
the north, was south-east of Paris and ready to fight again. From the
6th to the 9th the German right flank was counter-attacked in the
Battle of the Marne and driven back forty miles to the Aisne. A series
of attempts by each side to outflank the other to the north developed
into a race for the coast; by mid-November the line from Verdun to
Flanders was stabilised, and four years of trench warfare began. Paris
was never in danger again until the spring of 1918; but the French had
lost five hundred thousand men.

Among those who fled to Bordeaux, not in fear but in tragic
defiance, was Ferdinand Bac, who on alighting saw none other than
Mme de Chevigné, exchanging embraces with the working-class
family who had made room for her in their third-class carriage. There
were no beds in the city; and as Bac and the countess settled in an
empty train, they saw an endless line of cattle-trucks pass, loaded with
haggard young men in clotted brown bandages, the wounded from
the north. Weeping bitterly, Mme de Chevigné threw to them all she
had: the remains of her modest dinner of rolls and gruyère, her silver
cigarette-case, the contents of her handbag; and Bac saw in her face not
only terror and despair, but an outburst of selfless love to which she
had been many years a stranger. Bac went on to Bayonne, where he
found Mme de Noailles at the hospital ("Here I am, it's all I'm good
for, I recite poetry to them and write to their mothers"). At Pau he
met Mme Straus; they walked past the cemetery, where a young
woman knelt by a grave: "will scientists ever invent pills to cure a
broken heart?" enquired Mme Straus.

Others, however, had left Paris in the opposite direction, to con-
front the enemy in their beloved, menaced châteaux. Mme Lemaire
and Suzette waited dourly at Réveillon, which for a single day, on 5
September, the eve of the Marne, was within the fringe of the German
advance. As they walked in the garden a German officer on horseback
jumped the hedge, clapped his monocle to his eye, cried: "I wanted to
see Madeleine Lemaire, and now I have!" and galloped away. That
night a German detachment billeted in the château. Memories of

Réveillon and Suzette in 1895 had already served for the Narrator's last visit to Tansonville and walks with Gilberte; and the courage of mother and daughter at Réveillon in 1914 suggested Gilberte's heroic lingering at Tansonville in the war, which involved the transfer of Combray from the distant Beauce to the front line. Certain rivals, however, pretended that Mme Lemaire's behaviour in the war was, somehow, defeatist rather than brave; and Proust seems to reflect this calumny when the Narrator reports that Gilberte fled to Tansonville 'because the incessant Taube raids had terrified her so', and makes her praise 'the perfect breeding' of the German officers whom she is forced to billet.[1]

Proust was now harrowed by ceaseless anxiety for his relatives and friends. In October Robert Proust's field-hospital at Étain near Verdun was bombarded, and shell-fragments struck the table on which he operated; he was mentioned in despatches, promoted to captain, and continued to seek posts of utmost danger. Proust's youngest Mayer cousin was killed in the summer of 1915. The son of his former sweetheart Antoinette Faure died at Charleroi; Mme Scheikévitch lost her brother, whom Proust had glimpsed at Larue's; Charles Catusse was wounded in the Vosges, Henri Bardac on the Marne, Jacques Rivière was taken prisoner at Éton near Verdun on 24 August 1914, and Rivière's brother-in-law Alain-Fournier, the miraculous author of Le Grand Meaulnes, disappeared for ever on 22 September. Reynaldo was posted with Fernand Gregh and Robert Dreyfus to a regimental depot at Albi in Provence; but in spite of Proust's entreaties—'my little Albigensian, you must try to remain such'—he demanded to be sent to the front, and succeeded in November 1914. At Vauquois in the Meuse Reynaldo saw and risked death every day, intrepid for himself but anguished for others; he listened to the music of bombardment with the same invariable cigarette in his lips as when, at Mme Lemaire's twenty years before, he listened to his own; and he composed a gay regimental march which all the soldiers in the 31st used to whistle. Cocteau, wearing a beautiful uniform specially created by Poiret, joined a fantastic ambulance unit organised by Misia Edwards and her third husband-to-be, the Spanish

---

[1] III, 751. Proust adjusts the chronology and topography of the battle when he makes the Germans reach Tansonville 'after beating our troops at La Fère'— presumably La Fère-Champenoise, about thirty miles east of Réveillon, where the Germans won a temporary success in counter-attacking Foch on 8 September.

painter José Maria Sert. René Blum was an interpreter at Amiens, Lucien Daudet worked in a canteen at Tours, Jacques Bizet served at the Hôpital Saint-Martin, Lauris joined Gide at the Foyer Franco-Belge, a relief centre for Belgian refugees, and Albufera was Joffre's chauffeur. Loche Radziwill organised a Polish brigade, and finding that every volunteer wanted to be an officer, issued a standing order: 'There will also be privates in the Polish Army'.

At moments Proust imagined that he, too, would like to be pronounced fit for military service; but usually he felt it would be a disaster not only for himself but for his country: 'not to speak of the incapacity caused by my health, I ask myself what chaos I might not introduce into the services,' he told Mme Catusse. Three years before, on 6 September 1911, he had at last been struck off the territorial army lists in the rank of administrative officer in the Health Service; but the wartime regulations demanded that he should undergo a new medical examination. For a whole year he awaited the summons, sometimes pulling wires (Dr Pozzi had been most helpful in the very first month of war), sometimes with anxious resignation. He was, and always had been, fearless of danger; we shall find him later taking the same delight in air-raids as Cocteau or Apollinaire in shell-fire. But he was by now permanently unfit, both in body and in mind, for any way of life other than insomnia, asthma, fumigation, and confinement to bed for six and a half days in every week. Antoine Bibesco had expressed the fantastic unthinkability of Marcel's going to the wars, in an unfeeling telegram sent on Mobilisation Day: 'Hope they put you in the shock troops,' he wired.

Nevertheless, the war became part of his life. He deeply loved his country, its people, his friends and all who were dear to them, and suffered with their suffering. 'I have assimilated the war so completely, alas, that I can't isolate it,' he wrote to Princesse Soutzo later; 'it is not so much an object, for me, in the philosophical sense of the word, as a substance interposed between myself and all objects. As people used to love in God, I live in the war.' Then, no less profoundly, absorption in the war became a duty, a curiosity, an aspect of the search for truth; the war was a mysterious entity, sinister yet exhilarating, which it was imperative though impossible to fathom, like love or death. In his letters he explored and shared the longings, the anxiety, the grief of everyone he knew; he read seven newspapers every day, striving to pierce to the reality behind the communiqués, and followed the battles on a General Staff map. Proust particularly admired Henri

Bidou's daily articles, '*The Military Situation*', in the *Journal des Débats* ('clear and remarkable, the only decent things I've read about the war')[1]; though when Bidou began to combine this sacred office with the secular post of dramatic critic on *Le Journal*, he remarked, a little shocked: "I wonder he doesn't get mixed up!" For Brichot's articles on the war, however, which Mme Verdurin ridicules ostensibly for their absurdity, but really because they have won him admittance to the salons of the noble Faubourg, Proust thought of Joseph Reinach's column in *Le Figaro*, under the pseudonym 'Polybe'.[2] 'The abuse of his ridiculous metaphors, his inability to forget anything he ever learned, his mock brevity, like a pinchbeck Michelet, prevent me from doing justice to his articles, though they are otherwise so serious and sound, so authoritative in their competence and inexhaustible knowledge,' Proust wrote to Mme Catusse in much the same language as the Narrator of poor Brichot, whose articles are 'decked with the paste jewels that we have seen him lavishing so often on the Faithful, yet rich in a very real erudition', and contain, exclaims the Narrator, 'such knowledge, such intelligence, such sound reasoning!' 'Polybe's friends laugh him to scorn,' reported Proust; and Mme Straus, for one, was not sorry to join in the fun against her former admirer, while M. Straus, all through the war, made a collection of 'Polybiana'.

Gaston de Caillavet was the first of Proust's friends to die during the war, though, as it happened, not in the war. Gaston had been painfully ill in Périgord since the summer, accepting his destiny with noble resignation; and Proust, to whose constant enquiries Jeanne had replied too reassuringly, was overwhelmed to read in *Le Figaro* on 14 January 1915 of his death. He wept, thinking of their friendship twenty-five years before, when Gaston's army year was nearly over and his own just beginning, of Gaston's first formal letters, which began 'Dear Sir', of their absurd rivalry for the love of Jeanne, and of Gaston's beautiful daughter Simone, whom he had not seen again,

---

[1] In conversation with the widowed Gilberte at the Princesse de Guermantes's matinée the Narrator regrets that Saint-Loup died too soon to read the article of Bidou ('for whom he had a profound admiration, and who visibly had a great influence on his military ideas') on the German offensive of March 1918 (III, 981).

[2] Characteristically Proust differentiates his character from the model by emphasising Brichot's anti-Dreyfusism, and mentioning that he never collected his articles into a volume; whereas Reinach, the arch-Dreyfusist, sedulously reprinted his in no fewer than nineteen volumes: *La Guerre de 1914. Les commentaires de Polybe* (1915-19). Cf. III, 789-93.

although whenever Gaston met him he would proudly say: "Come and see her, she's a marvel of intelligence!" He must talk to Jeanne; and soon after her return to Paris he arrived at 12 Avenue Hoche by taxi, after midnight, and was deeply hurt to find the house unlit, and deaf to his chauffeur's honking. Others, he darkly hinted, had a shorter memory than his for love and friendship, and there would be remarks on this subject in the next volume of his novel. Jeanne goodnaturedly arranged to visit 102 Boulevard Haussmann. As she entered in her widow's veils Marcel cried, bursting into tears: "My dear Gaston is dead!" and then, alternately sobbing and laughing at the images of Time Lost, took from a cardboard box laid ready on his bed the photographs of their past: Gaston as a soldier, himself as a soldier, himself at the tennis party in the Boulevard Bineau, Gaston again. "I must go, Marcel, I'm hurting you too much," said Jeanne as he wept still more bitterly at her account of Gaston's last days. Saint-Loup was dead, and Gilberte a widow. But Gaston was only the first in time of his Saint-Loups. Already Proust was alarmed for Fénelon, of whom no news had come since early in December.

After his return from Washington in October 1909 Bertrand de Fénelon had remained in Paris until May 1912, when he was transferred in succession to Rio de Janeiro, Havana and Christiania. He had served during 1908 at the French Legation in Peking, where he was photographed below a Chinese verandah, grave and bearded, with a Siamese cat on his shoulder. In April 1914, on his last leave in Paris, he asked to see the exquisite, seventeen-year-old Marguerite Lahovary, Princesse Marthe Bibesco's younger sister, whom he had met two years before and remembered; and all three visited the Musée Cernuschi, where he explained the beauty of Far-Eastern art to these Europeans of the Near East. 'A young girl passed by', wrote the princess later, 'on the bye-road which was leading Bertrand out of this life'. In August he was still in Christiania and could have stayed, for diplomats were exempt from mobilisation; but he demanded to be allowed to fight, and passed that autumn through England on his last journey. At the London embassy the young Paul Morand, who had recently read *Swann* with enthusiasm, questioned him about Proust, and was struck by the guarded manner in which Fénelon replied. 'He called up not so much Marcel's presence as his phantom,' said Morand, and he gave the impression that to know Proust was to belong to a particularly select secret society. But Fénelon was not entirely discreet; he remarked that Proust had "published two books at his own

expense, and no doubt will remain unknown", and added: "he is a
Saturnian, and a very difficult friend". 'Saturnian' had been the accepted slang for 'homosexual' in the Fénelon-Bibesco-Proust circle,
but its meaning was perfectly understood elsewhere.

Fénelon's new comrades in the army noticed the same faint, ironic
smile which his friends had known twelve years before. 'My constant
aim, my only thought, is the liberation of our territory, the salvation
of our nation and our country,' he wrote, 'and if I can make the least
contribution to it, though unnoticed in the multitude, I shall feel I am
happy and my task will be done.' Saint-Loup might have thought it
more elegant to leave this resolve unexpressed; but perhaps it was still
more elegant, when it came from the heart, to express it, and certainly
no one had better right than Fénelon. 'He was always to the front,
always in the post of most danger, always completely calm, even gay,'
reported his superiors. His regiment was hurled into the useless First
Battle of Artois in December 1914, and Fénelon was killed at Mametz
on the 17th. For several months his fate remained obscure, and it was
hoped he might have been taken prisoner. There was a mysterious
rumour about a person in a motor-car, who claimed to have seen him
alive, but could never be found again. At last, on 15 March 1915,
Proust read in his morning *Figaro*: 'The sad news we have just
received concerning Sub-Lieutenant de Salignac-Fénelon puts an end,
alas, to the lingering hope that he might be found alive. After a
desperate struggle, at the very moment when he was calling on the
enemy to surrender, he received a mortal wound from a bullet in the
head. The family photographs he carried on him seem to leave no
doubt as to his identity.'

Proust had seen Fénelon rarely since 1902, and hardly at all since the
party at *Le Circuit* on 27 November 1909. A last letter, in which
Bertrand displayed his typical plain-speaking, had 'cooled my friendship for him still further,' he told Lauris. But for Fénelon, who died
the death of Saint-Loup, he mourned as the Narrator for Saint-Loup:
'I am in tears, because they say now there is no hope of his being a
prisoner,' he wrote to Lucien Daudet; 'I shall mourn him for ever,' he
told Clément de Maugny. He had written his novel on the plan of his
life, but now, with the vanishing of Agostinelli and Fénelon, life was
beginning to write his novel.

Another heroic death that spring resembled the end of Saint-Loup.
Vicomte Robert d'Humières, the proud and talented translator of
Kipling and Conrad, who had helped Proust with Ruskin and

reviewed *La Bible d' Amiens*,[1] was 'one of the Robert de Montesquious of this world, if I may use the expression,' wrote Ferdinand Bac. Bac had visited his lonely villa near Grasse in Provence; he noticed Henri Bataille's portrait of his host in youth as a cavalry-officer, with plumed helmet but bare, epicene chest, and the inscription: 'to my very dear friend Robert d'Humières'; in the garden stood an antique statue of Narcissus, 'pointing with an unequivocal gesture to the part of his body which he loved best'; and Humières's silent and self-effacing wife, with her infant daughter, seemed (like Gilberte at Tansonville) 'to carry in secret the burden of a vast, disappointed illusion'. Montesquiou wrote, in one of his venomous little couplets:

> *'With Humières you've left your son?*
> *Better make sure the light's still on.'*

Overwhelmed by an impending scandal Humières demanded to be posted to a Zouave regiment in the front line, and took the first opportunity of charging to his death. Proust read the news in the *Journal des Débats* on 13 May 1915, and linked his name with Fénelon's in letters to his friends: 'I weep day and night for Fénelon and Humières, as if I had left them only yesterday,' he told Mme Catusse. Perhaps, although there were many such, Humières was the invert to whom, as Proust remarked later to Paul Morand, 'love of men brought virility, and virility brought glory'. 'There are certain deaths I should like to discuss with you,' he told Robert de Billy, 'which I admire none the less, but which differ from the picture-postcard manner in which they are usually represented.'

Proust's life was more solitary in 1915 than ever before. His friends were far away, his hostesses had turned their mansions and châteaux into hospitals and their daughters into nurses, and all social life had ceased. He had increased his solitude by giving up his telephone in December 1914, ostensibly because of his 'ruin'; instead, Céleste used the telephone in a neighbouring café for her master's messages. Often during the spring he thought of retiring for a year, at the end of which the war would surely be over, to Nice or even to Venice, but waited in Paris for his ever-delayed medical board. In March he was distressed

---

[1] In *Chronique des arts et de la curiosité*, 12 March 1904. In return Proust reviewed Humières's *L'Ile et l'Empire de la Grande Bretagne* in the same periodical on 13 August 1904 (this article has not previously been noticed). The translation of Barrie's *Margaret Ogilvie*, which Proust mentioned admiringly in his *Figaro* article of 20 March 1907, '*Journées de Lecture*', was also by Humières.

by a malicious rumour that he had been heard to remark: "I haven't had time to think about the war yet, I'm still studying the Caillaux Affair." On 30 May, the first anniversary of Agostinelli's death, he asked Mme Catusse, then at her villa in Nice, to arrange for a wreath to bei delivered to the dead man's sister and laid on his grave; but remembering the poor reception of the 400-franc wreath the year before, he po ntedly ordered one to cost 40 francs only, 'as showy as possible'. Mlle Agostinelli, he explained apologetically, was living in sin, but her union was otherwise highly respectable, and had lasted for twenty years.[1] Ever since November 1914 Proust had been begging his friends on the Riviera—Gautier-Vignal, Mme Catusse, even Reynaldo's former secretary's cousin—to find a job for the destitute Émile Agostinelli.[2] In this May he at last succeeded in persuading Edmond Rostand to take him as chauffeur, but not for long; for Italy joined the war on 23 May, and Émile was killed a few months later at Gorizia on the Isonzo. He continued to keep benevolent ward over Anna, finding her excellent jobs in which she never stayed long. In October 1916 he refused her obstinate request to be recommended to Jacques Bizet for work in a munitions factory: it was too tiring for her, he explained to Mme Straus, and he would not be a party to it, 'any more than I consented to her poor husband's flying over the sea'. After this, in his published letters, the living Agostinellis are heard of no more; but no doubt his benevolence continued. Poor Nicolas Cottin caught pleurisy at the front in 1916 and died. Céline in her grief made no secret of her belief that the stifling air of 102 Boulevard Haussmann had given him his weak chest: 'You accuse me of Nicolas's death!' wrote Proust bitterly.

In June 1915 Proust visited Jacques Émile Blanche at Auteuil, where he complained of the cold; his host obligingly closed the window, lent him his cloak, and in delicate allusion to the opening chapter of Swann warmed him with an infusion of lime-tea. Since April Proust had been kindly but meddlesomely correcting the proofs of Blanche's

---

[1] Her lover was a certain Baron Duquesne, about whom Proust had heard from Agostinelli, and had recently asked for more from Gautier-Vignal, who knew the Baron as an old friend of his father. Proust seems to have used this relationship for the episode in which the squinting page-boy at Balbec tells of his sister's liaison with a wealthy man: "once she wanted to come home instead of staying respectable, but mother took the silly fool back to her friend, and quick too!" (II, 979-80).

[2] It is said that Émile Agostinelli took his brother's place as Proust's secretary for a time, presumably in July and August 1914.

Cahiers d'un Artiste, a talented and scandalous series of letters on the war, which introduced many of their society friends under disguised names, and ultimately reached six volumes. They worked on the proofs for a time; Proust recited the names of his friends dead at the war, lamented the ill-health 'which prevents me from doing my duty', and cried: "I ought to have fought like them!" Then, until dawn, he explained 'the architectural construction' of his novel; and as he revealed the significance in it of Sodom and Gomorrah, his voice grew louder, and Blanche, appalled, rose to shut the door that led to his sleeping household.

Montesquiou now arranged to read his first volume of war-poems, *Les Offrandes Blessées*, to a group of lucky friends at the Palais Rose. '188 elegies on the war,' Proust wrote in awe to Mme Catusse, 'he must have started on Mobilisation Day!' Proust evaded the reading, but not a punitive visit to his bedside in July, when the Count promised to go after five minutes and stayed for seven hours, chattering with the most astonishing and fatiguing brilliance. Montesquiou's own impressions were not altogether favourable: 'he's always ill, or rather, invariably in bed,' he wrote in his vengeful memoirs a few years later, recalling this visit, 'and one also notices jampots, not to mention chamber-pots'. Proust and Count Robert were destined never to meet again.

After being adopted as a mascot by a company of marines in Flanders, recommended for the *croix de guerre*, arrested as a spy, and rescued in the car of a general who happened to be a friend of his father (the Marines were wiped out next day), Cocteau had returned to Paris. Since the death of her husband in 1911 Mme de Chevigné had taken an apartment in Jean's family home at 10 rue d'Anjou, with its antiquated lift—"it dates from the period before lifts were invented," said Cocteau—and her star guest Joseph Reinach nicknamed her affectionately 'the Comtesse d'Anjou'. When Cocteau hugged her lapdog Kiss on the stairs, and the countess shouted: "Look out! I don't want him smothered in your facepowder!", they became great friends. In August Proust called on them both, and Jean found him sitting at midnight in the darkness on the top landing. "Why didn't you wait in my room, Marcel, you know I always leave the door ajar?" "Dear Jean," replied Marcel, "Napoleon had a man *shot* for waiting for him in his room."

At last, towards the same time, Proust was twice visited by medical majors, who to his horror were quite unaware, despite all his pulling

of wires, that he was the invalid son of Dr Adrien Proust and the
brother of Dr Robert Proust. "You're an architect, aren't you?" they
said; but fortunately he was so obviously ill that they exempted him
for six months. 'This is a recommendation which is certain to become
more and more cogent until my death,' he commented grimly to
Lucien.

Soon afterwards, at the urging of Coco de Madrazo and Lucien, he
twice called on Comte Joachim Clary, a retired gentleman in waiting
of the exiled Empress Eugénie, in his apartment in the Rue Galilée.
Clary was half-blind, paralysed and slowly dying, and was tended by a
faithful Japanese valet named Mineguishi, whom he had found on his
travels working as a waiter in a hotel at Kyoto. No doubt Proust's
memory of this situation reinforced his impression of the last days of
the Prince de Sagan, when he wrote of Charlus stricken in sight and
limbs under the care of Jupien. He rewarded Mineguishi with a signed
copy of *Swann*, 'because I kept him up till the most unearthly hours'.

Two authors from whom Proust constructed a little of Bergotte
died in the first period of the war: Jules Lemaître on 2 August 1914,
and Paul Hervieu on 25 October 1915. With his red face and snow-
white beard Lemaître had come to resemble 'a hot-house strawberry,
nestling in January on a bed of cottonwool,' said Cocteau, whom
Lemaître had met at Mme Scheikévitch's, and called, as the wise
Prospero called his familiar spirit, 'my Ariel'. Lemaître's rôle as the
sovereign guest and recognised lover of Mme de Loynes was curiously
parallel to that of France in Mme Arman's salon, Hervieu's in Mme de
Pierrebourg's, and Bergotte's in Mme Swann's. Proust had met
Hervieu in the earliest days of his life in society, in the salons of Mmes
Straus, Aubernon, Baignères and Arman, and had last seen him at
Mme Straus's two months before. He remembered with remorse that
he had never forgiven Hervieu's voting against his novel for the
Académie Française prize in June 1914; and in one of his letters of
condolence to the heartbroken Mme de Pierrebourg he told her,
alluding to the death of Bergotte, that in his 'third volume' she would
find a discussion of 'death, or rather this discord between the survival
of the person we have lost and his apparent annihilation from the
universe', which would bring her both pain and comfort.

On the outbreak of war Proust's publisher Grasset, together with
most of his small staff and his printers, had been called to the army, and
the appearance of Proust's second volume, originally planned for
October 1914, was postponed for the duration of hostilities. Never-

theless, nearly the whole volume was already in print, in the proofs he
had received in June, and the final pages were typed, perhaps by Émile
Agostinelli, early in July. Proust had warned Grasset in April 1914 of
'the alterations which, knowing myself as I do, I am afraid I shall be
forced to make', and this revision probably occupied his last visit to
Cabourg and the autumn of 1914. The rewriting of the 'third' volume,
which continued till the end of his life, was a natural continuation of
the same process, and must have begun early in 1915. In April he confessed to Robert de Billy his hope that he would be rejected for military
service, 'because I know how useless I should be, and because my last
remains of health would be destroyed before I could finish my novel';
and in July he told Montesquiou: 'I am saving what little strength I
have for the novel which, if God wills, I am in course of finishing.' By
November 1915 he had completed a first version of *Albertine Disparue*,
for he then covered the blank pages of Mme Scheikévitch's copy of
Swann with a résumé of the whole Albertine episode, from the
Narrator's first meeting with her at Balbec to his final oblivion after
her death.[1] Proust's funeral march of separation and everlasting farewell has the note, more than any other section of his novel, of
immediate experience rather than Time remembered; for he began
Albertine Disparue when his grief for Agostinelli was still fresh, and
wrote of oblivion as he attained it.

As the end of 1915 approached he felt his old melancholy for the
dying year, but for a new reason. 'These sad days remind us,' he wrote
to Antoine Bibesco, 'that the years return laden with the same natural
beauty, but cannot bring back people. Alas, 1916 will have its violets
and apple-blossom, but never again will there be a Bertrand de
Fénelon.' Saint-Loup was dead, and youth and friendship lay with
him in his unknown grave by the Somme.

[1] Embedded in this summary are two extracts from the quarrel and reconciliation scene after Mme de Cambremer's visit to Balbec (II, 833, 835), followed by
seventeen passages on the Narrator's grief and jealousy after the death of
Albertine, in the very order in which they occur in the novel (III, 419, 420, 430,
447, 475, 478, 483, 484, 490, 520 (cf. also 1104, note on 519), 529, 531 (note,
p. 1104), 557, 558, 595-6, 601, 644).

Chapter 12

THE VINTEUIL SEPTET
(*February 1916 – March 1917*)

ON 21 February 1916 the atrocious agony of Verdun began, and persisted until 2 November. Of this, the longest and bloodiest battle of the war, Proust thought in the letter from Gilberte at Tansonville in 1916. The Battle of Méséglise has raged 'for more than eight months,' she remarks, 'the Germans have lost more than six hundred thousand men there', the obscure Roussainville has become a name as glorious as Austerlitz or Valmy, and the cornfield above the hawthorn path is now the famous Hill 307.[1] Perhaps Proust was unaware that nameless hills in the battle-zone were called after their height in metres; certainly, it was absurd to imply that the gentle eminence of the hawthorn path could be a thousand feet in height; but he knew that one of the focal points of the Verdun conflict, and the only significant objective of this altitude in all the Western Front north of the Vosges, was known as Hill 304.

On 25 February Gide called on Proust, whom he had not met since 1892. Among the subjects they discussed, besides homosexuality, were Proust's novel, the news that Rivière was rereading *Swann* with delight in his German prison-camp, and Grasset's inability to publish the second volume. Gide reopened the suggestion of migrating to the NRF, and Proust repeated that it was impossible, but with less conviction than two years before. A committee-meeting of the NRF on 14 April resulted in a new proposal to take over *A la Recherche*; and this unlooked-for second chance was another turning-point in Proust's long way to future fame.

Exactly two years had passed since the NRF's first repentant offer in the spring of 1914, and the situation was now fundamentally changed. It is likely that Proust had then refused not only out of loyalty to Grasset, but as a proud rebuke for their rejection of his novel in December 1912. By this second approach, however, the NRF had at last expiated their error. Moreover, since their printers

[1] III, 755-6.

were now at work again, they were able to propose immediate publication. Proust had resolved not to publish until the war was over; but even so, proofs could be printed and corrected meanwhile, and the volumes made ready for publication at the first suitable moment after the coming of peace. By deserting Grasset he might well gain as much as a year in his race against death. He resolved to accept, and to approach Grasset as before through the good offices of René Blum.

The negotiations with Grasset were difficult and painful. Moved by relentless determination in the higher cause of his novel, and suppressed guilt for abandoning the lesser duty towards his publisher, Proust for once displayed something less than his usual magnanimity. Remembering Grasset's almost excessive sympathy when told in July 1914 of his losses on the stock exchange, he decided to plead his imaginary ruin, and pretended that it was from need of money, and with the intention of publishing without delay, that he wished to accept the NRF's offer. He was convinced that he had behaved throughout with extraordinary generosity, that Grasset had failed him and was morally and financially in his debt. Owing to the moratorium imposed by the war Proust had received neither accounts nor royalties since April 1914. On the other hand, Grasset had already incurred considerable expense by printing nearly the whole of the second volume in proof, and making Proust's extensive corrections; he had given Proust an excellent contract, with 20 per cent royalties, for this and the rest of the work; and now he was expected to relinquish not only the future volumes but the already successful *Du Côté de chez Swann* without compensation, to sign away one of his most promising authors without protest, almost as an atonement for injury.

At first, however, Grasset was unfindable, for the two respectable ladies who now formed his only staff refused to give his address. As it happened, poor Grasset had fallen gravely ill with typhoid in the summer of 1915, and after six months in a military hospital had retired, semi-incognito, to a Swiss sanatorium at Neuchâtel. May and June were wasted in trying to trace him, with the aid of René Blum, Léon Bailby, Lauris, Albert Sorel's son, and a bribe to Grasset's concierge; and July and August passed in an exchange of letters through the slow posts to Switzerland. Grasset, though pained, was dignified and fair; he appealed to his illness, the war, the expenses he had already met for the second volume; he asked Proust to reconsider, but made no threat of standing on his legal rights. 'I have too much pride to retain an author who has lost confidence in me,' he told Blum, 'and I will facilitate the complete recovery of his freedom.' Even this was not enough. Sternly beginning 'Dear Sir' instead of his usual 'Dear Friend', Proust retorted with deep umbrage to fancied charges of egoism, shirking and lack of patriotism, resumed his strangely inaccurate wrangling over the proofs of vol. 2, and offered almost insultingly 'a small indemnity, though I don't see the reason for it'. Grasset saw that further argument would be useless, and made no effort to exculpate himself. 'The poor man makes me feel sorry for him, so I've been as conciliatory and cordial as I could,' he told Blum; and to Proust himself he wrote on 29 August; 'it was only natural that I should not renounce a valued author without showing my regret, and there was no reason here for your feelings to be hurt; but I do not wish to increase your troubles by any act of mine. Whatever the sacrifice, I forego publishing the second volume of *A la Recherche du Temps Perdu*.' Proust replied about 22 September, beginning once more 'Dear Friend'. Grasset had behaved admirably, Proust less so; but the transaction which was to enable him to perfect his novel and know the bliss of fame in his lifetime was accomplished.

A major reason for Proust's migration was the ever-increasing size of *A la Recherche*, which made the resumption of publication still more urgent. He had originally written two further volumes of the same length as *Du Côté de chez Swann*, but these, as he told Blum on 31 May 1916, had now become four. The evolution of his novel, from its premature completion in summer 1912 to its final published form, was already far advanced. The nature and significance of these changes must now be examined.

As to the extent of the alterations certainty is possible. *Du Côté de chez Swann* (525 pages in Grasset's edition) contains 170,000 words, and the remaining two volumes, each of approximately equal size and totalling about 340,000 words, would have brought the total of the 1912 version to 510,000 words. The second volume (originally called *Le Côté de Guermantes*) was intended to include what later became *A l'Ombre des Jeunes Filles en Fleurs* and *Le Côté de Guermantes*, comprising in the final version 445,000 words[1]: it was therefore considerably more than doubled. But the largest increase occurred in the last volume, containing the remainder of the novel, which ultimately reached 626,000 words, although as will be seen Proust transferred

---

[1] This and the following figures are reached by multiplying the number of pages in each section in the *Pléiade* edition by 400, the approximate number of words in each page.

two long episodes from it to positions earlier in the novel: it was therefore nearly quadrupled. The final version of *A la Recherche* contains
1,240,000 words; and the volumes after *Du Côté de chez Swann* were
enlarged from 340,000 words to 1,070,000.

The chapter-headings of the original second and third volumes
were printed opposite the title-page of *Du Côté de chez Swann* in 1913,
and give invaluable information on the contents and structure of the
1912 version. They read as follows: LE CÔTÉ DE GUERMANTES (Chez
Mme Swann.—Noms de pays: le pays.—Premiers crayons du baron
de Charlus et de Robert de Saint-Loup.—Noms de personnes: la
duchesse de Guermantes.—Le salon de Mme de Villeparisis.); LE
TEMPS RETROUVÉ (A l'ombre des jeunes filles en fleurs.—La princesse
de Guermantes.—M. de Charlus et les Verdurin.—Mort de ma
grand'mère.—Les intermittences du cœur.—Les "Vices et les
Vertus" de Padoue et de Combray.—Madame de Cambremer.—
Mariage de Robert de Saint-Loup.—L'Adoration perpétuelle).

The proofs of the second volume printed in June 1914 survive, and
although their present location remains unknown their contents have
been thoroughly studied by Professor Feuillerat, and can be compared in detail with the final version. They comprise 66 galleys,[1] each
containing the text of eight pages, a total of 528 pages.[2] The alterations
in the final version consist partly of retouching, in which Proust
clarifies, enriches and enhances his style and meaning, partly of
additions, which occur at almost every page and range from single
phrases to long new episodes. In *A l'Ombre des Jeunes Filles en Fleurs*,
which Proust enlarged from 98,000 to 210,000 words, the dinners with
Norpois and Bergotte, the Narrator's visits to Odette, Odette's tea-
party with Mme Cottard, the suppers at Rivebelle, the visits to Elstir's
studio at Balbec are greatly enlarged. New episodes include the meeting with Princesse Mathilde in the Bois,[3] the Narrator's glimpse of
Rachel in the brothel and his gift of Aunt Léonie's furniture to the
proprietress, his dinner with the Blochs at Balbec, and the superb
comparison of the glass-fronted restaurant at Rivebelle to an aqua-

---

[1] Galleys 15 and 16 are wanting, but once existed. Nos. 1-28 (224 pages)
comprise *Le Côté de Guermantes* (these, as already explained, were printed first
in order to supply the NRF extracts of July 1914); nos. 29-66 (304 pages)
comprise *A l'Ombre*.

[2] Proust's estimate that vol. 2 would be of approximately the same length as
Du Côté de chez Swann (525 pages) is thus confirmed.

[3] Proust was at work on this in April 1915, when he asked Lucien Daudet for
technical information on the Princesse's dress.

rium. None of these additions shows any intention to change the main narrative; still less, as some critics have maintained, do they inflate or disrupt it. Proust's revision, both here and throughout the remainder of his novel, springs from a new conception of the ideal scale of *A la Recherche*; his purpose, which he perfectly achieves, is not to expand it, but to bring it to its true magnitude.

Two further alterations in *A l'Ombre*, however, amount to major structural changes. The episode of the Narrator's quarrel with Gilberte, his sight of her at dusk in the Avenue des Champs-Élysées with a young man, (who long afterwards turns out to have been the actress Léa in disguise), and the 'irregular progress of oblivion', is absent from the 1912 version. By inserting it Proust not only deepens the significance of the Narrator's calf-love, but provides an indispensable link between Swann's love and oblivion of Odette at the beginning of *A la Recherche*, and the Narrator's of Albertine at the end. Most important and surprising of all is the omission from the 1912 version of all mention of Albertine and the little band; for the first visit to Balbec then included only the Narrator's relations with Mme de Villeparisis, Saint-Loup, Charlus and Elstir. The table of contents to Volume Three shows that originally there were three sojourns at Balbec, of which the meeting with Albertine and her friends was to form the second, situated in the summer after Mme de Villeparisis's matinée[1] and immediately before the Princesse de Guermantes's soirée. Proust now transferred most of this chapter[2] to the first visit to Balbec, into which he interwove it with consummate skill. The structural advantages of this change are manifest: the first visit to Balbec receives a new depth and beauty, it is fully counterpoised with what now becomes the second and last, and the great theme of the Narrator's love for Albertine ramifies throughout the novel instead of being confined to the last third.[3]

---

[1] This is why at Doncières (II, 124) and again at Mme de Villeparisis's matinée (II, 225, 276) the Narrator announces his next visit to Balbec for the following spring, whereas in the final version it takes place three years after the first.

[2] A meeting with Morel (then still called Santois) at a concert in the Casino was transferred to the later visit and situated at the railway-station at Doncières.

[3] With the same purpose in view Proust now inserted in *Chez Mme Swann* the first warning hints of the theme of Albertine. Gilberte remembers her at school: "she'll certainly turn out very 'fast' one day," adds Gilberte, "and meanwhile she has the most peculiar ways". Mme Bontemps at Odette's tea-party repeats her niece Albertine's insulting remark to the wife of the under-secretary of state for finance ("Your father was a dishwasher"—in the 1912 version the culprit is

Le Côté de Guermantes in the 1912 version totalled about 72,000 words, in the final version 235,000. Here, too, Proust added short or long passages to almost every page of the proof. These include the opening paragraph (beginning 'The twittering of the birds at dawn seemed insipid to Françoise'), the discussion of military strategy at Doncières with Saint-Loup and his friends, the marvellous rhapsodies on deafness, sleep and the Ladies of the Telephone, and the Narrator's first meeting with Morel. But the proofs end with Charlus escorting the Narrator home after Mme de Villeparisis's matinée, and the remainder of the volume, comprising the death of the grandmother, Albertine's visits, the Narrator's abortive longing for Mme de Stermaria, his dinner with Saint-Loup in the fog, the Duchesse de Guermantes's dinner, the quarrel with M. de Charlus, and the incident of the Duchesse's red shoes, constitutes an enormous addition of 120,000 words. The death of the grandmother was transferred, with a manifest gain in structural balance, from the third volume, where it occurred immediately before the third (afterwards the second) visit to Balbec; so, most probably, was the incident of Swann and the red shoes, since it forms a prelude to the story of the Princesse de Guermantes's soirée.

Grasset's proofs stopped short of the third volume, and the original manuscript, if it still survives, has not yet been revealed; but the 1912 version can still be reconstructed with a fair degree of probability by comparison of its chapter-headings (quoted above) with the final version, supplemented by inferences from *Jean Santeuil* and *Contre Sainte-Beuve*, where much of the same material had already been used.

The volume began, as we have seen, with the Narrator's early acquaintance with Albertine and the little band during a second visit to Balbec, which Proust afterwards incorporated, retaining its original title, in *A l'Ombre des Jeunes Filles en Fleurs*. Next came the Princesse

---

her unnamed daughter); and the Narrator, absorbed in his loss of Gilberte, refuses to accompany his father to an official dinner to which the Bontemps are bringing Albertine, 'a little girl still almost a child' (I, 512, 598, 626). A still more striking insertion links the yet-unknown Albertine with the last incident in her story: a description of Gilberte's handwriting (in which the letters Gi resemble an A, while the last syllable is 'indefinitely prolonged in a waving flourish') prepares for the telegram signed 'Albertine' and beginning 'My dear, you think I am dead, forgive me, I am very much alive . . .', which the Narrator receives at Venice after Albertine's death, and finds a few days later to have come from Gilberte (I, 502; III, 641, 656).

de Guermantes's soirée, which no doubt already included the discovery of the Baron de Charlus's homosexuality, the treatise on the
inhabitants of Sodom, and the Narrator's fear that he has not really
been invited, since these are already present in the corresponding
episode of *Contre Sainte-Beuve*. '*M. de Charlus et les Verdurin*' follows,
and evidently combined in a single episode the Baron's introduction
to the little clan, accompanied by Morel, and his final betrayal and
disgrace; and the whole must have taken place in Paris, since the chapter occurs in the interval between two visits to Balbec. If there was any
equivalent in this chapter of La Raspelière, it must have been in the
country near Paris, like Mme Aubernon's Cœur-Volant to which
Proust had travelled early in the 1890s on a little train, amid the
Charlus-like self-revelations of Baron Doasan. The scene in which the
Queen of Naples befriends the fallen Charlus had already appeared in
Jean Santeuil, though told of the hero Jean himself and the Duchesse
de Réveillon; but for reasons which will be seen shortly, the performance of the Vinteuil Septet did not originally form part of this chapter.
If we compare this primitive form of Charlus's tragedy with the final
version, it will be felt that here is one of the finest of Proust's structural
improvements. By interweaving the rise of the Baron's love for Morel
and his credit with the Verdurins into the second visit to Balbec, and
the decline and fall of both into *La Prisonnière*, Proust has transformed an isolated episode into one of the dominating themes of the
second half of *A la Recherche*, and has developed it in splendid and
terrible counterpoint to the parallel course of the Narrator's love for
Albertine.

The death of the Narrator's grandmother occurred next, im-
imediately preceding his grief for her in the following chapter. But in
this position her death was not only too far separated from the incidents which prepare it (the Narrator's cruelty when Saint-Loup
takes her photograph at Balbec, and the telephone-conversation at
Doncières), but too close to the episode of his grief, the significance of
which lies in its long delay. Proust saw the need for the transference of
this chapter to its final position immediately after Mme de Villeparisis's matinée as early as May 1914 (when he informed Rivière that
it would form the end of his second volume), and it duly appeared
there in the extracts in the NRF of July 1914.

The next chapter, '*Les Intermittences du cœur*', was enormously
lengthened: in the final version it covers nearly two thirds of *Sodome et
Gomorrhe*, the whole of *La Prisonnière*, and all but the last chapter of

Albertine Disparue, amounting in all to nearly 400,000 words, or much more than twice the whole of the original third volume of about 170,000 words. This enlargement was partly motivated, no doubt, by Proust's recent love, imprisonment, jealousy and loss of Agostinelli, to whose memory it is, in a sense, his monument. Yet the original version, as has been shown, must have taken much the same form—a summer at Balbec in which the Narrator falls in love with Albertine, and a winter in Paris in which he torments and loses her—and have had the same function, to prepare by a last and greatest disenchantment for the revelation of Time Regained. But the first size of this crucial episode was clearly far too meagre, and Proust's additions were justified not only because they included so many of the finest passages of *A la Recherche*, but because they were aesthetically and organically necessary for the scale of his novel. The first enlarged version was completed in 1915, in time for the excerpts dedicated to Mme Scheikévitch in November; but he continued his additions during the following years, and we shall find him still at work on the final text of *La Prisonnière* and *Albertine Disparue* at the time of his death.

'*Les "Vices et les Vertus" de Padoue et de Combray*' must have contained the Narrator's visit to Venice, which was already included in the 1908 version of his novel; moreover, the essential incidents of his arrival, sight of the Golden Angel, and quarrel at sunset with his mother, appear in *Contre Sainte-Beuve*; and in *Du Côté de chez Swann* the Narrator mentions Venice in the list of places where he has lived.[1] The chapter must at first have contained the Narrator's reflections on Giotto's Virtues and Vices in the Capella degli Scrovegni at Padua, and the new meanings they had acquired since Swann gave him photographs of these frescoes long ago at Combray. No doubt Proust decided that he had already exhausted the subject in *Du Côté de chez Swann*; and instead, he finally mentioned only the flying angels in the upper frescoes, which seemed to him in retrospect, as they looped the loop 'like the young pupils of Garros', to allude to Agostinelli's death and to the air-ace who in 1916 became Cocteau's great friend. But the long opening paragraph, in which the sunlight and shade of Venice seem to the Narrator a 'transposition in an entirely different and richer key' of Combray, is no doubt a relic of this earlier version.[2]

'*Madame de Cambremer*' described the unexpected marriage, soon after the Narrator's return from Venice, of Jupien's niece, now the

[1] I, 9.
[2] III, 648, 623-6.

adopted daughter of M. de Charlus who has given her the family title
of Mlle d'Oloron, to young Léonor de Cambremer, and her death a
few weeks later. In June 1915 Proust told Lucien Daudet that he
would find 'in the third volume of *Swann*' how 'a single unforeseen
alliance suffices to bring the whole *casus foederis* into play and start a
procession of great names', and would 'appreciate the official
announcement of the young Cambremer girl's death'.[1]

'*Mariage de Robert de Saint-Loup*' told the equally surprising union
of Saint-Loup to Gilberte, and the Narrator's visit to Tansonville. A
similar marriage had occurred in *Contre Sainte-Beuve*, that of 'the
young Marquise de Cardaillec, *née* Forcheville', whose passion for
Balzac comes, says the Narrator, 'from the Swann in her'; and both the
marriage and the sojourn at Tansonville were unobtrusively prepared
in the first pages of *Du Côté de chez Swann*, when the Narrator believes
he has awoken 'in my room at Mme de Saint-Loup's . . . at Tansonville'.[2] Gilberte, likewise, reads Balzac at Tansonville, 'to keep up
with my uncles'.[3]

The final episode, '*L'Adoration perpétuelle*', was an early version of
the Princesse de Guermantes's last matinée, and the title draws a
parallel between the Catholic rite of perpetual adoration of the Real
Presence in the Blessed Sacrament and the Narrator's discovery of the
undying truth of Time Regained, which he has been adoring unawares all through his life. Proust frequently maintained, by way of
illustrating the preordained architecture of his novel to foolish persons
(the tribe is not yet extinct) who thought he just put down anything
that came into his head, that he had written the last chapter immediately after the first. It is not quite certain whether this was literally
true, or whether he alluded only to the second preface to *Contre
Sainte-Beuve*, written in January 1909, in which the revelations of the
madeleine and the uneven paving-stone are told side by side, together
with the sight from a railway-carriage of trees striped with sunlight
and shade, and the tinkling teaspoon which restores the sound of a
hammer on the wagon-wheels. We have seen, however, that these and
other salient episodes of *Le Temps Retrouvé*—the paralysis of Char-

[1] Cf. III, 671, where the letter of intimation is summarised, with its procession
of great names, and the very phrase 'le *casus foederis* venant à jouer' is used.

[2] I, 6-7. Proust explained this passage to Lucien Daudet in August 1913, when
Lucien had just read it in the proofs of *Swann*: 'in the third volume Mlle Swann
marries Robert de Saint-Loup, whom you will meet in the second volume'.

[3] III, 706.

lus,[1] the Prince de Guermantes's library, the rediscovery of *François le Champi*, the Narrator's meditation on his future novel, the realisation that everyone he knew, including himself, has grown old, the apparition of Mlle de Saint-Loup—all date from the period 1909-12. In the first version, nevertheless, when the interval between the death of Albertine and the final matinée was at most ten years, his fellow-guests could only have aged a little, and Mlle de Saint-Loup could only have been a child. The intervention of war, and the consequent further ten years' delay which enabled Proust to revise his novel, aged his characters in the last chapter by two decades instead of one. Once again, just as he had used Agostinelli's death to reinforce the loss of Albertine, he took masterly advantage of a calamity unforeseeable when the first version was written. He inserted the magnificent chapter on 'M. de Charlus during the War', which contains the redemption of Saint-Loup, the ultimate degradation of Sodom, and the explanation of the long gap between the visit to Tansonville and the matinée of the Princesse de Guermantes. The Princesse's matinée became not only a revelation of eternal joy and salvation, but a danse macabre which warns of eternal damnation. The Narrator's elders totter along the precipice where Time falls into Death; by the narrowest margin the Narrator has time to write his work of art before he follows them; and the counterbalancing miracle of Time Regained is affirmed on the human plane by the sixteen-year-old Mlle de Saint-Loup, a personification of the continuity of youth and the spring of love.

In both quality and quantity Proust's additions to his novel were enormous and fundamental. The 1909-12 version stood only half-way in his progress to greatness, occupying a place as far above *Jean Santeuil* as below the final *A la Recherche du Temps Perdu*: it was no doubt a work of genius, but it was not yet a masterpiece. The alterations, however, were not directed primarily at the plot, plan or intention, which remained substantially the same; they were concerned mainly with textural enrichment, enlargement of scale, and structural unity. During the ten years of revision from 1913 to 1922 Proust achieved the ideal form towards which he had moved ever since *Les Plaisirs et les Jours*, and for which the 1909-12 version was only a preliminary study. He changed his novel into itself.

In the summer of 1916, however, this vast process of revision was still at an early stage—except, of course, for *Du Côté de chez Swann*, in

<hr />

[1] Written before 1913, for the manuscript once gives his name in its early form as 'M. de Guercy' (III, 1132-860).

which it was perfectly and irrevocably completed in the seven months
of proof-correction before publication, during April to October 1913.
From May 1914, when the campaign in which he organised reviewing
and publicity for *Swann* was closed, he worked on the revision and
prepublication of the second volume planned for October, and no
doubt continued despite the moratorium of the war. During the
winter, however, he probably 'jumped' from some point in *Le Côté de
Guermantes* to the middle of *Sodome et Gomorrhe*, preferring to write
of Albertine while his grief for Agostinelli was still fresh. The extracts
sent to Mme Scheikévitch in November 1915 show that a new version
of the enormous expanse from the second (and now the last) visit to
Balbec to the Narrator's oblivion of his dead mistress was by then
already written. In the spring of 1916, when he asked Lucien Daudet
in April for expert advice on the vanity-case which the Narrator gives
Albertine for use on the Little Train,[1] he had evidently returned to
Sodome et Gomorrhe. As yet he had only completed the first of many
revisions, whether sustained or piecemeal.

One of the crucial metamorphoses of *A la Recherche* was inspired by
experiences which began in 1907 and culminated in the spring of 1917.
It is time to tell the strange story of the Vinteuil Septet.

The passion for music which had subsided during the years of the
Dreyfus Affair and Ruskin had returned, momentarily with the violin
and piano recital with which Proust regaled his guests at the Ritz on 1
July 1907, and in full force with the Russian Ballet in 1910 and the
operas heard on the theatrophone in 1911. Next year, and until early in
1914, he became engrossed in the late quartets of Beethoven, which
(although this was not Proust's reason) had suddenly become fashionable in Paris, and were one of the specialities of the newly reconstituted
Quatuor Capet. Lauris accompanied him to the Salle Pleyel, where
they sat in the private audition-room of the proprietress, screened
from the public by a painted canvas partition; and after the concert
Proust expressed his emotions with subtle simplicity to the astonished
and delighted leader: never, Capet declared afterwards, had he heard

---

[1] Proust had already mentioned the subject to Mme Raymond de Madrazo
(Reynaldo's sister Maria) in a letter of 18 February 1916. Later in the year (for
the same letter mentions the recent death of Nicolas Cottin and Proust's efforts
to aid the widowed and destitute Céline and her infant son), Proust told Albert
Nahmias of his intention to consult him on 'the dresses girls wore when dining
out at the seaside during our first years at Cabourg', and on the nicknames given
to 'the little local train at Cabourg'.

so profound an appreciation both of Beethoven's genius and of the players' interpretation. One night, moved by an irresistable desire ('which perhaps concealed,' Lauris acutely remarked, 'some sign of a secret affinity between composer and hearer'), Proust summoned Capet and his colleagues to 102 Boulevard Haussmann, and listened in solitude to Debussy's quartet.

Among the most welcome features of the revival of the arts in the Paris of 1916, after two years of wartime austerity, was the foundation of the Quatuor Poulet, which specialised in the chamber music of César Franck, Fauré, Chausson, Ravel and Borodin. After a performance of the Franck quartet in November 1916 at the Concert Rouge in the Rue de Tournon, the viola player, Amable Massis, was approached by a pale, black-moustached stranger in a fur coat, who asked if the four musicians would be willing to play Franck's work privately in his apartment. Massis agreed; and a few days later, at the Mephistophelean hour of midnight, Proust arrived by taxi to rouse the young man from bed, despite the indignant resistance of his mother, and to claim his awful promise. Inside the taxi, while the chauffeur reassuringly winked and beamed, the alarmed Massis glimpsed a tureen of mashed potatoes, and a vast eiderdown beneath which Proust instantly crept. Off they drove to collect the leader and first violin, the twenty-year-old Gaston Poulet, the second violin Victor Gentil, and the 'cellist Louis Ruyssen, who made more fuss than anyone. Céleste, wearing formal black with white apron and starched cuffs, towering over her master, received them at 102 Boulevard Haussmann; "she wouldn't have much trouble in knocking *him* out," remarked Massis irreverently. Proust lay on his bed, with the manuscript of *A la Recherche* stacked and strewn on the floor beside him; the players propped their music on the furniture; and at one a.m., in the deep silence of the night and (as Poulet admitted) the superlative acoustics of the corklined bedroom, they performed the Franck quartet in D major. "Would you do me the immense kindness of playing the whole work again?" Proust entreated. The weary players, fortified with a supper of champagne and fried potatoes served by Céleste, did as he asked; and Proust, with cries of delight and congratulation, paid them on the spot from a Chinese casket stuffed with fifty-franc notes. Four taxis awaited them in the blacked-out street below; and next day, charmed with so courteous, appreciative and generous a listener, they sent him a round-robin of thanks. On other evenings they played Fauré's Piano Quartet in G minor, quartets by Mozart, Ravel and

Schumann, the late Beethoven quartets,[1] and the César Franck violin
sonata, of which Proust insisted on hearing the third movement again
and again. On 6 March 1917, at dinner with Morand and Princesse
Soutzo at Larue's, he asked: "Would you like to hear some César
Franck?" and, despite the head waiter's protests—"there's a war on,
Monsieur Proust, they won't allow music in restaurants!"—he went
off to round up the musicians. But at midnight he returned crestfallen
and alone; he had woken Poulet ("it was just like Wells's *Food of the
Gods*, I was nearly devoured by giant chickens (*poulets*)!" he cried);
but Ruyssen was in hospital with appendicitis. Through Dr Pozzi's
intervention he saved Massis, who was on convalescent leave after a
serious wound, from returning to the front. He plotted to take the
whole quartet to Venice, where he would live in a palace and listen to
their music while dawn broke over the Grand Canal; but the disaster
of Caporetto and the cooling of his enthusiasm put an end to this
chimerical plan.

Proust constructed *A la Recherche* from his remembrance of the
distant past, which he supplemented during the course of revision
from analogous incidents in the present. Occasionally, however, like
a scientist devising experiments to fill the gaps in his grand hypothesis, he deliberately sallied out to find the scenes and experiences he
needed for his novel. We have seen him visiting Falaise in 1907
in search of 'an unspoiled Balzacian town', and in 1912 the country-
side near Paris for the sight of Balbec apple blossom, and the
autumnal Bois de Boulogne for a new conclusion to his first volume.
But the most remarkable of all these quests was the obsessive
listening to chamber-music which enabled him to create the Vinteuil
Septet.

The Septet had long been present in *A la Recherche*, but in different
places and primitive forms. It was played at first as a quartet at the
Princesse de Guermantes's last matinée, where it is still faintly audible,
even in the final version, as the music played in the drawing-room
during the Narrator's meditation in the Prince's library: "the Princesse won't have the doors opened until it's finished," says the butler.[2]
Wisely perceiving that its function was already taken in his concluding
chapter by the revelations of the paving-stone and the tinkling saucer,

[1] In *A la Recherche* it is M. de Charlus who 'wanted to hear Beethoven's late
quartets again, and had some musicians come to play them once a week' (I,
751).
[2] III, 859, 868, 869, 918.

and that it must come, as a miraculous harbinger, somewhere earlier in
the novel, Proust then transferred it to the second of the visits to
Balbec which, at this time, still numbered three in all. It was now a
quintet, played incompetently at the Casino of Balbec by the very
ladies whose concerts on the beach had been the torment of Proust's
Cabourg evenings in 1911; and it was followed by an organ recital
during which, by a hideous irony, a figure based on the paralytic old
nobleman whom Proust had met there in 1908 (and who later became
Odette's ex-husband, Pierre de Verjus, Comte de Crécy) clambered
repeatedly up the steps to the organ, and turned out to be Vinteuil
himself, decrepit and deranged, claiming his rightful place as composer beside the organist. Still later, when most of this second visit to
Balbec was embodied in the first, the manuscript of this concert came
to rest arbitrarily gummed to part of the Narrator's dinner with the
Bloch family. Last of all, presumably in 1917, after his association with
the Quatuor Poulet, Proust decided to place the episode in its final
position, as the central feature of the soirée at which the Verdurins
break with Charlus, and entirely rewrote it in its supremely beautiful
last version.[1]

Like the Vinteuil Sonata, and like other fictional entities in Proust's
novel, whether person, place or work of art, the Septet had many
models. And yet, just as Swann borrowed lesser features from many
people but was basically Charles Haas, and Balbec from many places
but remained basically Cabourg, so the essential models of Vinteuil's
music can be distinguished from the non-essential. Proust took a sly
pleasure in multiplying the minor origins of the Sonata: he mentioned
to Antoine Bibesco in 1913 the prelude to Act One of Lohengrin, and
Fauré's Ballade, to Jacques de Lacretelle in 1918 both these and the
Good Friday Spell from Parsifal, and 'something by Schubert'. But to
each of these confidants he also revealed the profounder models, for
the 'little phrase' in Saint-Saëns's Sonata in D Minor, and for the
sonata as a whole in César Franck's Sonata in A Major.

The lesser originals of the Septet were not named by Proust, but the
reader can still hear and identify them beneath his detailed description
of the recital at the Verdurins'. The first movement evokes to the
Narrator a seascape from dawn to midday. It begins 'on continuous

---

[1] Even then Vinteuil's masterpiece was still a sextet, and still remains so in
uncorrected portions of Proust's manuscript (III, 1083-5, notes on 253-77;
1133, note on 878). Once (III, 1084, note on 263) it is 'a piece for ten instruments'
or even a concerto (III, 1102, note on 502).

plane surfaces like those of the sea, amid a harsh silence, an infinite
void', and constructs before him, 'in the pink light of dawn, a new
universe drawn from silence and night'; and it ends at noon, 'beneath a
scorching and transitory sun', with 'a peal of clangorous and liberated
bells'. Here, beyond doubt, is the first movement of Debussy's
symphonic poem *La Mer*—'*De l'aube à midi sur la mer*'—from its
mysterious opening chords in B minor to the last noonday carillon of
trumpets and cymbals. Early in the Septet a tune on seven notes is
heard, 'like a mystical cock-crow, an ineffable but over-shrill appeal to
the eternal morning'; and Debussy's Quartet opens with just such a
seven-noted cock-crow:

The same theme reappears, as 'a summons to a supraterrestrial joy', in
the last movement of both the Vinteuil Septet and the Debussy
Quartet.

But Proust himself revealed the deeper sources of the Septet. 'César
Franck's quartet will appear in one of the later volumes,' he told
Lacretelle. Franck's Quartet in D major, the very work for which
Proust first brought the Quatuor Poulet to his lonely bedroom, was
his last and greatest work, and its first performance, at the Salle Pleyel
in February 1890, was the only public triumph the disappointed composer ever knew. But Franck's Piano Quintet in F minor was an
equally important model. Unlike the Quartet it is haunted by exquisite, evanescent phrases which recall the Franck Sonata, or rather
predict it, for the Sonata was written seven years after the Quintet.
This is the work of which Proust thought when he imagined the Vinteuil Septet as pervaded by themes from the Vinteuil Sonata: 'in the
midst of this music that was so new to me I found myself in the very
heart of the Vinteuil Sonata,' says the Narrator; and in the last movement, 'again and again one phrase or another from the Sonata returned,
but always changed, with different rhythm and harmony, the same and
yet otherwise, as things return in one's own life'.[1] In the manuscript
draft of the Vinteuil recital at the Balbec casino Proust had written, by
way of a shorthand memorandum that this was indeed the work he had
in mind: 'Franck's Quintet (call it something else)'.

[1] III, 249, 259.

PARALLEL PASSAGES IN THE
FRANCK QUINTET AND SONATA

The origins of Vinteuil as a native of Combray and an outraged
father remain obscure.[1] But in his shy and noble character, with his
displays of alternate humility and innocent vanity, and his situation as
a composer, great, neglected, unique and unknown till after his death,
he resembles César Franck and no other. Proust would have learned
to revere Franck, as a recently dead and saintly master, in 1893 in the
salon of Henri de Saussine, where Franck's disciple Vincent d'Indy
reigned supreme.[2] He could have heard more from Gabriel Astruc,
who tells the pathetic story of Franck bringing a manuscript to his
music-publisher Enoch, and saying: "I know it won't sell, I'm forcing
you to make sacrifices for me, don't give me too much money." And
in a letter to Lucien Daudet of May 1916 Proust repeated the Vinteuil-
like anecdote of the indignation of Franck's pupils when he was
awarded the cross of the Légion d'Honneur not as a composer, but as
teacher of the organ at the Conservatoire. "Not at all," expostulated
Franck, "I'm very pleased"; and he added in a confidential whisper:
"they told me I had very good chances for next year's list". To Reynaldo's sister Maria in February 1916 Proust explained: 'Vinteuil
symbolises the great composer of César Franck's kind (*genre Franck*).'

The Queen of Naples, who champions the broken Charlus at the
end of his disastrous soirée, was a historical character, the 'glorious
sister of the Empress Élisabeth' of Austria and wife of Francis II, the
last King of Naples. During the siege of Gaeta in 1861 the young
queen manned the guns against the rebellious populace: "you know
how this arm held the rabble at bay at Gaeta long ago," she says, as she

---

[1] Possibly he was the father of the unfortunate Mlle Joinville d'Artois, the
original at Illiers of Mlle Vinteuil. The gentle and sad Ernest Guiraud, professor
of advanced composition at the Conservatoire (in which post he was succeeded
by Vincent d'Indy), wrote the recitatives for Bizet's *Carmen*, and frequented
the salon of Bizet's widow, Mme Straus. Proust used the story of his naïve
reply to Mme Straus, when asked if his natural daughter took after her mother
("I don't know, I never saw her dear mother without her hat on") in *A l'Ombre*
(I, 859), and the first night of his posthumous opera *Frédégonde* on 18 December
1895 is one of the scenes of *Jean Santeuil* (vol. 3, pp. 66-73). Guiraud died in
1892. Possibly Guiraud and his daughter were among the models of Vinteuil and
Mlle Vinteuil.

[2] Proust seems to have drawn many features which Franck and Vinteuil share
from d'Indy's monograph *César Franck* (1906), e.g.: 'Franck's language is
strictly individual, of an accent and quality hitherto unused, and recognisable
among all other idioms. No musician would hesitate as to the authorship of one
of his phrases, even if it were unknown to him.' D'Indy is here quoting an
article by Paul Dukas in *Chronique des arts*, 1904, no. 33, p. 273.

offers it to the Baron. In the height of his insolent pride Charlus had jested cruelly at her fallen majesty: "she's come to your fête all the way from Neuilly," he boasts to Mme Verdurin, "which she finds a great deal less easy than leaving the Kingdom of the Two Sicilies"; and the exiled Queen in fact lived, during the early 1900s, in poverty-stricken retirement at Neuilly. During the war she joined the German Red Cross, and took cigarettes to French prisoners: "she's a frightful spy," cries Mme Verdurin in 1916, "if we had a more energetic government, that sort'd find itself in a concentration camp". After Proust's death, and a little before her own in 1925, the aged Queen listened with deep interest to a reading from *La Prisonnière*. "It's odd," she declared, "I never knew this Monsieur Proust, but he seems to know me very well, because he's made me act precisely as I think I would have done."[1]

The soirée at Mme Verdurin's has clear analogies with the Delafosse recital organised by Montesquiou at Baronne Adolphe de Rothschild's on 5 June 1897, when Count Robert was insulted by the Régniers, and quarrelled for ever with poor Delafosse. But that occasion, the insult, the consequent duel, and the vindictive break with the pianist, seemed to Montesquiou himself a personal triumph. The origins of this central event in *A la Recherche* must be sought deeper, in the otherwise unknown humiliation which Proust endeavoured unsuccessfully to exorcise in the most deplorable chapters of *Jean Santeuil*, where, in a series of equally preposterous alternative versions, Jean is outraged by Mme Marmet, a prototype of Mme Verdurin, and supported by the strong arm of the Duchesse de Réveillon.[2] A still crueller dishonour is remembered in the scene where Morel rejects the Baron to remain with the Verdurins. In 1896, during the series of quarrels which ended their passionate love and began their lifelong friendship, Reynaldo had angrily refused to leave a musical evening, and left Proust to go home alone and bitterly hurt. There is no more striking sign of Proust's moral maturity than the selfrighteous resentment with which he used the same episodes in *Jean Santeuil*, and the tragic grandeur to which he transformed them in *La Prisonnière*. Even so, these humiliations buried in the past of twenty years ago were still

---

[1] III, 322, 274, 765.

[2] *Jean Santeuil*, III, 66-102, 93. Mme Verdurin's double-edged exclamation concerning Charlus quoted in the same episode (III, 278)— 'Quelle tapette il a! Quelle tapette!"—was uttered in all innocence by Mme Alphonse Daudet, to the deep embarrassment of all present, to Montesquiou at a tea-party. *Tapette* means both 'cheek' and 'homosexual'.

too shameful to be laid to the account of the Narrator. Proust transferred them to the broad, bowed shoulders of the Baron de Charlus;
and in the next chapter we shall find him casting upon the same mighty
scapegoat the burden of still graver sins, committed in the very
present, in the dark nights of war.

Chapter 13

THE PIT OF SODOM
(*March 1917 – November 1918*)

A NEW dynasty of friends was appearing, for whom Proust was inseparable from the novel for love of which they approached him; and he, in turn, cherished them partly for the sake of *A la Recherche du Temps Perdu*, which they would help to fame within his lifetime, and to immortality when he was dead. Proust had known Henri Bardac through Reynaldo for several years, but without realising, as he confessed to Lucien, that he was 'remarkably intelligent and excessively nice', until Bardac became an enthusiast for *Swann* and in September 1914 suffered a severe head-wound at the Battle of the Marne. In his hospital at Angers, where he was nursed by nuns of the Perpetual Adoration who also adored Proust's letters, Bardac received an enormous telegram beginning: 'Although the extent of my admiration for your heroism is equalled only by your antipathy towards myself', and continuing with a superb disquisition on the Perpetual Adoration, which at that time was the emblematic title of the last chapter of Proust's final volume. Bardac, an Oxford graduate, was soon posted to the French Embassy in London, where he spread the gospel of *Swann*. On leave in Paris in 1915 he became Proust's favourite visitor, though a little hard of hearing from his wound, and reduced him to helpless laughter with readings from Thackeray's *Yellowplush Papers*.[1] Bardac's was the wound-scar which the Narrator saw, 'more august and mysterious for me than a giant's footprint', on the forehead of Saint-Loup.[2]

London had received early news of *Swann* in an unsigned review by A. B. Walkley in the *Times Literary Supplement* for 4 December 1913. Walkley wrote with insight of Proust's 'images in which matter and memory are subtly combined in a sudden warm flood of life revived, without the intervention of the understanding'; he noticed the crucial

---

[1] The burlesque letter of the Narrator's literary young footman, Joseph Périgot, owes much to these readings (II, 566-7).
[2] III, 757.

significance of the Two Ways, and compared *Swann*, as a study of a child's contact with a corrupt adult world, to Henry James's *A Small Boy* and *What Maisie Knew*.[1] Perhaps the Master felt urged to read *Swann* for himself after seeing this article. He obtained a copy early in 1914 from his friend Edith Wharton, the distinguished American novelist in Paris, and was discovered immersed in it by Logan Pearsall Smith. 'His letter to me showed how deeply it had impressed him,' wrote Mrs Wharton, 'he seized upon *Swann* and devoured it in a passion of curiosity and admiration ... he recognised a new mastery, a new vision, and a structural design as yet unintelligible to him but as surely there as hard bone under soft flesh in a living organism.' He wrote Proust a magnificent letter, informing him that this was an extraordinary book for so young an author (Proust was then forty-two, and James seventy), and that it was a great pity he lived in advance of his time. *Du Côté de chez Swann* was the greatest French novel since *La Chartreuse de Parme*, he truly declared, but perhaps (and here James was fortunately in error), Proust would suffer the fate of Stendhal and not be recognised in his lifetime.[2]

Probably it was Mrs Wharton, for he was her lover (unless it was Mme Scheikévitch, for she was his friend), who introduced Walter Berry to *Swann*. Berry was a dignified, white-moustached, intelligent and elderly American ('like an American in a Henry James novel,' said Paul Morand), an expert in international law, an ardent propagandist for the entry of the United States into the war, and president of the American Chamber of Commerce in Paris. In May 1916 Berry was delighted to find, at Belin's bookshop on the Left Bank, a volume bound in 1709 with the arms of Paulin Prondre de Guermantes, and sent it to the equally delighted Proust. Berry called and stayed till dawn, learning the future history of the Guermantes family, and slyly quoting Remy de Gourmont's saying: 'One only writes well about things one hasn't experienced'—to which Proust, feeling that he must stress the imaginative aspect of his work rather than its foundation in

[1] It would be arguable, however, that in *Du Côté de chez Swann* the child is less innocent than the grown-ups.
[2] Proust proudly referred to this letter when he wrote to Lucien Daudet in April 1918, of Léon Daudet's well meaning portrait of him in *Salons et Journaux*, in which Proust is presented as a kind of eccentric, talented child: 'He doesn't know what Henry James, whom he admires, said about me.' Lucien's comment, that 'Henry James, despite his apparent benevolence, was in fact as I have been told rather malicious, and what he had been reported to Proust as saying was extremely unkind', is a sheer misapprehension.

reality, evasively replied: "That's my whole novel!" This prudent
Franco-American, whose steadying influence on the passionate Mrs
Wharton was mistakenly deplored by his rivals, became one of
Proust's most useful and valued friends.

Among the proselytes converted by Bardac at the London embassy
was the brilliant young Paul Morand, a friend of Cocteau, Giraudoux
and the Bibescos. His verdict on *Swann* was reported to the author:
"It beats Flaubert hollow!"; and in the spring of 1916, on leave in
Bardac's Paris flat, Morand was woken by a night-visitor who proclaimed, 'in a ceremonious, bleating voice': "I am Marcel Proust." In
August 1916 Morand was transferred to the Quai d'Orsay, and during
the winter began a series of frequent visits to 102 Boulevard Haussmann. Many of the anecdotes then told to Morand by Proust reappear
in *A la Recherche*. The bluff Grand Duke Paul, when taken to see the
distinguished actress Mme Bartet, had applauded like thunder and
roared: "Bravo, old girl!"—the very words with which, at the Princesse de Guermantes's soirée, the Grand Duke Wladimir his brother
expresses his joy, 'clapping his hands as if he were at the theatre', when
Mme d'Arpajon is drenched by the garden fountain.[1] The Marquise de
Ganay owned a superb Cézanne, which her husband had never seen,
because, he said: "It's in her bedroom, so I've never had occasion to!"
So the Duc de Guermantes, when Oriane explains her plans for
Swann's enormous photograph of the coinage of the Knights of
Malta, declares: "If it's in your room, I may manage never to see it",
'without thinking of the revelation he so indiscreetly made of the
negative character of his conjugal relations'.[2] The infatuation of
Comte Greffulhe for the Comtesse de La Béraudière was now public
property. Proust, wearing his wadded overcoat, had visited the
couple on a hot evening in June 1913 in search of material for his novel.
"He left as pleased as Punch," remarked the Count, "but he didn't
fool me, I could see what he was after, I'm no child!" Proust returned
in July 1915, to the fury of Montesquiou, whose pressing invitations
to the Palais Rose he had eluded on the plea of ill-health: 'I had no idea
my call on Mme de La Béraudière would cause me so much trouble,' he
told Gautier-Vignal. In 1917 the aged Comte Greffulhe tried to keep
his beloved a prisoner, with an unsuccess which reminded Proust of
Agostinelli's captivity; but she evaded him, sending her concierge's
wife to keep him company (Cocteau one day surprised the Count
reading Hugo's *Légende des Siècles* to this amiable woman), or

[1] II, 658.   [2] II, 593.

ordering her chamber-maid to pace the bedroom-floor over the waiting nobleman, while she herself went out to call on friends, and the
unsuspecting M. Greffulhe wrote gallant verses to greet her reappearance:

> '*When I hear your tiny tootsies*
> *Pitter-patter, pitter-patter . . .*'[1]

It is said that he left her far too much money in his will, and his death in
1932 at the age of eighty-four was followed by family litigation.
Similarly there are rumours during the war, Saint-Loup reports, that
Oriane intends to divorce her husband[2]; and Odette in *Le Temps
Retrouvé* has become the Duc de Guermantes's mistress, is forced to
lunch, dine and spend every evening with him, eludes her sequestration
to mock him with her friends, and 'is certain to be his principal
legatee'.[3]

On 4 March 1917 Proust was introduced at Larue's to Morand's
friend and future wife, the Roumanian-Greek Princesse Hélène
Soutzo: 'he studied her black wrap and ermine muff,' wrote Morand,
'like an entomologist absorbed in the nervures of a firefly's wing,
while the waiters fluttered in circles around him'. It was on this evening that he went in search of the Quatuor Poulet, 'so that we can hear
some César Franck', and returned crestfallen. Rain lashed the windows of the Princesse's apartment at the Ritz while Proust, huddled in
his fur coat, his face 'the colour of endives blanched in a cellar', gave an
hour's monologue on Flaubert, 'which, as a concert of chamber-
music,' wrote Morand, 'was quite as good as the one we missed'. The
Princesse was as beautiful and witty as Morand had foretold; at Bucha-
rest, where she was rivalled and surpassed only by the incomparable
Princesse Marthe Bibesco, people had called her 'Minerva'; and
Proust, for almost the last time, was captivated by a fascinating young
woman who belonged to a friend.

He had not set foot in the Ritz since his grand dinner-party in July
1907, but now he began to dine there several times a week; and when
the lights in the vast restaurant were extinguished at 9.30, as wartime
regulations demanded, he vanished mysteriously aloft to Princesse
Soutzo's room. On 23 April he dined at the Ritz with Morand, Princesse Soutzo, Cocteau, and Mme de Chevigné, whom he had aban-

---

[1]   '*Quand j'entends vos petits petons*
               Trotte-menu, trotte-menu . . .'

[2] III, 738.   [3] III, 1015-20.

doned after his regular calls of last summer, alleging that he 'never
went out in the evening'. In all innocence the Princesse mentioned his
nightly visits: "the lift-boy brings him straight up, he doesn't have to
be announced!" Mme de Chevigné was enraged, an 'appalling drama'
ensued, and Proust, who had not forgotten her cruelty in the Avenue
de Marigny twenty-five years before, wrote the poor lady a stern letter
beginning: 'When a person you once loved turns out to be stupid . . .'

One of his last incarnations began; he was now famous as 'Proust of
the Ritz'. The great hotel became his second home, a substitute for the
palaces of Cabourg, Venice and Évian which he would never see
again, and for the salons of the Faubourg, scattered by the war, whose
surviving inmates now dined in strange company round him. At the
Ritz he found again the movement and enigmas of a miniature world,
the comfort and security of family life, the satisfaction of his lifelong
craving for reciprocal service and gratitude. He wrote in his cork-lined
bedroom, but went to the Ritz to live. "They don't hustle me, and I
feel at home there", he said.

A group of very juvenile page-boys and very old waiters surrounded his table. "Who is the younger of the two ladies in the
corner?" he asked, "I have to find out, because she's just like one of the
characters in my book. I know the elder already—ah, if you could
have seen her in my time!" The chamberlain of this court approached:
"I haven't eaten anything for two days, Olivier," Proust declared,
"I've been writing; but first I want very strong black coffee, double
strength, so," he added earnestly, "you mustn't be afraid to charge me
double for it on my bill." When he left his pockets were empty, and all
but one of the staff had been fantastically tipped. "Would you be so
kind as to lend me fifty francs?" he asked the door-man, who produced
a wallet of banknotes with alacrity. "No, please keep it—it was for
you"; and Proust repaid the debt with interest next evening.

The head-waiter at the Ritz, the celebrated Olivier Dabescat, was a
Basque whom César Ritz had lured from Paillard's at the inauguration
of his hotel in 1898. Olivier was tall, handsome, distinguished, and
slightly sinister; in his devoted genius for his profession he displayed
the sanctity of a high-priest, the tact of a diplomat, the strategy of a
general, and the sagacity of a great detective. "I have given Monsieur
the best table," he would whisper, a dozen times each evening, whenever a favourite client entered; but of the Grand Duke Boris, impoverished after the Revolution, he remarked with disdain: "that sort
only drinks beer nowadays". 'For Proust Olivier was a kind of chief

of secret police, and replaced Montesquiou as an informer,' thought
the Duchesse de Clermont-Tonnerre, who saw them not only in
private conference at the Ritz, but walking together in the Bois de
Boulogne; 'I wonder what they found to talk about?' marvelled Mme
Ritz in her memoirs. Proust gave him a set of *A la Recherche* inscribed
'To my friend Olivier, with my compliments'. "People say you help
Monsieur Proust in his work, and that he owes a great deal of his novel
to you," observed the social butterfly Gabriel Louis Pringué; and
Olivier replied, proudly but discreetly: "So it is murmured." Aimé,
the head-waiter of the Grand Hôtel at Balbec, although he owes a
little also to Hector at the Hôtel des Réservoirs and to Charles at
Larue's, is based chiefly on this equivocal and indispensable personage.

For five weeks in the spring of 1917 Proust was visited by
Emmanuel Berl, a young writer-to-be, now invalided from the war,
and tormented between a mistress, a fiancée, and the lifelong spell of
the mysterious Sylvia. Berl was distantly related by marriage, as was
Proust himself, to Bergson; he was a cousin of the poet Henri Franck
who had loved Mme de Noailles and died in 1912; and he had read
Sésame et les Lys in the trenches, and written an enthusiastic letter in
which Proust, much moved, found grains of shrapnel embedded. As
he entered Proust laid the manuscript-book on which he was working
upon the tall bedside column of its companions, and taught, night
after night, the black gospel of human solitude and the emptiness of
human love. Berl, unconvinced, returned to Sylvia. He revisited
Proust with the good news, that the true union of human hearts is
possible; but Proust, towering like a thundercloud, turned upon the
refractory disciple in one of his rare fits of monstrous rage. "You are
stupid, stupider than Léon Blum!" he cried; and retiring to his frosted
bathroom to dress for the Ritz he hurled abuse, cries of "Get out!" and
at last even his slippers. The disciple left, for ever; but Berl was
destined nevertheless, for he was more Proustian in practice than in
theory, to work out for long years in his own person the ineluctable
tragedy of the Narrator and Albertine.

At a tragic and embarrassing time for Roumanians, whose country
declared war in August 1916 at the Allies' entreaty and was now
defeated and occupied by Germany, Antoine Bibesco had arrived in
Paris from London in January 1917. Antoine asked more questions
than ever, and answered fewer, always under seal of secrecy. "I see my
exports are getting bigger than my imports," Proust told him ruefully, and complained: "Even when Antoine's only quoting Dos-

toevsky, he always says: 'but that's strictly between ourselves, isn't it?' And whenever I tip too heavily, he hurls himself on the waiters to find how much it was, and then tells them I've made a mistake, just to ruin my effect." "Do you find me altered in the last five years?" asked Antoine, as they supped on 17 March with Morand off Céleste's cider and chipped potatoes. "Yes, you're less." "Less what? Less intelligent? Less good-looking?" "Just less," replied the implacable Marcel. A few days later Antoine left for a fortnight in Spain; and every evening an enormous and inexplicable dish of ravioli arrived at 102 Boulevard Haussmann, followed at ten o'clock by a waiter who asked: "Was there enough ravioli, Monsieur?" "I haven't any enemies," lamented Proust at the Ritz on 30 March, "so I'm bound to suspect my friends"; and he darkly recalled telling Antoine how easy it was for him to dine at home, 'just by sending out for some ravioli'. The Roumanian General Iliesco was at their table: "Who's that chap in the white tie and dinner-jacket?" he asked, greatly intrigued, and declared his immediate intention of reading *Du Côté de chez Swann*. "What's it like?" he enquired, and Morand replied: "It isn't like anything, General."

In England, a little before the War, Prince Emmanuel Bibesco had taken greatly to Antoine's friend, the young Enid Bagnold. One day, as she sat with Antoine, a mysterious hand appeared round the edge of the door, offering a bouquet of withered flowers: it was Emmanuel who had seized this ambivalent posy, by way of introduction, from a vase in the hall. Emmanuel paid this brilliant girl the supreme compliment of admitting her to his passion for old churches; but she remembers a day when he hurried ahead to visit a village church in the home counties and returned saying: "We'll go back now, it's too beautiful for you to see." "The Bibesco brothers were my university," Miss Bagnold has said. Those who value her novels and plays for the unique originality of their fantastic yet classic vision, may nevertheless recognise in them a strand of lucid French imagination which appears also in the work of the Bibescos' friends, Giraudoux, Cocteau and Morand, even in Proust himself, and is connected in its origins with the unwritten art of that 'cruel and miraculous pair'.

In the spring of 1914 Emmanuel returned from a visit to Japan already touched by the cold finger of paralysis, and henceforth shunned the light of day and of life. The left side of his face was distorted; he announced day after day for his suicide, jesting at death as he had jested at life, guarded and frustrated by the distracted Antoine.

Now, in April 1917, he joined his brother in Paris, and visited for the last time the ancient mansions of the Marais, which spoke kindly to his own decay. On the 12th Antoine called on Proust with Morand: "I've left Emmanuel down in the cab," he said, "because he doesn't want people to see him." They descended, and Antoine with gentle authority prevented Emmanuel from giving up his place in the back seat: "The Bibesco brothers face the driver!" he declared. Proust and Morand took the two tip-up seats; but Emmanuel, with a laugh which made sobs rise in Marcel's throat, cried: "Cabman, drive backwards, so that Marcel Proust and Paul Morand may think they are facing forwards!" Proust, divining that Emmanuel was doomed, wept all that night, observed by Céleste: so Françoise watches the Narrator's tears for the death of Saint-Loup.[1]

Early in August Proust heard reassuring news: Morand had lunched with Emmanuel in London, Étienne de Beaumont had visited a church with him; but on the 22nd the death-devoted invalid evaded his friends and killed himself at Datchet. Miss Bagnold walked with Antoine all night on the Embankment, below the house in Grosvenor Road which the brothers had shared, to persuade him not to join Emmanuel. "Don't speak to me of this ever," said Antoine finally, "and don't speak of your silence." Proust's suffering, as he told Princesse Marthe Bibesco in April 1918, was 'double, uncured, I hope incurable; for I felt the sorrow of Antoine, and I had to accept the idea that I should never again see one of those who were among my dearest companions on this earth'. His grief for Emmanuel joined his loss of Fénelon. The sunlight of youth in which they had gazed, fifteen years before, from the tower of Coucy over the flowering apple-trees of the Ile de France, was extinguished for ever, and the darkness of war had reached its nadir.

On 13 October proofs of *A la Recherche* began to arrive from the NRF's printers, the firm of La Semeuse at Étampes. Imagining that all five volumes would now go to press, but even so exaggerating fantastically, Proust told his friends that he had 5000 pages to correct ('or rather 15,000, as there will be three sets of each'). The new edition of *Swann* was postponed to await simultaneous publication with *A l'Ombre* after the coming of peace[2]; but only two-thirds of *A l'Ombre* had been printed when, early in December 1917, the compositors of

---

[1] III, 849.

[2] The *achevé d'imprimer* is 14 June 1919. The process of enrichment and enlargement, which Proust had decided to apply successively to every volume

La Semeuse were conscripted. Gallimard and Copeau had just left on a propaganda mission to the United States; Rivière, after a gallant attempt to escape from his prison-camp at Hülseberg, was now ill and interned in Switzerland; Proust could only harass their deputy, the brave Mme Lemarié, and complain to Gide.

Meanwhile, not without pride, he pointed out to Lucien and to a new young friend, Jacques de Lacretelle, that it was 'futile to write novels, because life catches up with one!' Louis de Talleyrand-Périgord, aged fifty, married on 17 November 1917 the wealthy widow Cecilia Blumenthal, aged fifty-four, promising according to rumour to adopt the son of her first marriage and to surrender to the young man his own title of Duc de Montmorency. Purists in the Faubourg Saint-Germain felt this title was hardly his to give. It had been bestowed as recently as 1862 by the usurping Napoleon III upon the bridegroom's father, Adalbert de Talleyrand-Périgord, on the death of Adalbert's mother Anne, the last of the true Montmorencys. Proust felt obliged to delete from his novel an involuntarily prophetic remark of M. de Charlus, lest people should think he alluded to young M. Blumenthal. "They might just as well give it to M. Bloch!" the Baron was to have remarked, in denying Adalbert de Montmorency's right to the name. But he had his revenge in a far more important incident of A la Recherche, the amazing marriage of Mme Verdurin to the Prince de Guermantes,[1] which is founded on the strange rise of Mme Blumenthal. The Faubourg, however, could do nothing, except to nickname the bridegroom 'Momorenthal'.[2]

Proust had many other anxieties in the last months of 1917. His

[1] III, 955-6.
[2] In the event M. de Talleyrand-Périgord did not adopt his stepson, and kept the title of Duc de Montmorency for himself. His father Adalbert de Montmorency (1837-1915) is twice mentioned in A la Recherche (I, 640; III, 862) as a friend of Swann and Charlus; while both the Duc de Guermantes (II, 531, 592) and Charlus (III, 267) cast aspersions on his title.

of his novel, was already complete for Du Côté de chez Swann in November 1913. The text therefore remained unaltered, except for a few insignificant verbal corrections, and two equally small but more important amendments necessitated by later developments in A la Recherche. Saint-Loup's garrison-town was named for the first time Doncières (I, 9, 959); and in order to prepare for the war-chapter in his last volume, in which Combray would be in the front line, Proust altered the place-name Chartres (where Odette and Gilberte were supposed to be staying on the day of the family walk to Tansonville) to Rheims and Laon (I, 136, 145, 961).

brother Robert, always seeking the post of greatest danger, left for the
Italian front in mid-November soon after the disastrous defeat of
Caporetto.[1] Montesquiou had ominously begun to write his autobiography, spreading consternation in everyone who had ever known
him. Proust providently offered 'my own humble contribution of
observed absurdities', together with a list of persons to whom he had
recently spoken highly of Count Robert, and an invitation to dinner
with Princesse Soutzo; but the Count sent only a peal of magnificent,
enraged and incomprehensible thunders of rebuke from the Hôtel
Garnier, 'which he seems,' Proust told Lucien, 'to have chosen for his
Mount Sinai'. Princèsse Soutzo was awaiting an operation for appendicitis, which she postponed month after month until Morand's
departure for the French Embassy in Rome on 10 December. Proust
gave her expert medical advice, visited her daily before and after her
operation, and made himself responsible for telegrams to the exiled
Morand. His relations with Mme Scheikévitch were permanently
strained by his resentment at a report of remarks she had made about
him to her friends after he dined with her at the Hôtel Crillon on 22
November, and by his concern, for which he thought her insuffi-
ciently grateful, at her financial losses from the October Revolution in
Russia. He mislaid his certificate of exemption from military service,
and feared arrest as a deserter during his midnight walks, or even at the
Ritz, where the police were showing an embarrassing interest in able-
bodied male diners. He was alarmed by new symptoms in his perpetual illness, on which Robert had warned him before departing: his
eyesight had been declining since early 1915, though he had never yet
risen early enough to see an oculist, and at times his heart seemed
about to burst from palpitations. Lastly, he must find ready money for
the interest-payments of 22,000 francs per annum on his 1911 shares-
loan of 275,000 francs,[2] for an old lady friend, 'whom it is my moral
obligation to assist in her great misfortune',[3] and perhaps for certain
obscurer purposes.

[1] Venice at this moment seemed in danger of capture, and Proust tried in vain
to induce one of the great daily newspapers to accept an article on Venice,
probably based on the Narrator's visit with his mother after Albertine's death.
[2] As he told Mme Catusse in 1916, this investment brought in about 32,780
francs, leaving the rather meagre net profit of 10,780 francs, or not quite 4 per cent.
[3] Not Mme Scheikévitch, to whom he mentioned this lady as an artist who
could no longer persuade the dealers to buy her work, but perhaps Mme
Lemaire, or Mme Hayman (now a talented sculptress), both of whom were in
reduced circumstances during the war.

Recently he had given away the less valuable portion of the family furniture, which had been stored for eleven years in a warehouse. 'I've made a crowd of unfortunates happy with it,' he told Mme Catusse. But the two best carpets of his parents' home were still at the Place Clichy store and the Bon Marché repository; and the dust-furred, disused dining-room of 102 Boulevard Haussmann contained a vast sideboard, crystal lustres, thirty leather chairs; he also had two tapestries, the family silver in unopened packing-cases, and a particularly precious suite of four Louis XVI armchairs and sofa. In November 1917 he enlisted the help of Walter Berry, Mme Catusse and Mme Straus, in one of those curious paroxysms of battening on his friends which intermittently formed part of the profound generosity of this most generous of men. Walter Berry ('he knows all the rich Americans') lost interest. Mme Catusse was indefatigable, but could only find a pair of antiquarian ladies, who opened the dining-room shutters at two in the afternoon ('such a thing has never happened since I came to live here,' he remarked with horror), and offered too little. The Strauses, however, sold the Louis XVI suite for the splendid sum of 10,000 francs, and the carpets, after storing them in their own home and displaying them to prospective purchasers, for 4000. Proust declared himself solvent again.

The last year of war began with a suave letter of New Year greetings from the grateful Olivier, and an exchange of wishes for victorious peace with Walter Berry: 'but meanwhile', Proust added, 'the universal anguish keeps us shut in the same Ark, and the Deluge is not yet over'. As on a New Year's Day nine years before, when he returned through white streets to eat the madeleine, snow had fallen on Paris; but now he emerged undaunted at midnight to walk alone, as was his strange new habit on evenings when he had dined at home. An oval moon, two days past the full, rode over the unlit city[1]; for this was the very night on which the Narrator walks through wartime Paris, when 'the rays of moonlight lay on the snow in the Boulevard Haussmann as if on a glacier in the Alps', and the boulevard seemed 'a field in Paradise, woven of petals from blossoming pear-trees'.[2] The first soldiers from the United States had arrived in Paris a week before; and as Proust trudged along this frozen meadow he was stopped by two American privates, who asked him the way to the Hôtel Bedford. In silence, for he could not speak English and they

[1] The moon was full on the night of 29/30 December 1917.
[2] III, 736.

spoke only broken French, and much moved at the thought of how far they had come to offer their lives, he led the young men (as he allusively told Berry) '*à la recherche de l'Hôtel Bedford*'. He pretended to them, and afterwards to Berry, that he was obliged to enquire the way, though he had good cause to know it well. The highly respectable Hôtel Bedford was, and is still, at No. 17 in the nearby Rue de l'Arcade, which runs from the Boulevard Haussmann opposite the Gare Saint-Lazare into the Boulevard Malesherbes by Proust's former home. At No. 11, only three doors further on, was Jupien's brothel, the Hôtel Marigny.

The proprietor was Albert Le Cuziat, a Breton born at Tréguier on 30 May 1881. As a boy of sixteen he had set out to seek his fortune, armed with a letter of recommendation from his parish priest to a brother-cleric in Paris, who found him a post as third footman with the Polish Prince D——. Albert was seen and appreciated by his master's friend and fellow-countryman Prince Constantin Radziwill, who begged him from Prince D—— and promoted him to first footman.

Prince Constantin, the father of Proust's friend Loche, was famous for the strength and beauty of his squad of twelve footmen, to each of whom he is said to have presented a pearl necklace. "Taking the good years with the bad," the Prince informed Montesquiou, "blackmail costs me 70,000 francs a year"; and Count Robert was fond of repeating the little epigram which has been quoted already:

> '*It is most uncivil
> To mention ladies to Constantin Radziwill.*'[1]

Prince Constantin was the evident original of the Prince de Guermantes, about whose activities Charlus is similarly indiscreet,[2] in his later aspect as an invert. He reappears in Jupien's brothel as the Prince de Foix, 'father of Saint-Loup's friend, and like his son a tall, handsome man, who gave his wife the impression that he passed a good deal of time at his club, but in fact spent hours at Jupien's gossiping to corner-boys about people in society'.[3]

While in his employment Albert spent a delightful evening with a young man who accosted him in the Rue Jouffroy, and behaved with the utmost kindness and generosity, but refrained from revealing his

---

[1]   '*Parler femmes est incivil
          Chez Constantin Radziwill.*'

[2] III, 306-7.

[3] III, 827-8.

identity. A few days later the Prince gave a soirée, at which it was Albert's duty to announce the guests; and among these he recognised, at the moment of enquiring his name, which Albert then bawled out with astonished pride, the terrified features of his recent admirer, the Comte de S—. Proust used the story of Albert's adventure, after he heard it many years later from Albert himself, for the young Duc de Châtellerault at the Princesse de Guermantes's soirée, when the usher, 'who knew his heraldry well enough to complete for himself a title that seemed too modest, shouted with professional vehemence softened by intimate affection: "His Highness My Lord the Duke of Châtellerault!" '[1]

During a succession of posts as footman to the Prince d'Essling, Comtesse Greffulhe, Count Orloff and the Duc de Rohan, Albert acquired a profound devotion to the French nobility, particularly to the minority (neither larger nor smaller than in other layers of society) whose vice he shared and loved to assist. Proust met him towards 1911, when he served Count Orloff, and, attracted intellectually rather than physically by the personality of this still handsome but no longer young man, invited him to spend the evening at 102 Boulevard Haussmann. "How very witty!" he exclaimed at some remark of Albert's as they climbed the stairs, and Albert capped it with: "No, it was only staircase wit!"[2] He discovered that Albert possessed an extraordinary erudition on the etiquette and genealogy of the nobility, and tested him with imaginary situations from his novel. "The Duchesse de Guermantes is giving a dinner for a general and a bishop: to which should she give the place of honour?" "The bishop takes precedence," replied Albert immediately, "and must sit on the Duchesse's right." "And suppose she invited the Duchesse d'Uzès, who is the first Duchesse in France, and Princesse Murat, whose family although more recent was once royal?" "The Duchesse de Guermantes," Albert answered with equal decision, "would *never* ask the Duchesse d'Uzès and Princesse Murat on the same evening!" "You are as learned as Pico della Mirandola, and as witty as Mme du Deffand," cried Proust; and he called Albert 'my walking *Almanach de Gotha*'. He produced his cheque-book: "Please let me give you a modest indemnity for your trouble, say a hundred francs." Albert

[1] II, 634-7.
[2] Albert's little joke consisted of reversing the usual meaning of '*esprit d' escalier*', which signifies the brilliant retort that only occurs to one on the stairs after leaving, when it is too late to make it.

refused. "You are quite right, it isn't enough, I'll make it a hundred and fifty"; and Albert, who was not grasping, was obliged to accept before the figure mounted still higher. Proust sent Odilon and his taxi evening after evening to fetch Albert, paid by cheque for his valuable conversation on each occasion, and wrote letters for which the first footman was teased unmercifully by his colleagues.[1] After Proust's death Albert possessed several hundred of these, most of which were stolen and hawked to visiting inverts in the gay Paris of the 1920s, while the rest, he said, "I gave to my doctor, and other acquaintances."

It was towards the spring of 1917, after their relationship had presumably lapsed for several years during the reign of Agostinelli and the beginnings of war, that Albert discovered his true vocation. He was thirty-six, and could no longer serve his beloved superiors as in the days of youth; but he could be the cause of others' serving them, and his wide experience made him uniquely able to select both customers and staff. He decided to open a male brothel, gave notice to his last employer, the Duc de Rohan, and with the financial help of Proust took over the Hôtel Marigny, 11 Rue de l'Arcade, from its former proprietor M. Plaghki. The new establishment was partly furnished, especially in the entrance-hall and Albert's own bedroom, with the second-best chairs, sofas and carpets of Proust's dead parents. This was the furniture which he had stored in a warehouse ever since his removal from the family home in 1906, and now gave away, as he told Mme Catusse truly in October 1917, 'to make a crowd of unfortunates happy'. Similarly the Narrator presents 'some of the furniture inherited from Aunt Léonie, notably a huge sofa' to the proprietress of Bloch's heterosexual brothel, 'because she needed furniture, and I wanted to show my appreciation'. 'I never set eyes on it, because for want of space at home it was all piled in a warehouse,' he says.[2] For the financing of Jupien's brothel,[3] and for many of the incidents which the Narrator sees there, Proust preferred to transfer the responsibility from himself to the Baron de Charlus.

Here the tall Albert sat stiffly enthroned at the reception-desk, engrossed as the client entered in some textbook of genealogy, with bald head from which the golden hair had receded, pale forehead, thin lips, strangely sharp profile, and blue eyes still bright as the sky of his

---

[1] Charlus embarrasses Mme Verdurin's footman in the same way (III, 259).
[2] I, 578.
[3] III, 817.

native Brittany. Upstairs was his private room, which he called the
Royal Chamber, because he was sovereign prince of this Sodom, or
the Vatican Library, because it contained his little collection of books
on history and heraldry. This is the room of which Jupien says, in
words which must surely have been spoken by Albert to Proust (since
in order to explain the allusion Proust is compelled to attribute his
own translation of Ruskin's *Sesame and Lilies* to the Narrator): "I
leave the light on in my little window to show that I'm at home, and
you can come in: it's my Sesame. But if it's Lilies you're after, you'd
better try elsewhere."[1] Partly because it amused him, partly out of
professional secrecy, Albert never called his customers by their real
names: one was Jean the Pole, another the Grand Duke,[2] and a particularly generous one was God's Gift on a Rainy Day ('*la Providence
des Jours creux*'). Jupien has the same habit: his guests are nicknamed
Monsieur Eugène, Monsieur Victor, Pamela the Enchantress, the Man
in Chains (M. de Charlus himself), and he refers to his establishment,
again probably in Albert's own words, as the Temple of Immodesty.[3]
Perhaps not Verdun nor the Somme, but the nocturnal Hôtel Marigny
in the Rue de l'Arcade, where zeppelins or gothas droned overhead in
the starlight, and poor soldiers and lonely civilians entered to perform
the ultimate act of hopeess men, was the true centre of the war.

Proust was virile himlelf, and had always preferred virility in young
men; but in this terrible period of his descent into hell he was led, by
certain long-quiescent and temporarily reviving impulses, to desire
also violence and cruelty. By an irony as inevitable in vice as in love,
these qualities were no less hard to find than the devotion and sympathy he had ceased to seek; and yet, on the other hand, it is clear that
he himself desired only the mimic image of cruelty, not the reality.

Albert brought him, since a genuine butcher could not be found, a
youth who was willing to pretend to be one. "Have you worked
today?" asked Proust; "Did you kill an animal? An ox? Did it bleed
much? Did you touch the blood?" So far the inarticulate young person
had only mumbled, again and again, an unsatisfactory "Yes"; but now,
gathering courage, he replied: "Of course I did, I put both hands
right in it!" "Show me your hands," commanded Proust. Albert took
him to a real butcher's shop, where Proust said to the apprentice: "Let

---

[1] III, 833. 'He alluded,' says the Narrator, 'to a translation of Ruskin's *Sesame
and Lilies* which I had sent to M. de Charlus.'

[2] For a hidden allusion to this person, see III, 817.

[3] III, 815, 816, 821, 864.

me see how you kill a calf." These incidents reappear on the morning of Albertine's captivity in the butcher's boy, 'very tall and slim, fair-haired', who as he cuts up and weighs the superior and inferior portions of a side of beef seems 'a beautiful angel on Judgment Day, preparing the separation of the Good and Bad and the weighing of souls'[1]; again in Françoise's protégé, the 'timid and bloodstained' butcher's boy, who 'has just started work in the abattoirs', and whom she is anxious to save from going to the war[2]; and lastly in the 'ox-slaughterer, the man from the abattoirs', whom Jupien proposes to the Baron in place of the over-gentle Maurice, and who turns out to be only a hotel-employee.[3] Proust himself was not deceived. It is the lamentable paradox of Jupien's brothel, as of Albert's, that genuine evil is not to be had in it. Maurice, who flogs the Baron in chains, and is presented by Jupien as a murderer, is in fact only an irredeemably soft-hearted jeweller's apprentice; 'one of the most dangerous apaches in Belleville' is a dairy-boy; the rest of the inmates are working-class soldiers and airmen on leave from the front, patriotic, humanitarian, and ingenuously innocent, plying their hideous trade 'from mechanical habit, neglected education, need of money, and a preference for gaining it by a method which they supposed, perhaps wrongly, to be less laborious than working'.[4]

The conscious motives of this deplorable episode—perhaps the only truly deplorable episode—in Proust's life are not difficult to divine. In this pit of Sodom he was following his vice, which had begun with love for his equals (Reynaldo and Lucien), progressed through platonic affection for social superiors (Fénelon, Antoine Bibesco, and the rest) to physical affection for social inferiors (Ulrich and Agostinelli), and now ended, disillusioned with all, in a sterile intercourse with professional catamites. He was experimenting with evil—an evil which perhaps does not exist anywhere in the realm of natural or unnatural sex, except as a moral nullity, a mirage for the desperate—and testing his power to associate with it unscathed. He was buying cheaply, for money and without expense of time or emotion, not only pleasure but human society, albeit in its basest form; for Albert-Jupien's brothel, like the Little Train, was 'a form of society like any other'. Furthermore, like Toulouse-Lautrec sojourning for many months in a disorderly house, among the fallen women who would accept his deformed presence without contempt, he sought and found the last great paintings which would complete his art.

[1] III, 138.   [2] III, 750, 756-7.   [3] III, 817-18.   [4] III, 817-21.

Céleste reproached her master for associating with 'so disgusting a person' as Albert, but his excuse, however lame, was certainly part of the truth. "You are quite right, my dear Céleste," he said with a laugh, "but it can't be helped; he's indispensable for the information he brings me." Twice in the war years Proust had deliberately sought and found the experiences which would give him, at opposite poles of heaven and hell, the missing corner-stones in the edifice of his novel: the Vinteuil Septet, and Jupien's brothel.

But the worst remains. Proust's search for cruelty in these young men was only in part a conscious craving for the imaginary beauty of youthful strength and amorality. He was also performing symbolic acts of revenge for an injury inflicted in remote childhood, perhaps even further back than the kiss refused and extorted on the moonlight night at Auteuil. It was when he was only twenty-two months old, and his brother Robert was born, that it became for ever impossible for him to possess his mother's undivided love. Robert was not to blame, and Marcel had almost entirely forgiven his brother in very early years; but a diabolical part of him had never forgiven his mother. The deepest secret of Proust's life, the ultimate root of the very tensions which had produced his greatness of soul, his goodness and courage, his novel and his vice, now came to the surface. It revealed itself in acts which are at once abominable and absurd, but should be absolved with awe and sympathy by all his sinful fellow-humans. Perhaps these sins were even necessary for his salvation. The hitherto unresolved abscess of infantile aggression burst, by a fistula cut through forty-four years of time, leaving him free at last and ready to die. From the manner in which these terrible deeds appear in his novel it is clear, although their motives came from the lowest recesses of his unconscious, that this profound self-analyst was fully aware of their meaning.

The first was his gift to Albert's brothel of the furniture which had belonged to his dead parents. When the Narrator presents the proprietress of Bloch's brothel with Aunt Léonie's chairs and sofa, he is stricken with remorse on seeing them used by the inmates, 'tortured by the cruel contact to which I had delivered them without defence!' 'If I had caused the body of a dead woman to be violated,' he adds, 'I should not have suffered more.' The dead woman whose body Proust made and saw to be outraged was his own mother. 'I returned no more to visit the bawd,' says the Narrator, 'because they seemed to be alive and to beseech me, like the apparently inanimate objects in the Arabian

Nights, in which human souls are imprisoned who undergo martyrdom and beg for deliverance.'[1] But Proust returned again and again to visit Albert.

Throughout his life Proust was accustomed, as a not wholly innocent social game, to display to new friends his collection of photographs. He had done so to Lucien Daudet in 1895, when Lucien first came to tea in his bedroom and said, so disconcertingly: "I'd rather we talked!", and recently, on 16 December 1916, to Paul Morand on his first visit. But now this practice took a more sinister aspect. Proust arrived at the Hôtel Marigny with a packet of photographs, as Albert later told Maurice Sachs, 'of dear or illustrious lady-friends'. The butcher-boy or telegraph-messenger who was his companion for the evening would certainly have treated these with utter respect, since the sacred rite of viewing family photographs is nowhere regarded with deeper instinctive courtesy than among the proletariat. Instead, the young person had been sternly briefed by Albert, and when he saw the portrait of Proust's favourite Princesse Hélène de Chimay he dutifully cried: "And who the hell's this little tart?" Sometimes the image thus profaned was that of Mme Proust herself; and the primal scene at Montjouvain, where Mlle Vinteuil induces her friend to insult her father's portrait, was thus repeated in his own life by Proust.[2] It is true, however, of Proust as of Mlle Vinteuil (who dedicates her life equally to her vice and to the memory of her dead parent), that this atrocious deed was a symptom not only of hatred, but of wounded, lifelong love.

The story of Proust and the rats is circulated to this day, in preposterously elaborated forms, among the inverts of Paris and their foreign visitors. But of its basic truth there can unhappily be no doubt, since it is confirmed by independent witnesses, and still more conclusively by its unmistakable though disguised appearance in his novel. Maurice Sachs heard it from Albert Le Cuziat; Gide and Bernard Fay and Boni de Castellane from Proust himself; and between the wars it was possible and fashionable to meet the very chauffeur who declared, with a proud and beaming smile: "It was I who used to take the rats to Monsieur Marcel!" The wretched creatures were

[1] I, 578.
[2] It is therefore possible that Proust had already begun this sadistic ritual in 1912 or earlier, before the Montjouvain episode was written. But it is equally possible that the scene in his novel represents only a latent impulse, and that he did not put it into practice until his period of moral abasement in 1917-19.

Theced with hatpins or beaten with sticks, while Proust looked on.[1]
pier scene and its meaning appear in the Narrator's disquisition at
Doncières on 'nightmares with their fantastic albums, in which our
parents who are dead have met with a serious accident, that does not
preclude a speedy recovery. Meanwhile we keep them in a little rat-
cage, where they are smaller than white mice, covered with big red
spots in each of which a feather is stuck, and address us with Cicero-
nian speeches.'[2] Here, alas, are the rats, their wounds and the hatpins,
the wiremeshed rat-trap in which they were caught and brought to
him,[3] and their very identity. No doubt his victims represented many
things; for rats are among the most powerful, universal and complex
symbols in the inferno of the unconscious, and are regarded with
special libido and dread by homosexuals as emblems of anal aggression
and anal birth.[4] But for Proust at this time they were chiefly his dead
parents, who thus met through his revenge with a 'serious accident',
and spoke to him, dwarfed by immeasurable time, of mysteries in-
audible to his conscious memory.

He could not refrain from alluding further to the rats, once in a
letter, and again in the episode of his novel to which they really

[1] According to Sachs, 'he had a live rat brought to him and stuck with hatpins
while he watched'. According to Fay, as reported by André Germain, the rats
had to be pursued and beaten by young men. Gide records: 'During a memorable
night conversation (we had so few that I can remember each one) Proust
explained to me his desire to conjoin the most disparate sensations and emotions
for the purpose of orgasm. The pursuit of rats, among other devices, was to be
justified in this intention; however that might be, Proust invited me to believe
so.'

[2] II, 87.

[3] Perhaps this wire trap is the clue to the occasion of Proust's temptation
and to the origin of the rats. Did they come from the rat-infested public abattoirs
of La Villette, brought in a taxi by 'the man from the abattoirs' in the very cage
in which they were caught? And had the man suggested, in the course of describing his work under Proust's cross-examination: "Would you like to see what we
do with the rats?"

[4] In this infantile regression he also returned to the day when Ernestine had
killed the chicken in the yard at Illiers, and thereby associated cruelty with the
life of the family. He may have recreated this early memory still more closely, if
there is any truth in a rumour recorded shortly after the war by Maurice Martin
du Gard: that Proust, in a little hotel in the suburbs, took pleasure in having a
chicken killed in the next room, with a young man dressed as a policeman beside
him for protection. The detail of the suburban hotel is not necessarily false, for
a tradition exists that Proust was interested in more brothels than one, like
M. de Charlus (III, 832).

belonged. 'I am not afraid of the cannons and gothas,' he wrote to Princesse Soutzo in April 1918, 'but I *am* afraid of much less dangerous things, such as mice'; and the Narrator, leaving Jupien's brothel under bombardment in this same spring of 1918, meditates: 'one can be afraid of not sleeping, without being afraid of a serious duel; one can fear a rat, and not fear a lion'.[1]

It is probable that M. de Charlus's flagellation in chains remotely represents this most heinous of Proust's aberrations, and that here as elsewhere in the brothel scene the Baron is a mere scapegoat for Proust's own experiences. The masochistic form taken by Charlus's vice, though no more abject or absurd, is the most foreign to Proust's own sadistic desires, and was no doubt chosen for that reason; but it is by no means an uncommon one, and may have been adopted by some other customer of Albert's. Possibly, too, Proust may have thought here of Jean Lorrain, his opponent in his duel in 1897, and a minor original of Charlus[2]; for Lorrain's nocturnal excursions notoriously used to end, though not altogether in accordance with his wishes, in his being beaten up by his brutal companions. But Proust may well have selected it from one of the naïve natural histories of perversion then still current, such as Kraft-Ebbing's *Psychopathia sexualis*, one of which he read at this time, not without disapproval. "It seems that even vice has now become one of the exact sciences," he commented with rueful irony to Paul Morand.

Albert's brothel, then, was Jupien's, and Jupien in this episode of the novel is Albert. In his origins, however, Jupien has nothing to do with Le Cuziat. He already exists as tailor-concierge in passages of *Contre Sainte-Beuve* written in the spring of 1909, two years before Proust met Albert, and even then probably taken from an earlier version of the novel. In this aspect, as we have seen, Jupien is connected with the tailor Eppler in the courtyard of 9 Boulevard Malesherbes in Proust's boyhood; as Charlus's factotum he is suggested by Yturri, and as the paralysed Baron's male nurse he resembles Comte Clary's Japanese valet Mineguishi. During the process of revision, however, Proust seems to have retrospectively tinged Jupien's other

[1] III, 834. Similarly, defending himself without being accused, he then protested to Maugny that his nights out, 'though dangerous to my health' were 'absolutely innocent', and to Princesse Soutzo that he never went 'to any place unfit to be named'.

[2] Neither of the two chief originals of Charlus took a downward course. Montesquiou in his later years became ever more prim, while Doasan after his flighty youth seems to have been all talk and no sin.

appearances with something of Albert's wit and personality. The common idea that Albert was one of the chief originals of Albertine is evidently absurd: the two characters have nothing in common, and Albert himself, though he would have boasted if the contrary had been the case, always stated that he never had physical or emotional relations with Proust. However, it is not impossible that his name was a minor ingredient in the name of Albertine, along with those of Albert Nahmias, Alfred Agostinelli, and various women. Similarly, the character of Andrée already existed in the 1905-6 version of *A la Recherche*, where Swann himself meets the little band, and again in the 1907-8 version, where the Narrator meets only two girls at the seaside. In an early passage of *Albertine Disparue* she was called Germaine.[1] But Albert had a young soldier-friend named André, who visited 102 Boulevard Haussmann with him, and caused a jealous conflict between Proust and Albert which towards 1921, as Albert himself stated, brought the end of their long association. It is quite possible that this André is responsible not only for Andrée's name, but for some of the enigmatic by-play between the Narrator and Albertine's friend during and after Albertine's captivity; though here Anna Agostinelli is no doubt a more important original.

Without looking back, for fear of being turned into a pillar of salt, the reader may now at last be led away from the Hôtel Marigny. During the twelve months between the summers of 1917 and 1918, however, its environs were visited by the fire from heaven; and the Narrator himself, as he quits the scene of his appalling discovery during an air-raid, is reminded of the word '*Sodoma*' scrawled on a wall in the doomed city of Pompeii.[2]

On 27 July 1917, the night of the first great Gotha raid on Paris, Proust had dined at the Ritz with Morand, Princesses Soutzo and Violette Murat, Joseph Reinach ('he looks like Consul, the chimp that could smoke, dine and pay the bill, and at times a glimmer of almost human intelligence crosses his face,' remarked Proust), Réjane's son Jacques Porel, Étienne and Édith de Beaumont, and Cocteau. Beaumont telephoned for the latest hypnotist, a M. Delagarde: "the man's a complete ass," he assured the company, "but his fluid's absolutely terrific!" Sure enough M. Delagarde put Beaumont to sleep in a jiffy, and invited the guests to stick pins in his body, adding jovially but with gruesome ignorance of anatomy: "Only *do* try not to prick him in an artery!" Next came Princesse Murat: "could you cure me of

[1] III, 1106, notes on 546, 547.   [2] III, 806-7, 833.

grinding my teeth?" she asked ("a modest request," commented Proust); but she tactlessly began to come to of her own accord, while the hypnotist raced through the gestures of waking the subject in order to get there first. In the midst of their laughter and glee came the dreadful warning from the sirens on the Eiffel Tower. "Someone's trodden on the Eiffel Tower's toe, it's complaining," cried Cocteau. For a moment Proust ignored the interruption, still absorbed in the séance: "people in a trance always ask to be told their future," he observed, "for fear of being made to confess their past". Then he went out on the balcony. The sky was full of stars, a sheaf of search-lights at the peak of the great tower pointed into limitless space, and far away, in the direction of Le Bourget, tiny points of light soared into the air as the defending fighters took off to protect the city, and made new constellations. For more than an hour Proust stood there, entranced, for the first time since the final sunset of Cabourg and for the last time but one in all his life, by a scene of material beauty. When they descended, however, he was reminded of El Greco's *Burial of Count d'Orgaz*, in which the events of heaven and earth are presented on two separate planes; for while this apocalyptic vision was enacted in the sky, in the hall of the Ritz alarmed ladies in nightgowns were roaming, clutching their ropes of pearls to their bosoms, as in Fey-deau's farce, *L'Hôtel du Libre Échange*." Among those recognised," remarks Saint-Loup in a conversation in which many of these images (constellations, apocalypse, El Greco, Feydeau) are repeated from a letter Proust wrote that night to Mme Straus, "the Duchesse de Guer-mantes superb in her nighty, the Duc de Guermantes indescribable in bath-robe and pink pyjamas".[1] Then came the merry cry of the bugles sounding the All Clear, the *berloque*:

'The *berloque*,' says the Narrator, 'like an invisible street-boy, dis-cussed the good news at regular intervals, and threw its cry of joy high in the air.'[2]

The next great raid began a little before midnight on 30 January

[1] III, 758-9.   [2] III, 777.

1918, at the moment when Proust was leaving Gabriel de La Roche-foucauld's home in the Rue Murillo after a performance of Borodin's Second Quartet. Once again Proust had the opportunity of enjoying the same sublime spectacle, for his taxi broke down in the Avenue de Messine for half an hour, while he paced the pavement. When at last they reached 102 Boulevard Haussmann he kindly suggested to the aged driver: "I could put you up for the night in my drawing-room, if you're afraid to go home." But the old man was deaf, and oblivious of the raid raging about them. "Oh, no," he replied, "I'm off to Grenelle, it's only a false alarm, they haven't reached Paris at all." At that moment a bomb exploded near by, a little to the east, in a direction which might well have been the Rue de l'Arcade, though Proust learned afterwards that it was in the Rue d'Athènes, just behind the Gare Saint-Lazare. This was no doubt the very bomb which fell a few moments after the Narrator left Jupien's brothel, 'perhaps now already reduced to ashes'.[1]

On and after 23 March 1918 the Germans shelled Paris from posi-tions seventy miles away, with the enormous naval guns which were collectively known as Big Bertha, after Krupp's wife. The Gothas stormed more violently than ever, and at each alert the lodgers at 102 Boulevard Haussmann trooped down to the cellar, headed by Céleste,[2] while Proust worked calmly upstairs, like the boy on the burning deck. "I don't know the way to the cellar," he said. Poor Céleste, dis-traught with fear and with the additional burden of nursing Odilon, who arrived in mid-April on sick-leave with quinsy, thought of leaving Proust's service. He threatened to replace her with the hated Céline, and annoyed her by refusing to take refuge in Mme Catusse's villa at Nice, or even at Cabourg. Céleste was ill all summer, but the bond between them was too strong to be broken by fear, or by any-thing except death.

The noble and intelligent Céleste had now served Proust for five and a half years, ever since the November of 1912 when she tied the parcel in which the typescript of Du Côté de chez Swann went to the NRF and returned rejected. She had married Odilon Albaret in March 1913, but during the reign of Céline had been summoned only for emergency tasks, such as the distribution of presentation copies of Swann in November 1913. When she first entered that dark bedroom,

[1] III, 833.
[2] 'The All Clear sounded as I reached home, where I met Françoise coming up from the cellar,' says the Narrator on his return from Jupien's brothel (III, 840).

filled with the smoke of Legras powders, she had felt a twinge of eery
dread, and thought of the gloomy metal-mines in her native Auxillac
in Auvergne, where she lived with her brother François-Régis Gineste
until 1904. Then Proust's profound goodness, reaching far deeper in
him than anything that was imperfect, called to her generosity, his
orphan need to her abnegation, and they were united in a strange and
pure tie for ever. Céline, whose star was waning, called her 'the
cajoler', 'l'enjôleuse'. This is the word used by the jealous Françoise[1] of
Marie Gineste and Céleste Albaret, the lady's maids at Balbec, to
whom Proust by way of compliment gave the real names of Céleste
and her unmarried sister, and the brilliant untutored conversation
which is a pastiche of Céleste's, who accompanied him to Cabourg on
his last visit in 1914.[2] From that time until his death she lived with
him, fed, nursed and comforted him, taking the place of the young
mother of his infancy. On the first Sunday of their life together she had
dressed to go to mass. "Where are you going, how can you leave me
all alone?" he had cried; "my dear Céleste, surely the good Lord is as
likely to send you to heaven for nursing a sick man as for deserting
him to go to mass!" And Céleste never went to mass again while
Monsieur was alive.

Céleste, now aged twenty-seven, was tall, beautiful, and stately,
'like Lady de Grey forty years ago,' said Proust, having met that lofty
English beauty, whom people called Ten Degrees below Freezing, at
Mme Straus's in his youth. His friends called her 'the beautiful
Céleste'; and hence, no doubt, the words "Look, there's the beautiful
Françoise," with which Albertine warns the Narrator of her unexpected approach 'when my friend was lying naked by my side'[3]—
words so inappropriate of the aged Françoise—were spoken in real
life when Proust was disturbed with a companion by Céleste. Her
voice was melodious, but in her not infrequent rages with husband or
master 'it kept,' as the Narrator observes, 'the rhythm of her native
torrents'.[4] 'Céleste sometimes reproached her husband with not
understanding her,' says the Narrator of the lady's maid at Balbec,
'whereas I was amazed that he could endure her.'[5] "At that time,

[1] II, 848; III, 154.
[2] Many years after Proust's death Marie Scheikévitch repeated this episode of
Sodome et Gomorrhe (II, 846-50) aloud to Céleste, who had never read her master's
novel. "I said all these things to Monsieur not once but many times," commented
the astonished Céleste.
[3] III, 822.   [4] II, 846, 850.   [5] II, 850.

Monsieur," the real Céleste told Proust of poor Odilon in the early days of their marriage, "he carried a bachelor-flat in his heart!" Proust was almost as proud as Céleste of the fact that her brother had married a niece of Monseigneur Nègre, Archbishop of Tours. He attributed the same archiepiscopal alliance to the lady's maid at Balbec in his novel,[1] and wrote in doggerel verses which he gave to Céleste:

> '*Tall, beautiful, refined and meagre,*
> *Now weary, now elate and eager,*
> *Charming prince alike and beggar,*
> *Scolding poor Marcel with rigour,*
> *Giving for honeyed words vinegar,*
> *Witty, brisk,* vitae integra,
> *She's the niece-in-law of Nègre!*'

Early in her service Céleste acquired, as had the unfortunate Agostinelli, a curious talent for poetic diction, and another peculiar to herself and her master for parody and impersonation, both of which she employed satirically against Monsieur and his friends.[2] "Monsieur Léger's verses are more like riddles than poems," she remarked of a volume by Morand's friend Saint-Léger Léger, the future Nobel Prize winner.[3] Of Morand himself she said: "You can see M. Morand's voice cutting out a silhouette of his face"; and of the hoarse-toned Mme de Chevigné: "That lady who has made Monsieur so unhappy has a voice like a railway-train when it goes into a tunnel." When Gide gave Proust a copy of his early work *Les Nourritures Terrestres*, in which all the sensual joys of the world are hymned in lyric prose to the imaginary friend Nathanaël, Céleste rose to the occasion. When Proust sent her to telephone Princesse Soutzo she returned saying: "Nathanaël, I will speak to thee of the lady-friends of Monsieur. First is she who has made him go out again after so many years, whence taxis to the Ritz, page-boys, tips, exhaustion. . . ." 'I had to explain to her the other day that Napoleon and Bonaparte were one and the same person, I can't teach her to spell, she's never had the patience to read

[1] II, 850.
[2] 'She inserted in her little report of what purported to be a communication from the manager or one of my friends,' says the Narrator at Balbec, 'fictitious words which slyly depicted all the faults of Bloch, etc. In the form of a simple message which she had obligingly undertaken to deliver, she presented an inimitable portrait' (II, 849).
[3] Repeated by Céleste the lady's maid at Balbec (II, 849).

half a page of my book,' he told Gide, 'but she is full of extraordinary gifts.'

At the very time, in 1917-18, when Proust's association with Albert Le Cuziat was closest, he also saw a good deal of the Abbé Mugnier. No doubt he took a scientific, aesthetic and malicious pleasure in this strange counterpoint between a priest of evil and a priest of good; but he also felt a genuine need in his period of moral fall for a spiritual healer, even though, as in his relations with doctors who cared only for his body, he would always refuse to abdicate his own free will. The Abbé, with his selfless instinct for a soul in danger, came eagerly to meet him.

The Abbé Arthur Mugnier (1853-1944) was born at the Château of Lubersac, where his father was the architect in charge of the restoration of the Marquis's home. He was educated at the seminary of Nogent-le-Rotrou, twenty miles west of Illiers,[1] and ordained in Paris soon after the Siege. "My mother was overjoyed when I became a priest," he would say, "because she thought I would find peace—but I haven't! I've only had other people's troubles!" In 1896 he became vicar of the fashionable church of Sainte-Clothilde, in the heart of the Faubourg, and was seen at noble dinner-parties everywhere and always.

The Abbé was a witty, rosy-faced little man, with forget-me-not blue eyes behind pale pince-nez, a tuft of grey, smoke-coloured hair which he would twirl on his finger when puzzled, and an expression of harassed benignity. He lived in the utmost poverty, with humble food and threadbare soutane; he loved and cherished the poor, and heard confession, as he said, not only in his parish church but "in railway-stations, on benches, in streets and public gardens". Yet his true missions were elsewhere, instilled by his strange infancy in a great château, and by his passion for literature, which taught him that a great writer, as much as a priest, carries a vast burden of grace and sin along a dolorous path which leads out of this world. The souls of the French aristocracy were neither more nor less valuable to God, and perhaps in even greater peril, than those of the poor; and like Saint Paul to the pagan Greeks, or Father Damien to the lepers, the Abbé Mugnier became an Apostle to the Faubourg Saint-Germain. But he was no meddlesome or militant fisher for converts, for this wise and holy man, one of the rare saints of the twentieth century to be numbered with Gandhi or Albert Schweitzer, brought comfort and for-

[1] 'It ought to be renamed Nogent-l'Abbé!' Proust wrote to him in 1919.

giveness only to those who needed it. "She was far too pious to need converting," he said of a good Jewish lady; and when asked if he believed in hell he answered: "Yes, because it is a dogma of the Church —but I don't believe there is anyone in it." His other mission began when he sent Huysmans to the Trappists in 1892, and henceforth he specialised no less in sinful writers than in sinful nobles. Paul Bourget, who had begun to feel more Catholic than the Pope, complained: "he throws communion-bread to the sparrows!"; but the Abbé remarked: "I have two soutanes, Monsieur Bourget, would you like one?" After his death was found, tied in green cardboard folders, his correspondence from, among many others, Montesquiou, Cocteau, Bergson, Mme de Caillavet, Mauriac, Montherlant, Barrès, and Proust himself. In 1909, however, he had unwittingly offended the Church, when he endeavoured to reconvert the unfrocked and married priest, Hyacinthe Loyson, and was insulted by Loyson's son. "Now I know why priests must not marry," he cried, "it is because they have such unpleasant children!" As penance he was banished from Sainte-Clothilde and made a mere almoner to the Missionary Sisters of Saint Joseph of Cluny in the Rue Méchain, where he lived at No. 7 until his death. "In 1910 I had a nice neighbour on the floor above, very quiet, very polite," he would say, "his name was Lenin!" He deplored the war: "we ought to be fighting the Prussians inside us, our deadly sins," he said; but when asked if the Apocalypse had now come, he answered: "Not yet."

It is certain that two such indefatigable diners-out as Proust and the Abbé had met long before, though it is possible that each, for different reasons, may at first have misunderstood and avoided the other. Proust must have been aware of the Abbé's notorious devotion to the great Chateaubriand, whom none in our century have loved and known so passionately as the Abbé, his lifelong friend and spiritual ward Princesse Marthe Bibesco, and Proust himself. Early in the war, if not before, they had begun to make contact. 'I've just read Ruskin's *Sésame et les lys*, with an enchanting preface by Marcel Proust,' wrote the Princesse significantly to the Abbé on 11 June 1915, 'do you see him sometimes?' The Abbé was a friend of many of Proust's present friends, the Princesses Bibesco, Soutzo, and Marie Murat, Mme Scheikévitch, Morand, Blanche, the Beaumonts, Mme de Chevigné, Cocteau, Pierre de Polignac. On 5 June and 6 July 1917 Proust attended dinners at the Ritz, given by Princesse Soutzo, at which several of these and the Abbé were present. The Abbé, 'his quiff rising like smoke from a censer,' said Morand, sportively produced an edition of *Les Fleurs du Mal* to which Bourget had written a preface, and remarked: "Now, with Bourget's preface, we shall have to call it *Les Fleurs du Bien!*" In April 1918 Proust met the Abbé at Mme Daudet's, saw him home, and a few evenings later met him again: 'I like him very much,' he wrote to Lucien. The Abbé began to visit 102 Boulevard Haussmann, and Céleste always remembered two of his typically profound sayings. When Proust asked his opinion of *Les Fleurs du Mal* he replied, placing his hand on his heart: "They are always with me, in here." And once when leaving for his convent, the Abbé remarked with a similar double meaning: "I must hear the confessions of my mystic flappers—*mes poules mystiques*." The Abbé regarded indulgently Proust's love of high society, now almost platonic: "He was a honey-bee of heraldic flowers," he told Lucien Descaves. Proust pretended to be unaffected by the Abbé's interest in his soul: "He talked to me about salvation," he told Blanche, "but I said: 'I'd rather you talked about Comte Aimery de La Rochefoucauld'." In fact, like every great writer, Proust had undertaken to win redemption through his work alone, to negotiate direct with God. But we shall find him remembering the Abbé, and the Church whose May-mass he had attended at Illiers, whose priests and cathedrals he had defended in the dark hour of the Combes laws, at the moment of death, in his own way.

All that spring and summer the Germans fought towards Paris and died, reaching Château-Thierry on the Marne, only fifty miles away, in June. As in 1914 many Parisians took refuge in the south. Princesse Soutzo returned to Biarritz, where Proust thought vaguely of following her, but decided Céleste was too ill. He quoted Swann, who 'had enough courage to stay, but not enough to go',[1] and longed regretfully 'to kiss your hand, and hear you assuring me that there isn't any sugar on my moustache'. Her brother was in Paris, and he felt for a moment his old curiosity to see 'this transposition into another sex of a face one has loved'. So he had sought out the Waru brothers in 1892, because they were Mme de Chevigné's nephews, and Jeanne Pouquet's nephew 'little Prémonville' in 1911; and he had always regretted never having met the brother of Marie de Benardaky ('she was, perhaps without knowing it, the intoxication and despair of my childhood,' he explained to the Princesse) before his death aged eighteen early in the war, especially, perhaps, because the boy was of

[1] I, 353.

The weeping angels, from Giotto's fresco of the Deposition
from the Cross, in the Arena, Padua

Odilon (at the wheel) and Agostinelli, Cabourg, 1907

Princesse Hélène Soutzo, in
her room at the Ritz

Paul Morand in diplomatic
uniform, 1916

Sydney Schiff

Violet Schiff

extraordinary beauty and in the habit of dancing naked before his
particular friends. Once again he was disquieted by new symptoms of
ill-health, which seemed imaginary to his doctors, but were in fact
premonitory visitations of death, now only four and a half years distant. He felt impediments in his speech, a hint of facial paralysis, and
decided his brain was affected. In June he consulted Dr Babinski, the
great neurologist, and asked him to perform a trepanotomy; but
Babinski refused and succeeded in reassuring him.

On 13 June 1918 poor Dr Pozzi was murdered by a deranged
patient. Proust thought with bewildered grief of the immense space of
time during which he had known this gayer, more intelligent original
of Dr Cottard, who had dined at 9 Boulevard Malesherbes when he
was only fifteen, had invited him to the first precocious 'dinner in
town' which his parents had been so reluctant for him to attend, had
shone as the star of Mme Aubernon's soirées and tended her so
devotedly in her last illness, and had rescued him in 1914 from military
service. There was something portentous and supernatural in this
abrupt calamity, and he wrote with magnificent imagery to Mme
Straus: 'as at the death of Calmette, that innocent and mystic sacrificial
victim, one felt the coming of war, so after the death of Pozzi one can't
help wondering whether peace is near, whether these men were not
the two bloodstained pillars which marked the beginning and end of
the war'. And so it was to be.

After four months' interruption the flow of proofs of *A l'Ombre*
from La Semeuse had begun again in mid-April. Even two years
before, when Gallimard and Copeau had called to negotiate his migration to the NRF, and he showed them his corrections to the Grasset
proofs of June 1914, Copeau had exclaimed: "Why, it's a new book!"
But Proust persisted with his customary superb enlargement and
enrichment of the text. This work continued until the autumn, and
printing was finally completed on 30 November 1918.

On 10 April 1918 Jacques Émile Blanche offered to dedicate to
Proust the first volume of his *Propos de Peintre*, a series of essays on
the impressionist painters entitled *De David à Degas*, and asked him
in return to introduce the book. Proust's preface, which he wrote in
May, caused months of bickering between these two very susceptible
friends. Proust, in a parable which was equally true of himself, represented Blanche as an artist who in his youth had preferred the
pleasures of society, had been unwillingly forced to work by banishment from noble drawing-rooms, and had now reached fame through

the law which grants recognition only after a generation of neglect.
Blanche, on the contrary, felt that he had always consecrated himself
to art alone, and was still by no means appreciated in accordance with
his merits. This was the first of a series of critical writings in which
Proust used material from the unpublished *Contre Sainte-Beuve*. He
introduced the episode of great-uncle Louis Weil's cider-glasses and
prismatic knife-rests,[1] and a concise version of his attack on Sainte-
Beuve for contaminating his judgements on writers with considera-
tions of their outward life, in which he accused Blanche of committing
the same error in his essay on Manet. In the end Proust had his way,
the proofs were passed by Blanche in January 1919, and the volume
was published in the following March.

It was also in the first half of 1918, and probably during the gap in
proof-reading from January to April, that Proust completed the war-
chapter in *Le Temps Retrouvé*, his last major addition to his novel.
The chapter is first mentioned in a letter to Grasset of 18 July, in
which Proust demanded once more the long overdue royalties on *Du
Côté de chez Swann* for the period since April 1914. Gallimard, during
a flying visit to Paris from America in June, had arranged with
Grasset to buy back *Swann* 'for a pretty high figure', and the remainder
of Grasset's edition was now issued in new wrappers, with the NRF's
own label affixed to the title-page; but Grasset naturally insisted on
withholding the royalties until the further question of an indemnity
for the remainder of the novel was settled. 'Two volumes called
Sodome et Gomorrhe[2] have been written since the war began, and there
is a section about the war,' Proust now told Grasset. Probably, however, the first half of this war-chapter, before the visit to Jupien's
brothel, was written in the summer of the previous year, since nothing
in it is based on events later than the first Gotha raid of 27 July 1917.
At this time Proust expected to adhere to his original plan, in which
the chapter was to describe the Narrator's visit to Paris in the summer
of 1916, with a brief interpolation on his earlier visit in August 1914.
The events of the war which he mentions here, such as the Battle of
Tannenberg,[3] the sinking of the *Lusitania*,[4] French pressure on

[1] Proust scattered elements of this passage far and wide in *La Prisonnière* and
Albertine Disparue. Cf. III, 168, 254, 411-12, 479.

[2] That is, *Sodome et Gomorrhe* as we now have it, and a further volume with
the same title which was later divided into *La Prisonnière* and *Albertine Disparue*.

[3] 26-30 August 1914 (III, 760).

[4] 7 May 1915 (III, 772).

Roumania to join the war,[1] usually belong to the correct period; though allusions to King Constantine's withdrawal of troops to the Peloponnese[2] and the entry of the United States into the war[3] belong to the first half of 1917. However, since the only air attacks on Paris in 1916 had been by Zeppelin, Proust carefully turned the air-raid which the Narrator discusses with Saint-Loup, though modelled on the Gotha raid of July 1917, into a raid by Zeppelins.[4] It was not until the autumn of 1917 that Albert Le Cuziat opened his brothel at the Hôtel Marigny, and thus provided Proust with the material for the second half of his war-chapter. Accordingly he now introduced in the latter half of the Narrator's conversation with M. de Charlus and the visit to Jupien's brothel the environing events of that winter and the following spring, when he himself frequented the Hôtel Marigny: the bomb of 30 January 1918,[5] the incessant Gotha raids,[6] the bombardment by Big Bertha,[7] the German advance on Paris and the flight of refugees from the capital,[8] the crowds sheltering in the Metro and complaints of their scandalous behaviour,[9] and Françoise taking cover like Céleste in the cellar.[10] But these and many other anachronisms in *A la Recherche* are far from impairing the reality of Proust's novel; and the reader, assailed like the Narrator on waking by the malaise of wondering in what year he is, feels only the fluidity of time, and the possibility of eddies in its stream.

The same letter of 18 July to Grasset contains the first mention of *Pastiches et Mélanges*, the collection of Proust's Lemoine parodies, Ruskin prefaces and selected *Figaro* articles[11] which he had hoped to publish ever since 1908. He had arranged for its publication with Gallimard during his recent visit; and in order to ensure its simultaneous publication with *Swann* and *A l'Ombre* at the first suitable

[1] III, 785. Roumania declared war on 27 August 1916 (cf. III, 787).

[2] January 1917 (III, 729). King Constantine's abdication on 12 June 1917 is mentioned in the later section (III, 845).

[3] 6 April 1917 (III, 761, 794). The murder of Rasputin, however (29 December 1916), is mentioned as being still in the future (III, 777).

[4] III, 758-9.   [5] III, 833.   [6] III, 762, 777, 802, 809.

[7] III, 802.   [8] III, 806, 811.

[9] III, 834.   [10] III, 840.

[11] 'Sentiments filiaux d'un Parricide' (1 February 1907) and 'Impressions de route en automobile' (19 November 1907). Since it too was about churches, he added the latter, together with an abridged version of 'La Mort des Cathédrales' (16 August 1904), to the preface to *La Bible d'Amiens*, and called the whole, in allusion to the cathedrals wrecked by the Germans, 'En mémoire des églises assassinées—In Memory of the Murdered Churches'.

time after the end of the war, Proust asked the NRF to send it to a
different printer, since La Semeuse was still busy with *A l'Ombre*. He
had not kept copies of his articles, and was compelled to enquire their
dates from Robert Dreyfus, who was again on the staff of *Le Figaro*,
and to borrow cuttings (which arrived on an evening when he dined at
the next table at the Ritz to Mr Winston Churchill) from Lucien
Daudet. He took the occasion to ask Alfred Capus, the editor of *Le
Figaro* during Flers's absence on war-work, to renew the project of
printing extracts from *A l'Ombre* which had been thwarted by the
outbreak of war; but Capus was on holiday and did not reply, and in
the end, although the feuilleton was actually announced in *Le Figaro*,
the extracts were bespoken by the NRF.

The Germans retreated, fighting grimly to the end, preparing the
terrible legend which would bring the next war, that they were not
defeated but betrayed by their government. A million American
soldiers were in France, and Céleste no longer said, as she had the year
before: "I don't think much of America!" Proust did not go to
Cabourg, although Mme Straus was at Trouville: 'I thought I would
go,' he told her, 'and that we would talk together about everything
that one day, so suddenly, became the past.' He dined at the Ritz alone
with Mme de Chevigné: 'I don't regret having exasperated you twenty
years ago,' he wrote, politely forgetting that it was six years longer
still, 'and annoyed you sometimes since; you were as beautiful then as
today, not more, for you haven't changed.' He was introduced to
Mme Ritz, and met Princesse Soutzo's brother at last, 'a young prince
of the East surrounded by all the beauties of the Arabian Nights'.
Robert Proust returned from the quiescent Italian front, where his
wife Marthe had joined him as a nurse in the spring, to take part in the
last great battles of the war; and in October, during Robert's convalescence from a motor-accident on the Western Front, the brothers
met affectionately every day. Proust was persuaded by Henri Bardac
to call on the famous society clairvoyant and palmist Mme de Thèbes
for a character-reading; but the wise woman, after glancing at his face
and hands, observed only: "What do you expect from me, Monsieur?
It is for you to reveal my own character to me."[1] In November came,
as he wrote to Princesse Soutzo, 'the miraculous and vertiginous
Peace'.

[1] "It's instinct, divination in the style of Mme de Thèbes (you follow me?)
that is the decisive point in a great general, as in a great doctor," Saint-Loup
tells the Narrator at Doncières (II, 114).

Chapter 14

THE PRIZE
(*November 1918 – June 1920*)

THE men of Europe had struggled during four years towards a receding goal, with death everywhere on the way. Some, like Prince Paul Mourousy, a cousin of Princesse Soutzo, had fallen at the very end: 'The dead of the eleventh hour, who had only a day to wait not to be killed, are those who grieve us most of all,' Proust wrote to her. He was shocked by the wild rejoicing of the Paris mob on Armistice Day: 'we are weeping for so many dead,' he remarked to Mme Straus, 'that gaiety like this is not the form of celebration one would prefer'. Proust, as much as any civilian, had suffered for others' suffering and mourned for slaughtered friends; and yet for himself he had been curiously indifferent. He spent that long gulf of years, which now had vanished like a day, in an enclave outside the war, in the silent peace of his cork-lined bedroom, in the oblivious relaxation of Ritz or male brothel. But on that day of armistice he started again from where he had halted in August 1914. His novel was finished, his last duty was to see it published. Proust's own war now began, as he in turn struggled for four years towards a distant goal, with death everywhere on the way, and fell in the hour of victory.

First of all, however, pressed by the obscure necessity which drove him to make money each November and to strip himself of his worldly goods, he resumed the inextricable saga of his furniture-selling. He gave the inferior articles stored in the mews and spare bedrooms of 102 Boulevard Haussmann to a collection for refugees returning to the liberated areas of the north-east. The Strauses sold his remaining Smyrna carpet for 3000 francs in December, and he decided to part even with the historic carpet which the Shah of Persia had given Dr Proust in 1869. He persuaded Walter Berry to house tapestries and other furniture in the cellars of the American Chamber of Commerce, where prospective buyers could view them without disturbing his daytime sleep. He recommended his efforts to realise the uncashable cheque of 30,000 francs on the banking firm of Warburg for the enemy securities which he had surrendered on the outbreak of war, and enlisted once more the help of his friends, Berry, Émile Straus, Raphael Georges Lévy, even Princesse Marie Murat, whose Christmas Eve dinner he attended at the Ritz. They went on to the flat of a member of the Italian armistice delegation, where Cocteau sang ditties of the 1900s to Coco de Madrazo's accompaniment, the enormous Hélène Vacaresco talked in verse to Jacques de Lacretelle, Princesse Marie was effervescently witty; but in the end everyone gathered round to listen to Marcel, while Jacques Émile Blanche egged him on. He forgot his treasured walking-stick, sheathed in tattered leather, a present from an old friend on the occasion of his wedding, and returned home with laryngitis. A few weeks later, at a dinner in honour of Lord Derby, he prudently kept his greatcoat on, but removed it when Lord Derby amiably teased him. Two years later he was flattered to hear that Lord Derby had declared: "Of all the impressions my wife and I took home with us from Paris, Monsieur Proust was the most indelible"; but he was chagrined to find that the English statesman had added: "Yes, he was the first chap we'd ever seen dining in a fur-coat."

La Semeuse, after completing A l'Ombre on 30 November 1918, had already produced in vain the first six proof-sheets of Le Côté de Guermantes before the final transfer of Proust's works to the press of Louis Bellenand at Fontenay-aux-Roses early in December. Pastiches et Mélanges went to press immediately, though he kept back the still unfinished Saint-Simon pastiche, on which he had been working since September. Except for the Balzac, which he nearly doubled in length, the Figaro pastiches of 1908 and 1909 remained unaltered[1]; but the Saint-Simon which he had written in 1904 as an ironical tribute to Montesquiou, and adapted to the Lemoine Affair in February 1909, was now transformed by further additions into a vast satire on Paris society at the end of 1918. The new sub-plot is based on the pretentions of the Murats, who had never forgotten their brief season of

[1] The new passages in the Balzac are p. 12, l.32-p. 14, l.14; p. 14, l.30-33; p. 15, l.11-21; p. 15, l.32-p.16, l.5; p. 16, l.32-p. 17, l.3; p. 17, l.27-p. 18, l.9, and include a mention of Paul Morand as 'one of our most impertinent embassy secretaries'. A reference in the Flaubert pastiche (p. 22) to 'cork padding in their bedrooms to muffle the noise of neighbours' is prophetic, since it appeared in Le Figaro on 14 March 1908, whereas Proust installed his cork walls only in August 1910.

royalty in the First Empire, to the rank of sovereign princes,[1] and
the counter-intrigues of 'Saint-Simon' to thwart them. Proust felt
compunction at taking the family name of his good friend Princesse
Marie Murat in vain, but decided not to ask her permission, since a
refusal would have ruined his pastiche. He might have answered that
the jest was really on Saint-Simon, and the titanic vanity which made
all attempts to break the cobweb of social precedence seem, to that
sombre genius, crimes against 'the most vital interests of the State,
which is founded on the rights of the Dukes'. But the inmost, gleeful
irony of the Saint-Simon pastiche is that Proust himself, the 'little
Proust' who had travelled the Guermantes Way and emerged far
beyond, is speaking of the Faubourg Saint-Germain from the stand-
point of a social superior, with the bitter diction and violent syntax,
and in the haughty person of the great memorialist. He took the
opportunity, however, to add compliments to old and new friends: to
Guiche, Albufera, Princesse Soutzo ('the only woman who, to my
misfortune, has succeeded in making me leave my retirement'), Mme
Straus, Olivier ('the King's head-butler, respectful and beloved by
all'), José Maria Sert, Boni de Castellane and the Beaumonts. The last
additions relate to incidents of January 1919, his meeting with Lord
Derby ('whose affability is of a kind that the French do not possess
and by which their hearts are won'), and Antoine Bibesco's engagement to Elizabeth Asquith. Antoine, to Marcel's enchanted embarrassment, brought Miss Asquith to his humble bedside, and 'Saint-Simon'
remarks: 'she was probably the most intelligent woman in the world,
and seemed like one of the beautiful portraits in fresco that one sees in
Italy'. He promised, 'in another part of these Memoirs which will be
chiefly consecrated to Mme de Chevigné', to speak further of Princesse Soutzo and Mme Straus, and the pastiche ends with the words 'to
be continued'. But this sequel, which he intended to publish at the
same time as Le Côté de Guermantes, mentioned frequently and probably began, remains still unknown.

In the middle of January 1919 arrived a calamity from which
Proust never entirely recovered. No. 102 Boulevard Haussmann, with
its memories of Great-Uncle Louis and Mme Proust, had seemed an
inseparable annexe to his lost family home, a continuation of a way of
life which reached back to his childhood. Now his aunt announced she
had sold the building to a banker, M. Varin-Bernier, for conversion

[1] The same theme occurs several times in A la Recherche in passages which
were presumably added about this time (I, 772; II, 518; III, 50, 275).

into a bank. To Marcel's protests she replied, with a deadly irony which shows that Mme Émilie Weil and her nephew-in-law had much in common, that she 'preferred the sweet name of aunt to that of land-lady', and that should his health ever improve sufficiently for him to see her again, 'my decision will have the advantage of enabling us to discuss literature instead of the house!' He had never signed an ex-tended lease; he owed her 20,000 francs for three years' rent, because in 1916 he had announced that he would be unable to pay her dues until the settlement of the famous Warburg cheque; and he feared that this debt would be claimed by the new proprietor. Encouraged by a newspaper-cutting sent by Albufera, which stated that civilian lodgers had a right to two years' notice, he thought of remaining; but prepara-tions for the conversion began in February, the inner courtyard was to be covered over, the staircase reconstructed, he would be unable to sleep. He consulted Guiche, who not only interviewed the banker in his lair, but cancelled the debt and extracted a stiff indemnity: 'it was the greatest service a friend has ever rendered me,' he told Robert Dreyfus.

Early in March, at about the same season as the year before, the impediment in his speech returned, perhaps because it was connected with his springtime asthma, probably also, as his doctor assured him, because his state of anxiety had induced him to take too much veronal. 'It can't be general paralysis,' he told Berry, 'because all my reflexes are excellent, and I've never had venereal disease'; but he feared he might have the same malady as his mother, that he too might die speechless, and resolved if need be to shut himself away from all human contact, and die when his novel was finished. After three weeks, however, the mysterious symptoms vanished as before.

On 2 March Proust had been a fellow-guest of Princesse Soutzo at the Ritz with the young Harold Nicolson, a friend of Morand and Berry, who was now peace-making in Paris. He asked how the English delegation worked. "We generally meet at ten in the morning," began Nicolson; but Proust interrupted: "No, you're going too fast, begin again. You take the official motor-car, you get out at the Quai d'Orsay, you climb the stairs, you enter the committee-room. What happens then?" Nicolson told all to this 'white, unshaven, grubby' diner, who listened enthralled, exclaiming from time to time: "But be precise, *mon cher Monsieur*, don't be in such a hurry!" They met again on 30 April. "My dear friend, make an effort, try to be less incom-prehensible!" Proust resumed, "you say an earl's daughter is called

Lady, and his brother Esquire?" "No, the Honourable." "So when
you speak to him, you call him Honourable Sir?" persisted Proust,
with a gaze of deep sadness and tortured perplexity. Nicolson suggested that this passion for detail was a sign of the literary temperament.
"Certainly not!" exclaimed Proust crossly, and blew a kiss across
the table to his favourite Gladys Deacon. Soon, however, they were
discussing homosexuality, which Nicolson supposed must be 'a
matter of glands or nerves'. "It is a matter of habit," replied Proust,
and when Nicolson demurred he added, still more obscurely: "No,
that was silly of me, what I meant was that it's a matter of delicacy." Nicolson decided that he was 'not very intelligent on the
subject'.

Whether from habit or delicacy, Proust had been suffering for seven
months from his first protracted love-affair since the passing of Agostinelli. 'I have embarked on a sentimental enterprise without possibility of joy or retreat, a perpetual source of fatigue, anguish and
absurd expense,' he had told Mme Straus in November 1918. Writing
to Walter Berry on the very night of the second dinner with Nicolson,
he spoke of 'an unhappy love which is now finishing'. And on 7 May
he invited Vaudoyer to dine at his bedside with Reynaldo and 'a youth
I've been sheltering for several months, who won't be in our way
because he never says anything'. This unloquacious young person
was Henri Rochat, a Swiss employee of the Ritz, whom Proust had
hired as secretary; and indeed he now occasionally dictated letters to
Rochat, who wrote in a clear hand but with shaky spelling. Proust
detected in his new captive 'an amazing gift for painting'. He took him
to see the little still-life of two apples by Fantin Latour which hung in
Jacques Émile Blanche's dining-room at Auteuil; but Blanche,
although it was past eleven o'clock, was still out. One of the few traits
of Rochat in Albertine as prisoner which can be differentiated from
those of Agostinelli is her talent for painting, 'a touching recreation of
the captive,' says the Narrator, 'which moved me so much that I complimented her'.[1] But Proust's belief that his 'unhappy love' was now
ending was only a false alarm, for Rochat's captivity was to last for
two years more.

Towards the middle of March Proust sent the final proofs of
Pastiches et Mélanges to press, with a dedication to Walter Berry.
"Why Berry?" asked Antoine Bibesco one evening at his bedside,

[1] III, 180, 68, 409. Morel, too, says the Narrator, had 'a magnificent handwriting, disfigured by the grossest spelling mistakes' (II, 1034).

and: "Because he won the war!" Proust replied. 'Antoine left full of
sound doctrine, and I was delighted at this education of the masses
through the spoken word,' Proust reported to Berry; for he liked to
believe that his friend had been chiefly responsible for America's
intervention, and therefore for victory.[1] Publication of his three books
was promised for early May, and he therefore refused a gratifying
request from Sydney Schiff for an extract to appear in the July number
of his magazine *Art and Letters*. On 25 April, however, Proust unwillingly consented to postpone publication until early June, to allow
Rivière to print the conclusion of the Narrator's love for Gilberte
from *A l'Ombre* in the *Nouvelle Revue Française* for 1 June 1919. The
NRF had ceased publication in August 1914, a month after the issue
of 1 July 1914 containing extracts from *Le Côté de Guermantes*; and
the gulf of nearly five years was thus appropriately bridged.

As the time for a decision on his new home approached, Proust flew
agitatedly in decreasing circles from impossible dreams to possible
realities. He thought of visiting Perugia, Siena and Pisa, of taking
Mme Catusse's villa at Nice from May to November, of accepting
Antoine and Elizabeth's invitation to stay with them in England (he
had attended the dinner in honour of their engagement in March, and
they were married on 30 April in London). He found a fifth-floor flat
in the Rue de Rivoli, conveniently near the Ritz; the proprietor called
on 10 May to ask his concierge: "Is M. Proust an honourable man and
a quiet lodger?", and was told that he was both indeed. Proust asked
the new manager of 102 Boulevard Haussmann to settle the lease,
arranged thriftily for Guiche to sell his cork walls to a manufacturer of
bottle-corks, and made Céleste burn 'precious autographs, manuscripts of which no other copy exists, photographs which have
become rare'. But no one who really knew him can have been surprised
when on 30 May, the day before his tenure of 102 Boulevard Haussmann expired, he suddenly resolved to move to 8 *bis* Rue Laurent-
Pichat, the home of the great actress Réjane.

Her son Jacques Porel, who had glimpsed Proust in his violet cloak
on the golf-course at Cabourg in 1911, and enthusiastically forced his
mother to plough through *Du Côté de chez Swann* in 1914, was now an
unemployed war-hero aged twenty-six. In May 1917, when Porel had
been invalided from the army after being gassed at Ypres, Proust

---

[1] The dedication reads: 'To Monsieur Walter Berry, who from the first day
of the war, before a still undecided America, pleaded the cause of France with
incomparable energy and talent, and gained it.'

heard from Morand of his admiration for *Swann*, and sent Céleste ('a long fragile lady with a fixed smile, like an angel in a cathedral', Porel remembered) to summon the proselyte. "I like him, but he seems a bit flighty," Céleste reported, and ever afterwards Proust called his friend 'Porel the Flighty', and would say: "See that all the windows are shut, Céleste, or Monsieur Porel will fly away!" On this first visit Proust recalled the day in September 1914 at Trouville when Réjane, "that woman I madly admire, called me a Boche at Mme Straus's, and nearly pushed me into a rosebush"; and on the third, Porel says, 'he knew me better than my most intimate friends did'. He spoke so vividly of Balzac one evening when they dined together that Porel had the eery impression that Balzac himself would soon enter the restaurant and sit at their table. Dickens's *Bleak House*, Proust declared, was one of his favourite novels.[1] Porel noticed the pale Henri in the background, but felt that Proust had retired from life and love, that 'he enjoyed giving himself the sight of a young creature to whom he did service, and that was all'. He spoke often of homosexuality, but with remote objectivity, in the manner of Charlus to Brichot at Mme Verdurin's soirée in *La Prisonnière*: "*They* are so numerous nowadays that one might say it's *they* who are normal. For instance, So-and-so is normal, you can take my word for it, but X is abnormal, he likes women." Proust knew very well that Porel, in this sense, was 'abnormal', and it was to him that Porel first confided his love for the beautiful Anne-Marie, a war-nurse divorcée, whom he married on 11 March 1918. "I fear for you," Proust said, "when I see you preparing to advance into life, so young, with this marvellous burden on your arm." Now, in May 1919, on the second floor of 8 *bis* Rue Laurent-Pichat lived the great Réjane, aged sixty-two, still immensely celebrated and popular, but dying in harness; on the third floor were Porel and his wife with their seven-months old baby girl; and on the fourth floor was a vast furnished flat which Réjane kept for her estranged daughter, should she ever return, and which Porel providentially offered to Proust. He came, feeling that a fragment of his destiny was calling. Was he not entering the home of the dying Berma and her children?

It was a step towards his own death. By a strange coincidence the first new proofs of *Le Côté de Guermantes* came on the day of his departure, containing the description of the Narrator's despair when

---

[1] So was *Great Expectations*, and Proust was delighted when Lucien Daudet pointed out that the relationship between Magwitch and Pip resembled that between Charlus and Morel.

his family moved to a new apartment in the Guermantes mansion, where 'the twittering of the birds at daybreak seemed insipid to Françoise'. It was a memory of the Proust family's removal to 45 Rue de Courcelles in October 1900; but as he writhed in the asthma which always accompanied a change of residence Proust could savour the Narrator's remark, that he 'always found it as difficult to assimilate new things as he found it easy to abandon old'.[1] He did not regret 102 Boulevard Haussmann, but he was now homeless and uprooted for ever.

The house was made of paper, he declared, and noisier than the Gotha raids. At first the air seemed pure, but soon he decided that the trees of the Bois de Boulogne, only a quarter of a mile away, were giving him hay-fever; and the deluge of water when the actor Le Bargy performed his toilet in the house next door was muffled only by the sound of his own gasping for breath. Workmen arrived in Porel's apartment, and he shuddered at every hammer-blow. The lift was out of order, and on the stairs he would meet Réjane, panting also with her tired heart. The two invalids exchanged only a few words, but next day he talked endlessly of her with Porel, summoning his friend in this theatrical house by knocking thrice on the floor, in imitation of the three raps with which the curtain rises at the Comédie Française.

Thirty years had passed since Proust in his schooldays saw Réjane in the first night of *Germinie Lacerteux*. She was still as supreme in comedy as her friend Sarah Bernhardt in tragedy, and Proust created his Berma from both; but now she played only old women, sold the Théâtre Réjane which she had founded, and surrendered her great rôle in Sardou's *Madame Sans-Gêne* at the rueful request of Robert de Flers, who had married Sardou's daughter. During Proust's stay in her house she was resting, exhausted but bored, longing to live again and die on the stage. In the winter, with the reluctant consent of Dr Audistère and her son, she was to make a sensational return in Henri Bataille's *La Vierge Folle*, and in the spring of 1920 to play in a film which killed her.

It was on the tragedy of the Rue Laurent-Pichat that Proust based the terrible episode at the end of *Le Temps Retrouvé*, when the aged Berma sacrifices her life to the avarice of her daughter and son-in-law in a last revival of *Phèdre*, and the guests invited to her tea-party desert her for the Princesse de Guermantes's matinée.[2] As so often when he used a situation from real life, in his alteration of minor

[1] II, 9.   [2] III, 856, 995-8, 1002-3, 1013-14.

details Proust meticulously alludes to the actual circumstances under
the pretext of disguising them. Instead of son and daughter-in-law
Berma's relatives are her daughter and son-in-law[1]; they live not in her
own house but next door; the hammer-blows of their house-
renovations, which 'interrupted the sleep of which the great tragic
actress had such need', are the same that disturbed the slumbers of a
great novelist; and for only the second time in the whole of *A la
Recherche* Proust here mentions Réjane herself by name.[2] In other
respects he reversed the real position, for Porel and his wife were
neither mercenary nor snobbish nor heartless; indeed, Porel's feckless
disregard for money, his intimacy on equal terms with such men as
Giraudoux, Morand, Cocteau, Fargue, his indifference to all but the
intellectual left wing of the nobility, his filial adoration of his mother,
were known to everyone. Proust can have had neither the fear nor the
intention of seeming to portray Porel and Anne-Marie, except by
contrast, and the appalling cruelty of the last days of Berma, the final
turn of the screw which completes the ruin of the Narrator's world,
was enforced by aesthetic necessity. And yet, just as the wounded
feelings which Proust cherished towards Montesquiou, Mme de
Chevigné and Fénelon form an essential part in the greatness of his
creation of Charlus, the Duchesse and Saint-Loup, so this incident is
bitterly leavened with his personal resentment for the annoyances of
his sojourn in the house of Réjane.[3]

Proust's discontent, however, was only intermittent. At the end of
the month for which he had agreed to come he decided to stay,
thought of taking a lease for three years, and in fact remained for four
months. 'He maintained that he was an unbearable lodger,' wrote
Porel, 'but in fact he was a charming neighbour.' He took a fancy to
Charmel, their eighty-year-old concierge, who dyed his hair yellow
and looked like an impoverished marquis, and delighted in Céleste's

---

[1] Even so, Proust forgets once and calls them 'her son and daughter-in-law'
(III, 995).

[2] III, 997. The other mention, a passing compliment, was no doubt added at
the same time (II, 495).

[3] It may be noted also that the description of Berma's son-in-law as 'ailing
and lazy' refers unkindly but not unfairly to Porel. Her doctor's excuse for
allowing Berma to return to the stage, that 'she enjoys it, so it will do her good'
(his real motive being that he is in love with the young wife), is founded on
Dr Audistère's reluctant decision, reported by Porel, that 'the worst danger of
all would be to impose upon this fearless and exacting woman a total cessation
of her activity' (III, 995).

reports of the old man's gallantry on the servants' staircase.[1] He received visits from Rivière, Morand, and Giraudoux, whose *La Nuit à Châteauroux* he greatly admired in the NRF for 1 June, but whose review of *A l'Ombre* he thought 'exquisite, crammed with wit, and utterly disappointing'. Soon he forgot his half-imaginary miseries in the proof-correction of *Le Côté de Guermantes* and the battle for his books.

Publication had been announced for 6 June, then for 15 June; and certain 'obstinate maniacs', as he severely informed Gallimard, had even called early in the month at the NRF offices in the Rue Madame hoping in vain to buy his new works. *A l'Ombre des Jeunes Filles en Fleurs*, *Pastiches et Mélanges* and the new edition of *Du Côté de chez Swann* appeared at last in the week beginning 23 June 1919.

The common belief that *A l'Ombre* was an instant success is almost as mistaken as the idea that the first publication of *Swann* was a failure. Whether on the NRF's advice, or from exhaustion, or because he had decided to leave his novel to find its destiny unaided, Proust had abandoned his practice of arranging to be reviewed by his friends. For old times' sake he made a single exception, and asked Robert de Flers for a front-page article in *Le Figaro*, suggesting the well-known names of Gide, Léon Blum, Louis de Robert, Edmond Jaloux and Francis de Miomandre as possible reviewers. But he unaccountably delayed even this proposal until the week before publication, and Flers could only offer a notice by Robert Dreyfus in the form of a front-page news-item, which appeared on Monday, 7 July. Proust gently complained that the print was too small, that Dreyfus had signed only with his pseudonym 'Bartholo', and had used the forbidden word 'meticulous'. He did not know until later that on the Sunday night Henri Vonoven, Cardane's successor as managing editor, had been horrified to find that the article had been printed by mistake on page 2, and stopped the presses and re-arranged the lay-out of the paper for Proust's and everyone's sake. During the first five months *A l'Ombre* was reviewed less promptly and little more extensively than *Swann* had been in the same period.[2] The NRF had issued six editions

---

[1] Proust gave Charmel's name to one of M. de Charlus's footmen (II, 559, 1062).

[2] Reviews appeared by Giraudoux in *Feuillets d'Art* for June, by Fernand Vandérem in *Revue de Paris* on 15 July, by Abel Hermant in *Le Figaro* on 3 and 23 August, by Francis de Miomandre in *Paris Magazine* and François Mauriac in *Revue des Jeunes* on 25 August, by André Billy in *L'Œuvre* on 26 August,

simultaneously, and these satisfied the brisk though not overwhelming demand until the beginning of December.

Nevertheless, Proust's situation had subtly but radically changed since 1913. With the end of the war, and the final signing of peace on 28 June 1919, came a universal feeling that France and the world were reborn, and the arts and intellectual life of mankind renewed. In fact the twentieth-century revolution in literature, as in music and painting, had taken place before and during the war, unnoticed except by the intelligentsia; but now at last it was possible for the new names to become famous and popular. The centre of gravity in French literature had shifted from Anatole France, Barrès, Bourget, Mme de Noailles, Rostand, to Gide, Claudel, Larbaud, Giraudoux, Valéry and Cocteau, all of whom were closely associated with and published by the NRF; and now Proust's name, thanks to his farseeing choice in 1916, was linked with theirs. *Swann* had won him passionate admirers, known and unknown, though few in number; and these, with his new comrades of the NRF, had enrolled an underground network of invisible converts. To all appearance *A l'Ombre* was a moderate success like *Swann*, the indolent reviewers blew hot and cold, and it seemed that the six editions would see the year out. In reality the air of Paris was saturated with his coming glory, as with an unnoticed inflammable vapour which awaited only the exploding spark; and Proust, with the uncanny insight into his destiny which he had shown throughout his life, but hitherto only in slow patience, divined what he must do. In September he informed Louis de Robert that he was applying for the Goncourt Prize.

Meanwhile he had passed the summer in lamenting that he had no first editions of *A l'Ombre* to send to Mme de Noailles, the Princesse de Chimay, Comtesse Greffulhe, Anatole France, Barrès, and many more. An undiscoverable bookseller had cornered them all, 'as if they were butter or coffee,' he complained. With strange procrastination he desultorily sent out third editions several months later. France, 'the first of my masters, the greatest and the best-loved', as Proust had inscribed in his copy of *Swann* six years before, was too old to appreciate his pupil: "Life is too short and Proust is too long," he sighed, and after Proust's death he declared not unkindly to a young

---

by Dominique Braga in *Crapouillot* on 1 September, by Jacques Émile Blanche in *Le Figaro* on 22 September, and by Gaston Rageot, Proust's former 'usurper', in *Le Gaulois* on 25 October.

friend: "I liked him, haven't seen him for twenty years, I don't understand his work, but that's my fault not his, I belong to the generation
before."

On 14 July, while Proust slept, the great victory procession of the
Allies marched down the nearby Avenue de la Grande Armée and
through the Arc de Triomphe, where Fernand Gregh watched with
Montesquiou. The Count had not relished his portrait in the Saint-
Simon pastiche, and later grumbled to Marcel about his third edition
of *A l'Ombre*: "But there's nothing rare about it!" Gregh introduced
his twelve-year-old son Didier; but Count Robert sharply announced:
"This boy reminds me of a person whom I loathed more than anyone
else in my life," and Gregh, looking in alarm at his child, recognised a
hint of the delicate features of Léon Delafosse.

On 24 July Proust asked Robert Dreyfus's advice on taking a
fourth-floor apartment in September at 156 Boulevard Malesherbes,
next door to Dreyfus himself, at the far northern end of the boulevard
and nearly a mile from the home of his youth; but on the 28th his
messenger found the 'To Let' notice gone. 'The foxes have holes, and
the birds of the air have nests, but the Son of Man hasnot where to lay
his head,' he quoted, and decided to apply to a house-agent. Jacques
Émile Blanche called on Réjane, unaware that Marcel lived in the same
house, and was astounded to hear old Charmel say: "Monsieur
Proust? Fourth floor!" "I've been at the point of death three times
today," Marcel began, but Blanche declared in a loud aside to Céleste:
"He looks the picture of health to me." "Oh, Monsieur," replied the
flustered Céleste, "we're too near the country!" It was true, however:
'I've put on weight,' Proust had told Princesse Soutzo last month,
'my eyes aren't so tired, I look a bit less old, now it's no use to me.'
And Blanche, as they talked gaily over wine and biscuits brought by
Céleste, decided that Marcel looked young indeed, about twenty-
nine, almost only twenty, like the innocent portrait by himself which
he had noticed on entering; 'but his cheeks were paler, bronzed by the
furnace in which he fused the metal of his book'. Proust arranged to go
to Cabourg on 15 August in a friend's car; but he dined the night
before at the Ritz with Berry, the champagne was all too good, he
went to the Bois, 'sublime in silence, solitude and moonlight' to
recover from its effects; and deciding he was happiest in Paris, he let
the motor-car and Cabourg go for ever.

Réjane and the Porels left for Venice in September, enabling him to
stay a few weeks longer and find a new apartment. Boni de Castellane

called, and though Proust refused his invitation to dinner because
Boni had been rude to his aunt Mme Thomson, he was amused to find
himself treated for these last few days with paternal affection by the
aged Charmel, who had been in service long ago with Boni's father,
the late Marquis. On 1 October, after the carpet-layers and electricians
had worked until one in the morning, he moved into his last home at
44 Rue Hamelin.

It was a quiet, narrow and gloomy street, running downhill from
the Avenue Kléber halfway between the Arc de Triomphe and the
Trocadéro, and dominated at its southern end by the incongruous
skeleton of the Eiffel Tower beyond the Seine. The Rue Hamelin
today seems shabby, even vaguely immoral; but in Proust's time it
was still considered a moderately distinguished address, and contained
one princess, five marquises, six countesses and a baron, not to mention Mme Standish in the Rue de Belloy just round the corner. Even
Monsieur Virat, the baker on the ground floor and proprietor of No.
44, had his château in Seine-et-Marne and his name in *Bottin Mondain*
with the nobs. Proust inhabited a small furnished apartment on the
fifth floor, 'a vile hovel just large enough for my bedstead', he told
Montesquiou, which cost 16,000 francs in rent. He made a present of
felt slippers to the children who ran about on the floor above. But in
the very discomfort of this bare, monastic dwelling there was something that comforted him, chimed with the sacrificial impulse which
had made him sell his parents' furniture, and left him with no desire to
change. He slept and worked in the brass bed of his childhood, with
his manuscript piled on the mantelpiece and on the little bamboo bedside table, 'my shallop'; at last he was alone with his book.

In September Reynaldo Hahn had spent a few days at the Daudets'
country house, La Roche, near Tours, with the mission of sounding
Proust's prospects for the Goncourt Prize. He reported that 'they
discussed the Prize a great deal, and Léon Daudet wouldn't even listen
to what was said about the other candidates, but said he would vote
for you whatever happened'. A few days later Rosny *aîné* wrote:
'Several of my fellow-members have asked me to find out whether, if
the Prize was offered to you, you would accept it,' and when Proust
politely demurred wrote again to insist. Proust sent *A l'Ombre* to each
of the Ten, asked Louis de Robert and Robert de Flers to use their
influence, and awaited developments. Léon Daudet undertook his
crusade with truculent enthusiasm, not only from a genuine admiration for Proust's work, but also from emotions of family piety; for

it was twenty-five years since 'little Marcel' had become the friend and
protégé of himself, his mother, his brother Lucien, and his venerated
father. Proust had maintained distant amicable relations with the
Rosny brothers (though Rosny *jeune* did not always vote on the same
side as Rosny *aîné*) since their meeting at Cabourg in 1910. "Proust is
something new," Rosny *aîné* told his fellow-members. Of his two
other wellwishers in 1913 only Céard remained, for Paul Margueritte
had died in 1918. He had three certain votes, Daudet, Rosny *aîné* and
Céard, and could only leave the rest to fortune.

The Goncourt Academy sat, or rather lunched, on 10 December,
and on that afternoon Proust was wakened by a triumphant Léon
Daudet bearing the following letter:

'*Monsieur et cher confrère*,
                    We have the honour and pleasure to inform
you that you have been nominated today for the Goncourt Prize.
Elémir BOURGES   Gustave GEFFROY   J. H. ROSNY, *aîné*
Léon HENNIQUE   Léon DAUDET   Paul AJALBERT
J. H. ROSNY, *jeune*   Henry CÉARD.'

Proust had received the narrow margin of six votes, while the remaining four had gone to *Les Croix de Bois*, a war novel by Roland Dorgelès.[1] Almost simultaneously up came Rivière, Gallimard, and the
NRF's editorial manager Tronche, bursting with congratulations,
and were introduced round Proust's bedside, on this historic but
uneasy occasion, to Léon Daudet, their literary and political opposite.
Next came hordes of journalists, eager one and all 'to offer you the
front page of my paper', whom Proust imprudently dismissed unseen
before subsiding into asthma.

The Prize brought the instantaneous explosion into fame towards
which Proust had striven for thirty years. Next day there were twenty-
seven articles in the newspapers, and the hundred-mark was passed
before the end of January. He was well aware that his celebrity was
due, at the moment, merely to the sensational award of the first postwar Goncourt Prize to an intellectual non-combatant of whom the

[1] Émile Bergerat and Lucien Descaves had voted by post. Bourges, Céard,
Daudet and Rosny *aîné* voted for Proust. The names of his two other supporters
have not been recorded, but (unless Rosny *jeune* was among them) they were
probably Geffroy and Bergerat, with both of whom Proust is later found on
good terms. Descaves and Hennique are known to have voted for Dorgelès, the
latter protesting that Edmond de Goncourt's will had stipulated that preference
should be given to younger writers.

general public had never heard: it was a tribute not to his genius but to his news-value. His name was familiar overnight to all the millions in France who read a daily newspaper. 'And I thought I was unknown,' he remarked ironically to Grasset. Many of the comments were preposterously irrelevant: the refusal of the prize to the ex-soldier Dorgelès was an insult to all patriotic Frenchmen, its award to Proust was a political recompense, engineered by the right-wing Daudet, for his services as an anti-Dreyfusard (!) and a supporter of the Church. He had been at school with Daudet at the Lycée Stanislas (of all places), he had bribed Bourges (whom he had never met) with sumptuous dinners; he was too rich to need the money; he was too old, for on the day of the Prize he was forty-eight, next day he was fifty-two, and by the end of the week he was fifty-eight—'I am resignedly awaiting the celebration of my hundredth birthday,' remarked Proust. Paul Morand arrived brandishing Dorgelès's novel with a paper band reading in large letters: 'Goncourt Prize', and in very tiny letters: 'Four votes out of ten'. "You must prosecute him for forgery, Marcel!" he cried; and Proust wrote in chagrin to Gallimard: 'I'm not sure whether this offence really comes under the law of forgery, but I do feel it's not playing the game.'

From the very beginning, however, there was no lack of more responsible comment. Rivière wrote in next day's *Excelsior*, Léon Daudet in his *L'Action Française* on the day after, Souday in *Le Temps* on 1 January 1920, that the Prize had never been given to a more distinguished novel.[1] The malice of the opposition journalists defeated its own ends by making him notorious. Even the voters for Dorgelès wrote apologetically: 'If you'd been a candidate for membership we'd have voted for you.' Several members of the Académie Française (though surely not as mnay as twenty, as Proust alleged) wrote: 'What a pity you have the Goncourt Prize, because we meant to award you our Grand Prix.' The NRF had been taken by surprise, and *A l'Ombre* instantly went out of print; but Gallimard made a rush order, and from 21 December onwards edition after edition was on sale, with the words 'Goncourt Prize', truthful this time, on the wrapper.

Henceforth Proust's fame was established, immense, and ever-growing. The immediate sensation, like the Prize itself, as he well

[1] In fact, with the sole exception of *Le Feu* (1917) by Henri Barbusse, Proust's former companion on *Le Banquet*, *A l'Ombre* was the only novel of lasting merit crowned by the Académie Goncourt from its foundation in 1903 until the award of the prize to Malraux's *La Condition Humaine* in 1933.

knew, was a vanity and a mockery, and unconnected with the reality of his novel; but its persistence was due to a widening and deepening conviction of his genius in the mind of the individual reader. In this aspect the Prize was an award of love, the closest possible earthly symbol of his dominion in eternity. 'I don't care if the Prize lowers me a little,' he defiantly told Souday, 'so long as it wins me readers.'

Proust spent the 5000 francs of the Prize within a few days on dinner-parties of gratitude. His financial position, however, had unexpectedly improved. In October he had mentioned to Robert de Billy, then on leave in Paris from his post as French plenipotentiary at Athens, his difficulty in realising the famous Warburg cheque. A pathetic misunderstanding ensued; for Billy, unaware that he was not the first but the last of Marcel's influential friends to be asked for help in the same affair, and believing Marcel was in real need of the money, promised to cash it through his own bank. Billy's bank, however, since the cheque was still under sequestration and not yet legal tender, would only accept it as security for an advance in which Billy must act as guarantor. In effect, Proust had unintentionally extorted a large and unwanted loan from Billy himself, and was as far as ever from cashing the Warburg cheque. In his embarrassment he further complicated their cross-purposes by writing: 'I have what I wanted, the proof that I was mistaken in you, and that you are the best and most generous of friends'; and Billy remained under the mistaken impression that Marcel had devised this request as a fantastic test of their friendship. Proust resumed his efforts in the New Year, but in vain; the law would not be hurried, and it was not until December 1920 that he received a first instalment, which he immediately turned over to Billy. A happier windfall was his discovery in December 1919 that he still possessed four Royal Dutch shares of the seventy he had sold in 1913, and that through subsequent bonus issues they had miraculously increased to twelve. Owing to the postwar rise in oil each was now worth 33,000 francs; and he bought Céleste a hat crowned with a stuffed bird of paradise on the strength of it.

In the *Nouvelle Revue Française* for 1 January 1920 appeared Proust's remarkable essay '*A propos du Style de Flaubert*', which he proposed to Rivière about 16 November 1919, delivered on 10 December, and intended for the never-published second volume of *Pastiches et Mélanges*. His appreciation of Flaubert, though severely limited ('he is a writer I do not greatly care for') is extraordinarily new and true, yet is directed to qualities (grammatical innovations, solidity of style, the substitution of impression for direct narrative, the sense of Time) which belong to his own work as much as to Flaubert's. His renewed attack on Sainte-Beuve for inability to detect genius in contemporary writers, his complaint that 'we have lost the ability to read', is secretly addressed to the readers and critics of *A la Recherche*; and he concludes by pointing out 'the rigorous though veiled construction' of his own novel, and quotes—as if knowing that otherwise he would never live to see their effect on his readers—the precedents for unconscious memory in Chateaubriand and Gérard de Nerval which were to appear in *Le Temps Retrouvé*. On 22 February Rivière suggested an article on Sainte-Beuve for the April NRF, and soon Proust received from the circulating library managed by Tronche a collection of Sainte-Beuve's works on loan; for his own books were now stored in a warehouse, and he had made the many quotations in '*A propos du Style de Flaubert*' from memory. But time was too short to fight again the long-won victory of *Contre Sainte-Beuve*, and after half-promising the article for July he abandoned the plan in May, though he was soon to return to the same subject elsewhere. He offered to lend money to Rivière, who was poor, anxious for his pregnant wife,[1] neurasthenic, exhausted by the toils of editing, and in need of a holiday; and he sent him to his cousin-in-law Dr Roussy, who gave excellent advice and refused a fee, saying; "I am only too happy to give Marcel this token of my friendship." Without informing Rivière Proust sent an honorarium of 100 francs, which Roussy gave to charity.

The proof-enrichment of *Le Côté de Guermantes* had been delayed by insomnia and fatigue, during which he could do nothing but play draughts with Henri Rochat, as does the Narrator with Albertine.[2] The mere correction of misprints, which for the ordinary writers of this world is the sole labour of seeing their books through the press, seemed more impossible than ever. In February he asked the NRF for help; and they appointed André Breton, then chieftain of the Dadaists and not yet king of the surrealists, who performed his task with the utmost negligence, but was so enraptured by the poetry of Proust's novel that he began to spread his fame among the Dadaist young. Late in March Gallimard asked Rivère to persuade Proust to publish the first volume of *Le Côté de Guermantes* separately, in order not to

[1] Alain Rivière, named after Rivière's dead brother-in-law Alain-Fournier, author of *Le Grand Meaulnes*, was born on 11 March 1920.

[2] III, 67, 71, 372.

keep the public waiting till past the end of the year. Proust consented and delivered the final proofs about 23 May. Meanwhile, early in April, appeared the *de luxe* edition of *A l'Ombre* which he had planned ever since February 1919. There were fifty copies at 300 francs apiece, each containing folding sheets of the manuscript or of the heavily revised Grasset proofs of 1914 from which the original edition had been printed, together with a reproduction of his portrait as a young man by Blanche. The Schiffs bought one, Princesse Soutzo another, Berry three, feeling that after he had pointedly asked their advice on its circulation they could do no less. All but twelve of the fifty copies, with their vital evidence on the evolution of Proust's text, remain still to be rediscovered.

On 4 May he attended the gala performance of the Russian Ballet at the Opéra. Bakst, his companions informed him, was now in hospital with general paralysis, Nijinski, whom he had seen dancing the negro slave at the first night ten years before, was insane; the glory seemed departed from *Schéhérazade*. Beside him sat a niece of Comte Othenin d'Haussonville; and there, in a nearby stall, was the old man himself, now seventy-seven, changed by the ocean of years from his slender, ironic affability into the virile figure of the hunting squire his father. 'I felt that the years had given his head, without modifying its curves, a majesty which it did not have to such a degree before,' he wrote to Mme Straus; and he used the model for the Duc de Guermantes at the end of his novel: 'lashed on all sides by the waves of suffering and anger at suffering,' says the Narrator, 'by the mounting tide of death that hemmed him in, his face, crumbling like a rock, kept the style and curves I had always admired'.[1]

He had kept in touch with Porel, and called at Rue Laurent-Pichat one evening, tottering and smiling in white tie and tails, when Ricardo Vinès was playing Debussy. Proust sat on the sofa with Léon Paul Fargue, while the pianist, his head buried in the keyboard, seemed to confide a secret to the composer; and glancing at the couple on the sofa Porel saw that Fargue, who became somnolent when supremely happy and was never happier than when Debussy was played, had fallen asleep on Proust's shoulder. When the news of the Goncourt Prize came Réjane had asked to be allowed to give him a present. "I'd like her photograph dressed as the Prince de Sagan in the Marquis de Massa's revue at the Épatant," declared Proust without hesitation, and Porel brought it next day. She wore full evening dress and top hat, with the Prince's white hair, white gardenia, and monocle with the surprisingly broad black ribbon, but in her ears were pearl ear-rings. "Admire the intelligence of her interpretation," exclaimed Proust, "she is playing a male impersonation, but she has had the elegance to keep her ear-rings!"

On 14 June the dying Réjane had planned to see the first night of *Antony and Cleopatra* in Gide's translation at the Opéra. When the evening came she said only: "You ought to have taken Anne-Marie," and Porel, for in real life the great actress's children did not desert their mother, lamely replied: "Oh, you know, Shakespeare in summer, and in French!" A few moments later Réjane called his name, and died in his arms. Proust was at the Opéra in Princesse Soutzo's box with Henri Bardac, who reproached him a few days later for talking incessantly to his friends and paying no attention to the play; but Proust, raising his hands in protest, delivered so brilliant a lecture on Shakespeare, on the acting of Ida Rubinstein and Édouard de Max, the lighting in the banquet-scene, the conversation in the neighbouring boxes and incidents among the spectators below, that Bardac realised once more that Marcel always paid attention to everything. The news of Réjane's death arrived during the last interval, and Proust hurried to Rue Laurent-Pichat.

At this terrible moment, while Porel raved with grief, Proust stood pale and silent; as Porel was now, so had he been fifteen years before. At last he offered mechanically his customary words of consolation, which in the case of the guiltless and devoted Porel were true: that when at last the wound of separation was healed his mother would return, young and happy, and live for ever. Proust meditated all night in tense anguish, and at dawn found release in weeping. 'Keep what I said to you for the day when you will be able to use it,' he wrote to Porel, 'at present my words are meaningless for you, and may perhaps contradict bitter thoughts; but you will find them true, consoling and strengthening when you have made the journey from parting to memory, of which no one, alas, can spare you the cruel meanders.' At Porel's request he offered a tribute to Réjane for the NRF, which Rivière accepted with enthusiasm; but on reflection he found himself incapable of writing it. His words to Porel were not yet wholly true of himself. In his novel, just as he had projected his own homosexuality upon the other characters, and left the Narrator free of this gravest of sins, he had reconciled the mutual hatred between his mother and himself which persisted at the root of their love; he had cancelled her death, and made her young and happy for ever. But the redemption which was valid in the eternal world of art was still incomplete in the world of things, on this side of the grave. At Le Cuziat's brothel in the pit of Sodom he had hated and slain her again. In this world the Two Ways would meet only in the bed of death; he had killed his mother twice over, and it only remained to let her avenging spirit kill him.

Chapter 15

THE DARK WOMAN
(*July 1920 – October 1921*)

IN the summer of 1920, thinking no more of Cabourg, Proust half
planned a holiday at Monte Carlo by royal invitation. Comte Pierre
de Polignac, a new young friend from the last years of the war, had
married Charlotte Grimaldi, Duchesse de Valentinois and adoptive
crown princess of Monaco, on 19 March 1920. Her grandfather, the
reigning Prince Albert (1848-1922) was a friend of the Strauses,
through whom Proust had sought his protection for Agostinelli's
widow in 1914; and Polignac, in allusion to an incident in the Saint-
Simon parody in *Pastiches et Mélanges*, had gracefully remarked
when announcing his engagement to Marcel: "Perhaps this will enable
me to meet the lady who made that pretty retort to M. de Noyon!"[1]
The match was made for dynastic reasons, for Prince Albert's second
marriage to the gay Princesse Alice, born a Heine, widow of the Duc
de Richelieu, and mother of Gabriel de La Rochefoucauld's wife
Odile, had remained childless and ended in divorce; and the young
Duchesse de Valentinois was the recently legitimised only child of his
bachelor son Prince Louis from a morganatic liaison with an actress
in 1898. In June the royal consort visited Proust, who found him
'still nicer than when he was only Polignac', and invited him to
Monaco; but next month Proust took offence at his omission to
order the *de luxe* edition of *A l'Ombre* and broke off their friendship.

Aided by the resemblance in the amiable levity of their lives
between Princesse Alice and the Princesse de Sagan, his model for the
Princesse de Luxembourg whom the Narrator meets at Balbec in *A*

---

[1] *Pastiches et Mélanges*, 79. Proust had quoted the anecdote of Mme Straus's
reply to Gounod's remark that a passage in Massenet's *Hérodiade* was 'perfectly
octagonal': "I was just about to say the same myself"; but for Gounod he
substituted the Saint-Simonian name of M. de Noyon. François de Clermont-
Tonnerre, Bishop of Noyon, was a frequent butt of Saint-Simon, who consistently alludes to him by his episcopal title.

l'Ombre,[1] Proust now added to the proofs of *Le Côté de Guermantes* a
series of links between the fictitious Luxembourgs and the royal
family of Monaco. Pierre de Polignac became the Comte de Nassau,
who writes so sympathetically during the illness of the Narrator's
grandmother, and whom the childless Grand Duke of Luxembourg
adopts as his heir after his marriage to the 'enchanting and excessively
rich' only daughter of another prince of the family.[2] The new heir is
said by the young nobles dining in the restaurant in the fog to have
announced to the Duchesse de Guermantes: "I make a point of everyone's getting up when my wife passes!" to which the Duchesse
replies: "Well, that makes a change from her grandmother, because
she expected the men to lie down"; and when staying at the Grand
Hôtel at Balbec, it is rumoured, he insisted on having the Luxembourg
flag flown on the seafront.[3] The conversation at the Guermantes
dinner is equally malicious on the subject; and although the Narrator
silently protests that 'all these stories were equally false', and that he
'never met a better, more intelligent, refined and in a word exquisite
person than this Luxembourg-Nassau',[4] the new Duc de Valentinois
must have cursed the day when he refused to subscribe to the *de luxe*
A l'Ombre.

Le Côté de Guermantes, indeed, is particularly rich in the private
allusions to the time of proofreading, more than twenty years later,
with which Proust embellished his story of the late 1890s. The Narrator at Doncières meditates on the new world which is created, by the
temporary loss of hearing, for 'the sick man whose ears have been
hermetically stopped up'. In May 1919, foreseeing that he would be
deprived for ever of his cork walls, Proust had decided, as he wrote to
Mme de Noailles, 'to transport the means of defence into my ears'.
Mme Simone the actress (whom he had met in 1903 when she was a
friend of Antoine Bibesco and still married to Le Bargy) and Mme de
Noailles herself recommended little balls of ivory, the Duchesse de
Guiche advised cotton-wool soaked in vaseline; he tried both, but
preferred the incomparable Boules Quies, those beneficent pellets of
cotton-wool impregnated with pink medicated wax. In his delicious

[1] I, 698-703.
[2] II, 329-30.
[3] II, 410.
[4] II, 533-4, 537-9. 'Everything people say about him (that he thinks he's
become a Little King, etc.) is stupid', Proust told Sydney Schiff, 'but unfortunately everyone says it and invents the most absurd tales'.

catalogue of sounds which are thus deadened the Narrator mentions the bathwater of Le Bargy (whose wife, by a Proustian coincidence, was thus responsible unawares for dulling the noise of her long-since-divorced husband) and the hammering at Rue Laurent-Pichat; the milk which he imagines 'a great writer' watching as it comes silently to the boil stands on the same bedside electric hot-point on which Proust made his coffee in the small hours; and it is in the voice of Céleste that his servant tells him, when the saucepan boils over and 'his books and watch are engulfed by the milky tidal-wave', that he 'has no more sense than a child of five'.[1] 'I shall regret the black and white flowers on a red background,' he had told Porel as he prepared to move to 44 Rue Hamelin, 'but I have described them in my book.' And sure enough, the Narrator's bathroom at Doncières is hung, like Proust's at Rue Laurent-Pichat, with 'a violent red wallpaper sprinkled with black and white flowers', whence he 'views the world as if from the heart of a corn-poppy'.[2]

On 25 September 1920 Proust was awarded the cross of the Legion of Honour. Various friends had asked if he would like it; he replied that he would indeed; and his sponsors in approaching the Minister of Public Education, André Honnorat, included Barrès, Regnier, Léon Blum, Robert de Flers, Léon Daudet, Céard, Reynaldo Hahn, and Paul Morand. Mme de Noailles and Colette received the same honour on the same day. A wealthy art-dealer whom he had met before the war at Cabourg sent him a superb cross set in brilliants, for dress-wear: 'at most it will serve only to adorn my hearse, as I'm too ill to attend royal dinners,' he told Mme Catusse. But now, in his glory, he was not only a receiver but a giver of prizes. Mme Georges Blumenthal, a relative of the lady whose marriage had inspired the last avatar of Mme Verdurin, invited him to join the committee for her newly founded Blumenthal Prize, on which his eminent fellow-members included Barrès, Bergson, the philosopher Émile Boutroux, Boylesve, Gide, Robert de Flers, Edmond Jaloux, Mme de Noailles and Valéry. Proust resolved to propose the noble-souled Rivière, who was in need of money but still more of self-confidence, and to whom the 12,000 francs and prestige of the prize would give a little of both. On 30 September he arrived late at the Blumenthal committee, in pain from otitis caused by his earplugs, swaying with the fatigue of his sleepless day, nearly falling at one moment on Bergson, at another on Boylesve,

[1] II, 75-8.
[2] II, 89.

and afflicted once again by the mysterious impediment in his speech.
'In appearance and smile he looked like a lady palmist,' wrote Boylesve cruelly. Proust secured a unanimous vote for his friend: Rivière,
less directly, had won a prize for him, and now he had won a prize for
Rivière.

The next instalment of *A la Recherche* had been promised for 15
August,[1] postponed till 1 October because it seemed unwise to publish
in the middle of the holiday season, reviewed from proofs by Léon
Daudet in *L'Action Française* on 8 October, and delayed again for the
printing of two pages of errata. *Le Côté de Guermantes I* at last
appeared about 25 October, and was reviewed as the work of an un-
questionably great writer, though with some foolish complaints about
snobism. In the same way reviewers of *Sodome et Gomorrhe*, *La
Prisonnière*, *Albertine Disparue* and *Le Temps Retrouvé* were to accuse
Proust successively of obsession with homosexuality, inability to love,
jealousy, and death; for it is the oldest trick in that parasitic trade to
blame an author for writing about the subject of his book. Souday,
however, deeply distressed Proust by calling him 'feminine' in *Le
Temps* on 4 November. He retorted fiercely that if Souday wished to
know whether or not he was effeminate he had only to ask the seconds
who had attended him in his duel; and when Souday tried to bury the
hatchet by sending a box of chocolates on New Year's Day, Proust
cried: "Put these on the fire, Céleste, the man who sent them is capable
of anything." But he magnanimously sent a grateful letter and a copy
of the *de luxe A l'Ombre* in return.

Early in 1920 Paul Morand had published a volume of free verse,
Lampes à arc, with a teasing and famous *Ode to Marcel Proust*:

> 'Shadow
> Born of the smoke of your fumigations
> Face and voice
> Eroded by the wear and tear of night
> Céleste
> With gentle rigour soaks me in the dark juice
> Of your room that smells of warm cork and dead hearth . . .
> Proust, to what revels do you go by night'

—for Morand evidently had some inkling of his friend's visits to
Albert's brothel—

[1] The date of the *achevé d'imprimer*, 17 August, is inconsistent with Proust's
remark to Walter Berry on 7 August that the volume was then already stitched.

'That you return with eyes so tired and lucid?
What terrors to us forbidden have you known
That you return so kind and so indulgent
Wise in the toil of souls and family secrets,
Wise in the wound of love?'

Not to be outdone, Proust contributed a preface to Morand's *Tendres stocks*, a volume of three short stories based on the love-affairs of the young diplomat in London during the early years of the war, which was to be published by the NRF in March 1921.[1] He wrote it in the first week of October 1920, after his alarming indisposition at the Blumenthal committee, and published it in the *Revue de Paris* on 15 November under the title '*Pour un ami. Remarques sur le style*'. Proust took as his text an article on Stendhal by Anatole France in the same magazine on 1 September, and respectfully but resolutely attacked the view of 'my dear master' that no good French had been written since the eighteenth century, and that style must be judged by a canon lost for ever in the French Revolution. For the third time he returned to the themes of *Contre Sainte-Beuve*, in particular to the arch-critic's misapprehension of Baudelaire. Style, Proust maintains, must be renewed in each new writer, since it consists not in adhesion to a classic model, but in the moment of identification between the author and his subject. He compared the writer, as does the Narrator in *Le Temps Retrouvé*,[2] to the optician who gives his patient a new vision of the world (for Proust had at last succeeded, after five years of failing sight, in consulting an optician), and pointed out, as does the Narrator to Albertine,[3] the unconscious symbolism with which Stendhal situated the prisons of Julien Sorel and Fabrice, where they attain spiritual freedom, in high places. He playfully represented Morand as a Minotaur devouring girls in the worldly labyrinth of luxury hotels, and offered to introduce him (it was a journey which Morand, with all his talent, was never quite to succeed in making) to the hotel of Balbec situated in the world of the imagination.

In the opening paragraph of his essay, however, Proust revealed the monster that lay in wait at the heart of his own labyrinth. 'A

[1] M. de Charlus refers during the war to 'the charming Morand, the delicious author of *Clarisse*' (III, 793)—*Clarisse*, which Proust had read in proof before appearance in the *Mercure de France* in May 1917, being the first story in *Tendres Stocks*.
[2] III, 1033.
[3] III, 377.

strange woman,' he wrote, 'has chosen to make her home in my brain. She came and went; soon, from the commotion she caused, I began to know her habits; and besides, as is the way of a too forthcoming lodger, she insisted on striking up a personal acquaintance with me. I was surprised to find that she was not beautiful. I had always believed that Death was so, for otherwise, how could she get the better of us? However this may be, she seems to be out today—but not for long, to judge from all that she has left behind. And it would be wiser to profit from the respite she gives me otherwise than by writing a preface for a wellknown author who does not need one.'

For the last fifteen years Proust had been announcing his imminent death to his friends, who were duly amused. Mme de Chevigné teased him on his '*moribondage*', and Morand had written in his Ode:

'*I say: "You seem the picture of health," you reply:*
"*Dear friend, I have nearly died three times since morning." *'

The death of his mother had shown that he too was mortal, his failure to regain health at Dr Sollier's sanatorium had destroyed his hope of recovery, the beginning of *A la Recherche* filled him with the apprehension natural to authors of being unable to see a long work through to the end; yet death had always seemed during these long years of reprieve to linger, receding rather than approaching, a little past the horizon of his novel. Now, however, recurrent warnings had convinced him that death was very near; and the preface for Morand marks Proust's irreversible realisation of his fate. His foreboding must be taken seriously, not only because it was sincere, but because it was true: he now had only two years to live. In his life as in his novel the white revelation of the madeleine was matched and concluded by the black revelation that salvation lies on the verge of the grave.

However, the deepest significance of the Morand preface lies not in the premonition of death, but in the form of Death's personification. That sombre noun, though masculine in Teutonic languages, is feminine in French, and it is natural that in France Death should seem a woman. But the hideous female lodging in Proust's brain took a strangely particular form, and may be recognised in other contexts in the final nightmares of his novel. The Narrator dreams during the captivity of Albertine that he is walking in a dark avenue; he hears a female cab-driver quarrelling with a policeman, 'reads in her voice the perfection of her features and the youth of her body', and hurries to take her cab: 'it was indeed a woman, but old, tall and stout, with white hair straying from under her cap, and a red leprosity on her face'.[1] Bergotte in his last illness has a hallucination of 'a hand with a wet towel, rubbed over his face by an evil woman'.[2] And the Narrator dreams he is talking to the dead Albertine, while 'at the far end of the room my grandmother moved to and fro, with part of her chin crumbled away like corroded marble'.[3] Nearly thirty years before, in his student days, Proust had written: 'Who knows whether, from our marriage with death, our conscious immortality may not be born?'[4] But now death, in a shape strangely but unmistakably like that of his own mother in her last years, had become a bride who did not accept the atonement of his novel, whose annihilating nuptials would be her final revenge for his crimes against her. 'This idea of death took up its abode in me as definitively as being in love. Not that I loved Death, I hated her,' says the Narrator at the end of *Le Temps Retrouvé*.[5] The real presence of death in Proust was now crystallised in the terrible figure known to psychoanalysts as the Dread Mother, whose monstrous image consummates and punishes the child's sin of love and hatred in the ultimate horror of the unconscious mind. It was with her that Proust would have to reckon in his last moments on earth, and we shall find the dark woman punctually reappearing at his bed of death.

During his October fever Proust composed another preface for a friend. In her leisure moments as a war-nurse Clément de Maugny's wife had prepared a volume of humorous drawings, *Au royaume du bistouri*, for which Proust had tried in vain to find a publisher in November 1917 and January 1919. He particularly appreciated the caption: "Wake up, there's a good boy, it's time for your sleeping-draught!"; and now, urged by the Maugnys who had secured a publisher in Geneva, he wrote a charming foreword, recalling his days by the lake with Clément in the distant summer of 1899, and describing the little train from Geneva to Évian in words he had used for the Little Train at Balbec. 'I have announced my death in a preface for Morand,' he told Mme de Maugny, coughing as he dictated to Rochat, and interrupted still further by poor Henri's question: "How do you spell cough?" Another old friend noted the significance of the Morand preface: 'The Strange Woman who took up her abode with you this winter is prowling around me,' wrote the ailing Mme Straus. How-

[1] III, 125.   [2] III, 184.   [3] III, 539.
[4] *Les Plaisirs et les Jours*, 187, first published in *Le Banquet*, July 1892.
[5] III, 1042.

ever, his otitis had been cured by the ear-specialist Dr Wicart; and he
had at last acquired a pair of reading-spectacles, which he wore only in
the privacy of his bedroom.

Early in January 1921 appeared the second volume of Jacques
Émile Blanche's *Propos de peintre*, entitled *Dates*, with a long dedica-
tory foreword, woven from roses and thorns, in which this exceedingly touchy friend replied to Proust's amiable strictures in his preface
to the first volume two years before. Blanche's eleven-page evocation
of Montesquiou and his influence upon their youth was calculated to
suggest to observant readers that the Baron de Charlus might be not
unconnected with Count Robert. Worse still, and quite mistakenly in
so far as concerned the volumes of *A la Recherche* then published,
Blanche remarked: 'It seems to me that sometimes, and in your most
beautiful pages, you borrow from one sex the features of the other;
that in certain of your characters there is a partial substitution of
gender, so that one might read "he" where you say "she".' But
Blanche made a less unkind use of inside knowledge when he prophesied: 'You will sit beneath the dome of the Academy with Jacques
Rivière, André Gide, Giraudoux and Morand when your fellow-
academician Paul Claudel is President of the Republic.'

"Marcel will belong to the Académie Française," Dr Proust had
declared long ago in moments of pride; and when his academician
friends wrote in December 1919 to congratulate him on his Goncourt
Prize, Proust began to cherish the vision of making his father's words
come true. In May 1920 he asked Rivière whether the NRF would
favour his candidature, 'supposing I had a good chance of success';
and Rivière, much taken aback, replied that they would be only too
flattered, but that the time seemed premature: 'you are too vigorous,
too positive, too truthful for these people, they are too fast asleep'.
Proust sounded his chances. The Academy was then divided, as usual,
into a hard core of retired politicians, generals, clerics, and fourth-rate
belles-lettrists, and an outer fringe of writers and intellectuals with real
merit; and several of the latter were his friends from early youth. Sure
enough, Boylesve and Bordeaux gave their enthusiastic support; his
cousin-in-law Bergson, Régnier and Barrès, whom he named to
Jacques Boulanger in December 1920 as 'my promotors for the
Academy', expressed encouragement. Half a dozen others, such as the
newly elected Robert de Flers, his aged host Comte Othenin d'Haussonville, his boyhood masters Bourget and Anatole France, his
father's colleague Gabriel Hanotaux, Darlu's friend the philosopher

Two photographs of Proust at the Jeu de Paume, after seeing Vermeer's *View of Delft*, May 1921

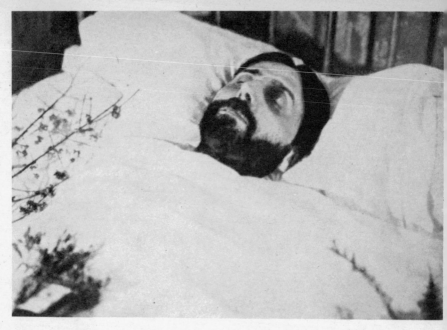

Proust on his deathbed, November 1922

Proust's bedroom, 44 rue Hamelin, with the manuscript of *A la Recherche du Temps Perdu* on bedside table and mantelpiece

Boutroux, Marcel Prévost, whom he had known ever since Louisa de Mornand acted in his *Les Demi-Vierges* fifteen years before, might well take a personal interest in him. Guiche, riding to hounds one day with Jacques Boulanger in the Forest of Ermenonville, was surprised to be informed (for though a duke, he was only a member of the Academy of Sciences, without influence on the Forty): "Marcel Proust says he'll have your help for the Academy!" Proust's willingness to sit on the Blumenthal committee, where Barrès, Bergson, Boutroux, Boylesve and Flers were his fellow-members, was doubtless part of his strategy; and in his Morand preface he meaningfully told the story of Baudelaire's abortive candidature and Sainte-Beuve's dissuasive perfidy; there was no need to point the moral.

Proust's dream was pathetic but not absurd: he would no doubt have obtained even in 1921 the preliminary token votes which are the time-honoured stepping-stone to eventual success, and if he had lived would have become an Academician not later than the 1930s. But death and his novel called more urgently; unless he could persuade the Academy to sit at midnight, how (as Barrès pointed out) could he attend its meetings?—and his project was last mentioned in a letter to Barrès in June 1921.

The publication of the second volume of *Le Côté de Guermantes* had been planned in July 1920 for December, and then, when the first volume was postponed till October, for February 1921. In January, however, Proust was still awaiting second proofs, *Sodome et Gomorrhe I* was still in manuscript, and he proposed 1 May as publication day. When the *Revue de Paris* had asked in August 1920 to print the volume as a serial, Proust refused, knowing the NRF's desire to keep their new great writer to themselves; but he was piqued by Rivière's apparent lack of zeal for extracts from the first volume,[1] and saw the opportunity to gain a wider public and extra money from occasional infidelities with other magazines. '*Une Agonie*', the episode of the grandmother's death, appeared in the NRF for 1 January 1921, attracting many new subscribers, and was followed in February by '*Un Baiser*', the story of Albertine's visit and her first kiss; but he reserved the dinner with Saint-Loup at the restaurant in the fog, which Rivière had also coveted, for the *Revue Hebdomadaire*, where it appeared on 21 January under the title '*Soirée de brouillard*'. He sent

---

[1] In fact Rivière had asked for extracts on 26 October 1919, Proust refused without giving reasons, and Rivière refrained from insisting, though he repeated the request, again without result, on 1 April 1920.

the manuscript of *Sodome et Gomorrhe I*, containing the meeting of Charlus and Jupien and the treatise on male homosexuality, to Gallimard on 20 January, swearing him to secrecy; but to make it legible to the printer Gallimard was compelled to have it typed, and it was on this typescript that Proust made his final modifications, including the deletion of a long, superb but superfluous introduction in an earlier manner.[1] There was no time for him to see a final proof of *Le Côté de Guermantes II*, or even a first proof of *Sodome et Gomorrhe I*. During the third week of April all other work was abandoned in the NRF offices, while Gallimard, Rivière and the deputy-editor Jean Paulhan, a devoted working-party, corrected the proofs on his behalf; and the volume was on sale, only one day late, on 2 May.[2]

The outcry that he had feared was not raised. The chapter on Sodom was praised or justified as being 'moral' or 'scientific'. Rivière himself, who first saw it only a fortnight before publication, declared himself 'profoundly overwhelmed', and confessed to 'a vengeful satisfaction in reading the terrible pages, made more terrible still by their very equitability, in which you describe the men of Sodom'. Rivière was still naïvely unaware that Proust was one of these, and Rivière's loyal admiration for Gide's genius did not extend to Gide's vice, still less to Gide's invert friends. 'I have listened too often to my acquaintances falsifying the idea of love,' he wrote, 'not to feel a delectable relief in hearing it discussed by someone as healthy and balanced as you.' Rivière's words were echoed by Roger Allard, the Gaston Rageot of the NRF, whose previous reviews had left Proust far from satisfied: 'These pages of such burning eloquence, such harsh and noble poetry,' wrote Allard in the NRF for September 1921, 'break the aesthetic spell of sexual inversion under which the arts and literature have lain so long bewitched.' It is strange to reflect that if his innocent friends had known the truth about Proust their opinion might have changed, yet his burning pages would still have remained the same, still have contained the moral fervour which they rightly discerned in them, without seeing that it sprang from self-accusation.

Gide himself, however, whom Proust summoned in Odilon's taxi on 13 and 17 May, was gravely displeased. To him this denunciation

---

[1] This passage, containing a vision of Balbec and Albertine called up by the heat of the day, and a meditation on the mysteries of pollen suggested by the Duchesse's rare shrub, was first published in BSAMP, tom. 6 (1956), 165-70.

[2] The *achevé d'imprimer* of 30 April is inconsistent with this fact, and must have been post-dated by several days, like that to *Le Côté de Guermantes I*.

of sodomy by a native of Sodom could only seem an act of both treachery and hypocrisy. He found Proust much altered, grown so fat that he looked vaguely like the deceased Jean Lorrain, and shivering in a stifling room. 'I used to suspect him of trading on his ill-health to protect his work, which I thought perfectly legitimate,' he noted, 'but now I was able to convince myself that he was really very unwell.' Proust, who enjoyed letting his hair down with this great invert, and relished still more the irony of shocking him, led the conversation immediately to the subject of homosexuality. He had never loved women otherwise than spiritually, he declared, and had never experienced love except with men. Baudelaire, too, was a practising invert, he rashly maintained, for "the manner in which he speaks of Lesbianism, and even his need to speak of it, would alone suffice to convince me". In order to provide material for the heterosexual part of his novel, he confessed, he had transposed to the budding grove of girls 'all that was graceful, tender and charming' in his homosexual memories. Gide sorrowfully reproached him for 'seeming to have intended to stigmatise uranism'; "Will you never portray this form of Eros for us in the aspect of youth and beauty?" he asked. Proust lamely replied that he felt Charlus and Jupien 'were not so repulsive as all that', that for him beauty had little to do with desire, and that he must reserve youth for his transpositions, because young people were the easiest to transpose. These unfortunate evenings exposed and perpetuated the incompatibility between those two inverts of genius. 'I've annoyed many homosexuals with my last chapter,' Proust told Jacques Boulanger, 'and I'm sorry for it; but it isn't my fault that M. de Charlus is elderly, and I couldn't suddenly make him look like a Sicilian shepherd boy.' Gide wrote later in his *Journal* of Proust's 'camouflage', 'this offence against the truth', and called him 'the great master of dissimulation'. More seriously still, Proust's biased avowals, made partly to tease and partly to mollify his friend, have been conveniently accepted by his critics as his final and total diagnosis of his own abnormality and its relation to his novel. Seen in their context, and compared with the known facts of his life, they form only a fraction of a far more complicated truth. In his novel Proust rejected his own inversion, and created the Narrator from the lost but real heterosexual part of his own divided nature; he used homosexuality, like snobism and cruelty, as a symbol of universal original sin; if he had told the literal truth and made the Narrator love men, he would have destroyed the symbolic truth of his work. Proust was a remorse-

ful, Gide a triumphant invert; and by Gide, whose art was based on
confession, the great opposing sexual tensions of *A la Recherche* were
mistaken for a figment of duplicity.

The publication of his latest two volumes had caused other and
quite different imbroglios with Proust's friends. Albufera had recognised in the quarrel of Saint-Loup and Rachel the memory of his own
brawls with Louisa at the Théâtre des Maturins in 1903, and severed
relations with Marcel. Mme de Chevigné had been well pleased with
her portrait in vol. 1 as the Duchesse de Guermantes with the corn-
flower hat and periwinkle eyes: 'all my next volume is about you,'
Proust had told her last summer, and: 'if you like the Duchesse half as
much as the Narrator does, who in the book is mad about her, I am
recompensed'. But the second volume, the vast dinner-party in which
the Duchesse displays her heartless vanity, the atrocious incident of
Swann and the red shoes, and Proust's suspicious delay in sending her
presentation copy, seemed a personal insult. Poor Mme de Chevigné
did not realise that here the model had changed, and the Duchesse had
temporarily become Mme Greffulhe, with a mixture, for her wit and
the red shoes, of Mme Straus. Proust himself unkindly contributed to
her misapprehension. At Mme Hennessy's dinner on 16 June, when
his hostess and Guiche correctly suggested Mme Greffulhe, he 'protested with the utmost vivacity', declaring mendaciously that Mme
Greffulhe was not the Duchesse, and truthfully that she was the Princesse de Guermantes. He spoke partly to avoid a dilemma, for Mme
Greffulhe was Guiche's mother-in-law, he liked her and appreciated
the obstinate goodwill with which during the last two decades she had
persisted in inviting him to dinners which he never attended; and she
could only be delighted to hear that she resembled the dazzling Princesse de Guermantes. But he was also determined that Mme de
Chevigné should not escape. 'Except that the Duchesse de Guermantes is virtuous,' he cruelly wrote a few days later to Guiche, 'she
resembles a little the tough hen whom I mistook long ago for a bird of
paradise, and who could only repeat like a parrot: "FitzJames is expecting me!", when I tried to capture her under the trees of the
Avenue Gabriel. By changing her into a mighty vulture, I at least
prevent people from thinking her an old magpie.' Word reached
Mme de Chevigné from malicious friends; in August she countered by
accusing Proust of snobism, and demanded her copy, four months
overdue, of this book about herself. 'Strange snobism,' he cried,
'which consists in never seeing anyone!' The book itself was his

present to her; what did it matter which of them paid for her copy? Duchesses had protested to him: "She's no duchess, she's only a lady for little Jewish drawing-rooms!"; but: "She has more breeding than you," he had replied. It was not his fault if she disliked her portrait: 'I had to show that Places and People lose from contact, Balbec for Places, and Guermantes for People.'[1] Mme de Chevigné was goaded to make the only completely effective retort: she declined to read his book. 'When I was twenty she refused to love me,' he lamented to their mutual friend Cocteau, 'will she refuse to read me now I am forty' (in fact he was now just fifty) 'and have made from her all that is best in the Duchesse de Guermantes?' 'Fabre wrote a book about insects,' replied Jean, 'but he did not expect the insects to read his book.'

Proust remained unconsoled. Indeed, the French nobility, whom he had loved all his life, and whose great obituary he had written, were not insects. In the final glory of their sunset, which coincided with the fifty years of his own existence, they had fashioned in miniature the last social culture that our world has seen, a beautiful, fugitive and irreplaceable thing that history produced and history has destroyed. In their drawing-rooms flourished a gay elegance, a fantastic individuality, a chivalrous freedom, a living interplay of minds, morals and emotions. They gave their last young blood in the war, then perished because they had served art instead of power. It is our duty as twentieth-century barbarians to salute the nineteenth-century civilisation which we have overwhelmed. So did Proust; and in the retrospective light of Time Regained, where beauty is restored to the past and disillusion itself is shown to be an illusion, the poetry of the Faubourg Saint-Germain remains in Time Lost as dazzling as the sunlight of Combray, Balbec and Venice.

As for Mme de Chevigné, although the injustice of time had changed her outward form into that of an ogrish, pearl-bedizened old lady—the 'sacred fish' with 'cheeks composite like nougat' into which the Duchesse de Guermantes is transformed in Le Temps Retrouvé[2]—

---

[1] By an unfortunate accident the chapter-headings were omitted from Le Côté de Guermantes I, and have never been restored, although they were given in June 1919 as part of the list of forthcoming volumes in Swann and A l'Ombre. They were: Noms de personnes: la duchesse de Guermantes; Saint-Loup à Doncières; Le salon de Mme de Villeparisis. The first of these corresponds to the title of the Balbec chapter in A l'Ombre, Noms de pays: le pays; and by its omission one of the chief structural themes of A la Recherche was obscured.

[2] III, 927, 937.

for Proust she was still the swift young noblewoman he had pursued
in the Avenue de Marigny, and his wounded feelings were unhealed.
'I remain as heartbroken as on the first day when she scorned me long
ago,' he told Guiche, and to herself he wrote: 'to be misjudged at
twenty years of distance'—again he minimised the date—'by the
same person, in the same incomprehensible way, without possible
excuse from the scandal-mongering of your too malevolent lady
rivals, is one of the only great sorrows which can affect at the end of his
life a man who has renounced everything'.

In his distress Proust felt resentment even against Mme de
Chevigné's son-in-law, the amiable, talented and ambitious Francis de
Croisset, who had married her daughter Marie in 1910. 'I'm not sending her my books,' he grumbled to Guiche, 'because as she met
Croisset in my house[1] and chose him for her son-in-law, I feel that
provides her with a sufficient fund of literature.' He had made a similar
complaint against Croisset to Paul Morand in 1917, and it was no
doubt at some time within this period that he used Croisset as his
model for the final aspect of Bloch in *A la Recherche*. Croisset, whose
real name was Franz Wiener, was a Belgian Jew born at Brussels in
1877 of a financier father and an English mother. Launched by Clemenceau and Octave Mirbeau, and assisted by his beautiful new name
(borrowed from Flaubert's country home near Rouen), he had cap-
tured literary and social Paris by storm in the early years of the
twentieth century, and had now taken the dead Gaston de Caillavet's
place as Robert de Flers' partner in the writing of popular light
comedies. 'Maeterlinck can't get into the Academy because he's a
Belgian, Mme de Noailles because she's a woman, Porto-Riche
because he's a Jew,' wrote Paul Léautaud in his journal, 'but Croisset's
certain to be elected, although he's all three.'[2] In memory of his
mother Croisset adopted an Anglophile attitude of distant, slightly
sinister hauteur, and formal English dress. Similarly Bloch is received
by Mme de Villeparisis as 'a young playwright, on whom she counted
to procure, free of charge, actors and actresses who would perform at
her next matinées'; and long afterwards, in *Le Temps Retrouvé*, he is

[1] This meeting was perhaps at Proust's tea-party on 6 March 1905, when
Mme de Chevigné was present. Croisset is not mentioned in the lists of guests
in the newspapers, but Proust was seeing him frequently at this time.
[2] On the other hand, Proust remarked to Lauris at Cabourg in August 1907:
'I see nothing at all of Croisset, entirely absorbed, I suppose, by his play, his
mistress, and a thousand other complications.'

married, has taken the exquisitely absurd name of Jacques du Rozier, his face is 'totally transformed by English *chic*' and by the hauteur of his monocle, and he is known as 'the Guermantes Bloch, the crony of the Guermantes'.[1]

But the most perplexing problem of all was Montesquiou. How could Count Robert fail to recognise his august person in the Baron de Charlus, who spoke in his voice and with his superhuman insolence, who was the cousin of the Duchesse de Guermantes just as he was the cousin of Mme Greffulhe, who conducted in this volume the same monumental quarrel with the Narrator as his own with Marcel in 1893, and had displayed since the beginning of the novel increasing symptoms of the homosexuality which he now finally revealed in his encounter with Jupien? True, Proust had observed his usual precaution of mentioning character and model side by side, as if to prove that they could not possibly be the same. "We have an Empire card-room that came to us from Quiou-Quiou and is a sheer marvel," says the Duchesse at dinner. M. de Charlus himself knows and feels a proper respect for Count Robert; he quotes to the Narrator ("as the only eminent man in our world has said") his saying about 'the supreme test of excessive amiability'; and in the next volume (which Montesquiou was destined not to live to see), when the Baron compliments the lovely son of Mme de Surgis on his unique knowledge of Balzac, he corrects himself: "No, I'm wrong, there's a Polignac and a Montesquiou as well."[2] In vain! At the first apparition of the Baron on the seafront at Balbec in *A l'Ombre*, as Proust had learned a year before from Henri Bardac, Count Robert had smelled a rat.

Even before the war, when he knew Proust only distantly as a friend of Reynaldo, Bardac had discussed him with Montesquiou. "It is strange," said the Count, "that it should fall to me to enlighten you concerning a person whose bourgeois rank and racial descent are so closely analogous to your own. He was a product of Mme Lemaire's garden, to the weeding of which the Empress of Roses did not always give proper attention. I do not allude particularly to little Proust, who has an original turn of mind, and whose deference to my person is all that it should be. Beneath a timid exterior he is by no means destitute of enterprise. Indeed he would have done better to devote himself to the field of big business, in which his cheek would have been aided by his fractional atavism. You, who have never advanced far into the country of the mind, might well profit by his company. But if you

[1] II, 189-90; III, 350, 823, 944, 952-3, 959, 965.   [2] II, 521, 556, 699.

want information about society, you must go to others. He thinks
Mme X is a fashionable lady!"—here the ceiling reverberated shrilly
with the exploding rockets of Count Robert's laughter. "Still, to him
and his friend Daudet I have shown benevolence which Heaven has
spared me from extending to the third thief, a certain Hahn. You
would do well," he concluded, "to give Proust the address of your
tailor."

More recently, a few months after the publication of *A l'Ombre*,
Bardac had found Montesuqiou filled with an enigmatic bitterness. He
spoke of 'shameless termites, burrowing their way through a world in
ruins', of 'barefaced opportunists, intriguing when everyone else is
weeping'. "And there's even talk of a Goncourt Prize!" he cried. Was
it not thanks only to his protection that certain distinguished persons
had taken an interest in a certain nobody? Had he ever grudged him
advice or instruction? And what did he get in return, but a note of
thanks for his congratulations, declining on grounds of alleged ill-
health the honour of his visit! "Who is that extraordinary fellow," he
hissed, "that incredible eccentric he meets on the promenade at Balbec?" Bardac tried to explain that each of the characters in Proust's
novel had several originals, which was true but uninformative. "I shall
leave you all my letters from Proust in my will!" screeched the Count
as he departed; but he forgot to do so. Bardac reported to Marcel, who
laughed, clasping his hands beneath his chin, and quoted grimly from
La Fontaine:

> " '*Romans, take heed, lest Heaven one day bestow*
> *On you our tears, on us your vengeful swords . . .*' "

Proust decided that his best policy was to defend himself before he
was attacked. On 9 March 1921, nearly eight weeks before *Le Côté de
Guermantes II* was published, with the fatal quarrel scene and encounter of Charlus and Jupien, he promised Count Robert 'to
send the two *Guermantes*, and tell you the only two spurious keys
in the whole work, which unlock only two chapters'. The Count
replied by making his own intelligent guesses: Saint-Loup, he presumed, was Albufera plus Guiche, Swann was Charles Ephrussi, and
as for the Duc and Duchesse: 'are they really the two persons who leap
to the eye? They are, whether you meant it or not'—he alluded, of
course, to M. and Mme Greffulhe. Charlus, he cleverly surmised,
though it seemed too good to be true that he should think this model
sufficient, must be based on Vautrin, the sinister and vaguely homo-

sexual master-criminal in Balzac; and he duly and gratefully recognised himself as 'the only eminent person in our world', complaining only that he would rather this eminent person had been named. In return Proust revealed that Saint-Loup, in his walk along the benches in the restaurant, was Fénelon, Swann was Haas, Mme de Villeparisis was Mme de Beaulaincourt, and Charlus—ah, Charlus, at the moment when he stared at the Narrator by the casino at Balbec, was Baron Doasan, 'habitué of Mme Aubernon's salon, where I dined with him twice or thrice, and rather of that kind'; but otherwise 'this character was constructed in advance and entirely invented'. Montesquiou, strangely pliant, acquiesced; he had 'never more than glimpsed the Baron, with his waxed moustaches and waxed hair, who lacked all the breeding you have bestowed on him'; how brave, and how rash, was dear Marcel, 'to dare for the first time to choose as a direct subject the vice of Tiberius or shepherd Corydon, the immense field of inversion, hitherto banned, which is capable of enriching art with perilous and beautiful works'. But Marcel was rich and famous, had a prize and a cross, while he—: 'Dear Marcel, you know I never wrote but for myself, and for those who understand me, as you always did so well. Solitude widens round my work, and so does my pride. . . .'

Moved by compunction and dread—could not this unwonted gentleness be a trap, devised to conceal who knows what horrible vengeance that the Count might be preparing in his Memoirs?—Proust planned a consolation and a bribe. He asked Jacques Boulanger in April and again in July to invite Montesquiou to contribute to *L'Opinion* or the *Revue de la Semaine*: 'he is a marvellous art critic,' he wrote, 'and portrays as no one else can the work of a painter or sculptor he likes'. Illnatured persons, Proust explained, had spread the rumour that Montesquiou was the model for Charlus, whereas, 'although I've known in high society an enormous number of inverts whom no one suspected, in all the years I've known Montesquiou I've never seen him show the least sign of it, whether alone or in company'; nevertheless, 'I believe he imagines, although he is too intelligent to show it, that I intended to portray him, and the kindness of his letters tortures me.' But Boulanger's invitation was too lukewarm, and Montesquiou, who could forgive an injury but not a benefaction, exploded at last in a letter of insane fury, in which he continued to be perfectly charming to Marcel, but said the most appalling things about Boulanger.

Meanwhile, all through May 1921, Paris had flocked to the loan exhibition of Dutch painting at the Jeu de Paume, which included two major works of Vermeer, the *Head of a Girl* and the *View of Delft*. Proust eagerly read the articles on Vermeer by Léon Daudet in the *Action Française* and by Vaudoyer in *L'Opinion*, probably also the essay on the exhibition by Clotilde Misme in the *Gazette des Beaux-Arts*. At last, about the 24th, he decided to go himself, and at 9.15 a.m., the hour when he usually retired to sleep, sent Odilon to fetch Vaudoyer as his escort. On the stairs of his home, seized by a terrifying giddiness, he swayed and paused, then pressed on. At the Jeu de Paume Vaudoyer had to take his arm and steer his tottering steps to the *View of Delft*. Proust had seen this painting, and 'knew I had seen the most beautiful picture in the world', at The Hague on 18 October 1902; he was perfectly capable of noticing the little patch of yellow on the wall unaided; but Vaudoyer's articles, in which he mentioned 'the gables like precious Chinese objects', and Mlle Misme's praise of 'the nuances of the bluish or red roofs, the pink walls, the sad green water and yellow river-bank', had no doubt served to guide his curiosity. In the lower right quarter of the painting, immediately to the left of the first turret on the shadowed water-gate, he saw a fragment of rooftop caught by the sunlight of that eternal summer evening, with the pent-roof of its distant attic window, and beneath it the 'little patch of yellow wall with a pent-roof', for which Bergotte dies and is redeemed.

Proust survived, and even found strength to proceed to the nearby exhibition of Ingres in the Rue de la Ville-l'Évêque—where he admired the view of Rome, long desired and never seen city, in the background of the portrait of François-Marius Granet—and to lunch at the Ritz. Then he returned home, still shaken and alarmed. "I don't know whether I shall ever be able to go out again," he said to Céleste, and then, seeing her distress and Odilon's, and remembering they were still hungry, he added: "Go and eat, you two. Take care of yourselves, I'm so fond of you. You are my children."

From the events of this day he added two incidents to *A la Recherche*, the warning of death that comes to the Narrator at the very end, when he 'narrowly escaped falling three times while going downstairs',[1] and the death of Bergotte, which the Narrator learns on the day of Albertine's visit to the Trocadéro. In all the details of Bergotte's illness Proust is thinking of his own. Bergotte suffers from an artificial malady which has become real, consults several doctors and ironically compares their conflicting advices, rarely goes out, takes sleeping-

[1] III, 1039-42.

drugs in excess, and is attracted to the fatal exhibition, after 'a slight attack of uraemia', by reading the article of a critic who compares the 'little patch of yellow wall' to 'a precious Chinese work of art'.[1] Only the manner of Bergotte's death, however, dates from May 1921, for the great writer's imminent extinction was already prepared by the long account of his illness, which coincides with the death of the grandmother, in *Le Côté de Guermantes II*.[2] This, however, is itself a late insertion, and must have been added to the text in 1920,[3] for Bergotte's symptoms at this stage are drawn from the breakdown of Proust's own health in that year. Already, like Proust, Bergotte stumbles on the stairs; his sight is failing, he has an impediment in his speech; some say he has a cerebral tumour—the same imaginary tumour for which Babinski had refused to open Proust's brain; and his works, 'with an extraordinary power of expansion', have at last become known to the general public, like Proust's after the Goncourt Prize.[4]

From the bare room of 44 Rue Hamelin the family furniture, except for a few sacred or indispensable objects, had vanished for ever; it only remained for Proust to rid himself of his last worldly possession, poor Henri. Once already, in the summer of 1920, Henri had fled, though we have found him again writing his master's letters from dictation in the following October. Now, however, the young man was in serious trouble from a broken engagement to the daughter of a concierge, and it seemed best for everyone's sake that he should leave the country. Henri's last semi-public appearance was in March 1921, when Mauriac dined at Proust's bedside, and was uncomfortably aware of the sinister darkness of the room, the ambiguous young captive, the fur coat spread by way of a coverlet on the bed, and the waxen mask, 'in which only the hair seemed alive', through which his host watched them eating.

[1] III, 182-8.

[2] And again in *Sodome et Gomorrhe*, when Mme Verdurin announces mendaciously that she expects him at La Raspelière, on the very day when 'the morning papers revealed that his health was giving cause for serious alarm' (II, 970-1).

[3] Partly, at least, as late as October 1920. Proust here elaborates (II, 327) the comparison in the preface to *Tendres Stocks* (pp. 33-4) of Renoir with the oculist—whom Proust had then recently visited—who gives us a new vision and says: "Now look"—'and behold, the world (which was not created once and for all, but is re-created as often as a new artist appears) seems completely different from the one we knew already, but perfectly clear'. Cf. also III, 911.

[4] II, 325-9.

It was only necessary to find Henri a suitable place. Proust wrote to Robert de Rothschild, to Mme de Noailles's newest friend Henri Gans, who visited him often in this spring, and to Horace Finaly, the comrade of his student days, now director of the Banque de Paris et des Pays-Bas. 'I have to confess that this young man is rather idle,' he declared, 'and hasn't much of a head for figures, but . . .' Moved by this recommendation Finaly found him a post in a United States branch of the Banque de Paris et des Pays-Bas, and Henri sailed into exile on 4 June. His last plaintive remark was: "My only regret is that I've never seen Princesse Soutzo!" So Morel plans, if he should succeed in seducing the niece of Jupien (who in the earliest versions of *A la Recherche* was a concierge), and again, when he has decided to break their engagement, to 'b— off to an unknown destination'.[1] Jupien's niece had existed in Proust's novel at least as early as the completion of *Du Côté de chez Swann* in 1912-13, when the Narrator's grandmother sees her during a visit to Mme de Villeparisis, mistakes her for Jupien's daughter, and remarks: "The child is a pearl!"[2] Her sole function at that time was to perform, at the end of the novel, her surprising marriage with young Léonor de Cambremer. But now, aided by the strange coincidence that Henri's jilted fiancée was likewise the daughter of a concierge, Proust was able to insert into the future *La Prisonnière* the sad episode of Morel's betrayal of the tailor's niece. Perhaps other details, such as Morel's terrible cry of *"grand pied de grue"*, belong to Henri's love-affair. Thus in Henri Rochat there was not only a fragment of Albertine, but also another of Charlie Morel.

On 16 June Proust attended Mme Hennessy's dinner to celebrate the sensational engagement of the Duke of Marlborough, whose first duchess, the former Consuelo Vanderbilt, had consented after nearly ten years of obduracy to allow him to marry Miss Gladys Deacon. Proust was attracted by Mme Hennessy's plump arms, protested, as we have seen, when she suggested that the Duchesse de Guermantes was Mme Greffulhe, and was startled by the extravagant delight with which the elderly Princesse de Polignac greeted his remark: "Paul Morand likes you very much." 'I must ask you not to contradict me,' he wrote that very night to Morand, and added scrupulously: 'Of course, I didn't tell her you were in love with her!' Marlborough took a fancy to his fiancée's old admirer, and invited him to Blenheim. Proust objected that he was bedridden. "I'll put you in a sleeper at the

[1] III, 51, 195.   [2] I, 20.

Gare du Nord," replied the Duke, "I'll tuck you up in a cabin on the boat, and you can stay in bed at Blenheim." Meanwhile Proust ought to try the Coué system: "Just repeat to yourself: 'I feel marvellous', because if you believe you're well, you'll be well!" Proust tried, but felt worse than ever, and stayed in bed for four months.

In the NRF for June 1921 appeared the last of Proust's critical essays, '*A Propos de Baudelaire*', written during the third week in April. A few ideas from the Baudelaire chapter of *Contre Sainte-Beuve* reappear, though without verbal reminiscences—a remark on the cruelty of *Les Petites vieilles*,[1] a comparison with Beethoven,[2] an unjustified complaint of the flatness of the last lines of *Le Voyage* and *Le Cygne*.[3] Once again, however, although no more profound and intuitively sympathetic study of Baudelaire has ever been written, Proust writes also of himself. He quotes Vigny's line '*La femme aura Gomorrhe et l'homme aura Sodome*', explaining that it sprang 'from the poet's jealousy caused by the friendship of Mme Dorval for certain women'; and here is the epigraph and subject of the next part of Proust's novel. 'Perhaps, alas,' he remarks, again alluding to his own situation, 'one must carry imminent death in one's own body, be threatened with aphasia like Baudelaire, to achieve his lucidity in the midst of real suffering'. He recalls for the last time the line from *Chant d'automne*, '*J'aime de vos longs yeux la lumière verdâtre*', and Fauré's melody, the leitmotivs of his love twenty-nine years before for Marie Finaly, who had died in the influenza epidemic of 1918. But he sensed a still more disturbing link between himself and Baudelaire in the poet's secret complicity with Lesbos, so unlike Vigny's angry horror, and in his enigmatic avowal:

'*Car Lesbos entre tous m'a choisi sur la terre*
Pour chanter le secret de ses vierges en fleurs.'[4]

In the future volumes of his novel, Proust confided, this link between Sodom and Gomorrah would be 'entrusted to a brute, Charles Morel'; but 'what is comprehensible in Charles Morel remains profoundly mysterious in the author of *Les Fleurs du Mal*'. Proust

[1] *Chroniques*, 220, *CSB*, 179-80.
[2] *Chroniques*, 221, *CSB*, 186.
[3] *Chroniques*, 219, *CSB*, 190.
[4] It is probably owing to a reminiscence of this line (in which the plural is required by the rhyme) that Proust called his second volume *A l'Ombre des Jeunes Filles en Fleurs*, whereas ordinary French might prefer '*en fleur*'.

refrained from announcing to the public the mistaken yet revealing explanation which he gave a few weeks later to Gide, that Baudelaire was himself a practising homosexual.[1] But the relations between male and female inverts, the affairs of Morel with Léa and Albertine,[2] which Proust perhaps inserted at this time and under the influence of these ideas, were to fulfil the circle of the mysterious round-dance of the sexes, and complete the unexpected but inevitable threads which join every character in *A la Recherche* to every other.

At the end of January 1921, when the printing of *Le Côté de Guer-mantes II* by Louis Bellenand at Fontenay-aux-Roses was still in progress, Proust proposed to Gallimard that *Sodome et Gomorrhe II* should be given to another press in order to save time, and printed not from the manuscript but from 'the detestable typescript', which had been made for him by a NRF typist. The first proofs, however, show considerable differences throughout from the surviving remains of this typescript. Proust must have devoted the intervals in the proof-revision of *Le Côté de Guermantes II* to these alterations, and the corrected typescript, now lost, cannot have gone to the new printer, F. Paillart of Abbeville, until March or April. Late in May Proust asked Gallimard to let him have the first proofs as soon as possible, 'because the volume will be the most difficult of all to recast', and on 5 June, the day after Henri's departure, he complained that he was still without proofs, 'although I sent you the text several months ago'. Proofs must have begun to arrive shortly afterwards, for at the end of August Rivière was able to read on holiday the first half of the volume in proof, up to the opening passages of the soirée at La Raspelière, and was aware that Proust was already well advanced with his corrections. This second stage of revision was even more important than the first, for the differences between the first proofs and the published volume, as we are told by the editor of the Pléiade text, 'extend not only to corrections of detail, but to the management of the narrative in general, and the order, length and form of its various elements'.

Among the additions, no doubt, was the appearance at La Ras-pelière of the Norwegian philosopher, who expounds Boutroux's and

[1] In fact few poets have been as exclusively heterosexual both in life and work as Baudelaire, whose obsession with Lesbianism was caused objectively by the homosexual infidelity of Jeanne Duval and other mistresses, and subjectively by its significance as one of the flowers of evil.

[2] III, 214-16, 598-600. These are certainly late additions, for Morel, who elsewhere appears in Proust's manuscript under his earlier name Santois, is here called Morel.

Bergson's views on soporifics, memory and immortality to the Narrator, and speaks French so haltingly but vanishes with such vertiginous rapidity.[1] This was the Swedish philosopher Algot Ruhe, a member of the Swedish Academy of Nine, the Swedish translator of Bergson, and the reviewer of *Du Côté de chez Swann* in the Stockholm *Var Tid* in 1917. Proust was introduced to him by Bergson, met him at Henri Bardac's, and tried in November 1921 to place a group of his prose-poems with Rivière, who found them 'not bad, but written in such uncertain French'. 'Let us hope,' wrote Proust to Rivière, 'that this eminent Swede will find no vestige of himself in the Norwegian philosopher, but I tremble for it.' The 'Norwegian' philosopher's reports on Bergson to the Narrator reflect a conversation between Proust and Bergson on insomnia and sleeping-drugs which was witnessed—probably during the Blumenthal Prize negotiations in September 1920 —by Edmond Jaloux. Jaloux listened with astonished admiration to these two supreme experts, Proust with his head thrown back and bulging chest, Bergson slender, bald and immaterial, 'like two black nightbirds', as they extracted from their malady such dazzling laws on the intellect and the unconscious, 'that insomnia seemed almost a blessing'.

In that autumn the seasonal relapse in Proust's health recurred. Towards 20 September he staggered and fell in his bedroom; soon afterwards he showed signs of uraemia, his mother's symptom and Bergotte's[2]; and early in October he poisoned himself accidentally by taking the enormous overdose of seven one-gramme cachets of veronal, dial and opium. He had thought each contained only a tenth of a gramme, he explained; but the ominous nature of such an error, in which a lapse of the conscious mind may well obey a destructive wish of the unconscious, is only too clear. This incident was not the first of its kind. A few years before, after Céleste had talked with her master until three in the morning, he had failed to ring at the usual time. All that day the bell remained silent; the chambermaid on the floor below urged her to go in, but Céleste did not dare to brave the wrath of her Ahasuerus and his cry from Racine's *Esther: "What reckless mortal comes to seek her death?"*[3] At two in the afternoon of the second day the summons sounded at last. "Ah, Monsieur, I was so worried about you!" she cried. "You had reason to be, Céleste." "I was afraid I'd never see you again." "You don't know how close you came to it." "I think he'd taken the largest possible dose of veronal he dared,"

[1] II, 930-1, 975-6, 984-5.   [2] III, 186.   [3] III, 120, 126.

Céleste told Miss Mina Curtiss many years later, "to be still sure of going on living while feeling and knowing what death was like." "We shall all meet again in the Valley of Jehoshaphat," Céleste would say, and: "Do you really believe people meet again when they're dead? If I thought I'd see Mother again I'd die this minute," her master replied. The heavenly scales, in which desire to complete *A la Recherche* was weighed against longing for the moment in which his sins would be instantaneously atoned and his mother's love eternally regained, trembled near the point of balance. So in these last years the visits of the Dark Woman punctually recurred in each spring and autumn, towards the times of his brother's birth and his mother's death; and Proust's life moved towards the brink in a slow and sinister rhythm, like the tolling of a great bell or the surging of an unknown sea.

Chapter 16

AN INDIAN SUMMER
(October 1921 – September 1922)

DURING the past fifteen years Proust must have been well aware of the existence in Paris of a coterie of charming and talented ladies who preferred their own society to that of men. The unjust stigma which condemned the natives of Sodom to a furtive or defiant criminality was spared them; they seemed to the world, as indeed they were, an innocent, proud, eccentric, indispensable leavening in a monotonous society. Their ranks were reconnoitred by the curious and benevolent, even temporarily joined by such eminent writers as Mme de Noailles and Colette. The great courtesans Liane de Pougy and Émilienne d'Alençon sought them for an idyllic holiday from professional duties. Certain repentant married ladies, including Proust's increasingly masculine friend Mme de Clermont-Tonnerre, the English feminist Anna Wickham, Yvonne Sabini, the drug-taking wife of the Italian commercial attaché in Paris, found them permanently preferable to their unsatisfactory husbands.

In the years before the war the nucleus of this little band was formed by Miss Natalie Clifford Barney, Lucie Delarue-Mardrus, Renée Vivien and her friend Evelina Palmer. Mme Delarue-Mardrus, a boyish brunette and a gifted poetess, was married to the fearsome, black-bearded Dr Mardrus, author of the magnificent translation of the *Arabian Nights* which the Narrator's mother, shocked by its impropriety and strange orthography, regrets having given to her son at Balbec.[1] Montesquiou, ravished by her poems and enraged by some lack of deference on the part of Mme de Noailles, invited both ladies to a grand fête. "A marvellous young Muse will now recite some of her verses!" he announced; but before Mme de Noailles could open her mouth she discovered she was not the Muse in question, for Mme Delarue-Mardrus had already begun to declaim. Count Robert henceforth took an avuncular interest in the whole group, and recorded in his secret diary a remark made to him by one of the sisterhood:"People

[1] II, 836-7.

call it unnatural—all I can say is, it's always come naturally to *me*!"
Renée Vivien, likewise ('a blonde young person with discouraged
shoulders', wrote Mme Delarue-Mardrus), was a talented Sapphic
poetess, and lived with her inseparable friend Miss Evelina Palmer, a
pre-Raphaelite American with auburn hair that reached to her ankles.
But the leader of them all was 'the wild girl from Cincinnati', as Joseph
Reinach's brother Salomon called her, the admirable Miss Barney.
Her father was an elegant clubman, descended from a Barney who
fought for France in the eighteenth century; she was educated at
the same odd boarding-school of Les Ruches in the Forest of
Fontainebleau (but several years later, when it was no longer under
the management of Mlles Souvestre and Dussaud) as her subsequent
friend, the wise and matchless authoress of *Olivia*; and she was and
remains celebrated as the Amazon, to whom the solitary and disfigured
Remy de Gourmont addressed his *Lettres à l'Amazone*. Mme Delarue-
Mardrus wrote of Miss Barney in her autobiography as 'the pure and
faithful companion whose pride, loyalty and greatness I esteem so
highly', and made her the heroine of her novel *L'Ange et les
Pervers*, 'where I have described and analysed at full length both
Natalie and the life into which she initiated me, in which it was not
until much later that I ceased to play more than the sexless rôle of the
angel'. Miss Barney had a feminine figure, golden hair, a pastel-
coloured skin, steely eyes, a biting smile, and a sudden blush.

The Amazon inhabited an ancient house at 20 Rue Jacob, once the
home of Racine's mistress the actress Champmeslé. Beneath the
garden trees stood an eighteenth-century pillared summerhouse,
called the Temple of Friendship and ambiguously barred, when it was
in need of repair, with a notice saying: 'DANGER'. Paul Morand visited
her in 1916, and commented: 'Very Fiesole 1895'. But after the
Armistice the headquarters of this little band became a brilliant salon,
and even Gide observed that "Miss Barney is one of the few people
one ought to see if one had time". Valéry, Rilke, Ezra Pound, T. S.
Eliot, Berenson, D'Annunzio and Pierre Louÿs were her friends.
She lived with the fearless purity of fire, devoted to the platonic
ideal of friendship which Proust had rejected, and wrote with an
intellectual passion and beauty of style for which posterity will
read and revere her. Her place among the great French women
writers of her time—Colette, Anna de Noailles, Princess Marthe
Bibesco—is assured, or at least deserved.

Proust and Miss Barney at last suspected they might have much in common, and at Morand's suggestion she sent him in September 1920 her *Pensées d'une Amazone* ('for Monsieur Marcel Proust, whose comprehension merits this unexpurgated copy'), and an invitation to the Temple of Friendship. Yet it seemed to him, rightly, that the realm over which Miss Barney was queen was a land of classic and literary idyll, Mitylene rather than Gomorrah. Nothing, he confessed, could be less like a response to her sweet singing than his coming *Sodome et Gomorrhe*: 'the divine peace of the *Eclogues* or *Symposium* does not reign there, but rather the dark despair of Vigny's line which I chose five years ago as an epigraph'[1]; and he prudently objected that the 'Temple of Love', as he cadlle it by a natural confusion, would be too draughty in October. Nevertheless, he declared, he would like to discuss 'all that' with her. For a year these two exceptional people contemplated one another from a distance. 'I'm apprehensive of what you will say about Gomorrah,' she wrote after reading *Sodome et Gomorrhe I*, and: 'My Sodomites are all horrible,' he replied, 'but my Gomorrhans will all be charming.' In his letters to her Proust wrote with the particular tone which he reserved for persons of high and vigilant intelligence; he did not 'talk down' to Miss Barney. Their meeting, however, when at last towards November 1921 he visited the Rue Jacob, was not a success. It was very late at night, long past Miss Barney's bedtime; she sat draped in the white ermine chasuble which she used as a bedspread, while Proust, in his white shirtfront and black tail-suit, his dark eyes 'ringed with black by the vampires of solitude', looked 'like a corpse laid out in a coffin'; and she was uncomfortably conscious that he was watching her steadily without seeming to see her. He would speak of nothing but persons in high society, and the Belgian carillon of Mme Greffulhe's laugh, and neither of them was willing to be the first to mention 'all that'. When Miss Barney read his later volumes she thought Albertine and her friends 'not so much charming as improbable': 'not everyone,' she grimly declared, 'is able to infringe these Eleusinian mysteries'. In fact, she could tell Proust nothing that he wished to know and did not know already; for the impenetrable enigma which veils the relations of Albertine with the natives of Gomorrah is not a sign of ignorance on the part of the author, but an essential symbol of the mystery of love and jealousy.

In October 1921 Proust received a copy of Montesquiou's last

---

[1] '*La femme aura Gomorrhe et l'homme aura Sodome*', from '*La Colère de Samson*'.

volume, *Élus et Appelés*, inscribed 'To Marcel Proust, author whom I
believe I judge rightly, friend whom I know I like truly'. This was
destined to be Count Robert's everlasting farewell to the 'dear
Marcel' whom, within his lights, he had respected and cherished for
nearly three decades. The Count's last years had been disenchanted
and sombre. 'I loved my fêtes better than my guests, who were perhaps
aware of the fact,' he confessed; and he never outlived the catastrophe
of his last grand pre-war party, a performance of Verlaine's *Les Uns et
les Autres* at the Palais Rose, when the few guests who turned up were
greatly outnumbered by the waiters. Alas, Mme Estradère, the gossip-
columnist of *Le Figaro*, who used the pen-name of Princesse de
Mésagne to which she was only vaguely entitled, had announced on
the authority of an anonymous letter that the fête was 'cancelled owing
to bad weather'.[1] "But here's the very letter!" cried the poor lady
when Montesquiou swooped for an explanation, "look, it begins
'Dear Princess'!" "Ah!—so you believed the rest!" exclaimed the
Count. He quarrelled with everyone, a process which he called
'widening, by cutting down the undergrowth of pointless friendships,
the avenues that lead to my solitude'. His despair of fame for his
writings was exacerbated by the incessant arrival of new names: 'no
sooner has one found leisure to enquire who André Gide is,' he complained, 'than one has to find out who André Suarès is!' He sold
Artagnan in 1919, after offering it in vain to all his rich, hated cousins.
In a last typically pure and remote love-affair he became enamoured of
the photograph of Prince Jean Sevastos, a clever, golden-haired boy
of seventeen, the stepson of his executor and physician Dr Paul-Louis
Couchoud, and courted him in a series of wary, melancholy and
moving letters, and with a box of crystallised violets. 'A photograph
is a mirror with a memory,' he wrote. Ought they to risk meeting? 'I
used to like being seen *very much*,' he admitted, 'but now I do not like
it *at all*. One only enjoys doing what one does well.' They met only
once, on 3 October 1920, when Montesquiou did the honours of the
Palais Rose for the young prince and his parents. But the boy was
bewilderingly reserved: was it shyness, or had he not understood
before that Count Robert was an elderly gentleman of sixty-six? 'You
will not know until later the meaning of that day,' wrote the Count, 'a
sad but human meaning, and not without beauty, if only the beauty
of sorrow.' "I'm looking for someone to close my eyes," he had

[1] M. de Charlus resolves to play this trick upon Mme de Mortemart (III,
271).

told Mme de Clermont-Tonnerre; but even that search had been in vain.

Montesquiou's final public appearance was in December 1920 at the baptism of his great-niece Corisande, the fifth and last offspring of Guiche and Élaine Greffulhe. "Are you the father of the child?" asked the verger, and "Certainly not!" cried the Count indignantly, muttering: "What a jazz-band baptism!" Then he approached Mme de Clermont-Tonnerre and spoke of their friend Marcel. "I, too, would like a little glory," he sighed, "I ought to start calling myself Montesproust." 'Guiche felt more exhausted after six hours of the Count's conversation,' she reported to Proust, 'than his wife after producing the baby.' Montesquiou retired to Dr Couchoud's clinic at Saint-Cloud with nephritis, emerged for his last amiable correspondence with Proust, and then, as summer ended, paced the Palais Rose taking his own blood-pressure and reading in it his death-warrant. "Shall I send for Dr Robin?" asked the faithful Henri Pinard. "What do you suppose Robin could do for me now?" replied Count Robert, "no, send for nobody, I'll die alone." He fled to the mimosas of Mentone—where Henri brought him *Élus et Appelés* fresh from the printer, saying: "Look, here is your newly-born!"—and died on 11 December 1921. A few loyal friends, Dr Couchoud who made a speech, Mme Delarue-Mardrus who recited a poem, Ida Rubinstein dissolved in tears, Mlle Breslau the painter, Mme de Clermont-Tonnerre, Coco de Madrazo, attended his funeral on the 21st. "We all owe him a great deal," said Mlle Breslau. He was buried in the Cimetière des Gonards at Versailles beside the waiting Yturri, beneath the statue of the Angel of Silence whose finger is ever on its lips.

The series of Proust's critical articles had been interrupted by a distressing contretemps. He had insisted, despite the author's justified forebodings, on arranging for the NRF to review Jacques Boulanger's ... *Mais l'Art est difficile!*, a volume of collected criticism which contained three laudatory articles on Proust's own work. To the horror of them both, Louis Martin-Chauffier's review in the NRF for June 1921 was hostile, and contained a gratuitous insinuation that Boulanger had praised the work of René Boylesve in the hope of winning his vote for the Académie Française. Urged by Proust, Boulanger had expostulated forcibly in the July NRF; but Rivière, allowing for once his editorial duty to override his sense of justice, repeated the offence by supporting his contributor. On 19 and 26 August the ruffled Boulanger published articles on Flaubert in the *Revue de la Semaine*, in which he took Proust to task for a harmless criticism of himself in '*A propos de Baudelaire*',[1] and attacked his '*A propos du Style de Flaubert*'. Proust immediately wrote a new article on Flaubert, replying to Boulanger and apologising for the NRF's discourtesy, and offered it to Rivière, who accepted with evident reluctance and with requests for modifications. Proust withdrew the article, which still remains undiscovered, remarking regretfully: 'it would have enabled me to produce a volume of criticism by enabling me to continue my Flaubert'. In fact, although we shall find him making other abortive attempts to resume, this unhappy affair put an end to Proust's career as a critic.

Fortunately Rivière had asked before the storm for 'the finest fragment of your next volume'. '*Les Intermissions du cœur*', the story of the Narrator's second arrival at Balbec, his delayed grief for his grandmother, and his recovery when he sees the appleblossom on a showery day in spring, appeared in the NRF for October 1921, and was followed in December by '*En tram jusqu'à La Raspelière*', the episode of the journey in the little train to Mme Verdurin's soirée, into which Proust temporarily transferred a number of incidents, such as the Norwegian philosopher, which belong to the later part of that evening. Proust insisted on dedicating the latter extract to Jacques Boulanger, while Rivière in turn stipulated that only Boulanger's name should appear, without Proust's embarrassing reasons for the dedication. But he magnanimously arranged for a favourable review of the second volume of Boulanger's . . .*Mais l'Art est difficile!* by Benjamin Crémieux in the January NRF. In December Proust gratefully lent Rivière money pending the payment of the last instalment of his Blumenthal prize. Meanwhile, however, others had profited from his irritation against the NRF. In July Boulanger had transmitted a request from Henri Duvernois, editor of the newly founded monthly *Les Œuvres Libres*, for a long extract from his novel. Proust accepted in September for the sake of independence, money, and the new readers who would be won by an occasional truancy from the closed shop of the NRF, and wrung Gallimard's reluctant consent. But Gallimard revealed immediately after that he was exceedingly distressed. 'Exclusivity is not laid down in the text of our agreement,' he admitted, 'but exists nonetheless in the mind of the contracting party!' 'I've never pronounced vows of obedience before Gallimard, nor even of

---

[1] 'And Jacques Boulanger, by far the best critic, and more than critic, of his generation, dares to tell us that Baudelaire's poetry is deficient in thought!' (*Chroniques*, 219).

chastity,' Proust grumbled to Boulanger, and called Gallimard and Rivière 'my two dear torturers'; but he promised not to repeat his dereliction, and privately resolved to do so never, or hardly ever. A 150-page extract from *Sodome et Gomorrhe II*, on the Narrator's love for Albertine at Balbec and his growing suspicions of her Lesbianism, appeared in the November *Œuvres Libres* under the disingenuous title: '*Jalousie. A complete, unpublished novel by Marcel Proust*'.

In September and October Proust worked incessantly on the second half of *Sodome et Gomorrhe II*, making his additions and corrections on the typescript already supplied by the NRF. At the end of November he sent the completed text to Gallimard, declaring that he passed it for publication without further proofs. He asked for larger type to be used, and thwarted Gallimard's protests by pointing out the economy gained by his abstention from proofs, and offering to allow any excess costs to be subtracted from his credit balance. The work was therefore printed, although this involved entirely resetting the first half, with the attractive large type in which *A la Recherche* was thereafter, until the Pléiade edition of 1954, most familiarly known to Proust's readers. In this new form it became necessary to produce *Sodome et Gomorrhe II* in three volumes instead of the usual two. Publication was planned for 1 May 1922.

Proust immediately began work on *Sodome et Gomorrhe III*, as the section afterwards called *La Prisonnière* was still entitled. At first he believed it would be an exceptionally short volume, though in fact it was to become one of the longest; in a moment of optimism he thought he might publish it in October 1922, though in moods of pessimism at the fancied slowness of the printers he feared that even *Sodome et Gomorrhe II* might have to be postponed till May 1923. At the New Year, after sending a present to the NRF lady typist, he decided to engage one of his own. Since Henri Rochat's flight Céleste had written many of Proust's letters from dictation, with spelling even more endearingly weak than Henri's; but now her young niece Yvonne came to live at 44 Rue Hamelin, where she typed his more formal correspondence and completed during the first half of 1922 a typescript of *La Prisonnière* and *Albertine Disparue*. This youthful Parisian was the very daughter of Françoise whose excruciating slang disconcerts the Narrator and corrupts the pure and original diction of her mother. She appears in her own typescript of *La Prisonnière*,[1] and is still with the Narrator some fifteen years later, apparently unaged, in the war-

[1] III, 154-5.

chapter of *Le Temps Retrouvé*, when Françoise proudly adopts her abominable catch-phrase '*et patatipatali et patatapatala*'.[1] But Proust had met Céleste's niece several years before, perhaps as early as the summer of 1919, when, as he told Princesse Soutzo, 'the Albaret family multiplies around me'; for she already appears with her repertoire of slang in *Le Côté de Guermantes I*, in the spring after the Narrator's visit to Doncières, and again in the early part of *Sodome et Gomorrhe II*, on the evening of Albertine's visit after the Princesse de Guermantes's soirée.[2] During these years Céleste's sister Marie Gineste had also been intermittently with him to share Céleste's errands, and now entered his home for the rest of 1922. Another occasional inmate was the infant daughter of the baker-concierge below, who toddled up with his letters and once, he suspected, lost them, when her mother sprained her arm in February 1922. In April, when the little girl had measles and whooping-cough, he cautiously ordered all his correspondence to be fumigated in a formol-stove. The same child, in 1950 a still-young woman in charge of the pastry-shop on the ground-floor of 44 Rue Hamelin, well remembered her first visit to his room. "It was so dark, and he was so kind but strange, and I ran away! You see, Monsieur, I was so little." This charming and intelligent lady is no doubt the youngest person alive who has seen Proust plain, and when the twentieth century draws to a close will perhaps be the last.

The gaiety of the 1920s had begun, in time for Proust to glimpse a new age which he found too incongruous to insert in *A la Recherche*. At the Princesse de Guermantes's last matinée the music is still a dying echo of the Vinteuil Septet; but the evenings of 1922 were danced away to the unfamiliar syncopations of tango and ragtime, which to survivors of a past epoch seemed to symbolise a dislocation not only of rhythm but of morals. "And what do they do after they've finished dancing?" enquired a great lady, after watching with deep interest a couple interlocked in the first tango she had ever seen. Proust sat benign, holding court; and Fernand Gregh's daughter Geneviève, noticing the band of maidens and men round his throne, was reminded of the aged Voltaire revisiting Paris on the eve of death. He stayed all night at the Beaumonts' ball on New Year's Eve, though he missed their next on 27 February, when Mlle d'Hinnisdäel, her sister and Princesse Marie Murat, dressed as picadors and matadors, slew a difficult bull who turned out to be Coco de Madrazo. He attended the Ritz

----

[1] III, 749.　　　　　　[2] II, 147-8, 331, 341, 726-8.

ball on 15 January, and received a promised demonstration of the latest steps from Mlle d'Hinnisdäel—'even when indulging in the most 1922 of dances, she still looks like a unicorn on a coat of arms!' He admired the chaste chivalry with which Morand, dancing with a lady in mauve, succeeded in disengaging his portliness from her person; he was introduced to the harpsichordist Wanda Landowska, 'just when she was in the act of biting Mlle Vacaresco in the buttock'; and then he fled to his private room upstairs and devoured a leg of lamb.

On 7 February he was observed by Maurice Martin du Gard at Princesse Soutzo's, tottering towards his dazzling hostess like a moth plunging into an electric light. Martin du Gard, the editor of *Les Écrits nouveaux*, had published last July a review of *Le Côté de Guermantes I* by André Germain, in which Proust was compared to 'an elderly governess who has become the mistress of the family footman'. Germain, a friend of Lucien Daudet, Montesquiou, Renée Vivien and Miss Barney, was a clever but hysterical young man who had never quite recovered from his brief mismarriage to Lucien's sister Edmée, and was tormented by the lifelong alternations of a fascinated liking and loathing for male and female inverts. In November Rivière had written a stern letter to Martin du Gard, announcing in the name of the NRF that 'we are all gravely displeased by M. André Germain's venomous article, and shall always regard any attack on Marcel Proust as an attack on ourselves'; but Proust himself, though determined to fight, had heard from Morand that the editor did not share his contributor's views, and specially asked the princess to invite him. "Proust wants a duel with sabres, but he doesn't want to take his overcoat off!" explained Morand, and disappeared. "It's true that this is hardly the weather for duelling," Proust agreed, "and supposing M. Germain goes to bed just when I get up? It's most awkward!" Reluctantly he allowed himself to be dissuaded from his homicidal intentions, but: "You and Morand are *most unkind*," he repeated. With a faint smile he cross-examined Martin du Gard on his most intimate beliefs—'a questioning that filled one with ecstasy, an absurd pride, and a tinge of terror'. He thanked Robert de Rothschild for a photograph of Fénelon—"the only one I have ever seen of that adorable person"—and tried to elucidate the mysteries of Fénelon's death to Martin du Gard; he declared that he himself was 'not just a novelist, but a moral poet', and insisted on sending his new acquaintance home in Odilon's taxi. "Number 8 *bis* Rue Laurent-Pichat," said Martin du Gard when asked for his address; for by a coincidence worthy of *A la*

Recherche itself he was a friend of Porel, and recently had taken Proust's place as lodger in the house of the dead Réjane.

The daily consequences of fame continued to amuse or exasperate Proust. He was annoyed when *Le Canard enchaîné* published an advertisement for 'the Swann pen, sole manufacturer Marcel Proust', but delighted when Mme Scheikévitch showed him a publicity item in *Le Figaro* which promised: 'You too can have the charming and supple figure of a young girl from "within a budding grove", if you buy our girdle!' When he noticed Morand's *Ouvert la Nuit* advertised in *Éve* as 'Not to be read by young girls' he commanded Gallimard to arrange the same publicity for himself; and on 28 May 1922 an announcement duly appeared in *Éve* of '*Sodome et Gomorrhe. Not to be read by young girls*'. Mme Bliss, he heard with mixed feelings, always kept the latest Marcel Proust on her drawing-room table, side by side with the latest Henry Bordeaux. An American girl wrote from the Villa Wolkonsky in Rome to inform him that she was extremely beautiful, and had read his works night and day for the past three years, but could not understand a word: 'Dear Marcel Proust,' she entreated, 'please tell me in two lines what you are trying to say.' An Italian journalist wrote: 'I enjoy everything in your books, but my wife has a marked preference for the meeting of M. de Charlus and Jupien, though she also likes the scene between Charlus and the cabman.' He was flattered by the comparison between himself and Einstein which Blanche had already suggested a year before in the preface to *Dates*, and on which the mathematician Camille Vettard had written an essay, '*Proust et Einstein*', published, after five months of effort on Proust's part, during which it was rejected by Rivière, accepted by Boulanger and withdrawn in a huff by the author, in the NRF for August 1922. Algot Ruhe, now an enthusiast for Einstein, as if egged on by his counterpart the 'Norwegian philosopher', wrote: 'You accelerate and decelerate the rotation of the earth, you are greater than God'. This, Proust himself felt, was going too far. 'Even if he'd merely said I was as great as God,' he objected to Guiche, 'it would still have been a bit much!' But the comparison with Einstein, if not with the Almighty, was attractive. *A la Recherche du Temps Perdu* was, indeed, the picture of a relativistic universe expanding and contracting in a curved space-time continuum; and when Benjamin Crémieux pointed out some apparent anachronisms in *Le Côté de Guermantes* Proust explained that these were due 'to the flattened form my characters take owing to their rotation in time'.

Proust continued his fruitless plans for articles. He had offered Rivière a 'burlesque obituary' on poor Joseph Reinach, who had died on 18 April 1921: 'what better service can one offer a dead man, than to make him live again?' When Léon Daudet dedicated his novel *L'Entremetteuse* to him in November 1921, Proust asked Boulanger to publish 'an extremely dithyrambic article' on his benefactor, which he wrote in the spring of 1922[1] but never submitted, for Daudet was political dynamite, and Boulanger could not be induced to accept with sufficient enthusiasm. He planned 'an anecdotic, high-society article' in memory of Montesquiou for an American magazine, but explained to Mme de Clermont-Tonnerre on 7 February 1922, with an unaccustomed lapse into callousness and bad taste, that he had abandoned it, fearing that Count Robert had only pretended to die, that his funeral was merely a last practical joke, and his coffin, like the Emperor Charles the Fifth's in the legend, was empty. The real reason for his abstention, no doubt, was the menace of the Count's posthumous memoirs, and the realisation that, if he should be compelled to ask for the suppression of any revelations concerning himself, it would be a tactical error to cast the first stone. If these memoirs were as many people, innocent and guilty, had reason to suspect, then indeed the terrible Count was not dead.

But the most important of these unprinted articles was an essay on Dostoevsky, which Proust proposed to Rivière in September 1921 and then abandoned, fearing it would interrupt his novel for too long. 'I am doing a great work,' he pleaded, quoting the prophet Nehemiah on the top of his ladder,[2] 'and I cannot come down.' Towards February 1922, however, when the centenary of the great Russian's birth was celebrated, he wrote a brief sketch,[3] which he developed into the superb monologue on Dostoevsky with which the Narrator interrupts Albertine at the pianola in *La Prisonnière*.[4] It was the last occasion but one on which he allowed an incident in the present to dictate an addition to his novel. The last of all, to anticipate a little, was in June 1922, when Paul Brach sent him a reproduction in *L'Illustration* of Tissot's painting of the Club in the Rue Royale in 1868, which was then being shown in an exhibition of Second Empire art at the

[1] *Contre Sainte-Beuve*, 438-41.
[2] *Nehemiah*, vi, 3.
[3] *Contre Sainte-Beuve*, 422-3, datable from the allusions to Gide's and Rivière's articles on Dostoevsky in the NRF for February 1922.
[4] III, 378-81.

Louvre.[1] 'Of the people in it I only knew Haas, Edmond de Polignac and Saint-Maurice,' he wrote, 'but what a pleasure to see them again!' And he added to *La Prisonnière* the apostrophe to 'dear Charles Swann' and the proud declaration; 'if everyone is talking of your presence in Tissot's painting of the balcony of the Club in the Rue Royale, along with Galliffet, Edmond de Polignac and Saint-Maurice, it is because people see there are several features which belong to you in the character of Swann.'[2]

His unavailing desire to write articles was to continue till the last months of his life. In June 1922 Robert de Flers asked him for a contribution on the centenary of Shelley's death, no doubt remembering the knowledge Marcel had shown of this subject long ago, in his Ruskin articles of 1900.[3] In July, realising that neither his Dostoevsky essay nor the Narrator's discourse to Albertine would be complete without mention of *The Possessed*, he arranged to borrow this novel from Morand, but without result. In the same month he offered Rivière an article in reply to remarks on his '*A propos du Style de Flaubert*' in Thibaudet's recently published biography, *Gustave Flaubert*, for which Rivière was still hoping as late as 20 September.

The publication of *Sodome et Gomorrhe II* on 2 May coincided with the Schiffs' long-awaited visit to Paris and the last but one of Proust's

[1] *L'Illustration*, 10 June 1922, p. 551.

[2] III, 200. Charles Haas himself had died just twenty years before, on 12 July 1902, a few months after his daughter's marriage. His funeral on the fifteenth at Saint-François-de-Sales (for he was a Catholic convert) was attended by the Ducs de Montmorency and de La Trémoille, the Marquis du Lau, Comte Othenin d'Haussonville, Baron Alphonse de Rothschild, Mme Meredith Howland, Comte Walewski (Proust's Prince de Borodino), and Comte Greffulhe. The obituary in *Le Gaulois*, in the style of Proust's parodied obituary of Swann (III, 199-200), called him 'one of the most sparkling conversationalists of his generation, and an art-connoisseur *di primo cartello*, whose place at the Jockey Club will be difficult to fill'. The aged Princesse de Polignac, during her exile in London in the Occupation, told the terrible and Proustian story of Haas sitting paralysed and speechless in his last illness, while his natural daughter Luisita scourged him with unnatural abuse. Proust himself intended to insert this incident, or something like it, in the visit to Gilberte at Tansonville in *Le Temps Retrouvé* (III, 697, 1118 *note*), where he wrote 'Cruelty on the death of her father (copy this from the manuscript-book in which it is written).'

[3] '*Pèlerinages ruskiniens en France*', in *Le Figaro*, 13 February 1900 (cf. *Chroniques*, 145) and '*Ruskin à Notre-Dame d'Amiens*', in *Mercure de France*, 1 April 1900 (cf. *Pastiches et Mélanges*, 102). In *Pastiches et Mélanges*, *loc. cit.*, Proust had shown his continued interest by adding a long footnote on Shelley's cremation.

spring and autumn accidents. He had begun to take adrenalin as a stronger substitute for cafeine when he wished to counteract the narcotic after-effects of veronal; and on the same day, to prepare himself for the Schiffs, he imprudently took an undiluted dose. His throat and stomach were burned as if with vitriol, he cried out with pain for three hours, and for a month lived on nothing but ice-cream and iced beer, which Odilon brought from the Ritz every morning and evening.

Violet and Sydney Schiff were a wealthy and highly intelligent English couple, patrons of art, literature and music, who had seen Proust briefly in the summer of 1920. Sydney Schiff, a talented novelist who dedicated his *Richard Kurt* (1919) to Proust before their first meeting, and translated *Le Temps Retrouvé* after the death of Scott-Moncrieff, was bald, thin, alarmingly brisk and slightly deaf, with piercing spectacled eyes and a bristling moustache. He was now fifty-two, a year senior to Proust, while his wife was several years younger. Both had read *Du Côté de chez Swann* with enthusiasm in wartime London, and were passionate admirers of Proust's genius. Mrs Schiff was tall and softly graceful, with brown doe-like eyes and slender hands, an unfading Edwardian beauty: 'the angel Violet,' Proust called her, 'retiring, fragrant and miraculous flower'. Those who saw Violet Schiff before her tragic illness in the summer of 1961 will remember for ever the extraordinary youth in face and mind of this gentle and noble lady, the wisdom of her heart and voice, the love and bereavement with which she spoke of Proust, as if he had died yesterday or was still somehow present. "People don't understand that he was good," she repeated, "he was such a good man"; and for an uncanny moment an innocent, affectionate and living Marcel seemed to look from her eyes which saw him always.

On 28 April, fortified with injections of adrenalin, Proust had sallied to the Ritz, expecting to see the newly arrived Schiffs; but they were staying at Foyot's, near the Luxembourg Gardens, where he had eaten delicious lunches thirty years before, on the days of his law-examinations. On 2 May a new appointment was made, and it was for their sake that he took his overdose and, when the pain subsided, followed Mrs Schiff to the Ritz, where Olivier had been ordered 'to see that every window in the restaurant and gallery is shut tight'. He drank astonishing quantities of iced beer, and reproached Sydney Schiff for drinking so much champagne. On another evening he invited them to meet his sister-in-law Marthe and his niece Suzy at 44

Rue Hamelin, after delicately confessing his anxiety lest Suzy, now aged eighteen, should read *Sodome et Gomorrhe*—"and my next book will be even more terrible for an innocent young girl!" Proust deeply loved his brother's child, who for sixty years, it is often said, has devotedly returned his love. 'I like to think,' he had told Mme Catusse long before, 'that a little of my father and mother survives in her.' "What would you like me to give you?" he asked, when she was only six. "A pink flamingo," she replied; but to her lifelong regret, when Uncle Marcel was on the point of promising one, her mother interrupted with: "Don't listen to the child, she's out of her mind!" From her cot she heard, evening after evening, his spontaneous laughter, his voice vibrating with an unearthly intelligence and sensibility, as he talked to her parents. He had sent Robert a de luxe *A l'Ombre des Jeunes Filles en Fleurs* 'for the darling girl', feeling that this book, at least, was fit for the young, and to herself, '*Ma chère petite Suzy*', he wrote that she would receive a huge volume if he sent her all the letters he wrote to her every evening in his thoughts. "She takes after Robert, she already has his kindness of heart," he told Paul Morand. The Schiffs invited her to stay with them in England, and both she and they were amused by his shocked indignation at the idea of her travelling alone, so young, to so distant a country. A few years after his death she spoke of her unconsoled loss to the Abbé Mugnier. "Marcel Proust," mused that good man, "why, no one is less dead than he is"; and she realised henceforth that she was mistaken, that her uncle was alive for ever.

On 18 May, after the first night of Stravinsky's *Renard*, the Schiffs gave an enormous supper-party to Diaghilev and the dancers, and to the four men of genius whom they most admired, Picasso, Stravinsky, Proust and James Joyce. Proust had delighted in Picasso's décor for Cocteau's *Parade*, and in 1918 had watched with amused appreciation the unpacking of a crate of astounding white and blue cubist pictures, a present from Biarritz, in the flat of the painter's patron Mme Errasuriz. He remembered the incident for his novel: 'These ladies, touched by art as if by heavenly grace,' he wrote in *Le Temps Retrouvé*, 'lived in apartments filled with cubist paintings, while a cubist painter worked only for them and they lived only for him.'[1]

[1] III, 946. In a letter to Walter Berry in 1917 Proust pointed out the affinity between prehistoric cave-painting and the art of Picasso. 'Picasso is an artist whose work and person are by no means unknown to me,' he declared to Blanche in 1919 ;and in his preface to Blanche's *De David à Degas* he wrote of

Stravinsky he had known before the war, with the Russian dancers at Larue's; and now Proust approached him with the most unfortunate question that can possibly be put to a great composer after an anxious first night. "Do you like Beethoven?" "I detest him!" "But surely, the late quartets?" protested Proust. "Worst things he ever wrote!" snarled Stravinsky, who explained later; 'I should have shared his enthusiasm for Beethoven, were it not a commonplace among intellectuals of that time, and not a musical judgment but a literary pose.' Stravinsky could not know that Proust's comprehension of the late quartets was, for a layman, no less profound than his own, nor that the imprudent question was not mere small-talk, but a request for information on the Vinteuil Septet.

Joyce arrived at midnight, already the worse for wear, and improperly dressed because he did not possess a suit of tails. He settled morosely down, head buried in hands, to drink champagne. In October 1920, newly descended in Paris from Zurich, he had written to a friend: 'I observe a furtive attempt to run a certain M. Marcel Proust of here against the signatory of this letter. I have read some pages of his. I cannot see any special talent but I am a bad critic.' But now, perhaps glimpsing in this nocturnal stranger a faint but deified apparition of Leopold Bloom, or even a peer of his own,[1] he moved shyly to the door when Proust departed with the Schiffs. As they set off in Odilon's taxi Joyce obliviously opened a window and lit a cigarette, and Sydney Schiff hurriedly shut the one and asked Joyce to throw away the other. Joyce complained of his eyes, Proust of his stomach. Did M. Joyce like truffles? He did. Had he met the Duchesse de X? He had not. "I regret that I do not know M. Joyce's work," remarked Proust. "I have never read M. Proust," replied Joyce. When they reached 44 Rue Hamelin Proust said to Schiff, politely but firmly: "Please ask M. Joyce to let my taxi drive him home." Thus the two greatest novelists of the twentieth century met and parted. "If only we'd been allowed to meet and have a talk somewhere . . .", remarked Joyce sadly afterwards. The failure of writers of genius to appreciate one another and one another's work is a common and unregrettable phenomenon of instinctive self-protection; for if one allowed himself

[1] In fact Joyce said later: "He looked like the hero of *The Sorrows of Satan*."

'the great and admirable Picasso, who has concentrated all Cocteau's features into a portrait of such noble rigidity that, when I contemplate it, even the most enchanting Carpaccios in Venice tend to take a second place in my memory'.

to be seized by the other's greatness he would risk contaminating his own. However, Joyce magnanimously embedded allusions to Proust's name and titles in *Finnegans Wake*,[1] a novel which like Proust's is circular or spiral in construction, and when it ends eternally begins again.

A new Blumenthal award was now imminent, and Proust again felt it his duty to secure at least one of the two prizes for a member of the NRF group. The first choice was Jean Paulhan, Rivière's assistant editor; but Proust begged Mme Blumenthal in vain to consider Paulhan's distinguished war-service, and to overlook his being two years beyond the age-limit of thirty-five. Proust next thought of the avant-garde poets André Salmon and André Breton, but finally fell back on Benjamin Crémieux and, for the second prize, the young, talented and impoverished George Gabory, who had corrected the proofs of *Sodome et Gomorrhe II* for a fee of 1000 francs, and was a protégé of Gide—'one of the most gifted of the young people I have had occasion to approach,' Gide assured Proust. At four in the afternoon of 13 Jnue, when the jury met, the absent Proust was sleeping off the effects of a party at Mme Hennessy's the night before. Walter Berry had told him there would be no voting, but only a registration of candidates; yet voting took place after all, Crémieux and Maurice Genevoix were elected, and poor Gabory, to Gide's keen distress, was left in the cold. Gide suggested that Proust was duty-bound to help the young man financially, and Proust did so, 'to show that I know how to forgive an injury,' he told Rivière ruefully, 'for Gabory left all the misprints in my book that he pretended to correct!'[2]

As soon as he entered Mme Hennessy's apartment the evening before, Proust realised that he had been asked not to her 'chic' party

---

[1] 'Prost bitte!' (*FW* 424: 9); 'the prouts will invent a writing' (*FW* 482: 31); 'swansway' (*FW* 450: 5, 465: 35); 'two legglegels in blooms' (*FW* 587: 26); 'pities of the plain' (*FW* 564: 28).

[2] Gide suspected Proust of treachery, but Proust's correspondence shows that his conduct was entirely correct and open. He sincerely believed on Berry's authority that voting was postponed till a later meeting, but in any case had voted by post for both Crémieux and Gabory. Gide himself was a little to blame as his second vote went to Genevoix. It seems that the partisans of Crémieux and Genevoix had done a deal, and that each gave his second vote to the other's candidate, so that only Gide and Proust could spare a vote for Gabory. Moreover, Gabory had imprudently applied for the same prize as Crémieux, so that Proust's vote for Gabory was not even valid. However, Gabory in turn showed his lack of resentment by writing his *Essai sur Marcel Proust* (1926), one of the earliest and most sympathetic of French studies of Proust's work.

but to her 'mixed' one. A lady was singing '*I must depart forthwith*', which seemed scarcely polite; Gustave Schlumberger was snorting like a buffalo as he stumped relentlessly towards Thérèse d'Hinnisdäel; the Princesse de Polignac, icy as a cold draught, was looking the image of Dante; and while Proust talked to Boni de Castellane he heard himself pointed out—"there, that dark man who looks ill and hasn't combed his hair, he's a genius!"—as "the famous Marcel Prévost, who wrote *Les Don Juanes*!" But Marcel Prévost himself, to whom letters intended for Proust had so often been misdirected, was there in person; and Proust half promised him *La Prisonnière* as a serial for his *Revue de France*, but withdrew the offer a few days later after an indignant outburst from Rivière.

A well-meaning friend, possibly Coco de Madrazo who adored her, had informed Laure Hayman, rather belatedly, that she was the original of Odette. While Proust was still suffering from his overdose of adrenalin she sent him a furious letter; he was a monster, she declared. He replied, without attempting to differentiate between their morals, that in her wealth of taste and intelligence she was the opposite of Odette, who was destitute of either; when he put Mme Straus's 'snowballs' in Odette's drawing-room, instead of accusing him of identifying her with Swann's wife, she had written to thank him; Odette in the Bois de Boulogne was Léonie Clomesnil; Mme Hayman was no more Odette than Baron Doasan was Charlus. Mme Hayman, after a mysterious sorrow towards 1900, had made a new career as a sculptress. She had lost her wealth and youth, but not her vitality and courage, and if she and Proust could have been reconciled these two old friends would have found much to say to one another. But Proust was deeply distressed by this pathetic incident, and complained to both Gabriel de La Rochefoucauld and Gallimard of the cruelty of 'a woman I loved thirty years ago'. 'Such letters, and having to reply to them, kill all work,' he wrote, 'not to mention pleasure, which I have long since renounced.'

The Schiffs had left a few days before Mme Hennessy's party. Proust posted to Sydney a sumptuous waistcoat he had admired, in grey velvet with a pattern of foliage, which Céleste insisted on sending first to the cleaner's ("it isn't good enough for Monsieur Schiff without!"). He recalled to them the two twin pageboys he had introduced to them at the Ritz, whose personality Sydney Schiff had thought so different ('but it's the same, and anyway perfectly null'), and revealed that one of them had gone off to Switzerland with Lord Northcliffe.

These brothers, alike in face but supposed unlike in nature, must
surely be connected with the tomato-twins at Balbec, whose dis-
similarity in character causes poor M. Nissim Bernard a black eye and
a permanent dislike for the fruit they resemble.[1]

'Every day more rapidly,' Proust had written to Edmond Jaloux in
the spring, when his real or fancied symptoms of uraemia had reappeared, 'I descend a rigid iron staircase that leads to the abyss.' But
during this final summer all omens of doom ceased, as he halted unaware on the last step of the stairs. 'My giddiness, the weakness in my
legs, my impediments of speech, have almost entirely vanished,' he
told the departed Schiffs. Again, but as chimerically as Aunt Léonie
when she thinks of visiting her beloved farmhouse at Mirougrain, he
dreamed of a holiday away from Paris. At his bedside he gave lessons
in French history to Céleste, Marie Gineste, Yvonne Albaret and
Odilon, scolding them when he was displeased with the awful menace:
"I'll drown you in an ocean of *merde*!" At the Ritz in his private room,
where the manager M. Elles had now arranged for him to dine in the
small hours, he held court for the last time with his retinue of pages.
One evening, when he was explaining Molière's *Amphitryon* to a
waiter who had studied the part of Sosie at the Conservatoire, the
appropriate sound of a deluge was heard in the next room, as though
an angry Jupiter had indeed arrived with his thunder; but no, Proust
was informed, it was only Sir Philip Sassoon taking a bath.[2] The staff
were proud of Proust's fame, and sometimes even gave him news of it.
Vespis, the Italian head waiter in the grillroom, announced one evening in July: "The *Corriere della Sera*, it say Monsieur Proust's books
are verra verra tiring, you must climb, climb always, but it's worth
while, because you see you so far from the top!" Vespis died a few weeks
later: 'poor Vespis,' wrote Proust to Paul Brach, 'or happy Vespis,
according to how you look at it—he's dead—is that a happy event?
I don't know.'

   On 15 July Proust allowed himself to be taken by Brach andf
Edmond Jaloux to the celebrated Bœuf sur le Toit, the night-resort o
artists which Cocteau had discovered and consecrated. Jaloux called
for him at the instant when Céleste was knotting her master's dress-tie

   [1] II, 854-5.
   [2] It was Sir Philip's mother, according to one of Montesquiou's favourite
stories, who enquired of a lady in the Faubourg Saint-Germain—as does Mme
Verdurin of M. de Charlus (II, 967): "Couldn't you recommend me some old
nobleman, I've a vacancy for a hall-porter."

and bringing a hot drink. It was lukewarm, he complained; and then, seeing her feelings were hurt, Proust immediately assured her that she was right, that the tepid tisane was just what he needed in his state of health at the moment. The service at the Bœuf sur le Toit, Proust felt, was less perfect than at the Ritz. The roast chicken was excellent, but it was hurled at their heads by a hideous waiter whom he uncomfortably felt he had seen somewhere before. He talked of the future volumes of his novel, and revealed that Saint-Loup would become an invert like his uncle Charlus, "at the same age and for the same reasons". At the moment of tipping Proust summoned a distant waiter and rewarded him regally. "But he didn't do anything for us," protested Brach, and Proust replied: "Oh, but I saw such a sad look in his eyes, when he thought he wasn't going to get anything!" Jaloux left to go on to a soirée, and the evening began to take a sinister turn. Brach was joined by drunken friends, who engaged in hostile banter with a band of 'unbelievable pimps and queers' at the other end of the bar. The waiters, alas, and even the proprietor Moyse—"the tables this Moses keeps are apparently not those of the Law," commented Proust—seemed to favour the other side. Suddenly a completely canned young reveller lurched across to Proust, astonished by his fur coat and bowler, perhaps misunderstanding his conversation about Sodom, and picked a quarrel. Like an aged warrior, exulting in the vision of a final combat, Proust went through the motions of challenging to a duel, and exchanged names and addresses: the drunk was named Jacques Delgado, and lived in the Rue Greuze near the Trocadéro. But the etiquette of the 1890s would not do for the 1920s; his friends hurried to part the foes, explaining that it was all a joke, that he had nothing to do with their brawl, that Marcel could not possibly fight a person so far beneath him. Proust was led crestfallen away; but that night he indomitably wrote a challenge to swords, which Odilon carried at dawn to the Rue Greuze. M. Delgado was now cold sober, and sent so courteous an apology that Proust could only reply in kind. 'You owed me no excuses,' he wrote, 'and it is only the more delicate and elegant on your part to offer them. . . . The elevated sentiments of your letter give me precisely the pleasure I should have had after a duel; I mean, sir, that of shaking you very cordially by the hand.'

Among the subjects discussed at the Bœuf sur le Toit was the menace of Count Robert's posthumous memoirs. Proust had written in alarm to Henri Pinard and received a charming letter of vague reassurance. Would he be entitled, he asked Brach, if the memoirs contained an attack on himself, to prosecute Pinard? Edmond Jaloux was now literary editor to Grasset, who at this time was proposing to publish the memoirs; and on 21 October, when he was already dying, Proust wrote to Jaloux: 'it would be best to delete everything, even my name, if I do not survive the strange illness I have at this moment. Since in that case I should have good reason for being unable to reply, I prefer not to be mentioned.' His anxiety, however, and that of so many others, was needless. Montesquiou's *Les Pas effacés* might have been a masterpiece of brilliant venom, yet turned out, when published in 1923 not by Grasset but by Émile-Paul, to be only the lame apology of a disappointed man. In an interminable waste-land of verbiage and vanity, illuminated only rarely by a blazing image or thrust of a flashing swordblade that recalled his former power, Montesquiou's three volumes deplored the neglect of his greatness, praised the perspicacity of his admirers, extolled the beauty of his interior decoration, and quoted in full all the flattering things that had ever been said about him. His only damaging revelation about 'my dear Marcel' was that he had an untidy bedroom. He did not dispute Marcel's genius; he lamented only that it should have been recognised at the expense of his own, that persons other than himself should have the effrontery to claim they had been the first to discover it. 'They say this dear young man is very nice,' he wrote, 'but we were already aware of the fact!' The dreadful truth emerged at last: Count Robert's memoirs were not scandalous, but merely boring. The verdict of his beloved cousin Mme Greffulhe was generally felt to meet the case: 'it's not quite what one expects of a dead man,' she decided.

Proust's oldest friends were beginning, unawares, to see him for the last time. Lucien Daudet had called in June, to talk of distant times and express his profound dislike for one of Marcel's newest acquaintances. "Sympathies and antipathies aren't transmissible," said Marcel, "that is the saddest thing about friendships." Lucien spoke of the little ivory coffer, carved with a girl leaning on an urn and the words 'To Friendship', which Marcel had given him on New Year's Eve, 1896. "God!" cried Proust, "How could you keep it? How hideous it must be! Can you see anything prettier here that you'd like?" But Lucien wanted no rival to his ivory box. As he departed, with sobs rising in his throat, he tried to embrace his friend; but Proust recoiled in his bed, exclaiming: "No, don't, I haven't shaved." Then Lucien seized his left hand and kissed it, and bore away with him for ever the image of Marcel's black-rimmed eyes, fixed silently upon him through the open doorway.

In this June, when Antoine Bibesco briefly visited Paris from his post at the Roumanian Legation in Washington, occurred the last imperfect 'conjunction' between Proust and the Bibescos. Princesse Marthe Bibesco had dined with Proust and Walter Berry at the Ritz in 1920, unable at first to recognise, in this supernaturally young man with the small moustache and eyes extraordinarily animated with new life, whom she now heard for the first time laughing, the bearded and melancholy apparition of the ball nine years before. About the same time he had called on Antoine and his wife Elizabeth—'to ask her some questions about certain passages in Shakespeare'—at their apartment on the prow of the ship-like Ile Saint-Louis, where the gilded walls reminded him of the golden mosaics of Saint Mark's at Venice. Now Antoine brought the two princesses, without warning, to 44 Rue Hamelin after the theatre, and rang for the last time the unmistakable double peal of their youth at the doorbell. Céleste, when she opened the door, seemed inclined to close it again. "Monsieur has just had a terrible attack of asthma," she said, in the formal manner she had learned from her master, "he can hardly breathe. I'm afraid he may not be able to receive anyone, not even Prince Antoine, whose visits always give him such immense pleasure." Proust called from within; Céleste retired and returned; Antoine was to enter, but the ladies were asked to wait in the outer drawing-room. "Monsieur is very much afraid," she explained, "of the scent of princesses."

At the end of one of his last evenings in society Proust sat with Jeanne de Caillavet, his old love, now Jeanne Pouquet again, for she had married her cousin Maurice, whom Proust had glimpsed thirty years before in her mother's house. The guests were leaving, she was tired and began to go. His face took a haunting expression of gentleness, irony and pain as he said: "Very well, Madame, goodbye." "No, dear Marcel, au revoir, I'll come and visit you very soon." "No, Madame, goodbye. I shall never see you again. You think I look well? I'm dying. Look well! That's too funny!" and he burst into a forced, uncanny laugh. "Don't come, don't be offended, you're kind, but I don't want to see my friends any more," he said, as his eyes filled with tears, "I have very urgent work to do."

Jeanne's daughter Simone, now grown into a beautiful woman and a gifted writer, for whom Anatole France, in turn, had written a preface, had married Georges Stoïcesco, a Roumanian diplomat whom Proust had seen and disliked at Princesse Soutzo's; though M. Stoïcesco, we are assured, was in point of fact intelligent and charming.

With his feelings still wounded by her mother Proust was enraged to
read in *Le Figaro* on 21 August that Mme Stoïcesco ('daughter of the
second grand passion of my adolescence, the first being Mlle de Benardaky' and 'wife of the most detestable of Roumanians') had given 'a
tea at Deauville in honour of the Shah of Persia and a *goûter* in honour
of Prince and Princesse Christopher of Greece'. What, he asked, was
the difference between a tea and a *goûter?* Why publish these delectable
meals to the world, when the next page of *Le Figaro* revealed that
millions were dying of famine in Russia after devouring the corpses of
their children? He added to the manuscript of *Le Temps Retrouvé* the
remark that Mlle de Saint-Loup 'later chose for husband an obscure
man of letters'[1]; for he was not to know that Simone de Caillavet's
second husband, at least, would be a most distinguished man of
letters, his own biographer and the discoverer of the English to themselves, M. André Maurois.

Proust's urgent work was the preparation of *La Prisonnière* and
Albertine Disparue. On 24 June he informed Gallimard that both were
now typed in duplicate, though his revision, 'in which I am making
changes and additions everywhere', was hardly begun. A fortnight
later he agreed to Gallimard's request for both volumes to be
announced for 1923, but still felt unable to fix a precise date. On 29
July he proposed to send in *La Prisonnière* for first proofs, with the
double purpose of revising it on the galleys, and of seeing whether it
would be short enough to publish simultaneously with *Albertine Disparue*. At the end of August he changed his plans, and re-engaged
Yvonne Albaret, whom he had dismissed in June, to retype *La
Prisonnière*. During the next ten weeks, which coincided with his last
illness and death, Mlle Albaret copied three successive versions of the
opening section of the volume, describing the morning of Albertine's
visit to the Trocadéro and the street-cries of Paris, and also a long
extract promised to *Les Œuvres Libres*, which gave an abridged
version of the whole volume, omitting, with much else, the Verdurin
soirée and the Vinteuil Septet, and was published posthumously in
February 1923 under the title '*Précaution inutile*'.

Early in May Tronche had suggested that *Sodome et Gomorrhe III*
and *Sodome et Gomorrhe IV* were inadequate titles for the coming
volumes. "When people see a book with the same title as the one
before," Tronche declared, "they'll say: 'Why, I've read that one
already!' " It was thus not until just before the eleventh hour that

[1] III, 1028.

Proust chose new titles for the story of Albertine's captivity and death. Still in doubt, he forbore to spread the news. 'I'm thinking of calling my next volume *La Prisonnière*,' he told Jacques Boulanger in mid-May; but Gallimard was not informed until 25 June, while as late as 3 September the astonished Rivière could confess that he was 'terribly curious' to know what Proust meant by *La Prisonnière* and *La Fugitive*. Early in July, however, Proust learned that a volume of Rabindranath Tagore's poems was about to appear, in a translation by Mme de Brimont, under his own newborn title of *La Fugitive*. He knew the lady slightly, and thought of appealing to her better feelings; but no, 'it would be caddish, and too late anyway', he told Gallimard. He now resolved to abandon his title, and early in October reiterated his decision to Gallimard. The *Pléiade* editors have justifiably retained the title *La Fugitive*, since it is the only one for which documentary evidence from Proust's lifetime survives. On the other hand, of all titles it is the only one which, as equally certain documentary evidence shlows, Proust would never have used. In the same October letter Proust revealed that he had made new plans for his title, and asked Gallimard to visit him to discuss the matter. Proust's published correspondence with Gallimard and Rivière during this month is incompete, and does not indicate whether or not the visit took place; but we need have little doubt that when the NRF announced the volume as *Albertine Disparue* only a year later, they were following Proust's declared wishes.[1]

In August the famous '*décades*', the ten-day periods of literary and philosophical discussion organised by Paul Desjardins in the former monastery of Pontigny, were resumed for the first time since the war. Proust himself, as has been seen, had thought of attending in 1910, and earlier still his own half-serious, half-visionary plans for a lay monastery, with Willie Heath in 1893, with Lauris and Mme de Noailles as 'admirable abbess habited all in white' in 1903, had no doubt owed their inspiration to Desjardins. More recently, in the supposed extract from the Goncourt *Journal* which the Narrator reads at Tansonville in *Le Temps Retrouvé*, Proust had introduced a sympathetic allusion to Pontigny in the guise of a sojourn in Normandy of the Verdurins and their friends; and his satire here is directed at the absurdity of Gon-

---

[1] For these reasons the title *Albertine Disparue* has been used throughout the present biography. It may also be noticed that the typescript from which *Albertine Disparue* was printed has disappeared, and that Proust would surely have entered in it his final decision as to the title.

court and Mme Verdurin, not at Desjardins's noble dream come true,
for which he kept a nostalgic affection. 'They lodged a whole colony
of artists in an admirable mediaeval dwelling, a former monastery
rented by them for a mere nothing; and my mouth waters,' cries the
pretended diarist,[1] 'at the thought of the life Mme Verdurin confessed
to leading down there, each one working in his cell, and joining the
rest before lunch in the drawing-room, so enormous that it had two
fireplaces, for altogether superior conversation mingled with paper-
games.'

Among the thirty-five decadists of 1922 were Rivière, Gide, Marc
Allégret, Jean Schlumberger, Roger Martin du Gard, Charles du Bos,
the critic Ernst Robert Curtius who had already begun to make
Proust known in Germany, and the young André Maurois—'a
charming mind, alert, courteous and very prettily cultivated', noted
Gide with approval. 'Please give my homage to the Desjardins
family,' Proust asked Rivière, 'they are and will remain one of the
dearest and most respected parts of the years I have lived.' Proust's
spiritual presence was felt throughout Pontigny that year. His work
was frequently discussed in the formal conversations; Charles du Bos,
walking in the neighbouring forest and noticing the changing position
of the abbey church, was reminded of the Narrator's essay on the
moving spires of Martinville; and Rivière, whenever a foreign visitor
asked him to name the greatest living French writer, invariably
answered: "Proust!"

Among the foreign Proustians at Pontigny was Dorothy Bussy,
elder sister of Lytton Strachey and Gide's matchless translator and
friend. Proust's English admirers now included such elder men of
letters as Conrad, Arnold Bennett, Arthur Symons, Logan Pearsall
Smith, Edmund Gosse and George Saintsbury, young writers of the
new generation such as Aldous Huxley,[2] Middleton Murry, Compton
Mackenzie and J. C. Squire, and the entire Bloomsbury group: Vir-
ginia Woolf, Clive Bell, Desmond MacCarthy, Arthur Waley, Roger
Fry and Lytton Strachey. The sun of his glory in England had risen;
Proust himself felt its distant rays and began to respond, but with a shy
reluctance which would soon be cut short by death. Since April he had

[1] III, 713-14.
[2] Hearing of this Proust had slipped a characteristic 'visiting-card' into
Sodome et Gomorrhe: 'The illustrious Huxley, whose nephew'—he should
have said grandson—'now holds a preponderant place in the world of English
literature . . .' (II, 637).

intended to thank Murry for a new article[1] and 'an extremely nice letter', but he hesitated, unsure whether or not his benefactor should be addressed as Sir Middleton Murry. He felt too ill to accept an invitation from Jaloux early in June to dine with Murry and Katherine Mansfield, herself so soon to die.[2] T. S. Eliot, then the London correspondent of the NRF, had requested an extract from *A la Recherche* for *The Criterion*, but waited in vain for a reply: 'I am in deep despair at not yet having written to M. Eliot,' Proust told Sydney Schiff in August.

His last thoughts of England were unhappy. In December 1919 a nameless English lady had offered to translate *A la Recherche*, and Proust himself had then proposed Gilbert Cannan, translator of Romain Rolland's *Jean Christophe*, a gifted but ill-fated novelist who soon afterwards became insane. Providentially, however, and unknown to Proust, Charles Scott-Moncrieff had already resolved to devote his life to the translation of *A la Recherche du Temps Perdu*. After unavailingly offering *Swann's Way* in January 1920 to the short-lived magazine *Land and Water* as a serial, he persuaded Chatto and Windus to accept the whole of his magnificent *Remembrance of Things Past*. Early in September 1922 the Schiffs took alarm from an advance announcement, and convinced Proust that the titles, at least, were hopelessly inaccurate; for they incomprehensibly supposed the words *Swann's Way* to mean 'in the manner of Swann', and failed to recognise in *Remembrance of Things Past* the bold but exquisitely appropriate quotation from Shakespeare's Thirtieth Sonnet through which Scott-Moncrieff symbolised the transplanting of Proust's novel into English literature.[3] In his distress Proust thought of stopping the publication. 'I cherish my work,' he told Gallimard, 'and I won't have it ruined by Englishmen.'

Swann's Way was published in England in the third week of Sep-

---

[1] '*Marcel Proust. A new sensibility*', in the *Quarterly Review*, New York, July 1922, pp. 86-100, of which Murry sent Proust advance proofs.

[2] However, he sent Murry inscribed copies of *Le Côté de Guermantes II* and *Sodome et Gomorrhe II*, the latter 'with admiring and grateful homage from a writer whom you have always protected and supported, and who would like to have an hour's good health in order to thank you less briefly'.

[3] The Schiffs, who had erred only from loyalty to Proust, were quick to make amends. They became ardent admirers and personal friends of Scott-Moncrieff, and Sydney Schiff dedicated his translation of *Time Regained*: 'To the memory of my friend Charles Scott-Moncrieff, Marcel Proust's incomparable translator'.

tember.[1] Proust, despite his shaky acquaintance with the half-learned and half-forgotten English language, was relieved a little as he struggled through his own copy by the beauty he dimly perceived, still more, perhaps, by his press-cuttings from London reviews, which tended, though they praised both highly, to declare the translation superior to the original. Even so, when he thanked Scott-Moncrieff on 10 October for 'the trouble you have taken', and complimented him on his 'fine talent', his tone was still grudging and prickly. 'The verses you have inserted, and the dedication to your friends,' he remarked, 'are no substitute for the intentional ambiguity of my *Temps perdu*, which corresponds to the *Temps retrouvé* that appears at the end of my work.' As for *Swann's Way*, all would have been well, he suggested, if his translator had called it '*To Swann's Way*'! Scott-Moncrieff, equally ruffled, replied stiltedly in English—'because my knowledge of French, as you have shown me with regard to my titles, is too imperfect, too stunted a growth for me to weave from it the chaplet that I would fain offer you'—and stood by his guns.[2]

But Proust's strange visitor, who had come to warn every year in May, the month of his brother's birth, and September, the month of his mother's death, had now come to stay.

[1] The British Museum copyright copy was received on 19 September, and the first review appeared in the *Times Literary Supplement* on the 21st.

[2] The memory of his unlucky skirmish with Proust perhaps played some part in the sturdy independence which makes, quite as much as its fidelity, the greatness of his translation. Curtius, when he visited Scott-Moncrieff in Rome in 1928, was amused by the 'sarcastic want of respect' which seasoned his profound devotion to Proust's work, and remarked: 'He generally received me with some strong abuse of Albertine, whose moods and vices were at that time keeping him very busy.'

Chapter 17

THE TWO WAYS MEET
(*September – November 1922*)

NEW and unusually violent attacks of asthma on 2 and 3 September were followed on the 4th by repeated fits of vertigo, in which he fell again and again to the floor. Whenever he dared to step from his bed he swayed, turned and dropped, and soon his speech and memory were again affected. 'I have been deprived successively of speech, sight and movement,' he told Jaloux and Curtius, adding to the latter: 'We must never be afraid to go too far, for truth lies beyond.'

The causes of the symptoms which during the past five years had marked the approach of Proust's death are mysterious and were probably complex. He had ceased to believe that his brain was affected; no doubt his doctors were justified in blaming his alternate abuse of narcotic and stimulating drugs, and Proust himself may well have been right a year before in diagnosing chronic uraemia, a disturbance of metabolism arising not from kidney disease but from a malfunctioning of the central nervous system, which could have been caused by his drugs and would account medically for all his signs of unco-ordination. But these symptoms, whatever their origin, combined to imitate, as he himself had noticed, those of his mother in her last illness. They included a psychosomatic factor which guided his physical ailments according to the self-destructive promptings of his inner guilt. The Dark Woman was punishing him with the sufferings he had caused; and conversely, by sharing his dead mother's torment he would be identified and united with her at last. For the present, however, Proust sought a more natural explanation. With some support from his doctors, he convinced himself truly or falsely that there were cracks in his chimney, and he was being poisoned by carbon monoxide fumes. Towards the middle of September he ventured several times to the Ritz for his four a.m. dinner, found his symptoms vanished when he left his unventilated bedroom, and felt his suspicions were confirmed. He gave orders that his fire must not be lit; and this most warmth-needing of men continued his journey to death in the still more dangerous environment of an unheated room. Henceforth all his actions combined to doom him. But the strange recurrent malady of his last years, though it had prepared for the end by undermining his powers of resistance, was not destined to be the cause of his death. He had sinned through his lungs when in childhood he used his asthma to compel his mother's love, and to punish her fancied refusal of love; and now he was to perish by his lungs, though not through asthma.

Never had he worked more obsessively at his novel. The opening section of *La Prisonnière* dissatisfied him, as has been seen, and from mid-August to late October he thrice rearranged the existing type-script, which Yvonne Albaret thrice typed again, until the themes of waking, the presence of Albertine, and the street-cries of Paris were interwoven and repeated in their final symphonic form.[1] The remain-der of the volume apparently contented him, as well it might, for only three minor additions were made to the typescript of the previous spring.[2] But the voice of duty to his editors sounded louder even than the knell of death. Early in August he had promised Rivière an extract on Albertine's sleep, '*Le Sommeil d'Albertine*', and another on the morning street-cries, '*Les Cris de Paris*', for the NRF. Towards the end of the month he wrung Gallimard's reluctant consent to the abridgement of *La Prisonnière*, '*Précaution Inutile*', in *Les Œuvres Libres*, for which the editor Henri Duvernois had offered the princely sum of 10,000 francs.[3] He began with the first NRF extract, adding, because it was too brief, another on the Narrator's waking entitled '*Mes Réveils*', and sent the contribution to Rivière on 24 September. "You're mad to work in a state like this," protested Dr Bize, and prescribed an injection of evatmine, for asthma, and cola as a heart stimulant. Readers of the November NRF must have been baffled to find that the naked girl slumbering at the Narrator's side was Gisèle;

---

[1] He was at work on the second of these revisions (which, counting the complete typescript as the first, he called the third) on 2 September, and on the third and last (which he called the fourth) on the 20th.

[2] Mme Verdurin's medicinal preparations for the torments of the Vinteuil Septet (III, 240-1), the quarrel with Albertine when she says, or nearly says, "*casser le pot*" (III, 338-40), and an enlargement of the final paragraph in which Françoise announces Albertine's departure (III, 415).

[3] Proust told Sydney Schiff in September that he had already lent 5000 francs in anticipation of this fee 'to help some infuriating unfortunates'. The last time he had lent money to 'unfortunates' was in November 1917, when he subsidised Albert Le Cuziat's brothel. Can Proust still have been assisting Albert, despite their break a year or two before? Or was he again helping Anna Agostinelli, or Céline Cottin?

for Proust had changed her name, and altered the title to '*La regarder dormir*', lest Duvernois should discover that his 'unpublished novel' had been shorn of one of its finest passages. The second extract, retitled '*Une Matinée au Trocadéro*', and enlarged by the death of Bergotte, appeared in January 1923 in the special number, *Hommage à Marcel Proust*, dedicated by the NRF to his memory. Next Proust began the still more formidable task of condensing his whole volume into 127 pages for *Les Œuvres Libres*, and of re-establishing the continuity he had broken by his NRF extracts. Even so, he found energy to negotiate from July to October with two collectors who competed to buy the manuscript and corrected proofs of *Sodome et Gomorrhe II*,[1] and to support Rivière's candidature for the Prix Balzac.[2]

Early in October, on a foggy evening, Proust attended a last soirée at the Beaumonts' and returned with a sore throat, which next day became a severe cold. The second stage of his last illness had begun. His fever rose, and bronchitis set in, with fits of incessant coughing. Towards the middle of the month, on Céleste's insistence, he sent for Dr Bize. "It's nothing serious yet," decided the good doctor, "I can

---

[1] Jacques Doucet offered 7000 francs in July. Proust hesitated, on learning that Doucet intended to bequeath his collection to the State. 'It isn't very agreeable,' Proust told the Schiffs, 'to think that when I am dead anyone who chooses will be able to study my manuscripts, compare them with the definitive text, and infer suppositions which will always be false on my method of work and the evolution of my thought ... but I wonder whether I wouldn't do better to diminish my absurd and useless expenses by these 7000 francs, than to let myself be sensitive about this posthumous indiscretion.' Proust no doubt foresaw the prejudiced and destructive fallacies of Professors Feuillerat and Vigneron, which have done lasting harm to Proustian scholarship, rather than the devoted work of the *Pléiade* editors André Ferré and Pierre Clarac, which is the greatest of all monuments to his memory. In any case, Proust's misgivings related only to his textual critics, and those who quote them against his biographers are not entitled to do so. Towards the end of August Serge André, the owner of the periodicals edited by Jacques Boulanger, offered 10,000 francs; but Proust was too scrupulous to sell anything to a personal friend. The negotiations with Doucet were still in progress at the end of October, but were cut short by Proust's death, when the manuscript passed with the rest of his literary property to his brother Robert.

[2] Rivière submitted his novel *Aimée*, which he dedicated to Proust, but his honourable refusal to allow Proust to approach his political enemy Léon Daudet cost him the prize. The jury, presided by Paul Bourget, included Barrès, Boylesve, Bidou, Marcel Boulanger, Léon Daudet, Henri Duvernois, Georges Duhamel and Gaston Chérau, all of whom except the last two were personal friends of Proust.

cure you in a week or ten days, but you'll have to stop work, and above all take nourishment." Proust would do neither of these things. Take nourishment! So the family doctor had ordered, more than forty years ago, on the night of *François le Champi*; and his mother had said: "My child, that doctor may be cleverer than I am, but I know what is right." "Mother always nursed me better than any doctors," he told Céleste, "and she knew that fasting is the only thing for a fever."

So he fasted, taking only fruit and milk, but the fever still rose and the helpless coughing persisted. Céleste kept the pathetic, peremptory notes her master now wrote to her when he was too breathless to speak. 'I'm so heated with this coughing that I'll probably try to drink a hot tisane. Hot, not warmed up. But no over-ripe fruit (so I'd better have your grapes). . . .' 'I've just coughed more than three thousand times, my back and stomach are done for, everything. It's madness. I need very hot sheets and woollen pullovers. Remember, all your sheets have a smell that starts my useless coughing. I hope you'll take strict account of my order, otherwise I shall be more than angry.' 'Have we a drop of that port from Voisin's, that the Comte de Polignac said was just like milk?' 'Céleste, I want an empty teacup and some sugar.' 'Can someone run and get me a peach or an apricot from the Ritz?' The sleepless Céleste grew as thin as her master, and Dr Bize's seven days were nearly over.

Late on the afternoon of the 19th Proust disobeyed his doctor and his fever, dressed and went out for the last time. His strength failed, and he returned almost immediately, cold to the marrow, shuddering, racked with fits of sinister sneezing. He rested for a moment on his chaise-longue, and returned to bed, too harassed even to work that night. "Death pursues me, Céleste," he said, "I shan't have time to finish my corrections, and Gallimard is waiting." Next day Céleste telephoned for Dr Robert Proust, who was out, and Dr Bize, who came. Proust himself suspected, prematurely, that he had pneumonia.

He sent Odilon for Rivière that evening, but Rivière was busy and unaware of danger. 'My dear Jacques,' wrote Proust, 'you will never guess why I sent for you, and I'd rather no one else knew. It was to ask you to write to your brother for some medical information.' Rivière came next day, and his brother Dr Marc Rivière, a clinician in the Faculty of Medicine at Bordeaux, replied on 25 October. 'Cocci,' he explained, 'are punctiform, slightly ovoid microbes. When they are grouped in twos we have diplococci, when in chains streptococci, when in clusters staphylococci. Pneumococci belong to the class of diplococci, being usually found in pairs in sputum. Each species of coccus is always grouped in the same way, thus permitting its identification...' Proust had written in time past to Emile Mâle for iconography, to François de Pâris for the heraldry of the Guermantes, to Louis Dimier and Henri Longnon for Brichot's etymologies of Normandy place-names; now he had verified the sources of his death.

On the 25th he had received the advance proof of his NRF extract. Finding that the ending of '*Mes Réveils*' was not to his liking, and forgetting that he had given Rivière no instructions for altering it, he upbraided his friend with an uncharacteristic cruelty which showed only the extent of his exhaustion. 'You have deceived me,' he wrote, 'leave me alone, my suffering today has touched the brink of despair. I have lost faith in you.' The loyal Rivière, bearing no malice, stopped the presses at Abbeville and obeyed his orders. The day before, on 24 October, Proust had completed *La Prisonnière*, and from now until his death worked on the revision of *Albertine Disparue*. On the 28th he learned the news of Rivière's rejection at the Prix Balzac committee,[1] without understanding it—'I happened to be a little delirious'; and it was not until about 2 November that he sent his condolences, with ironical thanks to Dr Marc Rivière for 'his graceful Bordelaisian pastoral, which proves that every microbe is a sign of health'. A few minutes later he wrote to Gallimard: 'the kind of fury with which I have worked at *La Prisonnière* (ready, but needs to be reread—the best would be for you to have first proofs made for me to correct), especially in my terrible state of these days, has made the following volumes recede. But three days of rest may suffice. Goodbye, dear Gaston.' A little before he had sent '*Précaution Inutile*' to Duvernois: 'if I have another hour of strength I shall write to my dear Robert de Flers, and ask him to spare me "after a long and painful illness valiantly borne".... Anyway, I think I may still come through.... And now, expect no more of me but silence, and imitate mine.' These three letters, as far as is known, were the last Proust ever wrote. "November has come," he said to Céleste, "November, that took my father." Towards 8 November Proust contracted the pneumonia he had already suspected and foretold.

The baffled Dr Bize summoned Robert Proust. "Your brother is impossible to treat," he exclaimed, "I decline all responsibility if he goes on like this. What's the use of my coming to see him? He defies

[1] The prize was shared by Émile Baumann with *Job le Prédestiné* and Giraudoux with *Siegfried et le Limousin*, with a minority vote for Rivière.

all my orders!" "Then I shall have him forcibly treated," exploded Robert, "as a doctor I have the right. I'll have him taken to the Piccini clinic."[1] For the first time since 1906, when Robert had un-selfishly refused to take his fair share of their mother's legacy, Proust quarrelled with his brother. Did Robert presume to save his life, which he must save unaided or not at all; did he dare to keep him from the rendezvous which lay at the end? "Let me alone," Marcel cried, blind with rage, "I won't leave my bedroom." Would he at least have a nurse, they pleaded. "I'll have no one but Céleste, she's the only one who understands me." Robert insisted, and Proust ordered his would-be saviours to leave. He rang for Céleste: "You are to promise not to let anyone in, neither doctor, nor nurse, nor my family. Everyone who might hinder my work must stay away. You are not to go out for a second, and if I get worse, you must stay by me. Do as I say, and don't torment me any more." In those days before the discovery of sulfa-drugs expert nursing was the only known treatment for pneumonia. Proust was now doomed.

Few persons were to see him again in this world. Tronche had called on 24 September to reveal that *Le Côté de Guermantes* and *Sodome et Gomorrhe II* were temporarily out of print—a form of news which seems gratifying to publishers but calamitous to authors. Rivière made a last visit to collect the typescript of *La Prisonnière* and, as Céleste believed, to receive instructions for *Albertine Disparue*, which may well have included the new title.[2] Reynaldo called every day to enquire, but left without being able to see his friend. The gay Morand came, and Proust was moved by his emotion. "I felt that Paul Morand has a heart of gold," he told Céleste, "though I didn't think so before. He must have found me much changed, he said such kind things, and I realised he was sad to see me like this. I didn't know he was fond of me; I am very fond of him too."

Proust began to prepare for the end. Remorseful for his unkindness to Dr Bize, and characteristically anxious to express repentance by a gift, he ordered Céleste to send the well-meaning doctor a basket of flowers. "That's one more thing put right, if I should die," he said.

[1] The Clinique Médicale de Paris, 6 Rue Piccini (only half a mile from 44 Rue Hamelin, on the far side of the Avenue du Bois de Boulogne), under the charge of Dr Louis Lamy.
[2] The title *Albertine Disparue* first appeared on the verso of the half-title of the first edition of *La Prisonnière*, which was printed and published in the autumn of the following year (*achevé d'imprimer* 14 November 1923).

Rather than explain why he had not asked his support for Rivière at the time of the Prix Balzac, he had not written to thank Léon Daudet for yet another article in his praise; so Daudet's wife, too, must have a present of flowers. In the summer of 1917 Marie Scheikévitch had given him a cigarette-lighter made from two English pennies, a present from her young brother at the front; "do you know," he remarked as he admired it, "you will find this in my novel."[1] Since the war his relations with Mme Scheikévitch had been strained; but now, as a gesture of reconciliation from beyond the grave, he told Céleste to return this sacred relic of their friendship after his death.

He thought of the saintly Abbé Mugnier's efforts to save his soul; he remembered, too, that he himself was a baptised and confirmed, though lapsed Catholic. Had he not fought against injustice to the Church in the dark days of the Combes laws, and expressed in his novel a profound love for the humble gothic churches which, perhaps, are a truer symbol of faith than the corrupt souls of men? Yet he could not show a conformity which he did not feel. "Send for the good Abbé Mugnier," he said with mingled irony and reverence, "half an hour after I die. You will see how he'll pray for me. And find the rosary that Lucie Faure brought me from Jerusalem, and put it between my fingers when I'm dead." He looked at Céleste's hands. "To think that those little hands will close my eyes," he said, "Céleste, you have nursed me as though you were my own mother."

Sleep had left him, and in his long hours of waking he imagined the sudden arrival in his bedroom of staff from the Piccini clinic, sent by Robert to take him away by force. He wrote to Reynaldo and Morand asking them to prevent this fell arrest; and poor Robert consented, on condition that he should be allowed to call every day. From the 15th Robert Proust was almost constantly near Marcel, sharing devotedly in Céleste's nursing. Another anxiety seized Proust: "Céleste, it is horrible to think that doctors insist on torturing a dying man. They will want to give me injections when I'm too weak to resist, just to prolong my sufferings for a few hours. You must swear to prevent them." Céleste hesitated, and he gave her a terrible look. "If you don't," he hissed, "I'll come back to haunt you."

Pneumonia, when uninterrupted by modern remedies, lasts for up

---

[1] In his list of wartime jewellery carried by fashionable ladies on the home front the Narrator mentions 'cigarette-lighters made of two English pennies, to which a soldier in his dugout had contrived to give so beautiful a patina that Queen Victoria's profile seemed traced by Pisanello' (III, 724).

to ten days, ending in a crisis followed by the death or rapid recovery of the sufferer; but the crisis is often preceded a day or two before by a 'false crisis', after which the patient's condition temporarily and illusorily improves. Proust's 'false crisis' came on 16 November, and on the 17th, declaring himself much better, he sent for Robert. "To-morrow will be the ninth day," he said, "and if I get past it I'll show my doctors what sort of a man I am. Five days more, and we shall see whether they were right in trying to prevent me from working. But it remains to be seen whether I can survive these five days." Robert asked him to take nourishment. Proust smiled. "If, like my doctors, you want me to eat," he told Céleste, "you can cook me a fried sole. I'm sure it won't do me any good, but I want to please you." But this ritual sole, which Mme Proust had prescribed for his convalescence at the time of *François le Champi*, was prudently forbidden by Robert, and Marcel gracefully acquiesced. "I'm going to do a good night's work," he said, as Robert departed, "and I'll keep Céleste by me to help."

At least two of the products of this last night have survived. One is written on the back of an envelope stained by a spilt tisane, in a tragically changed and quavering hand; only a few phrases are legible or intelligible, but enough to show that this was an expanded version of a few sentences in the Narrator's mother's conversation with her Combray friends on the marriage of Saint-Loup and Gilberte, near the end of *Albertine Disparue*.[1] Towards three in the morning, exhausted and suffocating, he called Céleste, in whose hand many of the November additions to the manuscript of *Albertine Disparue* are written, to take dictation. "Now I'm in the same condition myself, I want to add some notes to the death of Bergotte," he said. The only relic of these, written in the clear, unhurried, misspelt autograph of Céleste, is a satirical observation on the imbecility of doctors, drawn perhaps by Proust from the remarks of the previous day. 'And then one day everything changes. We are now allowed everything that was declared unsuitable, all that was forbidden us. "But I couldn't have champagne, for instance?" "Why, certainly, if you feel like it." Unable to believe our ears, we send for the very brands we had most strictly denied ourselves; and it is such things as this that impart a certain slight vulgarity to the unbelievable frivolousness of the dying.'

[1] '*Le vieux qui entretenait la mère . . . d'avoir épousé Mlle de Forcheville . . . cependant que la personne qui avait l'air de vouloir . . . trouva qu'elle était elle et était une autre (G. de Forcheville).*' Cf. III, 676.

His other insertions may have been less insignificant, for as he finished his face lit up with joy. "Céleste, I think what I've made you write was very good. Above all, don't forget to add it in the proper place." But Céleste forgot, or could not find the place, and the insertions were never made.[1] His strength suddenly failed, and the doctors told her next day that the abscess in his lungs must have burst at that moment. "I must stop, I can't do any more," he said. Céleste noticed that he was clutching at the bedclothes, drawing the scattered leaves of his manuscript towards him, and recognised, wise in peasant lore, the uncanny reflex action known as 'plucking', an infallible sign of the close and inevitable end.

When the dawn of Saturday, 18 November 1922, came he was still conscious. At six he asked for milk, adding with a smile: "Always just to please you." At ten he sent Odilon to the Ritz for iced beer: "Like everything else, it will come too late," he said. He drew breath with appalling difficulty; his face was white and emaciated, his black beard had grown again; and his eyes, with an extraordinary intensity, seemed to gaze on things invisible. "Leave me, I want to be alone," he murmured. Céleste stood by the inner door, concealed by the blue satin bedscreen, but he sensed her presence. "Why are you waiting, Céleste?" "I'm afraid to leave Monsieur." "Don't lie, Céleste, you know she's come." Proust was staring at the other door, the one through which visitors came, through which, indeed, a last visitor had just entered. "She's big, very big," he cried, "she's very big, very dark! She's all in black, she's ugly, she frightens me." "You needn't be afraid, I'm here, I'll make her go away." "No, don't touch her, Céleste! No one must touch her! She's merciless, she's getting more horrible every moment." It was more than time to send for the doctors.

Robert Proust hurried from his hospital, followed by Dr Bize, the long cortège of orderlies with cupping-glasses, bladders of oxygen, hypodermic syringes, and Odilon with the beer. With angry eyes Proust ignored the invaders, and murmured: "Thank you, my dear Odilon, for getting the beer." He submitted in silence to an injection from Dr Bize, while Robert clasped his hand; but as Céleste raised the bedclothes she felt his fingers, pinching her wrist till the blood came,

---

[1] In the *Pléiade* text of *La Prisonnière* (III, 182-8) the death of Bergotte is printed unchanged from the typescript made by Yvonne Albaret in the previous spring, while the passage on Gilberte is in the original version, without indication of any alternative.

and heard his voice whispering: "Ah, Céleste, why did you let them?"
The doctors performed their useless ritual in vain. The cupping-
glasses, intended to draw the broken abscess and stimulate his failing
heart, would not hold on his dying skin. At three in the afternoon
Robert raised his brother gently on the pillows: "I'm disturbing you,
my dear boy," he said, "I'm afraid I'm hurting you." "Oh, yes, my
dear Robert," replied Marcel, in his last conscious words; but a little
later he was heard to say: "Mother". The Dark Woman, raised five
years before by the unaccepted offering of his novel and his descent
into the final pit of Sodom, had come and gone. He had forgiven
Robert, who by his birth had hurt him indeed; and now only the
young mother, restored from before the beginning of Time Lost,
before she had ever seemed to withhold her love, remained. At half-
past five, calm and motionless, his eyes still wide open, Proust died.

Soon Reynaldo would come, to write hurried *pneus* to Marcel's
friends, and telephone; "Is that you, Lucien? Marcel has just died."
For two days more the endless, bewildered procession of mourners
would enter to see Proust for the last time and bid him farewell.
Morand and Gabriel Astruc, indeed, came the same evening, followed
a little before midnight by Fernand Gregh, who stayed to watch over
the dead man while Reynaldo rested, and the noises of the great city
gradually died away. Marcel, he reflected, was the first of the *Banquet*
group to die—the first, except for Jacques Bizet, who, fallen into alco-
holism and morphinomania and tortured by a cruel mistress, had shot
himself a fortnight before. But Gregh remembered most clearly the
young Marcel of thirty years ago, ringing from house to house in the
Boulevard Haussmann to find him in the first fervour of their friendship; in love with the enchanting Marie Finaly; and once at Trouville,
in the dark-room at the Manoir de la Cour Brûlée, inexplicably faint-
ing while Gregh and Jacques Bizet developed their negatives.

Marthe and Suzy Proust, Robert Dreyfus, Mme de Noailles, Lucien
Daudet, Lauris, Robert de Billy, Proust's cousins Valentine Thomson
and her sister Marguerite, Jaloux, Porel and Cocteau came next day.
When the weeping Céleste offered to lead him in, Dreyfus had not the
heart to see the body, and left with the kinder memory of the boy
Marcel in the Champs-Élysées, darting to meet Marie de Benardaky.
Mme de Noailles came with Henri Gans; Marcel's face was proud and
indolent, she thought, as though death had not succeeded in attracting
his attention. Lucien saw a smile of victory, Lauris Marcel's look of
infinite goodness—'never was so much goodness accompanied by so

much intelligence,' he wrote—while Billy noticed how each of the friends, stricken at heart, kept to himself rather than intrude on the suffering of the others. Porel slipped a cameo ring, given by Anatole France to Réjane after the first night of *Le Lys Rouge*, on Marcel's finger. Cocteau observed the twenty manuscript volumes of *A la Recherche du Temps Perdu*, piled neatly on the mantelpiece by Céleste, 'continuing to live, like the ticking watch on the wrist of a dead soldier'. But Jaloux, perhaps rightly, was struck by the impression that Proust 'was more dead than other dead men—he was totally absent'. Céline Cottin turned up and thought, with her streak of malice: "Thin and pale as ever, legs still like matchsticks." Helleu, Dunoyer de Segonzac, the sculptor Wlérick, the surrealist photographer Man Ray came at Robert's invitation to make portraits of the majestic head and folded hands. Helleu, who had been the Count's friend as well as Proust's, remarked to Céleste: "Why did he write like that about Montesquiou? Montesquiou died of it", and was horror-struck by the look of vengeful delight in Céleste's face.

Proust's funeral-service would be at noon on Tuesday, 21 November, at the nearby church of Saint-Pierre-de-Chaillot, with the military honours due to a chevalier of the Légion d'Honneur. In that enormous concourse, where Antoinette Faure-Berge stood with Comte Greffulhe, Pierre Lavallée with Princesse Marie Murat, Reynaldo's sister Maria with Diaghilev, he was surrounded by all the friends of all his life, as though a throng of ghosts had risen to do honour to a living man. Ravel's *Pavane for a Dead Infanta* was played, the Abbé Delepouve pronounced absolution, the bells tolled, and the mourners waited for their carriages. Barrès, bowler-hatted, his umbrella dangling from his elbow, said to Mauriac: "Ah, well, he was our young man." Reynaldo recognised a familiar face in the crowd: "Good Lord, there's Céline," he thought. Astruc and Léon Daudet, sworn enemies for thirty-five years since Astruc had written disrespectfully of Alphonse Daudet in *L'Évènement*, hailed the same taxi and pardoned one another. Fernand Gregh's little dog Flipot had escaped and taken refuge, amid the vulgar laughter of sightseers, under Proust's hearse; and suddenly the desperate animal darted away through the torrent of motor-cars, never to be seen again. They buried Proust with his father and mother, beneath Marie Nordlinger's plaque of the bearded Doctor Proust, at the summit of Père Lachaise. For a few years, until no one came, the Abbé Mugnier held an anniversary mass in his memory at Saint-Pierre-de-Chaillot.

Meanwhile, however, the dead writer lay on his white bed, with a bunch of violets in his clasped hands, holy water and a sprig of box at his side. Daylight and fresh air flooded his bedroom for the first time, and funereal flowers which did not rouse his asthma surrounded him. The look of peace and returned youth, the faint smile left his face, replaced by the hollow cheeks and stark grin of dissolution. But the great circle commenced by his birth, which the spiritual triumph of *A la Recherche du Temps Perdu* had left still imperfect, was now at last entire. His novel, by leaving his deepest guilt unatoned, had led to his most terrible sin; but salvation is completed only in the material world, at the moment of forgiveness and being forgiven, which for Proust was the moment of death. Now not only his work but his life was eternally alive. As he predicted, the Two Ways had met. The Méséglise and Guermantes Ways, the self we are born with and the self which we acquire, always join at last, for the rarest and greatest in a work of art, in death for everyone; but to find their point of unity we must first travel them, in the world of people, places and things, in Time.

THE END

BIBLIOGRAPHY

MARCEL PROUST. VOLUMES ONE AND TWO

This bibliography is limited to books and articles containing the primary sources on which the present biography is based. Each entry is preceded by the abbreviated form used for the source-references given in the Notes.

MAJOR WORKS BY PROUST

BA   *La Bible d'Amiens* (Mercure de France, Paris, 1904).

C   *Chroniques* (Gallimard, Paris, 1927).

CG   *Correspondance générale.* 6 vols. (Plon, Paris, 1930-36).

CSB   *Contre Sainte-Beuve* (Gallimard, Paris, 1954).

I., II, III *A la Recherche du Temps Perdu.* Ed. Pierre Clarac and André Ferré. 3 vols. (*Bibliothèque de la Pléiade*, Gallimard, Paris, 1954.)

JS   *Jean Santeuil.* 3 vols. (Gallimard, Paris, 1952).

PJ   *Les Plaisirs et les Jours* (Gallimard, Paris, 1924).

PM   *Pastiches et Mélanges* (Gallimard, Paris, 1919).

SL   *Sésame et les Lys* (Mercure de France, Paris, 1906).

LETTERS AND MINOR WORKS OF PROUST, MEMOIRS, MISCELLANEOUS WORKS, ARTICLES

Abraham Abraham, Pierre. *Proust* (Rieder, Paris, 1930).

Adam *Adam International Review*, no. 260 (1957). *Marcel Proust. A world symposium.* ed. Miron Grindea.

Adam (Barney) *Adam International Review*, no. 269 (1963). *The Amazon of Letters. A world tribute to Natalie Clifford Barney.* ed. Miron Grindea.

Adam, A. Adam, Antoine. 'Le Roman de Proust et le problème des clefs', *Revue des sciences humaines*, jan. mars 1952, 49-90.

Adam, H. P. Adam, H. P. *Paris sees it through* (Hodder & Stoughton, London, 1919).

Adelson Adelson, Dorothy. 'The Vinteuil Sonata', *Music and Letters*, vol. 23 (July 1942), 228-33.

Albalat Albalat, Antoine. *Trente ans de Quartier Latin* (Malfère, Paris, 1930).

Alden Alden, Douglas W. *Marcel Proust and his French Critics* (Lymanhouse, Los Angeles, 1940).

Ambrière Ambrière, F. 'Gaston Calmette et les écrivains du Figaro', *Nouvelles littéraires*, 17 Sept. 1932.

Amiel Amiel, Denys. 'Une Lettre inédite de Proust (à Denys Amiel)', *Nouvelles littéraires*, 31 Dec. 1927.

Amphitrion Amphitrion. 'Marcel Proust à la recherche d'un bastone perduto', *Nuova antologia*, 16 March 1935, 319-20.

Astruc Astruc, Gabriel. *Le Pavillon des fantômes* (Grasset, Paris, 1929).

Augustin-Thierry Augustin-Thierry, A. *La Princesse Mathilde* (Albin Michel, Paris, 1950).

Autret Autret, Jean. *L'Influence de Ruskin sur la vie, les idées et l'oeuvre de Marcel Proust* (Droz, Genève, 1955).

Bac (A) Bac, Ferdinand. *Intimités de la Troisième République*, 2 vols. (Hachette, Paris, 1935).

Bac (B) ——, ——. *La Princesse Mathilde* (Hachette, Paris, 1928).

Baedeker Baedeker, Karl. *Le Nord-Ouest de la France*. 8me éd. (Baedeker, Leipzig, 1908).

Balsan Balsan, Consuelo Vanderbilt. *The Glitter and the Gold* (Heinemann, London, 1953).

Bardac (A) Bardac, Henri. 'Madeleine Lemaire et Marcel Proust', *Revue de Paris*, août 1949, 137-42.

Bardac (B) ——, ——. 'Proust et Montesquiou,' *Revue de Paris*, sept. 1948, 142-6.

Barney (A) Barney, Natalie Clifford. *Aventures de l'esprit* (Émile Paul, Paris, 1929).

Barney (B) ——, ——. *Souvenirs indiscrets* (Flammarion, Paris, 1960).

Barrès Barrès, Maurice. *Mes cahiers*. 14 vols. (Plon, Paris, 1929-57).

Baumont Baumont, Maurice. *L'Affaire Eulenbourg et les origines de la guerre mondiale* (Payot, Paris, 1933).

Bell Bell, Clive. *Old Friends* (Chatto & Windus, London, 1956).

Benda Benda, Julien. *La Jeunesse d'un clerc* (Gallimard, Paris, 1937).

Benoist-Méchin Benoist-Méchin, Jacques. *Retour à Marcel Proust* (Amiot, Paris, 1957).

Bérence Bérence, Fred. 'Une Héroine de Proust. Souvenirs inédits sur la reine Marie de Naples', *Nouvelles littéraires*, 26 sept. 1946.

Bergson Bergson, Henri. 'Rapport sur un ouvrage de M. Marcel Proust: *La Bible d'Amiens* de Ruskin', *Académie des Sciences morales et politiques, Séances et travaux*, vol. 162, juillet 1904, 491-2.

Berl (A) Berl, Emmanuel. *Sylvia* (Gallimard, Paris, 1952).

Berl (B) ——, ——. 'Une Lettre de Marcel Proust à Emmanuel Berl', *Table ronde*, sept. 1953, 9-11.

Berl (C) ——, ——. *Présence des morts* (Gallimard, Paris, 1956).

Bertaut Bertaut, Jules. *L'Opinion et les mœurs* (Éditions de France, Paris, 1931).

Bibesco, A (A) Bibesco, Prince Antoine. 'The Heartlessness of Marcel Proust', *Cornhill Magazine*, no. 983 (summer 1950), 421-8.

Bibesco, A (B) ——, ——. *Lettres de Marcel Proust à Bibesco* (Éditions de Claire-fontaine, Lausanne, 1949).

Bibesco, M (A) Bibesco, Princesse Marthe. *Au Bal avec Marcel Proust* (Gallimard, Paris, 1928).

Bibesco, M (B) ——, ——. *La Duchesse de Guermantes. Laure de Sade, comtesse de Chevigné* (Plon, Paris, 1951).

Bibesco, M (C). ——, ——. *Le Voyageur voilé* (La Palatine, Genève, 1947).

Bibesco, M (D) ——, ——. 'Marcel Proust et la mémoire', *Hommes et mondes*, jan. 1956, 183-93.

Bibesco, M (E) ——, ——. *La vie d'une amitié*. 3 vols. (Plon, Paris, 1951-7).

Billy Billy, Robert de. *Marcel Proust. Lettres et conversations* (Éditions des Portiques, Paris, 1930).

Bisson Bisson, L. A. 'Deux inédits de Proust', *French Studies*, vol. 2, no. 4 (Oct. 1948), 341-7.

Blanche (A) Blanche, Jacques Émile. *Mes modèles* (Stock, Paris, 1928).

Blanche (B) ——, ——. *La Pêche aux souvenirs* (Flammarion, Paris, 1949).

Blanche (C) ——, ——. *Propos de peintre*. 3 vols. (Émile Paul, Paris, 1919-28).

Blanche (D) ——, ——. 'Souvenirs sur Marcel Proust', *Revue hebdomadaire*, 21 juillet 1928, 259-70.

Blanche (E) ——, ——. *Portraits of a Lifetime* (Dent, London, 1937).

Blum Blum, René. *Comment parut Du Côté de chez Swann. Lettres de Marcel Proust à René Blum, Bernard Grasset et Louis Brun* (Kra, Paris, 1930).

Boigne Boigne, Comtesse C. de. *Récits d'une tante.* 5 vols. (Plon, Paris, 1907-8).
Bonnefont Bonnefont. *Les Parisiennes chez elles* (Flammarion, Paris, 1895).
Bonnet Bonnet, Henri. *Marcel Proust de 1907 à 1914* (Nizet, Paris, 1959).
Bordeaux (A) Bordeaux, Henry. *Histoire d'une vie* (Plon, Paris, 1951-00).
Bordeaux (B) ——, ——. 'Souvenirs sur Proust et Boylesve', *Œuvres libres*, no. 288 (juillet, 1951), 98-146.
Bourcet Bourcet, M. *Un Couple de tragédie. Le duc et la duchesse d'Alençon* (Perrin, Paris, 1939).
Bourdet (A) Bourdet, D. *Pris sur le vif* (Plon, Paris, 1957).
Bourdet (B) ——, ——. 'Images de Paris (César Ritz)', *Revue de Paris*, sept. 1948, 152-3.
Boylesve Boylesve, René. *Feuilles tombées* (Dumas, St. Étienne, 1947).
Brach Brach, Paul. *Quelques lettres de Marcel Proust* (Flammarion, Paris, 1928).
Briand (A) Briand, Charles. *Le Secret de Marcel Proust* (Lefèbvre, Paris, 1950).
Briand (B) ——, ——. 'Lettres inédites à Marcel Proust', *Combat*, 17 nov., 1 déc. 1949.
Brousson Brousson, J. J. *Les Vêpres de l'avenue Hoche* (Cadran, Paris, 1932).
BSAMP *Bulletin de la Société des amis de Marcel Proust.*
Buffenoir Buffenoir, H. *Grandes dames contemporaines* (Librairie du Mirabeau, Paris, 1893).
Bugnet Bugnet, Charles. 'Lettres de Proust au capitaine Charles Bugnet', BSAMP, III, (1953), 5-22.

Casa-Fuerte Casa-Fuerte, Marquis Illan de. 'Marcel Proust et les parfums', *Revue hebdomadaire*, août 1935, 355-62.
Castellane (A) Castellane, Marquis Boniface de. *L'Art d'être pauvre* (Crès, Paris 1926).
Castellane (B) ——, ——. *Comment j'ai découvert l'Amérique* (Crès, Paris, 1925).
Castillon Castillon du Perron, M. *La Princesse Mathilde* (Amiot-Dumont, Paris, 1953).
Cattaui (A) Cattaui, Georges. *Marcel Proust. Documents iconographiques* (Cailler, Genève, 1956).
Cattaui (B) ——, ——. *L'Amitié de Proust* (Gallimard, Paris, 1935).
Cattaui (C) ——, ——. *Marcel Proust* (Julliard, Paris, 1952).
Catusse Catusse, Mme A. *Marcel Proust. Lettres à Mme C.* (Janin, Paris, 1946).
Chalupt Chalupt, René. 'Petite musique de nuit à la façon de Marcel Proust', *Revue internationale de musique*, no. 11 (aut. 1951), 497-500.
Chapman Chapman, Guy. *The Dreyfus Case* (Hart-Davis, London, 1955).
Charavay Librairie Charavay, Paris. *Lettres de Marcel Proust à Reynaldo Hahn. Vente 16, 17 déc. 1958.*
Charensol Charensol, G. 'A Combray à la recherche de Marcel Proust', *Nouvelles littéraires*, 29 août 1946.
Clermont-Tonnerre (A) Clermont-Tonnerre, Duchesse Élisabeth de. *Marcel Proust* (Flammarion, Paris, 1948).
Clermont-Tonnerre (B) ——, ——. *Mémoires.* 4 vols. (Grasset, Paris, 1928-35).
Clermont-Tonnerre (C) ——, ——. *Robert de Montesquiou et Marcel Proust* (Flammarion, Paris, 1925).
Cocteau (A) Cocteau, Jean. *La Difficulté d'être* (Morihien, Paris, 1947).
Cocteau (B) ——, ——. *Journal d'un inconnu* (Grasset, Paris, 1953).
Cocteau (C) ——, ——. *Opium* (Stock, Paris, 1930).
Cocteau (D) ——, ——. *Poésie critique*, vol. 1 (Gallimard, Paris, 1959).
Corpechot Corpechot, Lucien. *Souvenirs d'un journaliste.* vol. 3 (Plon, Paris, 1937).
Couvreur Couvreur, J. 'Avec Céleste Albaret', *Le Monde*, 9 juillet 1953.

Craft Craft, R. *Conversations with Stravinsky* (Faber & Faber, London, 1959).

Crémieux Crémieux, Benjamin. *Du Côté de chez Marcel Proust* (Lemarget, Paris, 1929).

Crosland Crosland, Margaret. *Jean Cocteau* (Nevill, London, 1955).

Curtiss (A) Curtiss, Mina. *Letters of Marcel Proust* (Chatto & Windus, London, 1950).

Curtiss (B) ——, ——. 'Céleste', *Cornhill Magazine*, vol. 164 (spring, 1950), 306-17.

Daudet, Mme A. Daudet, Mme Alphonse. *Souvenirs de famille et de guerre* (Charpentier, Paris, 1920).

Daudet, Léon (A) Daudet, Léon. *Au temps de Judas* (Nouvelle Librairie Nationale, Paris, 1920).

Daudet, Léon (B) ——, ——. *Devant la douleur* (Nouvelle Librairie Nationale, Paris, 1915).

Daudet, Léon (C) ——, ——. *Écrivains et artistes*, vol. 3 (Capitole, Paris, 1928).

Daudet, Léon (D) ——, ——. *L'Entre-deux-guerres* (Nouvelle Librairie Nationale, Paris, 1915).

Daudet, Léon (E) ——, ——. *Fantômes et vivants* (Nouvelle Librairie Nationale, Paris, 1914).

Daudet, Léon (F) ——, ——. *Paris vécu*. 2 vols. (Gallimard, Paris, 1929, 30).

Daudet, Léon (G) ——, ——. *Salons et journaux* (Nouvelle Librairie Nationale, Paris, 1917).

Daudet, Léon (H) ——, ——. *Vers le roi* (Nouvelle Librairie Nationale, Paris, 1921).

Daudet, Léon (I) ——, ——. *Quand vivait mon père* (Grasset, Paris, 1940).

Daudet, Lucien (A) Daudet, Lucien. *Autour de soixante lettres de Marcel Proust* (Gallimard, Paris, 1929).

Daudet, Lucien (B) ——, ——. *Dans l'ombre de l'Impératrice Eugénie* (Gallimard, Paris, 1935).

Davray Davray, Jean. *Collection J. D. . . . Vente à Paris 6, 7 déc. 1961*.

DBF *Dictionnaire de biographie française* (Letouzey & Ané, Paris, 1933-00).

Défense *Défense de Marcel Proust* (Rouge et le Noir, Paris, 1930).

Deffoux Deffoux, Léon. *Chronique de l'Académie Goncourt* (Firmin-Didot, Paris, 1929).

Delarue-Mardrus Delarue-Mardrus, Lucie. *Mes mémoires* (Gallimard, Paris, 1938).

Delattre Delattre, Floris. 'Bergson et Proust', *Études bergsoniennes*, vol. 1 (1948), 7-127.

Delay Delay, Jean. *La Jeunesse d'André Gide*, vol. 2 (Gallimard, Paris, 1957).

Descaves Descaves, Lucien. *Deux amis. Huysmans et l'abbé Mugnier* (Plon, Paris, 1946).

Dreyfus (A) Dreyfus, Robert. *De Monsieur Thiers à Marcel Proust* (Plon, Paris, 1939).

Dreyfus (B) ——, ——. *Souvenirs sur Marcel Proust* (Grasset, Paris, 1926).

Drumont Drumont, Édouard. *La France juive*. 2 vols. (Flammarion, Paris, 1886).

Du Bled Du Bled, Victor. *La Société française depuis cent ans*. vol. 2. *Mme Aubernon et ses amis* (Bloud & Gay, Paris, 1924).

Du Bos Du Bos, Charles. *Journal, 1921-1923* (Corréa, Paris, 1946).

Dujardin Dujardin, Marie. 'Proust à Venise', *Le Figaro*, 10 oct. 1931.

Dumesnil Dumesnil, René. 'L'Abbé Mugnier', *Mercure de France*, mars 1949, 398-409.

Duplay (A) Duplay, Maurice. 'Proust avant Proust', *Nouvelles littéraires*, 3 oct. 1957.

Duplay (B) ——, ——. 'Marcel Proust tel que je l'ai connu', *Figaro littéraire*, 19 nov. 1960.

Duplay (C) ——, ——. 'Marcel Proust. Lettres à M. Duplay', *Revue nouvelle*, juin 1929, 1-13.
Dupont Dupont, Alfred. *Précieux autographes composant la collection de M. Alfred Dupont. Vente 22 nov. 1962. Paris.*

East East, C. J. *The Armed Strength of France* (War Office, London, 1877).
Elkin Mathews Elkin Mathews Ltd. *Catalogue* no. 117 (July-August 1950).
Ellman Ellman, Richard. *James Joyce* (Oxford University Press, London, 1959).

Fauchier-Magnan Fauchier-Magnan, A. *C'était hier* (Scorpion, Paris, 1960).
Fernandez Fernandez, Ramon. *A la gloire de Proust* (Nouvelle Revue Critique Paris, 1944).
Ferré (A) Ferré, André, *Les Années de collège de Marcel Proust* (Gallimard, Paris, 1959)..
Ferré (B) ——, ——. *La Géographie de Marcel Proust* (Sagittaire, Paris, 1939).
Feuillerat Feuillerat, Albert. *Comment Marcel Proust a composé son roman* (Yale University Press, New Haven, 1934).
Flament Flament, Albert. *Le Bal du Pré Catelan* (Fayard, Paris, 1946).
Flament (B) ——, ——. 'Souvenir de l'abbé Mugnier', *Revue des deux mondes*, mars 1950, 144-51.
Fleury Fleury, Maurice de. 'Deux lettres inédites de Marcel Proust à Maurice de Fleury', BSAMP, V(1955), 6-8.
Fouquier Fouquier, Baron Marcel. *Jours heureux d'autrefois* (Albin Michel, Paris, 1941).
Fouquières (A) Fouquières, Comte André de. *Cinquante ans de panache* (Horay, Paris, 1951).
Fouquières (B) ——, ——. *Mon Paris et ses parisiens* (Horay, Paris, 1953-00).
Fouquières (C) ——, ——. 'Fantômes du Faubourg Saint-Honoré', *Œuvres libres*, no. 353 (déc. 1956), 75-112.

Gabory Gabory, Georges. *Essai sur Marcel Proust* (Le Livre, Paris, 1926).
Gaillard Gaillard, Roger. *Vie d'un joueur* (Calmann-Lévy, Paris, 1953).
Garver Garver, Milton. 'An Unpublished Letter of Proust', *Modern Language Notes*, vol. 47 (1932), 519-21.
Germain (A) Germain, André. *La Bourgeoisie qui brûle* (Sun, Paris, 1951).
Germain (B) ——, ——. *Les Clés de Proust* (Sun, Paris, 1953).
Germain (C) ——, ——. *Les Fous de 1900* (Plon, Paris, 1954).
Germain (D) ——, ——. *De Proust à Dada* (Sagittaire, Paris, 1924).
Germain (E) ——, ——. *La Vie amoureuse de D'Annunzio* (Fayard, Paris, 1954).
Ghika Ghika, Prince Matila. *Couleur du monde*. 2 vols. (Éditions du Vieux-Colombier, Paris, 1956).
Gibbs-Smith Gibbs-Smith, Charles H. *The Aeroplane* (H.M. Stationery Office, London, 1960).
Gide (A) Gide, André. *Journal, 1889-39. Bibliothèque de la Pléiade* (Gallimard, Paris, 1941).
Gide (B) ——, ——. *Marcel Proust. Lettres à André Gide* (Ides et Calendes, Neuchâtel, 1949).
Goncourt Goncourt, Edmond and Jules de. *Journal*. 4 vols. (Imprimerie Nationale, Monaco, 1956).
Goron Goron, Lucien. 'L'Horizon de Combray', BSAMP, I(1950), 19-33.
Gramont Gramont, Armand, duc de. 'Souvenirs sur Marcel Proust,' BSAMP, VI (1956), 171-80.
Grandjean Grandjean, Charles. 'Lettres de Marcel Proust à Charles Grandjean', BSAMP, VI (1956), 137-57.

Grasset (A)   Grasset, Bernard. 'Souvenirs sur Émile Clermont', *Revue hebdomadaire*, 9 avr. 1938, 129-51.

Grasset (B)   ——, ——. *Textes choisis* (Table Ronde, Paris, 1953).

Gregh (A)   Gregh, Fernand. *L'Age d'or* (Grasset, Paris, 1947).

Gregh (B)   ——, ——. *L'Age d'airain* (Grasset, Paris, 1951).

Gregh (C)   ——, ——. *L'Age de fer* (Grasset, Paris, 1956).

Gregh (D)   ——, ——. *Mon amitié avec Marcel Proust* (Grasset, Paris, 1958).

Grigoriev   Grigoriev, S. L. *The Diaghilev Ballet* (Constable, London, 1953).

Guichard (A)   Guichard, Léon. *Introduction à la lecture de Proust* (Nizet, Paris, 1956).

Guichard (B)   ——, ——. 'Un Article inconnu de Marcel Proust', RHLF, vol. 39 (1949), 161-75.

Guillot de Saix   Guillot de Saix. 'Trente ans après. Céleste servante au grand cœur nous raconte les derniers jours de Proust', *Nouvelles littéraires*, 20 nov. 1952.

Guth   Guth, Paul. 'A l'ombre de Marcel Proust. Comment Céline . . . et Nicolas Cottin voyaient leur maître', *Figaro littéraire*, 25 sept. 1954.

Gyp (A)   Gyp (pseud. of Comtesse M. A. de Martel). *Du temps des cheveux et des chevaux* (Calmann-Lévy, Paris, 1929).

Gyp (B)   ——. *La Joyeuse enfance de la Troisième République* (Calmann-Lévy, Paris, 1931).

Hahn (A)   Hahn, Reynaldo. *La Grande Sarah* (Hachette, Paris, 1930).

Hahn (B)   ——, ——. *Marcel Proust. Lettres à Reynaldo Hahn.* ed. Philip Kolb. (Gallimard, Paris, 1956).

Hahn (C)   ——, ——. *Notes. Journal d'un musicien* (Plon, Paris, 1933).

Hahn (D)   ——, ——. 'Proust et Ruskin', *Le Figaro*, 21 avril 1945.

Hahn, M.   Hahn, Maria. 'Huit lettres inédites de Marcel Proust à Maria Hahn', BSAMP, III (1953), 23-8.

Halévy   Halévy, Daniel. *Pays parisiens* (Grasset, Paris, 1932).

Halicka   Halicka, Alice. *Hier. Souvenirs* (Pavois, Paris, 1946).

Hayman   Hayman, Laure. *Lettres et vers de Marcel Proust à Mesdames Laure Hayman et Louisa de Mornand* (Andrieux, Paris, 1928).

Hermant (A)   Hermant, Abel. *Souvenirs de la vie frivole* (Hachette, Paris, 1933).

Hermant (B)   ——, ——. *Souvenirs de la vie mondaine* (Hachette, Paris, 1935).

HLB   *Harvard Library Bulletin.*

Hommage   *Hommage à Marcel Proust* (NRF) (Gallimard, Paris, 1927).

Hommage (DV)   *Hommage à Marcel Proust* (Disque Vert, Bruxelles, 1952).

Hommage (RN)   *Hommage à Marcel Proust* (Rouge et le Noir, Paris, 1928).

Humières   Humières, Comte Robert d'. *Le Livre de la beauté* (Mercure de France, Paris, 1921).

Indy   Indy, Vincent d'. *César Franck* (Alcan, Paris, 1930).

Jaloux   Jaloux, Edmond. *Avec Marcel Proust* (Palatine, Genève, 1953).

Jammes   Francis Jammes & Arthur Fontaine. *Correspondance* (Gallimard, Paris, 1959).

Jones   Jones, Stanley. 'Two Unknown Articles by Marcel Proust', *French Studies*, vol. 4, no. 3 (July 1950), 239-51.

Joyce   Joyce, James. *Letters of James Joyce.* ed. Stuart Gilbert (Faber & Faber, London, 1957).

Keim   Keim, Albert. *Le Demi-siècle* (Albin Michel, Paris, 1950).

Kolb (A)   Kolb, Philip. *La Correspondance de Marcel Proust* (University of Illinois Press, Urbana, 1949).

Kolb (B)   ——, ——. 'The Genesis of Jean Santeuil', *Adam*, 112-9.

Kolb (C) ——, ——. 'An Enigmatic Proustian Metaphor', *Romanic Review*, vol. 54, no. 3 (Oct. 1963) 187-97.

Kolb (D) —— ——. 'Le "Mystère" des gravures anglaises recherchées par Proust', *Mercure de France* (1 août 1956), 750-5.

Kolb (E) —— ——. 'Proust et Ruskin: nouvelles perspectives', *Cahiers de l'Association Internationale des Études Françaises* XII (1961), 259-73.

Labori Labori, Marguerite. *Labori* (Attinger, Paris, 1947).

Lacretelle Lacretelle, Jacques de. *Les Maîtres et les amis* (Wesmael-Charlier, Paris, 1959).

La Faye La Faye, J. de. *La Princesse Mathilde* (Émile Paul, Paris, 1928).

Landau Landau, Baron Horace de. *Sale Catalogue, Sotheby's, 12-13 July 1948.*

Lannes Lannes, Roger. *Jean Cocteau* (Seghers, Paris, 1945).

Larcher Larcher, P. L. *Le Parfum de Combray* (Mercure de France, Paris, 1945).

Larnac Larnac, Jean. *La Comtesse de Noailles* (Sagittaire, Paris, 1931).

La Rochefoucauld La Rochefoucauld, Comte Gabriel de. *Constantinople avec Loti* (Éditions de France, Paris, 1928).

La Sizeranne La Sizeranne, Comte Robert de. *Ruskin et la religion de la beauté* (Hachette, Paris, 1897).

Lauris (A) Lauris, Marquis Georges de. *A un ami* (Amiot-Dumont, Paris, 1948).

Lauris (B) ——, ——. *Souvenirs d'une belle époque* (Amiot-Dumont, Paris, 1948).

Léautaud Léautaud, Paul. *Journal littéraire* (Mercure de France, Paris, 1954-00).

Leclercq Leclercq, Paul. 'Marcel Proust au temps de la bicyclette', *Figaro littéraire*, 7 fév. 1931.

Le Goff Le Goff. M. *Anatole France à la Béchellerie* (Albin Michel, Paris, 1947).

Le Masle Le Masle, Robert. *Le Professeur Adrien Proust* (Lipschutz, Paris, 1935).

Le Masle (B) ——, ——. 'Un Familier de Proust (Odilon Albaret)', *Nouvelles littéraires*, 17 nov. 1960.

Levaillant Levaillant, J. 'Note sur le personnage de Bergotte', *Revue des sciences humaines*, jan.-mars 1952, 33-48.

Lieven Lieven, Prince P. *The Birth of the Ballets Russes* (Allen & Unwin, London, 1936).

Lifar Lifar, Serge. *A History of Russian Ballet* (Hutchinson, London, 1954).

Lister Lister, Barbara. *The House of Memories* (Heinemann, London, 1929).

Louÿs Louÿs, Pierre. *Poésie*. 2 vols. (Albin Michel, Paris, 1945).

Lowery Lowery, Bruce. *Marcel Proust et Henry James* (Plon, Paris, 1964).

Lubbock Lubbock, Percy. *Portrait of Edith Wharton* (Cape, London, 1947).

Marquis Marquis, Chanoine Joseph. *Illiers* (Archives Historiques du Diocèse de Chartres, Chartres, 1907).

Martin du Gard Martin du Gard, Maurice. *Les Mémorables*. vol. 1 (Flammarion, Paris, 1957).

Massis Massis, Henri. *Le Drame de Marcel Proust* (Grasset, Paris, 1937).

Maupassant Maupassant, Guy de. *Correspondance inédite* (Wepler, Paris, 1951).

Mauriac, C. Mauriac, Claude. *Marcel Proust par lui-même* (Éditions du Seuil, Paris, 1954).

Mauriac, F. Mauriac, François. *Du côté de chez Proust* (Table Ronde, Paris, 1947).

Maurois Maurois, André. *A la recherche de Marcel Proust* (Hachette, Paris, 1949).

Maurois (B) ——, ——. *Mémoires*. vol. 1 (Flammarion, Paris, 1948).

Mérimée Mérimée, Prosper. *Lettres à Mme de Beaulaincourt* (Calmann-Lévy, Paris, 1936).

Mérode Mérode, Cléo de. *Le Ballet de ma vie* (Horay, Paris, 1955).

Mille Mille, Pierre. *Mes trônes et mes dominations* (Éditions des Portiques, Paris, 1930).

Missoffe Missoffe, Michel. *Gyp et ses amis* (Flammarion, Paris, 1932).

Mondor Mondor, Henri. *Vie de Mallarmé* (Gallimard, Paris, 1941).

Monnin-Hornung Monnin-Hornung, J. *Proust et la peinture* (Droz, Genève, 1951).

Montesquiou (A) Montesquiou, Comte Robert de. 'Cahiers secrets', *Mercure de France*, vol. 211 (15 avr. 1929), 296-322.

Montesquiou (B) ——, ——. 'Netzkés', *Mercure de France*, vol. 221 (juillet 1930), 48-64.

Montesquiou (C) ——, ——. 'Papillotes mondaines', *Mercure de France*, vol. 212 (juin 1929), 557-9.

Montesquiou (D) ——, ——. *Les Pas effacés*. 3 vols. (Émile Paul, Paris, 1923).

Montesquiou (E) ——, ——. *Les Quarante bergères* (Librairie de France, Paris, 1925).

Montesquiou (F) ——, ——. 'Lettres inédites au prince Sevastos', *Revue de Paris*, juillet 1947, 128-42.

Montesquiou (G) ——, ——. *Le Chancelier des fleurs* (Privately printed, Paris, 1908).

Montfort Montfort, Eugène. *Vingt-cinq ans de littérature française*. 2 vols. (Librairie de France, Paris, 1922-5).

Morand (A) Morand, Paul. *Journal d'un attaché d'ambassade* (Table Ronde, Paris, 1949).

Morand (B) ——, ——. *Le Visiteur du soir* (Palatine, Genève, 1949).

Morand (C) ——, ——. *L'Eau sous les ponts* (Grasset, Paris, 1954).

Morand (D) ——, ——. *Mes débuts* (Cahiers libres, Paris, 1933).

Morand (E) ——, ——. *Tendres stocks* (Gallimard, Paris, 1921).

Morand (F) ——, ——. 'Une Agonie', *Nouvelles littéraires*, 25 nov. 1922.

Mornand Mornand, Louisa de. 'Mon amitié avec Marcel Proust', *Candide*, 1 nov. 1928.

Mourey Mourey, Gabriel. 'Proust, Ruskin et Walter Pater' *Monde Nouveau*, août-sept. 1926, 702-14, Oct. 1926, 896-909.

Nichols Nichols, Beverley. *The Sweet and Twenties* (Weidenfeld & Nicolson, London, 1958).

Nicolson (A) Nicolson, Sir Harold. *Peacemaking* (Constable, London, 1933).

Nicolson (B) ——, ——. 'Proust et l'Angleterre', *Figaro littéraire*, 15 oct. 1955.

Nicolson (C) ——, ——. 'Marcel Proust et l'Angleterre', *Revue hebdomadaire*, juin 1936, 7-21.

NNRF *Nouvelle nouvelle revue française.*

Nordlinger (A) Riefstahl-Nordlinger, Marie. *Marcel Proust. Lettres à une amie* (Éditions du Calame, Manchester, 1942).

Nordlinger (B) ——, ——. 'Proust as I knew him', *London Magazine*, Aug. 1954, 51-61.

Nordlinger (C) ——, ——. 'Et voici les clefs du Jean Santeuil de Marcel Proust' *Figaro littéraire*, 14 juin 1952.

Nordlinger (D) ——, ——. 'Proust and Ruskin', *Wildenstein*, 57-63.

Nordlinger (E) ——, ——. 'Memories of Marcel Proust', *The Listener*, 28 April 1960, 749-51.

Nordlinger (F) ——, ——. 'Fragments de journal', BSAMP, VIII (1958), 521-7.

Nordlinger (G) ——, ——. 'Chez Céleste', *Studies in French Literature presented to P. Mansell Jones* (Manchester University Press, Manchester, 1961), 263-5.

NRF *Lettres à la NRF* (*Cahiers Marcel Proust*, VI), (Gallimard, Paris, 1932).

Oberlé Oberlé, Jean. *La Vie d'artiste* (Denoel, Paris, 1956).

Paléologue   Paléologue, Maurice. *Journal de l'Affaire Dreyfus* (Plon, Paris, 1955).
Paléologue (B)   ——, ——. *Journal, 1913-1914* (Plon, Paris, 1947).
Patin   Patin, J. 'Mme Madeleine Lemaire', *Figaro littéraire*, 10 avril 1928.
Péguy   Péguy, Charles. *Notre jeunesse* (Ollendorff, Paris, 1910).
Penrose   Penrose, Roland. *Picasso: his life and work* (Gollancz, London, 1958).
Peter (A)   Peter, René. *Claude Debussy* (Gallimard, Paris, 1931).
Peter (B)   ——, ——. *L'Académie Française et le xxe siècle* (Librairie des Champs-Élysées, Paris, 1949).
Peter (C)   ——, ——. *La Vie secrète de l'Académie Française*. 5 vols. (Librairie des Champs-Élysées, Paris, 1934-40).
Pierre-Quint   Pierre-Quint, Léon. *Marcel Proust. Sa vie, son œuvre* (Kra, Paris, 1925).
Pierre-Quint (B)   ——,——. 'Deux lettres de Marcel Proust', *Europe*, nov. 1947, 67-9.
Poniatowski   Poniatowski, Prince Stanislaus. *D'un siècle à l'autre* (Presses de la Cité, Paris, 1948).
Porel (A)   Porel, Jacques. *Fils de Réjane*. 2 vols. (Plon, Paris, 1951-2).
Porel (B)   ——, ——. 'Proust locataire de Réjane', *Figaro littéraire*, 22 juin 1957.
Porto-Riche   Porto-Riche, Georges de. 'Lettres de Marcel Proust à Porto-Riche', *Table ronde*, juin 1954, 93-101.
Pouquet (A)   Pouquet, Jeanne Maurice. *Quelques lettres de Marcel Proust* (Hachette, Paris, 1928).
Pouquet (B)   ——, ——. *Le Salon de Madame Arman de Caillavet* (Hachette, Paris, 1926).
Pringué   Pringué, Gabriel Louis. *Trente ans de dîners en ville* (Édition Revue Adam, Paris, 1948).
Proust, Mme   Proust, Mme Adrien. *Marcel Proust. Correspondance avec sa Mère*. ed. Philip Kolb. (Plon, Paris, 1953).

Rachilde   Rachilde (Mme Alfred Vallette). *Portraits d'hommes* (Mercure de France, Paris, 1930).
Radziwill   Radziwill, Princesse Marie. *Lettres au général de Robilant*. 4 vols. (Plon, Paris, 1933-4).
Regnier (A)   Regnier, Henri de. *De mon temps* (Mercure de France, Paris, 1933).
Regnier (B)   ——, ——. *Nos rencontres* (Mercure de France, Paris, 1931).
Reinach   Reinach, Joseph. *Histoire de l'Affaire Dreyfus*. 7 vols. (Fasquelle, Paris, 1901-11).
Renard   Renard, Jules. *Journal* (Gallimard, Paris, 1948).
RHLF   *Revue d'histoire littéraire de la France.*
Ritz   Ritz, Marie L. *César Ritz* (Tallandier, Paris, 1948).
Rivière   Rivière, Jacques. *Marcel Proust et Jacques Rivière. Correspondance, 1914-1922*. ed. Philip Kolb. (Plon, Paris, 1955).
RL   *Renaissance Latine.*
Robert (A)   Robert, Louis de. *Comment débuta Marcel Proust* (Gallimard, Paris, 1925).
Robert (B)   ——, ——. *De Loti à Proust* (Flammarion, Paris, 1928).
Robert (C)   ——, ——. *Lettres à Paul Faure* (Denoël, Paris, 1943).
Rose   Rose, Sir Francis. *Saying Life* (Cassell, London, 1961).
Rosny   Rosny, J. H., aîné. *Portraits et souvenirs* (Compagnie Française des Arts Graphiques, Paris, 1945).
Rostand (A)   Rostand, Maurice. *Confessions d'un demi-siècle* (Jeune Parque, Paris, 1948).
Rostand (B)   ——, ——. 'Rencontre avec Marcel Proust', *Revue de Paris*, fév. 1948, 95-8.

Sachs (A)   Sachs, Maurice. *Le Sabbat* (Corréa, Paris, 1946).
Sachs (B)   ——, ——. 'L'Air du mois', *NRF*, 1 juillet 1938, 863-4.
Salmon   Salmon, André. *Souvenirs sans fin* (Gallimard, Paris, 1955-00).
Scheikévitch (A)   Scheikévitch, Marie. *Souvenirs d'un temps disparu* (Plon, Paris, 1935).
Scheikévitch (B)   ——, ——. 'Marcel Proust and his Céleste', *London Mercury*, vol. 37 (April 1938), 601-10.
Scheikévitch (C)   ——, ——. 'Marcel Proust et Céleste', *Œuvres libres*, no. 168 (1960), 37-52.
Schiff   Schiff, Violet. 'A Night with Proust', *London Magazine*, Sept. 1956.
Schiff, S.   Schiff, Sydney. *Céleste* (Blackamore Press, London, 1930).
Schlumberger   Schlumberger, Gustave. *Mes souvenirs*. 2 vols. (Plon, Paris, 1934).
Scott-Moncrieff   Scott-Moncrieff, C. K. *Memories and Letters* (Chapman & Hall, London, 1931).
Seillière   Seillière, Baron Ernest. *Marcel Proust* (Nouvelle Revue Critique, Paris, 1931).
Sert   Sert, Misia. *Misia* (Gallimard, Paris, 1952).
Sévrette   Sévrette, J. *Cabourg et ses environs* (Hachette, Paris, 1882).
Sorel   Sorel, Cécile. *La Confession de Célimène* (Presses de la Cité, Paris, 1949).
Souday   Souday, Paul. *Marcel Proust* (Kra, Paris, 1927).
Souza   Souza, Sybil de. 'Un des premiers états de *Swann*', *French Studies*, vol. 3, no. 4 (Oct. 1949), 335-44.
Suffel   Suffel, Jacques. *Anatole France* (Éditions du Myrte, Paris, 1946).

Tharaud (A)   Tharaud, Jérôme, and Jean. *Mes années chez Barrès* (Plon, Paris, 1928).
Tharaud (B)   ——, ——. *Le Roman d'Aissé* (Self, Paris, 1946).
Thomas   Thomas, Louis. *Le Général de Galliffet* (Dorbon, Paris, 1910).
Thomson   Thomson, Valentine. 'My Cousin Marcel Proust', *Harpers Magazine*, vol. 164 (May 1932), 710-20.

Univers   *L'Univers de Proust.* (*Le Point*, no. 55/56.) (Le Point, Mulhouse, 1959).
Uzès   Uzès, Anne, Duchesse d'. *Souvenirs* (Plon, Paris, 1939).

Vandérem   Vandérem, Fernand, *Gens de qualité* (Plon, Paris, 1938).
Védrines   Védrines, Louis. 'Séjours vénitiens', BSAMP, IV (1954), 57-60.
Vigneron   Vigneron, Robert. 'Genèse de Swann', *Revue d'histoire de la philosophie et d'histoire générale de la civilisation*, 15 jan. 1937, 67-115.
Viollet-le-Duc   Viollet-le-Duc, Eugène E. *Dictionnaire raisonné d' architecture française* (Paris, 1863).

Wharton   Wharton, Edith. *A Backward Glance* (Appleton-Century, New York, 1934).
Wildenstein   Wildenstein Gallery, London. *Marcel Proust and His Time* (1955).
Wisely   Wisely, G. A. K. *Handbook of the French Army* (War Office, London, 1891).

Yeatman   Yeatman, Léon. 'Lettre de Marcel Proust à Léon Yeatman', *Nouvelles littéraires*, 25 juillet 1936.

Zillhardt   Zillhardt, M. *L.-C. Breslau et ses amis* (Éditions des Portiques, Paris, 1932).
Zola   Zola, Émile. *Livre d'hommage des lettres françaises à Émile Zola* (Société Libre d'Éditions des Gens de Lettres, Paris, 1898).

REFERENCES TO SOURCES

The sources used in each paragraph are grouped separately, preceded by the page number and first words of the paragraph. For the full titles of the works cited, see Bibliography. Volume numbers of these are given in roman numerals, page numbers in arabic.

VOLUME ONE

CHAPTER 1 THE GARDEN OF AUTEUIL

Page and Paragraph

1 *The doorway* . . . Larcher, 41; *Le Masle*, 9, 32-3.
1 *The heroic* . . . Le Masle, 33-5.
2 *Adrien Proust* . . . Le Masle, 34-6, 38, 40, 43; CG, VI, 218.
3 *Mlle Weil* . . . Proust, Mme, 5; Cattaui (B), 188.
3 *Within* . . . JS, I, 172, 174; Briand (A), 19.
4 *After* . . . Le Masle, 36-7.
4 *At first* . . . Curtiss (A), 3; Lauris (A), 24; Daudet, Lucien (A), 180.
4 *Their Paris* . . . Proust, Mme, 86, 123.
5 *The first* . . . Le Masle, 37; Hommage, 17; Cattaui (A), 5; Daudet, Lucien (A), 21 Proust, Mme, 6, 49.
6 *The other* . . . Curtiss (B), 164; I, 52, 77; Proust, Mme, 75.
7 *Auteuil* . . . Goncourt, 24 May 1871.
8 *It was* . . . Blanche (C), I, vi; Proust, Mme, 36, 221; Thomson, 713-4.
8 *During* . . . Blanche (C), I, vii-viii, xii; Le Masle, 37; III, 411-12.
10 *He wrote* . . . I, 27-43; CSB, 125-6; Proust, Mme, 176; JS, III, 306-11; Le Masle, 37.
12 *During* . . . Hommage, 18.

CHAPTER 2 THE GARDEN OF ILLIERS

13 *Marcel's* . . . Le Masle, 11-12, 32; Mauriac, C, 147.
13 *Her daughter* . . . Le Masle, 21, 40; Larcher, 43.
13 *They took* . . . JS, I, 135-6, 140; C, 114; I, 63.
14 *His bed* . . . PM, 230-6.
15 *Marcel* . . . PM, 226-30; JS, I, 140, 160, 176; I, 122.
16 *It was* . . . Le Masle, 22, 24; Goron, 32.
16 *Gradually* . . . I, 69, 105-7; Lauris (A), 63; Le Masle, 13, 16; Goron, 21; Marquis, 210.
17 *Ernestine* . . . Le Masle, 23; Goron, 20; JS, I, 139-41; I, 54.
18 *The door* . . . I, 12, 72; Le Masle, 19-20; PM, 227; JS, I, 161-2.
19 *The garden* . . . I, 14; Larcher, 51.
19 *Past* . . . I, 43, 45, 49, 56, 83, 135; Le Masle, 16; Larcher, 43, 46; PM, 230.
20 *In the* . . . Larcher 42; I, 58.
21 *The church* . . . I, 63-6; PM, 229; CSB, 289.

21 *The church* ... I, 61-2, 105; *Le Masle*, 12-13, 16-18; *Larcher*, 17, 18, 32, 34; *Goron*, 29; *Marquis*, 200; JS, I, 230.
23 *As they* ... JS, I, 144, 155, 174, 217; *Larcher*, 58, 109; CSB, 64-6; I, 12, 58; *Le Masle*, 16; *Goron*, 20.
24 *After* ... *Larcher*, 55; II, 154.
25 *Up the* ... *Goron*, 47-8; I, 139, 922; JS, I, 204; *Larcher*, 86-7.
25 *Uncle* ... PM, 236; JS, I, 144-5, 168, 174, 189, 201; *Larcher*, 87; *Le Masle*, 27.
26 *Above* ... *Larcher*, 87; *Le Masle*, 27-8; I, 135; *Goron*, 48, 53; JS, I, 183-4, 189, 193, 202, 211.
27 *There is* ... *Goron*, 32.
27 *Sometimes* ... I, 133-5, 147; III, 691; *Larcher*, 48; *Le Masle*, 53; JS, III, 310.

CHAPTER 3 THE TWO WAYS

29 *A few* ... *Larcher*, 91.
30 *Méréglise* ... II, 473-4.
30 *The church* ... *Larcher*, 87, 90.
31 *The Méréglise* ... I, 134; *Goron*, 23, 30; JS, I, 206-7
32 *At Combray* ... *Larcher*, 102-3; *Charensol*.
32 *Her name* ... *Larcher*, 99-100; *Charensol*.
33 *In his* ... *Goron*, 30; *Larcher*, 100-1; I, 147-8.
33 *Saint-Éman* ... *Larcher*, 104.
34 *At* ... *Goron*, 29; *Larcher*, 106-7.
35 *It was* ... I, 48, 58, 109, 146, 904; II, 531; *Ferré* (B), 88; *Larcher*, 41; *Hommage*, 190.
36 *The most* ... *Blanche* (C), I, xi; *Proust, Mme*, 125; PM, 226, 228-30.
37 *It was* ... *Le Masle*, 26.
37 *Sometimes* ... *Curtiss* (A), 336; *Daudet, Léon* (E), 114-15; *Nordlinger* (B), 54; *Schlumberger*, II, 171; *Peter* (B), 22; *Mondor*, 814.
38 *Illiers* ... JS, I, 86, 137-8, 149, 163-4.
38 *But Illiers* ... *Proust, Mme*, 5; JS, I, 201, 221; PM, 236-7; *Lauris* (A), 63; III, 692.

CHAPTER 4 THE GARDEN OF THE CHAMPS-ÉLYSÉES

40 *Marcel's* ... *Cattaui* (A), 16, 12, 19, 14, 15.
41 *For the* ... *Dreyfus* (B), 340.
41 *His parents* ... *Dreyfus* (B), 19-22.
41 *There is* ... *Briand* (A), 167-8; *Dreyfus* (B), 23; JS, I, 117-21; *Cattaui* (A), 37.
43 *Perhaps* ... *Hommage*, 191; *Bibesco, M* (C), 102; *Morand* (B), 81; I, 405; *Dreyfus* (B), 16-17; *Maurois*, 20.
43 *Lucie* ... *Gyp* (B), 204-7; BSAMP, VII (1957), 272.
44 *Marie* ... CG, V, 190-1; *Clermont-Tonnerre* (A), 92; *Flament*, 230; *Fouquières* (B), I, 113; *Germain* (A), 186.
45 *Except* ... *Dreyfus* (B), 11; *Dreyfus* (A), 42-4; *Hommage*, 191; *Abraham*, pl. VI; I, 492-4; II, 310.
46 *In the* ... *Dreyfus* (B), 14, 16; JS, I, 90; *Gyp* (B), 206-7.
46 *Soon* ... *Dreyfus* (B), 12; C, 101; JS, I, 89-90, 97-8; I, 396-9.
47 *In December* ... JS, I, 94-6; *Hommage*, 191; I, 398-9.
47 *Every* ... JS, I, 93; I, 400-1.
48 *In February* ... JS, I, 98-9, 104; CSB, 111-12, 115; *Germain* (B), 139-40.
49 *In the* ... JS, I, 101-9; CG, V, 190-1; PJ, 185.

CHAPTER 5 BALBEC AND CONDORCET

51 *An inventory* . . . *Cattaui* (A), 20.
51 *His* . . . *Cattaui* (A), 20.
52 *Illiers* . . . *Hommage*, 7; *Proust, Mme*, 5; *Maurois*, 21; *Cattaui* (A), 34; C, 135; *Gide* (A), 694.
53 *In 1887* . . . *Catusse*, 13-15.
54 *In the* . . . JS, I, 118-19; *Dreyfus* (B), 24; *Clermont-Tonnerre* (A), 16; *Proust, Mme*, 1-3; *Catusse*, 132.
55 *In October* . . . CG, IV, 169, 171.
55 *Maxime* . . . CG, IV, 3, 171-2; *Maurois*, 33-5; *Astruc*, 25-6; *Dreyfus* (B), 30; *Daudet, Léon* (A), 115.
56 *In the* . . . *Dreyfus* (B), 25; CG, IV, 169, 171; *Gregh* (A), 136.
56 *There is* . . . *Cattaui* (A), 25; *Dreyfus* (B), 24; *Wildenstein*, no. 231.
57 *Early* . . . *Proust, Mme*, 4-7.
57 *The servants* . . . *Proust, Mme*, 5; CG, IV, 178-80; CG, V, 222; *Hommage*, 191; *Astruc*, 132.
58 *He was* . . . *Proust, Mme*, 6, 8; *Dreyfus* (B), 48.
59 *In October* . . . PJ, 16; *Gregh* (A), 141-3; JS, I, 241-5; CG, IV, 252; *Hommage*, 18.
60 *Meanwhile* . . . *Gregh* (A), 142; *Dreyfus* (B), 68-72.
61 *The most* . . . *Dreyfus* (B), 56-9; *Pierre-Quint*, 30.
62 *His school* . . . *Halévy*, 122-3; *Curtiss* (A), 3-4; *Blanche* (D); CG, IV, 173-4.
63 *He might* . . . *Briand* (A), 161; CG, VI, 202; CG, III, 101-2; CG, I, 108.
63 *The key* . . . *Gregh* (A), 169, 185-7; *Germain* (B), 50; *Dreyfus* (A), 20; CG, VI, 3.
64 *When the* . . . *Dreyfus* (B), 23, 46, 55.

CHAPTER 6 BERGOTTE AND DONCIÈRES

65 *Proust* . . . CG, IV, 137; *Pouquet* (A), 5, 6; *Gregh* (A), 175-6; I, 547.
65 *His hostess* . . . *Pouquet* (B), 4, 9-10.
65 *In 1889* . . . *Gregh* (A), 175; *Germain* (B), 54.
66 *Like* . . . *Pouquet* (B), 8, 228-31.
66 *Her husband* . . . *Gregh* (A), 179; *Morand* (A), 224; *Scheikévitch* (A), 55-7; *Mille*, 95.
67 *Mme* . . . *Pouquet* (B), 49-53; *Du Bled*, 233.
67 *For a* . . . *Pouquet* (B), 55, 57, 121, 123; *Suffel*, 190-1; *Morand* (A), 223-4; *Clermont-Tonnerre* (A), 140.
68 *Anatole* . . . *Pouquet* (B), 58; *Billy*, 90-1; *Wildenstein*, no. 360; *Clermont-Tonnerre* (A), 100; *Levaillant*, 38, 43, 45; I, 474.
69 *To the* . . . *Cattaui* (A), 37.
70 *On* . . . *Clermont-Tonnerre* (B), I, 4; *Regnier* (A), 42; *Gregh* (A), 173, 182.
71 *Perhaps* . . . *Pouquet* (B), 15, 66, 84-105; *Pouquet* (A), 24; CG, IV, 137
71 *The period* . . . *Wisely*, 5; *East*, 16-18; *Cattaui* (A), 28-9; *Wildenstein*, no. 230.
72 *His way* . . . *Hommage*, 18; *Proust, Mme*, 28, 36; *Clermont-Tonnerre* (A), 27; *Lauris* (B), 83; *Guichard*, 175; JS, III, 59-62; *Wildenstein*, no. 27.
73 *In theory* . . . *Proust, Mme*, 89; JS, II, 287-91, 316.
73 *In February* . . . *Billy*, 21-3.
74 *Incredible* . . . *Proust, Mme*, 21, 44, 64; *Curtiss* (A), 101; JS, II, 316; *Dreyfus* (B), 150; *Gregh* (A), 218-19.
75 *Meanwhile* . . . *Proust, Mme*, 10-14, 16-19, 26, 29, 31, 36, 43-4.
75 *His* . . . *Proust, Mme*, 9, 17, 20, 27.
76 *Almost* . . . CG, IV, 137-8; *Pouquet* (A), 9-10.
77 *One* . . . *Pouquet* (A), 11, 16.

77 *Soon* . . . *Pouquet* (A), 12-16; CG, IV, 141-2.
78 *In the* . . . *Proust, Mme*, 36; *Daudet, Lucien* (A), 152; *Cattaui* (A), 30-33.
78 *That* . . . *Proust, Mme*, 31-2, 36-7, 45; *Blanche* (B), 173; *Goncourt*, 28 Jan. 1895; *Maupassant*, 243-67.
79 *For the* . . . *Proust, Mme*, 45, 49; *Bugnet*, 12; *Maurois*, 49; *Hahn* (B), 225.

CHAPTER 7 THE STUDENT IN SOCIETY

On 20 . . . *Proust, Mme*, 51; *Billy*, 23-6, 89; *Delattre*, 39; *Le Masle*, 36; *Daudet, Léon* (E), 297; *Hommage*, 25.
81 *Meanwhile* . . . *Pouquet* (A), 18-21.
81 *That winter* . . . *Pouquet* (A), 16, 20-1; *Maurois*, 53-4.
82 *In the* . . . *Pouquet* (A), 17; *Cattaui* (A), 38, 39; CG, IV, 119.
82 *After* . . . *Pouquet* (A), 22; *Suffel*, 216-17; *Clermont-Tonnerre* (B), I, 12.
83 *In September* . . . *Maurois*, 21; *Blanche* (C), I, v-vi; *Seillière*, 9, 189; *Clermont-Tonnerre* (A), 105.
84 *Another* . . . *Blanche* (C), I, iv-vi; *Morand* (A), 239; *Cattaui* (A), 49; *Wildenstein*, no. 170; *Hommage*, 61.
85 *Towards* . . . *Hommage*, 29; *Pouquet* (A), 17.
85 *Laure* . . . *Fouquières* (B), I, 139-41; *Poniatowski*, 257; *Flament*, 213; *Dreyfus* (B), 249.
86 *When* . . . CG, V, 222; *Poniatowski*, 257-9; *Dreyfus* (B), 44-6; *Maurois*, 42; *Flament*, 213; *Wildenstein*, no. 97, 343; CG, V, 210; I, 616; *Pouquet* (A), 17.
87 *Unlike* . . . CG, V, 209, 211, 215, 219; CG, VI, 15; *Blanche* (A), 119; NRF, 213.
88 *Jeanne* . . . CG, VI, 4-6, 11, 14.
89 *The social* . . . *Clermont-Tonnerre* (B), I, 200, II, 112, 198, 200, 203; *Blanche* (A), 103; *Dreyfus* (A), 20; CG, VI, 126; *Hahn* (B), 220.
89 *Émile* . . . *Gregh* (A), 168-9; *Dreyfus* (A), 18-20; *Clermont-Tonnerre* (A), 99; *Lauris* (B), 156; *Schlumberger*, I, 303-4.
90 *Mme* . . . *Gregh* (A), 168-9; *Hermant* (B), 236; *Clermont-Tonnerre* (B), II, 200; *Dreyfus* (A), 21, 27, 30; CG, VI, 84, 263; CG, I, 237.
91 *Mme* . . . *Hermant* (B), 233; *Gregh* (A), 168; *Flament*, 156.
91 *In the* . . . *Blanche* (A), 109; *Lauris* (B), 153-5; *Hommage*, 49; *Dreyfus* (A), 22-3; *Clermont-Tonnerre* (B), II, 198-9; *Gregh* (A), 195; *Goncourt*, 25 March 1894; *Schlumberger*, I, 305; *Schlumberger*, II, 163-4; CG, VI, 250.
92 *Among* . . . *Clermont-Tonnerre* (A), 99; *Clermont-Tonnerre* (B), II, 198, 201 *Schlumberger*, I, 305.
92 *Charles* . . . *Seillière*, 128; *Clermont-Tonnerre* (A), 59; *Gregh* (A), 160; *Gyp* (B), 42, 90-100, 116-19; *Halévy*, 80-2; *Dreyfus* (B), 249-50; *Cattaui* (A), 104-9, 113-4, 117, 120; *Wildenstein*, no. 78; *Brach*, 9; *Schlumberger*, I, 322, 379; *Astruc*, 155, 307; *Clermont-Tonnerre* (C), 237; *Gregh* (A), 160; *Le Gaulois*, 16, 17 July 1902.
93 *Haas* . . . *Clermont-Tonnerre* (C), 236; *Fouquières* (A), 75; *Montesquiou* (D), II, 87; *Clermont-Tonnerre* (A), 60; *Gregh* (D), 45; *Astruc*, 90; *Seillière*, 128; *Hahn* (C), 189.
94 *In some* . . . *Germain* (B), 79; *Blanche* (A), 116.
94 *In his* . . . CG, VI, 167; *Astruc*, 310; *Clermont-Tonnerre* (A), 61; C, 19.
95 *Another* . . . *Augustin-Thierry*, 232; *Billy*, 42; *Hahn* (C), 11, *Hermant* (B), 169-70; *Regnier* (A), 23; *Scheikévitch* (A), 47; C, 14-18; I, 338.
96 *The Princess* . . . *Hermant* (B), 175-7; *Augustin-Thierry*, 302; *Schlumberger*, II, 159; *Blanche* (A), 53; *La Faye*, 267.
97 *In* . . . C, 14-27; *Goncourt*, 18 Sept. 1890; *Augustin-Thierry*, 307-9; *Bac* (B), 207-10; *Hermant* (B), 180.
98 *Mme Lydie* ● . . . DBF, vol. 4, col. 1, 2; *Vandérem*, 15, 25; *Du Bled*, 159, 162-3,

243; *Pouquet* (B) 51; *Goncourt,* 22 May 1895; *Gregh* (A), 243, 266; *Hermant* (B), 97.

99 *Mme Aubernon* ... *Gregh* (A), 266, 268; *Lauris* (B), 150; *Montesquiou* (D), II, 301; *Du Bled,* 159, 188-92; *Vandérem,* 15; *Billy,* 44.

100 *Mme* ... *Lauris* (B), 150; *Du Bled,* 160, 163, 171, 173, 208, 234, 264; *Fouquier* 117; *Gregh* (A), 268; *Vandérem,* 20-23; *Blanche* (A), 109.

100 *In some* ... *Montesquiou* (D), II, 301.

101 *The doctor* ... *Daudet, Léon* (G), 220; *Du Bled,* 231, 236, 248; *Clermont-Tonnerre* (A), 147.

101 *The pedant* ... *Blanche* (A), 101; *Vandérem,* 37; *Du Bled,* 233, 238; *Gregh* (A), 145; *Daudet, Léon* (B), 251-5.

102 *Brochard* ... *Du Bled,* 181-2, 251; *Blanche* (B), 169-71; *Blanche* (A), 102-3; *Gregh* (A), 266; *Vandérem,* 20-23; CG, I, 282, 284; CG, V, 221-2.

103 *The train* ... *Vandérem,* 49-51; *Du Bled,* 162-3.

104 *Mme* ... CG, VI, 205, 261.

104 *To complete* ... *Gregh* (A), 263; *Du Bled,* 230; *Lauris* (B) 258; *Clermont-Tonnerre* (B), I, 207.

105 *The last* ... C, 29-32; *Wildenstein,* no. 203-12.

106 *She was* ... *Flament,* 55, 104; *Bardac* (A), 140; *Gregh* (A), 271; *Cattaui* (A), 99; *Fouquières* (A), 69; PJ, 11; *Curtiss* (A), 337.

106 *As a* ... *Bardac* (A), 139; C, 37; *Scheikévitch* (A), 45; *Clermont-Tonnerre* (A), 208; *Clermont-Tonnerre* (C), 136.

107 *If a* ... *Fouquières* (A), 198-9; PM, 78; *Hahn* (B), 48; C, 37.

CHAPTER 8 THE DUCHESSE AND ALBERTINE

109 *Either* ... *Dreyfus* (A), 17; *Lauris* (B), 157; *Flament,* 156-7; C, 31.

109 *He had* ... *Hahn* (B), 47; *Bibesco, M* (B), 153; I, 178; II, 12; *Billy,* 45, 78-9, 106; *Pierre-Quint,* 46; *Bibesco, M* (C), 111; *Blanche* (A), 108; *Bibesco, M* (A), 46.

111 *Mme de* ... *Lister,* 76-7; *Bibesco, M* (B), 20, 32, 38, 73, 79-80, 99, 101; *Hahn* (C), 87; *Schlumberger,* II, 198-9.

112 *Comtesse* ... *Flament,* 156; *Sert,* 118; PJ, 74-5; *Bibesco, M* (B), 12, 13, 49-50, 67 *Bibesco, M* (C), 111; *Montesquiou* (E), 88-9.

113 *In May* ... PJ, 74-5.

113 *Le Banquet* ... *Hommage,* 36; *Gregh* (A), 148-9; *Dreyfus* (A), 16.

114 *Le Banquet* ... *Dreyfus* (B), 73, 82-3; NRF, 57-8.

115 *And yet* ... PJ, 68, 75, 185-6, 216, 236; C, 135.

115 *She was* ... *Proust, Mme,* 10-14; 17; *Gregh* (A), 164; *Billy,* 65; *Clermont-Tonnerre* (A), 33; *Poniatowski,* 523.

116 *Mme Hugo* ... *Landau,* 1; *Gregh* (A), 163-5; CG, V, 156; *Astruc,* 5-6.

117 *Early* ... *Billy,* 40-1; CG, IV, 184; *Gregh* (A), 165-6; *Cattaui* (A), 44, 56; CG V, 158, 160, 167.

117 *Horace* ... *Gregh* (A), 164-7; *Gregh* (B), 256; *Billy,* 46; *Proust, Mme,* 143.

118 *A curious* ... CG, V, 158; *Billy,* 44-5, 105.

CHAPTER 9
FIRST GLIMPSES OF THE CITIES OF THE PLAIN

120 *In the* ... *Bibesco, A* (B), 81

121 *His new* ... *Billy,* 37-9, 43, 48, 51, 101; *Bibesco, A* (B), 123.

122 *The three* ... *Billy,* 43, 48

122 *In August* ... *Billy,* 39, 43, 48, 53.

122 *Instead* ... *Billy,* 40, 43, 102-3, 106; CG, IV, 29.

123 *It was* ... *Billy,* 53; PJ, 12, 15.

123 *They* . . .   PJ, 11-13; CG, IV, 4; *Billy*, 29, 52; BSAMP, VII (1957), 276.
124 *Meanwhile* . . .   CG, I, 3, 97.
124 *Montesquiou* . . .   *Montesquiou* (D), I, 17-88; *Gregh* (A), 205; *Daudet, Lucien* (A), 200.
125 *Montesquiou* . . .   *Clermont-Tonnerre* (C), 25-6, 59; *Montesquiou* (D), II, 15-78, 87-95, 107-27, 185-91; *Mondor*, 434-5.
127 *Montesquiou was* . . .   *Clermont-Tonnerre* (C), 22-4, 34, 68; CG, I, 200, 225; *Régnier* (B), 180.
127 *Montesquiou had* . . .   *Morand* (A), 312; *Castellane* (B), 334; *Zillhardt*, 134, 136; *Clermont-Tonnerre* (C), 57-8, 154-5; *Corpechot*, 39; *Montesquiou* (G), 119-34.
128 *The conversation* . . .   *Clermont-Tonnerre* (C), 23, 48, 82, 85, 213; *Corpechot*, 36; *Gregh* (A), 204; *Daudet, Léon* (E), 282; *Blanche* (A), 121; *Blanche* (B), 195; *Montesquiou* (D), I, 80; *Schlumberger*, II, 172; *Morand* (A), 312.
129 *Montesquiou* . . .   *Clermont-Tonnerre* (C), 39, 59-60, 74, 167; *Montesquiou* (D), II, 105-6; *Germain* (B), 10; *Clermont-Tonnerre* (A), 167; III, 214, 818.
129 *The first* . . .   *Clermont-Tonnerre* (C), 54-5; *Blanche* (A), 102; *Montesquiou* (D), I, 279, II, 168; *Montesquiou* (G), 13, 16, 34; *Gregh* (A), 203; *Germain* (B), 8; *Clermont-Tonnerre* (A), 167.
130 *In one* . . .   *Zillhardt*, 140-2; *Blanche* (B), 195; *Blanche* (A), 7; *Montesquiou* (D), II, 229-31; *Goncourt*, 7 July 1891; *Cattaui* (A), 142.
131 *Montesquiou* . . .   *Montesquiou* (D), II, 296-300, III, 66-8; *Blanche* (B), 199.
132 *For a* . . .   *Clermont-Tonnerre* (B), II, 137-8; *Blanche* (B), 196-9.
133 *Early in* . . .   CG, I, 3-4; *Blanche* (B), 195; *Montesquiou* (D), II, 183, 198, 210-11; CSB, 434.
134 *It was* . . .   CG, I, 5-6; *Goncourt*, 7 July 1891, 15 Aug. 1896; *Montesquiou* (D), II, 209.
134 *The reasons* . . .   CG, I, 20, 23, 26, 35-7, 97, 250, 286-7; *Goncourt*, 21 March 1895; *Blanche* (B), 198; *Corpechot*, 235; *Montesquiou* (D), III, 287; *Daudet, Lucien* (A), 185.
135 *The quarrel* . . .   *Billy*, 49-51, 106, 145; PJ, 223-5; *Gregh* (A), 278, 297.
136 *In September* . . .   CG, VI, 51, 56; *Proust, Mme*, 53-4.
137 *With an* . . .   *Proust, Mme*, 52-3; BSAMP, VI, 141-53; *Billy*, 51; CG, VI, 195-6; *Pierre-Quint*, 33; *Fouquier*, 17.
138 *His progress* . . .   *Gregh* (A), 187-8; *Billy*, 52-4.
138 *Any attempt* . . .   PJ, 113-34, 211-15, 222-7.
139 *Another* . . .   *Revue Blanche*, Dec. 1893; PJ, 49-55; *Proust, Mme*, 142.
140 *It was* . . .   *Billy*, 76-7; *Gregh* (A), 226-7, 231; *Peter* (B), 25-8; *Delay*, II, 130.
141 *In November* . . .   CG, I, 43-6, 49, 51; *Renard*, 141.
141 *With all* . . .   CG, I, 8-9, 47, 111-12.
142 *Meanwhile* . .   *Montesquiou* (D), III, 25; *Goncourt*, 10, 17 Jan. 1894; CG, I, 85, 132; CG, IV, 212.
143 *In February* . . .   CG, I, 14, 50; *Rachilde*, 214; *Montesquiou* (D), II, 286-91; *Wildenstein*, no. 287; *Le Ménestrel*, 29 April 1894.
144 *Léon* . . .   *Rachilde*, 215-16; CG, I, 52-3; *Montesquiou* (D), II, 288, 294-5; *Gregh* (D), 35-6.
145 *Meanwhile* . . .   *Montesquiou* (D), II, 294-5; CG, I, 52-3, 67, 89-90, 96-8.
145 *He was* . . .   *Montesquiou* (D), II, 283, 292-4; *Régnier* (B), 161-3; *Bisson*, 342-4; *Goncourt*, 31 May, 17 June 1894; CG, I, 69, 98.

CHAPTER 10 THE GUERMANTES WAY

147 *The agate* . . .   *Blanche* (B), 201-2; *Fouquier*, 50; *Fouquières* (A), 35; *Flament*, 105-6; *Montesquiou* (D), I, 238; *Mondor*, 767; *Seillière*, 172.

148 *Her* . . . *Blanche* (B), 203.
148 *He was* . . . *Blanche* (B), 202-5; *Clermont-Tonnerre* (B), II, 25-7; *Morand* (A), 300; *Flament*, 259.
149 *Comtesse* . . . *Blanche* (B), 202; *Clermont-Tonnerre* (B), II, 24-5, 131; *Morand* (A), 289; *Montesquiou* (C), 558; *Clermont-Tonnerre* (A), 47; *Goncourt*, 5 Feb. 1894; *Flament*, 182; *Wildenstein*, no. 122, 123 *bis*; *Montesquiou* (D), II, 145-9.
149 *The Countess* . . . *Germain* (B), 129; *Montesquiou* (D), II, 147, 154; *Goncourt*, **25** April 1891, 20 June, 6 July, 8 August 1894; *Clermont-Tonnerre* (B), II, 22-3; *Fouquières* (A), 283.
150 *As we* . . . *Clermont-Tonnerre* (C), 136; *Clermont-Tonnerre* (B), II, 18-21, 24. 27; *Clermont-Tonnerre* (A), 87; *Hommage*, 191; *Schlumberger*, II, 218; *Castellane* (B), 97; *Fouquières* (B), I, 243; *Seillière*, 193; *Morand* (A), 59.
151 *Another* . . . *Thomas*, 65-6, 84-101, 119-37, 226-30; *Schlumberger*, II, 184; *Blanche* (B), 54; *Fouquières* (A), 49-50; CG, VI, 47; *Castellane* (B), 152.
152 *In several* . . . CG, IV, 124-7; *Wildenstein*, no. 122.
152 *A later* . . . *Clermont-Tonnerre* (B), II, 68; *Germain* (B), 129-30.
153 *For the* . . . *Fouquières* (A), 79-80; *Montesquiou* (D), I, 275-9; *Gramont*, 175; *Montesquiou* (A), 305; *Morand* (A), 112.
154 *The Prince* . . . *Fouquières* (A), 48-9; *Castellane* (A), 25, 59-60, 75-6; *Fouquier*, 53, 58; *Castellane* (B), 92-7; *Astruc*, 82.
155 *The Princesse* . . . *Fouquières* (A), 48-9; *Seillière*, 9, 189; *Drumont*, II, 178.
156 *The Prince* . . . *Clermont-Tonnerre* (A), 109; *Seillière*, 149; *Fouquières* (A), 50; *Castellane* (B), 110.
156 *In 1895* . . . *Castellane* (B), 1-37, 198; *Clermont-Tonnerre* (B), I, 151, II, 65-6.
156 *Boni* . . . *Clermont-Tonnerre* (A), 92, 165-6; *Clermont-Tonnerre* (B), II, 64; *Bibesco*, M (B), 150; *Schlumberger*, II, 197; *Seillière*, 133; *Castellane* (B), 100, 185; *Goncourt*, 21 Sept. 1887; CG, I, 282, 284; *Hommage*, 30; *Mérimée*, xxxi; *Blanche* (A), 121.
158 *Mme de* . . . *Seillière*, 132-3; CG, I, 212, 282, 284; *Clermont-Tonnerre* (C), 220.
159 *In real* . . . *Clermont-Tonnerre* (A), 166; *Blanche* (B), 165; *Clermont-Tonnerre* (C), 60-1; *Hahn* (B), 38.
159 *The gratin* . . . *Schlumberger*, II, 179-80; CG, I, 47; *Seillière*, 191; *Fouquières* (B), I, 104-5; *Germain* (B), 31-2.
160 *Another* . . . *Fouquier*, 120-4; *Schlumberger*, II, 81; *Lister*, 83.
160 *When* . . . *Castellane* (B), 110; *Clermont-Tonnerre* (B), II, 62, 72-3; *Montesquiou* (D), II, 230; *Schlumberger*, II, 196.
161 *Another* . . . *Fouquières* (A), 75, *Schlumberger*, II, 177; *Clermont-Tonnerre* (B), II, 48; *Hahn* (B), 164; *Fouquières* (B), I, 47-8; *Germain* (B), 138; *Germain* (A), 185-6; *Fouquier*, 125.
161 *Comtesse* . . . *Fouquières* (A), 59-60; *Poniatowski*, 26; *Hahn* (C), 100; *Catusse*, 47; *Castellane* (B), 98-9; *Germain* (B), 138.
162 *One of* . . . *Fouquières* (A), 97-8; *Fouquières* (B), I, 169; PM, 80, 83; *Clermont-Tonnerre* (B), I, 90; *Morand* (A), 312, 315.
163 *Next* . . . *Uzès*, vii, ix, xiv, xvii, xix, xxv, xxvii, xxxiii-iv, 7, 88; *Fouquier*, 29, 47; *Castellane* (B), 112; *Clermont-Tonnerre* (B), I, 149.
164 *One of* . . . *Clermont-Tonnerre* (C), 236; C, 40-5; *Blanche* (B), 249; *Goncourt*, 18 April 1894.
164 *Another* . . . *Clermont-Tonnerre* (B), I, 109; *Fouquières* (A), 73; *Fouquier*, 113-16; *Bibesco*, M (B), 104; C, 52-3; *Proust, Mme*, 120; CG, III, 86.
166 *One of* . . . *Blanche* (B), 145, 158-65, 171-3; *Flament*, 280-1; *Du Beed*, 198; *Fouquier*, 123; C, 56-9; *Hahn* (C), 267.

CHAPTER 11 DESCENT INTO THE CITIES OF THE PLAIN

169 *During* . . . CG, I, 28, 62, 72, 77; *Hahn* (B), 23.
169 *Before* . . . *Schlumberger*, II, 226; *Gregh* (A), 191-2; *Drumont*, II, 213; *Daudet, Léon* (E), 237; *Astruc*, 81, 177; *Billy*, 89.
170 *In August* . . . *Clermont-Tonnerre* (C), 24-5; CG, I, 28.
170 *Hahn* . . . *Hahn* (B), 13-14; *Goncourt*, 18 Dec. 1893; C, 36-7; *Flament*, 51, 159.
171 *Réveillon* . . . *Baraac* (A), 139-40; *Hommage*, 33-4.
172 *Proust's stay* . . . *Hahn* (B), 24-9; CG, I, 9-10; CG, IV, 11-12; PJ, 48; *Proust, Mme*, 56-7; *Catusse*, 136.
172 *Proust's mention* . . . *Nordlinger* (A), vi; CG, IV, 10; *Wildenstein*, no. 142, 293 *bis*; *Flament*, 206-8; CG, I, 48.
173 *Hahn's* . . . CSB, 328-31; NRF, 66-8.
173 *It was* . . . *Hahn* (C), 141; *Hommage*, 190; *Bibesco, A* (B), 153; *Hahn, M*, 28; *Adelson*, 232; JS, III, 146-151, 212-27; *Louys*, II, 541; *Germain* (B), 105.
175 *Meanwhile* . . . PJ, 11, 16; BSAMP, VI, 151, 155; CG, I, 24-5, 99-100.
176 *La Confession* . . . PJ, 141-159; JS, I, 189, 198, 211.
177 *By the* . . . CG, I, 18-20, 27, 32-3; *Hahn* (B), 45; *Clermont-Tonnerre* (B), II, 56; *Kolb* (A), 13; *Le Gaulois*, 29 May 1895; CG, IV, 16; PJ, 135-40.
178 *Proust* . . . CG, IV, 4, 12, 13; *Hahn* (C), 139; *Blum*, 60; PJ, 177-9; CG, I, 14.
179 *In June* . . . *Hahn* (B), 15, 35, 37; NRF, 278-80; *Suffel*, 158, 160; CG, IV, 15; CG, I, 107; *Daudet, Lucien* (A), 18; *Porto-Riche*, 95-6.
180 *Early* . . . *Billy*, 95-7, 194; *Kolb* (A), 244.
180 *After* . . . *Hahn* (B), 24, 48, 51; CG, I, 16; CG, IV, 13; PJ, 17-48.
181 *Soon* . . . *Hahn* (B), 48-50; *Hahn, M*, 24; *Le Gaulois*, 24 Aug. 1895; PJ, 232-4; *Proust, Mme*, 64.
182 *No doubt* . . . CG, IV, 54; CG, I, 58; *Hahn* (A), 135; *Yeatman*; III, 173; *Kolb* (B), 113; JS, II, 171-3.
183 *Their* . . . *Nordlinger* (B), 52-3; *Nordlinger* (C); *Billy*, 96-7; CG, I, 58-9; JS, II, 182, 186-7, 189, 193, 210.
183 *Among* . . . *Nordlinger* (B), 53; *Nordlinger* (C); JS, I, 34-6, II, 194-207; *Lauris* (A), 83; *Flament*, 70
184 *His return* . . . *Hahn* (A), 135; CG, IV, 25; NRF, 278-9.
185 *Whether* . . . JS, II, 241, 243, 245-6, 298, 302, 332-7; *Hahn, M.*, 24; NRF, 280.
185 *Another* . . . *Flament*, 39-42; *Goncourt*, 12 Dec. 1895.
186 *After* . . . *Daudet, Lucien* (A), 10-12; *Renard*, 181; *Germain* (B), 17-18, 165-8.
187 *In the* . . . *Daudet, Lucien* (A), 14, 18-19, 27.
187 *Lucien* . . . *Daudet, Lucien* (A), 26-7, 30-32, 41; CG, I, 51-2; *Hahn* (B), 29; *Germain* (B) 13, 19, 26; *Bardae* (B), 144.
189 *Meanwhile* . . . *Hahn* (B), 54-6.
189 *Only* . . . CG, I, 90-1; CG, VI, 15; PJ, 8, 9.
190 *Les Plaisirs* . . . *Revue Blanche*, 1 July 1896, 46-8; *Revue de Paris*, 15 July 1896; *Revue encyclopédique*. 22 Aug. 1896, 582-4; *Suffel*, 194-6; *Kolb* (A), 300.

CHAPTER 12 THE EARLY YEARS OF *JEAN SANTEUIL*

192 *The appearance* . . . *Kolb* (A), 169; CG, V, 212; *Catusse*, 36; CG, VI, 62.
192 *In* . . . CG, V, 212-14; *Wildenstein*, no. 82, 85.
193 *Next* . . . *Le Figaro*, 2 July 1896; *Cattaui* (A), 5; I, 12; *Crémieux*, 99; *Blanche* (C), I., xi; *Proust. Mme*, 67-9, 243; JS, I, 107-8, III, 125, 245; CG, I, 55, 124; *Hahn* (B), 60.
216 *Although* . . . *Castellane* (B), 163-6, 178; *Hahn* (B), 59.
216 *M. Groult* . . . *Flament*, 138, 159-63; *Clermont-Tonnerre* (C), 79-80; *Hahn* (C), 15; *Zillhardt*, 162-6; *Fouquier*, 122-3.

194 *In August* . . . *Hahn* (B), 61-2, 66, 68; JS, II, 214-221.

194 *On the* . . . *Proust, Mme,* 63, 95; *Hahn* (B), 57, 60, 62, 65-6, 68.

194 *In September* . . . *Proust, Mme.* 71-5, 78, 80-2.

195 *Early* . . . *Proust, Mme,* 76; *Flament,* 85-6; *Times,* 7 Oct. 1896, 3; *Clermont-Tonnerre* (B), II, 13; I, 431, 458, 460.

196 *Another* . . . *Clermont-Tonnerre* (A), 220.

196 *On 19* . . . *Daudet, Lucien* (A), 32; *Daudet, Léon* (F), I, 135; *Daudet, Léon* (G), 301; *Daudet, Léon* (C), 20-2; *Proust, Mme,* 84-101; JS, II, 177.

197 *On 20* . . . *Proust, Mme,* 84-5, 88, 91; *Bibesco, A* (B), 65; JS, II, 178-81; II, 132-6.

198 *Proust* . . . *Kolb* (B), 114-15; *Hahn* (B), 53, 66; *Proust,* Mme, 75, 77, 95; *Dreyfus* (B), 150.

200 *The narrative* . . . JS, I, 78, 125-31.

201 *The Easter* . . . JS, I, 136, 140, 146, 163-4, 167, 174, 176, 181, 184, 188-9, 203-10, 219-22.

202 *Part IV* . . . JS, II, 11-15, 31.

204 *Most* . . . JS, II, 263, 276; *Proust, Mme,* 95.

205 *I mean* . . . *Hahn* (B), 53.

206 *Henri's* . . . JS, II, 242.

206 *And so* . . . *Proust, Mme,* 75.

206 *In December* . . . *Nordlinger* (A), v-vi; *Wildenstein,* no. 58, 60, 280; *Cattaui* (A), 130; *Nordlinger* (B), 51, 54; *Hahn* (B), 66; *Hahn* (C), 19, 31.

208 *Lorrain* . . . *Astruc,* 81; *Renard,* 241; *Gregh* (A), 213; *Germain* (C), 58; *Hahn* (C), 43.

208 *It was* . . . *Montesquiou* (D), III, 79-80; *Flament,* 228.

209 *It was* . . . *Wildenstein,* no. 238; *Dreyfus* (B), 152; *Pouquet* (A), 28; C, 73-4; CG, III, 133; *Hahn* (C), 154; *Robert* (A), 79.

210 *After* . . . *Montesquiou* (A), 316; *Kolb* (A), 17; *Bourcet,* 297; *Uzès,* 69-72; *Fouquières* (B), I, 72-4; *Montesquiou* (D), III, 9-16, 81-2, 294-6; *Clermont-Tonnerre* (C), 85-6; *Regnier* (B), 163-5.

212 *The recital* . . . *Montesquiou* (D), II, 292, 295; *Gregh* (D), 36; *Germain* (B), 17; *Pierre-Quint,* 64; CG, I, 113-14; *Rachilde,* 214-15; *Blanche* (E), 157; *Chapman,* 52-3.

213 *Meanwhile* . . . *Dreyfus* (B), 116, 119-29; *Gregh* (A), 250, 272; *Daudet, Léon* (F), I, 117; *Daudet, Léon* (A), 116-20; *Keim,* 87; *Pouquet* (A), 24.

214 *A few* . . . *Flament,* 109-113.

214 *On 24* . . . *Le Figaro,* 26 May 1897; *Le Gaulois,* 25 May 1897; CG, I, 129-30; CG, VI, 15.

215 *It was* . . . *Proust, Mme,* 103; *Guillot de Saix.*

216 *Proust* . . . See after 193 above, 216 *Although.*

216 *M. Groult* . . . *Ibid.*

217 *Later (In July)* . . . *Nordlinger* (B), 60; CG, I, 108, 128.

217 *During* . . . *Mondor,* 416-17; *Montesquiou* (D), III, 174-5.

218 *It was* . . . *Regnier* (A), 76; *Nordlinger* (B), 54.

218 *Mme* . . . *Regnier* (A), 74; *Mondor,* 485-6, 780-1, 802; *Hahn* (C), 66; *Nordlinger* (A), 34, 85.

219 *In August* . . . *Proust, Mme,* 109, 121; *Kolb* (B), 117.

219 *On 16* . . . *Daudet, Lucien* (A), 13, 129, 179; CSB, 339-42; *Lauris* (A), 34.

220 *For three* . . . *Daudet, Lucien* (A), 34; NRF, 69-70; *Daudet, Léon* (F), I, 42.

CHAPTER 13 THE DREYFUS CASE

221 *On 26* . . . *Paléologue,* 1-52, 65, 186; *Chapman,* 45-111.

221 *The case* . . . *Chapman,* 53-7, 65, 97, 117, 152, 367.

222 *In July* . . . *Chapman*, 117-142.
223 *Suddenly* . . . *Chapman*, 155-79; *Reinach*, II, 36, 373; *Paléologue*, 79-81.
223 *I was* . . . CG, III, 71; *Gregh* (A), 290-1; *Nordlinger* (B), 52; II, 152; *Chapman*, 181; *Reinach*, III, 244-5; *Zola*, II, 34-7, 43, 52, 54; *Mondor*, 760; *Regnier* (B), 107.
224 *From 7* . . . *Chapman*, 190, 194-5; *Reinach*, II, 413.
224 *A few* . . . *Maurois*, 95; JS, II, 117, 134; *Robert* (B); CG, VI, 49; *Catusse*, 114; *Billy*, 126.
225 *Zola* . . . *Chapman*, 187, 189, 195; *Paléologue*, 109; JS, II, 123, 134, 142-8; *Hahn* (B), 69.
226 *The intervention* . . . *Chapman*, 197, 203.
226 *Already* . . . *Billy*, 150.
226 *The split* . . . *Gregh* (A), 288; CG, I, 100-1.
227 *The bourgeois* . . . *Clermont-Tonnerre* (B), I, 202; *Chapman*, 30, 91-2; *Daudet, Léon* (C), 23; *Daudet, Léon* (A), 13-16; *Blanche* (A), 115; *Gregh* (A), 286, 293; *Schlumberger*, I, 306-8.
228 *Mme* . . . *Paléologue*, 102-5, 120-4, 134, 146; *Gregh* (A), 169.
228 *For Mme* . . . *Paléologue*, 60-1, 89-91; *Vandérem*, 27-8, 53-4; *Du Bled*, 241, 266; DBF, vol. 4, col. 2; CG, VI, 205.
229 *For Mme* . . . *Clermont-Tonnerre* (A), 76; *Hermant* (B), 146-7; *Daudet, Léon* (A), 132-5; *Schlumberger*, II, 148-9; *Vandérem*, 41; *Du Bled*, 175-6; *Lauris* (B), 169; *Suffel*, 257, 263
230 *Mme* . . . *Flament*, 155-9.
230 *At* . . . *Nordlinger* (A), 3; CG, I, 59-60; *Lauris* (A), 108; *Catusse*, 22-4; CG, IV, 186; *Proust, Mme*, 104.
231 *Proust* . . . *Proust, Mme*, 104; *Jones*, 243; CSB, 382-5.
231 *In August* . . . *Paléologue*, 126-7; *Chapman*, 212-13, 221-8.
232 *At last* . . . *Chapman*, 233, 236, 238, 258-65.
232 *Meanwhile* . . . *Chapman*, 240-2; CG, VI, 16-17; *Schlumberger*, I, 301; *Wildenstein*, no. 250.
233 *Even* . . . CG, VI, 17; *Chapman*, 228, 247; *Reinach*, IV, 439-42.
233 *In* . . . *Chapman*, 250; *Gregh* (A), 259-62; *Hermant* (B), 163; *Castellane* (B), 221.
234 *In* . . . *Nordlinger* (A), 1-3.
235 *On the* . . . *Paléologue*, 174-6; *Chapman*, 253-7.
235 *On 25* . . . *Flament*, 198-9; CG, IV, 107-8; *Pouquet* (B), 193; *Pouquet* (A), 29; *Kolb* (A), 128.
236 *He had* . . . *Flament*, 202.
236 *On 16* . . . *Flament*, 217-19; *Suffel*, 273.
237 *Proust* . . . *Flament*, 219, 22.
237 *The next* . . . *Flament*, 261-2; *Kolb* (A), 20; CG, I, 104-5.
238 *Proust* . . . *Pouquet* (B), 196.
239 *The decision* . . . *Chapman*, 264, 269, 272, 275, 375; *Thomas*, 99, 247; *Radziwill*, II, 340.
239 *The new* . . . *Chapman*, 277, 285-305; *Paléologue*, 194-5; *Péguy*, 63-4.
240 *Meanwhile* . . . *Curtiss* (A), 92; *Hermant* (B), 220-6; *Labori*, 121.
241 *At* . . . *Bordeaux* (A), II, 47-8; *Bordeaux* (B), 100-2; *Hermant* (B), 202; CG, V, 131; *Proust, Mme*, 123.
241 *Other* . . . *Hermant* (B) 226; *Proust, Mme*, 119-23; CG, V, 89-90, 121-2, 131; *Hahn* (B), 69.
242 *The weeks* . . . *Proust, Mme*, 119, 121-3, 126, 129-30, 140-1, 150.
243 *We have* . . . *Proust, Mme*, 158, 161; CG, V, 122-3.
243 *Dr and* . . . *Proust, Mme*, 105, 110, 112, 115, 146, 153.
244 *On the* . . . *Proust, Mme*, 113, 116, 118, 128, 133-4, 136; *Kolb* (B), 118.

245 *One of* ... *Proust, Mme,* 106, 128, 138-9, 143; *Hermant* (B), 227; *C,* 51; *Daudet, Léon* (G), 221-3; II, 1005-6; *Bibesco, M* (B), 125.
246 *Autumn* ... *Proust, Mme,* 153, 157-8, 160.
246 *Proust* ... *Proust, Mme,* 156-7; *Pouquet* (B), 125.
247 *Early* ... *Proust, Mme,* 150, 158, 160-1; *CG,* V, 129-31.
247 *The Dreyfus* ... *Chapman,* 303, 312, 320, 343, 375; *Benda,* 202; *Clermont-Tonnerre* (B), I, 202; *CG,* VI, 84; *Barrès,* II, 209; *Proust, Mme,* 106.
248 *The enchanting* ... *Morand* (A), 299; *Schlumberger,* I, 326; *Hahn* (C), 268; *Proust, Mme,* 143; *CG,* IV 243; *Germain* (B), 43; *Blanche* (B), 257; *Blanche* (A), 116.

CHAPTER 14 SALVATION THROUGH RUSKIN

256 *Except* ... *Autret,* 15, 170; *Proust, Mme,* 111; *Nordlinger* (A), 32, 83, 85, 117.
256 *In 1897* ... *Hommage,* 279-80; *Billy,* 128; *PM,* 150.
257 *In 1898* ... *Billy,* 111.
257 *Marie* ... *Nordlinger* (D), 58-9; *Nordlinger* (A), 93.
258 *In the* ... *Proust, Mme,* 148-9, 156; *CG,* V, 121-2, 130-1; *La Sizeranne,* 23, 71, 106, 130, 135-7; *CG,* IV, 21; *Nordlinger* (A), 8, 10, 20, 114.
259 *On 5* ... *Nordlinger* (A), 5, 6; *Nordlinger* (D), 59.
260 *Ruskin* ... *PM,* 110-12, 116-17.
261 *It was* ... *PM,* 68-70, 111-12, 117, 120-4; *CSB,* 76; *BA,* 286-8.
262 *The visit* ... *PM,* 115; *C,* 147.
262 *On 20* ... *Nordlinger* (A), 9.
263 *He was* ... *Daudet, Léon* (G), 42; *Daudet, Léon* (D), 162.
264 *He did* ... *C,* 145-9.
264 *Early* ... *Scheikévitch* (A), 127.
265 *On the* ... *PM,* 173-4.
265 *Proust* ... *Scheikévitch* (A), 127-8; *PM,* 162, 174-6; *Nordlinger* (A), 19; *Kolb* (A), 303-4.
266 *Thanks* ... *NRF,* 280-3; *CG,* I, 57-8; III, 419; *Proust, Mme,* 150; *CG,* V, 130.
268 *He had* ... *Proust, Mme,* 161; *Nordlinger* (B), 56; *Kolb* (A), 305.
268 *It was* ... *Nordlinger* (A), ix, 20-1; *Nordlinger* (D), 61; *CSB,* 119-20, 122, 270; *Dujardin; Gide* (B), 56; *Kolb* (A), 305; *PM,* 109; *CG,* 123.
269 *In the mornings* ... *BA,* 245; *CSB,* 122-3; III, 625.
269 *In the afternoon* ... *Nordlinger* (B), 56; *BA,* 306-7; *Nordlinger* (A), ix; *PM,* 184-5; *Ruskin, Stones of Venice,* II, iv, 71.
270 *In the* ... *Nordlinger* (A), 91-2, 106; *Nordlinger* (B), 56; *Nordlinger* (E), 751.
271 *Influenced* ... *Nordlinger* (A), 21; I, 388, 390; *BA,* 219; *Kolb* (A), 305; *Lauris* (A), 131.
272 *Leaving* ... III, 648; *CG,* I, 12.
272 *By the* ... *Kolb* (A), 305.
273 *A few* ... *Nordlinger* (A), 15; *Autret,* 23, 26; *CG,* IV, 44-5.
274 *The validity* ... *Lauris* (A), 22; *Nordlinger* (A), viii, 23; *CG,* V, 35; *CG,* III, 13, 56; *Autret,* 38; *NRF,* 248-9; *Adam,* 48; *Wildenstein,* no. 259, 260, 301; *Lauris* (A), 21-2; *Bibesco, A* (B), 124; *Nordlinger* (D), 59; *Billy,* 129-30; *Proust, Mme,* 278-9; *Hahn* (B), 37; *Hahn* (D); *SL,* 7.
275 *Such are* ... *Autret,* 32, 39, 58, 76; *Nordlinger* (A), 14.
277 *The first* ... *PM,* 153-6; III, 890.
278 *In* ... *C,* 147; *Wildenstein,* no. 303.
279 *If Bergotte* ... *Levaillant,* 44-5, 51; *JS,* I, 125; *PM,* 193.
282 *At the* ... *PM,* 180; *Nordlinger* (A), 14; *Billy,* 137.

283 *Soon* . . . Proust, Mme, 163-70; *Fouquières* (B), I, 59-60; *Germain* (B), 140; Maurois, 156.
284 *He* . . . Proust, Mme, 155-6, 161, 169-70; *Dujardin; Védrines*, 59-60.
285 *The business* . . . Proust, Mme, 170; CG, IV, 22.
286 *This is* . . . Castellane (B), 137-8; C, 89; *Daudet, Lucien* (A), 14.
287 *Proust* . . . II, 19; Proust, Mme, 204.

CHAPTER 15 SAINT-LOUP

288 *At 45* . . . Le Figaro, 21 June 1901; *Duplay* (C), 4; *Lauris* (A), 27; *Hommage*, 64, 191; Proust, Mme, 156, 173; *Kolb* (A), 22, 69; *Hahn* (A), 170-3; CG, II, 32-3; Le Gaulois, 12 May, 1901; *Daudet, Léon* (G), 302-3; *Daudet, Léon* (A), 66.
289 *Throughout* . . . Daudet, Léon (F), I, 182-4; *Daudet, Léon* (A), 51; *Daudet, Léon* (G), 298, 300-1, 304.
290 *Sometimes* . . . Daudet, Léon (G), 312-13.
290 *Another* . . . Peter (A), 98-9; *Daudet, Léon* (G), 308-9; *Hahn* (B), 227.
291 *On 9* . . . Bibesco, A (B), 35; C, 39-44; *Morand* (A), 112; Proust, Mme, 176.
292 *By this* . . . Proust, Mme, 172-5, 177, 179, 181; C, 146.
293 *The first* . . . Hommage, 63-4; *Clermont-Tonnerre* (C), 207.
294 *Gabriel* . . . Clermont-Tonnerre (B), I, 105; C, 59; *La Rochefoucauld*, 25; *Montesquiou* (A), 313.
295 *A few* . . . Bibesco, A (B), 29-30, 160; *Bibesco, M* (A), 63; *Hermant* (B), 212.
296 *In 1900* . . . Bibesco, A (B), 31-2; *Cattaui* (A), 157; *Billy*, 172-3.
296 *In the* . . . Bibesco, M (A), 31; *Flament*, 221; *Vandérem*, 42; *Lauris* (A), 9, 10; Lauris (B), 105; *Clermont-Tonnerre* (A), 35; *Billy*, 121; *Kolb* (A), 295.
297 *Proust* . . . Bibesco, M (A), 11, 12, 18, 25-7, 54.
298 *But the* . . . Bibesco, M (A), 15, 18; *Bibesco, A* (B), 78, 80-2.
298 *For a* . . . Bibesco, M (A), 20, 169; *Bibesco, A* (A), 424; CG, I, 281.
300 *Early* . . . Nordlinger (D), 59, 61; *Nordlinger* (F), 521.
300 *The first* . . . Bibesco, M (A), 31, 128-9; *Bibesco, A* (B), 97.
300 *At* . . . Bibesco, A (B), 97.
301 *On the* . . . Bibesco, A (B), 86-7.
301 *It was* . . . Bibesco, M (A), 38, 196-7.
301 *On a* . . . Bibesco, M (A), 39.
302 *The other* . . . Billy, 122; *Lauris* (A), 18-20; *Bibesco, M* (A), 37, 47, 49; *Hommage*, 41; Proust, Mme, 215; *Nordlinger* (D), 59; *Adam*, 18; BA, 296, 326; *Catusse*, 27-8.
303 *On the* . . . Billy, 122; *Hommage*, 41; *Lauris* (A), 19-20; *Viollet-le-Duc*, VI, 114.
304 *By the* . . . CG, II, 39-40; *Lauris* (A), 11.
304 *He now* . . . Lauris (A), 21; *Bibesco, A* (B), 71, 144-5.
304 *On 29* . . . CG, II, 43-4; CG, IV, 189; Proust, Mme, 186-91; *Bibesco, A* (B), 122.
305 *However* . . . CG, VI, 261; CG, V, 158; CG, IV, 148-9; PJ, 238.
306 *Early* . . . Proust, Mme, 197-202; *Bibesco, A* (B), 88; *Wildenstein, no. 182; Jones*, 245; PM, 254-6; *Hahn* (B), 70; CG, IV, 86.
307 *He returned* . . . Bibesco, A (B), 59-60; 64-5, 70-2, 94-6, 99-100; *Bibesco, M* (A), 85-6.
308 *Antoine* . . . Kolb (A), 272; Proust, Mme, 202-4; *Bibesco, A* (B), 84-5.
309 *Fénelon* . . . Proust, Mme, 203-4; *Hommage*, 80.
309 *Saturnian* . . . Bibesco, A (B), 30, 47, 119; *Clermont-Tonnerre* (A), 36; *Morand* (A), 227; *Morand* (B), 26.
311 *Two* . . . Bibesco, A (B), 66, 68, 71; Proust, Mme, 200, 204-5; CG, IV, 189.
311 *The ceremony* . . . Thomson, 717; *Catusse*, 19-20; *Bibesco, A* (B), 83-5.
312 *Since* . . . Bibesco, M (A), 23, 126-7; *Bibesco, A* (B), 100; *Briand* (A), 351-3, 372.

313 *Spurred* ... *Proust, Mme,* 194, 208; *Bibesco, A* (B), 39-40, 71, 102, 104; C, 14-27; PJ, 207-10.
314 *In March* ... *Proust, Mme,* 206-10.

CHAPTER 16 TIME BEGINS TO BE LOST

315 *By the* ... *Bibesco, M* (C), 10, 13, 15, 21; *Clermont-Tonnerre* (A), 36, 38; C, 58; *Gramont,* 171; *Bibesco, A* (B), 98-9.
316 *Prince* ... *Poniatowski,* 610; *Castellane* (A), 41; *Hommage,* 309-13; *Montesquiou* (C), 558; *Montesquiou* (B), 60; *Halicka,* 66.
317 *At that* ... CG, I, 202; *Proust, Mme,* 213; C, 45; *Briand* (A), 372-3; *Clermont-Tonnerre* (A), 35; CG, V, 149-51, 181; *Bibesco, A.* (B), 135-6.
318 *A few* ... *Bibesco, A* (B), 100, 104, 107-8; C, 34; CG, IV, 115.
319 *Since* ... *Bibesco, A* (B), 120, 123, 126, 128-9; *Gregh* (A), 161; *Hommage,* 36; CG, V, 176.
321 *During* ... *Proust, Mme,* 213.
321 *On 9* ... *Nordlinger* (B), 57-8; *Clermont-Tonnerre* (C), 71-2, 94.
322 *The return* ... *Proust, Mme,* 212, 214-16.
322 *Early* ... *Clermont-Tonnerre* (C), 11-14.
323 *On 29* ... *Lauris* (A), 23, 62, 66, 70.
324 *Two* ... *Le Masle,* 31-2, 62-4; *Lauris* (A), 23, 65, 69, 71, 84.
325 *Early* ... *Proust, Mme,* 218, 220-1, 224, 226-8.
325 *Meanwhile* ... *Bibesco, A* (B), 123, 127-8, 137; *Nordlinger* (A), 22-3; *Proust, Mme,* 225; *Lauris* (A), 45, 82-3.
326 *Feverish* ... *Lauris* (A), 46-7; CSB, 102; I, 655-8; *Proust, Mme,* 229; *Duplay* (A).
327 *After* ... *Lauris* (A), 48-9; *Billy,* 121, 145; CG, II, 53-4; PM, 256, 268; *Nordlinger* (A), 24; *Catusse,* 121; CG, V, 202.
328 *The energetic* ... CG, V, 72; *Le Masle,* 39-44, 57-9; *Bibesco, A* (B), 143; *Proust, Mme,* 136, 149.
329 *His* ... *Crémieux,* 166; *Morand* (A), 56; *Thomas,* 168; *Maurois,* 156.
330 *Dr Proust's* ... *Daudet, Léon* (G), 40-1; *Hahn* (B), 142; *Daudet, Léon* (B), 81-4; *Le Masle,* 51; *Montesquiou* (D), II, 193-5; *Schlumberger,* II, 149, 152; *Clermont-Tonnerre* (A), 147; *Bac* (B), 205; *Astruc,* 307; *Gregh* (A), 202; *Morand* (A), 122; *Keim,* 84; CG, II, 140; *Daudet, Lucien* (A), 36; *Guichard,* 176; *Clermont-Tonnerre* (C), 146; *Goncourt,* 7 June 1896; *Robert* (A), 74-5.
332 *Time* ... *Le Masle,* 48-50; *Cattaui* (A), 55; *Mauriac, C,* 9; *Thomson,* 712; *Fleury,* 6-7.
333 *Despite* ... I, 36; *Le Masle,* 50-2; *Pierre-Quint,* 60; *Clermont-Tonnerre* (A), 29.
333 *On at* ... *Le Masle,* 31, 55.
334 *On Sunday* ... CG, II, 49-50; *Le Masle,* 49.
334 *On Monday* ... *Le Masle,* 44; CG, V, 215; *Hahn* (B), 223; CG, II, 190.
335 *Dr Proust's* ... *Le Masle,* 45, 49; *Nordlinger* (F), 527; *Nordlinger* (B), 58.
335 *Montesquiou* ... CG, I, 121; CG, II, 48-9, 51-2; CG, IV, 190; *Catusse,* 40, 4-34, 56.
336 *Life* ... CG, II, 51.
336 *The old* ... I, 36.

CORRECTIONS AND ADDITIONS TO VOL. I

xi: 18 *For* moment. *read:* moment, **xv: 10** *For* two *read:* six **xv: 31** *For* 1954 *read:* 1945 **3: 4, 10, 11** *For* Nathée *read:* Nathé *et passim.* **5: 6-8** *For* a canopy . . . lion's head *read:* a carved stone shield, framed in oak-leaves and bearing the number Nine. **6: note 2** *For* I, 486 *read:* I, 52, 77, 486 **8: 17** Aunt Laure was Mme Proust's distant cousin Mme Charles Nathan, *née* Laure Rodrigues-Ely. See *Proust, Mme,* 36, note 2, 221. **13: 9** *For aggrégation* read: *agrégation* **23: 35, 38** *For* Catalan *read:* Catelan *et passim.* **26: 21** *For* seek. *read:* seek, **39: 4** *For d'Angleterre* read: *de l'Angleterre* **44: 10** *For* Gramont *read:* Grammont **66: 18** *For* Greffuhle *read:* Greffulhe *et passim.* **73: 29** *Delete:* first **73: 35** *Delete:* Comte **73: 35** *For* 39th *read:* 30th **78: 22** *For* three *read:* four **79: 17** *For* trooper *read:* private. As Proust was in an infantry regiment, he was not strictly speaking a 'trooper'; but the nickname was given him by his family, no doubt because his training included riding exercises. **83: 37** *For* Laure Baignère's *read:* Charlotte Baignères's **84: 11** *For* two *read:* three **87: 12** *For* October *read:* December **94: note 3** *Read:* III, 200 **95: 4** *For* founded *read:* edited **96: note 3** *Add:* Cf. I, 338 **110: 8** *For* Comtesse Rosa *read:* Comte Robert **111: 38** *For* Joseph du *read:* Joseph de **116: 9** *For* France *read:* Paris **116: 29** *For* who *read:* and **121: 7** *For* Herrengasse *read:* Rue des Granges **126: 23** *For* Huysmans *read:* Mallarmé **126: 35** *For* Neuilly *read:* Passy **127: 6** *For* Larochefoucauld *read:* La Rochefoucauld. The Cirque Mollier was a charity display organised by sponsors in high society; and this gymnastic La Rochefoucauld was no mere commoner, but a member of the ducal family. **130: 2-3** *For* about 1868 *read:* on 12 March 1864 **130, note 1** *For* Rue de *read:* Rue du **132: 13** *For* bequest *read:* request **134: 21** *For* Neuilly *read:* Passy **135: 12** *For* only the year before Yturri had felt *read:* in March 1895 Yturri felt **135: 14** *For* had been *read:* was **137: 40** For *licenciat* read: *licence* **140: 12-14** Proust first met Gide at the home of Gabriel Trarieux on 1 May 1891. See *Delay,* II, 130. **143: 5** For *Près* read: *près* **150: 21** *For* d'Aigle *read:* de l'Aigle **150: 30** *For* Comte *read:* Marquis **153: 33-6** So the story is invariably told; but as the head of the La Rochefoucauld family was traditionally named François, it is probable that Comte Aimery really said: "François Premier". **157: 30** The archivist M. Vallenères, who on the afternoon of Mme de Villeparisis's matinée is helping her with her Memoirs and with the distribution of *petits fours* (II, 189, 231), was a M. Guérineau, whom Boni sent to his great-aunt with an immense chart showing the genealogical tree of the Castellane family from Carolingian times. "You've missed something out," she commented sardonically, "you haven't mentioned Adam de Castellane, who married that Eve Thingummy—do try and find out her surname for me!" See *Castellane* (B), 186. **159: 31** *For* idol *read:* vase **159: 34-5** *For* Chevruel *read:* Chevreul **170: 34-5** *Delete:* and Saint-Saëns **172: 16** *Delete:* comma after friend **179: 4** *For* 1915 *read:* 1913 **182: 38** *For* Pierre *read:* André **184: 17** *For* funeral *read:* funereal **186: 15** *For* Laure *read:* Charlotte **194: 7** *Insert:* p. 216 *infra,* line 1—p. 217, line 2. **198, note 3** *For* Pierre *read* André **206: 9** *For* 867 *read:* 887 **207: 24** *For* Premier *read:* Première **208: 14** For *de* read: *des* **209: 33** *For* Villebonne *read:* Villebon **216: 1** *For* Proust was *read:* Although he keenly followed its events in the newspapers, Proust was unable through mourning to be **216: 1-217: 2** *Transfer* to after 194: 7. **217: 3** *For* Later that month *read:* In July 1897 **217: 23-4** *Delete:* and accompanied by Marie Nordlinger **218: 7-8** *Delete:* and Marie Nordlinger **224: note 2** *For* Schwarzkoppen *read:* Schwartzkoppen; for *faux-Henry* read: *faux Henry* **226: 36** *For* Forain *read:* Caran d'Ache **228: 15** *For* 7 *read:* 5 **229: 6** *For* 7 *read:* 2 **230: 4** *For* 28 *read:* 25 **231: 34** *For* August *read* July **231: 36:** *For* the 30th *read:* 30 August **241: 20** *For* Henri *read:* Henry **242: 10** *For* confidents *read:* confidants **246: 30** *For* twenty-eight *read:* eighteen **246: note 3** *Delete:* Jean de Tinan . . . her father. The girl rescued by Tinan was not Suzanne France, but a daughter of Rosny *aîné:* see *Goncourt Journal,* 10 May, 17 May, 28 June 1896. I deeply regret this error, which was caused by a misleading source; and I am grateful to M. Lucien Psichari, the son of Suzanne France by her second marriage, for the courtesy with which he accepted my explanation and apology, which I here repeat. **248: 28** *For* Marquise *read:* Marquis **250: 40** *For* music *read:* music, **254: 36** For *Recherhe* read: *Recherche* **258: 21** *For* beyond *read:* behind **272: 37** For *Saint* read: *Sainte* **275: 31** *For* excerise *read:* exercise **276: 21** *For* production; *read:* production. **280: note 2** For 171 *read:* 193 **283: 16-17** *Delete:* (whose son Maurice was to become Proust's friend a year or two later) **284: 20** *For* Lazzaro *read:* Lazaro. In a letter of May 1859 to Charles Eliot Norton, which Proust probably read in Norton's preface to the Brantwood edition of *Stones of Venice. Traveller's edition,* New York, 1891, vol. 1, p. ix, Ruskin particularly praised the view of Venice from San Lazaro. **290: 18** *For* Jean Paul *read:* Paul Jean **295: 18-19** *Delete:* hundred; *for* 177 *bis read:* 69 **296: note 2** *For* 1898 *read:* 1899 **298: 20** *For* Henri *read:* Henry **300: 3** *For* Samuel *read:* Siegfried **310: 16** *For* Antoine Bibesco *read:* Antoine and Emmanuel Bibesco **310: 18** *For* later married *read:* later, all except Emmanuel Bibesco, married **310: 18-23** *Delete:* Two, however . . . beyond liking. **310: 39** *For* only thrice more *read:* still more seldom **312: 18-20** *Delete:* who may be . . . Dr Simon Duplay. Whoever Proust's friend 'M.' may have been, he was not Maurice Duplay, with whom I 'conjecturally identified' him. I have since been informed that the autograph original of at least one of Proust's letters to 'M.' is in fact addressed to Loche Radziwill. In any case, the letters show quite clearly that this friendship was entirely platonic, and reflect no blame whatever on the anonymous 'M.' I regret this error of identification, and the pain which it caused M. Maurice Duplay; and I am grateful to him for the kindness with which he accepted my apology, which I here repeat. **317: 22** *Delete:* was of Jewish birth **319: 16** For *Sieur* read: *Sire* **320: note 1** In a letter of 1904 or 1905 to Louisa de Mornand (CG, V, 176) Proust wrote: 'I'm having a morphine injection, which no doubt will get me some sleep at last'.

Note.—The corrections called for above, with the exception of those relating to pp. **216-18, 283** and **310,** have been made in the third and subsequent impressions of Volume One.

REFERENCES TO SOURCES
VOLUME TWO

CHAPTER 1 VISITS FROM ALBERTINE

Page and Paragraph
1 *Life has* ... CG, II, 48-50; *Proust, Mme*, 145, 235.
1 *Not unreluctantly* ... CG, II, 49, 56-7; *Bibesco, A* (A), 425; RL, 15/11/1904.
2 *With a* ... CG, II, 51; *Proust, Mme*, 231-2.
2 *In some* ... *Proust, Mme*, 196; *Nordlinger* (A), 26-40; *Nordlinger* (B), 57-9; *Nordlinger* (D), 59, 62; *Hommage*, 39; CG, II, 57; *Daudet, Lucien* (A), 48, 51, 239; *Maurois*, 128.
3 *Towards* ... *Nordlinger* (A), ix-x, 3, 28-30, 32, 35, 116-18; *Nordlinger* (B), 57-9; *Nordlinger* (D), 62; *Adam*, 18; *Montesquiou* (D), II, 209.
4 *Meanwhile* ... CG, II, 59; *Bibesco, A* (B), 105; *Kolb* (A), 73; *Annuaire diplomatique*, 1914, 291.
4 *The other* ... CG, II, 58-64, 70-2; *Clermont-Tonnerre* (A), 34; *Gregh* (B), 55-9; *Gregh* (D), 96-100; *Montesquiou* (A), 314.
5 *It is* ... CG, I, 84-5, 106, 148-9; *Castellane* (A), 77-88; *Nichols*, 215-16; *Hahn* (B), 39, 40; *Montesquiou* (A), 314; *Montesquiou* (D), II, 86, III, 116-19; *Montesquiou* (G). 80; *Kolb* (A), 23; *Bac* (A), II, 89, III, 119-32; *Fouquières* (C), 107-9; *Zillhardt*, 147-8; *Clermont-Tonnerre* (C), 90-2.
6 *By sheer* ... CG, I, 157, 172, 216-17; CG, II, 72, 100-5; NRF, 49; PM, 73-8; C, 39-54; *Montesquiou* (G), 82.
7 *Although* ... *Nordlinger* (A), 55-8; *Kolb* (A), 126.
7 *Another* ... CG, II, 103-5; CG, IV, 96-7, 185; *Billy*, 32-3; *Curtiss* (A), 101; *Duplay* (C), 1-3; *Alden*, 6, 160; *Nordlinger* (A), 79; *Bergson*; PM, 241; CG, II, 185; *Gregh* (D), 89-91.
8 *La Bible* ... PM, 195.
9 *In his* ... PM, 182-92.
11 *Proust* ... PM, 193, 195.
11 *Copies* ... CG, IV, 29. *Maurois*, 116.
12 *In April* ... CG, V, 152-4; *Wildenstein*, no. 81, pl. 8; *Mauriac*, C, 59.
12 *For some* ... CG, V, 172-4, 176-7, 181, 188, 198, 203; *Curtiss* (A), 87; *Mornand*.
13 *His* ... CG, V, 174.
13 *In her* ... CG, V, 152.
14 *Meanwhile* ... *Nordlinger* (A), 26-7, 31, 37-9, 41-8, 55-8, 62-7.
15 *In April* ... *Nordlinger* (A), x, 45, 118-19; *Nordlinger* (B), 58.
15 *On 16* ... CG, I, 78-9; *Montesquiou* (D), I, 204, 206, 208; *Clermont-Tonnerre* (C), 119; *Zillhardt*, 139-40.
16 *Ever since* ... CG, II, 73.
16 *The theme* ... CG, II, 73-92; CG, VI, 187; *Clermont-Tonnerre* (B), II, 217; *Bibesco, M* (E), I, 77; *Morand* (A), 200; *Lauris* (B), 173.
17 *The Paris* ... CG, II, 93; CG, V, 197, 202; *Clermont-Tonnerre* (B), I, 134, 165; *Clermont-Tonnerre* (C), 14-15; *Bibesco, A* (B), 89; *Hahn* (B), 140; *Morand* (A), 188-9; *Montesquiou* (D), II, 46-7; BSAMP, VI, 175-7.
18 *For a* ... *Bibesco, A* (B), 89.

18 *Albufera* . . . CG, V, 196-203.

19 *When on* . . . CG, II, 83, 89; Noailles, *Nouvelle espérance*, 266.

19 *Nothing* . . . *Barrès*, II, 108; *Blanche* (A), 53; *Tharaud* (B), 12-14, 58.

20 *Proust* . . . *Dreyfus* (B), 108-11; *Gregh* (B), 259.

21 *The rift* . . . CG, II, 93-4, 109-10, 134; CG, IV, 199-200; *Bibesco, A* (B), 89-91; *Kolb* (A), 76.

22 *On Tuesday* . . . *Proust, Mme*, 237-45; *Billy*, 72, 136, 143-4, 147, 181; CG, VI, 22; *Nordlinger* (A), 70-2.

23 *On 16* . . . C, 150-69.

23 *Towards* . . . *Proust, Mme*, 247-75.

24 *Mlle Nordlinger* . . . *Nordlinger* (A), 61-2, 68-78, 120-1; *Proust, Mme*, 246, 294; *Kolb* (A), 312; CG, V, 167, 216-7.

25 *During* . . . CG, I, 125, 131-2; CG, V, 174-5, 184; *Bibesco, A* (B), 144-5; C, 170-1; *Gregh* (D), 107-9; *Cattaui* (C), 40; HLB, II (1949), 257-67; *Jones; Proust, Mme*, 143-4.

26 *The first* . . . CG, V, 168, 172-3; *Bibesco, A* (B), 160-70; *Bibesco, M* (C), 27; *Proust, Mme*, 251, 273, 276-7.

26 *The noble* . . . *Bibesco, M* (C), 25-46; BSAMP, VI, 177; *Montesquiou* (D), II, 155; *Proust, Mme*, 247; *Wildenstein*, no. 240.

27 *For Proust* . . . CG, V, 167, 171-3; *Gregh* (D), 109-13.

CHAPTER 2 DEATH OF A MOTHER

29 *It was* . . . CG, VI, 20, 25; *Montesquiou* (D), II, 243-62; *Nordlinger* (A), 82-5; *Nordlinger* (F), 525-6; *Proust, Mme*, 279.

30 *On 9* . . . *Proust, Mme*, 257-8; *Clermont-Tonnerre* (B), I, 105; BSAMP, VI, 175; *La Rochefoucauld*, 1, 6.

30 *In mid-February* . . . CG, I, 221-4; CG, V, 181-4; CG, VI, 17-18; *Kolb* (A), 300-1; *Clermont-Tonnerre* (C), 89, 107-9.

31 *Poor* . . . CG, I, 215; CG, VI, 18-28.

32 *He made* . . . CG, V, 162-3, 165-6, 168-9, 182-4, 188-9, 198.

32 *Towards* . . . CG, I, 74-6, 125-9, 133-46, 156-8, 215-7; CG, VI, 29, 33; *Kolb* (A), 27; *Montesquiou* (D), II, 284-5, 301.

34 *While* . . . CG, I, 216; CG, IV, 193, 196-8; CG, VI, 27, 35; *Bibesco, A* (B), 124; *Billy*, 130; *Autret*, 62; *Mourey; Nordlinger* (A), 84; SL, 7.

34 *My only* . . . PM, 226, 244, 250, 252; SL, 7.

36 *For five* . . . PM, 254.

37 *Sur la* . . . CG, II, 111-33, 147-9; CG, IV, 208; CG, VI, 27, 36; *Lauris* (A), 59, 77.

37 *Meanwhile* . . . *Nordlinger* (A), x, 86; *Nordlinger* (B), 61; *Proust, Mme*, 293.

38 *On 15* . . . CG, I, 245-7; CG, II, 124; *Lauris* (A), 60, 77; *Nordlinger* (A), 86-91, 94; BSAMP, VIII, 455; *Proust, Mme*, 293-6.

38 *Louisa* . . . CG, V, 155-65.

39 *On 24* . . . CG, V, 42; *Clermont-Tonnerre* (A), 40-1; *Proust, Mme*, 298.

40 *The third* . . . CG, I, 42, 152, 157, 216, 246; *Hommage* (RN), 11-12; *Garver*, 519-20.

40 *It had* . . . CG, I, 149-52; *Clermont-Tonnerre* (C), 110-12; *Germain* (B), 10; *Montesquiou* (G), 185-219; *Morand* (A), 199; *Zillhardt*, 136-7.

42 *Proust* . . . CG, I, 152-6, 159.

42 *On 25* . . . CG, II, 138-42; CG, V, 161; *Hommage*, 191.

43 *In Proust's* . . . CG, V, 161; *Bibesco, A* (B), 131-2; SL, 7-8; *Nordlinger* (A), 79-80, 89-91, 93, 96-7; *Proust, Mme*, 262.

44 *Sufficient* . . . CG, II, 140; *Maurois*, 153-4.

69 *Cardane* ... CG, IV, 273; *Ambrière; Dreyfus* (B), 202; *Bibesco, A* (B), 179; *Hahn* (B), 127-30.

69 *After* ... PM, 223-4.

CHAPTER 4 BALBEC REVISITED

72 *The nervous* ... *Lauris* (A), 87-125.

72 *All was* ... CG, I, 192; CG, VI, 68-75; *Catusse*, 87, 89-93; *Maurois*, 129.

73 *Meanwhile* ... C, 83-91.

74 *The five* ... *Boigne*, I, 256, 413; C, 89-90.

76 *Proust* ... CG, I, 159, 199-201, 225-6; CG, IV, 164; *Briand* (B); *Hahn* (B), 123; *Nordlinger* (A), 109; *Lauris* (A), 143-5; *Robert* (A), 39-41, 45-6.

77 *In the* ... CG, V, 186-7; *Duplay* (B); *Hahn* (B), 125-6, 128; *Léautaud*, III, 379.

78 *On* 11 ... *Hahn* (B), 132-4.

78 *It was* ... CG, I, 184; *Billy*, 31; *Casa-Fuerte; Elkin Mathews; Germain* (E), 200 HLB, VII (1953), 152.

79 *Proust* ... *Hahn* (B), 131-2.

80 *The impact* ... CG, I, 198-9, 226; *Germain* (B), 20-1.

80 *The publication* ... CG, II, 170-3; C, 86-7.

81 *Proust's* ... CG, I, 202; CG, II, 164-9; CG, VI, 78; C, 177-92; *Lauris* (A), 126.

82 *His review* ... CG, II, 174-6; CG, VI, 75-85.

82 *The dinner* ... CG, IV, 111-12, 216-17; CG, VI, 75-85; *Billy*, 171-2; *Brach*, 9; *Clermont-Tonnerre* (C), 137, 139; *Hahn* (B), 136-8, 237; *Morand* (B), 40.

83 *On* 23 ... C, 67-72.

83 *Dr Bize* ... CG, VI, 50, 56, 58; *Catusse*, 99; *Hahn* (B), 57; *Proust, Mme*, 224; *Sévrette*, 87, 157.

84 *The visitor* ... *Sévrette*, 43-4, 48-69, 120-131.

85 *Cabourg* ... CG, VI, 250; *Baedeker*, 221-2; *Clermont-Tonnerre* (C), 234; I, 385.

86 *In this* ... CG, III, 298; *Lauris* (A), 63; *Marquis*.

87 *In* ... *Hahn* (B), 142; *Sévrette*, 224.

88 *For the* ... *Lauris* (A), 122-3, 130-5.

88 *The penance* ... CG, VI, 86-7; *Bibesco, A* (B), 42-3; *Billy*, 112-17; *Hahn* (B), 139-40; *Lauris* (A), 131; *Le Masle* (B).

89 *Alfred* ... *Adam*, 81; *Cattaui* (A), 63; *Curtiss* (A), 220; *Vigneron*, 102.

89 *The next* ... CG, I, 220; *Bibesco, A* (B), 43; *Lauris* (A), 130-1; PM, 96-7.

90 *His first* ... *Bibesco, A* (B), 42; *Billy*, 115-17, 153; *Catusse*, 17; *Daudet, Lucien* (A), 229; *Lauris* (A), 131-3; *Le Masle* (B); II, 825.

91 *Proust* ... *Astruc*, 308; *Brach*, 37; *Corpechot*, 63-73; *Curtiss* (A), 353; *Daudet, Léon* (I), 248; *Flament*, 178-82; *Fouquières* (B), I, 225; *Goncourt*, 4/6/1890, 5/2/1894; *Hahn* (B), 145-6; BA, 32; *Lauris* (A), 131-2; I, 850; *Clermont-Tonnerre* (B), II, 114.

92 *Proust* ... *Billy*, 117, 153, 212; *Hahn* (B), 144-6.

93 *His daily* ... CG, VI, 85, 88; *Annuaire des châteaux*, 1906-7, II, 175; *Billy*, 153; *Hahn* (B), 113, 138, 146; *Lauris* (A), 133.

94 *Towards* ... CG, III, 5-6; CG, IV, 219-20; CG, VI, 85-90; *Billy*, 153, 212-3; *Catusse*, 99; *Clermont-Tonnerre* (C), 101-5, 139; *Clermont-Tonnerre* (B), IV, 9; *Hahn* (B), 135, 143-4, 148, 150; *Hommage*, 190; PM, 91; *Zillhardt*, 147-50.

95 *Towards* ... PM, 91-9.

96 *At the* ... CG, VI, 171; *Billy*, 175; *Catusse*, 102, 104.

97 *On* 26 ... C, 73-4.

CHAPTER 5 PURIFICATION THROUGH PARODY

98 *In January* ... *Times, Figaro*, Jan.-March, 1908.

98 *At first* ... *Billy*, 138; *Hahn* (B), 86-7, 98, 100, 112-13, 115; PM, 11, 37.

99 *Proust's* . . . *Lauris* (A), 243-4; C, 204; PM, 108.
100 *He had* . . . PM, 15, 20-1, 49, 57.
102 *Other* . . . III, 708; PM, 22.
103 *It was* . . . CG, IV, 228-30; BSAMP, VIII, 457-9; *Wildenstein*, no. 360.
103 *Perhaps*... CG, IV, 115-19; *Dreyfus* (B), 234; *Gregh* (D), 140; *Lauris* (A), 181, 206.
104 *The Lemoine* . . . CG, VI, 96; *Clermont-Tonnerre* (B), II, 62-8; *Fouquier*, 164; *Hahn* (B), 151-2; *Morand* (A), 162; *Morand* (B), 105; *Porel* (A), II, 29.
105 *The third* . . . *Baumont*, 240, *et passim*.
106 *Proust* . . . *Billy*, 175-6.
106 *Since* . . . CG, IV, 234-5; CG, VI, 97; *Dreyfus* (B), 239; *Vigneron*, 73-9.
108 *The other* . . . CG, IV, 230-4; CG, VI, 103-5; *Billy*, 72, 143, 168, 174, 208, 219; *Dreyfus* (B), 239; *Gregh* (A), 273; *Gregh* (B), 13; *Kolb* (A), 251; *Sachs* (A), 64; *Uzès*, 163.
108 *In June* . . . CG, VI, 198-202; *Porto-Riche*, 96; *Schlumberger*, II, 113-16, 190.
109 *The young* . . . *Hahn* (B), 171-2; *Lauris* (A), 195.
109 *Nearly* . . . *Bac* (A), II, 190-8; *Bertaut*, 388; *Clermont-Tonnerre* (C), 112; *Figaro*, 28, 29/6/1908; *Germain* (B), 11; *Montesquiou* (D), III, 45, 75; *Montesquiou* (G).
111 *Proust* . . . CG, I, 171-5, 226-7; *Hahn* (B), 153; *Lauris* (A), 128-9.
111 *He arrived* . . . *Catusse*, 113-14; *Daudet, Lucien* (A), 202; *Hahn* (B), 98-100 112-13, 154-6, 185; *Kolb* (A), 44; *Kolb* (F).
112 *Once more* . . . *Clermont-Tonnerre* (C), 133-5, 139; *Hahn* (B), 156.
113 *He passed* . . . CG, V, 194; *Billy*, 209.
113 *Louisa* . . . CG, V, 179-80, 193-5; *Bottin mondain*, 1910, 805; *Hommage*, 56-9; NRF, 90; *Sévrette*, 57, 220.
114 *Proust* . . . CG, V, 195; *Hahn* (B), 156-7; *Hommage*, 58-9; *Mérode*, 66-9.
115 *It was* . . . CG, IV, 98; CG, V, 180; *Bibesco, A* (A), 164; *Bottin, Paris*, 1907, 647; *Fouquières* (B), I, 259; *Lauris* (A), 151, 176.
115 *Perhaps* . . . *Leclercq: Dreyfus* (B), 17.
116 *Once more* . . . CG, VI, 105-9; *Billy*, 114, 116, 160-1; CSB, 284-8; *Clermont-Tonnerre* (C), 105; *Hommage*, 190; *Kolb* (A), 272; *Lauris* (A), 147, 150-2.
116 *At the* . . . CG, VI, 105-9; *Billy*, 160-1; *Hahn* (B), 162; *Lauris* (A), 147, 150-2.

CHAPTER 6 BY WAY OF SAINTE-BEUVE

118 *After* . . . CG, VI, 108; *Lauris* (A), 150-2.
118 *Early* . . . *Lauris* (A), 146-9, 155-7.
118 *As early* . . . CG, II, 45-6; CG, IV, 227; *Lauris* (A), 158.
119 *By way* . . . *Lauris* (A), 15-16, 154, 160
119 *In December* . . . *Lauris* (A), 138, 154, 161; C, 226.
120 *Sainte-Beuve* . . . *Lauris* (A), 153-4, 160.
121 *Meanwhile* . . CG, I, 204-5; CG, IV, 244; *Billy*, 169-70; *Lauris* (A), 154, 163, 170-1; CSB, 15; PM, 32-5.
122 *Early in March he* . . . CG, I, 210, 217-8; CG, IV, 237-8; *Briand* (B); *Dreyfus* (B), 244-5; *Daudet, Lucien* (A), 58; PM, 32-5.
123 *Early in March Proust* . . . *Clermont-Tonnerre* (A), 163; *Lauris* (A), 170; *Lauris* (B), 63-6; *Schlumberger*, II, 370, 393.
123 *In June* . . . *Lauris* (A), 166, 176, 181, 199.
124 *Proust's* . . . CSB, 14-15.
124 *On a* . . . CSB, 14-15.
125 *Proust's* . . . CSB, 136-9, 172-4.
126 *The section* . . . CG, IV, 229-30; CSB, 301-13.
127 *Once again* . . . CG, II, 45-6; *Lauris* (A), 158.

CHAPTER 7 THE TEA AND THE MADELEINE

129 *With the* . . . CSB, 53-4; *Figaro,* 30/12/1908—3/1/1909.
129 *He now* . . . CSB, 53-9.
130 *Such is* . . . CSB, 56-7.
131 *Early in* . . . CSB, 15.
131 *The first* . . . *Flament,* 41; NNRF, 1/2/1953, 377-84.
134 *In Chapter* . . . *Proust, Mme,* 91.
135 *From Balzac* . . . *Billy,* 97; *Daudet, Lucien* (A), 37-8.
137 *Yet again* . . . *Schlumberger,* II, 200.
138 *At this* . . . CSB, 15.
141 *The origins* . . . CSB, 29.
142 *Like* . . . JS, I, 114-15.
143 *Set* . . . *Maurois,* 153-9.
144 *Meanwhile* . . . *Lauris* (A), 139, 164-7, 173, 176, 180-1, 208.
145 *In the* . . . CG, VI, 118; *Hahn* (B), 173-5; *Nordlinger* (B), 60-1.
145 *Proust* . . . CG, IV, 238, 241; *Dreyfus* (B), 248-50; CSB, 15; *Hahn* (B), 174.
148 *The beginning* . . . CG, IV, 239, 244-5; *Lauris* (A), 180-1, 196-7.
148 *For the* . . . CG, II, 68; CG, VI, 115; *Duplay* (C), 9-10; *Kolb* (A), 265; *Hahn*
     (B), 175-6; *Lauris* (A), 182-3; I, 878.
148 *A distressing* . . . *Hommage* (DV), 11-20.
149 *Another* . . . *Fouquier,* 288-9; *Fouquières* (C), 82-4.
149 *Proust's* . . . CG, IV, 37; *Clermont-Tonnerre* (A), 123-4.
150 *Meanwhile* . . . CG, IV, 246-9; CG, VI, 116-17; *Lauris* (A), 181.
151 *Mme Straus* . . . CG, IV, 248; CG, VI, 115-18.
151 *When the* . . . *Lauris* (A), 32, 169, 177-8.
151 *As it* . . . *Lauris* (A), 32, 169, 177-8.
152 *The contents* . . . *Lauris* (A), 177-8, 186.
152 *Meanwhile* . . . CG, I, 224; CG, II, 67; CG, IV, 203-4; CG, VI, 162; *Annuaire
     diplomatique,* 1914, 291; *Bibesco, A* (B), 139-40; *Lauris* (A), 168-9.
153 *In his* . . . *Lauris* (A), 168.
153 *I nearly* . . . *Bibesco, A* (A), 424.

CHAPTER 8 MADEMOISELLE DE SAINT-LOUP

154 *Early in* . . . *Billy,* 180-1; *Kolb* (E).
155 *For nearly* . . . CG, IV, 123; *Maurois,* 135; *Pouquet* (B), 249-53; *Scheikévitch*
     (A), 64, 67-73; *Suffel,* 297-305.
156 *On 28* . . . CG, IV, 108, 121; *Bac* (A), III, 82; *Pouquet* (B), 253-68; *Scheikévitch*
     (A), 73-4.
157 *Now he* . . . CG, IV, 120, 141-4.
157 *The Seine* . . . *Times,* Jan. 1910; *Schlumberger,* II, 124-6.
158 *But when* . . . CG, I, 168-9; CG, VI, 123-5; *Gregh* (A), 204; *Gregh* (B), 242;
     Hahn (B), 176-7; *Lauris* (A), 202-3.
159 *He was* . . . *Guth.*
160 *In June* . . . CG, IV, 35-7; *Hahn* (B), 188; *Lauris* (A), 209.
160 *Meanwhile* . . . *Cocteau* (A), 50; *Corpechot,* 247-56; *Hahn* (B), 203; *Lieven,* 121;
     Montesquiou (D), III, 122-4.
161 *In the* . . . CG, V, 70, 133; *Cocteau* (A), 47; *Daudet, Lucien* (A), 181-2; *Fouquier,*
     240, 296; *Hahn* (B), 144-5; *Jaloux,* 16-17; *Morand* (A), 38; *Morand* (B), 110;
     Porel (A), II, 113; RHLF, avril-juin 1930, 305-6; *Sert,* 131-40.
162 *After* . . . *Astruc,* 133, 308; *Bibesco, M* (A), 181-2; *Cocteau* (C), 64; *Hahn* (B),
     142, 146; *Morand* (B), 110; *Sert,* 131-40.

182 *Towards* ... CG, V, 225-6; CG, VI, 112-13.

183 *About* 16 ... CG, VI, 131-2.

183 *The novel* ... NRF, 96, 99-100, 107; *Robert* (A), 26.

184 *At first* ... CG, IV, 45; CG, VI, 133-44; *Robert* (A), 23-6.

184 *In February* ... CG, IV, 53; *Hahn* (B), 227; *Lauris* (A), 235.

185 *While* ... *Robert* (A), 23-8; *Robert* (B), 161-3.

185 *Nevertheless* ... CSB, 15; *Lauris* (A), 177; NRF, 89-106; III, 1116, 1242.

186 *Again Proust* ... *Bibesco, A* (B), 174-7, 181.

187 *Du Côté* ... CG, VI, 132-3, 137-8, 140-1.

187 *In these* ... CG, VI, 144-53; *Robert* (A), 37-9; *Figaro*, 21/12/1912.

188 *At last* ... *Bibesco, A* (B), 178-80; *Bonnet*, 127; BSAMP, VII, 307-9, VIII, 517-20; *Gide* (B), 9-11; *Kolb* (C); NRF, 98; *Robert* (A), 52.

189 *While he* ... CG, VI, 134, 142, 154-6; NRF, 106-7; *Robert* (A), 29-33, 37.

189 *Only a* ... CG, VI, 154-5; CG, II, 192-3; *Bibesco, A* (B), 179; *Blum*, 38; *Robert* (A), 34-5, 37, 51.

189 *Robert* ... *Robert* (A), 12-13, 35-6, 44.

190 *On the* ... CG, VI, 155, 157, 159-60, 162-3; *Hahn* (B), 239.

190 *To another* ... CG, VI, 157-8; *Daudet, Lucien* (A), 89-90; *Hahn* (B), 237; *Rostand* (B), 55.

190 *Towards* 10 ... *Robert* (A), 13-15, 50-1, 55-9.

191 *Proust* ... CG, IV, 57-8, 62-3; *Bibesco, M* (A), 29; *Blum*, 28-55, 228-9; *Grasset* (A), 9; *Grasset* (B), 194; *Massis*, 7-8; *Robert* (A), 15, 52-3, 59.

192 *For many* ... CG, V, 90.

192 *One day* ... CG, VI, 242, 244-5; CG, II, 193; *Robert* (A), 63-4.

193 *Real* ... CG, II, 198; CG, VI, 122, 145; *Billy*, 191; *Blum*, 47, 51.

194 *Immediately* ... CG, IV, 56, 58; *Blum*, 51; *Robert* (A), 62-3; *Duplay* (C), 10.

194 *The last* ... CG, IV, 56; *Blum*, 49; *Daudet, Lucien* (A), 69, 79-80; *Lauris* (A), 184-5; *Robert* (A), 16-17, 63, 65-7, 75; *Robert* (C), 79; NRF, 95, 100-1, 105; *Vigneron*, 107.

195 *Meanwhile* ... CG, VI, 132, 145-6, 164; *Robert* (A), 84; *Robert* (B), 175.

196 *At this* ... *Robert* (A), 64, 83-6; *Robert* (C), 65-78.

196 *Maurice* ... CG, IV, 4; CG, V, 226-7; *Blum*, 60; *Hahn* (B), 237; *Robert* (A), 46, 53, 59-60; *Rostand* (B), 55-7; *Scheikévitch* (A), 136-7.

196 *Proust's* ... *Hahn* (B), 240-1.

197 *For a* ... *Daudet, Lucien* (A), 68-9, 74; *Kolb* (A), 51; *Lauris* (A), 223-4.

197 *In the* ... *Lauris* (A), 168, 223.

CHAPTER 10 AGOSTINELLI VANISHES

199 *Proust* ... *Cocteau* (A), 103; *Daudet, Lucien* (A), 65-6, 74, 76, 78; *Duplay* (C), 10-11; *Lauris* (A), 224.

199 *Early in* ... *Blum*, 59; *Cocteau* (A), 105-6; *Daudet, Lucien* (A), 65-6, 68-80; *Robert* (A), 62-77; *Robert* (B), 166-8.

199 *The final* ... CG, IV, 99; *Dreyfus* (B), 294-7; I, xxxix, 959.

200 *Proust* ... *Blum*, 75-7; *Dreyfus* (B), 285-94; *Scheikévitch* (A), 139-41.

200 *Swann* ... CG, IV, 98-9, 260-1; *Ambrière*; *Dreyfus* (B), 294-9; *Daudet, Lucien* (A), 81.

201 *Lucien* ... *Daudet, Lucien* (A), 80-6; *Robert* (A), 80.

201 *Cocteau's* ... *Alden*, 10; *Daudet, Lucien* (A), 73; *Hahn* (B), 188; *Rivière*, 19; *Robert* (A), 80.

202 *The loyal* ... CG, I, 188-9, 201-2; *Blum*, 129-30.

202 *Paul* ... CG, I, 265; CG, III, 62-3; CG, IV, 64-5; CG, V, 229-30; *Scheikévitch* (A), 141; *Souday*, 7-16.

202 *Swann* . . . CG, IV, 62-4; *Blum*, 44; *Daudet, Lucien* (A), 73; *Billy*, 72; *Robert* (A), 78-82; *Robert* (B), 170-1.
203 *Having* . . . *Briand* (A), 523; *Cocteau* (B), 112; *Gide* (B), 14-15, 21, 41.
204 *My dear* . . . *Gide* (A), I, 398; *Gide* (B), 9-12; *Kolb* (C), 187-97.
204 *He replied* . . . CG, VI, 251-2; *Blum*, 150-9, 169; *Gide* (B), 13-17, 19-23, 30, 36.
204 *This was* . . . CG, IV, 62-4; *Blum*, 151, 171; *Gide* (B), 20.
205 *Proust's* . . . *Astruc*, 309; *Blum*, 178, 209; *Gide* (B), 30.
205 *In February* . . . CG, VI, 165-6, 203; *Bordeaux* (A), III, 353; *Daudet, Léon* (F), I, 109; *Gregh* (B), 159-61; *Lauris* (B), 222-3; *Morand* (A), 153; *Schlumberger*, II, 239.
206 *It is* . . . CG, I, 248; CG, II, 204; CG, IV, 60-2, 65; CG, V, 228; III, 1032; *Robert* (A), 77; *Figaro Littéraire*, 25/11/1939; CG, VI, 189; *Astruc*, 310; *Blum*, 123; *Daudet, Lucien* (A), 95.
206 *Proust's* . . . CG, VI, 244; *Maurois*, 140-1.
207 *There are* . . . CG, VI, 189, 242; *Cocteau* (A), 105-6; *Gide* (B), 39; III, 372-3, 382-3.
208 *The main* . . . III, 501, 902; *Jammes*, 286-7; *Rivière*, 3.
209 *Soon after* . . . CG, III, 321; *Gibbs-Smith*, 84-7; *Paléologue* (B), 208; *Schlumberger*, II, 242.
210 *Before long* . . . CG, III, 321; RHLF, Jan.-March, 1933, 159.
210 *It was* . . . CG, IV, 61, 64-5; CG, V, 228; CG, VI, 242, 245; *Daudet, Lucien* (A), 95; *Jammes*, 286-7.
211 *In the* . . . CG, VI, 242; *Bonnet*, 165; *Dupont*, no. 137; PM, 97.
212 *Agostinelli* . . . CG, VI, 247; *Bordeaux* (A), III, 186; *Gide* (B), 38; III, 406-7.
212 *But the* . . . CG, VI, 242-245; III, 321; PM, 95-6; *Vigneron*, 100-1.
212 *Joseph* . . . *Vigneron*, 100-1.
213 *Proust* . . . CG, VI, 241-2; *Adam*, 81, 83; *Figaro*, 31/5/1914.
213 *Boats* . . . CG, VI, 241-7; *Bordeaux* (A), III, 87; *Vigneron*, 107-8.
213 *On Sunday* . . . *Catusse*, 133-5; *Vigneron*, 107-8.
214 *In his* . . . CG, I, 270-1; *Astruc*, 310-11; *Bordeaux* (A), III, 87; *Daudet, Lucien* (A), 109; *Gide* (B), 43.
214 *Jealousy* . . . CG, V, 41; *Blum*, 155-7, 207; *Gide* (B), 34; NRF, 103.
215 *As before* . . . CG, VI, 166-7; *Gide* (B), 36-7, 45; *Feuillerat*, 5, 23-107; I, xxiii; *Rivière*, 3-18.
216 *Only* . . . CG, IV, 263; CG, V, 95-6.

CHAPTER 11 THE DEATH OF SAINT-LOUP

217 *The sky* . . . *Bac* (A), III, 177-87; *Bardac* (A), 141; *Daudet, Lucien* (A), 135
217 *Bac called* . . . *Bac* (A), III, 197-211.
218 *The catastrophe* . . . CG, VI, 171; *Guth; Hahn* (B), 249-50; *Nordlinger* (G), 265; *Scheikévitch* (C), 41.
218 *The French* . . . *Hahn* (B), 250.
219 *Céleste* . . . *Bordeaux* (A), III, 87; *Catusse*, 115, 118; *Hahn* (B), 250; *Kolb* (A), 290; *Figaro*, 5/9/1914; *Scheikévitch* (C), 43.
219 *He emerged* . . . BSAMP, III, 28; BSAMP, V, 15; *Catusse*, 117.
219 *One day* . . . CG, VI, 172-3; *Clermont-Tonnerre* (C), 178-81; *Bac* (A), III, 298; *Dreyfus* (A), 33.
220 *Proust* . . . *Catusse*, 119; *Gregh* (A), 168; *Daudet, Lucien* (A), 109-10; *Hermant* (B), 243; *Kolb* (A), 290; *Morand* (A), 175; *Porel* (A), I, 270, 317, 320; *Porel* (B); I, 431.
220 *Meanwhile* . . . *Le Masle*, 24.
221 *Among* . . . *Bac* (A), III, 229-286, 313-14.

221 *Others* . . .   Bardac (A), 141-2; Gregh (A), 271; Patin; Schlumberger, II, 157.
222 *Proust* . . .   CG, III, 318, 320; CG, V, 230-1; CG, VI, 171-2; Astruc, 313; Bardac (B), 143; Billy, 195; Blum, 165; Crosland, 40-1; BSAMP, III, 29; Daudet, Lucien (A), 100, 107, 113, 133; Gregh (B), 165-8, 173-81; Catusse, 115-27, 140; Gide (A), 514, 527, 534, 537; Lannes, 27-8; Lauris (A), 240, 242, 248; Lauris (B), 187-90; Halicka, 66; Guth; Poniatowski, 610; Sert, 199.
223 *At moments* . . .   CG, III, 317; CG, VI, 127, 171-2; Billy, 197; Catusse, 116, 120, 124; Daudet, Lucien (A), 104; Morand (A), 200; Morand (B), 15.
223 *Nevertheless* . . .   CG, VI, 175-7, 189, 193-5, 206; Daudet, Lucien (A), 106, 135, 141; Catusse, 137; Hahn (B), 255; Hommage, 82; Lauris (A), 240; Morand (A), 39, 173, 314; Morand (B), 81-2.
224 *Gaston* . . .   Pouquet (A), 75-82; CG, IV, 109, 129-36.
225 *After his* . . .   CG, IV, 131, 134; Annuaire diplomatique, 1914, 291; Bibesco, A (B), 47, 119; Bibesco, M (A), 136-8; Billy, 137; Hommage, 80; Morand (B), 13.
226 *Fénelon's* . . .   Bibesco, M (A), 137; Pouquet (A), 64, 77-8.
226 *Proust* . . .   CG, V, 92; Billy, 195; Daudet, Lucien (A), 140; Lauris (A), 241-7.
226 *Another* . . .   CG, V, 92, 159; Bac (A), III, 91-7; Billy, 194; BSAMP, III, 29-30; C, 87; Catusse, 135; Figaro, 4/8/1915; Montesquiou (C), 558; Morand (A), 301; Proust, Mme, 211; Humières, 15-19; Wharton, 288-9; Porel (A), I, 283-4.
227 *Proust's* . . .   CG, III, 317, 322; CG, VI, 168-9, 248; Adam, 82; Billy, 198; Blum, 199, 206; Catusse, 124-7, 133-6; Daudet, Lucien (A), 111, 135-6, 139-45; Guth; Hahn (B), 255; Lauris (A), 244.
228 *In June* . . .   CG, III, 112-15; Hommage, 52.
229 *Montesquiou* . . .   CG, I, 252; CG, III, 255-6; Catusse, 137; Montesquiou (D), II, 286.
229 *After being* . . .   CG, III, 320; Bibesco, M (B), 15; Crosland, 41; Cocteau (C), 163; Porel (A), I, 349.
229 *At last* . . .   CG, III, 112, 116, 126, 317-18, CG, IV, 67, 135; CG, V, 231-2; BSAMP, III, 27; Daudet, Lucien (A), 123-4, 137; Catusse, 116, 120, 124-5.
230 *Soon* . . .   Adam, 51; BSAMP, IV, 86-7; Daudet, Lucien (A), 96, 115, 137, 148.
230 *Two authors* . . .   CG, VI, 248-9; Astruc, 314; Bac (A), III, 79-90; Gide (A), I, 514; Lauris (A), 236-7, 249-51, 259-69; Lauris (B), 243-79; Scheikévitch (A), 89-90.
230 *On the* . . .   CG, I, 257; CG, V, 233-41; Billy, 197; Blum, 156, 163; Lauris (A), 236-7.
231 *As the* . . .   Bibesco, A (B), 149-50.

CHAPTER 12 THE VINTEUIL SEPTET

232 *On 25* . . .   Blum, 166-71, 205; Gide (A), 543, 553; Gide (B), 52-3.
232 *Exactly* . . .   Blum, 169-70.
233 *The negotiations* . . .   Blum, 166-70, 178-9, 224.
233 *At first* . . .   Blum, 174-219.
234 *A major* . . .   Blum, 169.
235 *The chapter-headings* . . .   I, xxiii.
235 *The proofs* . . .   Daudet, Lucien (A), 143, 145; Feuillerat, 2-5, 23-68, 275-92; Lauris (A), 184; Robert (A), 67.
236 *Two further* . . .   Feuillerat, 36-42, 68, 140-50, 282-4, 290-2; I, 981-2, II, 861-3.
237 *Le Côté* . . .   Feuillerat, 69-70, 77-80, 107, 292, 294-6, 302.
237 *The volume* . . .   CSB, 247-66; JS, III, 93.
238 *The death* . . .   Rivière, 7.
238 *The next* . . .   CG, V, 233-41.

CHAPTER 13 THE PIT OF SODOM

259 *Meanwhile* ... *Daudet, Lucien* (A), 203; *Germain* (B), 55-6; *Lacretelle*, 116; III, 1141; *PM*, 59.

259 *Proust* ... *CG*, I, 234-5, 254, 257, 267, 269-70; *CG*, IV, 151; *CG*, V, 6, 20-1, 33, 36-7, 97, 105, 249-50, 253-7, 261; *CG*, VI, 184, 187; *Blum*, 187, 217; *Catusse*, 129, 132, 145, 152, 173, 200; *Daudet, Lucien* (A), 153-4, 209; *Lacretelle*, 115; *Morand* (B), 66-79.

261 *Recently* ... *CG*, V, 21-2, 250-1; *CG*, VI, 180-8, 196, 198, 201; *Catusse*, 152-74; *Morand* (B), 66-8.

261 *The last* ... *CG*, V, 33-8; *Adam*, 68; *Bottin, Paris*, 1916-7, II, 1129; *Daudet, Lucien* (A), 233; *Morand* (B), 66, 76-7.

262 *The proprietor* ... *Bottin, Paris*, 1919, II, 756, 1129; *Guichard* (A), 168; *Sachs* (A), 280.

262 *Prince* ... *Barney* (B), 123-4; *Clermont-Tonnerre* (A), 209-10; *Clermont-Tonnerre* (C), 142-3; *Fouquier*, 272-3; *Halicka*, 66; *Montesquiou* (B), 60; *Montesquiou* (C), 558.

262 *While* ... *Sachs* (A), 281-2.

263 *During* ... *Guichard* (A), 168-9; *Sachs* (A), 280-1; *Sachs* (B).

264 *It was* ... *Bottin, Paris*, 1916-7, II, 1129; *Guichard* (A), 169-70; *Sachs* (A), 280-3.

264 *Here the* ... *Sachs* (A), 279-80; *Sachs* (B).

265 *Albert* ... *Guichard* (A), 169-70; *Sachs* (A), 285; *Sachs* (B), 864.

266 *The conscious* ... *Adam*, 80-1; II, 1110.

268 *Throughout* ... *Daudet, Lucien* (A), 15; *Germain* (B), 71, 149; *Hommage*, 188-9; *Morand* (A), 112; *Sachs* (A), 285; *Sachs* (B), 864.

268 *The story* ... *Germain* (B), 71-2; *Germain* (C), 248; *Gide* (A), II, 1123; *Martin du Gard*, 244; *Rose*, 118; *Sachs* (A), 285.

269 *He could* ... *CG*, V, 105; *Morand* (B), 76, 82.

270 *It is* ... *Goncourt*, 3 June 1891; *Morand* (C), 54; *Rachilde*, 79-92.

270 *Albert's* ... *CSB*, 14, 15, 86, 232; *Guichard* (A), 170-1; *Maurois*, 153; *Sachs* (A), 282-3.

271 *On 27* ... *CG*, VI, 176-9; *Adam, H. P.*, 316; *Curtiss* (A), 249; *Morand* (A), 324-5.

272 *The next* ... *CG*, VI, 197-8.

273 *On and* ... *CG*, V, 98; *Blum*, 224-5; *Catusse*, 175-6; *Daudet, Lucien* (A), 98; *Morand* (B), 80, 82, 87-8.

273 *The noble* ... *Couvreur; Curtiss* (B), 313; *Morand* (A), 111; *Scheikévitch* (B), 607-8; *Scheikévitch* (C), 40.

274 *Céleste* ... *CG*, VI, 278, 280; *Castellane* (B), 6; *Clermont-Tonnerre* (C), 207; *Daudet, Lucien* (A), 138, 187; *Fouquier*, 161-2; *Fouquières* (A), 96; *Gregh* (D), 43; *Guillot de Saix; Hahn* (B), 83, 145; *Montesquiou* (A), 300, 311; *Morand* (A), 306; *Morand* (B), 54.

275 *Early in* ... *Gide* (B), 61-2; *Morand* (A), 243, 277, 299.

276 *The Abbé* ... *Bibesco, M* (E), I, 2, 4.

276 *The Abbé was* ... *Bibesco, M* (E), I, 1, 6, 28, 174, 181, II, 7; *Clermont-Tonnerre* (B), II, 52-3, 202; *Descaves*, 41, 131, 139-40; *Dumesnil; Flament* (B); *Fouquières* (A), 127-9; *Germain* (B), 217, 219; *Lauris* (B), 197-201; *Morand* (A), 299.

277 *It is* ... *Bibesco, M* (E), I, 6, 12-17, 326; *Bibesco, M* (D), 192-3; *Blanche* (A), 137-8; *Curtiss* (B), 313-14; *Descaves*, 152; *Daudet, Lucien* (A), 214; *Fouquières* (A), 72; *Morand* (A), 283, 306.

278 *All that* ... *CG*, III, 147; *CG*, IV, 126, 143; *CG*, V, 102, 190-1, 256-8; *CG*, VI, 193; *Bibesco, M* (A), 46; *Clermont-Tonnerre* (A), 91-2; *Daudet, Lucien* (A), 224; *Fouquières* (B), I, 114; *Morand* (B), 80-91; *Nouvelle Revue Française*, 1/1/1928, 87-8; *Pouquet* (B), 246.

279 *On* 13 ... CG, III, 102; CG, VI, 202-7.
279 *After* ... *Daudet, Lucien* (A), 224, 227; *Lacretelle*, 110-1; NRF, 115.
279 *On* 10 ... CG, III, 121-5, 127-58; *Blanche* (C), I, vii-viii; CSB, 78-9; *Daudet, Lucien* (A), 231.
280 *It was* ... *Blum*, 179, 220-31; NRF, 37.
281 *The same* ... CG, IV, 263; CG, V, 44; CG, VI, 206, 224; *Blum*, 228; *Daudet, Lucien* (A), 211, 220-1; *Lacretelle*, 112.
282 *The Germans* ... CG, III, 150; CG, V, 97; CG, VI, 206, 224; *Bibesco, M* (B), 162-4; *Daudet, Léon* (G), 271; *Daudet, Lucien* (A), 229; *Catusse*, 143-4, 176; *Fernandez*, 205; *Hommage*, 91; *Morand* (A), 305; *Morand* (B), 91-3.

CHAPTER 14 THE PRIZE

283 *The men* ... CG, VI, 214; *Morand* (B), 93.
283 *First* ... CG, III, 213-14; CG, V, 6-20, 45-9, 136; CG, VI, 212-27; *Billy*, 202; *Blum*, 204; *Clermont-Tonnerre* (C), 204-5; *Guth*.
284 *La Semeuse* ... CG, V, 13; CG, VI, 207, 210-11, 215, 218, 224, 233, 257, 263; *Bibesco, A* (B), 52; *Bibesco, M* (A), 157; *Morand* (B), 105-6; NRF, 114; PM, 15, 22, 69-72, 79-80, 82-6; *Rivière*, 27-8.
285 *In the* ... CG, IV, 77, 270; CG, V, 6-10, 16, 51, 54, 102-3; CG, VI, 226-8, 256-7, *Billy*, 119; *Catusse*, 177.
286 *Early in* ... CG, IV, 74, 77, 264; CG, V, 29-31; *Catusse*, 177; *Morand* (B), 100-3.
286 *On* 2 ... *Bibesco, M* (A), 197; *Nicolson* (A), 275-6, 318-9; *Nicolson* (B); *Nicolson* (C).
287 *Whether* ... CG, III, 205; CG, IV, 75; CG, V, 55-7; CG, VI, 220; *Blanche* (A), 136-7; *Blanche* (B), 127; *Pierre-Quint*, 113-14; *Rivière*, xvii, 48, 70, 103, 105.
287 *Towards* ... CG, III, 3-5; CG, V, 52-4; *Rivière*, 21-2, 26-33.
288 *As the* ... CG, II, 213; CG, III, 6-8; CG, IV, 76-8; CG, V, 29, 32, 56; *Cattaui* (B), 184; *Catusse*, 178-80, 183-4, 186, 188-92; *Scheikévitch* (B), 604; *Scheikévitch* (C), 44.
288 *Her son* ... CG, V, 60; *Catusse*, 186; *Hommage*, 88-9; *Morand* (A), 175, 278; *Morand* (B), 18, 41; *Porel* (A), I, 317-31, 334; *Porel* (B).
289 *It was* ... NRF, 121.
290 *The house* ... CG, III, 7-8; CG, IV, 268, 273; CG, V, 60-1; *Catusse*, 193; *Martin du Gard*, 201-2; *Porel* (A), I, 330-1, 364, II, 77; *Porel* (B).
290 *Thirty* ... CG, VI, 3; *Porel* (A), I, 364, 370-3.
290 *It was* ... *Porel* (A), I, 372.
291 *Proust's* ... CG, III, 193, 221; CG, V, 61; *Catusse*, 186; HLB, VII (1953), 157-60; NRF, 121; *Porel* (A), I, 330-1, II, 77.
292 *Publication* ... CG, V, 56; *Kolb* (A), 217; NRF, 122-3; *Rivière*, 32.
292 *The common* ... CG, IV, 266-78; *Dreyfus* (B), 210-36; NRF, 111-12.
293 *Nevertheless* ... *Robert* (B), 169-72.
293 *Meanwhile* ... CG, I, 276-8; CG, III, 11; CG, IV, 79; *Astrue*, 314; *Blum*, 244; *Bibesco, A* (B), 156; *Catusse*, 194, 196; *Le Goff*, 243, 332; *Lacretelle*, 102; *Suffel*, 381.
294 *On* 14 ... CG, I, 276-9; *Gregh* (A), 205; *Gregh* (B), 249; *Gregh* (D), 37.
294 *On* 24 ... CG, I, 275; CG, IV, 273-7; CG, V, 66; *Blanche* (C), II, xxxvii-xl; *Billy*, 202; *Morand* (B), 109, 112.
294 *Réjane* ... *Charavay*, no. 102; HLB, VII (1953), 157-60; *Porel* (A), I, 365-7.

295 *It was* ... CG, I, 287-8, 290; *Abraham*, pl. XXXVI; *Bottin, Paris*, 1919, II, 1370; *Bottin-Mondain*, 1919, 1125, 1608, 1653; *Catusse*, 197; *Daudet, Lucien* (A), 48, 239; *Maurois*, 128, 320; *Pierre-Quint*, 112-13.

295 *In September* ... CG, III, 71, 214, 216, 218; *Billy*, 72; *Daudet, Lucien* (A), 161; *Deffoux*, 121-3; *Maurois*, 292; *Robert* (B), 169-72; RHLF, jan.-mars, 1932, 160.

296 *The Goncourt* ... CG, III, 71, 200, 216, 230; CG, IV, 159; *Alden*, 32, 162; *Deffoux*, 121-3, 136; *Lacretelle*, 123, 125; *Montfort*, II, 25; NRF, 217; *Rivière*, 73; *Wildenstein*, no. 257.

296 *The Prize* ... CG, III, 71, 166-7, 200-1, 216-17; *Alden*, 29-36, 176-8; *Blum*, 237; NRF, 127.

297 *From the* ... CG, III, 70, 201; NRF, 129, 229; *Rivière*, 76-7.

297 *Henceforth* ... CG, III, 71.

298 *Proust* ... CG, V, 7-9, 14-15, 23, 28, 31-2, 56-7; CG, VI, 195-6, 198-9; *Billy*, 233-43; *Catusse*, 201-2; *Pierre-Quint*, 109.

298 *In the* ... CG, III, 208, 298; C, 193-211; *Rivière*, 60-77, 80, 86-7, 89, 91-4, 99, 101-3, 106, 142.

299 *The proof-enrichment* ... CG, III, 8-11, 15-16, 18-20, 209; CG, V, 59-60, 68; *Bibesco, M* (B), 154; BSAMP II, 36; *Gide* (B), 78; *Lacretelle*, 112-13; *Morand* (B), 132-3; NRF, 124, 130; I, xxiv; *Rivière*, 85, 103, 108.

300 *On* 4 ... CG, VI, 234-5.

300 *He had* ... BSAMP, VII, 278-9; *Castellane* (B), 197; *Porel* (A), I, 331-2, 342-3.

301 *On* 14 ... *Hommage*, 92-3; *Porel* (A), I, 332, 374.

301 *At this* ... CG, V, 105; *Lacretelle*, 121; *Porel* (A), I, 332; *Rivière*, 109-10, 116, 118, 120, 127.

CHAPTER 15 THE DARK WOMAN

303 *In the* ... CG, III, 17, 20, 24-5; CG, VI, 232; *Fouquières* (C), 84-5; *Germain* (B), 101; *Morand* (A), 306; *Morand* (B), 117; *Rivière*, 91, 137; *Schlumberger*, II, 55-8; *Wildenstein*, no. 124.

303 *Aided* ... *Clermont-Tonnerre* (A), 105.

304 *Le Côté* ... CG, II, 214-5; CG, III, 21-2, 219; CG, V, 87; CG, VI, 137; *Billy*, 119; III, 137; RHLF, avril-juin, 1930, 306; *Rivière*, 108.

305 *On* 25 ... CG, III, 21-2, 81-3, 217; CG, IV, 100, 280; CG, V, 72, 82, 106; *Bibesco, A* (B), 54; *Boylesve*, 266-7; *Catusse*, 201; *Jaloux*, 134-6; *Journal officiel*, 1920, 14250; *Daudet, Lucien* (A), 238; NRF, 133-4; *Rivière*, 136-7; *Porto-Riche*, 100.

306 *The next* ... CG, III, 86-91; CG, V, 69; *Alden*, 54-6; NRF, 39, 119; *Rivière*, 147-8; *Scheikévitch* (B), 604.

306 *Early in* ... CG, III, 77; CG, V, 71, 120-1; *Morand* (A), 222-3; *Morand* (B), 41, 58, 115; *Morand* (C), 46; *Morand* (D), 56-7.

307 *In the* ... *Morand* (E), 9-11.

308 *For the* ... CG, I, 198; CG, IV, 38, 203; CG, VI, 81, 106; *Bibesco, M* (B), 119, 123; *Billy*, 160; *Hahn* (B), 196; *Lauris* (A), 186.

309 *During* ... CG, III, 21-2, 256; CG, IV, 105, 263; CG, V, 95-7, 102-6, 117-24; CG, VI, 272; *Blum*, 217; *Catusse*, 200; *Curtiss* (A), 281; BSAMP, XII, 530; *Mauriac, F*, 24; NRF, 132; *Morand* (B), 79.

310 *Early in* ... CG, III, 159-62, 170-3; *Blanche* (C), II, xv, xli; *Rivière*, 167.

310 *Marcel* ... CG, III, 228; CG, V, 159, 169; *Bordeaux* (A), III, 88; BSAMP, VI, 178; *Écrits de Paris*, jan. 1951, 108; *Le Masle*, 50; *Morand* (E), 16-22; *Rivière*, 105-7, 167; *Tharaud* (A), 180-3.

311 *Proust's* ... *Écrits de Paris*, jan. 1951, 108.

CHAPTER 16 AN INDIAN SUMMER

333 *Proust* ... CG, III, 33-5, 174, 181, 184, 283; CG, IV, 136-7; CG, V, 25, 267; *Billy*, 203; *Maurois*, 309; *Morand* (B), 109, 130-1; NRF, 178, 185-6, 199, 203, 224; *Rivière*, 251.

334 *The gaiety* ... CG, V, 25; *Bibesco, M* (C), 104; *Gregh* (B), 257; *Morand* (B), 125-6, 130; NRF, 193; *Schlumberger*, II, 342.

335 *On 7* ... CG, III, 273; *Germain* (A), 59-72, 95-111; *Germain* (B), 207-10, 234-5, 247; *Germain* (D), 13-14; *Martin du Gard*, I, 195-202; *Morand* (B), 126-7; NRF, 218-9; *Rivière*, 229-30.

336 *The daily* ... CG, III, 182-94, 284-6, 289-92; CG, V, 25, 77; *Bibesco, M* (C), 105; *Blanche* (C), II, xliii; *Crémieux*, 167-8; *Kolb* (A), 227; *Morand* (B), 129; NRF, 181, 210, 215, 232, 237, 244; *Riviere*, 242, 244-9, 256-9; *Scheikévitch* (A), 161.

337 *Proust* ... CG, III, 274-8, 281-5, 287, 289, 292; CG, V, 80; *Clermont-Tonnerre* (C), 244-5; *Rivière*, 189.

337 *But the* ... *Brach*, 27-8; *Cattaui* (A), 106-7; *Gaulois*, 16/7/1902; NRF, 173-4; *Proust, Mme*, 71; *Rivière*, 218.

338 *His unavailing* ... CG, IV, 103; NRF, 225, 236, 242, 246; *Rivière*, 263, 266 268, 277, 284.

338 *The publication* ... CG, III, 38; CG, IV, 90; CG, V, 23-4, 84, 113-15; NRF, 214, 224; *Rivière*, 251.

339 *Violet* ... CG, III, 20, 51. 57; *Adam*, 6-12; *Hommage*, 274; *Schiff*.

339 *On 28* ... CG, III, 31-3, 36-8, 51; *Adam*, 11-12; BSAMP, IX, 18-24; *Catusse*, 42; *Morand* (B), 33; *Schiff; Wildenstein*, no. 258, 316.

340 *On 18* ... CG, III, 158; CG, V, 40; *Bell*, 179-80; *Blanche* (C), I, xxii; *Cocteau* (C), 165-6; *Craft*, 89; *Monnet-Hornung*, 14-16; *Penrose*, 208; *Porel* (A), II, 321; *Schiff*.

341 *Joyce* ... *Adam*, 64-5; *Bell*, 179-80; *Ellman*, 523-4; *Joyce*, 148.

342 *A new* ... CG, V, 81-5; *Crémieux*, 161-3; *Gabory*, 36; *Gide* (B), 86-96; *Jaloux*, 132-3; NRF, 203, 206, 209, 221; *Rivière*, 252, 254-7; *Salmon*, III, 73-5.

342 *As soon* ... CG, III, 42, 221-2, 293; CG, V, 84-6, 134; *Bibesco, M* (C), 100, 115-17; NRF, 221, 253; *Rivière*, 257, 259-60; *Robert* (A), 26.

343 *A well-meaning* ... CG, V, 221-3; *Hayman; Hommage*, 70; NRF, 213-14; I, 634.

343 *The Schiffs* ... CG, III, 42; *Adam*, 11; *Wildenstein*, no. 239.

344 *Every day* ... CG, III, 45, 301; CG, V, 82, 134; *Brach*, 27-8, 32-3; *Crémieux*, 165; *Jaloux*, 138, 140, 143-4; *Montesquiou* (A), 313; *Pierre-Quint*, 114-15.

344 *On 15* ... *Brach*, 33-8; *Briand* (A), 515-16; BSAMP, VI, 135; *Hommage*, 150; *Jaloux*, 11, 13, 86, 149-51; *Kolb* (A), 230; NRF, 231, 243; *Oberlé*, 108-10.

345 *Among* ... *Brach*, 38; *Clermont-Tonnerre* (C), 192; *Jaloux*, 152; *Mauriac, F*, 49-56; *Montesquiou* (D), 111, 285-94; *Pierre-Quint*, 211.

346 *Proust's* ... *Daudet, Lucien* (A), 27, 241.

347 *In this* ... CG, III, 45; *Bibesco, A* (B), 52-5; *Bibesco, M* (A), 153-60, 195-200; NRF, 220.

347 *At the* ... *Pouquet* (A), 94-5.

347 *Jeanne's* ... CG, III, 55; *Adam*, 12; *Bibesco, M* (C), 101-2; *Bibesco, M* (E), II, 62; *Kolb* (A), 97; *Maurois* (B), I, 210-19, 230-7; *Morand* (B), 111.

348 *Proust's* ... CG, IV, 161; *Abraham*, LII-LVI; BSAMP, III, 17-18; *Crémieux*, 169; NRF, 224-5, 234-5, 246, 256, 265; *Œuvres Libres*, février 1923, 235-6; III, 1057-8; *Rivière*, 284.

348 *Early in* ... CG, III, 290-1; I, xxxii-iii, III, 1094; NRF, 225, 235, 271; *Rivière*, 272, 275, 277, 278.

349 *In August* ... CG, II, 54; *Lauris* (A), 49, 209; PJ, 12-13.

350 *Among the thirty-five* ... *Du Bos*, 164; *Gide* (A), I, 741; *Maurois* (B), I, 185-91; *Rivière*, 271, 274.

INDEXES

Two separate indexes are provided, the first of real persons and places, the second of fictitious characters and places in Proust's novel, A la Recherche du Temps Perdu. In order to facilitate the tracing of discussions in the text of Proust's models in real life, cross-references from each index to the other have been given, where applicable, in capitals and parentheses. For this special purpose the two indexes should be used in conjunction with one another, and with the corresponding indexes in Volume One.

I. PERSONS AND PLACES

II. CHARACTERS AND PLACES

ABOUT THE AUTHOR

GEORGE D. PAINTER was born in Birmingham, England and educated in Classics at Trinity College, Cambridge. From 1938 until his retirement in 1974 he was a curator at the British Museum in London. He is the author of *André Gide: A Critical Biography; William Caxton, A Biography;* a forthcoming three-volume biography of Chateaubriand; and numerous translations, including *Marcel Proust: Letters to His Mother.*